5 **TH EDITION**

Governing Texas

★ ★

5TH EDITION

Governing Texas

Anthony Champagne
UNIVERSITY OF TEXAS AT DALLAS

Edward J. Harpham
UNIVERSITY OF TEXAS AT DALLAS

Jason P. Casellas
UNIVERSITY OF HOUSTON

W. W. NORTON & COMPANY
NEW YORK · LONDON

W. W. NORTON & COMPANY has been independent since its founding in 1923, when William Warder Norton and Mary D. Herter Norton first published lectures delivered at the People's Institute, the adult education division of New York City's Cooper Union. The firm soon expanded its program beyond the Institute, publishing books by celebrated academics from America and abroad. By midcentury, the two major pillars of Norton's publishing program—trade books and college texts— were firmly established. In the 1950s, the Norton family transferred control of the company to its employees, and today—with a staff of five hundred and hundreds of trade, college, and professional titles published each year—W. W. Norton & Company stands as the largest and oldest publishing house owned wholly by its employees.

Editor: Peter Lesser

Associate Editor: Anna Olcott

Project Editor: Laura Dragonette

Manuscript Editor: Ellen Lohman

Managing Editor, College: Marian Johnson

Managing Editor, College Digital Media: Kim Yi

Production Manager: Stephen Sajdak

Media Editor: Spencer Richardson-Jones

Media Editorial Assistant: Lena Nowak-Laird

Media Project Editor: Marcus Van Harpen

Marketing Manager, Political Science: Ashley Sherwood

Design Director: Rubina Yeh

Director of College Permissions: Megan Schindel

College Permissions Assistant: Patricia Wong

Text Design: Tamaye Perry

Photo Editor: Thomas Persano

Information Graphics: Kiss Me I'm Polish LLC, New York

Composition: Achorn International, Inc.

Manufacturing: Transcon

Permission to use copyrighted material is included in the credits section of this book, which begins on p. A47.

Library of Congress Cataloging-in-Publication Data

Names: Champagne, Anthony, author. | Harpham, Edward J., author. |
    Casellas, Jason Paul, 1977- author. author.
Title: Governing Texas / Anthony Champagne, Edward J. Harpham, Jason P. Casellas.
Description: 5th edition. | New York, N.Y. : W. W. Norton & Company, 2021. |
    Includes bibliographical references and index.
Identifiers: LCCN 2020053065 | ISBN **9780393427004** (paperback) | ISBN 9780393539707 (epub)
Subjects: LCSH: Texas—Politics and government.
Classification: LCC JK4816 .C48 2021 | DDC 320.4764—dc23
LC record available at https://lccn.loc.gov/2020053065

W. W. Norton & Company, Inc., 500 Fifth Avenue, New York, N.Y. 10110
www.wwnorton.com

W. W. Norton & Company Ltd., 15 Carlisle Street, London W1D 3BS

1 2 3 4 5 6 7 8 9 0

Contents in Brief

Contents

★ ★ ★ ★ ★ ★ ★ ★ ★

5 • Campaigns and Elections 151

6 • Interest Groups and Lobbying 185

7 • The Legislature 215

8 • The Executive Branch 253

13 • Crime, Corrections, and Public Safety 447

14 • Building the Future: Public Policies for a Changing Texas 487

Preface

OUR GOAL in this text is to offer readers a broad understanding of the factors that are reshaping political processes and institutions in the Lone Star State in the first two decades of the twenty-first century. We are particularly concerned with explaining how the principles underlying constitutional government in Texas are being reworked in the face of new political, economic, and demographic changes. By supplementing our institutional analysis with concrete examples from everyday political life in Texas, we hope to show the reader that politics and government in Texas are not only important to their lives but endlessly fascinating as well. Texas has been dramatically affected by a pandemic that has caused tensions between the state and local governments, conflicts within and between the political parties, and disagreements among state officials. The pandemic has also caused major economic problems for Texans and for state and local governments. This text explores the effect of this public health crisis on Texans, the state's politics, and Texas political institutions.

In recent years, how we talk about racial and ethnic minorities has received increased attention. Debates about which words to use to describe groups are ongoing and fluid, and for the sake of clarity, we would like to explain which terms we use in this book and why. In the past, we used the terms "African American" and "black" to describe individuals who have descended from Africa. In recent style guide changes, the Associated Press, the *New York Times*, Fox News, the *Washington Post*, and others have decided to capitalize "Black" when describing this group. We have decided to adopt this standard as well. Accordingly, we also describe Whites with a capital letter. When describing individuals with descent from Latin America or Spain, we will continue to use "Latinos," as this is a term that is widely used by people from this community. We do recognize other terms have emerged to describe this group to take into account all aspects of gender expressions. When we use "Latinos," however, we are thinking of the term as widely encompassing all gender expressions. In accordance with new guidance, we will also change the terms "slave," "slaves," and "slaveholder" to "enslaved person," "enslaved people," and "slaveowner," respectively, to acknowledge the humanity of those whose freedom was denied during this history and to more accurately describe the institution of slavery.

Features of the Fifth Edition

Another, related goal of the book is to provide students with extensive pedagogical support throughout each chapter. In every chapter, several features engage students' interest and help them master the learning objectives for the topic.

- **NEW Citizen's Guide features in every chapter** highlight critical issues and provide students with questions and resources to become more informed voters on, and participants in, these issues. Periodic online updates highlight the new developments on the issues and provide instructors with helpful current events assignments for students.

- **What Do Texans Think? features in every chapter** highlight fascinating public opinion data in Texas. The features allow students to compare their opinions on major issues with those of people across the state and the nation. Accompanying PowerPoint slides make it easy for instructors to poll their own classrooms on hot button topics in Texas government and politics.
- **Updated "What Government Does and Why It Matters" chapter introductions** draw students into the chapter by showing them why they should care about the chapter's topic.
- **Chapter Goals** appear at the start of the chapter and then recur at the start of the relevant sections throughout the chapter to create a more focused, active reading experience.
- **Core Objectives are woven into every chapter**, helping students gain proficiency with critical thinking, effective communication, personal and social responsibility, and quantitative reasoning.
- **Updated Who Are Texans? infographics** engage visually oriented students with a "statistical snapshot" of the state related to each chapter's topic. Through accompanying quantitative reasoning questions, these features help students grasp the political implications of demographic, political, economic, and regional diversity in Texas. Related exercises in the online coursepacks and slides in the instructor PowerPoints make it easy for instructors to bring these graphics into their online or face-to-face classrooms.
- **Updated Texas and the Nation infographics** enable students to compare Texas's government and politics to other states'. Critical thinking questions accompany each Texas and the Nation graphic and encourage students to engage deeply with the graphics and draw their own conclusions. InQuizitive features a dedicated learning objective to the Who Are Texans? and Texas and the Nation graphics, and slides in the PowerPoints make it easy for instructors to bring these graphics into their online or face-to-face classrooms.
- **"Future of Texas" sections at the end of every chapter** examine how Texas government and politics are likely to change in light of Texas's shifting demographics and economy.
- **Extensive end-of-chapter review sections organized around Chapter Goals** include section outlines, practice quiz questions, and key terms. Students have everything they need to master the material in each section of the chapter.

Revisions to the Fifth Edition

In the Fifth Edition of *Governing Texas*, we have tried to provide students with the most up-to-date account of Texas government and politics. Every chapter was scrutinized with help from dozens of outside reviewers, and we have tried to provide the most current examples and data throughout the text. Highlights of the Fifth Edition include the following:

- Chapter 1 (The Political Culture, People, and Economy of Texas) has been fully updated with the most recent available economic and demographic data. Material has also been added to help students understand the complexity of political culture in Texas and the impact of changing demographics and the coronavirus pandemic in the state.

- Chapter 2 (The Texas Constitution) has been updated and refined to include more material on the Texas Founding and the transformation of the Texas Constitution.
- Chapter 3 (Texas in the Federal System) has been revised to discuss how federalism is structured in the United States and how it has evolved in Texas over time, including recent decisions in the Texas legislature.
- Chapter 4 (Political Parties) has been updated throughout with particular attention to the influence of the Tea Party in state Republican Party politics. The chapter also highlights the role of the Latino community in changing Texas and Democratic Party competition.
- Chapter 5 (Campaigns and Elections) includes a new opener highlighting congressional races in 2020, emphasizing why students should care about what happens in elections. This chapter also includes a revamped and updated section on recent changes to electoral practices, including redistricting, voter ID litigation, early voting, straight-ticket voting, and the role of mail-in voting during the coronavirus pandemic.
- Chapter 6 (Interest Groups and Lobbying) includes many updated examples and stories to highlight the changing role of interest groups in state politics, and devotes considerable attention to recent attempts at ethics reform.
- Chapter 7 (The Legislature) begins with a new opener highlighting the changing composition of the Texas legislature after the 2018 elections. It includes updated data to reflect the 2020 elections and Dennis Bonnen's speakership.
- Chapter 8 (The Executive Branch) has been significantly rewritten to take into account all the officials in the Executive Branch and recent executive actions during the 2019 legislative session and the coronavirus pandemic. Considerable discussion is directed toward the expansion of executive power during the COVID-19 crisis.
- Chapter 9 (The Judiciary) begins with a new opener highlighting the new judges elected to the Harris County judiciary in 2018. It has been updated throughout, with new content added regarding judicial ethics and misconduct, and the role of the judiciary during the coronavirus pandemic.
- Chapter 10 (Local Government) has been significantly updated to account for changes in local governments and local officials, and the impact of COVID-19 on local governments.
- Chapter 11 (Public Finance) has been fully updated with the data made available to political leaders for the 2019 legislative session. An enhanced discussion of the challenges of both budgetary surpluses and deficits is also included, especially with regard to the coronavirus pandemic.
- Chapter 12 (Public Policy) has been fully updated. New discussions of the problems facing policy makers in education and health care have been added focusing on the importance of recent court decisions. Explicit linkages have also been made between theories of the policy-making process and the substantive policy areas.

- Chapter 13 (Crime, Corrections, and Public Safety) has been extensively revised to include more on policing in Texas—including controversies around recent instances of alleged racial profiling and police brutality in Texas and around the country—and open carry laws.
- Chapter 14 (Building the Future: Public Policies for a Changing Texas) includes new updates on policy areas like transportation, higher education, immigration, and water resources in Texas.

We believe that these changes will assist professors in teaching students the nuts and bolts of Texas government and politics, as well as the broad themes and issues that will shape the Lone Star State in the coming decades.

A Cohesive, Flexible Set of Teaching and Learning Resources

Norton's study tools, featuring InQuizitive, help students understand the reading, master key concepts from each chapter, and apply what they've learned. This ensures they arrive better prepared for lecture. Assessing students on the Texas Student Learning Objectives (SLOs) is easy with the Texas SLO test bank, InQuizitive (with questions tagged to SLOs), and a variety of activities built specifically to complement the book. And creating dynamic classroom and online presentations is easy with the variety of instructor resources written by instructors who teach this course.

- InQuizitive is Norton's award-winning, easy-to-use adaptive learning tool that personalizes the learning experience for students and helps them master—and retain—key learning objectives. It helps students think critically about recent political events and controversies.
- InQuizitive is proven to increase students' scores on exams. Norton recently conducted a within-subjects efficacy study (designed by Dustin Tingley, *Harvard University*) of InQuizitive for American government, and among the students who did not earn a perfect score on the pretest, Norton saw an average InQuizitive Effect of +17 points on the posttest.
- InQuizitive personalizes student learning paths based on their success in answering questions linked to learning objectives.
- Answer-specific feedback and the opportunity for students to keep working until they reach their desired mastery level makes InQuizitive a fun, efficient, low-stakes learning environment.
- New Learning Objectives focused on the Who Are Texans? and Texas and the Nation infographics give students more practice with analyzing the data presented in these features.
- InQuizitive skills modules like How to Read Charts and Graphs, as well as the **NEW How to Evaluate Sources** allow students to practice fundamental skills necessary to succeed in the Texas politics course.
- Each question in InQuizitive is tied to one of the Texas SLOs, and instructors can run a report that measures class performance on the SLOs.

- The InQuizitive course for *Governing Texas*, Fifth Edition, expands upon the Fourth Edition's by offering more questions that focus on the following:
  - Concepts and term comprehension
  - Concept application
  - Critical thinking (linked to text features)
- The convenience of learning management system (LMS) integration saves you time by allowing InQuizitive scores to report right to your LMS gradebook. (LMS integration with InQuizitive is provided by a Norton specialist for qualified adoptions.)
- After students complete a chapter's **InQuizitive** assignment (Cory Colby, *Lone Star College*), instructors can further assess and enhance their learning by assigning **book-specific activities right from their LMS**. Each activity is aligned with at least one Texas SLO and Core Objective. A chart of these alignments is provided for instructors. Activities include the following:
  - Simulations, with related assessments, explore the perspectives of political actors and participants in Texas politics.
  - **NEW Texas News Analysis Activities** will be available every other week. Using news articles, videos, and podcasts from a variety of Texas media sources, the Texas News Analysis Activities provide a current look at an issue in the news and helps students connect it to their everyday lives.
  - Animated Who Are Texans? and Texas and the Nation infographics examine Texas demographics and how Texas politics compare with the politics of other states.
  - **NEW "A Citizen's Guide to the Future of Texas"** short-answer questions ask students to understand and apply current debates in Texas government and politics. These questions and hundreds of other questions from the test bank can be easily customized and exported to an instructor's learning management system.
  - What Do Texans Think? features allow students to answer polling questions via learning management system survey tools.
- The **test bank** (Rachel Walker, *University of Texas, Tyler*), available within a learning management system in addition to traditional formats, is sorted by Texas SLOs and Bloom's taxonomy. It was thoroughly revised for the Fifth Edition and includes more conceptual questions.
- To round out students' experience in lecture, Norton provides high-quality teaching resources for instructors. A new **Interactive Instructor's Guide** (Emily Erdmann, *Blinn College*) offers a wealth of teaching materials, including discussion questions, suggested multimedia lecture launchers, and tips for teaching with InQuizitive or other student assessment tools. **Lecture PowerPoints** ease lecture prep by providing all of the photos, graphs, tables, and infographics from the text, as well as new What Do Texans Think? clicker questions.

About the Authors

OVER THE PAST 25 years, we have worked together on a number of books that have studied various aspects of government and political life in Texas. We come to the study of Texas politics and government from very different backgrounds.

Anthony Champagne was born in Louisiana, as the French surname suggests. His mother's family, however, were pioneer farmers and ranchers in Hopkins County, Texas. It was growing up with Louisiana and Texas connections that gave him a lifelong interest in politics. When he moved to the University of Texas at Dallas in 1979, he immediately visited the Sam Rayburn Library in Bonham. Sam Rayburn was one of Texas's most influential political figures. He was elected to the U.S. House of Representatives in 1912 and served until his death in 1961. During that time, he was chairman of one of the most influential committees of the House and was majority leader, the Speaker, and minority leader of the House. He is responsible for much of the major legislation in the New Deal and for his key role in the politics of the Truman, Eisenhower, and early Kennedy administrations. A chance meeting at the Sam Rayburn Library with H. G. Dulaney, Sam Rayburn's secretary for 10 years, led to the opportunity to do over 130 oral histories with persons associated with Sam Rayburn. As a result, Champagne was completely hooked on studying Texas politics. He was particularly interested in the transformation of the state from an overwhelmingly Democratic state to a Republican bulwark. And he was interested in how Texas changed from being a key partner with the national government in the cooperative federalism of the New Deal period to a state whose leaders are frequent critics of national power today. Political change in the state from the Sam Rayburn era to today is a key research focus of his.

Edward Harpham, in contrast, was born in Montreal to second-generation Canadian parents who immigrated to the United States soon after his birth. His family's migration over the last 100 years from Sheffield to Toronto (1919) to Delaware (1952) to Texas (1978) and the industries that employed the family (the auto service industry, chemical industry, and academia) mirror the demographic changes that have reshaped much of the population movement in the United States and Texas throughout the twentieth century. Trained as a political theorist with a deep interest in political economy, Harpham's move to Texas sparked an interest in how economic changes in the late twentieth century were changing the contours of the state's traditional political life in new and unexpected ways. At the heart of his work lies an abiding interest in the role that ideas play in shaping the growth and development of political institutions and public policies in the modern information age.

Jason Casellas was born in New Orleans and has always had an interest in state and local politics. His grandfather was a professor of Spanish literature at Our Lady of the Lake University in San Antonio. He inspired Harpham to pursue a career as a professor. After graduating from Loyola University in New Orleans, Harpham attended graduate school at Princeton University, where he earned a Ph.D. in politics. His dissertation and book examined Latino representation in state legislatures and Congress, with Texas as one of the key states in his study. Even though he was not born in Texas, he got there as fast as he could. He moved to Texas in 2005 to take an assistant professorship at the University of Texas at Austin, where he continued his immersion in all things Texas. In 2013, he moved not very far to the University of Houston, where he is now an associate professor. Most of his extended family fortuitously reside in all parts of the Houston area. He has continued to teach, research, and comment on Texas politics with a specific expertise in the growing Latino population, and how it might transform the state in the future.

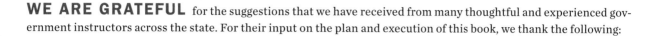

Acknowledgments

WE ARE GRATEFUL for the suggestions that we have received from many thoughtful and experienced government instructors across the state. For their input on the plan and execution of this book, we thank the following:

Jason Abbott, *Hill College*

Lee Almaguer, *Midland College*

Natasha Altema McNeely, *University of Texas–Rio Grande Valley*

Alicia Andreatta, *Angelina College*

Mark Arandia, *Dallas College–North Lake*

Ellen Baik, *University of Texas–Rio Grande Valley*

Robert Ballinger, *South Texas College*

David E. Birch, *Lone Star College–Tomball*

Robin Marshall Bittick, *Sam Houston State University*

Walt Borges, *University of North Texas at Dallas*

Patrick Brandt, *University of Texas at Dallas*

Gary Brown, *Lone Star College–Montgomery*

Lee Brown, *Blinn College*

Jonathan Buckstead, *Austin Community College*

Daniel Bunye, *South Plains College*

Jack Byham, *Texas A&M International University*

James V. Calvi, *West Texas A&M University*

Michael Campenni, *Austin Community College*

Larry Carter, *University of Texas at Arlington*

Dina Castillo, *San Jacinto College*

Max Choudary, *Northeast Lakeview College*

Mark Cichock, *University of Texas at Arlington*

Adrian Clark, *Del Mar College*

Jennifer Clark, *University of Houston*

Andrew Clayton, *McLennan Community College*

Cory Colby, *Lone Star College–Tomball*

Tracy Cook, *Central Texas College*

Cassandra Cookson, *Lee College*

Leland M. Coxe, *University of Texas at Brownsville*

Sandra K. Creech, *Temple College*

Philip Crosby, *Central Texas College*

Kevin Davis, *North Central Texas College*

Steve Davis, *Lone Star College–Kingwood*

Henry Dietz, *University of Texas at Austin*

Brian K. Dille, *Odessa College*

John Domino, *Sam Houston State University*

Douglas Dow, *University of Texas at Dallas*

Jeremy Duff, *Midwestern State University*

David Edwards, *University of Texas at Austin*

Matthew Eshbaugh-Soha, *University of North Texas*

Lou Ann Everett, *Trinity Valley Community College*

Victoria A. Farrar-Myers, *University of Texas at Arlington*

John P. Flanagan, *Weatherford College*

Ben Fraser, *San Jacinto College*

Joey Fults, *Kilgore College*

Frank J. Garrahan, *Austin Community College*

David Garrison, *Collin College*

Will Geisler, *Collin College*

Patrick Gilbert, *Lone Star College–Tomball*

Mandi Gilligan, *Dallas College–El Centro*

Shaun M. Gilligan, *Dallas College–Cedar Valley*

Terry Gilmour, *Midland College*

Randy Givens, *Blinn College*

Donna Godwin, *Trinity Valley Community College*

Elsa Gonzalez, *Texas State Technical College–Harlingen*

Larry Gonzalez, *Houston Community College–Southwest*

Christine Gottemoller, *Del Mar College*

Paul Gottemoller, *Del Mar College*

Kenneth L. Grasso, *Texas State University*

Heidi Jo Green, *Lone Star College–CyFair*

Sara Gubala, *Lamar University*

Yolanda Hake, *South Texas College*

Sabrina Hammel, *Northeast Lakeview College*

Jeff Harmon, *University of Texas at San Antonio*

Tiffany Harper, *Collin College*

Billy Hathorn, *Laredo Community College*

Ahad Hayaud-Din, *Dallas College–Brookhaven*

Virginia Haysley, *Lone Star College–Tomball*

Tom Heiting, *Odessa College*

John Hitt, *Dallas College–North Lake*

Kevin Holton, *South Texas College*

Nathan Hosey, *Dallas College–Mountain View*

Taofang Huang, *University of Texas at Austin*

Casey Hubble, *McLennan Community College*

Gregory Hudspeth, *St. Philip's College*

Glen Hunt, *Austin Community College*

Tammy Johannessen, *Austin Community College*

Catherine Johnson, *Weatherford College*

Annie Johnson-Benifield, *Lone Star College–Tomball*

Doris J. Jones, *Tarrant County College*

Joseph Jozwiak, *Texas A&M Corpus Christi*

Michael Kelley, *Central Texas College*

David Kennedy, *Lone Star College–Montgomery*

Edward Korzetz, *Lee College*

Melinda Kovacs, *Sam Houston State University*

Heidi Lange, *Houston Community College–Southwest*

Boyd Lanier, *Lamar University*

James Lantrip, *South Texas College*

Kalan Laws, *Texas Southern University*

David Lektzian, *Texas Tech University*

Raymond Lew, *Houston Community College–Central*

Frank Lewis, *Texas State Technical College–Harlingen*

Bob Little, *Dallas College–Brookhaven*

Robert Locander, *Lone Star College–North Harris*

Nicholas Long, *St. Edward's University*

George Lyon, *El Paso Community College*

Mitzi Mahoney, *Sam Houston State University*

Lynne Manganaro, *Texas A&M International University*

Sharon Manna, *Dallas College–North Lake*

Prakash Mansinghani, *Laredo College—Ft. McIntosh*

Bobby J. Martinez, *Northwest Vista College*

David McClendon, *Tyler Junior College*

Mike McConachie, *Collin College*

Larry McElvain, *South Texas College*

Elizabeth McLane, *Alvin Community College*

Lindsey McLennan, *Kilgore College*

Phil McMahan, *Collin College*

Eddie Meaders, *University of North Texas*

Gay Michele, *Dallas College–El Centro*

Tom Miles, *Texas Woman's University; University of North Texas*

Banks Miller, *University of Texas at Dallas*

Eric Miller, *Blinn College–Bryan*

Patrick Moore, *Dallas College–Richland*

Sherri Mora, *Texas State University*

Dana Morales, *Lone Star College–Montgomery*

Amy Moreland, *Sul Ross State University*

Rick Moser, *Kilgore College*

Mark R. Murray, *South Texas College*

James Myers, *Odessa College*

Sugumaran Narayanan, *Midwestern State University*

Sharon Navarro, *University of Texas at San Antonio*

Jalal Nejad, *Northwest Vista College*

Glynn Newman, *Dallas College–Eastfield*

Matthew Newton, *Lone Star College–Kingwood*

Timothy Nokken, *Texas Tech University*

James Norris, *Texas A&M International University*

John Osterman, *San Jacinto College*

Cissie Owen, *Lamar University*

William Parent, *San Jacinto College*

Hyung Park, *El Paso Community College*

David Putz, *Lone Star College–Kingwood*

Himanshi Raizada, *Lamar University*

Prudencio E. Ramirez, *San Jacinto College*

John Raulston, *Kilgore College*

Daniel Regalado, *Odessa College*

Darrial Reynolds, *South Texas College*

Donna Rhea, *Houston Community College–Northwest*

Laurie Robertstad, *Navarro College*

Mario Salas, *University of Texas at San Antonio*

Larry Salazar, *McLennan Community College*

Michael Sanchez, *San Antonio College*

Raymond Sandoval, *Dallas College–Richland*

Gilbert Schorlemmer, *Blinn College*

Mark Shomaker, *Blinn College*

Dennis Simon, *Southern Methodist University*

Shannon Sinegal, *Temple College*

Steve Slagle, *Texas State Technical College–Harlingen*

Brian William Smith, *St. Edward's University*

Michael Smith, *South Plains College*

Thomas E. Sowers II, *Lamar University*

John Speer, *Houston Community College*

Debra St. John, *Collin College*

Jeff Stanglin, *Kilgore College*

Jim Startin, *University of Texas at San Antonio*

Andrew Teas, *Houston Community College–Northwest*

Erica C. Terrell, *Dallas College–Richland*

John Theis, *Lone Star College–Kingwood*

Sean Theriault, *University of Texas at Austin*

James Thurmond, *University of Houston*

Rosalyn Tinnin, *Houston Community College–Northwest*

John Todd, *University of North Texas*

Delaina Toothman, *Texas State University*

Steven Tran, *Houston Community College*

Agostine Trevino, *Temple College*

Homer D. Trevino, *McLennan Community College*

Christopher Turner, *Laredo Community College*

Ronald W. Vardy, *University of Houston*

Linda Veazey, *Midwestern State University*

Albert Waite, *Central Texas College*

David Watson, *Sul Ross State University*

Reed Welch, *West Texas A&M University*

Clay Wiegand, *Cisco College*

Geoffrey Willbanks, *University of Texas at Tyler*

Neal Wise, *St. Edward's University*

Christy Woodward Kaupert, *San Antonio College*

Kathryn Yates, *Dallas College–Richland*

Ozum Yesiltas, *Texas A&M University–Commerce*

Michael Young, *Trinity Valley Community College*

Tyler Young, *Collin College*

Rogerio J. Zapata, *South Texas College*

We thank the following University of Texas at Dallas students for their assistance on the Fourth Edition, which reverberates in this Fifth Edition: Lisa Holmes, Josh Payne, Ali Charania, Alan Roderick, Basel Musharbash, Liza Miadzvedskaya, and Sachi Dave.

At W. W. Norton, Peter Lesser provided editorial guidance throughout the process of developing and publishing the book. Project editor Laura Dragonette, media project editor Marcus Van Harpen, and associate editor Anna Olcott kept everything organized. Copy editor Ellen Lohman helped polish the text. Production manager Stephen Sajdak made sure we ended up with a high-quality book, right on schedule. Media editor Spencer Richardson-Jones and media editorial assistant Lena Nowak-Laird worked with the authors of accompanying resources to develop useful tools for students and instructors. Our sincere thanks to all of them.

Anthony Champagne
Edward J. Harpham
Jason P. Casellas
December 2020

Governing Texas

★ ★

5TH EDITION

The role of local government took on newfound importance during the coronavirus pandemic of 2020. Texans looked to their mayors, city councilmen, county judges, and their governor for information on public health, statewide stay-at-home orders, the growing economic crisis and unemployment benefits, and the reopening of Texas businesses.

The Political Culture, People, and Economy of Texas

WHY TEXAS'S GOVERNMENT MATTERS The history of American government in the twentieth and early twenty-first centuries is one of an expanding and centralizing nation. International conflicts, economic crises, and movements for social and economic quality have tended to increase the power of the national government. By the early twenty-first century, interest in state and local politics had decreased significantly. This all changed in 2020, when a global health crisis pushed state and local governments to the forefront of American political life.

On January 7, 2020, Chinese officials identified a new coronavirus, COVID-19, and by January 20, cases were being reported in Thailand, Japan, and South Korea. The next day, the first case of COVID-19 was identified in Washington state. As the virus spread across the United States and the world, investors became concerned, and the stock market began to drop. By the end of February, the Trump administration announced travel restrictions on China and Iran and warnings on travel to Italy and South Korea. On March 11, the World Health Organization declared a pandemic. By the end of March, stay-at-home orders and suspensions of nonessential business caused national unemployment to rise at a phenomenal rate. And, most importantly, people were becoming seriously ill with the virus, and many were dying. While citizens expected the federal government to act swiftly in response to the virus, the Trump administration left many responsibilities to states and localities.

In the early stages of the pandemic in Texas, the responses of public officials were decidedly mixed. Perhaps the boldest and most courageous response to the emergency came from Travis County judge Sarah Eckhardt and Austin mayor Steve Adler. The popular international music and culture festival South by Southwest, with a combined attendance of 417,000 generating $356 million for the city's economy,[1] was scheduled for mid-March. Officials were facing pressure to cancel the event from attendees, performers, sponsors, and vendors despite the fact that at the time there were only a small number of cases in Texas. Eckhardt and Adler cancelled the event, and by early April, the wisdom of this early action by proactive local officials was clear: going ahead with South by Southwest would likely have led to a health care disaster.

Other county judges and city mayors declared health emergencies, cancelling major events, like Houston's Livestock Show and Rodeo, a huge event for the local economy. Counties throughout the state imposed shelter-in-place or stay-at-home orders throughout the spring, trying to slow the spread of the virus.

Governor Abbott, usually skeptical of policy making at the local level, deferred to those officials for several weeks rather than imposing a statewide shelter-in-place restriction. Abbott had taken other measures to deal with the virus, such as closing gyms, bars, and restaurant dining areas. He had required 14-day self-quarantines for air travelers from virus hot spots and he imposed self-quarantines on road travelers from Louisiana.[2] He had, however, been unwilling to take the major step of closing nonessential businesses in the state. Abbott argued that many parts of the state had not been affected by the virus, but it also seems that Abbott did not want to be the person responsible for harming business interests unless absolutely necessary. President Trump's extension of social distancing guidelines on March 29 gave both Abbott and other governors the political cover to take drastic statewide action.

While some officials acted swiftly and decisively, there were also some significant failures in state and local responses to the pandemic. The Texas Workforce Commission was woefully unprepared for the economic shutdown. Phone lines were jammed with applicants seeking to apply unemployment compensation. Local food banks began running low on food to distribute to people who had lost their jobs. Public schools and local libraries were closed throughout the state and many low-income students lost access to free lunches and the internet. Throughout the early spring, fear grew that if the spread of the coronavirus was not stopped, the entire public health care system might be overwhelmed.

State and local governments in Texas (and across the nation) emerged at the center of the coronavirus crisis, sometimes as a source of innovation and leadership, sometimes as an example of ineptitude and failure. The life and livelihood of every Texan were literally in the hands of these local officials.

Texas's political culture has traditionally stressed limited government, free markets, and personal responsibility in the making of public policy. In light of the coronavirus pandemic, state leaders may have to rethink their assumptions about how to govern a large, dynamic state like Texas, especially in times of crisis. Whether or not politics in Texas change after the coronavirus pandemic, one thing is clear: Texas government matters, perhaps now more than ever.

CHAPTER GOALS

- Describe the defining characteristics of political culture in Texas (pp. 5–7)

- Explain how Texas's geography has influenced its political culture (pp. 7–12)

- Trace the evolution of Texas's economy (pp. 12–21)

- Explain how the population of Texas has changed over time (pp. 21–29)

- Describe Texas's shift from a rural society to an urban one (pp. 29–35)

Texas Political Culture

Describe the defining characteristics of political culture in Texas

Political scientists have long recognized the importance of **political culture**, that is, the broadly shared values, beliefs, and attitudes about how the government should function and politics should operate. American political culture is traditionally viewed as emphasizing the values of liberty, equality, and democracy. These terms have meant a variety of things to Americans in different times and places.

States often exhibit a distinctive political culture that is the "product of their entire history."[3] Presumably the political culture of a state has an effect on how people participate in politics and how individuals and institutions interact.[4] Often, Texas is categorized as having a **"traditionalistic individualistic" political culture** in which deference is shown to political elites by the masses and hard work and self-interest are valued as core virtues in the economic life of the state.[5] Taxes are kept low, and social services are minimized. Political elites, such as business leaders, have a major voice in how the state is run. In spite of the difficulty in measuring this concept of "traditionalistic individualistic" political culture in any empirical way, it is widely regarded as useful in explaining fundamental beliefs about the state and the role of state government.

The political culture of Texas can change over time, and it is difficult to classify the political culture of a state as large and as diverse as Texas in any one category. The liberal cultural norms of urban areas such as Houston, Dallas, and Austin often stand in sharp contrast to those found in the conservative suburban (places outside a city) and exurban (places beyond the suburbs) areas of these cities. These, too, differ from the political cultures found in south Texas along the border or in the rural Panhandle of west Texas. In fact, Texas has many different political cultures or subcultures.[6]

This chapter will investigate the economic, social, and demographic changes that transformed Texas's political culture during the twentieth century and have continued to shape it in the second decade of the twenty-first century. To understand the complexity of political culture in Texas today, it is useful to consider three long-lasting patterns in Texas politics and the changes that they are undergoing: the one-party state, the idea of provincialism, and business dominance.

political culture broadly shared values, beliefs, and attitudes about how the government should function and politics should operate; American political culture emphasizes the values of liberty, equality, and democracy

"traditionalistic individualistic" political culture the belief that government should be dominated by political elites and guided by tradition, influenced by the culture of the South, combined with the belief that government should limit its role in providing order in society so that citizens can pursue their economic self-interest, influenced by the culture of the mid-Atlantic states

One-Party Dominance

For over 100 years, Texas was dominated by the Democratic Party. Winning the Democratic primary was tantamount to winning the general election. The pattern was broken in 1978 when Republican William Clements first won the governorship to the surprise of many, and again in 1986 when he won his second term. During the 1990s, substantial competition also emerged between the parties for control of the state legislature. Following redistricting in 2002 the Republicans secured a 7-vote majority in the state Senate and a 24-vote majority in the state House. They continued to expand these majorities for the next 15 years. Between 2002 and 2020 all major statewide elected offices were controlled by Republicans. (One Court of Criminal Appeals justice switched to the Democratic Party in December 2013 after being elected as a Republican, but was defeated in the November 2016 general elections.) Few observers doubt that Republicans and conservative values will continue to dominate state politics in the near future. But changes are in the wind. A powerful Republican Party controls most suburban, exurban, and rural areas and has grown increasingly conservative and divided. Moderate pro-business Republicans have begun to clash with a strident group of cultural conservatives championing such issues as traditional marriage, border security, and school choice. The Democratic Party that controls Texas cities has become a party of liberal Whites and people of color seeking to promote a progressive agenda emphasizing pro-choice, LGBTQ rights, and public education. Democrats see in the expanding young Latino population a route back into political prominence. It may be difficult to predict the full impact of these changes on the "traditionalistic individualistic" political culture in Texas. But impact it they will.

Provincialism

provincialism a narrow, limited, and self-interested view of the world often associated with rural values and notions of limited government

A second pattern that once defined Texas political culture is **provincialism**, a narrow view of the world that is often associated with rural values and belief in limited government. The result often was an intolerance of diversity and a concept of the public interest that dismissed social services and expenditures for education. Some of the more popular politicians in Texas in the past have espoused such attitudes, along with corn pone—a rural rejection of the cosmopolitanism found in large urban areas. Racism and intolerance of other cultures played important roles in defining provincialism in the traditional Texas political culture. Increasing urbanization, the growing influence of minorities, women, and LGBTQ people in politics, and the state's rising importance in the global economy have undercut some of Texas's traditional provincialism. But recent episodes of intolerance toward transgender individuals, minority religious groups, and new immigrants from Asia, the Middle East, and Latin America show a resurgence in some of the values associated with provincialism in Texas, at least in some parts of the population.

PERSONAL RESPONSIBILITY: WHAT WOULD YOU DO?

- Do you agree with the popular myth that Texas is overly provincial—that is, intolerant, narrow minded, and overly critical of government? Do you think that there has been a resurgence of provincialism in recent years?

- What are the economic and political consequences of provincialism in modern America? What do you think government and the people should do to foster more open-mindedness in Texas?

Business Dominance

A third pattern that defined Texas's political culture is its longtime dominance by business. Business groups are the major players in Texas politics, in terms of campaign contributions, organized interest groups, and lobbyists. The concerns and values of business groups continue to shape political culture in Texas today. Increasingly, business interests are not limited to state and local business concerns but include national and international business concerns as well. National and international corporations are often more cosmopolitan in their orientation than traditional Texas business interests, having to be concerned with workers and customers living outside Texas. Business influence is

Ties between business and politics have always been close in Texas. Here, Governor Greg Abbott signs a bill allowing craft breweries in Texas to sell their goods directly to customers.

being challenged by a powerful social conservative wing in the Republican Party that is less concerned with business interests than expanding gun owner rights and curtailing abortion, immigration, and LGBTQ rights.

The Land

Explain how Texas's geography has influenced its political culture

Much of Texas's history and political life has been shaped by its land. When Texas became a republic in 1836, it claimed 216,000,000 acres (approximately 350,000 square miles) of unappropriated land as its own. At its founding, Texas was land rich but money poor, having only $55.68 in its treasury. Texas was the only state other than the original 13 colonies to keep control of its public lands when it entered the Union, in 1845. Privatizing these public lands was probably the most important ongoing public policy pursued by the state in the nineteenth century. **Privatization of public property** established the property rules and regulations under which economic development would take place in the state. And although Texas turned a large portion of its public lands over to private ownership, it retained ownership of the minerals under some of this land, including land containing oil and natural gas. This would provide funding for elementary and secondary education as well as higher education for the next 160 years.

Privatization was not the only political issue surrounding land in Texas in the nineteenth century. The exact boundaries of Texas were contentious throughout the 1840s and 1850s. Following the Mexican-American War, the Treaty of Guadalupe Hidalgo in

privatization of public property the act(s) by which Texas gave public land owned by the state over to private individuals for cultivation and development

Confederate Monuments in Texas

1 Why removing Confederate monuments and symbols matters

Historical memory plays an important role in political culture. Constructing and building historical memory can bring the people of a state together. But it can also divide those very people when disagreements emerge as to what should be remembered, and how.

For over 150 years, the memory of Texas's participation in the Confederacy has been an important element of Texas's political culture. Secession drove pro-Union governor Sam Houston from office in 1861. Although there were pockets of pro-Union sentiment in the state, the large majority of (White) Texans supported secession and the Confederacy. Almost 90,000 Texans served for the Confederacy during the Civil War, and 24,000 were killed or wounded.

Following the Civil War, numerous histories about the "Lost Cause"—the idea that the fight for secession was a legendary and heroic but, ultimately, doomed cause—were written celebrating the bravery and patriotism of Texans during the war. Counties, towns, schools, and highways were named after prominent Confederates. Historical markers identifying important Civil War events were placed around the state. The state capitol itself included a portrait of the president of the Confederacy, Jefferson Davis, in the Senate Chamber. In addition, the notorious "Children of the Confederacy Creed" monument, erected in 1959 and located in a corridor of the first floor of the capitol, read: "The war between the states was not a rebellion nor was its underlying cause to sustain slavery."

2 What's the debate?

The cultural consensus about Texas and the Civil War unraveled throughout the civil rights revolution of the 1960s. African Americans, Latinos, and liberal Democrats began calling for a new awareness of Texas's historical memory, particularly about the legacy of the Civil War, Reconstruction and its aftermath, and the pre-1965 segregation era that had effectively removed African Americans from participating in state and local politics. The myth of the Confederacy and Texas's place in it distorted the past and caused harm in the present. Many of the monuments had been erected between 1900 and 1940 not just to remember the past, but to celebrate the White community that had triumphed in Texas following the Civil War.

Accompanying this new historical awareness was a demand for new monuments and paintings celebrating the lives and action of Texans who had been marginalized in the past. In the twenty-first century, new monuments were built on the capitol grounds and across Texas commemorating Texas African Americans and Tejanos.

But there were problems in Texas's historical memory that simply adding new memorials couldn't resolve. African American children were attending schools named after Confederate heroes who had died supporting the institution of slavery. People encountered statues every day that many saw as wrong historically and out of touch with the values of current Texans. After considerable commotion, the "Children of the Confederacy Creed" memorial was taken down in 2019 from the capitol corridor.

Who should have the power to remove, modify, or relocate Confederate monuments and memorials in the state? Should the state develop uniform policies governing all monuments, memorials, or building names, or should localities be empowered to build a historical memory that reflects local political sensibilities?

In 2019, the power of monument removal or modification on state property rested with the legislature, the Texas Historical Commission, and the State Preservation Board and with appropriate county, city, and school board jurisdiction locally. In 2019, the Texas Senate passed a bill that would have created new rules forbidding the removal of any monument or memorial on state and local property over 40 years old and providing for additional guidelines for assuring historical accuracy of monuments under 40 years old. The bill passed through committee in the House but died in the Calendars Committee. The murder of George Floyd by Minneapolis police in the spring of 2020 spurred protests in cities across the nation and rekindled the debate over Confederate monuments in public places in Texas cities. There is a good chance that the debate over replacing these monuments will be an important one during the 2021 legislative session.

In 2017 the city of Dallas removed a statue commemorating Confederate general Robert E. Lee.

Dedication of Confederate Symbols in Texas by Year

YEAR DEDICATED	NUMBER
Pre-1880	12
1880–99	15
1900–39	93
1940–69	29
1970–2015	7
Unknown	92

3 What do the numbers say?

Monuments celebrating the Confederacy in Texas were built at different rates over the last 100 years, reflecting changing public sentiment about race relations. The majority of monuments were erected between 1900 and 1939. This era followed the removal of African Americans from the voting rolls and the intense segregation of public facilities and schools in Texas. In contrast, between 1970 and 2015, the decades following the full implementation of civil rights and voting rights protections for all Texans, only seven were built. Since 2015, more Confederate symbols and monuments have been removed in Texas than in any other state. Between 2014 and 2018, 33 monuments, statues, or symbols were removed. Calls emerged for more removals, but these calls were countered by Republicans in the legislature of more conservative inclinations who felt that removing monuments was an attempt to deny the past or to rewrite it incorrectly. There remain approximately 200 monuments or symbols of the Confederacy found in Texas public spaces, including monuments, highways, schools, and counties.

Communicating Effectively: What Do You Think?

- Do you believe that Confederate monuments are a problem and should be removed from public places?

- Who should decide what monuments remain in their public spaces—local governments or the state? Should local governments be able to decide what monuments remain in their public spaces?

- Does it make sense to allow any statue or monument to remain in place if it is over 40 years old?

WANT TO LEARN MORE?

- Texas Historical Commission. *Texas in the Civil War: Stories of Sacrifice, Valor, and Hope.* Austin: 2013.

- Baylor University, "The Civil War and Texas: A Guide to Manuscript Collections in the Texas Collection." www.baylor.edu/lib/texas/index.php?id=870271.

- Southern Poverty Law Center. *Whose Heritage? Public Symbols of the Confederacy.* 2nd ed. February 1, 2019. www.splcenter.org/20190201/whose-heritage-public-symbols-confederacy.

1848 established the Rio Grande as the southern border of the state. After Texas threatened to use military force to reassert its land claims in the west, the Compromise of 1850 established Texas's current western borders. In exchange for $10 million in federal bonds, Texas gave up claims to 67,000,000 acres of land in what are now New Mexico, Wyoming, Colorado, Kansas, and Oklahoma. The Compromise of 1850 enabled Texas to pay off the public debts incurred during the Republic and to retain 98,000,000 acres in public lands.[7]

Today, Texas is the second-largest state, next to Alaska, and its size is perhaps the most distinctive characteristic of its geography. To understand the dynamics of political life and governance in Texas demands an appreciation of the vast spaces and topography that define the state. The longest straight-line distance across the state from north to south is 801 miles; the longest east–west distance is 773 miles. To put this into perspective, the north–south distance between New York City and Charleston, South Carolina, is 763 miles, cutting across seven different states. The east–west distance between New York City and Chicago is 821 miles, cutting across six different states.

Distances alone, though, do not tell the whole story of the state's diverse geography. There are four distinct physical regions in Texas (Figure 1.1)[8] whose distinctive features have shaped its politics.

The Gulf Coastal Plains

The Gulf Coastal Plains extend from the Louisiana border and the Gulf of Mexico, along the Rio Grande up to Del Rio, and northward to the line of the Balcones Fault and Escarpment. As one moves westward, the climate becomes increasingly dry. Forests become less frequent as post oak trees dominate the landscape until they too are replaced by the prairies and brushlands of central Texas.

The eastern portion of the Gulf Coastal Plains—so-called east Texas—is hilly and covered by forests of pine and hardwoods. Almost all of Texas's timber production takes place here, which is also the home of some of the state's most famous oilfields. To the west is the Blackland Belt. Rolling prairie soil made the Blackland Belt a prime farming area, especially for cotton, during the late nineteenth and early twentieth centuries. Today, it is the most densely populated area of the state and has a diversified economy.

The Coastal Prairies around Houston and Beaumont were the center of the state's post–World War II industrial boom, particularly in the petrochemical industry. Winter vegetable and fruit production plays a major role in the Lower Rio Grande Valley, while livestock is important in the Rio Grande Plain.

Texas's political life grew out of the Gulf Coastal Plains. The land grants offered to Americans willing to come to Texas in the first half of the nineteenth century were in this region, which was the birthplace of plantation slavery and, after the Civil War and Reconstruction, of Jim Crow segregation in the state. East Texas also saw the first oil booms in Texas in the early decades of the twentieth century. The Dallas–Fort Worth area in the northwestern part of this region was once a bastion of a small Republican Party. A union movement grew out of the industrialized areas along the coast, providing support to a liberal wing of the Democratic Party. For the most part, though, the Gulf Coastal Plains were dominated by rural conservative values, whether in the Democratic Party (from the end of Reconstruction in 1876 to the early 1990s) or the Republi-

FIGURE 1.1

The Physical Regions of Texas

SOURCE: Dallas Morning News, *Texas Almanac 2000–2001* (Dallas: *Dallas Morning News*, 1999), p. 55.

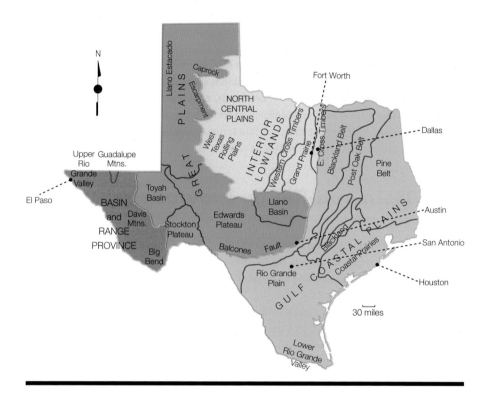

can Party (from the 1990s to today). Urbanization and suburbanization in Houston and Dallas have added new dimensions to the political life of this region. In the twenty-first century, urban areas have become increasingly Democratic, while suburban areas have become more Republican.

The Interior Lowlands

The Interior Lowlands are an extension of the lowlands that run south from Canada through the Midwest. Extending west from Fort Worth, the Interior Lowlands have a predominantly agricultural economy and rural population. In the western portion, which rises from 750 to 2,000 feet in elevation, the West Texas Rolling Plains contain much level, cultivable land, along with a large cattle-raising industry. Many of the state's largest ranches are located here. Like other rural areas of Texas today, this region is dominated by conservative politics and the Republican Party.

The Great Plains

The Great Plains define the terrain in much of western Texas. The major city on the northern plains is Amarillo. Ranching and petroleum production dominate the economy. Farther to the south, the economy centers on agriculture and cotton production, with Lubbock as the major city. Large-scale irrigation from underwater reservoirs, particularly the Ogallala Aquifer, has played a major role in the economic development of this region. The aquifer is being pumped out faster than it is being replenished, however, raising questions about the viability of basing future growth on current irrigation practices. We will return to a discussion of the problem of aquifer depletion in Chapter 14.

As in east Texas and the Interior Lowlands, conservative political values have a home in the Great Plains. Although politicians from this area have played a major role in Texas government over the last 100 years, their power has been ebbing in the face of the expanding population of urban areas elsewhere.

The Basin and Range Province

In the Basin and Range Province, one finds Texas's mountains in the Guadalupe Range along the border with New Mexico, including Guadalupe Peak (8,749 feet) and El Capitan (8,085 feet). To the southeast is Big Bend country, so named because the Rio Grande surrounds it on three sides as the river makes its southward swing. Rainfall and population are sparse in this region.

The area along the Mexican border, running from the Basin and Range Province through the southern Great Plains and Gulf Coastal Plains to the Lower Rio Grande Valley and the Gulf of Mexico, has always had a distinctive political culture, dominated by the economic and demographic connections between Texas and Mexico. The population in this region is overwhelmingly Latino. In the twenty-first century, the Border region, including the cities of El Paso, McAllen, and Brownsville, has remained a Democratic Party stronghold.

Economic Change in Texas

 Trace the evolution of Texas's economy

Over the last 150 years, three great waves of technological change defined and redefined the state's economy. The first centered on the production of cotton and cattle and their distribution by an extensive railroad system. The second grew out of the oil industry. The third and most recent is tied to the development of the high-tech digital economy.

Cotton

Cotton is one of the oldest crops grown in Texas.[9] Missions in San Antonio in the eighteenth century are reported to have produced several thousand pounds of cotton annually, which were spun and woven by local artisans. Large-scale cultivation began in 1821 with the arrival of White Americans. Political independence, state-hood, and the ongoing removal of the Native American "threat" in the years before the Civil War promoted the development of the cotton industry. By the mid-nineteenth century, production soared under the expanding institution of slavery, placing Texas eighth among the cotton-producing states in the Union. By 1880, Texas led all states in the production of cotton in most years.

Three technological breakthroughs further stimulated the cotton industry in Texas. First, in the 1870s barbed wire was introduced, enabling farmers to cordon off their lands and protect their crop from grazing cattle. Second, the building of railroads brought Texas farmers into a national market. Finally, a newly designed plow made it easier to dig up the prairie soil and significantly increased farm productivity.

Throughout the 1870s immigrants from the Deep South and Europe flooded the prairies of Texas to farm cotton. Most of these newly arrived Texans became tenant farmers or sharecroppers. Tenants lived on farms owned by others, providing their own animals, tools, and seed. They generally received two-thirds of the final value of the cotton grown on the farm, while their landlord received the other third. Sharecroppers, a subset of tenant farmers, furnished only their labor and received only half the value of the final product. By the turn of the century, almost half of the state's farmers were tenants.[10]

Two important consequences resulted from the tenant and sharecropping system. First, it condemned many rural Texans to lives of social and economic dependency. Under the notorious "crop lien" system, developed by landlords and merchants to extend credit to farmers who did not own their land, farmers profited from their work only after their debts had been paid or new loans had been made to pay off old debts. The result often was to trap farmers in a debt cycle from which they could not escape. Second, the tenant and sharecropping system helped fuel radical political discontent in rural areas, sparking both the Grange and Populist movements. These movements played a major role in defining the style of Texas politics throughout much of the late nineteenth and early twentieth centuries.

Cotton production cycled up and down during this period as farmers experienced a series of crises and opportunities, ranging from destructive boll weevils to an increased demand brought on by World War I to a collapse in prices following the war. Overall, however, the cotton culture began a decline that continued after World War II. The 1930 Census reported that 61 percent of all farmers in Texas were tenant farmers and that one-third of these were sharecroppers. These numbers fell throughout the Great Depression and beyond. By 1987 only 12 percent of all farmers were tenants.[11] In 2019, 98.6 percent of Texas farms and ranches were family farms, partnerships, or family-held corporations.[12]

During the late nineteenth century, in most years Texas produced more cotton than any other state. But although over one-third of the cotton produced in the United States still comes from Texas, the importance of the cotton industry to the state's economy has declined since the 1920s. This photo shows land and machinery used to farm cotton.

Cattle

The history of ranching and the cattle industry parallels that of cotton.[13] Their origins extend back to the late seventeenth century, when the Spanish colonial authorities brought livestock to the region to feed their missionaries, soldiers, and civilians. During

Cattle ranching is another of Texas's important industries. The most famous ranch in Texas is the King Ranch, shown here in 1950. Currently covering almost 1,300 square miles, it is larger than the state of Rhode Island.

the periods of Mexican rule and independence, ranching offered immigrants an attractive alternative to farming. In the 1830s traffic in cattle was limited to local areas, but over the next two decades cattle drives and railroads began opening new markets in the east.

Following the Civil War, the cattle industry took off, expanding throughout the state. As with cotton, the invention of barbed wire helped, closing off ranch lands used for grazing. By the end of the century, open range had given way to fenced pasturing. As a result, conflicts over land often broke out between large and small ranchers as well as between ranchers and farmers. As cattle raising became a more specialized and efficient business, conflicts also arose between ranchers and their employees. Even into the first two decades of the twenty-first century, ranching remained a cyclical industry, struggling when national and international prices collapsed and thriving during upturns in the economy.

Ranching and cotton production remain important industries in the state, although increasingly dominated by big agribusiness companies. Today, Texas normally leads the nation in both livestock and cotton production. About 37.5 percent of the cotton produced in the United States comes from Texas. In 2018 the cotton crop was over 6.8 million bales valued at over $2.4 billion, most of which was exported to China, Turkey, and Mexico. Production has fluctuated over the last decade because of the severe drought that plagued parts of the state.[14]

Today, however, neither cotton production nor ranching drives the Texas economy. The number of people making a living from agriculture has dropped significantly over the last 50 years as agribusiness has pushed out the family farm and ranch. In 1940, 23 percent of the population lived on farms and ranches. Another 17 percent were suppliers to farms and ranches or helped assemble, process, or distribute agricultural products. Currently, less than 2 percent of the population lives on farms and ranches, with an additional 15 percent providing support, processing, or distribution services to agriculture.[15]

In the early twentieth century, a new set of technological breakthroughs challenged the nineteenth-century dominance of cotton and cattle. These breakthroughs focused not on what grew on the land, but on what lay beneath it.

Oil

Spanish explorers first sighted oil oozing out of the ground in the mid-seventeenth century.[16] Because there was then no market or demand for it, however, nothing was done to develop this natural resource. Over a century later, encouraged by a growing demand for petroleum products following the Civil War, a scattering of entrepreneurs dug wells, but they proved not commercially viable. The first economically significant oil discovery in Texas was in 1894 in Navarro County near Corsicana. By 1898 the state's first oil refinery was operating at the site.

What catapulted Texas into the era of oil and gas was the discovery at Spindletop on January 10, 1901. Located three miles south of Beaumont along the Gulf Coast, the Spindletop discovery produced the state's first oil boom and encouraged large numbers of speculators and entrepreneurs to try their luck in the new business. Within three years, three major oilfields had been discovered within 150 miles of Spindletop. As a result, oil fever spread throughout Texas in the early twentieth century with major oilfields developed all across the state.

The oil and gas industry transformed Texas. A cheap new source of energy helped farms and factories operate more efficiently, reducing the need for farm workers and stimulating manufacturing. This encouraged people to escape rural unemployment by moving to cities with growing numbers of industrial jobs. In addition, cheap oil encouraged automobile production and the building of roads. The Interstate Highway System built during the 1950s and 1960s changed fundamentally the transportation patterns that had shaped the movements of people and goods in Texas. The triangle formed by I-35 from San Antonio to Dallas–Fort Worth, I-45 from Dallas–Fort Worth to Houston, and I-10 from Houston to San Antonio became the heartland of the Texas economy and the location of an increasing percentage of the state's population.

The oil and gas boom brought a new rhythm to economic life in the state. When the economy was tied to cotton and cattle, prices of products could rise and fall, bringing prosperity or gloom to local economies. But there were natural seasonal and annual cycles in these agricultural activities, and a bond existed between the land and the people and the communities that formed around them. Oil and gas, on the other hand, introduced a boom-and-bust mentality that carried over into the communities that sprang up around oil and gas discoveries. Rural areas were often unprepared for the population explosion that followed such discoveries: housing was often inadequate or nonexistent, schools quickly became overcrowded, and living conditions were poor as people sought to "make it big." Importantly, a major discovery that brought large amounts of new oil and gas to market could lead to a sudden collapse in prices. Local prosperity could then quickly turn into depression. And when particular fields were tapped out, boomtowns could quickly become ghost towns.

The oil and gas industry also transformed Texas government and its role in the state's economy. In 1890, after considerable controversy fueled by hostility to railroad companies, a constitutional amendment was passed to create a regulatory agency, the Texas Railroad Commission. In 1917 the commission's powers were extended to regulation of energy, to ensure that petroleum pipelines were "common carriers" (that they transported all producers' oil and gas on equal terms) and to promote well-spacing rules (which controlled production by limiting how closely packed together oil wells could be in a particular field). In the 1930s, in an attempt to limit price fluctuations brought on by the glut of oil on world markets and to avoid wasteful production, the commission won the authority to determine how much every well in Texas was allowed to produce. Through the late 1960s the Texas Railroad Commission was one of the most important, as well as one of the few democratically elected, regulatory bodies in the nation.

Expanding the power of state government in the economy through the Railroad Commission was only one political effect of the oil and gas industry in Texas. The industry also had an important fiscal effect. Beginning in 1905 the state collected oil production taxes, which rose from $101,403 in 1906 to almost $6 million in 1929. For the 2020–21 biennium, it was estimated that such taxes, known as severance taxes, would contribute $7.8 billion to the state budget, up 7 percent from $7.3 billion in 2018–19. Natural gas production taxes in 2020–21 added another $3 billion to the state budget, similar to the $3.1 billion in 2018–19.[17] These revenue numbers have fluctuated wildly in recent years, particularly during the months of the coronavirus pandemic. As we will see in Chapter 11 on public finance in Texas, oil and natural gas production plays an important role in the state's finances through the severance tax.

Higher education in Texas has also benefited from the oil and gas industry. What many thought was worthless land at the time had been set aside by the state constitution of 1876 and the state legislature in 1883 as the Permanent University Fund to support higher education. As luck would have it, oil was discovered in the West Texas Permian Basin in 1923 on university land. Soon, 17 wells were producing oil there, sparking a building boom at the University of Texas. In 1931 the income of the Permanent University Fund was split between the University of Texas at Austin and Texas A&M University, with the former receiving two-thirds and the latter one-third. In 1984 the income was opened up to all University of Texas and Texas A&M schools. Along with the royalties from other natural resources on university land, oil and gas royalties created one of the largest university endowments in the world. In June 2019, the Permanent University Fund held title to 2.1 million acres in 24 counties, primarily in west Texas, and the market value of the fund was calculated to be $22.6 billion.[18]

At the end of the twentieth century, the oil and natural gas industry was no longer as important to the state's economy as it once had been. Production of oil had fallen to below 400,000 barrels in 2008, despite high world prices for oil (see Figure 1.2). Beginning in 2008, new technologies such as horizontal drilling and fracking led to a new boom era of oil and gas production in Texas. Through 2017 a large share of the new production came from the Permian Basin region in west Texas, which may be the second-largest oilfield in the world. The result of this most recent boom is that oil and gas have emerged again as mainstays of the Texas economy, although it is an economy that is far more diversified than in any earlier era. With the boom came greater resources for the state's budget. But the boom also brought new demands for vast water supplies—an essential component of the new drilling and fracking technologies—and new concerns about the effects of this technology on the environment.[19]

In the spring of 2020, two events posed new challenges to the oil and natural gas industry in Texas. First, in the late spring there was glut of oil on world markets. The price of oil collapsed, driving many oil producers out of business. Second, in response to the COVID-19 pandemic, shelter-in-place policies were put into effect throughout the state and nation, driving the economy into a serious recession. The demand for oil products fell significantly in Texas and around the world. No one was sure how deep or how long this recession might be or what the long-term impact would be on the oil and natural gas industry in Texas.

FIGURE 1.2

Oil Production in Texas

Note that these data refer to onshore production in Texas.

SOURCE: Texas Railroad Commission and Macrotrends.

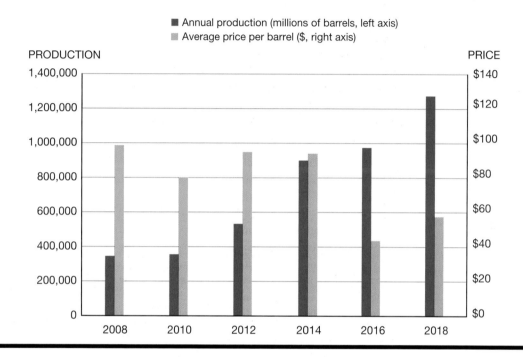

High-Tech Industry

By the last decade of the twentieth century, new industries and technologies were assuming significant roles in the state's economy. The 1990s were a period of rapid growth in the Texas economy. At the heart of this boom was a fast-growing manufacturing sector tied to high tech. In the 1990s, Texas went from seventh in the nation in total manufacturing employment to second. In 2018, 13 percent of the total output in the state came from manufacturing, and 7 percent of the workforce was employed in manufacturing.[20]

The Austin–San Marcos area is the home of the computer giant Dell and has become a production center for computer chips, personal computers, and related computer hardware with such companies as Google, Facebook, Flex, Apple, Oracle, and IBM. Seven of the area's largest employers are part of the computer or semiconductor industry. The Dallas metropolitan area, particularly north of the city, is the home of a number of important electronic and electronic-equipment companies, including Texas Instruments. Houston also has become known worldwide for its medical center and expanding research facilities in the medical field.

Houston has become an important center of medical research. Here Dr. C. Huie Lin of Houston Methodist Research Institute displays a 3-D printed medical model of a patient's heart, which is used to test surgical techniques.

NAFTA, USMCA, and the International Economy

North American Free Trade Agreement (NAFTA) trade treaty among the United States, Canada, and Mexico to lower and eliminate tariffs among the three countries

Texas's place in national and international markets has been shaped by its central location within the United States, its border with Mexico, and its sophisticated transportation infrastructure. Since the signing of the **North American Free Trade Agreement (NAFTA)** by the United States, Mexico, and Canada, international trade has grown in importance to the Texas economy. The following statistics from 2019 put the importance of Texas's international trade, particularly with Mexico and Canada, into perspective:[21]

- Texas exports totaled $330.5 billion, up from $207 billion in 2012. Texas exports were 20.1 percent of all U.S. exports.
- The North American market (Mexico and Canada) was the destination for 41.5 percent of these exports.
- Mexico was the top importer of Texas exports at almost $108.6 billion in 2019, up from almost $73 billion in 2012.
- Canada's imports from Texas totaled $28.4 billion in 2013, up from $19 billion in 2010.

The Trump administration's concerns over undocumented workers in the United States and terrorism have added a new dimension to the debate over NAFTA and global trade in Texas. Most Texas political and business leaders continue to believe that expanding trade with Mexico and other countries is a good thing. A free flow of people across the border, however, is another issue. An increasing number of people, particularly conservative Republicans, now question the benefits to Texas of a porous border. During the 2016 election campaign, Donald Trump, as well as leading Texas Republicans, portrayed the large numbers of undocumented workers in Texas as a burden upon the state's social

The signing of NAFTA in 1992 (left) created a free-trade zone in North America. Although many Texas workers were adversely affected by the availability of cheaper labor in Mexico, NAFTA appears to have had a beneficial effect on the state's economy as a whole. In 2018, President Trump (right) negotiated a new trade deal between the United States, Mexico, and Canada that addressed the concerns of many conservatives over NAFTA.

NAFTA and International Trade

The North American Free Trade Agreement (NAFTA) was an important part of national economic policy from when it was signed in the early 1990s. At both the state and national levels, Democrats and ideological liberals generally supported the agreement. But Republicans and conservatives, once strongly in favor of free-trade agreements like NAFTA, grew to oppose the agreement. In the fall of 2018 the Trump administration negotiated a new trade agreement, the United States-Mexico-Canada Agreement (USMCA) with Mexico and Canada, which mostly addressed the concerns of conservatives.

NAFTA: Mostly Good or Bad for Economy?

TEXANS				
	LIBERAL (%)	MODERATE (%)	CONSERVATIVE (%)	DON'T KNOW/ REFUSED (%)
Good	57%	52%	29%	36%
Bad	13	19	38	10
Don't know/refused	30	29	33	54
NATIONWIDE				
	BAD (%)	GOOD (%)	DON'T KNOW/NO RESPONSE (%)	
All	33%	56%	11%	
Democrat/Leaning Democrat	18	72	10	

SOURCES: (top) 2017 Texas Statewide Survey, the Texas Lyceum, April 18, 2017, 1,000 respondents; (bottom) Pew Research Center Survey, October 25–30, 2017, 1,504 respondents.

services. President Trump has claimed that undocumented immigrants have brought crime and drugs across the border with them. Moreover, fears of Islamic terrorists accompanying Mexicans and other Latin Americans seeking work in the United States have led to calls for building walls and fences that will make illegal immigration a thing of the past. Conceding that immigration is a national issue, numerous Texas politicians have called for a stricter policing of the border by state authorities. It is hard to imagine a new stricter border policy not having negative effects on the trade that has followed from NAFTA and expanding global trade (see the What Do Texans Think? feature).

NAFTA was replaced by a new trade agreement among the United States, Mexico, and Canada (USMCA) in the fall of 2018. Among the changes demanded by the Trump administration were provisions to protect American workers in the car industry from low wages, increased intellectual property protections, and an opening up of the Canadian milk market. Initial fears that free trade among the three nations might be a thing of the past were set aside as they agreed that increased trade under the proper conditions benefited all parties and that tariffs served no one.

The Military in Texas

Since Texas's annexation by the United States, its economic development has been closely tied to the establishment of military bases. As population pressures pushed westward, a series of federal forts were built to protect Texans from Native Americans, who were perceived to be alien threats to the expanding Anglo-American culture. Seizing federal forts for the Confederacy was one of the first and most important acts of the Texas government following secession. And Texas provided a major military training center during both world wars. Strong leadership in Congress from Texas politicians such as Sam Rayburn and Lyndon Johnson during the New Deal and the post–WWII years brought much-needed jobs and money into the state through the building of one military installation after another (see Figure 1.3).

It is hard to overestimate the importance of these military bases to local communities. For example, Fort Bliss is the U.S. Army's second-largest base in size, covering over 1.1 million acres in Texas and New Mexico. In partnership with the city of El Paso, Fort Bliss created the world's largest inland desalination plant, providing fresh water to the base and city. Fort Hood is today the army's largest active-duty armored post. Taking up more than 217,000 acres, Fort Hood has been responsible for deploying and redeploying over 852,000 soldiers since 2003. Fort Hood is the home to over 43,000 military and civilian personnel, making it the largest single-site employer in the state. According to a study conducted by the Texas Comptroller's Office, the base generated $21 billion for the state's economy.[22]

Today, military installations continue to be important to the economic well-being of the state. In 2019, 150,000 active-duty, reserve, and civilian personnel employed by

---

FIGURE 1.3

Major U.S. Military Bases in Texas

*In October 2010, Fort Sam Houston, Lackland Air Force Base, and Randolph Air Force Base were merged into Joint Base San Antonio under the jurisdiction of the U.S. Air Force 502nd Air Base Wing, Air Education and Training Command, in accordance with the recommendations of the federal Base Realignment and Closure Commission.

SOURCE: *Texas Almanac* online, Major Military Installations, texasalmanac.com. Taken from U.S. Department of Defense, "Base Structure Report 2018."

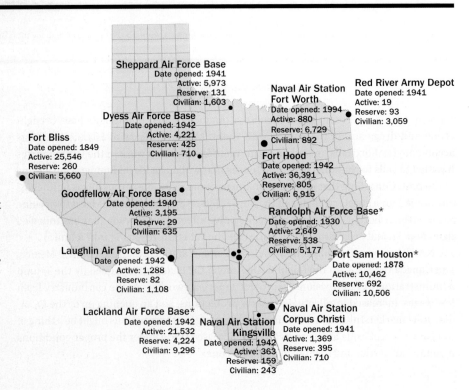

Sheppard Air Force Base
Date opened: 1941
Active: 5,973
Reserve: 131
Civilian: 1,603

Naval Air Station Fort Worth
Date opened: 1994
Active: 880
Reserve: 6,729
Civilian: 892

Red River Army Depot
Date opened: 1941
Active: 19
Reserve: 93
Civilian: 3,059

Dyess Air Force Base
Date opened: 1942
Active: 4,221
Reserve: 425
Civilian: 710

Fort Bliss
Date opened: 1849
Active: 25,546
Reserve: 260
Civilian: 5,660

Fort Hood
Date opened: 1942
Active: 36,391
Reserve: 805
Civilian: 6,915

Goodfellow Air Force Base
Date opened: 1940
Active: 3,195
Reserve: 29
Civilian: 635

Randolph Air Force Base*
Date opened: 1930
Active: 2,649
Reserve: 538
Civilian: 5,177

Laughlin Air Force Base
Date opened: 1942
Active: 1,288
Reserve: 82
Civilian: 1,108

Fort Sam Houston*
Date opened: 1878
Active: 10,462
Reserve: 692
Civilian: 10,506

Lackland Air Force Base*
Date opened: 1942
Active: 21,532
Reserve: 4,224
Civilian: 9,296

Naval Air Station Kingsville
Date opened: 1942
Active: 363
Reserve: 159
Civilian: 243

Naval Air Station Corpus Christi
Date opened: 1941
Active: 1,369
Reserve: 395
Civilian: 710

---

the U.S. military were living in Texas. The military, along with the many businesses that provide consumer services to its members, is big business in Texas. Expanding the military stimulates economic growth and employment in Texas.

Who Are Texans?

 Explain how the population of Texas has changed over time

The population of Texas has grown rapidly since 1850, when it stood at a little more than 210,000 people, more than one-quarter of whom were enslaved African Americans. According to the 1900 U.S. Census, there were only 470 American Indians still residing in Texas, the others having been driven out during the Indian Wars. Today Texas is the home to over 65,000 American Indians. Although there are three recognized reservations, most live in urban areas, including over 20,000 in Dallas–Fort Worth.[23]

Texas in 1850 was an overwhelmingly rural state. Only 4 percent of the population lived in urban areas. By 1900 the population had increased to more than 3 million, with 83 percent living in rural areas. The 1980s began as boom years for population growth, with increases running between 2.9 percent and 1.6 percent per year from 1980 through 1986. After a brief slowdown, a recovering economy spurred population growth, which surged in the 1990s and has continued to do so into the twenty-first century.

Three factors account for the population growth in Texas: natural increase as a result of the difference between births and deaths; international immigration, particularly from Mexico; and domestic immigration from other states. The makeup of the growth in population shifted in significant ways in the late twentieth and early twenty-first centuries. In 1991 almost two-thirds of population growth was accounted for by natural increase. A little more than 20 percent was a result of international immigration, while less than 14 percent resulted from domestic immigration. By 2017 natural increase accounted for only a little over half the growth, while international immigration accounted for about 17 percent and domestic immigration for about 30 percent.[24] In the early decades of the twenty-first century, Texas was being redefined not by native-born Texans but by outsiders coming to benefit from and contribute to the state's diversified economy.

In 2017, it was estimated that 400,000 new residents were added to the state, bringing the total population to 28.3 million people. The majority of this increase came from a natural increase. Of the 189,580 people who migrated into Texas during 2017, there was a sharp change in the numbers of international migrants (from outside the United States) and domestic migrants (from inside the United States). In 2016, 91,839 came to Texas from abroad while 125,703 came from other states. In 2017, the trend lines reversed: 110,417 migrated from abroad while 79,163 immigrated from other states. The immediate impact of this would mean that there would be more Latinos and fewer Whites making up the Texas population in coming years.[25]

For a deeper understanding of the roles that changing demographics have played in Texas's culture and politics, we must look closer at the major racial and ethnic groups that have constituted the population over time (see Figure 1.4).

FIGURE 1.4

The Changing Face of Texas, 1850–2018

*Latinos were not counted as a separate group until 1990 and were included in the White census count.

SOURCES: *Statistical Abstract of the United States: 1994* (Washington, D.C.: U.S. Department of Commerce, Bureau of the Census, 1994); see also *Texas Almanac 2014–15* (Denton: Texas State Historical Association, 2014), 15; 2010 U.S. Census. *Texas Almanac 2018–19* also consulted. These are available online.

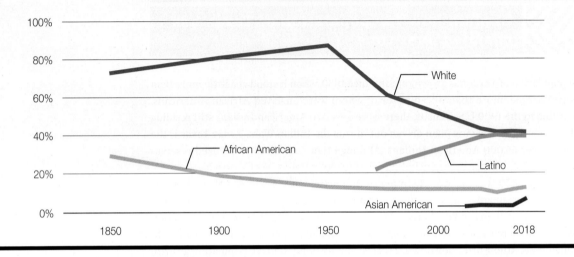

Whites

empresario Spanish word for an individual who promotes, organizes, or helps to finance a particular endeavor

For most of the nineteenth and twentieth centuries, the largest ethnic group was non-Hispanic Whites, also referred to as Whites or Anglos. Whites comprise a wide range of European ethnic groups, including English, Germans, Scots, Irish, Czechs, and European Jews. The first wave of Whites came to Texas before the break with Mexico. Encouraged by **empresarios** such as Moses Austin and his son Stephen F. Austin, who were authorized by the Spanish and later the Mexican leaders to bring people to Texas, these newcomers sought inexpensive land. And they brought along a new set of individualistic attitudes and values about democratic government that paved the way for the Texas Revolution. Following the revolution, a new surge of White immigrants came from the Deep South. Like their predecessors, they too sought cheap land, but they brought with them new cultural baggage: slavery. By the time of the American Civil War, this group had come to dominate the political culture of the state. Although most Texas farmers were not slaveowners themselves, the vast majority supported the institution as well as secession from the Union.

Defeat in the Civil War shattered temporarily the dominance of the traditional White power structure in the state. By the end of Reconstruction, however, it had reasserted itself, establishing the three patterns that defined Texas politics for the next hundred years: the one-party Democratic state, provincialism, and business dominance. Whites continued to dominate and define Texas's political culture throughout much of the twentieth century, but by the end of that century much had changed. As a percentage of the total, White population peaked at 74 percent in 1950. This percentage began to fall, reaching 41.5 percent in 2019, and will likely continue to fall (see Figure 1.5).[26]

FIGURE 1.5

White Population in Texas Counties, 2018

SOURCE: U.S. Census Bureau, "QuickFacts," www.census.gov/ (accessed 4/27/20).

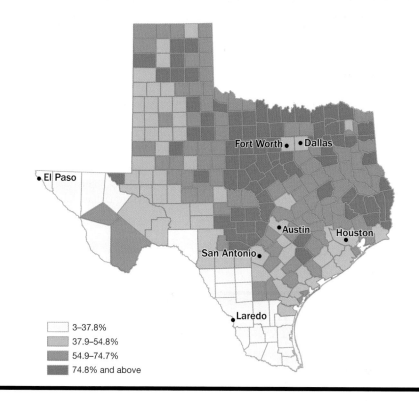

Legend:
- 3–37.8%
- 37.9–54.8%
- 54.9–74.7%
- 74.8% and above

Furthermore, numbers alone do not tell the whole story. A new wave of White immigration into Texas over the past 40 years has redefined the political culture of White Texans. No longer can one assume that a White Texan lives on a farm, holds culturally conservative values, and is firmly tied to the Democratic Party. On the contrary, he or she may not have been born in Texas and furthermore may be an urbanite with progressive values or a suburbanite who votes Republican.

Latinos

The use of *Hispanic* and *Latino* can be confusing. The terms are often used interchangeably to refer to people of Spanish descent or people from Latin America. In asking about ethnic identity and reporting the results, the U.S. Census generally uses the term *Hispanic* in its databases, but we will generally use the terms *Latino* and *Latina*.

Most Latinos and Latinas in Texas are of Mexican descent.[27] Prior to independence from Spain, this group included people born of Iberian (Spanish) parents as well as mestizos (people of mixed Spanish and Native American ancestry). In the early nineteenth century, approximately 5,000 people of Mexican descent were living in Texas.

Although their number fluctuated considerably over the years, by 1850 it was estimated that 14,000 Texans were of Mexican origin. Over the next 75 years, Texas became for many a refuge from the political and economic instability that troubled Mexico from the late 1850s to the 1920s. Subsequently, despite periodic attempts to curtail the growth of the Mexican American population in Texas, it grew from an estimated 700,000 in 1930 to 1,400,000 in 1960 and to 5.1 million in 2000. Immigration from other Latin American countries intensified as well. In 2019 there were approximately 11.5 million Latinos and Latinas residing in Texas, who constituted over 19 percent of all Latinos in the United States.[28]

Until 1900, Latinos were concentrated in south Texas, constituting a majority along the border with Mexico and in certain border counties of west Texas. During the first few decades of the twentieth century, many migrated to northwest Texas and the Panhandle to work as laborers in the newly emergent cotton economy. Labor segregation limited the opportunities available to them before World War II. After the war, however, many Latinos left agricultural work and took jobs in the rapidly growing urban areas of Texas. By the end of the century, Latinos and Latinas constituted majorities in the cities of San Antonio and El Paso and sizable minorities in Houston, Dallas, Austin, and Fort Worth (see Figure 1.6).

FIGURE 1.6

Latino Population in Texas Counties, 2018

SOURCE: U.S. Census Bureau, "QuickFacts," www.census.gov (accessed 4/27/20).

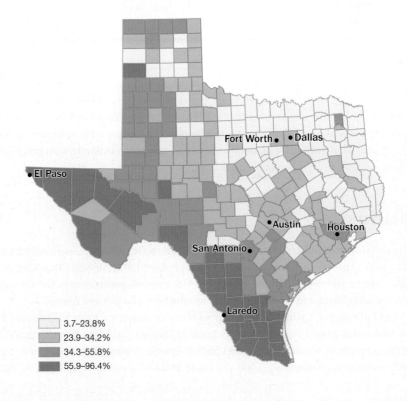

- 3.7–23.8%
- 23.9–34.2%
- 34.3–55.8%
- 55.9–96.4%

How Is the Texas Population Changing?

The face of Texas is changing rapidly and will continue to change well into the future. The figures below show projections of how the Texas population will change over the next 30 years. The state's population will continue to grow quickly, especially as the number of Latino Texans increases. Further, most of the population growth in the state will happen in metropolitan areas—Dallas–Fort Worth, Houston, San Antonio, and Austin.

Race and Total Population

= 250,000 people

	1980		2010		2050	
White	66%	White	45%	White	28%
Latino	21%	Latino	38%	Latino	54%
African American	12%	African American	12%	African American	10%
Other	1%	Other	6%	Other	8%

Total population =	14,229,191	25,145,561	41,311,221

Geography (projected population growth from the year 2010, by metropolitan area)

Area	2010	2020		2050	
San Antonio	2,142,508	2,481,286	+16%	3,445,603	+61%
El Paso	804,123	929,478	+16%	1,301,438	+62%
Dallas–Fort Worth	6,426,214	7,445,492	+16%	11,147,784	+73%
Houston	5,920,416	6,934,564	+17%	10,273,617	+74%
Brownsville	406,220	478,974	+18%	729,461	+80%
Austin	1,716,289	2,090,278	+22%	3,338,673	+95%
McAllen	774,769	953,069	+23%	1,589,783	+105%

SOURCES: Texas Demographic Center, demographics.texas.gov; (accessed 6/15/16).

NOTE: Numbers do not always add up to 100 percent due to rounding.

QUANTITATIVE REASONING

- Based on your reading of the data, how many Latinos were added to the state population between 1980 and 2010? How many Whites? How is the projected 2050 population different from the population in 2010?

- Given the metropolitan population projections for 2020 and 2050, how might the balance of political power shift over the next 40 years?

Most Latinos and Latinas in Texas are Mexican American. During the first half of the twentieth century, Mexicans immigrated to Texas to work in the emerging cotton industry. Today, Latinos play a central role in Texas politics. In 2019 former El Paso county judge Veronica Escobar became one of the first Latinas to represent Texas in the U.S. Congress.

poll tax a state tax imposed as a requirement for voting; poll taxes were rendered unconstitutional in national elections by the Twenty-Fourth Amendment, and in state elections by the U.S. Supreme Court in 1966

The political status of Latinos in Texas has changed considerably over the past hundred years. Well into the twentieth century, their ability to vote, particularly among the lower economic classes, was tightly controlled or actively discouraged by the White primary and the **poll tax**. Only after World War II were Latino politicians able to escape some of the strictures that had been imposed on them by the dominant White political culture. A more tolerant atmosphere in urban areas enabled some to assume positions of importance in local political communities. In 1956, Henry B. González became the first Mexican American elected to the Texas Senate since the nineteenth century. In the mid-1960s a political movement emerged in the La Raza Unida Party, which confronted many of the discriminatory practices that isolated Texas Latinos from the political and economic mainstream. By the 1980s, Latino political leaders were playing a growing role in state politics, and Latino voters were courted heavily by both political parties. The number of Latinos and Latinas elected to public office rose from 1,466 in 1986 to 2,521 in 2011. In 2016 the National Association of Latino Elected and Appointed Officials reported that 1 Latino served in the U.S. Senate from Texas, 5 Latinos represented Texas in the U.S. House of Representatives, 7 Latinos were in the Texas Senate, and 35 Latinos were elected to the state legislature. In addition, the association reported that 2,477 Latinos and Latinas served as local officials in Texas.[29]

African Americans

People of African descent were among the earliest explorers of Texas.[30] Most African Americans, however, entered Texas as enslaved people brought by Whites from the upper and lower South. At first, antislavery attitudes among Spanish and Mexican authorities kept the population of enslaved people down. However, independence from Mexico lifted the restrictions on slavery, creating an incentive for southerners to expand the system westward. The number of enslaved people in Texas rose from 5,000 in 1845 to 58,000 in 1850. By the Civil War, over 182,000 enslaved people lived in Texas, approximately one-third of the state's entire population.

Emancipation for African Americans living in Texas came on June 19, 1865, when federal troops landed in Galveston to take formal control of the state. On that day, the federal commander, General Granger, released General Order No. 3, which proclaimed "The people of Texas are informed that, in accordance with a proclamation from the Executive of the United States, all [enslaved people] are free. This involves an absolute equality of personal rights and rights of property between former masters and [enslaved people], and the connection heretofore existing between them becomes that between employer and hired labor." With this order, over 250,000 enslaved people in Texas were granted their freedom, two and a half years after Lincoln's Emancipation Proclamation and six months before the Thirteenth Amendment to the U.S. Constitution was ratified by the states on December 18, 1865. This day is now celebrated by African Americans across the country as "Juneteenth" and commemorates the official end of slavery in the United States. However, emancipation did not bring anything approaching equality. Between 1865 and 1868 both the state legislature and various cities passed a series of so-called Black Codes that restricted the rights of formerly enslaved people. But federal military occupation of the state and congressional reconstruction of its government opened new opportunities for formerly enslaved people, who supported the radical wing of the Republican Party. Ten African American delegates helped write the Texas Constitution of 1869, and 43 served in the state legislature between 1868 and 1900.

The end of Reconstruction and the return to power of the Democratic Party in the mid-1870s, however, reversed much of the postwar progress made by Black Texans. In 1900 over 100,000 African Americans voted in Texas elections. By 1903 the number had fallen to under 5,000, largely because of the imposition of the poll tax in 1902 and the passage of an early version of the White primary law in 1903. In 1923 the legislature explicitly banned Blacks from voting in the Democratic primary. Segregation of the races became a guiding principle of public policy, backed by the police power of the state and reinforced by lynching and race riots against African Americans. Between 1885 and 1942, 339 African Americans were lynched in Texas, with most lynchings taking place in the eastern portion of the state.[31] For all intents and purposes, African Americans had become second-class citizens, disenfranchised by the political system and marginalized by the political culture.

As in most former slave states, there was initial resistance to the civil rights movement in Texas. These signs (left) appeared in Fort Worth's Riverside section in September 1956 during a protest over a Black family's moving into a previously all-White block of homes. Today, Eric Johnson (right) serves as the mayor of Dallas.

In the 1940s and 1950s federal court decisions offered some hope of relief to African Americans living in Texas. The U.S. Supreme Court decision in *Smith v. Allwright* (1944) outlawed the White primary. *Sweatt v. Painter* (1950) guaranteed African Americans admission to graduate and professional schools at state colleges and universities. Finally, *Brown v. Board of Education* (1954) outlawed the segregation of public schools.

Political progress was much slower. The Civil Rights Act of 1964 and the Voting Rights Act of 1965 helped to open the political system in Texas to African Americans, and in 1966 a small number of African American candidates began to win political office in the state. In 1972, Barbara Jordan became the first African American woman from Texas to be elected to the U.S. House of Representatives.

The state's African American population remains concentrated in east Texas, where the plantation and sharecropping systems were dominant during the nineteenth century. Large numbers of African Americans have also migrated to Houston and Dallas, where they form sizable minorities in both central-city and suburban areas (see Figure 1.7). African American political leaders have come to play major roles in these areas as members of Congress, the state legislature, and city councils, as well as mayors of Houston and Dallas beginning in the late 1990s.

FIGURE 1.7

African American Population in Texas Counties, 2018

SOURCE: U.S. Census Bureau, "QuickFacts," www.census.gov (accessed 4/27/20).

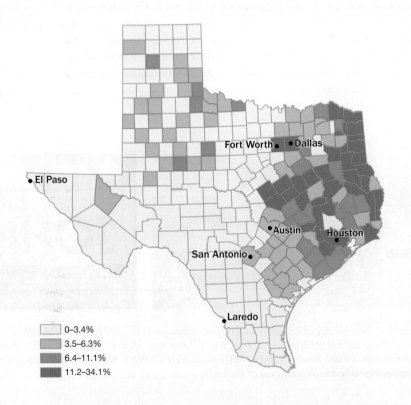

- 0–3.4%
- 3.5–6.3%
- 6.4–11.1%
- 11.2–34.1%

Asian Americans

Although considerably smaller than the groups already discussed, the Asian population has grown in Texas in recent years. It includes individuals from many countries, but particularly India, Vietnam, China, Pakistan, Korea, and Japan. In 2017 the U.S. Census Bureau estimated that over 1 million Asian Americans resided in Texas, or about 5 percent of the state's population.[32] Asian Americans tend to be concentrated in certain cities and their suburbs, particularly in west Houston and Fort Bend County, the western and northern suburbs of Dallas, Arlington, and Austin and its suburbs. Sizable pockets of Asian Americans also live along the Gulf Coast.[33]

Age

When compared with the rest of the nation, the population of Texas is younger. In 2019, 32.9 percent of the population was estimated to be under 18 years old, compared with 28.5 percent nationally. In addition, only 12.6 percent of Texans were 65 or older, compared with 16.0 percent nationally.[34] Its relatively young population presents Texas with a variety of both problems and opportunities, as we shall see in later chapters.

Poverty and Wealth

Younger populations tend to be poorer, as income and poverty statistics bear out. Even taking into account the Great Recession (2008–09), the late twentieth and early twenty-first centuries were a period of rapid economic growth in Texas. Although the state continued to lag slightly behind the nation as a whole, its per capita income rose from $17,366 in 1990 to $52,504 in 2019 (see Table 1.1), ranking Texas at 25 among the 50 states. The percentage of the population in Texas with incomes below the poverty level—as defined by the federal government—was 13.6 percent in 2019.[35]

TABLE 1.1

Per Capita Personal Income in Texas and the United States

	1990	2019
United States	$19,611	$56,663
Texas	$17,366	$52,504

SOURCE: U.S. Department of Commerce, Bureau of Economic Analysis.

Urbanization

Describe Texas's shift from a rural society to an urban one

Urbanization is the process by which people move from rural to urban areas. Suburbanization is the process by which people move out of central city areas to surrounding suburban areas. Much of Texas's history is linked to ongoing urbanization. By the twenty-first century, this process was largely complete, as 85 percent of the population now resides in urban areas (see Figure 1.8). Suburbanization, however, continues as city populations spill over into surrounding suburban areas.[36] Urbanization has transformed Texas political life.

urbanization the process by which people move from rural to urban areas

FIGURE 1.8

Urbanization in Texas, 1850–2010

SOURCE: *Statistical Abstract of the United States: 1994* (Washington, D.C.: U.S. Department of Commerce, Bureau of the Census, 1994); *Texas Almanac 2001–2002* (Dallas: Dallas Morning News, 2001); U.S. Department of Agriculture, Economic Research Service, U.S. Census Bureau, "Texas: 2010, Population and Housing Unit Courts, 2010 Census of Population and Housing" (September 2012), p. 16.

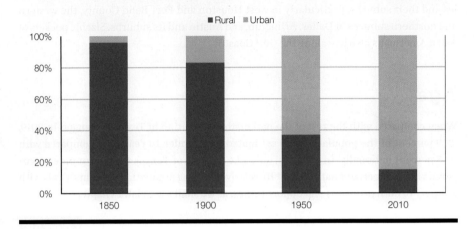

Urban Political Life

Understanding the complexity of the government and politics in Texas today demands having some sense of how Texas's major metropolitan areas compare with each other (see Table 1.2). We will look briefly at four of the most important.

Houston Houston, located in Harris County, is the largest city in Texas and—with a population of 2.3 million—the fourth-largest in the United States, behind New York, Los Angeles, and Chicago. Its metropolitan area encompasses eight counties, with an estimated population of 6.1 million in 2011. Houston grew by 7.5 percent during the first decade of the twenty-first century.

In the late nineteenth century, Houston's economic well-being depended on cotton and commerce. Railroads played an integral role in placing the city at the hub of the Texas economy, and the opening of the Houston Ship Channel further enhanced its position by helping to turn it into the second or third largest deep-water port in the United States. But it was oil that fundamentally transformed the Houston area in the twentieth century. Oil refineries opened along the ship channel and a petrochemical industry emerged, making Houston one of the leading energy centers in the world. Today, Houston continues to rank first in the nation in the manufacture of petroleum equipment.

SOCIAL RESPONSIBILITY: GET INVOLVED

- Based on the population growth, urbanization, and economic change of the last two decades, what do the next two decades hold for Texas? Which areas will grow in population, and will government be ready for that growth?

- If you wrote a letter to the governor or your state legislators, what advice would you give them to strengthen the Texas economy? Would you want them to focus on supporting rural or urban communities? Why?

TABLE 1.2

Race and Ethnic Breakdown of Texas and Its Largest Counties, 2019 (major cities indicated in parentheses)

	WHITE (%)	BLACK (%)	LATINO (%)	ASIAN (%)	MULTIPLE RACES (%)	TOTAL
Texas statewide	39.6%*	12.8%	39.6%	5.2%	2.0%	28,995,881
Harris (Houston)	29.1	19.9	43.3	7.4	1.9	4,713,325
Dallas (Dallas)	28.6	23.5	40.5	6.7	1.9	2,635,516
Tarrant (Fort Worth)	45.9	17.5	29.2	5.8	2.5	2,102,515
Bexar (San Antonio)	27.4	8.5	60.5	3.3	2.4	2,003,554
Travis (Austin)	48.8	8.9	33.9	7.3	2.6	1,273,954
Collin (Plano)	55.9	10.5	15.4	15.9	2.7	1,034,730
El Paso (El Paso)	11.6	3.9	83.0	1.3	1.5	839,238

*Columns may not add to 100 percent as a result of multiple counting. These are estimates projected from the 2019 Census.
SOURCE: U.S. Census Bureau, 2019.

By 1930, Houston had become the largest city in Texas, with a population of around 292,000 people. The population continued to expand in the next half century, assisted by a liberal state annexation policy that enabled the city to incorporate into itself many of the outlying suburban areas. Although the oil bust in the mid-1980s slowed the city's growth, that growth continued in the early twenty-first century.

Dallas–Fort Worth Metroplex The Metroplex is an economic region encompassing the cities of Dallas and Fort Worth as well as a number of their suburban cities, including Arlington (population 398,112 in 2018), Mesquite (142,816), Garland (242,507), Richardson (120,981), Irving (242,242), Plano (288,061), McKinney (191,645), Carrollton (136,879), Grand Prairie (194,614), Frisco (188,170), and Denton (138,541).[37] The major counties in the area are Dallas, Tarrant, and Collin. The Metroplex is joined together by a number of interlocking highways running north–south and east–west and by a major international airport strategically located in the national air system.

Dallas was founded as a trading post in 1841, near where two roads were to be built by the Republic.[38] By the 1850s it had become a retail center servicing surrounding rural areas, with a population that reached 3,000 by 1870. The coming of the Houston and Texas Central Railway in 1871 and the Texas and Pacific Railway in 1873 made Dallas the first rail crossroads in Texas and transformed forever its place in the state's economy. Markets now beckoned east and north, encouraging entrepreneurs and merchants to set up shop. As cotton became a major cash crop, the city's population more than tripled by 1880, to more than 10,000 people. By the turn of the twentieth century, Dallas had grown to more than 42,000 people.

Houston is a large metropolitan area with a growing minority population. Here, recent immigrants take a class on English as a second language in Fort Bend County, near Houston.

As with Houston, the oil economy changed the direction and scope of the city's economic life. With the discovery of oil in east Texas in 1930, Dallas became a major center for petroleum financing. By the end of World War II, the economy had diversified, making Dallas a minor manufacturing center in the nation. In the 1950s and 1960s technology companies such as Ling-Temco-Vought (LTV) and Texas Instruments were added to the industrial mix, transforming Dallas into the third-largest technology center in the nation. The high-tech boom of the 1990s was built from the corporate infrastructure laid down in the 1950s and 1960s. Dallas grew from 844,401 people in 1970 to 1,341,075 in 2017.

Although locked together in important ways economically, Dallas and Fort Worth are as different as night and day. Whereas Dallas looks to the east and embodies a more corporate white-collar business culture, Fort Worth looks to the west. Fort Worth originated as an army post in 1849,[39] but by 1853 the military had abandoned it as new forts were built to the west. Although settlers replaced the soldiers, population growth was slow through the early 1870s. The spark that set off the town's prosperity was the rise of the cattle industry. Because Fort Worth was a convenient place for cowboys to rest on their cattle drives from southern Texas to Kansas, cattle buyers established headquarters in the city. By 1900, Fort Worth was served by eight railroad companies, most of them transporting cattle and related products to national markets.

The two world wars encouraged further economic development in Fort Worth. Over 100,000 troops were trained at Camp Bowie during World War I. World War II brought an important air force base and, along with it, the aviation industry. The Consolidated Vultee Aircraft Corporation, which was later bought by General Dynamics, became the largest manufacturer in the city. Between 1900 and 1950, Fort Worth's population grew from 26,668 to 277,047. By 2017 the population was 874,168. The overall metropolitan area of Dallas–Fort Worth included 6.954 million people in 2014.

How Does Texas's Population Compare to Other Major States'?

Texas is more diverse than many states in the country, which has important implications for the future of the state's politics. Also, the Texas population has increased dramatically, while some states are not growing as fast. In fact many states in the Midwest such as Ohio and Pennsylvania have seen population declines in recent years.

Racial Diversity

Texas		California		Florida		New York		Ohio	
White	44%	White	39%	White	56%	White	57%	White	80%
Black	13%	Black	7%	Black	17%	Black	18%	Black	13%
Latino	39%	Latino	39%	Latino	24%	Latino	19%	Latino	4%
Asian	4%	Asian	14%	Asian	3%	Asian	9%	Asian	2%

Percent Change in Population, 2000–10

9.7%: overall U.S. change

Gain

- 50% +
- 25.1 to 49%
- 9.7 to 25%
- 0 to 9.6%

- -10 to -0.1%
- -50 to -10.1%

Loss

- Data not available

CRITICAL THINKING

- In what ways are California and Texas similar in terms of demographic makeup? How are they different?

- In what ways will Texas politics change in the future based on its racial and ethnic makeup?

SOURCES: U.S. Census Bureau, QuickFacts 2014, www.census.gov; demography.cpc.unc.edu.

NOTE: Numbers do not always add up to 100 percent. Black Latinos may be counted in both categories

San Antonio San Antonio, in Bexar County, grew out of the Spanish presidio San Antonio de Béxar, which was founded in 1718.[40] In 1773 it became the capital of Spanish Texas, and by the Civil War, it was the largest city in Texas.

Following the war, San Antonio continued to grow rapidly, stimulated by the building of the San Antonio Railroad in 1877. By 1880 the population was more than 20,000, mostly White Americans from southern states. By 1920 it had reached 161,000. Mexican immigration increased significantly following the Mexican Revolution of 1910 and the building of a city infrastructure that provided paved roads, utilities, water, telephones, and hospitals. By midcentury, San Antonio had become a unique blend of Latino, German, and southern Anglo American cultures.

Today, San Antonio is Texas's second-largest city (third if you consider Dallas and Fort Worth together). The population of the city was estimated to be 1,532,233 in 2018. San Antonio's population has become increasingly Latino. In San Antonio in 2018, approximately 64.2 percent of the people were Latino, 24.8 percent were White, and 6.9 percent were African American.[41]

Unlike Houston or Dallas, San Antonio lacks high-paying manufacturing jobs, and average metropolitan income is lower than in Houston and Dallas. The economy rests on four legs: national military bases, educational institutions, tourism, and a large medical research complex.

Austin Located in central Texas in Travis County on the eastern edge of the Hill Country, Austin had an estimated population of 964,254 in 2018. Per capita income was $40,391—33 percent higher than the state average. Median household income was $67,462—13 percent higher than the state amount. Almost half of adults living in Austin had a bachelor's degree or higher.[42] Along with Round Rock and San Marcos, Austin is part of the 31st largest metropolitan area in the country and 4th largest in the state (behind Houston, Dallas–Fort Worth, and San Antonio).

Austin's economy rests on three solid foundations. First, as the state capital, Austin is the hub of governmental business in the state. Although the legislature only meets for 140 days every two years, state agencies are a year-round activity as are the lobbying activities of special interests. Second, Austin is the location of the University of Texas at Austin, the flagship institution of the University of Texas system and home to more than 50,000 students and faculty. In 2012–13 it was estimated that the school generated $8.8 billion in Texas business activity.[43] Third, Austin has a thriving high-tech industry. Grown from seeds planted by governmental and university activity, Austin's computer and electronics businesses are the core of one of the most vibrant regional economies in the country. Through them, the city continues to attract people and businesses at a remarkable pace.

Having settled its status as the government hub in the state in 1846, Austin began to gradually grow, reaching a population of 3,546 in 1860. The emergence of the Houston and Texas Central Railroad in 1871 linked Austin to the eastern part of the state and turned it into a trading center in central Texas. By 1880 the city's population had grown to 11,013.

Compared with that of Dallas–Fort Worth or Houston, Austin's economic base was narrow for the early decades of the twentieth century. Except for the benefits gleaned from the university's endowment, Austin missed out on much of the economic development flowing from the rise of oil and gas production. The population of the city was 22,258 in 1900 and 132,459 in 1950.[44] Austin's population began to surge in the second

Urban areas like Austin, Houston, and Dallas have become bastions of liberal politics. Here, demonstrators rally to protest the separation of families at the U.S.-Mexico border outside the Texas capitol building in Austin.

half of the twentieth century, growing to 656,962 in 2000. Driving this increase was a rapidly diversifying economy led by the high-tech sector. IBM located to Austin in 1969 and was soon followed by Texas Instruments and Motorola. Other high-tech firms followed in the 1980s, including Dell Computers and Sematech. By the 1990s there were estimated to be 400 high-technology businesses located in Austin.[45] In 2017, Austin's 100 largest digital tech companies employed almost 60,000 people. Amazon and Facebook have increased their presence in the city with plans to expand.[46]

★ ★

Political Culture and the Future of Texas

WE BEGAN this chapter by highlighting the importance of the coronavirus outbreak in Texas and the nation in early 2020. What began as a public health crisis soon morphed into an economic crisis of cataclysmic proportions. As shelter-in-place policies were implemented by local governments across the state to protect the further spread of the virus, economic activity collapsed, spot market oil prices (that is, the price of oil to be delivered within two days of sale) for west Texas crude fell below $0.00, unemployment rates escalated rapidly, and tax revenues began to decline sharply. Partisan controversies broke out among state and local officials regarding how best to balance public health against getting the economy going again. The stakes were high, not just in public health or private wealth but in determining which party might control the levers of power in the state for the coming decade.

The public health crisis brought on by the coronavirus is likely a short- or medium-term problem that will be resolved when an effective vaccine is developed along with treatments that can manage or even cure infections. Over the next few years, this public health problem could prove damaging to the state's economy, and popular frustration with elected officials could grow if state and local governments are unable to alleviate the suffering brought on by the pandemic. But economic recovery will take place. The political future of Texas will be created not by COVID-19, but by long-term demographic and economic changes in the state.

Three great technological revolutions have in turn reshaped the economic life of the state over the last 150 years. Accompanying and fueling these economic transformations have been ongoing demographic changes, which have redefined who the "typical" Texan is and where this person lives. No longer can it be said that a "typical" Texan is simply an extension of White American culture rooted in southern tradition. No longer does this person reside in a small town, living life close to the land much as his or her ancestors did. Like the economy, the people of Texas have become diversified. Increasing numbers of Latinos from Mexico and farther south and Whites from other parts of the United States as well as immigrants from Asia have created a new melting pot of cultures and concerns throughout the state, especially in the big metropolitan areas.

The future of Texas likely will continue to be defined by economic and demographic change. For almost 40 years, a diversifying economy fueled by international trade and a rejuvenated oil and natural gas industry has integrated the state more closely into a burgeoning world economy. President Trump's call to reevaluate international trade agreements, particularly NAFTA, and to rethink our trade relationship with China may negatively affect Texas's connection to the world economy. However, it is hard to imagine Texas in the twenty-first century without a thriving export-driven economy. Similarly, calls to build a wall to keep out undocumented workers may slow down the flow of Latinos into Texas, but it is hard to imagine Texas without a growing population fueled by loose immigration rules. Trump's initiatives aside, Latinos will come to play an increasingly important role in the economic and political life of the state as the Latino population ages and works its way through the educational system. Over the next 30 years, both political parties will have to adjust their expectations and ideologies to meet the demands of an electorate increasingly dominated by young Latino voters.

Use 🐰 INQUIZITIVE to help you study and master this material.

Texas Political Culture

- **Describe the defining characteristics of political culture in Texas (pp. 5–7)**

Texas political culture can best be characterized as individualistic and traditional. Texans have great pride in their state and have adopted a famous phrase, "Don't mess with Texas," for those external forces wishing to change the state's way of doing things. Texas is a low-tax state with distrust for large government programs. Business plays a major role in defining the political culture of the state.

Key Terms
political culture (p. 5)
"traditionalistic individualistic" political culture (p. 5)
provincialism (p. 6)

Practice Quiz

1. In terms of area, how does Texas rank among the 50 states?
   a) first
   b) second
   c) third
   d) fifth
   e) seventh

2. *Provincialism* refers to
   a) a narrow view of the world.
   b) a progressive view of the value of diversity.
   c) a pro-business political culture.
   d) an urban society.
   e) a group of counties.

The Land

- **Explain how Texas's geography has influenced its political culture (pp. 7–12)**

Because of Texas's immense size, the state's topography is diverse, with east Texas's flatlands, west Texas's arid climate, and central Texas's Hill Country all representing diverse ecosystems and land patterns.

Key Term
privatization of public property (p. 7)

Practice Quiz

3. Which of Texas's physical regions is characterized by the presence of many of the state's largest ranches?
   a) Gulf Coastal Plains
   b) Great Plains
   c) Interior Lowlands
   d) Basin and Range Province
   e) Rio Grande Valley

4. Which of Texas's physical regions is found in the westernmost part of Texas?
   a) Gulf Coastal Plains
   b) Great Plains
   c) Interior Lowlands
   d) Basin and Range Province
   e) Pine Belt

Economic Change in Texas

- **Trace the evolution of Texas's economy (pp. 12–21)**

The Texas economy has undergone a series of technological transformations over the past 150 years. Once, the Texas economy was grounded in cotton and ranching. Oil production came to play an important role in the twentieth century. Today, high technology and international trade play important roles in the state's economy. Texas appears to have weathered the Great Recession better than most other states.

Key Term

North American Free Trade Agreement (NAFTA) (p. 18)

Practice Quiz

5. Which of the following statements is true?
- **a)** Cotton no longer plays an important role in the Texas economy.
- **b)** Less than 2 percent of the population in Texas live on farms and ranches.
- **c)** The Texas Railroad Commission regulates the internet.
- **d)** Higher education has not benefited from the oil and gas industry.
- **e)** All are true.

6. Which industry controlled the politics and economy of Texas for most of the twentieth century?
- **a)** cotton
- **b)** cattle
- **c)** railroad
- **d)** oil
- **e)** technology

7. Which of the following statements is true?
- **a)** Oil production in Texas is less today than it was 10 years ago.
- **b)** Oil production no longer plays an important role in the state's economy.
- **c)** Oil has been almost totally drained from Texas oil fields.
- **d)** The border region has become a major producer of oil in the early twenty-first century.
- **e)** Fracking and horizontal drilling have reinvigorated Texas's oil industry.

8. Unlike earlier eras, the Texas economy of the twenty-first century features
- **a)** computers, electronics, and other high-tech products.
- **b)** transportation, oil and natural gas, and banking.
- **c)** insurance, construction, and banking.
- **d)** ranching, oil, and tourism.
- **e)** education, the military, and agriculture.

9. NAFTA refers to
- **a)** an oil company.
- **b)** an independent regulatory commission.
- **c)** an interstate road network.
- **d)** an interest group.
- **e)** an international trade agreement.

10. U.S. military bases in Texas
- **a)** have only a small impact on the Texas economy.
- **b)** are no longer important in Texas.
- **c)** are important features to many local economies across the state.
- **d)** generate less than $1 billion in the state economy.
- **e)** promote unemployment in the state.

Who Are Texans?

* **Explain how the population of Texas has changed over time (pp. 21–29)**

Texas demography has changed over the last century. Once dominated by Whites, Texas now has a large Latino population that, when combined with the African American population and other minorities, makes Texas a majority-minority state. Despite considerable overall wealth in Texas, Texans tend to be younger and poorer than the average American.

Key Terms
empresario (p. 22)
poll tax (p. 26)

Practice Quiz
11. Which of the following accounts for most of Texas's population growth today?
   a) immigration
   b) natural increases as a result of the difference between births and deaths
   c) domestic immigration
   d) NAFTA
   e) movement from rural to urban areas

12. Which of the following is not true?
   a) Latinos are increasing as a percentage of the population in Dallas.
   b) More African Americans live in east Texas than in west Texas.
   c) San Antonio has a larger White population than Latino.
   d) Houston's largest minority population is Latino.
   e) The Latino population in Texas has grown rapidly in recent decades.

Urbanization

* **Describe Texas's shift from a rural society to an urban one (pp. 29–35)**

Initially a rural state, Texas has urbanized, with Houston, San Antonio, Dallas–Fort Worth, and Austin representing the largest metropolitan areas in the state. This process of urbanization has changed the state's economy from an agricultural powerhouse to a high-tech and innovative economy.

Key Term
urbanization (p. 29)

Practice Quiz
13. *Urbanization* refers to a process in which
   a) people move from rural to urban areas.
   b) people from the north and west move to Texas.
   c) people move out of urban centers to the suburbs.
   d) people move out of urban centers to rural areas.
   e) minorities assume political control of a city.

14. The four major metropolitan areas in Texas are
   a) Houston, Dallas–Fort Worth, San Antonio, and Austin.
   b) Houston, Dallas–Fort Worth, San Antonio, and El Paso.
   c) El Paso, Houston, Lubbock, and Austin.
   d) San Antonio, El Paso, Houston, and Brownsville-Harlingen-McAllen.
   e) San Antonio, El Paso, Dallas–Fort Worth, and Brownsville-Harlingen-McAllen.

AQUÍ Vote HERE

The Texas Constitution has become a long and detailed document. Texans vote on constitutional amendments every two years. Voter turnout is usually very low, and most amendments pass.

The Texas Constitution

WHY THE TEXAS CONSTITUTION MATTERS The Texas Constitution is the legal framework within which government works in Texas, just as the U.S. Constitution is the legal framework for our national institutions. Perhaps even more than the U.S. Constitution, however, the Texas Constitution has an immediate and enormous impact on citizens' everyday lives. Its Article 1 guarantees to Texans rights that go far beyond those guaranteed to Americans in the U.S. Constitution, addressing numerous specific issues related to Texans' private lives. For example, Article 1, Section 7, stipulates that no money will be appropriated or drawn from the treasury that benefits a sect, religious society, or religious seminary. Section 7 also clearly lists the conditions that the state must meet if it wants to take, damage, or destroy the private property of individuals. Section 30 provides a detailed list of the rights of crime victims, including the rights to be treated with dignity and privacy in the criminal process and to confer with representatives of the prosecutor's office. Section 31—now rendered inoperable by a U.S. Supreme Court decision in 2015—defines a marriage as consisting "only of the union of one man and one woman." Section 33 guarantees Texans a right to access and use public beaches. One could argue that each of these issues is more a matter of policy preference than of constitutional right. By being placed in the Texas Constitution, however, particular policy positions take on a protected status, because it is more difficult to change a right enshrined in a constitution than a policy backed only by ordinary, statutory law.

Given the length and detail of the Texas Constitution, the constitutional amendment process assumes a central role in the state's political process. There are some important differences between processes for amending the Texas Constitution and the U.S. Constitution. For example, voter approval is necessary for proposed amendments to the Texas Constitution to take effect. After passage during a regular or special session, the Texas legislature presents to the voters a list of proposed amendments for their approval. Whereas the U.S. Constitution has been amended 27 times since it was adopted in 1789, as of 2019 the Texas Constitution has been amended 507 times. The number of proposed amendments and their frequency of approval have varied over the years, although recently most have been approved.

Occasionally, amendments deal with structural issues of government. In 1979, for example, an amendment gave the governor limited authority to remove appointed statewide officials. A 1995 amendment abolished the office of the state treasurer, placing its duties in the Texas Comptroller's Office. In such cases, amendments to the Texas Constitution function like those to the U.S. Constitution. There are many more ➤➤

amendments, however, that deal with technical problems in the Texas constitution, reflecting efforts to clean up specific language that has become out-of-date. In 2007, for example, an amendment passed that eliminated the county Office of the Inspector of Hides and Animals.[1] Although the office had been effectively abolished with the passage of a new Agricultural Code in statutory law,[2] the constitution needed to be brought up to date with the law.

Other amendments to the Texas Constitution grapple with pressing policy matters. This gives voters the chance to approve certain policy initiatives directly, something that is inconceivable at the national level. In 2009 amendments were passed protecting certain private property from being taken by the state through eminent domain. Among the amendments passed in 2013 and 2015 were ones creating funds to help finance important water and transportation projects. Without the passage of these amendments, effective public policy in a variety of areas central to the future of Texas would have ground to a halt. In 2019, Texas voters approved a constitutional amendment that prohibited an income tax on individuals in Texas (see this chapter's Citizen's Guide). Far more than the U.S. Constitution, the Texas Constitution is involved with the nuts and bolts of public policy and must be taken into account frequently by Texas legislators seeking to address problems in new and innovative ways.

CHAPTER GOALS

- Identify the main functions of state constitutions (pp. 43–45)
- Describe the seven Texas constitutions and their role in Texas political life (pp. 45–59)
- Analyze the major provisions of the Texas Constitution today (pp. 59–69)
- Describe modern efforts to change the Texas Constitution (pp. 69–73)

The Role of a State Constitution

State **constitutions** perform a number of important functions. (1) They justify and make legitimate state political institutions by clearly explaining the source of their power and authority. (2) State constitutions also delegate power, explaining which political powers are granted to particular institutions and individuals and how those powers are to be used. (3) They are responsible for the establishment of local governments, including counties, municipalities, and special-purpose districts. (4) They prevent the concentration of political power by providing mechanisms that check and balance the powers of one political institution or individual officeholder against another. (5) They define the limits of political power. Through declarations of rights, state constitutions explicitly forbid the intrusion of certain kinds of governmental activities into the lives of individuals.

Since its first constitution, the idea of constitutional government in Texas has been heavily indebted to the larger American experience. Five ideas unite the U.S. and Texas constitutional experiences. First, political power in both the United States and Texas is ultimately derived from the people. The Preamble to the U.S. Constitution begins with the clear assertion that it is "We the People of the United States" who ordain and establish the Constitution. Echoing these sentiments, the Preamble to the Texas Constitution proclaims that "the people of the State of Texas, do ordain and establish this Constitution." In both documents, political power is something that is artificially created through the constitution by a conscious act of the people.

Second, the U.S. and Texas constitutions feature **separation of powers**. The legislative, executive, and judicial branches of government have their own unique powers derived from the people. Each branch has its corresponding duties and obligations.

Third, the U.S. and Texas constitutions structure political power in such a way that the power of one branch is checked and balanced by the powers of the other two branches. The idea of **checks and balances** reflects a common concern among the framers of the U.S. Constitution and the authors of Texas's various constitutions that the intent of writing a constitution was not just to establish effective governing institutions but also to ensure that these institutions would not tyrannize the very people who established them. In this theory of checks and balances, both the U.S. and Texas constitutions embody the ideas articulated by James Madison in *The Federalist Papers*, nos. 10, 47, and 51. There, Madison argued that one of the most effective ways of preventing **tyranny** (the concentration of power in one branch of government) was to pit the self-interest of officeholders in one branch against that of officeholders in the other branches. Good intentions alone would not guarantee liberty in either the United States or Texas. Rather, constitutional means combined with self-interest would ensure that officeholders had an interest in preserving a balance among the different branches of government.

The concern for preventing the emergence of tyranny is also found in a fourth idea that underlies the U.S. and Texas constitutions: the idea of individual rights. Government is explicitly forbidden from violating a number of particular rights that the

constitution the legal structure of a government, which establishes its power and authority as well as the limits on that power

separation of powers the division of governmental power among several institutions that must cooperate in decision making

checks and balances the constitutional idea that overlapping power is given to different branches of government to limit the concentration of power in any one branch

tyranny according to James Madison, the concentration of power in any one branch of government

people possess. Some rights, such as freedom of speech, freedom of assembly, and freedom of religion, are guaranteed by both the U.S. Constitution and the Texas Constitution. Interestingly, the Texas Constitution also guarantees other rights not found in the U.S. Constitution, such as certain victims' rights and the right to have an "efficient system of public free schools."

federalism a system of government in which power is divided, by a constitution, between a central government and regional governments

The final idea embodied in both the U.S. and Texas constitutions is that of **federalism**, the division of government into a central government and a group of regional governments (see Chapter 3). Both kinds of government exercise direct authority over individual citizens, of both the nation or state and a particular region within it. The Tenth Amendment to the U.S. Constitution also recognizes the importance of the idea of federalism to the American political system. It reads, "The powers not delegated to the United States by the Constitution, nor prohibited by it to the States, are reserved to the States respectively, or to the people." According to the U.S. Constitution, enormous reservoirs of political power are thus derived from the people who reside in the states themselves.

supremacy clause Article VI of the U.S. Constitution, which states that the Constitution and laws passed by the national government and all treaties are the supreme law of the land and superior to all laws adopted by any state or any subdivision

Despite the similarities, some important differences distinguish the constitutional experience of Texas from that of the United States. Most important is the subordinate role that Texas has in the federal system. Article VI of the U.S. Constitution contains the **supremacy clause**, declaring the Constitution and the laws of the United States to be "the supreme Law of the Land." The supremacy clause requires all judges in every state to be bound by the U.S. Constitution, notwithstanding the laws or constitution of their particular state. In matters of disagreement, the U.S. Constitution thus takes precedence over the Texas Constitution.

One of the major issues of the Civil War was how the federal system was to be understood. Was the United States a confederation of autonomous sovereign states that were ultimately independent political entities capable of secession (much like the current European Union)? Or was it a perpetual union of states that were ultimately in a subordinate relationship to the central government? The results of the war and the ratification of the Fourteenth Amendment to the U.S. Constitution in 1868 ultimately resolved this debate in terms of the latter idea, an outcome that would have profound implications for constitutional government in Texas. A series of court cases determined that because of the language of the Fourteenth Amendment, much of the Bill of Rights to the U.S. Constitution applies to the states, a finding that became a dominant theme of constitutional law in the twentieth and twenty-first centuries. The Fourteenth Amendment thus effectively placed restrictions on Texas government and public policy that went far beyond those laid out in Texas's own constitution.

necessary and proper clause Article I, Section 8, of the U.S. Constitution; it provides Congress with the authority to make all laws "necessary and proper" to carry out its powers

Another major difference between the U.S. and Texas constitutions lies in the **necessary and proper clause** of Article I, Section 8, of the U.S. Constitution. Section 8 begins by listing in detail the specific powers granted to Congress by the Constitution. The Founders apparently wanted to limit the scope of national government activities. But Section 8 concludes by granting Congress the power "necessary and proper" to accomplish its constitutional tasks. The net effect of this clause was to provide a constitutional basis for an enormous expansion of central government activities over the next 200-plus years.

Drafters of Texas's various constitutions generally have been unwilling to grant such an enormous loophole in the exercise of governmental power. Although granting state government the power to accomplish certain tasks, Texas constitutions have generally denied officeholders broad grants of discretionary power to accomplish their goals.

Finally, Texas's power to establish local governments has no analogous feature in the U.S. Constitution. States such as Texas are sovereign entities unto themselves, deriving power directly from the people in the state through the state constitution. Texas is not created by the U.S. Constitution, although it is subject to it, as we shall see in Chapter 3. Local governments within Texas, on the other hand, derive their authority directly from the state constitution and the people of Texas as a whole, not from the people in the locality. Self-government for local governing bodies in Texas ultimately means self-government to the extent allowed by the Texas legislature under the state constitution.

The Texas Constitutions: 1836–1876

 Describe the seven Texas constitutions and their role in Texas political life

Many myths surround the origins of Texas as a state. Some trumpet its unique origins as an independent republic that fought to attain its own independence from an oppressive regime much like the United States did. Others suggest that Texas has a certain privileged position as a state given the way that it entered the Union or that it reserved for itself a right to break up into separate states. To separate the myth from the reality, it is necessary to understand how the constitutional regime operating in Texas today is the product of a long course of political and legal development in the state.

Texas has operated under seven constitutions: one when it was part of a state under the Mexican political regime prior to independence, one as an independent republic, one as a member of the Confederacy, and four as a state within the United States. Each was shaped by historical developments of its time and, following the first constitution, attempted to address the shortcomings of each previous constitution. To understand constitutional government in Texas today demands a clear understanding of the founding of Texas out of its war of independence with Mexico and the specific historical circumstances that gave rise to each constitution.

The Texas Founding

Political scientists refer to "the Founding" as that period in American history when the foundational principles of American political life were established, roughly the period of time from the Declaration of Independence in 1776 through the ratification of the Constitution (1790) and the Bill of Rights (1791). Texas too has a founding period and on the face of it, Texas's road to independence appears to mirror that of the United States. Like the United States, Texas had a period of discontent with the governing regime that culminated in a Declaration of Independence. However, Texas's march toward independence was much longer and more convoluted than the United States'.

The Constitution of Coahuila y Tejas, 1827 Texas was part of New

Spain until the Mexican War of Independence,[3] which grew out of a series of revolts against Spanish rule during the Napoleonic Wars. Burdened by debts brought on by a crippling war with France, Spain sought to extract more wealth from its colonies. The forced abdication of King Ferdinand VII in favor of Napoleon's brother Joseph in 1808 and an intensifying economic crisis in New Spain in 1809 and 1810 undermined the legitimacy of Spanish rule. Revolts broke out in Guanajuato and spread throughout Mexico, including its Texas province. Although these rebellions were initially put down by royalist forces loyal to Spain, by 1820 additional local revolts and guerrilla actions had helped to further weaken Spanish rule. On August 24, 1821, Mexico was formally granted independence by Spain.

The first federal constitution that Texas operated under was thus the Mexican Constitution of 1824. At the national level, it provided for two houses of Congress, a president and vice president elected for four-year terms by the legislative bodies of the states, and a supreme court. Although the Mexican Constitution mandated separate legislative, executive, and judicial branches, no attempt was made to define the scope of states' rights within the Mexican confederation, and local affairs remained independent of the central government. This constitution embodied many of the ideas found in the U.S. Constitution, but there was one important difference: Catholicism was established as the state religion and was supported financially by the state.[4]

Under the Mexican Constitution, the state of Coahuila and the sparsely populated province of Texas were combined into the state of Coahuila y Tejas, with Saltillo, in Coahuila, as the capital. More than two years were spent drafting a constitution for the new state. It was finally published on March 11, 1827.

The state of Coahuila y Tejas was formally divided into three districts, with Texas composing the District of Bexar. Legislative power for the state was placed in a **unicameral** legislature composed of 12 deputies elected by the people, including 2 representing Bexar. Along with wide-ranging legislative powers, the legislature was also empowered to elect state officials when no majority emerged from the popular vote, to serve as a grand jury in political and military matters, and to regulate the state's army and militia. Executive power was vested in a governor and a vice governor, each elected by the people for a four-year term. Judicial power was placed in state courts. The Constitution of 1827 formally guaranteed citizens the right to liberty, security, property, and equality. Its language also supported efforts to curtail the spread of slavery, an institution of vital importance to planters who were immigrating from the American South. The legislature was ordered to promote education and freedom of the press. As in the Mexican federal constitution, Catholicism was the established state religion.[5]

Political instability in Mexico in the late 1820s and early 1830s largely undercut the provisions and protections of both the federal and the state constitutions under which Texans lived. But these constitutions were important to political debate at the time as discontent against the central government built up. At least in the early stages of the Texas rebellion against Mexico, many Texans could, and did, see themselves as defending these constitutions and most of the political principles that they represented. The turn away from defending the Mexican Constitution of 1824 and the state constitution of 1827 to articulating a new constitutional regime relying more on American political and cultural values was a fundamental step on the road to independence for Texas.

unicameral comprising one body or house, as in a one-house legislature

The Constitution of the Republic of Texas, 1836

Texas's break with Mexico was in large part a constitutional crisis that culminated in separation. Americans had come to Texas for a variety of reasons. Some, like Stephen F. Austin, had come in the service of the Mexican state as empresarios, whose goal was to encourage American immigration into Texas by distributing land made available by the Mexican government. They saw themselves as Mexican citizens working with the constitutional regime of 1827. Americans who had come to Texas in the early 1830s still wanted the land and economic opportunities offered by Texas, but they, as part of America's move westward, were far less committed to integrating themselves into the Mexican political community. For these people, separation from Mexico, either as an independent republic or as part of the United States, was the ultimate political objective.

Recognizing the dangers to Mexican authority from Americans coming into Texas, Mexican officials made various attempts to limit the influx. These restrictions, along with other grievances, led to growing discontent among Texans over their place in the Mexican federal system. Ultimately, Texans called for political conventions in 1832 and 1833 to discuss new constitutional forms of government. Along with demands for a more liberal immigration policy for people from the United States and for the establishment of English- and Spanish-speaking primary schools, calls for separate statehood for Texas emerged from the conventions. The 1833 convention actually drafted a constitution and sent Stephen F. Austin to Mexico City to petition the central government for reform. Austin's mission failed and led to his imprisonment, which in turn pushed Texas closer to open rebellion.

On November 7, 1835, a meeting of Texas political leaders at San Felipe adopted a declaration stating the reasons Texans were beginning to take up arms against the Mexican government. The declaration proclaimed that Texas was rising up in defense of its rights and liberties as well as the republican principles articulated in the Mexican Constitution of 1824. But though it was one thing to call for a defense of republican principles under the Mexican Constitution of 1824, it was something else to call for separation from Mexico. In the end, the declaration was but a prelude to the formal Texas Declaration of Independence that emerged out of the Convention of 1836 held at Washington-on-the-Brazos.

Of the 59 delegates attending the Convention of 1836, only 10 had lived in Texas prior to 1830, and 2 had arrived as late as 1836. Two-thirds of the delegates—39—were from southern slave states, 6 were from the border state of Kentucky, 7 were from northern states, 3 were from Mexico (including 2 born in Texas), and 4 were from other English-speaking lands.[6] The final products of the convention—the Texas Declaration of Independence and the Constitution of 1836—reflected the interests and values of these participants.

The Texas Declaration of Independence Like the Founders during the American Revolution, leaders of the Texas Revolution felt they needed to justify their actions in print. Written by George C. Childress and adopted by the general convention at Washington-on-the-Brazos on March 2, 1836, the Texas Declaration of Independence stated why the signers believed it was necessary to separate from Mexico and create an independent republic (see appendix, pp. A1–A3). Not surprisingly, the

FIGURE 2.1

The Republic of Texas 1836–45

This map shows the Republic of Texas with its large claimed territory. Texas's current boundaries were not established until 1850. Even then, minor controversies persisted along the Red River.

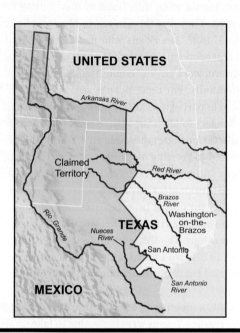

document draws heavily on the ideas of John Locke and Thomas Jefferson for inspiration. The description of the role of the government, "to protect the lives, liberty, and property of the people," repeated verbatim Locke's litany of the primary reasons for establishing government. And like Jefferson's Declaration for the United States, Texas's declaration catalogs a list of grievances against the Mexican regime which they said failed to provide freedom of religion, a system of public education, and trial by jury. It proclaimed that the federal constitutional regime they had been invited to live under by the rulers of Mexico had been replaced by a military tyranny that combined a "despotism of the sword and the priesthood."

The "melancholy conclusion" of Texas's declaration echoed ideas that Locke and Jefferson would have understood well: any government that stripped a people of their liberty was unacceptable to those raised on principles of self-government. Self-preservation demanded "eternal political separation" from the very state (Mexico) that had invited them to settle in Texas (see Figure 2.1).

The Provisions and Values in the 1836 Constitution
After declaring Texas a separate republic independent from Mexico, the convention proceeded to draft and pass a new constitution reflecting these republican sentiments. Resembling the U.S. Constitution in being flexible and brief (fewer than 6,500 words), the

1836 Constitution established an elected chief executive with considerable powers, a **bicameral** legislature, and a four-tiered judicial system composed of justice, county, district, and supreme courts.[7] Power was divided among these three branches, with a system of checks and balances between them. The constitution also included complicated procedures for amendments, along with a bill of rights.

bicameral having a legislative assembly composed of two chambers or houses

The values of American democracy percolated through the document in other ways as well, such as a guarantee that all White males could vote. Checks and balances were established between the three branches of government. On the other hand, a number of important provisions from Spanish-Mexican law were adapted for the Texas Republic in the constitution, including the idea of community property in which property acquired by either spouse during a marriage would be jointly owned, homestead protections in which one's home would be protected during bankruptcy proceedings, and debtor relief.

While giving these Spanish-American legal provisions constitutional status, Texas moved closer to the Anglo-American model of jurisprudence in other ways. By 1840 the Republic of Texas formally adopted the rules of English Common Law to replace Spanish Law in most civil and criminal matters. But there was one notable exception. Following Spanish and Mexican law, Texas initially retained ownership of all minerals under the

The Texas Declaration of Independence was written by George C. Childress and adopted at the Convention of 1836. Childress modeled the document on the American Declaration of Independence (see appendix, pp. A1–A3).

ground even as land grants provided for individual ownership of the land itself. Until the Constitution of 1866, a consensus existed that the best model for developing Texas and its mineral resources was through direct government ownership of all mineral rights. Under the constitutions of 1866, 1869, and 1876, a new model was adopted granting ownership of mineral rights to the individuals who owned the land under which minerals were found. The state retained some claims to mineral rights, largely in western parts of the state, to fund public schools and higher education. But the new idea was that private entrepreneurs would do a better job developing the state's natural resources than would state officials. The complicated history of mineral rights and oil and gas law (as well as the entire oil and natural gas industry) in the nineteenth and twentieth centuries follows directly from the decisions made in later constitutions to replace the original mineral rights provisions of the constitutions of 1836, 1845, and 1861.

One of the most important aspects of the Constitution of 1836, at least from the perspective of newly immigrated Americans from the South, was its defense of slavery as an economic and political institution with constitutional protections. The Constitution of Coahuila y Tejas of 1827 had challenged, albeit unsuccessfully, the existence of slavery. Although the 1836 Constitution outlawed the importation of enslaved people from Africa, it guaranteed that slaveowners could keep enslaved people as property and that new slaveowning immigrants could bring enslaved people into Texas with them. The results of this constitutional protection were monumental. In 1836, Texas had a population of 38,470, including 5,000 enslaved people. By 1850 the population of enslaved people had grown to 58,161, over one-quarter of the state's population. By 1860 there were more than 182,566 enslaved people, accounting for more than 30 percent of the population.[8] The Constitution of 1836 not only saved slavery as an institution in Texas but also provided the protections needed for slavery to flourish.

Writing a constitution is one thing; putting it into effect is another. Texas really became an independent state with a working constitution only after the Battle of San Jacinto, where on April 21, 1836, Sam Houston's force of 900 men overran the 1,300-man force of Antonio López de Santa Anna and captured Mexican dictator Santa Anna himself. And still many questioned whether the Lone Star Republic would survive given the dismal state of its finances, an army that couldn't protect the Republic's sweeping land claims to the west and the south, a hostile Mexico that only reluctantly accepted Texas's secession, and a United States that appeared to be unwilling to bring Texas into the Union.[9] Annexation to the United States in 1845 ended such questions and brought into being a new constitution, this time a state constitution that would operate within the framework of the U.S. Constitution.

The Texas State Constitution of 1845

The next phase of Texas's Founding took place from 1845 to 1861. Although the 1836 Constitution called for annexation by the United States, Texas remained an independent republic for nine years. The reasons included American concerns that if Texas were admitted to the Union as a slave state, the move could alter the delicate balance between slave and free states and further divide the nation over the sensitive subject of slavery. Additionally, it was feared that annexation by the United States would lead to war with Mexico. Santa Anna had repudiated the Treaty of Velasco, which had ended the war between Texas and Mexico, and Mexico thus still claimed Texas as part of its territory.

Though both of these fears proved justified, hesitation over annexation was overcome by the mid-1840s. On March 1, 1845, the U.S. Congress approved a resolution that brought Texas into the Union as a state (see appendix, pp. A5–A6). The annexation resolution had a number of interesting provisions. First, the Republic of Texas ceded to the United States all military armaments, bases, and facilities pertaining to public defense. Second, Texas retained a right to all "its vacant and unappropriated lands" as well as responsibility for its public debts. This was no small matter, because Texas claimed an enormous amount of land that extended far beyond its present state boundaries. The boundary issues were not resolved until Congress passed the Compromise of 1850, which among other provisions established Texas's present boundaries in exchange for a payment from the federal government, some of which was used to pay the state's debts. Finally, Texas was given permission to break up into four additional states when its population proved adequate. Considerable controversy surrounds this provision, and no serious attempt has been made to put it into effect.

On July 4, 1845, Anson Jones, fourth and final president of the Republic of Texas, called a convention in Austin to draft a state constitution. Drafters of the constitution relied heavily on the Constitution of 1836, although the final document ended up being almost twice as long. The familiar doctrines of separation of powers, checks and balances, and individual rights defined the basic design of government.

Under the Constitution of 1845, the legislature would be composed of two houses. The House of Representatives would have between 45 and 90 members, elected for two-year terms, and the Senate between 19 and 33 members, elected for four-year terms. (Half of the Senate would be elected every two years.) As in the U.S. Constitution, revenue bills would have to originate in the House. In a separate article on education, the legislature was ordered to establish a public school system and to set aside lands to support a Permanent School Fund. Another power granted to the legislature was the authority to select the state treasurer and comptroller in a joint session.

This constitution provided for an elected governor and a lieutenant governor. The governor's term was set at two years, and a governor could serve only four years in any

The lowering of the Republic flag marked Texas's annexation to the Union on March 1, 1845. A state constitution was drafted shortly thereafter to reflect Texas's new role.

six-year period. Among the executive powers granted to the governor were powers to convene and adjourn the legislature, to veto legislation (vetoes could be overturned by a two-thirds vote of each house of the legislature), to grant pardons and reprieves, and to command the state militia. The governor also had the power to appoint the attorney general, secretary of state, and district and supreme court judges, subject to the approval of the Senate.

The Constitution of 1845 established a judicial branch consisting of a supreme court composed of three judges, district courts, and lower courts deemed necessary by the legislature. Judges on the higher courts were to be appointed to six-year terms and could be removed from office subject to a two-thirds vote of each house of the legislature.

Amending the Constitution of 1845 was difficult. After being proposed by a two-thirds vote of each house, amendments had to be approved by a majority of the voters and then by another two-thirds vote of each house in the next legislature in order to be ratified. Only one amendment was ever made, an 1850 provision for the election of state officials who were originally appointed by the governor or by the legislature.[10]

The Constitution of 1861: Texas Joins the Confederacy

While slavery had made it difficult for Texas to get into the Union in the early 1840s, slavery drove Texas from the Union twenty years later. By 1860 slavery, concentrated in east Texas and along the Gulf Coast, had become a vital institution to the Texas economy. However, in large sections of the state, particularly in the north and west, the economy was based on ranching or corn and wheat production rather than cotton. There, slavery was virtually nonexistent. The question of whether Texas should secede from the Union along with other southern slave states was a controversial one that divided the state along regional as well as party lines.

Pressure to secede mounted following the November 1860 election of President Abraham Lincoln, who was committed to resisting the further expansion of slavery. A staunch Unionist, Governor Sam Houston refused calls to convene a special session of the legislature to discuss secession (see appendix, pp. A7–A10). Seeking to bypass Houston, a number of influential political leaders in the state, including the chief justice of the Texas Supreme Court, called for a special convention in January 1861 to consider secession. Giving in to the pressure, Houston called a special session of the legislature in the hopes of undercutting the upcoming secession convention. The legislature, however, had other ideas, validating the call for the convention and turning its chambers over to the convention delegates.

Lawyers and slaveowners dominated the secession convention, with lawyers composing 40 percent of the delegates and slaveowners 70 percent. The Texas Ordinance of Secession, produced by the convention on February 2, 1861, reflected this proslavery membership (see appendix, pp. A11–A12). In striking language, it proclaimed that the northern states had broken faith with Texas, particularly regarding the institution of slavery, and that Northerners had violated the laws and constitution of the federal Union by appealing to a "higher law" that trampled on the rights of Texans. The Ordinance of Secession proclaimed,

We hold as undeniable truths that the governments of the various States, and of the confederacy itself, were established exclusively by the [W]hite race, for themselves and their posterity; that the African race had no agency in their establishment; that they were rightfully held and regarded as an inferior and dependent race, and in that condition only could their existence in this country be rendered beneficial and tolerable.[11]

Texas voters approved secession from the Union on February 23, 1861. The secession convention then reconvened to enact a new constitution to guide the state as it entered the **Confederacy**. This constitution was surprisingly similar to the Constitution of 1845 except that references to the United States of America were replaced with references to the Confederate States of America. Public officials had to declare allegiance to the Confederacy, and slavery and states' rights were defended. A clause in the 1845 Constitution that provided for the possible emancipation of enslaved people was eliminated, and freeing enslaved people was declared illegal. But more controversial proposals, such as resuming the African slave trade, were rejected. The move out of the Union into the Confederacy may have been a radical one, but the new constitution was conservative insofar as it reaffirmed the existing constitutional order in the state.[12]

This image shows what the Texas State Capitol, which burned in 1881, looked like in the 1870s. Texas's first constitution after joining the Union as a state was ratified in 1845. It lasted until 1861 when Texas seceded from the Union along with other southern states.

Confederacy the Confederate States of America, those southern states that seceded from the United States in late 1860 and 1861 and argued that the power of the states was more important than the power of the central government

The Constitution of 1866: Texas Rejoins the Union

Defeat in the Civil War led to the writing of another state constitution in 1866. The provisional governor, pro-Union Andrew Jackson Hamilton, called a constitutional convention on November 15, 1865, a little over six months after the surrender of Robert E. Lee's army in Virginia essentially ended the Confederacy's existence. Delegates were elected on January 8, 1866, and the convention was held February 7. Under the provisions of President Andrew Johnson's "**Presidential Reconstruction**," few former secessionists were excluded from voting. As a result, the convention was dominated by former secessionists, many of whom had held commissions in the Confederate army.

The delegates took a number of actions to bring the state into compliance with Presidential Reconstruction, including the rejection of the right to secession (see appendix, p. A11), a repudiation of the war debt incurred by the state, and an acceptance of the abolition of slavery. Formerly enslaved males were granted fundamental rights to their persons and property as well as the right to sue and be sued and to contract with others. However, they were not allowed to vote and were banned from holding public office. The various amendments to the Constitution of 1861 passed by the convention came to be known as the Constitution of 1866.

As in the two previous constitutions, the size of the House was set between 45 and 90 members, and that of the Senate between 19 and 33. Terms of office remained the same as under the 1845 and 1861 constitutions, although salaries were increased. Reapportionment was to be based on the number of White male citizens, who would be counted in a census every 10 years.

Presidential Reconstruction a reconstruction plan for reintegrating former Confederate states back into the Union and freeing the enslaved people that placed mild demands upon the existing White power structure

The salary was also increased for the governor, whose term was extended to 4 years, with a limit of 8 years in any 12-year period. The governor was also granted, for the first time, a line-item veto on appropriations. The comptroller and the treasurer were to be elected by the voters for 4-year terms.

Under the new constitution, the state supreme court was expanded from three to five judges, whose terms were increased to 10 years, and whose salaries were also increased. The chief justice was to be selected from among the five judges on the supreme court. District court judges were to be elected for 8-year terms, and the attorney general for a 4-year term.

Voters ratified the Constitution of 1866 in June in a relatively close referendum, 28,119 to 23,400. The close vote was attributed to a widespread unhappiness with the salary increases for the various state officers,[13] but there were other sources of opposition as well. Many unionists who had been driven from the state during the war rejected the constitution, arguing it was the product of a convention dominated by former secessionists. They appealed to the increasingly Radical Republican Congress in Washington, D.C., for redress, arguing that former secessionists should be disenfranchised and forbidden from holding office. Their arguments gained force when the first legislature elected under the provisions of the Constitution of 1866 passed laws including the Black Codes, which limited the social, political, and economic status of African Americans in Texas. In response, Radical Republicans in Washington passed the **Congressional Reconstruction** Acts of 1867.

Congressional Reconstruction the reconstruction program put forward by Radical Republicans in Congress in 1867 that disenfranchised former Confederates and granted formerly enslaved people American citizenship and the right to vote

The Reconstruction Constitution of 1869

Republicans in Congress had come to see the initial efforts of reintegrating Texas and other southern states back into the Union as a failure. Under the direction of Congress, General Winfield Scott, the commander of the Union military force that was still occupying Texas and Louisiana, summarily dismissed most state officials elected to office under the 1866 Constitution and called for a new convention to write a new constitution in Texas in 1868. This time, however, former secessionists would be banned from voting or holding office. Against limited Democratic opposition, **Radical Republicans** easily won the vote to hold a convention by 44,689 to 11,440. Of the 90 delegates to the convention, only 6 had served in the previous constitutional convention. Ten were African American. The vast majority represented the interests of various wings in the Republican Party. The convention was a rancorous affair as delegates argued over a wide range of issues, including railroad charters, lawlessness in the state, and whether laws passed during the war years were legal. In the final days of the convention, delegates finally got down to the constitutional matters and the challenges of accepting the Thirteenth and Fourteenth Amendments to the United States Constitution, which abolished slavery, provided full citizenship to African Americans, and restricted former secessionists from holding office. Although delegates never completed their task of reworking the Constitution of 1866, the results of their efforts were published under orders by military officials, without being submitted to the voters, and became the Constitution of 1869.

A number of features of the Constitution of 1869 stand out.[14] The U.S. Constitution was declared to be the supreme law of the land. As in the 1866 Constitution, slavery was forbidden. But now African Americans were given the right to vote. Fourteenth Amendment guarantees of the privileges and immunities of citizens, due process under law, and

Radical Republicans a bloc of Republicans in the U.S. Congress who pushed through the adoption of African American suffrage as well as an extended period of military occupation of the South following the Civil War

equal protection under the law were recognized. Additionally, the constitution altered the relationship among the three branches of government.

The House of Representatives was set at 90 and the Senate at 30 members. Senatorial terms were extended to six years, with one-third of the seats to be elected every biennium. Legislative sessions were to be held annually. The most critical changes, however, were in the executive branch and the courts. The powers of the governor were vastly expanded. Among other things, the governor was given wide-ranging appointment powers that included the power to appoint judges. The state supreme court was reduced from five to three judges, and their term was reduced to nine years, with one new judge to be appointed every three years. Salaries for state officials were increased.

Underlying and fueling the debate over the Constitution of 1869 was another deeper constitutional debate about the meaning of the Secession Ordinance of 1861, the Constitution of 1861, and the Texas government that had functioned under the Confederacy. From the perspective of the U.S. Constitution, had Texas ever "left the union"? Was the Constitution of 1861 "illegal"? And what about the laws that had been passed by the legislature under the powers granted by the 1861 Constitution? Were they the law of the land, or did they have no legal force? Were all laws that had been written and all contracts that had been made during the period of rebellion "null and void"? This debate came to an end with the U.S. Supreme Court decision *Texas v. White et al.* (1869). Here, the court ruled that Texas had never left the Union, which was "perpetual, and as indissoluble as the union between the original states." The Ordinance of Secession of 1861 and all acts of the legislature that gave effect to that ordinance were considered to be "null" (see appendix, pp. A11–A12).

The first governor elected under the Constitution of 1869 was Edmund Davis, a Republican affiliated with the Radical faction of the party and a former Union general. Davis had vast authority, since the constitution had centralized power in the executive while reducing local governmental control. The popular perception at the time was that he presided over a corrupt, extravagant administration that eventually turned to the state police and the militia to attempt to maintain its control. Closer to the truth may be the fact that Davis sought to maintain his rule by relying on formerly enslaved people who had become a bulwark of the Republican Party in the state, and by limiting the reintegration of former Confederates into state politics.

In 1872 the Democrats regained control of the legislature, and in 1873 the Democrat Richard Coke was elected governor. Davis attempted to maintain control over the governor's office by having his handpicked supreme court invalidate Coke's election. He refused to give up his office and surrounded himself with state police in the capitol. However, when Democrats slipped past the guards and gathered upstairs in the capitol to organize a government, Davis was unable to obtain federal troops to maintain him in office and finally had to leave.

The Constitution of 1876

The final phase of Texas's Founding began with the passage of the Constitution of 1876. To prevent another government such as Davis's, efforts were made to write a new constitution, but in 1874 a proposed constitution was rejected by the legislature.[15] Finally, in 1875, a new constitutional convention was called, with 3 delegates selected by popular vote from each of the 30 senatorial districts. The final composition of the convention

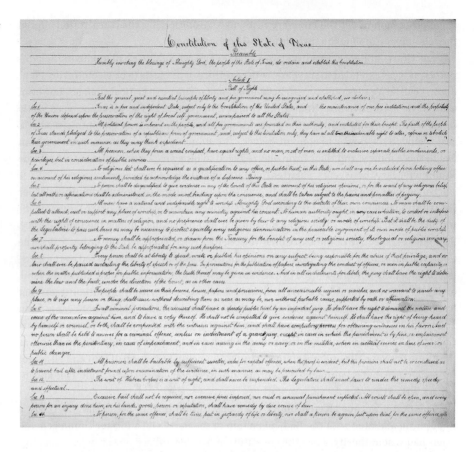

The example of Edmund Davis's reign motivated the revision of executive branch power in the Constitution of 1876. The framers of that constitution sought popular control of state government in order to limit the appointment powers of the governor as provided by the Constitution of 1869.

Grange a militant farmers' movement of the late nineteenth century that fought for improved conditions for farmers

included 75 White Democrats and 15 Republicans, 6 of whom were African American. Not one of the elected delegates had participated in the constitutional convention of 1868–69. Forty of them were farmers, and 40 were members of the **Grange**, a militant organization that had emerged to improve the financial plight of farmers.

The document that emerged from this convention, the Constitution of 1876, is still the basis for Texas government today. In an era of agriculture when prices and incomes were low and when little was demanded or expected from government, much in the 1876 Constitution made sense. However, one might question whether a constitution designed primarily by White males for Whites in a rural agrarian society—and for the purpose of keeping the likes of Edmund Davis from ever controlling the state again—is the best foundation for government in the modern era.

The framers were committed to a constitution with four major themes. First, they wanted strong popular control of state government; second, they believed that a constitution should seriously limit the power of state government; third, they sought economy in government, by which they meant government would spend as little as possible and as efficiently as possible; and fourth, they sought to promote agrarian interests, particularly those of small farmers, who formed the basis of support for the Grange movement.

Popular control of state government meant that the governor's previously vast appointment powers were limited by making judges and other public officials subject to election. But it did not mean broadening the electorate. When the framers of the 1876 Constitution thought of popular control of government, they thought of control by White males.

In the effort to limit the powers of state government, the constitution placed great restrictions on governmental actions, restrictions that could be modified only through a complex constitutional amendment process. Executive authority was diffused among numerous officeholders, rather than concentrated in the hands of the governor. Although subsequently changed by constitutional amendment, an initial provision further limited gubernatorial power by setting a two-year term limit for the office. The legislature was part-time, ordinarily sitting for a prescribed time period every other year, in contrast to the annual sessions provided for in the 1869 Constitution.

Limiting the power of state government was accomplished in several other ways. The constitution restricted the extent of government debt and of government's power to tax. In addition, there were limits on the salaries of state officials, especially legislators. A major economic depression had begun in 1873, and many Texans were experiencing economic hardship. One way money was saved was by decentralizing public education. The constitution provided for racially segregated schools and eliminated compulsory education laws. By gaining local control over education, White landowners could avoid paying taxes for the education of African American students.

Texas at that time was an agricultural state. Wishing to protect agrarian interests, the framers wrote provisions protecting homesteads from bankruptcy proceedings and restricting institutions that were perceived to be harmful to farmers, such as banks and

TABLE 2.1

The Changing Texas Constitutions, 1836–1876

The common perception of major constitutional provisions is that they are fixed in time and never to be changed. In Texas, however, constitutional changes took place frequently in the nineteenth century.

	1836	1845	1861	1866	1869	1876
LEGISLATURE						
Session frequency	annual	biennial	biennial	annual	annual	biennial
House term length	1 year	2 years	2 years	2 years	2 years	2 years
Senate term length	3 years	4 years	4 years	4 years	6 years	4 years
SUPREME COURT						
Size	*	3	3	5	3**	3†
Term length	4 years	6 years	6 years	10 years	9 years	6 years
Method of selection	elected††	appointed†	elected	elected	appointed	elected
GOVERNOR						
Term length	2 years	2 years	2 years	4 years	4 years	2 years††

*Chief justice and district judges acting as associate judges. The constitution provides for 3–8 district judges.
**Increased to 5 in 1874 by constitutional amendment.
†Amended. Currently 9 members.
††Elected by joint ballot by the Texas congress.
†Election made selection method in 1850 by constitutional amendment.
††Amended. Currently 4 years.

TABLE 2.2

A Constitutional Timeline, 1836–1876

DATE	MAJOR FEATURES
1836 The Constitution of the Republic of Texas following the revolution.	Adopted U.S. Constitution as a working model, including separation of powers, checks and balances, bill of rights. Rejected Catholicism as state religion. Defended slavery.
1845 The first Constitution of the State of Texas after annexation by the United States.	Affirmed many of the institutional features of the U.S. Constitution and the 1836 Constitution of Texas. Made amendment process difficult. Texas retained ownership of all public lands and minerals under these lands.
1861 The constitution following secession from the Union.	Affirmed broad features of the 1845 Constitution. Strongly defended slavery as an institution and the existing White-dominated political and economic system.
1866 Embodied values of Presidential Reconstruction. Suspended by military rule under Radical Reconstruction.	Affirmed broad institutional features of the 1845 and 1861 constitutions. Reflected values of former secessionists. Accepted results of Civil War and an end to slavery. Rejected equality before the law or the franchise for formerly enslaved people.
1869 The product of Radical Reconstruction. Never completed and went into effect without approval by the people.	Affirmed U.S. Constitution as the "Supreme Law of the Land." Affirmed Thirteenth Amendment (ending slavery) and the Fourteenth Amendment (granting equality under the law and due process to all formerly enslaved people). Greatly expanded powers of governor. Increased salaries of state officials.
1876 Texas's current constitution. Amended 491 times.	Backed away from radical features of Reconstruction including the acceptance of the dominance of the national government over the state. Reflected a break with activist constitution of 1869. Promoted traditional agrarian interests like the Grange in Texas. Promoted values of "economy" and "efficiency." Curtailed powers of governor and legislature. Provided for election of judges. Provided for future regulation of railroads.

railroads. There were also detailed regulations on railroad competition, freight and passenger rates, and railroad construction incentives.

The Constitution of 1876 was a conservative document with a distinctly populist flavor. On the one hand, it broke with the more activist government model laid out by the two Reconstruction constitutions of 1866 and 1869. On the other hand, it sought to protect those being harmed by the social and economic changes that transformed Texas after Reconstruction. The debates of the Constitutional Convention of 1875 drew attention to the fact that Texas was undergoing rapid change. New social and economic conditions, particularly the aggregation of capital in "immense railroad systems," gave rise to new social and political problems. These, in turn, demanded the institution of new restrictions on the powers of state government to prevent corruption. A new constitution with new provisions that restricted the activities of government became the bulwark of a conservative White social and political order in the state throughout the late nineteenth and early twentieth centuries (see Governor Richard Coke's inaugural address in 1876, appendix, p. A13).

Even in its earliest stages, the Texas Constitution of 1876 was a lengthy, rigid, and detailed document, and purposely so. Regulations curtailing government power were placed not in statutes where they could easily be reversed, but in the body of the constitution. The goal of this design was to ensure that the Radical Republicans and Edmund Davis would never again be able to control the state. They never did, although over the years the constitution became an increasingly unwieldy document (see Tables 2.1 and 2.2).

The Constitution of Texas Today

 Analyze the major provisions of the Texas Constitution today

The U.S. Constitution has two great virtues: brevity and flexibility. Neither of these can be said to characterize the Texas Constitution. The U.S. Constitution is limited to 7 short articles and 27 amendments. Much in the federal document is left unsaid, allowing lawmaking to be accomplished by statute. In contrast, in 2020 the Texas Constitution contained 16 articles (see Table 2.3; another article that concerned Spanish and Mexican land titles was deleted from the constitution in 1969). Six hundred and ninety amendments have been proposed by the legislature. Five hundred and seven have been approved by the electorate, while 180 have been defeated. (Curiously, three amendments were proposed by the legislature, but for obscure historical reasons never voted on by the electorate.[16]) Many of the articles are lengthy, complex affairs, but it is not just the length that differentiates the two constitutions. There is a difference in tone. The Texas Constitution reflects the writers' fears of what government could do if the principle of **limited government** was not clearly established.

In addition to its severe limits on executive power, the Texas Constitution also addresses a number of specific policy problems directly in the text, turning what might appear to be matters of public policy into issues of constitutional authority. By granting a variety of boards and districts a special place in the constitution, the framers created additional checks and balances that make it difficult for governors to exercise power effectively. Quite unintentionally, the Texas Constitution became a place where special interests could promote and protect their own agendas, even in the face of considerable political opposition.

The contrasts in character between the federal and Texas constitutions are a direct reflection of the differences in their framers' underlying goals. The U.S. Constitution was written to overcome the liabilities of the Articles of Confederation and create a government

limited government a principle of constitutional government; a government whose powers are defined and limited by a constitution

TABLE 2.3

The Texas Constitution: An Overview

Article 1: The Bill of Rights

Article 2: Separation of Powers in State Government

Article 3: The State Legislature

Article 4: The Plural Executive

Article 5: The Judicial Department

Article 6: Suffrage

Article 7: Public Education

Article 8: Taxation and State Revenues

Articles 9 and 11: Local Government, Including Counties and Municipal Corporations

Article 10: Empowering the State to Regulate Railroads and to Create the Texas Railroad Commission

Article 12: Empowering the State to Create General Laws for Corporations

Article 13: Concerning Spanish and Mexican Land Titles, Now Deleted from the Constitution

Article 14: Creates the General Land Office to Deal with Registering Land Titles

Article 15: Impeachment Provisions

Article 16: General Provisions Covering a Wide Range of Topics

Article 17: Amendment Procedures

that could act effectively in the public welfare in a variety of policy areas. The Texas Constitution was written to prevent the expansion of governmental authority and the return of a system of political power that was perceived as acting against the interests of the people.

The Preamble

The Preamble to the Texas Constitution is surprisingly short: "Humbly invoking the blessings of Almighty God, the people of the State of Texas, do ordain and establish this Constitution." This brevity is more than made up for in what follows.

Article 1: Bill of Rights

Article I of the U.S. Constitution establishes and delegates power to the legislative branch of government. One of the overriding concerns of the Founders was to create a legislature that could act effectively in public affairs. What came to be known as the Bill of Rights—the first 10 amendments to the Constitution—was added after the original Constitution was drafted and approved.

How Should We Balance Civil Rights and Religious Freedom?

Constitutional protections can clash with one another. The right to practice one's conservative religious beliefs can come into conflict with the civil rights of another person to get married. In Texas, Democrats, Republicans, and self-identified members of the conservative Tea Party movement disagree sharply on how these protections should be balanced with one another. In the context of controversies around same-sex marriage and transgender rights, a recent poll in Texas asked respondents to evaluate the following statement:

"A sincerely held religious belief is a legitimate reason to exempt someone from laws designed to prevent discrimination."

	AGREE (%)	DISAGREE (%)	DON'T KNOW (%)
All	30%	51%	19%
Republicans	40	39	21
Democrats	14	72	13
Tea Party	57	29	14

SOURCE: UT/TT poll, June 2017. Margin of error +/− 2.83 percent.

In contrast, the Texas Constitution puts its Bill of Rights up front as Article 1, well before any discussion of the legislature, the executive, or the courts. From the beginning, the purpose of the Texas Constitution was not simply to create a set of institutions that could wield political power. It was to limit the way political power is used and to prevent it from being abused.

Section 1 of the Bill of Rights proclaims that "Texas is a free and independent State, subject only to the Constitution of the United States, and the maintenance of our free institutions and the perpetuity of the Union depend upon the preservation of local self-government, unimpaired to all the States." On the face of it, this proclamation would seem to be relatively noncontroversial, as it appears to accept the Constitution of the United States and the perpetuity of the Union. Put into proper historical context, however, it meant something very different.

The Constitution of 1869, written under the watchful eyes of Radical Republicans in Texas and in the U.S. Congress, had rejected the "heresies of nullification and secession" and explicitly acknowledged that the U.S. Constitution was "the supreme law of the land" and that the Texas Constitution was "subject to national authority." Article 1, Section 1—the product of a constitutional convention in 1876 that was hostile to many of the efforts of Reconstruction—concedes two very different things: (1) that Texas is free and independent, "subject" to the U.S. Constitution, and (2) that free institutions and the perpetuity of the Union depend upon local self-government that is "unimpaired." No mention is made of the supremacy of the U.S. Constitution over the state constitution.

The idea of a "perpetual Union" is made to depend upon "the preservation of local self-government," meaning an independent and autonomous state government freed from an intrusive national authority. Texas may have lost the Civil War, but Article 1, Section 1, claims an autonomy of the state from outside forces that would have surprised many politicians outside the state. Such sentiments continue to resonate throughout parts of Texas today.

The Texas Bill of Rights embodies certain ideas captured in earlier state constitutions and the U.S. Bill of Rights. All "free men" are declared to have equal rights (Section 30) that cannot be denied or abridged because of sex, race, color, creed, or national origin (Section 3a). Freedom of religious worship is guaranteed (Section 6), and religious tests for office are prohibited (Section 4). Liberty of speech and liberty of the press are guaranteed (Section 8). Individuals are protected from unreasonable search and seizure of their homes and property (Section 9), from excessive bail (Section 11), from bills of attainder (imposing punishment for an action without holding a trial) and ex post facto laws (making an action into a crime retroactively) (Section 16), and from double jeopardy (being prosecuted twice for the same crime) (Section 14). Article 1 also guarantees an individual a right to trial by jury (Section 15) and the right to bear arms "in the lawful defense of himself or the State; but the Legislature shall have the power, by law, to regulate the wearing of arms, with a view to prevent crime" (Article 1, Section 23).

republican government a representative democracy, a system of government in which power is derived from the people

Article 1 also contains some ideas that move beyond those guaranteed by the first 10 amendments to the U.S. Constitution. The right to **republican government**, something clearly stated in the main body of the U.S. Constitution but not in the U.S. Bill of Rights, is powerfully articulated in the first two sections of Article 1. These sections declare that all political power is inherent in the people, and that the people of Texas have at all times the "inalienable right to alter, reform or abolish their government in such manner as they may think expedient" (Article 1, Section 2).

The differences between the Texas Bill of Rights and the U.S. Bill of Rights are not simply matters of where best to articulate a philosophy of republican government. They also involve very concrete matters of public policy. Section 26 of the Texas Bill of Rights, for example, forbids monopolies that are contrary to the public interest, and states that the law of primogeniture and entail (a law designed to keep large landed properties together by restricting their inheritance to the firstborn child) will never be in effect in the state. Although monopolies remain a public concern today, primogeniture and entail are not.

Section 11 in the Texas Bill of Rights grapples with the complicated issue of bail and under what specific circumstances an individual can be denied it. Significantly, Section 11 has been the subject of three major constitutional revisions: in 1955, 1977, and 1993. Section 30, adopted in 1989, provides a long list of the "rights of crime victims," including the right to be treated fairly and with dignity, the right to be protected from the accused, and the right to restitution. Although these are important matters of public policy for Texas today, they could hardly be considered proper material for the U.S. Constitution.

Article 2: The Powers of Government

Like the U.S. Constitution, Article 2 divides the power of government in Texas into three distinct branches: the legislative, the executive, and the judicial. It also stipulates that no one in any one branch shall be attached to either of the other branches, except where explicitly permitted (as in the case of the lieutenant governor's role in the Senate). The article—one short paragraph of text—assures that a version of the separation of powers doctrine found in the U.S. Constitution will be embodied in Texas institutions.

Article 3: Legislative Department

Article 2 is one of the shortest articles in the Texas Constitution. Article 3 is the longest, making up almost one-third of the original text of 1876. Like Article I of the U.S. Constitution, Article 3 of the Texas Constitution vests legislative power in two houses: a Senate of 31 members and a House of Representatives of no more than 150 members. It stipulates the terms of office and qualifications: House members serve two-year terms, whereas senators serve four-year terms, half being elected every two years. House members must be citizens of the United States, must be at least 21 years of age, and must have resided in the state for two years and in their district for one year. Senators must be citizens of the United States, must be at least 26 years old, and must have resided in the state for five years and in their districts for one year. In addition, Article 3 provides for the selection of officers in both houses of the legislature, states when and for how long the legislature shall meet (Section 5), and explains how the legislative proceedings will be conducted (Sections 29–41) and how representative districts will be apportioned (Sections 25, 26, and 28).

Like Article 1 (Texas Bill of Rights), Article 3 moves well beyond the U.S. Constitution, putting limits on what the legislature can do. For example, it puts limits on legislators' salaries and makes it difficult to increase those salaries. Article 3 also creates a bipartisan Texas Ethics Commission, whose job, among other things, is to recommend salary increases for members of the legislature and to set per diem rates for legislators and the lieutenant governor. Article 3, Section 49a, also subjects the legislature to the actions of the comptroller of public accounts, whose duty is to prepare a report prior to the legislative session on the financial condition of the state treasury and to provide estimates of future expenditures by the state. This provision of the Texas Constitution effectively limits the state legislature to the financial calculations and endorsements of the comptroller, a check on the legislature all but unimaginable to the writers of the U.S. Constitution.

Putting constraints on certain legislative actions is only part of the story. The largest portion of Article 3 (Sections 47–64) is dedicated to addressing a variety of policy issues, including lotteries, emergency service districts, debt creation, the Veterans' Land Board and the Texas Water Development Board, Texas park development, the creation of a state medical education board, and even the establishment of an economic development fund in support of the now-defunct superconducting supercollider.

Article 4: Executive Department

Article II of the U.S. Constitution concentrates executive power in the presidency. Under the U.S. Constitution, cabinet members such as the secretary of state, the attorney general, and the secretary of agriculture are appointed by the president (and confirmed by the Senate). "Executive power" is "vested," or placed, in the hands of the president (see U.S. Constitution, Article II, Section 1). Vested executive power, in this regard, is a broad-ranging term that covers a wide range of activities. The goal of the framers was to create a more effective and more responsible executive than had been possible under the Articles of Confederation.

In contrast, there is no "vesting" of executive power in any one executive office in Texas (see Table 2.4). Article 4 of the Texas Constitution states that the executive shall consist of six distinct offices: the governor, who serves as the chief executive; the lieutenant governor, who serves as the president of the Senate; the secretary of state, who keeps the official seals of the state; the comptroller of public accounts; the commissioner of the General Land Office; and the attorney general, who acts as the state's chief legal officer. With the exception of the secretary of state, who is appointed by the governor and approved by the Senate, all other offices are elected by voters every four years. Besides creating a **plural executive** (see Chapter 8), Article 4 guarantees its members will have independent political bases in the electorate. This arrangement provides an additional check against any concentration of powers in the hands of any one person.

plural executive an executive branch in which power is fragmented because the election of statewide officeholders is independent of the election of the governor

Article 5: Judicial Department

Article III of the U.S. Constitution succinctly provides for a Supreme Court and empowers Congress to create any necessary lower courts. As such, it could not be further from the detailed discussion of the state courts found in Article 5 of the Texas Constitution. Besides creating a supreme court to hear civil cases and a court of criminal appeals to hear criminal cases, Article 5 provides for such lesser courts as courts of appeal, district courts, commissioner's courts, and justice of the peace courts, and empowers the legislature to establish other courts as deemed necessary. It also goes into such details as the retirement and compensation of judges, the jurisdictions of the various courts, and the duties of judges; it states what to do in the case of court vacancies; and it includes a series of discussions on particular issues involving the lower courts.

An even greater difference between the federal and the Texas constitutions in their treatment of the judiciary is the crucial role Texas gives to elections. Federal judges are appointed by the president and approved by the Senate. In Texas the people elect state judges. Nine supreme court and nine court of criminal appeals judges are elected at large in the state, and lower court judges are elected by voters in their respective geographic locations. Much like the U.S. Constitution, the Texas Constitution seeks to create an independent judiciary that can check and balance the other two branches of government. However, it seeks an additional check as well, in that it wants the people to in turn watch over the courts.

Article 6: Suffrage

Article 6 contains a short but detailed discussion about who may vote in Texas. It also empowers the legislature to enact laws regulating voter registration and the selection of electors for president and vice president.

Article 7: Education

The concerns found in the Texas Declaration of Independence over the need for public schools to promote a republican form of government are directly addressed in Article 7 of the constitution, which declares, "A general diffusion of knowledge [is] essential to

TABLE 2.4

Major Constitutional Officers in Texas

OFFICE/POSITION	ELECTED BY/APPOINTED BY	DUTIES
LEGISLATIVE (ARTICLE 3)		
Speaker of the House	Elected by House members	Leads the House
President Pro Tempore of the Senate	Elected by Senate members. Most senior member of the Senate from either party.	Leads the Senate in absence of the lieutenant governor
EXECUTIVE (ARTICLE 4)		
Governor	Elected by Texas voters for 4-year term	Acts as chief executive of the state
Lieutenant Governor	Elected by Texas voters for 4-year term	Acts as governor in absence of the governor and presides over the Senate
Secretary of State	Appointed by the governor by and with advice and consent of Senate	Acts as the chief election officer of Texas
Comptroller of Public Accounts	Elected by Texas voters	Acts as chief steward of state finances
Commissioner of the General Land Office	Elected by Texas voters	Manages state assets, investments, and mineral rights from state lands and serves as chair for numerous state boards and commissions
Attorney General	Elected by Texas voters	Represents the state in cases where it is a party
JUDICIAL (ARTICLE 5)		
Justice of Supreme Court	9 positions elected by Texas voters for 6-year terms	Decides on civil cases reaching the Texas Supreme Court
Judge of Court of Criminal Appeals	9 positions elected by Texas voters for 6-year terms	Decides on criminal cases reaching the Texas court of criminal appeals
Justice of the Court of Appeal	80 justices in 14 courts of appeal elected by Texas voters for 6-year terms from multimember districts	Decides on cases reaching the Texas court of appeal
District Court Judge	456 district court judges elected by Texas voters for 4-year terms from a mixture of multi- and single-member districts	Decides on cases in Texas district court

Other county-level court officials are also elected for 4-year terms on a county or precinct basis. Municipal court judges are usually appointed.

OFFICE/POSITION	ELECTED BY/APPOINTED BY	DUTIES
OTHER IMPORTANT OFFICES		
Texas Railroad Commissioner (Article 13, Section 30)	3 officers elected by Texas voters for 6-year overlapping terms	Regulates the oil and gas industry, gas utilities, pipeline safety, and surface coal and uranium mining (no longer regulates railroads)
State Board of Education Member (Article 7)	15 members elected by Texas voters from single-member districts for 4-year terms	Makes statewide policies for public schools
Agricultural Commissioner (office established under Agricultural Code, not the constitution)	Elected by Texas voters for a 4-year term	Regulates state agriculture and administers state agriculture policy

the preservation of the liberties and rights of the people." Section 1 makes it a duty of the state legislature to support and maintain "an efficient system of public free schools." The Texas Supreme Court's interpretation of this provision as applying to school funding in the state has led to political battles over school finance for 40 years. Sections 2–8 provide for the funding of public education and the creation of a State Board of Education to oversee the operations of elementary and secondary education. Article 7 also provides for the establishment and funding of a "University of the first class" to be called "The University of Texas" as well as an "agricultural and mechanical college" (Texas A&M University). Provisions were later included to fund other state universities and colleges. State universities are the subject of over half of Article 7, where detailed discussions of the funding and operations of particular state institutions are put directly into the text.

Article 8: Taxation and Revenue

The complex issue of taxation is the subject of Article 8, where once again we find a highly detailed account of several important policy issues built directly into the text of the constitution. One of the most controversial sections of the Texas Constitution during the 2019 session centered on the issue of the income tax. Section 1 of Article 8 of the 1876 Constitution enabled the legislature to tax the income of individuals and businesses. But, as we will discuss in the Citizen's Guide to this chapter, the legislature refrained from doing so. In 1993 a constitutional amendment was passed (Article 8, Section 24) which required that a personal income tax be approved by the voters and that the proceeds from it be dedicated to education and tax relief. In 2019, Article 8, Section 24 was replaced by another amendment which repealed Section 24 entirely by prohibiting any income tax on individuals. As with other portions of the constitution, the net effect of Article 8, Section 21a provisions was to curtail severely what the state legislature can do and how it can do it. If Section 24a of Article 8 is any indication, the public fear of unresponsive and potentially tyrannical governme nt is as alive today as it was in 1876.

Articles 9 and 11: Local Government

These articles provide highly detailed discussions of the creation, organization, and operation of counties and municipal corporations.

Articles 10, 12, 13, and 14

These heavily revised articles deal with a series of specific topics: the railroads (10), private corporations (12), Spanish and Mexican land titles (13), and public lands (14). Article 10 empowers the state to regulate railroads and to establish the Railroad Commission. Article 12 empowers the state to create general laws creating private corporations and protecting the public and individual stockholders. Article 13, now entirely repealed, dealt with the nineteenth-century issue of Spanish and Mexican land titles. Article 14 created a General Land Office to deal with the registration of land titles.

Which State Has the Longest Constitution?

State Constitution Length (estimated)

- ● < 19,999 words
- ● 20,000–39,999 words
- ● 40,000–59,999 words
- ● 60,000–79,999 words
- ● > 79,999 words

Vermont
8,565 words
Shortest

Alabama
402,852 words
Longest

Texas
92,025 words
Second longest

The Texas Constitution is the second-longest state constitution in the United States. The framers of the Texas Constitution gave the state government very specific powers so that the government could not use ambiguity to expand its powers. As a result, the Texas Constitution requires frequent amendments to address situations not covered specifically in the original constitution. The Texas Constitution has been amended 507 times as of 2019, third most of any state.

SOURCE: Book of the States, 2019, Council of State Governments; data for 2019 compiled by the authors.

Amendments Added to Constitution

- ● < 75 amendments
- ● 75–149 amendments
- ● 150–224 amendments
- ● 225–300 amendments
- ● > 300 amendments

Rhode Island
12 amendments
Fewest

Alabama
946 amendments
Most

Texas
507 amendments
Fourth most

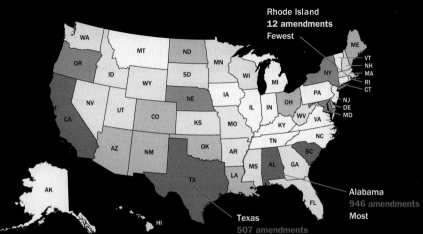

CRITICAL THINKING

- After examining the two maps, do you see any relationship between the length of a state constitution and the number of amendments to the constitution? Why do you think that there might be such a relationship in some states?

- Do different regions in the country seem to favor short rather than long state constitutions? What factors might account for such similarities?

Article 15: Impeachment

impeachment under the Texas Constitution, the formal charge by the House of Representatives that leads to trial in the Senate and possible removal of a state official

In the U.S. Constitution, **impeachment** is one of the major checks Congress holds against both the executive and judicial branches of government. The House of Representatives holds the power to impeach an individual; the Senate is responsible for conducting trials. A two-thirds vote in the Senate following impeachment by the House leads to the removal of an individual from office.

A similar process is provided for in Article 15 of the Texas Constitution. The House has the power to impeach. The Senate has the power to try the governor, lieutenant governor, attorney general, land office commissioner, and comptroller, as well as judges of the supreme court, the courts of appeal, and district courts. Conviction requires a two-thirds vote of the senators present. In contrast to the U.S. Constitution, the Texas Constitution rules that all officers against whom articles of impeachment are proffered are suspended from their office. The governor is empowered to appoint a person to fill the vacancy until the decision on impeachment is reached.

Despite these similarities to the impeachment procedures in the U.S. Constitution, the Texas Constitution has its own caveats. Most notably, the Texas Constitution does not explicitly define impeachable offenses in terms of "Treason, Bribery, or other high Crimes and Misdemeanors," as the U.S. Constitution does. The House and Senate (and the courts) decide what constitutes an impeachable offense.[17] In addition, the supreme court has original jurisdiction to hear and determine whether district court judges are competent to discharge their judicial duties. The governor may also remove judges of the supreme court, courts of appeal, and district courts when requested by the two-thirds vote of each branch of the legislature. Significantly, the reasons for removing a judge in this case need only involve a "willful neglect of duty, incompetence, habitual drunkenness, oppression in office, or other reasonable cause" (Article 15, Section 8). The barriers to removing a judge by political means are thus, at least on paper, much lower in Texas than in the national government.

In 1980, Section 9 was added to Article 15, providing a new way to remove officials appointed by the governor. With the advice and consent of two-thirds of the members of the Senate present, a governor may remove an appointed public official. If the legislature is not in session, the governor is empowered to call a special two-day session to consider the proposed removal.

Article 16: General Provisions

Article 16 is one of the lengthiest in the Texas Constitution and has no parallel in the U.S. Constitution. It is literally a catchall article tackling a variety of issues ranging from official oaths of office to community property to banking corporations and stock laws to the election of the Texas Railroad Commission to the state retirement systems. Here, perhaps more than anywhere else, we see the complexity and confusion of the philosophy reflected in the Texas Constitution.

Article 17: Amending the Constitution

Like the U.S. Constitution, the Texas Constitution explicitly delineates how it can be amended. Essentially, to be adopted, an amendment must undergo a four-stage process. First, it must be proposed by the legislature meeting in either regular or special session. Second, it must be approved by a two-thirds vote of all the members elected to each house. Third, a brief statement explaining it must be published twice in each recognized newspaper in the state that meets the publication requirements for official state notices. Finally, it must be approved by a majority of the state's voters in a statewide election.

Recent Attempts to Rewrite the Texas Constitution

 Describe modern efforts to change the Texas Constitution

Given the difficulty of amending the state constitution, a surprising number of amendments have been proposed by the legislature and approved by the people. By 2019, 690 amendments had been passed by the legislature and 507 had been adopted. Following a major stock fraud scandal in the 1970s, there was an attempt to rewrite the entire constitution by calling a constitutional convention in 1974 that lasted 150 days. Bitter politics, coupled with the intense demands of highly mobilized special interest, made it impossible to reach an agreement. In the end, proponents of a new constitution failed to achieve the necessary two-thirds majority by three votes (118–62 with 1 abstention). Attempts to rewrite the constitution through eight constitutional amendments in 1975 failed as well, as the voters rejected all eight in a special election in November 1975. Demands for amending the Constitution have intensified in recent years, as legislators have dealt with the problem of making changes in public policy while being constrained by an unwieldy constitutional document.

Recent Amendments

One thing that is clear about Texas elections dealing with constitutional amendments is that voting participation is invariably low. Who Are Texans? on p. 71 compares the percentage turnout of registered voters in November special elections on constitutional amendments with the percentage turnout in presidential elections (which tend to produce the highest turnout). There are two likely reasons for the low voter turnout in constitutional amendment elections: first, constitutional amendment elections are usually held in "off" years—following the general session of the legislature (and most special sessions)—when there are no elections with candidates on the ballot. Without candidates to generate voter turnout, the political parties take a less active role in getting out their voters. As a result, advertising campaigns about the election are frequently limited to those of interest groups that support or oppose the issues on the ballot. Second, many of the amendments are relatively insignificant to most voters.

While most proposed constitutional amendments are uncontroversial, such was not the case in 2011 when 3 of the 10 amendments presented to the voters were turned down. The controversial ones were those that the Tea Party and other antitax groups saw as increasing the financial burden on Texans. For example, Proposition 4 was defeated because it would have expanded the ability of counties to issue bonds to finance the development of unproductive areas where those bonds were to be repaid with property tax revenues. Critics of the proposal argued that it would clear the way for new toll roads. Proposition 7 was defeated because it would have given El Paso new borrowing authority. Proposition 8, which passed the legislature with bipartisan support, was defeated because it would have given property owners the opportunity to opt out of agricultural or wildlife conservation property tax exemptions in favor of water conservation property

---

TABLE 2.5

Passed Constitutional Amendments, 2019

Proposition 2	The constitutional amendment providing for the issuance of additional general obligation bonds by the Texas Water Development Board in an amount not to exceed $200 million to provide financial assistance for the development of certain projects in economically distressed areas. (Passed 65.6%)
Proposition 3	The constitutional amendment authorizing the legislature to provide for a temporary exemption from ad valorem taxation of a portion of the appraised value of certain property damaged by a disaster. (Passed 85.1%)
Proposition 4	The constitutional amendment prohibiting the imposition of an individual income tax, including a tax on an individual's share of partnership and unincorporated association income. (Passed 74.41%)
Proposition 5	The constitutional amendment dedicating the revenue received from the existing state sales and use taxes that are imposed on sporting goods to the Texas Parks and Wildlife Department and the Texas Historical Commission to protect Texas's natural areas, water quality, and history by acquiring, managing, and improving state and local parks and historic sites while not increasing the rate of the state sales and use taxes. (Passed 88%)
Proposition 6	The constitutional amendment authorizing the legislature to increase by $3 billion the maximum bond amount authorized for the Cancer Prevention and Research Institute of Texas. (Passed 64%)
Proposition 7	The constitutional amendment allowing increased distributions to the Available School Fund. (Passed 74.1%)
Proposition 8	The constitutional amendment providing for the creation of the flood infrastructure fund to assist in the financing of drainage, flood mitigation, and flood control projects. (Passed 77.8%)
Proposition 9	The constitutional amendment authorizing the legislature to exempt from ad valorem taxation precious metal held in a precious metal depository located in this state. (Passed 51.6%)
Proposition 10	The constitutional amendment to allow the transfer of a law enforcement animal to a qualified caretaker in certain circumstances. (Passed 93.8%)

Who Votes in Texas Elections Amending the Constitution?

Turnout of Registered Voters in Texas Constitutional Amendment Elections Compared with Presidential Elections*

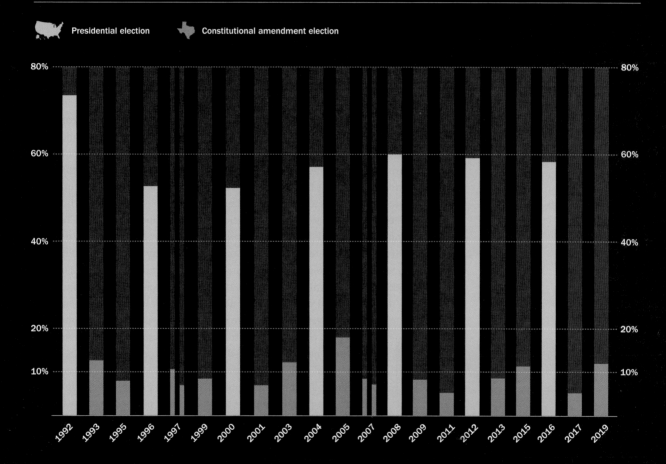

Presidential election   Constitutional amendment election

Since 1983, Texans have voted to amend the state's constitution dozens of times. Turnout in these elections is always low, even when well-publicized amendments are on the ballot. For example, in 2005, 17 percent of registered voters voted on Proposition 2, which banned same-sex marriage in the state.

* 1997 elections in August and November; 2007 elections in May and November.

SOURCE: Texas Secretary of State, www.sos.state.tx.us/ (accessed 2/27/20).

QUANTITATIVE REASONING

• What is the difference between participation rates in presidential elections and constitutional amendment elections? What might account for this difference?

• What could be done to increase turnout in constitutional amendment elections?

tax exemptions. The Tea Party successfully opposed the proposition on the grounds that it would shift the tax burden to others.[18] While the Tea Party and other anti-tax groups could not defeat all of the propositions they opposed, low voter turnout enabled them to exert a significant influence. Indeed, their defeat of three proposals broke the modern pattern in which amendments are routinely approved. For example, between 2001 and 2010, 77 of 79 proposed amendments were approved. In the 2019 constitutional amendment elections, voters were asked to consider ten proposed amendments. Nine of the ten amendments passed (see Table 2.5). The one that failed was a minor proposition enabling people to hold more than one municipal judgeship at a time. Twelve percent of the registered voters went to the polls, 6 percentage points higher than in the 2017 constitutional amendment elections. Still, turnout was far behind the 2016 presidential elections when 59 percent of the voters turned out or 2018 when 53 percent of the registered voters turned out to vote in a toughly fought senatorial campaign.

Participation in the 2005 constitutional amendment election may appear to be abnormally high (see Who Are Texans? on p. 71). Most of the 2005 proposed constitutional amendments were, like the previously discussed propositions, of significance only to a narrow group of people. For example, one of the nine proposed amendments provided for clearing land titles in Upshur and Smith counties. Another authorized the legislature to provide for a six-year term for a board member of a regional mobility authority. Yet the turnout in this election was much higher than is typically seen in constitutional amendment elections. The reason was Proposition 2, which defined marriage in Texas as the union of one man and one woman. The proposition also prohibited the state or any political subdivision of the state from creating or recognizing any legal status identical to or similar to marriage. The proposition generated a strongly favorable vote—1,723,782 in favor versus 536,913 against. Unlike Proposition 12 in 2003, this was not an economic battle involving interests concerned with tort law; rather, this was an issue pitting social conservatives against those more sympathetic to gay rights. The strength of the social conservative vote in the state was, of course, remarkable, since the amendment carried by more than a 3-to-1 margin. Many churches and religious organizations strongly supported the proposed amendment. Their activities probably generated the relatively high voter turnout. The proposition was unusual in that people felt it was important to their lives because it affected their value systems. Although it is doubtful the amendment was necessary to support the traditional concept of marriage and although the ambiguity of the provision rejecting any legal status similar to marriage is disturbing, a significant part of the voting population apparently believed that it was important to vote their moral values, even if the proposal was largely symbolic.

Although most constitutional amendments are not of great importance, there are some notable exceptions. Table 2.6 identifies some of those amendments that, like Proposition 12 in 2003 or Proposition 2 in 2005, have had great significance in the public policy of the state.

Amendments to the state constitution affect many areas of Texans' lives. In 2019, Proposition 10 allowed for law enforcement animals to be adopted by qualified caretakers upon retirement from the force. Lobos, pictured here, retired from Texas law enforcement after working for eight years to stop the shipment of illegal drugs through Texas.

TABLE 2.6

Some Important Constitutional Amendments

1894 An amendment providing for the election of railroad commissioners. In later years, when Texas became a major oil producer, the railroad commission gained the authority to regulate oil production and became the most powerful elected regulatory agency in the country.

1902 An amendment "requiring all persons subject to a poll tax to have paid a poll tax and to hold a receipt for same before they offer to vote at any election in this state, and fixing the time of payment of said tax." The poll tax required a payment of money prior to voting. The effect was to reduce the size of the electorate, limiting the opportunity of those with lower incomes to vote.

1966 Repealed the poll tax as a voting requirement in the face of pressures from the U.S. Supreme Court and from a national constitutional amendment that eliminated the poll tax in national elections.

1972 A constitutional amendment "to provide that equality under the law shall not be denied or abridged because of sex, race, color, creed or national origin." This amendment was seen as primarily banning sex discrimination, since federal civil rights statutes largely dealt with discrimination on other grounds. It was the state version of a proposed sexual equal rights amendment that was never ratified and made part of the U.S. Constitution.

2005 An amendment "providing that marriage in this state consists only of the union of one man and one woman and prohibiting this state or a political subdivision of this state from creating or recognizing any legal status identical or similar to marriage." The amendment was passed in response to the movement toward the recognition of civil unions and same-sex marriage in some states.

2009 An amendment establishing "the national research university fund to enable emerging research universities in this state to achieve national prominence as major research universities." The amendment was a recognition that the Texas economy would benefit by the development of more nationally recognized research universities in the state.

2009 An amendment "to prohibit the taking, damaging, or destroying of private property for public use unless the action is for the ownership, use, and enjoyment of the property by the State, a political subdivision of the State, the public at large, or entities granted the power of eminent domain under law or for the elimination of urban blight on a particular parcel of property, but not for certain economic development or enhancements of tax revenue purpose." This was passed in reaction to a U.S. Supreme Court decision involving eminent domain—the taking of private property for public use—that was seen as unsympathetic to property rights.

2019 An amendment to prohibit the passage of a state income tax on individuals in Texas.

Prohibiting an Income Tax through the Constitution

1 Why prohibiting an income tax through the constitution matters

Constitutions are about choices: the choices people make about their governing institutions, about the political processes that govern these institutions, and about restrictions on the powers of government. In 2019, the legislature passed a constitutional amendment that prohibited a state income tax. This was approved overwhelmingly by the voters in November, making it part of the Texas Constitution under Article 8, Section 21a. The constitutional prohibition on the income tax was an important choice about how the legislature could grapple with fiscal challenges in the state.

Passing the constitutional amendment prohibiting an income tax was difficult because it required a two-thirds vote of all the members of both houses of the legislature and had to be approved by a majority of the voters during a state-wide election. These difficulties were overcome (barely) when 100 members of the Texas House and 22 members of the Texas Senate supported a constitutional prohibition on a state income tax on May 27, 2019. Sixty-five percent of the Democrats in the legislature opposed the prohibition. The constitutional amendment was approved by 74.4 percent of the voters on November 5, 2019. Anyone wanting to pass an income tax in Texas would first have to pass another constitutional amendment overturning the ban and then pass a statute putting an income tax into place. Neither of these is likely in the foreseeable future.

Many business groups in Texas are ardent supporters of Texas's no-income-tax policy.

2 What's the debate?

The state legislature originally was granted the power to impose an income tax under Article 8, Section 1 of the 1876 Constitution. There were no judicial rulings on this power because an income tax had never been imposed through statute. As the debate over funding public education picked up in the 1980s, some state leaders, including powerful Lieutenant Governor Bob Bullock, began floating the idea that maybe an income tax could be a solution to the state's recurring fiscal woes. Bullock's idea, however, touched off a firestorm that led him to propose a constitutional amendment that would restrict any income tax passed by the legislature to funding public schools or easing tax burdens. It was this constitutional provision that was essentially overturned by the prohibition of an income tax in 2019.

For supporters of the ban, it was not enough to limit any income tax initiative to funding public schools or easing tax burdens. The very idea of having an income tax for any purpose had to be rejected out of hand. They also argued that denying the state legislature the power to impose an income tax keeps the tax burden on citizens in the state low and constrains government growth. Opponents of the prohibition argued that such constitutional provisions needlessly constrained the power of the legislature to confront problems facing the state, particularly in times of fiscal distress. Opponents argued that what should be an open policy debate about taxes in the legislature was being turned into a constitutional debate over the limits of government. Not being able to raise taxes quickly and efficiently means that important programs like public education and health care might have to be cut to balance the budget.

The constitutional debate over prohibiting an income tax in Texas is largely symbolic, at least today. There was no (and never has been any) serious support for an income tax in either the electorate or the legislature. Nevertheless, political leaders in the Republican Party felt that a statement had to be made about the depth of the opposition to an income tax in the state. Texas had the reputation of having a low tax burden and leaders in the legislature felt that the best way to protect this reputation was to make it more difficult to pass new taxes.

3 What do the numbers say?

Two issues lie at the heart of the debate over the constitutional banning of an income tax across Texas. Does not having an income tax mean that Texas's overall tax burden is lower than other states'? Second, is banning an income tax through constitutional amendment a popular way in other states to accomplish the policy objective of keeping taxes low? What do the numbers say?

There are only seven states with no income tax: Alaska, Florida, South Dakota, Wyoming, Texas, Washington, and Nevada. Two other states, Tennessee and New Hampshire, have no income tax proper, but do impose taxes on interest and dividends and are considered to be "nearly no income tax" states. As the accompanying table shows, the overall tax burden (as a percent of income) in states without an income tax does appear to be lower than the tax burden in states with one. Constitutional prohibitions on income taxes appear to be associated with lower tax burden rankings.

Interestingly, five of these states prohibit income taxes through constitutional provisions. (Alaska and South Dakota, in contrast, have constitutional provisions for an income tax but have passed laws restricting the imposition of an income tax.) In other words, 43 states have rejected the idea of having constitutional prohibitions on income taxes, relying instead upon the legislative process for controlling the tax burden in a state.

Comparison of States with No Income Tax

NO-INCOME-TAX STATE	TAX BURDEN AS A % OF INCOME	TOTAL TAX BURDEN RANK (1=LOWEST)
Alaska	5.10%	1
Tennessee	6.28%	3
Florida	6.56%	4
New Hampshire	6.86%	5
South Dakota	7.28%	8
Wyoming	7.51%	10
Texas	8.18%	18
Washington	8.20%	19
Nevada	8.26%	22

SOURCE: Adam McCann, "Tax Burden by State," Wallethub, www.wallethub.com.

Communicating Effectively: What Do You Think?

- Are you in favor of or against an income tax in Texas? Why or why not?

- Should the question of an income tax in a state be a policy matter controlled by the legislature or a matter addressed specifically in the constitution?

- Is the question of the income tax ultimately a policy or a constitutional issue or both?

WANT TO LEARN MORE?

- Tax Foundation is a leading tax policy nonprofit organization providing data and information about tax policy across the United States. www.taxfoundation.org

★ ★

The Constitution and the Future of Texas

IN THIS CHAPTER, we explored the Texas Founding and the story of constitutional government in Texas. We analyzed the seven constitutions under which Texas has been governed and explained the similarities and differences between the U.S. Constitution and Texas's current constitution (the Constitution of 1876). We also discussed successful attempts to amend the constitution and some of the constitutional issues that face Texas today.

It has been decades since there was any serious effort to change the Texas Constitution in any way other than by adding to its numerous amendments. This pattern likely will continue: more and more amendments will be added to an already lengthy and cumbersome document. Many of these amendments will address technical problems often related to the operations of various state agencies and local governments. Some may create additional funding sources for major state initiatives as we have seen recently in water and transportation policy. Other amendments might be adopted in response to such controversial social issues as abortion or the free exercise of religion. Turnout in constitutional amendment elections will remain low, unless there is a highly controversial amendment on the ballot. Though narrow interests have outsized influence on the proposing and passage of constitutional amendments, the constitution and its amendments will continue to reflect the values and goals of the people of Texas and the political system that the people have put into place through the constitution.

Use ☖ INQUIZITIVE to help you study and master this material.

The Role of a State Constitution

- **Identify the main functions of state constitutions (pp. 43–45)**

The state constitution is the governing document of the state much in the same way the U.S. Constitution sets up the framework for the nation as a whole. Many of the ideas found in the U.S. Constitution are also found in Texas's constitutions, including republican government, separation of powers, checks and balances, and individual rights.

Key Terms
constitution (p. 43)
separation of powers (p. 43)
checks and balances (p. 43)
tyranny (p. 43)
federalism (p. 44)
supremacy clause (p. 44)
necessary and proper clause (p. 44)

Practice Quiz
1. Which idea is contained in both the U.S. and Texas constitutions?
   a) separation of powers
   b) Keynesianism
   c) laissez-faire economics
   d) rebus sic stantibus
   e) none of the above

2. Which of the following is *not* an important function of a state constitution?
   a) prevents the concentration of political power
   b) delegates power to individuals and institutions
   c) allows government to intrude in the lives of businesses and individuals
   d) legitimizes political institutions
   e) limits application of the U.S. Constitution

3. Which part of the U.S. Constitution reserves power to the states?
   a) Article I
   b) Article VI
   c) First Amendment
   d) Tenth Amendment
   e) Nineteenth Amendment

4. Under the U.S. Constitution, the government of Texas is most limited by
   a) Article IV of the U.S. Constitution.
   b) the implied-powers clause and the Tenth Amendment of the U.S. Constitution.
   c) the Fourteenth Amendment of the U.S. Constitution.
   d) all of the above equally.
   e) none of the above

The Texas Constitutions: 1836–1876

- **Describe the seven Texas constitutions and their role in Texas political life (pp. 45–59)**

Texas has had seven constitutions reflecting the concerns of the historical periods in which they were written. The Civil War and Reconstruction played a major role in shaping Texans' attitudes toward the dangers of strong state government. The Constitution of 1876 sought to limit the powers that had been wielded under the previous constitution by Republican governor Edmund Davis. It remains, though much amended, the existing state constitution of Texas.

Key Terms
unicameral (p. 46)
bicameral (p. 49)
Confederacy (p. 53)
Presidential Reconstruction (p. 53)
Congressional Reconstruction (p. 54)

Radical Republicans (p. 54)
Grange (p. 56)

Practice Quiz

5. The Constitution of 1861
   a) generally accepted the existing constitutional framework.
   b) guided Texas's entry into the Confederate States of America.
   c) supported slavery.
   d) defended states' rights.
   e) all of the above

6. A unique feature of the Constitution of 1869 was that
   a) it explicitly rejected the power of the federal government in Texas.
   b) fewer than 1 percent of voters opposed it.
   c) it was less than four pages long.
   d) it was never submitted to the voters.
   e) it is considered the best of Texas's constitutions.

7. A new Texas Constitution was written
   a) when Reconstruction ended.
   b) when the Compromise of 1850 was adopted.
   c) at the start of World War I.
   d) in 1999.
   e) none of the above

8. The present Texas Constitution
   a) is well organized and well written.
   b) is considered to be one of the best of the 50 state constitutions.
   c) delegates a great deal of power to the governor.
   d) severely limits the power of the governor and other state officials.
   e) all of the above

9. The Constitution of 1876 was a reaction to the Reconstruction Constitution of 1869 because
   a) the 1869 Constitution was too short.
   b) the 1869 Constitution forbade slavery.
   c) the 1869 Constitution increased state officials' salaries.
   d) the 1869 Constitution was seen as giving the governor too much power.
   e) none of the above

10. When the framers of the Constitution of 1876 wrote of "the people," they meant
    a) all adult citizens of Texas.
    b) all adult male citizens of Texas.
    c) all men and women over the age of 21.
    d) all citizens except carpetbaggers and scalawags.
    e) none of the above

The Constitution of Texas Today

- Analyze the major provisions of the Texas Constitution today (pp. 59–69)

The Texas Constitution is composed of 16 articles (one of the original 17 articles has been deleted). The articles lay out the complex structures of power that define government in Texas.

Key Terms

limited government (p. 59)
republican government (p. 62)
plural executive (p. 64)
impeachment (p. 68)

Practice Quiz

11. The *separation of powers doctrine* refers to
    a) the idea that the United States is composed of 50 individual states.
    b) local government being autonomous from state rules and regulations.
    c) power being divided in Texas into three distinct branches of government: the legislature, the executive, and the judiciary.
    d) the process that sees the secretary of state appointed by the governor.
    e) none of the above

12. *Impeachment* refers to
    a) the power of the Court to declare a legislative act unconstitutional.
    b) the power of the House to charge a state official of inappropriate behavior leading to a trial by the Senate to remove him or her from office.
    c) the power of the governor to remove a judge from office.
    d) the result of an election.
    e) none of the above

13. Which of the following statements is true?
 a) Today the Texas Constitution authorizes the passage of an income tax in Texas.
 b) In 2019 a constitutional amendment was passed that eliminated the gasoline tax in Texas.
 c) In 2019 a constitutional amendment was passed that prohibited an income tax in Texas.
 d) The Texas Constitution makes no mention of taxation in any form.
 e) All statements are true.

Recent Attempts to Rewrite the Texas Constitution

Describe modern efforts to change the Texas Constitution (pp. 69–73)

The Texas Constitution has been changed 507 times since 1876 through the amendment process. In recent years, the vast majority of proposed constitutional amendments have been approved by the people. But occasionally, they have been turned down for a variety of reasons.

Practice Quiz
14. Why is there such low participation in constitutional amendment elections?
 a) The elections are unimportant.
 b) These elections are held in "off" years.
 c) They are generally held before special sessions of the legislature.
 d) They are held during a regular session of the legislature.
 e) none of the above

Environmental regulations by the national government sometimes raised issues of federalism. When the federal government promulgated a rule affecting surface mining, Texas and other states sued, claiming that the rule was an example of federal overreach that interfered with the powers of states.

Texas in the Federal System

WHY FEDERALISM MATTERS Federalism involves the distribution of power between the states and the national government. Although at times there is cooperation between the two levels of government, there has also been nearly constant tension between the two. Often, these conflicts over the proper role of the states versus the national government have been fraught with partisan political battles. Such partisanship in conflicts between the state and national government was common in the Obama administration when Republicans Greg Abbott and Ken Paxton sat in the attorney general's office.

It was during this intense mixture of federalism and political partisanship that the Obama administration put in place the "Stream Protection Rule." The rule was designed to reduce the levels of coal waste that surface strip-mining tossed into nearby streams. It would have required companies to restore streams and return the strip-mined areas to uses that the areas were capable of supporting prior to the mining and to replant the mined areas with native trees and vegetation. Essentially the rule updated regulations for surface coal mining that had been in existence for over 30 years.

The coal industry opposed the rule. The industry claimed that the rule would create a huge expense for the industry and would cause companies to cut jobs. One of the most vocal critics was Robert Murray, the CEO of Murray Energy, who considered the rule the most expensive regulation of the coal industry that existed.

In contrast, environmental groups supported the rule.[1] Appalachian Voices, an environmental group, estimated that coal companies had buried over 2,000 miles of streams through surface mining since the 1990s, and the group was concerned about the health effects of coal waste in the water. Supporters of the rule claimed that it would improve water quality in about 263 miles of streams each year going forward to 2040.[2]

Texas was one of the affected states. Texas is the sixth-largest coal-producing state in the country and is the largest producer of lignite coal—a poor-quality coal that is produced through strip mining.[3] Most of the lignite is used in electrical power generation, and it is a major pollutant. Because natural gas is an inexpensive alternative to coal, and there is increased use of wind energy and solar energy in electrical generation, lignite mining in Texas is a fast-fading industry. Still, surface strip mining is a significant business in Texas and Attorney General Ken Paxton decided to sue the federal government over the Stream Protection Rule.

Paxton joined a lawsuit against it with eleven other states. In filing the suit, Paxton said he "wanted to give it one last shot" prior to Donald Trump becoming president, believing this would be

Paxton's last chance to sue over an Obama administration policy. The state's argument in the suit was that the rule had been adopted without participation by the states. It was necessary to sue, said Paxton, because "yet again we must fight federal overreach. This rule tramples states' retention of sovereign authority under the Tenth Amendment and seeks to destroy an entire industry, displacing hardworking men and women and setting a precedent to disregard states' own understanding of major industries within their borders."[4]

The rule went into effect on December 20, 2016. Exactly one month later, Donald Trump was inaugurated as president along with a Republican-controlled House and Senate. Donald Trump, of course, had campaigned on stopping the decline of the coal industry. While Paxton's lawsuit was in the courts, the Trump administration acted. Repealing the rule was an easy way to quickly show the coal industry that President Trump meant to keep his campaign promises to it. Although repeal would not save the declining industry, it would provide it with a boost. On February 1, 2017, only days after Trump was inaugurated, the House of Representatives passed a resolution to repeal the rule. The next day, the Senate passed the repeal resolution and on February 16, less than a month into his presidency, Donald Trump signed the resolution.

The lifetime of the Stream Protection Rule was exceptionally short. With the rule voided, the lawsuit by Texas and the other states could be dismissed—there was no longer anything to sue about. Paxton could claim victory and President Trump could claim an early and easy fulfillment of his campaign promise to revitalize the coal industry. For his part, Attorney General Paxton, putting this partisan battle within the context of federalism, crowed, "Fighting federal overreach and protecting Texas sovereignty is a cornerstone of my office."[5]

During the Obama presidency, Texas sued the national government nearly 50 times and Paxton was clear in expressing the connection between federalism and partisanship when he said, "A lot of people are concerned about my mental health—now that Obama is leaving office, what is he going to do with his time? Some people have suggested maybe taking a day off, a week, maybe some counseling. But I want you to know that everything's going to be OK because I can still sue the city of Austin."[6] There is no doubt that tensions between the state of Texas and other levels of government will continue.

CHAPTER GOALS

- Understand the basics of the U.S. federal system (pp. 83–85)
- Explain how the Constitution and court decisions have shaped the federal system (pp. 85–92)
- Describe the major theories and mechanisms of American federalism (pp. 92–98)
- Analyze how federalism shapes key policy debates today (pp. 100–108)

What Is Federalism?

Understand the basics of the U.S. federal system

Federalism is a system of government in which power is divided between a central government and regional governments. In the United States, the balance between the powers of the states and those of the national government has been the subject of intense political dispute since the American Revolution. States have always done much of the routine governance in the United States. State laws provide the regulations for birth, death, marriage, divorce, and most crime and punishment. Most commercial law is regulated by the states, and states manage education, prisons, highways, welfare, environmental issues, corporations, and professions. The many conflicts that have been fought over the proper roles of states versus the national government include disputes over the states' rights to leave the Union, the power of government to regulate business, the implementation of political reforms, and responses to problems of race, poverty, and abortion.

federalism a system of government in which power is divided between a central government and regional governments

The Pros and Cons of Federalism

There are both advantages and disadvantages to federalism, although federalism has been essential to American government. It has proven enormously flexible in the United States. It has adapted to vast changes in the geographic size of America, to large increases in its population, and to changes in the racial, religious, and ethnic background of its population. It has also adapted to vast economic changes in the nation.[7] It should be noted that there are degrees of federalism—that is, regional governments can have substantial power in relation to the national government or they may have quite limited powers. Federalism in the United States, for example, is vastly different now than it was early in the twentieth century when the states had far more power in relation to the national government than they have now. Even though the states have far less power than they once did, the United States is still not a centralized system of government and there are continuing debates over the strengths and weaknesses of federalism.

The sharing of powers means that both the national and state governments have limits on their powers—attempts at overreach by one government can be checked by the other. These limits can be seen as an advantage because there is no all-powerful government that can intrude upon and potentially restrict the liberties of the people. Of course, advocates of stronger centralized government would make the contrary argument—that a decentralized government makes it harder for government to act in a clear and uniform manner to deal with the problems that are facing people.

Advocates of federalism often claim that the best government is the one closest to the people because it will be more accountable and responsive to the people's interests. Those who believe this take the position that the Texas state government is in a better position to know what Texans need and want from government than a distant national government trying to respond to the needs of all fifty states. An advocate of centralization might respond by pointing out times when the state government was not responsive

In recent years, Texas conservatives have clashed with the federal government's policies on key social issues, like abortion rights. Antiabortion protesters demonstrated outside an abortion clinic in McAllen, Texas.

to the needs of its people and the federal government had to step in. For example, Texas (and some other states) had legally imposed segregation—a policy clearly unresponsive and unaccountable to the needs of its African American citizens in their efforts to ensure racial equality. It was only action by the national government that ultimately brought an end to that lengthy era of state-imposed racial segregation.

Another major argument for federalism is that it allows freedom for policy experimentation. As Justice Louis Brandeis noted many years ago, it is federalism that allows the states to function as "laboratories of democracy." Rather than a one-size-fits-all national policy that would exist with a completely centralized national government, states may pursue different approaches to dealing with problems. Those different approaches would reflect the different needs and cultures of the states. States can then learn from each other in crafting their own policies.

An advocate of centralized government would argue that under a centralized government, there could still be national policies that allow flexibility and room for experimentation—national policies do not necessarily have to be uniform throughout the nation. Though advocates of centralization would argue that many policies should actually be uniform throughout the nation. For example, it seems more reasonable for Social Security payments to the elderly to be the same throughout the nation rather than for payments to vary significantly or perhaps not exist in some states under a decentralized system.

Polling data shows, however, that Texans seem to have a more favorable impression of the direction taken by the state than they do of the national government. The What Do Texans Think? feature shows that Texans were asked if they thought the state and the national government were going in the right direction. Based on polling of Texas voters every February from 2013 through 2020, Texans consistently have a more

Is the United States headed in the right direction? Is Texas?

Polling suggests that Texans are more convinced that their state is moving in the right direction than believe the nation is moving in the right direction. Why do you think Texans are more supportive of the direction of the state versus the nation? If state government was dominated by Democrats, how do you think these numbers would change? Why?

**PERCENTAGE OF TEXANS WHO THINK TEXAS
AND THE NATION ARE HEADING IN THE RIGHT DIRECTION**

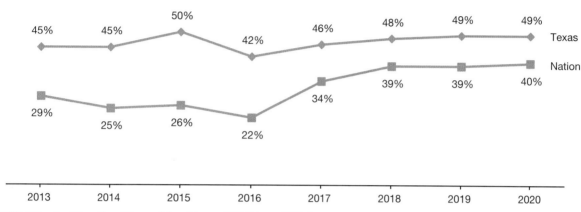

SOURCE: University of Texas *Texas Tribune* poll from February 2013–February 2020. Respondents were asked if they thought Texas and the country were moving in the right direction or wrong direction or if they had no opinion.

positive view of the direction the state is going compared with the direction of the country at large. That consistently more positive view of the direction of the state compared with the nation seems to provide support for the argument that one benefit of federalism is that state-level governance is closer to the people and is preferable to government at the national level.

Federalism in the Constitution

Explain how the Constitution and court decisions have shaped the federal system

Understanding federalism requires an understanding of why the framers shaped the system in the unique way they did. In many ways, the federal system in the Constitution emerged out of practical decisions made by the framers, who were dealing with an overly decentralized system of government under the Articles of Confederation that was not working. And as we will see, the debates the framers tackled over state and national power are ones we continue to face today.

State Power under the Articles of Confederation

For several years after the United States won its independence from Britain, the Articles of Confederation gave states the primary role in governance, and the national government was small and had limited powers. Its relative weakness meant that the states functioned as nearly independent entities rather than as a unified nation. By the mid-1780s, the states' diversity and self-serving policies appeared to be splitting the new nation apart. An economic decline in the 1780s worsened the divisions in the country. Daniel Shays led a rebellion of Massachusetts debtors who attacked towns and burned courthouses, and the new nation seemed on the precipice of revolt. George Washington criticized the state governments for the new nation's problems, saying the states' pursuit of narrow self-interest was making "the situation of this great country weak, inefficient and disgraceful."

It was hard for the national government under the Articles of Confederation to act. The Confederation Congress had limited powers, and the rules allowed a few states—in some cases a single state—to block congressional action. It took 9 states (out of 13) to enact any defense or economic policy. The Congress could not tax; it had to request money from the state governments, and it could not compel payment. By 1786 the Con-

During the American Revolution, the lack of a strong central government made it difficult for the United States to fund a strong military, as exemplified by terrible conditions for the troops at Valley Forge.

gress was broke because states were not paying their share of expenses for the national government. The Confederation also had no executive or court system and could not defend the nation because it could not pay for an army or a navy. Moreover, the Articles of Confederation could not easily be amended, because a unanimous vote of the states was required for amendment.[8]

By 1786 it was becoming clear that something had to be done to increase the power of the national government. A meeting was held that year in Annapolis, Maryland, that called for a convention of states to meet in Philadelphia the following year to "render the constitution of the Federal Government adequate to the exigencies of the Union." That call led to the Constitutional Convention in 1787, where 55 delegates met and designed the new U.S. Constitution.[9]

The Federal System under the Constitution

Under the U.S. Constitution, a federal system was created in which the national government was **sovereign**, deriving its power directly from the American people. One of the most important parts of the Constitution was the **supremacy clause** in Article VI. That clause provided that the Constitution, federal laws, and treaties were the supreme law of the land. If state laws or state constitutions were contrary to the Constitution, federal laws, or treaties, the state laws or state constitutional provisions were invalid. State courts were required to be bound by the U.S. Constitution and federal laws. The supremacy clause prevented states from acting in ways that were inconsistent with the U.S. Constitution and national laws, and thus the clause was a unifying national provision that was sorely lacking under the Articles of Confederation.

sovereign possessing supreme political authority within a geographic area

supremacy clause a provision in Article VI of the Constitution that provides that the U.S. Constitution, federal laws, and treaties are superior to state constitutions and laws and provides that state courts must adhere to the U.S. Constitution and federal laws

The immediate effect of the Constitution was to increase national power and to delegate to the national government distinctive powers and responsibilities such as national defense and foreign policy. Individual states were also sovereign, however, deriving their power from the people in their state through their state constitutions and having their own separate powers and responsibilities, such as protecting public safety.[10] Under this system, local governments were created by state governments, and their powers are granted (and can be revoked) by state governments (see Chapter 10).

State interests were protected under the new Constitution in a variety of ways, and one of the most important was that each state would get equal representation in the Senate. At the time, state legislatures chose the U.S. senators from that state, and so the senators were agents of state interests in the national government. States also retained their power to tax and to maintain a militia, and they had commercial powers, such as the power to regulate commerce within states. Several provisions of the Constitution are especially important in understanding the nature of American federalism. Among those provisions are the Tenth Amendment, the elastic clause, and the full faith and credit clause of the Constitution.

The Tenth Amendment In the debates over ratification of the Constitution, there was great concern that the national government had been made too powerful and that, if ratified, the Constitution would foster a centralized tyranny that would destroy the rights of the people and the states. In an effort to alleviate these concerns, the Bill of Rights was added to the Constitution in the form of the first ten amendments. The **Tenth Amendment**, commonly called the States' Rights Amendment, provides the greatest support in the U.S. Constitution for protecting states against national power. It says, "The powers not delegated to the United States by the Constitution, nor prohibited by it to the States, are reserved to the States respectively, or to the people." The problem with the amendment is that it does not specify national and state powers, and so rather than settle conflicts over federalism, the amendment has become a source of conflict over the meaning of federalism.[11]

Tenth Amendment a provision in the Constitution's Bill of Rights that says, "The powers not delegated to the United States by the Constitution, nor prohibited by it to the States, are reserved to the States respectively, or to the people"; used by states to challenge actions of the national government

The Elastic Clause

For its part, the national government under the Constitution had taxing authority, military powers, and commercial authority such as the power to regulate commerce between states. And it had flexible powers that could be expanded in the future through Congress's constitutional power "to make all Laws which shall be necessary and proper for carrying into Execution the foregoing Powers, and all other Powers vested by this Constitution in the Government of the United States."[12] This provision, sometimes called the **elastic clause**, provides support for implied national powers and this exercise of implied national powers often comes in conflict with state powers guaranteed by the Tenth Amendment.

elastic clause clause in Article I of the Constitution that gives Congress power "to make all Laws which shall be necessary and proper for carrying into Execution the foregoing Powers, and all other Powers vested by this Constitution in the Government of the United States"; the source of implied powers for the national government

Full Faith and Credit Clause

Article IV, Section 1 of the Constitution contains the **full faith and credit clause**, which provides that each state must recognize the "public Acts, Records, and judicial Proceedings of every other State." Congress does have the authority under this provision to pass laws regulating state recognition of the acts of other states. The clause is a unifying force in creating a nation out of multiple sovereign states. Generally, the acts of one state are accepted by another. If a couple is married in Arkansas, that marriage is recognized in Texas and so moving from Arkansas to Texas would not require the couple to marry again in Texas. There are exceptions, however, to one state recognizing the acts of other states. The classic example involved same-sex marriage prior to the Supreme Court's decision in *Obergefell v. Hodges* (2015) which recognized same-sex marriage as a constitutional right. Before *Obergefell*, Hawaii was on the verge of recognizing same-sex marriage and Congress passed the Defense of Marriage Act in 1996 which allowed states to refuse to recognize same-sex marriages from other states.[13]

full faith and credit clause a constitutional requirement that each state must generally recognize the law and judicial actions of other states

One of the main exceptions to the full faith and credit clause is not congressional action allowing states to reject the acts of other states, it is a vague concept known as the **public policy exception**. A state may refuse to give full faith and credit to the actions of another state if those actions are deemed against the public policy of the state. Ultimately, the public policy exception is determined by the federal courts. Colorado, for example, has legalized the purchase and use of marijuana, but Texas does not have to follow Colorado's lead. Legal marijuana in Colorado is illegal in Texas, as many Texans have learned the hard way. A number of states have entered into reciprocal agreements with Texas where Texas recognizes their concealed carry permits for firearms and those states recognize Texas's permit. However, a Texas concealed carry permit is not recognized in all states. The position of states not recognizing Texas's concealed carry permits is that concealed carry (at least as legislated by Texas) is against the public policy of those states.

public policy exception the concept that states do not have to give full faith and credit to the actions of other states where those actions violate a state's public policy

Early Constitutional Debates over Federalism

Controversy over the exact nature of the federal system has been long-standing. During the Nullification Crisis in 1833, South Carolina tried to assert the right to veto (or nullify) national legislation passed by Congress. The prominent South Carolina politician John C. Calhoun, then vice president under President Andrew Jackson, argued that a strong national government was a threat to the sovereignty of states and called for a federal system along the lines of the original Articles of Confederation. When Jackson responded by threatening to use military force in support of federal law, however, South Carolina backed down.

Although the national government imposed its will successfully during the Nullification Crisis, the question of the exact relationship between it and individual states was still open. In spite of the forces of decentralization, most notably coming from the South, the Supreme Court under Chief Justice John Marshall (1801–35) issued a number of important opinions that promoted national power at the expense of state power.

In *McCulloch v. Maryland* (1819), for example, one issue was whether Congress had the power to incorporate the Second Bank of the United States. Writing for a unanimous Court, Marshall noted that Article I, Section 8, of the Constitution enumerated the powers of Congress. Nowhere in Article I, Section 8, is specifically found the power to incorporate a bank. However, because a Bank of the United States could be a means to accomplish some of Congress's enumerated powers, such as carrying out the power to borrow money, the Court found that Congress did have the implied power to incorporate the bank. Thus, the "necessary and proper" clause (the elastic clause) of Article I, Section 8, provided a source of implied powers for the national government. Marshall further noted in his opinion that unlike the Articles of Confederation, the U.S. Constitution had no provision that excluded the recognition of implied powers. He even made the case that the Tenth Amendment recognized that Congress had implied powers because it said "The powers not delegated to the United States" rather than "The powers not *expressly* delegated to the United States." This was a vastly important decision favoring national power at the expense of state powers.[14]

Another major Marshall Court decision that expanded national power by broadly defining Congress's power to regulate interstate commerce was *Gibbons v. Ogden* (1824), which dealt with a dispute over the operation of steamboats in New York waters. Robert Fulton and Robert Livingston obtained a monopoly from New York to operate steamboats in its waters, and they granted a license to Aaron Ogden to operate steamboats between New Jersey and New York. When Thomas Gibbons then obtained a license from the national government to operate steamboats between New Jersey and New York, Ogden went to New York courts to get an injunction against Gibbons. Marshall wrote that one of the powers of Congress in Article I, Section 8, was the "power to regulate commerce with foreign nations, and among the several states."[15] Ogden argued that such power was limited to the interchange of commodities and did not include navigation, but Marshall broadly defined commerce to include navigation and wrote that interstate commerce "cannot stop at the external boundary line of each state, but may be introduced into the interior." While the completely internal commerce of a state could be considered reserved to the states for regulation, he wrote, if commerce was not

A major power of the national government is the power to regulate interstate commerce. Gibbons v. Ogden (1824) was a key case that expanded national power. It held that Congress had the power to regulate interstate commerce, such as shipping between New York and New Jersey, pictured here.

completely internal to a state, then it was interstate commerce and could be regulated by Congress.[16] This decision, providing a broad definition of interstate commerce, was to be the primary source of the most important regulatory power of Congress: the power to regulate interstate commerce.

Marshall was consistent when deciding cases in expanding the power of the national government and weakening the power of states. However, he was unwilling to make the Bill of Rights apply to the states as well as the national government, a step that would require the ratification of the Fourteenth Amendment in 1868. In Marshall's time, it was clear that the Bill of Rights was not a restriction on the powers of states; it was intended to limit the powers of the national government.

The Constitution was created out of a fear of disunity. Seventy-five years after the ratification of the Constitution, an observer of American federalism would have concluded that it was a failure. America faced a massive rebellion and a bloody civil war.[17] Texas played a major part in the tensions between the North and the South that threatened the Union when Texas sought statehood and was ultimately admitted to the Union as a slave state. Only sixteen years after its admission to the Union, Texas seceded and joined the Confederacy. With secession of southern states came the Civil War, which was, in part, a struggle over the meaning of the federal system and the proper relationship between the national and the state governments. Southern states, including Texas, feared that a national government controlled by northern states would move to end slavery, an institution that the southern states felt was essential to their social, political, and economic way of life. They saw the creation of the Confederacy as a movement back to the older system embodied in the Articles of Confederation, wherein the central government in Richmond was weak and the individual states were strong. This vision of a confederation effectively came to a close in 1865 with General Robert E. Lee's surrender to Union general Ulysses Grant at the Appomattox Court House.

The Civil War Amendments and Increased National Power

Reconstruction the period after the Civil War when much of the South was under military occupation

The end of the Civil War brought an era of **Reconstruction**. With the end of the Civil War, a key constitutional question remained, previously unanswered by the Supreme Court: Can a state secede from the Union? In 1869, Texas was a party to the case in which the Supreme Court resolved this question. The case, *Texas v. White*, dealt with the legality of a bond sale sponsored by the state that had occurred under its Confederate government. In rejecting the legality of the sale, Chief Justice Salmon Chase's opinion stated that the Constitution "in all its provisions, looks to an indestructible Union, composed of indestructible states." Secession was void and Texas had remained a U.S. state during the Civil War; it had not had a lawful government during the Confederacy, and so the bond sale was void. Additionally, the Court ruled, the national government could create a government in Texas after the war where no legitimate government existed because Article IV, Section 4, of the Constitution provided, "The United States shall guarantee to every State in this Union a Republican Form of Government."[18]

Three amendments to the Constitution were also ratified in the aftermath of the Civil War. Those amendments, the Thirteenth, Fourteenth, and Fifteenth amendments, are together known as the **Civil War Amendments**. The Thirteenth Amendment banned slavery and was important after the Civil War in ending slavery as a basis of the southern economy. The Fifteenth Amendment has been used as a source within the Constitution for legislation dealing with voting rights. It has been the Fourteenth Amendment that has had the most dramatic effect on the nature of federalism. However, with the exception of the Thirteenth Amendment, the Civil War Amendments had little immediate effect because of an unwillingness on the part of Congress and the president to enforce the amendments and because of Court interpretations that limited the impact of the amendments. However, as time went by, the amendments, especially the Fourteenth Amendment, began to have great significance in guaranteeing civil rights and liberties.

The most significant provision of the **Fourteenth Amendment** states, "nor shall any State deprive any person of life, liberty, or property, without due process of law; nor deny to any person within its jurisdiction the equal protection of the laws." With few exceptions, in the nineteenth century the Fourteenth Amendment offered little promise of being a U.S. constitutional restriction on the states. Its importance in this regard began to increase early in the twentieth century due to two developments: (1) the Supreme Court's incorporation of the Bill of Rights into the Fourteenth Amendment and (2) the use of the equal protection clause in the Fourteenth Amendment to combat racial discrimination.

The **incorporation of the Bill of Rights** meant that the Court ruled that some of the rights guaranteed in the Bill of Rights are fundamental—so essential they are incorporated (held to be part of) in the "liberty" guaranteed in the Fourteenth Amendment, which states, "nor shall any State deprive any person of life, *liberty* [emphasis added], or property, without due process of law." Over the years, more and more rights were found by the Court to be fundamental ones that were held to apply to the states. Most recently, in 2010 the Court held that the Second Amendment right to "keep and bear arms" applied to the states.[19] There are now very few rights in the Bill of Rights that have not been held to be fundamental.

In the 1930s the Supreme Court began to use the equal protection clause to chip away at state laws promoting racial discrimination. In 1950 a Texas case heralded the end of segregated higher education. Heman Sweatt was denied admission to the University of Texas Law School because he was African American. He refused to attend a Black law school that Texas had set up to provide what the state claimed to be a **"separate but equal"** legal education for Black Texans. Texas claimed that its provision of the two separate law schools complied with the Supreme Court's interpretation of the equal protection clause in *Plessy v. Ferguson* (1896), when it upheld a state requirement of racially segregated train cars in Louisiana. Sweatt's argument was that the Black law school was not equal to the University of Texas Law School but was inferior and, therefore, to require him to attend it would deny him the equal protection of the laws. The Supreme Court agreed, pointing out that there were vast differences in the facilities as well as differences in the prestige of the schools, the reputation of the faculty, the experience of the administration, and the influence of the alumni. While the Court stopped just short of declaring "separate but equal" requirements to be unconstitutional, after *Sweatt* it was hard to see how the doctrine could survive,[20] and it did not. In 1954 in *Brown v. Board of Education of Topeka*,

Civil War Amendments the Thirteenth, Fourteenth, and Fifteenth amendments, ratified after the Civil War

Fourteenth Amendment ratified in 1868, the amendment that protects persons from state action denying them due process or the equal protection of the laws

incorporation of the Bill of Rights the Supreme Court ruling that rights that are deemed to be fundamental rights are considered part of "liberty" in the Fourteenth Amendment and apply to the states as well as the national government

"separate but equal" an interpretation of the Fourteenth Amendment's equal protection clause that held that states could segregate races as long as equal facilities were provided; it was overturned in 1954

Heman Sweatt (right) walks with a White student at the University of Texas. Sweatt refused to attend a separate, all-Black law school.

the Supreme Court unanimously held that segregated public schools were inherently unequal.[21] The doctrine of "separate but equal" was dead, though resistance to the decision in many states, including Texas, would delay for decades the end of legally created segregation in public schools.

How Does Federalism Work?

Describe the major theories and mechanisms of American federalism

There has not been a singular theory of how federalism works in the United States. Instead, there have been different ideas about federalism over time and different mechanisms for putting those ideas into practice.

Dual Federalism

dual federalism, or **layer-cake federalism** a form of federalism in which the powers and responsibilities of the state and national governments are separate and distinct

Following the end of Reconstruction and into the early twentieth century, the court embraced **dual federalism**, which was described by political scientist Morton Grodzins as **layer-cake federalism** (see Figure 3.1). Like the layers on a cake, the powers of the national government and state governments were largely separate and, one might add, the layer that was the national government's powers and responsibilities was smaller than was the layer that represented the powers and responsibilities of state governments.[22] Under layer-cake federalism, there were still clear limits to the sovereignty of states. States could not nullify national legislation, nor could they secede from the Union. But states had a major role to play in governance that was quite distinct from the role of the federal government.

Prior to the late 1930s the Supreme Court was using dual federalism to strike down regulation of the economy by the national government. Congressional power to regulate interstate commerce was narrowly defined, Congress was powerless to forbid the distribution of the products of child labor in interstate commerce, and it could not regulate aspects of the manufacture of goods, such as monopolies on production or working conditions in factories.

Dual federalism had tremendous effects on Texas. For example, the Railroad Commission of Texas established rules that, among other things, limited the number of oil wells that could be drilled on a particular amount of land and the amount of oil that could be pumped from those wells. Such regulations were seen as a matter for state rather than national regulation until the discovery of the East Texas Oil Field in 1930, which then

FIGURE 3.1

Dual versus Cooperative Federalism

In layer-cake federalism, the responsibilities of the national government and state governments are clearly separated. In marble-cake federalism, national policies, state policies, and local policies overlap in many areas.

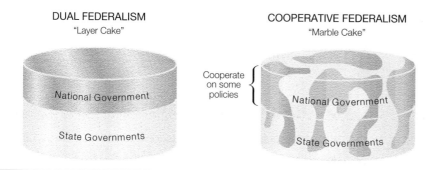

DUAL FEDERALISM
"Layer Cake"

COOPERATIVE FEDERALISM
"Marble Cake"

Cooperate on some policies

National Government

State Governments

National Government

State Governments

was the largest oil field in the world. As a result of this discovery, such overproduction of oil occurred that national legislation was needed to prevent an interstate market in oil produced in violation of state regulations.

Dual federalism was also used to prevent national intervention into acts of racial violence in Texas, because enforcement of criminal laws was seen as a state matter. Texas did pass an anti-lynching law in 1897 that was used to prevent some lynchings by authorizing the governor to call out the state guard. Nevertheless, Texas and other states were remarkably ineffective in preventing lynching. It is hard to identify the precise number of victims, but the Equal Justice Initiative has identified 3,959 lynchings between 1877 and 1950 whose purpose was to enforce racial separation and segregation laws. Of those, 376 occurred in Texas.[23] It was only in the 1960s that national laws began to be used to successfully prosecute these crimes.

Dual Sovereignty
Dual sovereignty is not to be confused with dual federalism. **Dual sovereignty** means that both state governments and the national government have powers to make laws. The national government's power is limited to the lawmaking authority granted in the Constitution to the national government. The lawmaking authority of state government is the **police power**—the power of states to pass laws to promote the health, safety, and welfare of people. As long as the state can show it is reasonably exercising its police power, it has the authority to, for example, require businesses to close or people to wear masks in public in order to reduce the spread of the coronavirus.

Sometimes the national government passes laws that regulate or forbid actions that are also regulated or forbidden by state laws. In such a situation, the question often becomes whether a person charged with a state crime can also be charged with the same crime under federal laws. That situation happened to Terance Gamble, who pled guilty to a state charge of violating Alabama's law against a felon possessing a firearm. Then

dual sovereignty the principle that states and national government have the power to pass laws and, in the case of overlapping laws, both the state and national government can enforce their laws

police power the power of states to pass laws to promote health, safety, and public welfare

The U.S. and Texas flags that fly in front of many government buildings in Texas (including the Texas state capitol, pictured here) reflect the nature of federalism. Both the national government and the state government are sovereign.

cooperative federalism, or **marble-cake federalism** a way of describing federalism where the boundaries between the national government and state governments have become blurred

categorical grants congressionally appropriated grants to states and localities on the condition that expenditures be limited to a problem or group specified by law

federal prosecutors charged Gamble with the federal crime involving a felon possessing a firearm. Gamble took his case all the way to the Supreme Court arguing that he was being tried for the same crime twice which was double jeopardy and violated that provision of the Fifth Amendment. The Court, however, cited 170 years of Court precedent in explaining that unlike the United Kingdom, the United States is not a unitary government. Instead, it is a federal system where both the state and the national government have the power to pass laws and so Alabama could prosecute and convict Gamble for the firearm charge and the federal government could do so as well without any problem of double jeopardy.[24]

Cooperative Federalism

With the presidency of Franklin Roosevelt (1933–45)—when America faced the Great Depression and then World War II—the relationship between the national government and the states changed dramatically. This new relationship was called **cooperative federalism**, or **marble-cake federalism**, in which the boundaries between the national and state governments became blurred. In the initial form of cooperative federalism, national and state governments worked together to provide services—often with joint funding of programs or state administration of programs mostly funded by the national government.

In fighting the Great Depression, Roosevelt pursued a variety of such programs. The Social Security Act of 1935, for instance, changed the existing system of federalism in a number of fundamental ways. First, it put into place a national insurance program for the elderly (now known as Social Security), wherein individuals in all states were assessed a payroll tax on their wages and upon retirement received a pension check. Second, the act put into place a series of state-federal programs to address particular social problems, including unemployment insurance, aid to dependent children, aid to the blind and disabled, and aid to impoverished elderly people. The basic model for these programs was that the federal government would make money available to states that established their own programs in these areas, provided they met specific administrative guidelines. Although the federal dollars came with these strings attached, the programs were state run and could differ from state to state. This type of funding system was common in the early days of cooperative federalism. The federal grants made using this model were called **categorical grants**.

During the New Deal period, the idea was abandoned that the Tenth Amendment was a barrier to national power and that the national government could not involve itself in areas that had previously been reserved only to the states. As the Supreme Court case *Wickard v. Filburn* (1942) suggested, the regulatory power of the national government under the interstate commerce clause was so broad that there seemed no boundaries on national power.[25] National government regulation under the interstate commerce clause even included regulating the wheat grown by a farmer for his personal use.[26]

In the 1960s, during the Great Society policies of President Lyndon B. Johnson, a former U.S. senator from Texas, new programs were added to the Social Security Act.

Federal Funds to Texas versus Other States

Many factors affect how much federal funding a state receives. Federal money can go directly to individuals, such as Social Security or Medicare. Federal money can also go to the states, which then decide how best to use the funds to benefit their constituents, such as for highway funding. In the graph below, we can compare how much federal money Texas and Texans receive compared to California, Florida, New York, and Ohio.

Federal Funds Received by States, 2005–18

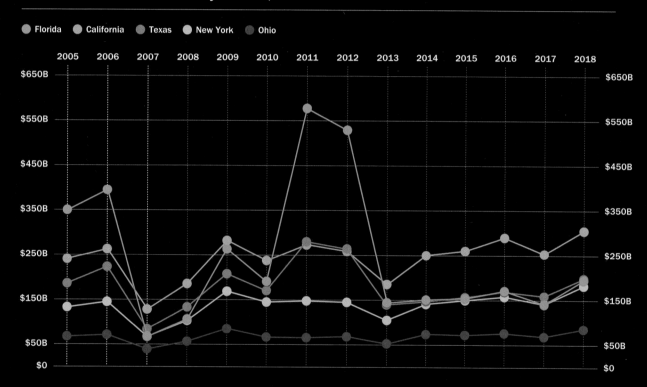

Federal Funding as a Percentage of State Revenue, 2017

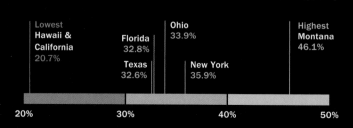

Lowest Hawaii & California 20.7%	Florida 32.8%	Ohio 33.9%		Highest Montana 46.1%
	Texas 32.6%		New York 35.9%	

20% 30% 40% 50%

SOURCES: "Spending by Geography, 2019," USASpending.gov; Janelle Cammenga, "Which States Rely the Most on Federal Aid?," February 12, 2020 (accessed 6/17/2020).

CRITICAL THINKING

- What might explain why certain states receive more funding than others at different time periods?

- Florida and Texas received about the same amount of federal funding in 2018, even though the population of Texas is much larger. Why do you suppose Florida receives proportionally more federal funds than Texas?

During the 1930s, Texans were affected by unemployment and drought that led to massive poverty across the state. The federal government stepped in to help, employing people in public works projects. Here, people make copper utensils for a Texas hospital.

Medicare was established to provide health insurance for the elderly, paid for through a payroll tax on current workers. Medicaid was added to provide health care funding for individuals enrolled in the state-federal Aid to Families with Dependent Children (AFDC) program. Medicaid's funding and administration were based on the same state-federal principles as AFDC and unemployment insurance: the federal government provided funding for approved state programs. Federalism continued to evolve with the passage of civil rights legislation in the 1950s and '60s, when the role of the national government was expanded to protect the rights of minorities. In the process, the national government was often thrown into conflict with southern states such as Texas that persisted in trying to maintain a segregated society.

After his election in 1968, President Richard M. Nixon briefly tried to reduce the power of the national government and increase that of the states with a program known as **New Federalism**. Nixon introduced a funding mechanism called **block grants**, which allowed the states considerable leeway in spending their federal dollars. In the 1980s, President Ronald Reagan adopted Nixon's New Federalism as his own, and block grants became an important part of state-federal cooperation.

New Federalism's biggest success, however, came during President Bill Clinton's administration, when in 1996 major reforms were passed that gave the states a significant decision-making role in welfare programs. By the 1990s liberals and conservatives were in agreement that welfare in America was broken. Replacing the state-federal system with a system of grants tied to federal regulations and guidelines lay at the heart of the Clinton welfare reforms, the most important since the New Deal.

New Federalism the attempts by Presidents Nixon and Reagan to return power to the states through block grants

block grants federal grants that allow states considerable discretion on how funds are spent

Coercive Federalism

coercive federalism federal policies that force states to change their policies to achieve national goals

In recent years some national actions have been described as **coercive federalism**, in which federal regulations are used to force states to change their policies to meet national goals. For example, until the 2012 Supreme Court decision involving the 2010 Affordable Care Act (commonly called Obamacare) struck down the provision, states were threatened with the loss of all Medicaid funding if they did not expand their Medicaid coverage to comply with the legislation.

Perhaps the most disturbing aspect of coercive federalism for states are federal **unfunded mandates**, which are federal requirements that the state (or local) governments pay the costs of federal policies.[27] For example, the federal Americans with Disabilities Act requires that street curbs be accessible to wheelchairs, but the federal government does not pay for the curbs. That cost is passed on to state and local governments. The Congressional Budget Office reported that from 2006 through 2016 Congress passed 167 laws that imposed mandates on state and local governments, with 27 passed in 2015–16. A study of the costs of unfunded mandates from 1994 through 1998 claimed they would cost states and localities $54 billion. In recent years, however, the costs of unfunded mandates have lessened. No mandate with costs exceeding $77 million has been imposed since 2010.[28]

unfunded mandates federal requirements that states or local governments pay the costs of federal policies

Along with unfunded mandates, federal **preemption** is another aspect of coercive federalism. Preemption is based on the supremacy clause in Article VI of the U.S. Constitution, which states, "This Constitution and the Laws of the United States which shall be made in Pursuance thereof; . . . shall be the supreme Law of the Land." Preemption does not force expenditures upon the states, but it does prevent the states from acting in areas that the Constitution exclusively reserves to the national government. In 2008 the city of Farmers Branch, Texas, passed an ordinance that prohibited persons who were not citizens or legally in the United States from renting a residence inside the city. Violations of the ordinance were criminal offenses which applied to both the renter and the landlord. The federal Fifth Circuit Court of Appeals struck down the ordinance on preemption grounds, holding that the law interfered with the national government's constitutional power over immigration.[29]

preemption an aspect of constitutional reasoning granting exclusive powers to act in a particular area to the national government

The States Respond States have begun to fight back against coercive federalism and centralization of government in general. This has often had a partisan tinge, in which Republican-controlled states opposed actions of the Obama administration and Democratic-controlled states opposed actions of the Trump administration. As coercive federalism became more common, concerns were increasingly expressed in the last few decades of the twentieth century, particularly among conservative Republicans, that the federal government was becoming too strong in the federal system. In response, not surprisingly, a more conservative Supreme Court rethought its doctrines on federalism. Beginning in the 1990s, although not dramatically reinterpreting constitutional law, the Court's rulings did begin to place limits on Congress's ability to legislate under the interstate commerce power, and the Court resurrected the Tenth Amendment as a protection for the rights of states.

There have been several more recent examples of increased pushback by states against federal power. Numerous state leaders were critical of the Affordable Care Act and refused to initiate the state health insurance exchanges intended under the act or expand Medicaid. Politicians in Texas and elsewhere also criticized what they called the Obama administration's weak efforts to enforce immigration laws, and thus states have become involved in aspects

SOCIAL RESPONSIBILITY: GET INVOLVED

- Do you think the federal government should be allowed to impose "unfunded mandates" on the states?

- What state issues, if any, do you feel the federal government should be involved in? Why these and not others?

of immigration enforcement. State officials in Texas, Mississippi, and Oregon vowed to reject attempts by the federal government to impose new gun laws.[30] And the Tenth Amendment is now being used by some jurisdictions in an effort to prevent the federal government from forcing localities to end "sanctuary cities" and comply with federal immigration requirements.

Reflecting this rebellion against coercive federalism and centralized government, a number of states, including Texas, have filed lawsuits against the federal government. As then attorney general Greg Abbott put it in defending such suits against Obama administration policies by his office, "When Texas challenges the federal government, it's about more than money. It's about principles—fundamental principles enshrined in the Constitution and recently reaffirmed by the U.S. Supreme Court when it said: 'The national government possesses only limited powers; the states and the people retain the remainder. The independent power of the states serves as a check on the power of the federal government.' Defending the constitutional principles that have made the United States truly exceptional: That's priceless."[31]

Independent State Grounds

independent state grounds a constitutional concept allowing states, usually under the state constitution, to expand rights beyond those provided by the U.S. Constitution

In addition to Supreme Court decisions in recent years that are more favorable to the claims of states versus federal legislation, states do have leeway to expand rights of their residents through a concept known as **independent state grounds**. State constitutions can provide greater constitutional guarantees to a state's citizens than the U.S. Constitution. Independent state grounds are a characteristic of federalism in that states are free to add to the rights guaranteed at the national level. Some states, such as Massachusetts, relied on their state constitutions to invalidate laws against same-sex marriage.[32] Under the U.S. Constitution, Texas's very inequitable property tax–based system for funding public education was held to be constitutional. In 1973 the U.S. Supreme Court held that education was not a fundamental right and so Texas only needed a rational justification—that is, local control of schools—for the funding system to be upheld.[33] However, in *Edgewood v. Kirby* (1989), the Texas Supreme Court relied on the Texas Constitution to strike down the system on the grounds that it did not provide "what the [Texas] constitution commands—i.e., an efficient system of public free schools throughout the state."[34]

In the 1970s there was a major effort to gain ratification of an Equal Rights Amendment to the U.S. Constitution. If ratified, the key part of the amendment would have stated, "Equality of rights under the law shall not be denied or abridged by the United States or by any state on account of sex." Although the amendment was not ratified nationally, in 1972 Texas adopted its own version of the Equal Rights Amendment, which is Article 1, Section 3a, of the Texas Constitution: "Equality under the law shall not be denied or abridged because of sex, race, color, creed, or national origin." U.S. Supreme Court decisions have provided major protection against sex discrimination under the equal protection clause of the Fourteenth Amendment to the U.S. Constitution; however, it is the Texas Constitution, rather than the U.S. Constitution, that contains an explicit ban.

How Do Federal Funds Flow to Texas?

Federal grants provide states with money for programs that range from Medicaid and school lunches to tuberculosis control and immunization programs. As the chart below indicates, federal grants make up a majority of the money the state of Texas spends on health care and a large share of the money spent on natural resources, education, and general government.

2018–19 Texas Budget

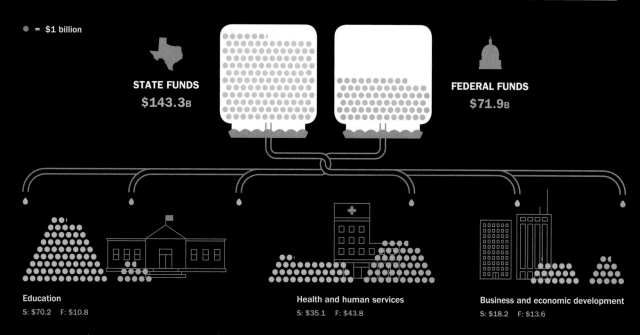

● = $1 billion

STATE FUNDS
$143.3B

FEDERAL FUNDS
$71.9B

Education
S: $70.2   F: $10.8

Health and human services
S: $35.1   F: $43.8

Business and economic development
S: $18.2   F: $13.6

Public safety and criminal justice
S: $11.7   F: $0.6

General government
S: $5.0   F: $1.2

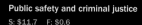

Natural resources
S: $2.6   F: $1.9

Other (regulatory, judiciary, legislature, general provisions)
S: $0.5   F: $0.1

SOURCE: Legislative Budget Board, "Fiscal Size-Up 2018–2019," pp. 2, 6.

QUANTITATIVE REASONING

- According to the data, what proportion of the Texas budget consists of federal funds? How might the presence of this federal money affect the relationship between the state and federal governments?

- Suppose federal funds for health and human services were eliminated. How might Texas reallocate state funds to avoid drastically reducing these services?

Current Issues Involving Federalism

Analyze how federalism shapes key policy debates today

Federalism is at the heart of political controversies in the United States. Many of the issues on the contemporary political agenda involve often bitter partisan disagreements over the relationship between the states and the national government. Some of those issues of federalism include Texas and involve questions such as state regulation of voting, the Affordable Care Act, immigration, and the effect of the coronavirus pandemic on Texas and its relationship to the nation.

State Regulation of Voting

preclearance the requirement under Section 5 of the Voting Rights Act that the U.S. Department of Justice or a Washington, D.C., federal court had to approve any voting changes from states (including Texas) covered by the provision; this is no longer required due to a Supreme Court decision

The federal Voting Rights Act required **preclearance** by federal officials for states, such as Texas, that were covered under the act. Those covered states could not change voting procedures such as requiring voter identification laws, redrawing political district boundaries, or changing the times and locations of polling places without getting federal approval. The formula for determining which states were covered under the act was challenged in an Alabama case, *Shelby County, Alabama v. Holder*.

Texas filed an amicus curiae or "friend of the court" brief supporting Shelby County's claim that the Voting Rights Act went beyond Congress's powers and placed substantial enough costs on federalism that it violated the Tenth Amendment. Texas's brief noted that the act was based on voting conditions in Texas in the distant past. Unlike then, Texas now has bilingual ballots, and the brief pointed out that in every federal election between 1996 and 2004, African Americans in Texas had registered and voted at higher rates than Whites, while between 1980 and 2002, Latinos in Texas had registered to vote at higher rates than Latinos in jurisdictions not covered by the act. The remainder of the brief essentially argued that the preclearance requirement created substantial costs to federalism because it had prevented the implementation of Texas's 2011 voter ID law.[35]

In 2013 the Court issued a 5–4 decision striking down the formula for determining the jurisdictions covered under the preclearance requirement. Finding that the formula was based on decades-old data, the Court held that Shelby County was correct in its position that they were too outdated to be valid. Congress could, the Court said, draft another formula to cover jurisdictions under the act, but that formula must be based on current voting conditions. The Court emphasized two important points about the federal system: (1) all states enjoy equal sovereignty, and (2) under the Tenth Amendment, states have broad power to regulate elections. Only exceptional conditions, it said, such as the racial discrimination in voting at the time of the initial passage of the Voting Rights Act, justified intrusion on the equality and the powers of states. The Court's view was that the outdated data provided insufficient evidence that such conditions still existed and thus, absent a valid formula to determine which jurisdictions must go through a preclearance procedure, none had to do so.[36] Given this decision, Texas no longer has to obtain pre-clearance to change aspects of its system of elections.

The Affordable Care Act

Since Congress passed, and President Obama signed, the Affordable Care Act (Obamacare) in 2010, it has been one of the most contentious recent issues regarding federalism. From the beginning, Obamacare has been a partisan issue. When the Senate voted on Obamacare, every Republican senator (except one who did not vote) voted against it and every Democrat, along with two independents, voted for it. In the House, all 178 Republicans, who were joined by 34 Democrats, voted against Obamacare. Republicans have consistently opposed the Affordable Care Act since that 2010 vote and have tried to repeal Obamacare over 70 times. Their argument is that Obamacare is too expensive, that it imposes a tax, that it is a harmful federal regulation, and that it is a violation of individual liberty by requiring individuals to buy health insurance. A central argument against Obamacare was that state action regarding provision of health care was preferable to national action. In fact, one major Republican idea that involved an important part of Obamacare was that Medicaid—the health care program for poor persons—which had been substantially expanded by the Affordable Care Act should be converted into block grants to the states.

Republicans came close to repealing the act in 2017. President Trump had been vocal in his opposition to the act which he has called a "disaster," and Governor Abbott and Attorney General Paxton have been strong opponents as well. Texas is one of the states that have not taken advantage of a provision of the act that allows the expansion of Medicaid for low-income persons, although Texas has the highest rate of uninsured people in the country (currently estimated at 18 percent). With the passage of the Affordable Care Act, the uninsured rate in Texas did drop from 22.1 percent in 2013 to 16.6 percent in 2016.[37] The pandemic, along with the attacks on the program and limitations placed on accessing the program by the Trump administration, has caused the uninsured rate to rise in Texas.

With the failure of Congress to repeal Obamacare, Attorney General Paxton has taken the lead in using litigation to gain the law's repeal. He explained that while the Affordable Care Act was claimed to be health care reform, it stopped the fifty states from experimenting with ways to provide health care to their citizens because with Obamacare the states needed Congress's approval before proceeding with their own health care policies. By getting Obamacare struck down as unconstitutional, Paxton argued, "legislators across the country can get back to crafting policies that address the needs, and conform with the values, of their own residents." Thus, claimed Paxton, "If California wants to experiment with socialized medicine, let them do it. Texas will focus on maximizing competition and putting choice back in the hands of consumers." Paxton noted, "It's time the courts returned control over health care to the laboratories of democracy the founders established." Indeed, Paxton wrote, different states had developed different solutions to the provision of health care before Obamacare. Massachusetts, for example, had a state-level health plan much like what was created with Obamacare. In contrast, Texas handled the problem of people with preexisting conditions by establishing

Federal Oversight of Texas Voting Rights

1 Why state or federal control of voting rights matters

The right to vote is fundamental to democracy. The Fifteenth Amendment, ratified in 1870, and the civil rights movement of the 1950s and '60s were efforts to ensure that voting rights extended to all racial and ethnic groups. In 1965 in an implementation of the Fifteenth Amendment, the 1965 Voting Rights Act was passed. It contained mechanisms by which state control over elections can be overridden by the federal government when states are found to discriminate on the basis of race or ethnicity.

One aspect of the Voting Rights Act was Section 5, which required that states covered under the provision, including Texas, would have changes in their voting procedures approved by the Department of Justice or a federal court in the District of Columbia. This process was called *preclearance*. Section 5 was there to ensure that the national government would have oversight over voting procedures in states that had excluded racial and ethnic minorities from the political process.

The Voting Rights Act, including Section 5, has been used to prevent states, including Texas, from drawing legislative districts and making other changes in voting procedures that disadvantaged minority voters. However, the Supreme Court in *Shelby County v. Holder* (2013) declared the formula used for determining the states that were covered under Section 5 was outdated and therefore unconstitutional. As a result, states now have greater freedom to change voting procedures in matters such as redistricting and voter ID requirements.

2 What's the debate?

Supporters of Section 5 of the Voting Rights Act say that Texas, with its strict voter ID laws, discriminates against racial and ethnic minorities in voting. Supporters say that without Section 5 states have too much leeway over voting procedures and will limit early voting, close polling places, impose stricter and stricter voter ID requirements, and engage in racial gerrymandering when drawing legislative and congressional districts.

Opponents of Section 5, such as former attorney general (now governor) Greg Abbott, have argued that it is unfair to single out only some states to comply with the law, that the Voting Rights Act exceeded the bounds of federal authority by violating the Tenth Amendment, and that voter discrimination in Texas is no longer an issue.

Opponents of Section 5 also argue that there is another provision of the Voting Rights Act—Section 2—that allows civil rights groups or individuals to file suits challenging allegedly discriminatory voting laws. It is the case that since Section 5 was eliminated, numerous suits against state voting practices have been brought under Section 2. However, supporters of Section 5 argue that the problem with reliance on Section 2 is that it is expensive and time-consuming to litigate such suits.

3 What do the numbers say?

In the aftermath of the elimination of Section 5, Texas and several other states passed voter ID laws which require some form of governmental identification such as a driver's license, a concealed carry permit, or a passport in order to vote. In response to a court decision, Texas modified its voter ID law so that it is possible to vote in Texas without the required identification if voters sign a statement saying they were reasonably unable to obtain the identification and they can provide some other identification such as a birth certificate or a utility bill. However, voter ID laws in Texas and elsewhere have been the most controversial state regulations of voting in the aftermath of the elimination of Section 5. Key to the debate over whether Section 5 is needed is a dispute over whether there is continued discrimination against racial and ethnic minorities in voting.

Since it was no longer possible to challenge Texas's voter ID law under Section 5, civil rights groups and individuals sued under Section 2 and argued the voter ID law discriminated against minorities. Texas, on the other hand, argued that the law was necessary to prevent voter fraud.

In the early litigation over Texas's voter ID law, Harvard professor Stephen Ansolabehere performed a statistical analysis of voting where he found that Latino voters were 195 percent more likely than White voters to lack voter ID and Black voters were 205 percent more likely than Whites to lack voter ID (see the figure below).

Ratio of those without ID

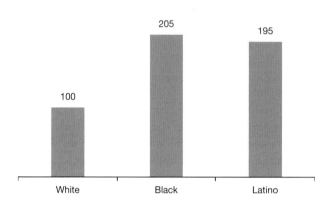

Communicating Effectively: What Do You Think?

● Do the data in the figure persuade you that the Texas election system discriminates on the basis of race and ethnicity? Why or why not?

● Texas's new voter ID law—which was passed after the studies in the figure—allows persons lacking state-required voter ID to vote if they sign a statement that they were reasonably unable to obtain ID and if they provide some alternative ID such as a utility bill or birth certificate. Do you think this resolves any problems associated with denying the right to vote?

● Is requiring voter ID in order to prevent voter fraud a sufficient reason for the law? Do you think it would be beneficial for Congress to pass new, constitutional legislation that allowed for preclearance under Section 5, or do you think it is unnecessary?

WANT TO LEARN MORE?

While there are deep, partisan divisions around voting rights, several nonpartisan organizations also study the issue.

- FiveThirtyEight
  www.fivethirtyeight.com

- Lawyers' Committee for Civil Rights under Law
  www.lawyerscommittee.org

- Brennan Center for Justice
  www.brennancenter.org

Health care is a key federalism issue. Texas senator Ted Cruz has been among the key figures who have advanced states' opposition to the federal Affordable Care Act.

a high-risk insurance pool,[38] though Paxton did not mention that only 28,000 people signed up for this costly program.[39]

Given the strong Republican opposition to Obamacare as well as the ideological commitment to state action regarding health care rather than national legislation, Paxton led 19 other states in a federal lawsuit challenging the constitutionality of the entire act. Their argument was the Tax Cuts and Jobs Act of 2017—the major tax legislation of the Trump administration—had eliminated the tax for the failure to buy insurance. In 2012, the U.S. Supreme Court had held in *National Federation of Independent Business v. Sebelius* that the payment required from those who did not buy insurance was a tax and was therefore constitutional.[40] Without that tax, Paxton asserted, the **individual mandate** (the requirement to buy insurance) was unconstitutional and the individual mandate was such a fundamental part of the law that the entire law had to be struck down as unconstitutional.

individual mandate a requirement of the Affordable Care Act that health insurance be purchased

The case, *Texas v. United States* (2018), was argued in federal district court in Fort Worth before Judge Reed O'Connor. The Trump administration defended only part of the law. It argued that the individual mandate was unconstitutional and so the coverage for preexisting conditions, which was tied to the individual mandate, was also unconstitutional. However, argued the Trump administration, the rest of the law, such as unmarried persons being covered under their parents' health insurance until age 26, was constitutional. Sixteen other states plus the District of Columbia also participated in the case. Their position was that the entire law was constitutional.

Judge O'Conner agreed with Paxton's argument and struck down all of Obamacare as unconstitutional. He delayed implementing his decision pending the outcome of an appeal before the Fifth Circuit Court of Appeals.[41] That court held the individual mandate was unconstitutional and asked the district court to assess how much of the law could stand without an individual mandate. Paxton was, of course, thrilled by his initial success before the district court, saying that the case "demonstrates that the 2017 repeal of the individual mandate's tax penalty renders the whole mess unconstitutional."[42] Not everyone was so pleased. The California attorney general commented that the district court decision "is an assault on 133 million Americans with preexisting conditions, and the 20,000,000 Americans with preexisting conditions who rely on the ACA's consumer protections for health-care."[43]

A group of states led by the California attorney general appealed the Fifth Circuit decision to the Supreme Court. The case pits a California-led group of states against the Trump administration and a Texas-led group of states. The California group's position is that the individual mandate is constitutional and, if not, the rest of Obamacare is still constitutional. In contrast, the Trump administration and the Texas-led group of states has the position that all of Obamacare is unconstitutional. The death of Ruth Bader Ginsburg and the elevation of Amy Coney Barrett to the Court increases the likelihood that the Affordable Care Act will be struck down as unconstitutional in whole or partly.

There is no question the district court and Court of Appeals decisions were great ideological victories for Texas and the Trump administration. However, if Obamacare is declared unconstitutional by the Supreme Court, Texas will have to deal with about 1,200,000 people who currently receive subsidized health insurance coverage.

The state will also have to determine how preexisting conditions are covered and whether vaccines and physicals will continue to be provided, as well as deciding whether unmarried children are still covered under parents' policies until age 26. Currently, the state has done no planning for action if Obamacare ends except for a proposal to initiate another high-risk insurance pool for those with preexisting conditions, though the incoming Biden administration may be able to shore up the law.[44]

At this point, the case can best be seen as an early victory for Paxton and Republicans in the lengthy partisan wrangling over the Affordable Care Act. Significantly, that wrangling has taken the form of a battle over federalism—should each state decide how to deal with access to health care or should there be a national solution?

Immigration

Another highly contentious issue connected to federalism is immigration. During the Obama administration, Texas once again clashed with the federal government over immigration, this time over the question of how to deal with young people who were brought to the United States illegally by their parents. During the Obama administration, the secretary of Homeland Security established a policy called **Deferred Action for Childhood Arrivals (DACA)**. DACA offers immigrant youths who came to the United States when they were children relief from deportation. It gives them protection from deportation and a work permit. Not all immigrant youth are eligible; there are detailed requirements for participation in the program.

DACA raises a federalism issue because several states took the position that DACA was overreach by the national government. With Donald Trump in the White House, Texas took the lead with a group of other states challenging the legality of the DACA program. Then on September 5, 2017, then–attorney general Jeff Sessions announced the government was terminating DACA. Additionally, on September 5, the acting secretary of Homeland Security directed that all new DACA applications and related work authorizations received after September 5 should be rejected and applications for renewal of

Deferred Action for Childhood Arrivals (DACA) an administrative decision of the Obama administration that certain undocumented immigrants brought to the U.S. as children would not be deported

The Trump administration took a hard stance against undocumented immigration at the U.S.–Mexico border. Here, Trump speaks to reporters in Mission, Texas, flanked by Senators Ted Cruz and John Cornyn, who have supported the administration's policies.

DACA status should be rejected after October 5, 2017.[45] That decision led to multiple lawsuits where two federal district courts stopped the Trump administration's decision to end DACA.

The continuation of DACA led Texas and six other states[46] to restart their lawsuit challenging the legality of the DACA program itself.[47] Initially, Texas requested a preliminary injunction to stop the implementation of DACA. The court noted that nationwide, there were an estimated 1,500,000 people who were potentially qualified for the DACA program and 800,000 had applied for and been accepted into it. Texas alone had about 100,000 DACA recipients. Because of such a widespread impact on people and the fact that the program had been in existence since 2012, the judge decided it was "not in the public interest" to issue an injunction and terminate the program at that point.

In evaluating the arguments favoring and opposing the DACA program, the judge made it clear that he believed the plaintiffs (those opposed to the program) would win at trial. The fundamental argument of the defendants was that the DACA program was an exercise in administrative discretion. That is, enforcement of immigration laws was focused not on children, but on other groups of immigrants, such as persons who came to the United States as adults. They argued that if, for example, a police officer has the legal discretion to give someone a warning rather than a speeding ticket, immigration officials also have the discretion to focus on immigrants other than those who came to the United States as children. The judge, however, supported Texas's argument that the DACA program was an overreach of executive power. Congress had made no provision in its immigration laws for the administration to award huge numbers of people a lawful presence in the United States and work authorization. The judge wrote, "If the nation truly wants to have a DACA program, it is up to Congress to say so."[48]

Although the judge's thinking in this case did not bode well for the future of the DACA program without congressional action, the case was put on hold because of another

DACA-related case. On June 18, 2020, the Supreme Court decided that the Trump administration had failed to follow proper procedures in ending DACA by not providing adequate reasons for their actions. The decision does not mean the DACA program cannot be ended, only that the administration must give sufficient justification for doing so.

The Coronavirus, Texas, and Federalism

The coronavirus pandemic was an enormous shock to the American political system, and in only a few short months it decimated the economy of Texas and of the nation. It also drastically changed the relationship between the states and the national government. As the disease spread, it caused a new form of federalism to emerge, one imbued with intense political partisanship, but also a hybrid of several different models of how states and the national government interact.

Cooperative federalism played a major role in the initial response to the health and economic crisis brought on by the coronavirus in such programs as Medicaid and unemployment insurance. In the spring of 2020, the national government assumed a larger financial role in paying for health care and underwriting unemployment insurance. These funding initiatives ran against the grain of prior Trump administrative policies cutting back federal involvement in health and welfare programs. Despite the enormous federal investment, state and local government budgets were strained to the breaking point by the pandemic and the sums provided to states were not sufficient for the states most ravaged by COVID-19.

The ideas underlying New Federalism also found a prominent role in the Trump administration's arsenal to combat the economic catastrophe. The various coronavirus bailouts targeted at smaller businesses and higher education, particularly state institutions of higher education, are powerful examples of the federal government directly transferring monies to organizations at the state and local level and leaving considerable discretion as to who might receive these emergency funds.

One also sees elements of coercive federalism in the response to the pandemic, particularly in President Trump's efforts to pressure the states to agree to a timetable for reopening the economy. Although President Trump initially claimed that the federal government was a backup to the states and the onus was on state governors to deal with the pandemic, he asserted that he had "total" authority to nullify state and local restrictions and to open the economy.[49] Reaction to that claim was so strongly negative that the president then stated, "Governors will be empowered to tailor an approach that meets the diverse circumstances of their own states."[50] While telling governors that they were "going to call your own shots," he did emphasize that the federal government would be involved to support states in reopening the economy, and the administration released guidelines on when the economy should be reopened.[51] The president opposed restrictions imposed by several Democratic governors and supported protests against those restrictions, showing that governors would not call their own shots free from critical treatment by the national government.

One of the most unusual features about the early governmental response to the coronavirus crisis was the articulation of a strategy that almost seemed to revive major aspects of the dual-federalism model. Through most of February, March, and April, the Trump administration appeared to argue that the responsibility for providing health care was primarily a state and local responsibility, not a national one. The business of acquiring testing kits, ventilators, and protective equipment for health care workers was left to the states, who were encouraged to go out into national and international markets to get what they needed.[52] The failure of Congress to agree on another coronavirus aid package in September and October 2020, in effect, also left substantial responsibility to the states for further responses to the pandemic. Essentially, the response to the pandemic has created a hybrid system of federalism that is more complex than previous models of state-national relationships.

Federalism and the Future of Texas

IT HAS BEEN a frequent refrain for Texas politicians to want the states to have greater power. Their argument is that the national government is too distant, controlling, expensive, and unresponsive. With Republicans in control of Texas's statewide offices, especially the office of the governor and the attorney general, the Obama administration was frequently challenged in the courts. In voting rights, health care, and immigration, Texas's position was one that promoted state over national power. With the Trump administration, Texas found an ally for its state power argument. The pandemic, however, complicated the dispute between state versus national power. While the Trump administration tended to be deferential to the states in responding to the pandemic, that was not always the case. For example, the Trump administration pressured states for a rapid reopening of the economy. It also became clear that there were limits to the states' abilities to deal with the virus, and at least to some degree, it was clear there was a need for a national response that was more than funding efforts to deal with the disease. What the future holds for federalism is unclear. Will this hybrid system of federalism, combining aspects of cooperative, coercive, New Federalism, and dual federalism with the states in a front-line role and the national government generally functioning as a source of funding, continue beyond the pandemic or beyond the Trump administration? While that remains to be seen, it is clear that in the highly polarized political environment of modern America, many of our political controversies will be framed as battles over federalism. ★

Use 🐰 INQUIZITIVE to help you study and master this material.

What Is Federalism?

- **Understand the basics of the U.S. federal system (pp. 83–85)**

Along with many other countries, the American system of government has divided power between national and regional or state governments. That division of power has varied over time, and America's notion of federalism has evolved through a number of forms.

Key Term
federalism (p. 83)

Practice Quiz

1. *Federalism* refers to
  a) a system of powerful local governments.
  b) a system where state governors are the primary decision makers.
  c) a system of government in which there is a national government as well as a number of regional governments.
  d) a system of government dominated by Congress.
  e) a system of government based on strong state legislatures.

2. An advantage of federalism is that it
  a) creates uniformity in policies.
  b) strengthens the powers of the national government.
  c) encourages a strong two-party system.
  d) allows experiments to determine the best policies.
  e) provides a check on the power of the president.

3. Texans have a more favorable view of the direction of
  a) the state over the national government.
  b) the national government over the state.
  c) the Obama administration over the Trump administration.
  d) state government over local government.
  e) the U.S. Congress over the Texas legislature.

Federalism in the Constitution

- Explain how the Constitution and court decisions have shaped the federal system (pp. 85–92)

The Constitution contains key provisions that are important to our understanding of federalism. Additionally, the Supreme Court played a major role in defining American federalism through its interpretations of those key provisions.

Key Terms

sovereign (p. 87)
supremacy clause (p. 87)
Tenth Amendment (p. 88)
elastic clause (p. 88)
full faith and credit clause (p. 88)
public policy exception (p. 88)
Reconstruction (p. 90)
Civil War Amendments (p. 91)
Fourteenth Amendment (p. 91)
incorporation of the Bill of Rights (p. 91)
"separate but equal" (p. 91)

Practice Quiz

4. The Articles of Confederation
   a) established a loose confederation of independent states that operated in the 1820s.
   b) were never accepted by a majority of the states.
   c) derived their power directly from the state governments.
   d) replaced the Constitution of 1787.
   e) outlawed ineffective state constitutions.

5. The relationship between the states and the national government
   a) has been a matter of continuing controversy throughout the nation's history.
   b) was finally settled when the Articles of Confederation were rejected in favor of the U.S. Constitution.
   c) was resolved for all time by the Civil War.
   d) was resolved by Article I, Section 8, of the U.S. Constitution.
   e) was not a problem in a federal system.

6. The Supreme Court under John Marshall expanded national power partly through
   a) rejecting the Articles of Confederation.
   b) expanding the meaning of interstate commerce.
   c) expanding Congress's war-making powers.
   d) ignoring the Tenth Amendment.
   e) increasing the powers of the president.

7. Prior to the ratification of the Fourteenth Amendment, the Bill of Rights
   a) applied only to states.
   b) applied only to the national government.
   c) applied to states and the national government.
   d) was essential in protecting racial minorities.
   e) was used to ensure the right to vote.

8. *McCulloch v. Maryland* (1819) was important
   a) in establishing that the national government had implied powers.
   b) in establishing that state governments had implied powers.
   c) in showing that the state and national governments could cooperate.
   d) in preventing national banks from operating.
   e) in destroying corrupt state banking systems.

9. The Fourteenth Amendment
   a) required states to give full faith and credit to the decisions of other states.
   b) banned slavery.
   c) declared secession unconstitutional.
   d) guaranteed to each person the equal protection of the laws.
   e) guaranteed judicial supremacy.

How Does Federalism Work?

American federalism has gone through major changes over the history of the country. In the late nineteenth century there was a strict division between the powers of the states and the powers of the national government. That division was called *dual federalism* or *layer-cake federalism*. During Franklin Roosevelt's New Deal, federalism was dramatically redefined and there was greater involvement of the national government in all areas of American life. Cooperative federalism or marble-cake federalism became the new approach to state and national relationships. In recent times, many believe federalism has taken a new form and has become coercive, with the national government compelling states to act in ways that achieve national priorities.

Key Terms
dual federalism (p. 92)
layer-cake federalism (p. 92)
dual sovereignty (p. 93)
police power (p. 93)
cooperative federalism (p. 94)
marble-cake federalism (p. 94)
categorical grants (p. 94)
New Federalism (p. 96)
block grants (p. 96)
coercive federalism (p. 96)
unfunded mandates (p. 97)
preemption (p. 97)
independent state grounds (p. 98)

Practice Quiz
10. *Dual federalism*
   a) refers to a system of government in which states do most of the governing.
   b) existed in the United States following World War II.
   c) rejected the idea that states were sovereign political entities.
   d) is the idea that there are two branches to the national legislature.
   e) drained all power from state governments.

11. Layer-cake federalism switched to marble-cake federalism
   a) after the Civil War.
   b) during World War I.
   c) during the New Deal.
   d) after the fall of the Soviet Union.
   e) because of President Ronald Reagan's efforts.

12. The use of categorical grants was a way of promoting
   a) cooperative federalism.
   b) dual federalism.
   c) coercive federalism.
   d) bipartisan federalism.
   e) civil rights.

13. Independent state grounds
   a) allow state laws to be superior to the national laws under certain conditions.
   b) allow states to provide more state constitutional protections than does the U.S. Constitution.
   c) allow states to remain independent of the national government.
   d) prevent the national government from overriding the Tenth Amendment rights of states.
   e) limit the power of the national government to pass economic regulations.

14. The national government can preempt state laws because
   a) the national government is weaker than any state.
   b) the Tenth Amendment to the Constitution specifically allows state laws to be overridden by federal laws.
   c) the supremacy clause of the Constitution makes national laws supreme over state laws.
   d) the Sanford dictum established preemption.
   e) the Constitution was adopted mainly to do just that.

Current Issues Involving Federalism

- Analyze how federalism shapes key policy debates today (pp. 100–108)

Many of the major political controversies today involve issues of federalism. The dispute over the role of states versus the national government is often infused with high levels of political partisanship and these issues tend to be at least temporarily resolved by the federal courts.

Key Terms

preclearance (p. 100)
individual mandate (p. 104)
Deferred Action for Childhood Arrivals (DACA) (p. 105)

Practice Quiz

15. *Shelby County v. Holder* (2013) is an important case because
    a) it guaranteed voting rights for African Americans.
    b) it required changes in voting practices in Shelby County to be precleared by the Department of Justice.
    c) it found that Alabama discriminated on the basis of race in its voting procedures.
    d) it struck down the formula that was used to determine if states needed to preclear their voting procedures.
    e) it held that the Voting Rights Act was constitutional.

16. The Affordable Care Act
    a) was a major national reform of health insurance in the United States.
    b) drastically reduced the cost of prescription drugs.
    c) is now, like Social Security or Medicare, a fairly uncontroversial federal program.
    d) currently requires people to pay a tax if they do not buy health insurance.
    e) has helped Texans become one of the most insured state populations in the United States.

17. The DACA program
    a) was passed by Congress in spite of strong Republican opposition.
    b) is an administrative decision to avoid deporting certain undocumented persons brought to the United States as children.
    c) is one of the immigration reforms proposed by the Trump administration.
    d) has led to the construction of a border wall with Mexico.
    e) is the regulation used to deport large numbers of undocumented young people.

Voters' support in the primary election for state representative Sarah Davis, a rare pro-choice Republican, illustrates that the Republican Party in Texas may not be as united as it seems.

Political Parties

WHY POLITICAL PARTIES MATTER Sarah Davis is a moderate Republican who represented a suburban, wealthy district in Houston that includes Rice University and the ritzy Galleria. Davis was first elected to the legislature in 2010, narrowly defeating Houston city council member Ellen Cohen, a liberal Democrat. Davis was re-elected in 2012 against Democrat Ann Johnson. While in the legislature, Davis has toed an independent line, failing to cooperate with the Tea Party wing of the Republican Party on issues ranging from the "bathroom" bill to abortion legislation. As the only pro-choice Republican in the Texas House, she has caught the attention of statewide elected officials, including Governor Greg Abbott. In an unprecedented move, Abbott endorsed Davis's Republican opponent in the March 2018 primary. Abbott reasoned that Davis was not sufficiently supportive of his agenda in his first term as governor. Davis's opponent, Susanna Dokupil, had also worked under Abbott when he was attorney general of the state. Davis went on to defeat Dokupil in the primary and her Democratic opponent, Allison Lami Sawyer, in the November 2018 election. The new speaker, Dennis Bonnen, took note of these Republican primaries by warning members of the House Republican caucus not to endorse primary opponents in 2019. This practice, Bonnen feared, would lead to the nomination of even more conservative Republicans who could not hold on to these suburban districts.

What does this story about Sarah Davis tell us about the state of political parties in Texas? On the surface, Republicans dominate Texas politics. Since 1994 every statewide elected official has been a member of the Republican Party. Since 2002 the Texas legislature has been controlled by Republicans. Yet there remain intra-party tensions between the more conservative wing of the party and the few moderates remaining in the party. In a district such as Davis's, Republican divisions could possibly yield an opening for Democrats who could field a candidate who would be more in tune with the district, which voted for Hillary Clinton in the 2016 election. Indeed, in the 2020 elections, Democrat Ann Johnson defeated Davis in the increasingly Democratic district in Houston, which also went for Joe Biden in the presidential race.

In reality, there are three political parties in modern-day Texas politics: business-oriented mainstream Republicans, Tea Party conservative Republicans, and the Democratic Party. In the George W. Bush era during the 1990s, the Republican Party was dominated by business-oriented mainstream Republicans who were interested in low taxes, less regulation, and tort reform. By 2012 the party had become more conservative. That year the business-oriented Lieutenant Governor David Dewhurst lost the U.S. Senate primary to Ted Cruz, who positioned himself to the right of Dewhurst. This competitive primary resulted from the retirement of mainstream Republican senator Kay Bailey Hutchison.

In the two most recent legislative sessions, the clash between factions of the Republican Party were readily apparent. Speaker Joe Straus, a moderate Republican, clashed with Lieutenant Governor Dan Patrick (a Tea Party favorite) on a host of issues, including the bathroom bill as well as SB 4, a ban on sanctuary cities in the state. Governor Greg Abbott began his career as a mainstream Republican but arguably has moved to the right to avoid the fate of Dewhurst and other Republicans who were defeated in primaries by more conservative firebrands.

The Democratic Party has sought to gain power in the state by trying to capitalize on the internal divisions within the Republican Party. But based on the state's current voter profile, the Democrats face an uphill battle, at least in the short term. Democrats believed they had a chance to unseat Senator Ted Cruz in 2018 with the nomination of El Paso's U.S. representative Beto O'Rourke, a White liberal representing a heavily Latino district. They believed he would unite the party's urban, nonwhite, and labor bases to unseat a relatively unpopular incumbent. Though O'Rourke lost, the margin was razor thin, with Cruz winning 51 percent of the vote to O'Rourke's 48 percent. Democrats might have more success, however, fielding candidates in suburban districts such as Davis's in Houston, Austin, San Antonio, and Dallas. Republican primaries might produce candidates in the general election who are too far to the right for these areas.

These examples demonstrate a couple of important facts about parties in Texas. All too often, we hear about Texas being a solidly Republican state, but this masks the internal diversity within the party. The observation that Republicans hold all statewide offices does not tell the whole story. In addition, internal divisions affect not only the Republican Party, with its Tea Party and mainstream business factions, but the Democratic Party as well. As the Democratic Party in Texas becomes more Latino, we might see more Democratic primary races pitting Latino candidates against White or African American incumbents.

Because parties play such a large role in government processes, we must know how parties are organized, how candidates are selected, and how partisanship influences public policy. This chapter will address the history of political parties in Texas, the current party system in the state, and what the future may hold for parties.

CHAPTER GOALS

- Describe the main functions and structure of state party organizations (pp. 117–32)
- Trace the evolution of the party system in Texas (pp. 132–39)
- Analyze how ideological divisions and demographic change affect Texas political parties (pp. 139–45)

The Roles and Structure of Political Parties in Texas

Describe the main functions and structure of state party organizations

In the narrowest sense, a political party refers to an organization of people established to win elections. This can include people holding or running for office who identify formally with the party. It can also refer to the professionals and volunteers who actively work for the election of their party's candidates. In a broader sense, a political party can refer to those people in the electorate who identify with a particular party and vote for that party's candidates on a regular basis.

Political parties help candidates win elections and assist voters in making their electoral choices. Perhaps the most important function of parties in Texas is that they provide a label under which candidates can run and with which voters can identify. Each party develops a **party platform** by which voters can get a better sense of what the party stands for. While candidates can and often do deviate somewhat from their party platform, voters wishing to know a candidate's basic political philosophy can consult the state party platform. Because Texas elects large numbers of officeholders, it is unlikely that voters will be familiar with the views or the qualifications of every candidate. However, Texas voters overwhelmingly identify with or lean toward either the Republican Party or the Democratic Party.[1] Thus, for many voters, without other information, the party label becomes the standard they apply in casting a ballot for a candidate. Voters often use the party label as a cue to the ideology of candidates. A voter may assume that,

party platform a statement of principles and political philosophy that a political party promises to enact if elected to office

One of the most important functions of political parties is to select candidates to run for office under the party label. Here, then–state senator and congressional candidate Sylvia Garcia (Houston) speaks at the Democratic Party's 2018 convention in Fort Worth, where the party officially announced its candidates for office.

for example, a Republican candidate is a "conservative" and may vote for or against that candidate because of the ideology that a party affiliation implies.[2]

In addition, parties help in raising money for candidates' campaigns and in assisting candidates with legal requirements and training for a campaign. They sometimes recruit candidates for political races, although in Texas any candidate may run in a party primary and if victorious in the primary will become the party nominee. Parties also assist in "getting out the vote" for candidates through phone banks, door-to-door contacts, and other efforts.

Once a candidate is elected to office, party affiliation helps in organizing the government. Governors usually appoint members of their own party to positions within the government, and the Texas legislature is increasingly divided by party as well. Public officials may also feel a greater sense of loyalty and cooperation toward other public officials of their party. After all, they often campaign together and make appearances at the same political events, and their fortunes often rise and fall together based on the popularity of the party. In that sense, the banding together of officeholders with the same party affiliation provides voters an opportunity to hold the party accountable for its successes or its failures.

Texas Party Politics

As the nation has become more divided along party lines, voters have elected fewer moderates to office. This created more friction in government, including gridlock in Congress. If we only observed national politics, we would come away with the impression that politics at the state and local levels mirrors the national partisan battles. However, this has not always been the case. As explained in the introduction, in Texas the dominant Republican Party has its own internal divisions. Even though the majority party controls committee assignments, chairs of committees sometimes include a mix of Democrats and Republicans. This has historically been true in Texas. For example, the former speaker of the Texas House, Joe Straus from San Antonio, was considered a moderate Republican and owed his election to the speakership to many Democrats in the legislature who voted to elect him speaker. In recognition of their support, Straus made some Democrats committee chairs. This situation would never happen in the U.S. Congress, as parties are much more salient in national politics. In Congress the majority party gives leadership positions like committee chairs only to its own loyal party members. As the Republican Party in Texas has moved further to the right, the bipartisan tradition there will likely change to the partisan polarization prevalent nationally. Indeed, when conservative Republican Dan Patrick took over as lieutenant governor, he ended the previous lieutenant governor's practice of appointing Democrats as committee chairs.

Why might these partisan divisions we see in Washington be less pronounced at the state and local levels? Tip O'Neill, the former Speaker of the U.S. House, used to say that "all politics is local," and this certainly rings true in Texas. Local issues are usually not ideological in nature. They often deal with who is most effective at creating jobs and providing public works projects within the district. Voters in state races are therefore likely to be influenced as much or more by these concerns than by hot-button issues such as abortion and same-sex marriage. Hence, partisanship is not always a major concern in running the everyday business of the state. To be sure, ideological issues might matter in certain state-level elections during some election years. In addition, **partisan polarization**, the degree to which Republicans have become more conservative and Democrats more liberal, is beginning to become more pronounced in the Texas legislature. Partisan polarization in politics means that it is increasingly difficult for politicians to compromise on important policy issues, since compromise becomes seen as a sign of weakness and caving in to the other side.

partisan polarization the degree to which Republicans have become more conservative and Democrats have become more liberal

Party politics in Texas is similar to that in some other southern states, but there are important differences in its racial and ethnic aspects. Historically, other southern states have had larger African American populations than Texas. African Americans, who are generally loyal Democrats, constitute nearly 30 percent of the population in Mississippi and Louisiana, for example. In Texas, they represent only 12 percent, and most are concentrated in east Texas and the state's major urban areas. Another major difference between Texas and some other southern states is Texas's large Latino population, which is about 40 percent of the state total. Like African Americans, Latinos tend to be Democrats, but not to the same degree.

To a certain extent, Texas is similar to New Mexico, Arizona, and Colorado in terms of its large Latino population. In contrast with the Latino population in Arizona, however, Tejanos (Texans of Mexican descent) are more likely to have resided in the state for generations. In Arizona, the Sonoran Desert region is the largest U.S. gateway for Mexican immigration, and new immigrants in Arizona exhibit political behavior that differs from that of their Tejano counterparts in many ways. For example, they are more likely than Tejanos to identify as Democrats and to see the Democratic Party as more supportive of immigrant rights.

Public Attitudes about Parties

Texans, like many other Americans, are increasingly identifying as independent. However, in practice many self-identified independents lean toward either Democratic or Republican affiliation. What is the source of these political leanings? The process of **political socialization** occurs throughout our early years, when our parents, religious leaders, teachers, and others influence our partisan identifications. Although this identification can change over time, we often retain the same political beliefs as those of our parents.

political socialization the introduction of individuals into the political culture; learning the underlying beliefs and values on which the political system is based

We are also profoundly shaped by our geographical environment. For example, Texans living in rural areas are more likely to vote for Republicans than Texans living in cities and suburbs. In the 2018 election, Senator Ted Cruz was re-elected due to strong support from voters in the state's rural areas. In addition, Texas has a long history of state pride, independence, and individualism. People growing up in the state become accustomed to these values and thus often incorporate them into their political ideologies and partisan preferences. Visitors to Texas are often surprised at how much state pride native Texans display. For example, the very notion of a state pledge of allegiance like the one recited by many Texas schoolchildren is a practice that surprises people from other states.

In Texas, as in the country as a whole, partisanship has increasingly become correlated with ideology. That is, Texans who identify as conservative are more likely to identify as Republican, while Texans who identify as liberal are more likely to identify as Democrats. According to the *Texas Tribune* poll, in 2008, 35 percent of Texas Democrats identified as liberal. By 2018, 60 percent of Texas Democrats identified as liberal. Seventy-three percent of Texas Republicans identified as conservative in 2008. By 2018 the percentage of Texas Republicans identifying as conservative had risen to 85 percent. Perhaps the greatest shift has been in Texas moderates, with 55 percent of Texas Democrats identifying as moderate in 2008. By 2018, 28 percent of Texas Democrats identified as moderate. Self-described Republican moderates have decreased from 25 percent to 11 percent in the same time period. Partisanship and ideology have converged so much that few voters identify as a liberal Republican or conservative Democrat. How does partisan affiliation affect Texas voters? According to a February 2019 *Texas Tribune* poll, 45 percent of respondents in Texas said they were going to vote in the 2020 Republican primary for president, while 40 percent said they would vote in the Democratic primary. This gives us a sense of the state's political leanings, which has shown some gains for Democrats building on Beto O'Rourke's narrow loss to Senator Ted Cruz in 2018. For the most part, when we see an "R" or a "D" next to a candidate's name, we make certain assumptions about the positions the candidate takes. Of course, other characteristics of candidates matter too; voters also cite the candidate's record, stated positions on issues, and character as important considerations in their voting choices.[3]

The Contemporary Republican Party in Texas

The Texas Republican Party diminished in strength during Donald Trump's term in office. According to a 2018 *Texas Tribune* poll, 54 percent of voters in Texas would support a generic Republican candidate for Congress, while roughly 46 percent would support a generic Democratic candidate. This leaves a remainder of about 15 percent that are the "swing" voters who ultimately decide elections. However, in a February 2020 poll by *Texas Tribune*, 46 percent would support a generic Democratic candidate and 43 percent would support a generic Republican candidate with 11 percent uncertain. While Republicans are still in control of state government, the tightness of the 2018 elections and recent trends might suggest that Democrats can crack Republican dominance in the future.

Texas Republicans currently hold all of the major statewide elected offices. The governor, lieutenant governor, comptroller, attorney general, members of the state supreme court, the Court of Criminal Appeals, and railroad commissioners are all Republicans, as are both U.S. senators. Texas Democrats have attempted to recruit successful challengers for these offices but have come up short. The major competition for important statewide offices has occured during the Republican primaries, much in the same way the Democratic primaries used to fulfill this role when Texas was a Democratic state. Given the increasingly competitive nature of recent Texas elections, this might change in the near future.

Republican primaries often pit conservatives against moderates, reflecting a major division in the Republican Party. Pro-business "establishment" Republicans have dominated the party along with state politics in recent years, but the Tea Party movement has had a strong influence on state legislative races as well as major statewide races. The Tea

Party movement is particularly strong in Texas. In an October 2018 *Texas Tribune* poll, 14 percent of respondents said they would vote for a Tea Party candidate if the movement organized as a third party. When asked about the Tea Party's influence on the state Republican Party, respondents were split: 28 percent felt that the Tea Party had too much influence, 17 percent thought its degree of influence was about right, and 27 percent thought it had too little influence.[4]

These dynamics have been seen in many races across the state, but one of the most prominent was the lieutenant governor's race in 2014. In the Republican primary, incumbent lieutenant governor David Dewhurst had the endorsement of then-governor Rick Perry and many of the state's other political leaders. However, state senator Dan Patrick, a darling of the Tea Party movement, and several other Republicans challenged Dewhurst because they sensed a weak candidate who had lost the U.S. Senate primary in 2012 to now senator Ted Cruz. Patrick ran to the right of Dewhurst and all the other candidates, especially on immigration issues. In a debate in early 2014, he called for an end to the "invasion" of illegal immigrants from the southern border. Patrick also criticized Dewhurst for being too moderate and a political insider, turning his endorsements from the state's political establishment against him. In a low-turnout primary, he forced Dewhurst into a runoff by winning 41 percent of the vote to Dewhurst's 28 percent, and in the runoff he received 65 percent to 35 percent for Dewhurst. (Patrick went on to win the general election over Democrat Leticia Van de Putte, a Latina state senator from San Antonio, with 58 percent of the vote.) It was remarkable that an incumbent lieutenant governor would be defeated so badly in his own party primary, but Patrick successfully positioned himself to the right of Dewhurst in an increasingly conservative party. Although Dan Patrick was re-elected lieutenant governor in 2018, he faced minor opposition in the Republican primary and then beat his opponent in the general election, Democrat Mike Collier, but only by a relatively slim 51 to 46 percent margin.

While running for lieutenant governor in 2014, Dan Patrick positioned himself as more conservative than his opponent, fellow Republican David Dewhurst. Here, Patrick celebrates his victory over Dewhurst in the primary on election night.

The Contemporary Democratic Party in Texas

The Republican Party and conservative politics have not always been so powerful in Texas. Prior to 1994, Democrats held many statewide offices, and many of those Democrats were liberals. Ann Richards, the state's last Democratic governor, was a proud liberal, as was former U.S. senator Ralph Yarborough, who championed the Bilingual Education Act in 1968, which provided federal funds for states and localities to implement bilingual education programs. However, in recent years Democrats have had difficulty recruiting quality candidates for political office at the state level. In 2017 national Democrats were hopeful that former Health and Human Services secretary Julián Castro would enter the race for governor but he decided against it. Instead, he waited and launched a presidential campaign alongside Beto O'Rourke in a crowded Democratic primary. Democrats were scrambling to find a challenger to Governor Greg Abbott in 2018 and settled on Dallas County Sheriff Lupe Valdez. In the general election, Abbott defeated Valdez, winning 55 percent of the vote. Despite the loss in the gubernatorial race, Texas Democrats remained hopeful considering the close senatorial and lieutenant governor's races, as well as the gain of twelve seats in the State House. The only statewide race on the 2020 ballot was the senatorial race with incumbent Republican senator John Cornyn seeking re-election with Donald Trump at the top of the ticket. Though several Democrats launched bids to unseat Cornyn, Democrats were hoping to recruit a highly visible candidate like congressman Joaquin Castro or Beto O'Rourke. After a runoff between a military veteran MJ Hegar and state senator Royce West of Dallas, Democrats chose MJ Hegar, who went on to lose against Cornyn in November 2020.

Most Texas Democrats today would be classified as liberal. The party's base is made up of African Americans, Latinos, and White liberals in urban areas. Most White liberals are located in Austin, Houston, Dallas, and San Antonio, and they have often moved to Texas from other parts of the country. This coalition, however, is currently not large

Recently, the Democratic Party in Texas has been shut out of statewide offices. Democrats continue to believe that mobilizing Latino voters and White urban liberals will help their chances. Here, MJ Hegar campaigns in Austin for the U.S. Senate seat held by Republican John Cornyn.

enough to win elections in statewide races, although Texas Democrats are trying to change that by launching significantly more voter registration drives and harnessing the tech industry to improve data analytics to more effectively target potential Democratic voters. In what is termed the "Texas Model," Texas Democrats have said that they have flagged 600,000 potential Democratic voters in the state who, if they turn out to vote, might make a difference in some election outcomes.[5] Most rural Whites in Texas have settled into the Republican Party, and Republicans have won all recent statewide elections. Latinos are the fastest-growing group in the state, however, and Democrats hope to mobilize more Latinos to vote. Sixty-nine percent of Texas Latinos are American citizens by birth, but a large proportion of these are under age 18 and cannot vote. Moreover, voter turnout rates among Texas Latinos are much lower than among their Anglo counterparts. To change this pattern will require extensive efforts to register Latino voters and bring them to the polls in force.

No Democrat has won Texas in a presidential race since Jimmy Carter in 1976. In 2020, Republican president Donald Trump won 52.2 percent of the vote in Texas, while Democrat Joe Biden won 46.4 percent. This 5.8 percentage point margin in favor of the Republican candidate meant that Trump underperformed relative to his performance four years earlier, when he won the state by 9 percentage points. Democratic candidates have also fared poorly in recent U.S. Senate races. For example, in the 2012 election to replace retiring senator Kay Bailey Hutchison, Ted Cruz, the Republican nominee, won easily. Democrat Beto O'Rourke, a congressperson from El Paso, challenged Cruz in 2018, and narrowly lost to him in the most competitive statewide race in decades. However, in 2020, Republican senator John Cornyn easily defeated MJ Hegar with 53.6 percent of the vote, while Hegar received 43.8 percent.

Texas Democrats do have influence in certain localities. In Travis County, the home of Austin, Democrats dominate city government. Other major cities, including Houston and San Antonio, have Democratic mayors and city councils. However, this influence does not extend to statewide elections.

Eleven of the 13 Democrats representing Texas in the U.S. Congress are either Latino or African American. Lloyd Doggett of Austin and Lizzie Fletcher of Houston are the only White Democrats representing Texas in Congress. This could suggest that the majority of Texas Democrats are people of color, and the growth of the nonwhite population in the state suggests that the party's makeup will become steadily more nonwhite. This demographic change in Texas is making the state more similar to its neighbors in the Deep South, where the Democratic Party is mostly an African American party. In contrast, in the Northeast and on the West Coast, White Democrats are a larger proportion of the electorate.

Democratic and Republican Party Organization

Although many Texans proclaim that they are "registered Republicans" or "registered Democrats," Texas does not have a system of party registration. Registered voters may vote in either the Democratic or the Republican primary. When they do vote in a primary, their voter registration card is stamped "Democrat" or "Republican" to prevent them from voting in the other primary as well.

One of the most important functions of political parties is to select candidates to run for office under the party label. During the nineteenth century, candidates were nominated at party conventions, but early in the twentieth century the state began using primary elections to select candidates. If several candidates are running for the party nomination in a primary, it may be that none receives a majority vote. In that case, the party holds a runoff election to determine its nominee.

To understand how the parties are organized, think first in terms of the permanent organization of the party and then in terms of the temporary (campaign) organization (see Figure 4.1). In each election **precinct**, a **precinct chair** is elected in the party primary. The precinct chair will head the precinct convention and serve on the party's **county executive committee**, whose main responsibility is to run the county primary and plan the county conventions. Also elected in the primary is a **county chair** to head the county executive committee, which includes all the precinct chairs. There may be other district committees as well for political divisions that do not correspond to the county lines.

At the state level, there is a state executive committee, which includes a **state chair and vice chair**. These officers are selected every two years at the state party conventions. The **state executive committee** accepts filings by candidates for statewide office and also helps raise funds for the party and establish party policy. Both the Democratic and the Republican parties also employ professional staff to run day-to-day operations and to assist with special problems that affect the party.

The temporary organization of the party includes the precinct conventions. The main roles of the **precinct conventions** are to select delegates to the **county conven-**

precinct the most basic level of political organization at the local level

precinct chair the local party official, elected in the party's primary election, who heads the precinct convention and serves on the party's county executive committee

county executive committee the party group, made up of a party's county chair and precinct chairs, that is responsible for running a county's primary elections and planning county conventions

county chair the county party official who heads the county executive committee

state chair and vice chair the top two state-level leaders in the party

state executive committee the committee responsible for governing a party's activities throughout the state

precinct convention a meeting held by a political party to select delegates for the county convention and to submit resolutions to the party's state platform; precinct conventions are held on the day of the party's primary election and are open to anyone who voted in that election

county convention a meeting held by a political party following its precinct conventions, for the purpose of electing delegates to its state convention

FIGURE 4.1

Party Organization in Texas

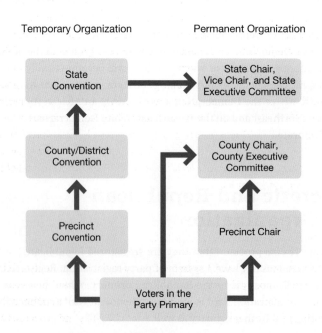

Political parties in Texas are organized at the precinct level, the county level, and the state level. This photo shows members of the Anderson County Democratic Party organization.

tion and possibly to submit resolutions that may eventually become part of the party platform.

Delegates chosen by the precinct convention then go to the county conventions (or in urban areas, to district conventions), which elect delegates to the **state convention**. Both the Democratic and the Republican parties hold a state convention every other year. These conventions certify the nominees of the party for statewide office; adopt a platform; and elect a chair, a vice chair, and a state executive committee. In presidential election years, the state conventions also select delegates for the national party conventions, elect delegates for the national party committee, and choose presidential electors, who, if the party's choice for president carries the state in the election, will formally cast the state's electoral votes for the president in the electoral college.

Battles for control of a state party have often been fought in Texas politics, where rival ideological and other interest groups have struggled to control precinct, county, and state conventions and to elect their candidates for precinct chair, county chair, and state executive committee. In the 1950s struggles between liberals and conservatives for control of the Democratic Party were fierce. On the other hand, sometimes apathy has been so great that precinct conventions have been sparsely attended and offices such as precinct chair have gone unfilled.

state convention a party meeting held every two years for the purpose of nominating candidates for statewide office, adopting a platform, electing the party's leadership, and in presidential election years selecting delegates for the national convention and choosing presidential electors

Third Parties in Texas

In Texas, as in many other states, the two major parties have made it difficult for third parties to gain power, mostly through onerous requirements for ballot access. In essence, Democrats and Republicans agree that a third competitor is not a net positive for either of them. As a result of the major parties dominating the rules and processes of elections, third-party candidates rarely win elections in Texas. Since they are seen as inevitable losers at the ballot box, voters prefer to "go with the winner."

The third parties that have gained some success at certain points in Texas history have done so mainly because they emphasized a particular issue. In the late nineteenth century, two farmers' movements—the Grange and the Populists—provided alternatives to the two major parties in various elections. In 1948 opposition to racial integration led the States' Rights Party, or **Dixiecrats**, to rally behind segregationist Strom Thurmond for president instead of Democratic candidate Harry Truman. Interestingly, while Thurmond carried some southern states, they did not include Texas, which voted for Truman. Segregation spurred a third-party candidacy again in 1968 when Alabama governor George Wallace ran against the liberal Democratic candidate Hubert Humphrey. Echoing Thurmond's results, Wallace carried a number of southern states but failed to win Texas, which supported Humphrey.

The civil rights movement in the 1960s planted the seeds for an independent Latino movement named **La Raza Unida**, meaning "united race." José Ángel Gutiérrez led the party at its inception, which was concentrated in Zavala County. La Raza Unida developed into a third party that was able to win races in Crystal City and other small towns in south Texas by taking advantage of the system of nonpartisan elections used in many Texas municipalities. (Even today, many cities, such as Austin, conduct nonpartisan elections.) Actually, "nonpartisan" does not mean that the candidates for office do not belong to political parties; it just means that their party affiliation is not listed on the ballot. Reformers in many cities pushed for this change so that voters would choose candidates on the basis of their qualifications rather than their party. La Raza Unida won so many of these races in Zavala and surrounding counties that at one point the party was able to take control of some city councils, school boards, and even two mayor's offices. Statewide, in 1972 the La Raza Unida candidacy of Ramsey Muñiz nearly cost Democrat Dolph Briscoe the governorship. While the party ultimately faded away, as most third-party movements do, it marked the growing influence of Latinos in the state.

In recent years, the Libertarian Party in Texas has emerged as a third-party alternative to the two major parties. While running candidates for a wide range of offices across the state, the party has had little impact on Election Day. For the most part, it has been a party of protest through which people dissatisfied with politics in the state can express their discontent at the polls. Libertarians believe in limited government and can be considered fiscal conservatives and social liberals. Former U.S. representative Ron Paul of Lake Jackson, nominally a Republican, ran for president in 1988 as a Libertarian and subsequently as an unconventional Republican espousing libertarian views. His son, U.S. senator Rand Paul of Kentucky, has followed in the footsteps of his father by advocating libertarianism albeit as a Republican. Libertarians are particularly active in some of the major cities, including Austin. While they do not win many elections, they can influence politics in other ways. For example, the major parties may adopt some of the positions promoted by Libertarians (or members of other minor parties) in order to win their support in runoff elections.

The most recent significant threat to major-party dominance of Texas politics came in the 2006 election for governor. Rick Perry was seen as a vulnerable incumbent, especially during a year that was not particularly favorable for Republicans. Chris Bell, a former Houston member of Congress, won the Democratic nomination, but two major independent candidates also ran for governor: former comptroller Carole Keeton Strayhorn and musician and humorist Kinky Friedman, whose slogan was "Why the hell not?"

Dixiecrats conservative southern Democrats who abandoned the national Democratic Party in the 1948 presidential election over the issue of racial integration

La Raza Unida former political party created in 1970 in Texas in order to bring attention to the concerns of Mexican Americans

How Republican Is Texas?

The South has become a solidly Republican region, and Texas is no exception to this. Indeed, former President Clinton official Paul Begala once called the state "South Carolina on steroids." Since the 1960s, South Carolina has been a reliable Republican state in presidential elections. On the other hand, California has become a solidly Democratic state since the 1990s largely due to its growing Latino population and its relatively high population of White liberals. How does Texas compare with other key states on political partisanship?

Percentage of Residents Who Identify as Republicans*

Wyoming 59%	Utah 56%	North Dakota 55%	Alabama 52%	South Dakota 51%	Alaska 51%	Idaho 50%	West Virginia 49%	Mississippi 48%
Tennessee 48%	Arkansas 48%	Missouri 47%	South Carolina 47%	Kansas 47%	Montana 46%	Indiana 46%	Oklahoma 46%	Kentucky 45%
Ohio 45%	Louisiana 45%	Wisconsin 43%	Nebraska 43%	Georgia 42%	Iowa 42%	North Carolina 42%	Texas 42%	Florida 41%
Arizona 41%	Colorado 40%	Pennsylvania 40%	Virginia 39%	Michigan 39%	New Mexico 38%	Oregon 38%	Minnesota 38%	Nevada 38%
Maine 37%	New Hampshire 36%	Rhode Island 36%	New Jersey 35%	Washington 35%	Delaware 35%	Illinois 34%	Connecticut 33%	Maryland 31%
California 31%	Vermont 30%	New York 30%	Hawaii 29%	Massachusetts 27%				

* Or who identify as independents but say they lean Republican.

SOURCE: 2019 Gallup Organization.

CRITICAL THINKING

- How does Texas compare with other states in terms of partisanship?

- How might demographic change, especially the growing Latino population, change Texas's political preferences?

Independent candidates face considerable challenges in elections. Although the musician and writer Kinky Friedman's 2006 candidacy for governor attracted major media attention, Friedman received only 12.4 percent of the vote.

"first past the post" an election rule that states that the winner is the candidate who receives a plurality of the votes

single-member district an electorate that is allowed to elect only one representative for each district

proportional representation a multimember district system that allows each political party representation in proportion to its percentage of the total vote

When all the ballots were counted, Perry was re-elected, but with only 39 percent of the vote. While it is not clear that a two-way race between Bell and Perry would have ensured a Bell victory, the candidacies of Strayhorn and Friedman damaged whatever mandate Perry could claim from a victory without a majority.

Why don't people vote for third parties? In general elections, Texas, like most of the United States, employs what is known as a **"first past the post," single-member district** electoral system. Under a first past the post system, only the candidate who wins the plurality of votes, that is, the most votes, is elected. This type of voting system tends to favor a two-party system because a vote for a third-party candidate generally does not result in a win and many American voters believe that their votes would be wasted if they voted for a third-party candidate. This expectation is rational, as the history of elections shows that a Republican or Democrat will almost always win. So most voters logically decide that it makes more sense to vote for the major-party candidate whose ideology is closest to their own. This is not to say that a vote for a third-party candidate is "wasted," because major-party candidates as well as the parties themselves often adapt their rhetoric and policies in response to voters who support a third-party candidate. Winning candidates often would like to appeal in future elections to constituents who might not have supported them in the past.

In contrast, some other countries use a system of **proportional representation** that encourages third-party voting because even if a party wins only 10 percent of the vote in an election, it will still win 10 percent of the seats in the legislature or other representative body. Voters in

PERSONAL RESPONSIBILITY: WHAT WOULD YOU DO?

- Do you think Texas should make it easier for minor parties to gain political power? Why?

- What changes would you make in order to improve the visibility and power of minor parties?

these countries are more likely to vote for third and minor parties because they will almost certainly be able to elect at least one of their preferred candidates.

The Tea Party Movement in Texas

The **Tea Party movement** became prominent nationwide and in Texas during the presidency of Barack Obama. Tea Party advocates have had a great deal of influence in Texas mainly because of their libertarian antitax message, which resonates with many Texans. The implications of these antitax policies in Texas mean less funding for K–12 and higher education and fewer social services such as children's health care programs.

Tea Party organizers have not sought to run a third-party candidate in elections, however. Instead, they have been successful at influencing Republican primary elections. They believe that they can have more influence in state politics if they become powerful within the Republican Party. Undoubtedly, this is a wise strategy given the history of defeat for third parties, not only in the state but nationwide. Tea Party groups have focused their efforts on key statewide races. They have campaigned against incumbents, such as former speaker Straus of San Antonio, whom they deemed to be too moderate. Straus's retirement from the House in 2018 paved the way for a more conservative speaker, Representative Dennis Bonnen (R-Angleton), who announced in November 2018 that he had secured enough votes from his colleagues to ensure his election as speaker in early 2019, though he only served for one session. The Tea Party has had success in defeating incumbents and nominating preferred candidates, making it fairly clear that the Republican Party is dominated by this more conservative faction. Dan Patrick's reelection for lieutenant governor in 2018 suggests that the Tea Party movement and the Republican Party in Texas are increasingly converging.

Tea Party movement reaching prominence after Barack Obama's election, a political movement that advocates lower government spending, lower taxes, and limited government

In 2020, Republicans tapped Representative Dade Phelan of Beaumont, Texas, to be the new Speaker of the House. Phelan received support from both Republicans and Democrats, and hopes were that his leadership would promote moderation and a spirit of bipartisanship in the House of Representatives.

Which Party Reflects Your Political Beliefs?

1 Why parties matter

In Texas, the majority of state legislators and all members of the executive branch are members of the Republican Party. However, in recent years, the Democratic Party has strengthened in certain parts of the state, especially the major cities. The Republican Party has seen some internal divisions between the Tea Party faction, which has successfully garnered a large share of state and local offices. As Texas becomes more competitive between the two major parties at the state level, it is important to consider what the parties stand for and how this affects you. It is through the political parties that we, as citizens, can get involved in politics and make a difference in our communities. In this citizen's guide, we hope to provide you with the information you need to determine which political party best represents your views and give you a road map to get involved in politics.

2 What's the debate?

The Democratic and Republican parties in Texas have strongly divergent views on nearly every policy, from funding of public schools, to criminal justice reform, to voting rights.

- *Democrats* emphasize expanding health care access and education funding at all levels. They tend to oppose the death penalty and support abortion rights. Democrats in the legislature have also argued for laws protecting the LGBTQ community, as well civil rights legislation protecting African Americans and Latinos. Democrats have opposed Republican efforts to ban sanctuary cities and spend state resources on increased security along the U.S.-Mexico border.
- *Republicans* generally prefer stronger state, rather than federal, control over most major issues. Texas Republicans have most recently emphasized border security and the banning of sanctuary cities in the state. Generally, most Republicans prefer limited government, lower taxes, and fewer regulations on business. They also tend to oppose abortion. In Texas, however, the Republican Party has two major factions, which often come into conflict:

- The *Tea Party* faction of the Republican Party is more concerned about immigration and other social policy issues, such as abortion, and ensuring that individuals can only use restrooms that correspond to their gender assigned at birth. The Tea Party faction's most visible state leader is Lieutenant Governor Dan Patrick, who has championed a more socially conservative push in the state Senate since his election.
- *"Establishment" or "pro-business" Republicans* pre-date the Tea Party wing, and are more interested in emphasizing the party's fiscal conservatism. That is, they are more likely to pursue policies aimed at lowering taxes, cutting regulations, and making Texas business-friendly. Former Speaker Joe Straus was part of this wing when he was Speaker. Establishment Republicans are more pro-immigration and less interested in pursuing policies aimed at restricting abortion, immigration, or who can use which bathrooms in the state.
- *Libertarians* are the third-largest party in the state, but have been unable to win elections statewide or to the

The results of the 2018 senatorial race showed deep divides along the lines of age and race. While older, White voters tended to vote for incumbent senator Ted Cruz, younger voters favored Congressman Beto O'Rourke.

legislature. Libertarians support fiscal conservatism just like establishment Republicans. Libertarians, however, are more socially liberal, generally supporting abortion rights, gay marriage, the legalization of marijuana, and rights for the LGBTQ community.

One of the most important considerations in Texas politics today is the tensions between the two factions of the Republican Party. Do these divisions mean that there will be more opportunities for Democrats to gain power? There is no question that the path to victory in the state for Democrats is to mobilize and turn out Latino voters—who are not registered at the same rates as their Anglo counterparts and do not turn out to vote at the same rates. In 2017, Democrats made a strong effort to oppose SB 4 (the bill cracking down on sanctuary cities) and characterized the law as racially discriminatory against the state's large Latino population. Will legislation such as SB 4 mobilize Latinos to punish Republicans? This remains to be seen, as some commentators point to Donald Trump's election as evidence that Latinos did not realize their potential power in the 2016 election to stop his candidacy.

3 What do the numbers say?

In Texas, as in most of the country, there are clear patterns in terms of the demographic makeup of the political parties. These patterns are reflected in the most recent exit polls from the 2018 hotly contested Senate election between Senator Ted Cruz and Beto O'Rourke. In that race we see a clear gender gap, with 54 percent of women in Texas supporting O'Rourke and 56 percent of men in Texas supporting Cruz. An even more striking difference can be seen in terms of age. Seventy-one percent of 18- to 29-year-olds supported O'Rourke, while 58 percent of Texans 65 and older supported Cruz. There are also racial differences in partisanship, as 66 percent of White Texans voted for Cruz, while 89 percent of African Americans voted for O'Rourke. The state's growing Latino electorate supported O'Rourke over Cruz by a 64 to 35 percent margin.

Communicating Effectively: What Do You Think?

- Politically, which do you identify most closely with, Democrats, Tea-Party Republicans, establishment Republicans, or Libertarians? Why?

- If you had to come up with bumper stickers to represent each of these groups, what would they say and how would they be designed?

- If you identified as a Libertarian and were advising the Libertarian Party on how to win elections in Texas, what would you say? How would you respond to those who say you are wasting your vote?

WANT TO LEARN MORE?

Political parties are very interested in having you as a member. They will ask you to contribute to candidates, volunteer for campaigns, and attend rallies and events. The parties' websites provide in-depth information on the issues these parties care about the most, and opportunities for participation. The CNN exit poll data includes a breakdown of voting by income, educational level, and other criteria.

- Texas Republican Party Platform
  www.texasgop.org/platform

- Texas Democratic Party Platform
  www.texasdemocrats.org/our-party/texas
  -democratic-party-platform

- Texas Libertarian Party Platform
  www.lptexas.org/platform

- 2018 Texas Exit Poll Data
  www.cnn.com/election/2018/exit-polls/texas

Parties and Digital Media

Traditionally, parties relied on newspapers, television, and radio to disseminate their messages to voters and to raise funds from and mobilize their supporters. However, in the digital age, parties have established active presences on social media platforms such as Facebook, Twitter, and Snapchat. They hire digital media professionals to monitor social media and respond to criticisms, publicize the other party's faults, and advertise for their candidates.

Social media are also an important fund-raising tool. Before the internet, parties relied on snail mail and phone calls to solicit campaign contributions, but now they can raise funds more easily and cheaply using email blasts and posts on social media.

Parties use digital media for voter mobilization as well. Parties can urge their supporters who follow them on Facebook or Twitter to turn out to vote. They can also encourage their friends to pass on these messages. In addition to social media, the Texas Democratic Party website (txdemocrats.org) and the Texas Republican Party website (texasgop.org) provide Texans an opportunity to learn more about party positions, contribute money, volunteer, and make inquiries.

Texas's History as a One-Party State

Trace the evolution of the party system in Texas

In order to understand the present partisan environment in Texas, let us look at the history of partisanship in Texas since the end of the Civil War. With the defeat of the Republican governor Edmund J. Davis in 1873, Texas entered a period of Democratic dominance that would last for over a century. Often the Republican Party would not contest major state offices, and other parties, such as the Populist or People's Party, exerted some influence for brief periods but lacked staying power. In general elections, it was a foregone conclusion that the Democratic nominee would win. Any meaningful election contest would have been in the Democratic Party primary.

Republicans tended to have a limited role in Texas politics. Most commonly, people remained Republicans in the hope of gaining political patronage (usually local postmaster or rural mail carrier positions) when Republican presidents were in office. Other Republicans were businesspeople unhappy with the liberal policies of Democratic presidents such as Franklin Delano Roosevelt or Harry Truman. However, Republicans were never numerous enough to make their party a threat to Democratic dominance in the state. Indeed, Republicans interested in patronage positions from the national government may have had an incentive to keep the party small, as the fewer the Republicans, the less the competition. When the father of the late U.S. senator Lloyd Bentsen first moved to the Rio Grande Valley, he visited R. B. Creager, then state chairman of the Republican Party, and told him that he wanted to get involved in the party because his father had been a devoted Republican in South Dakota. Rather than welcoming Bentsen,

When Did Texas Become Republican?

The Republican Party is the dominant party in Texas. However, this is a fairly recent development. Before the 1970s, Texans were less likely than the rest of the nation to support Republican presidential candidates. And it was only in the 1990s and the early 2000s that Republicans came to hold a majority of seats in the Texas delegation to the U.S. House and in the Texas legislature.

Republican Share of the Presidential Vote

■ Texas   ■ National

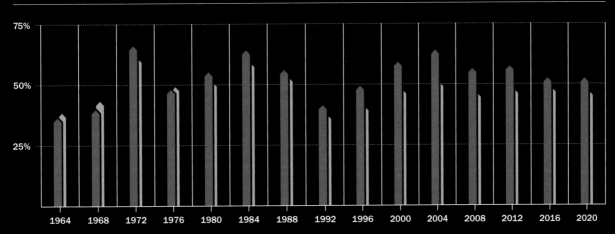

SOURCES: First figure: 1960-2004 data from the CQ Elections and Voting Collection. 2008 data and beyond from the Associated Press. Second figure: 1986-2002 data from the Republican Party of Texas. 2004–18 data calculated by author from election results archived at the Texas Secretary of State.

Republican Share of Office Held

Texas statewide offices   100%

4%

Texas House   55%

37%

Texas Senate   61%

19%

Texas delegation to U.S. House   64%

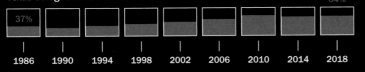

37%

1986   1990   1994   1998   2002   2006   2010   2014   2018

QUANTITATIVE REASONING

- Based on these data, how has the Republican share of the presidential vote in Texas changed compared to the rest of the nation? Why?

- Describe the trend in the growth of the Republican Party in Texas according to the data shown here. What factors might have shaped this trend? Do you think it will continue in the future?

Sr., as a Republican, however, Creager told him, "You go back to Mission [Texas] and join the Democratic Party, because what's best for Texas is for every [other] state in the union to have a two-party system and for Texas to be a one-party state. When you have a one-party state, your men stay in Congress longer and build up seniority."[6]

In 1952 and 1956, however, the conservative Democratic governor Allan Shivers led a rebellion within Democratic ranks, which became known as the **Shivercrat movement** and presaged a dramatic change in party alignments a quarter century later. Shivers, widely regarded as one of the most able Texas governors of the twentieth century, supported Republican Dwight Eisenhower for the presidency against the Democratic nominee, Adlai Stevenson. In addition, he and all statewide officeholders except the agriculture commissioner, John White, ran on the 1952 and 1956 ballots as both Democrats and Republicans. Stevenson opposed the Texas position on the Tidelands, offshore lands claimed by both Texas and the national government, which were believed to contain oil. Additionally, Stevenson was much more liberal than Shivers, and Eisenhower was a famous and popular hero of World War II. Nevertheless, the Shivercrats' party disloyalty was condemned by Texas Democrats such as Sam Rayburn, Speaker of the U.S. House of Representatives, and it led to much tension in the state party between liberal and conservative Democrats as well as between party loyalists and the Shivercrats.

The Shivercrat movement sent a strong message that many conservative Texas Democrats were philosophically opposed to the national Democratic Party and that, although unwilling to embrace the Republican Party fully, they found the Republican Party more compatible with their views. A pattern in voting known as **presidential Republicanism** was strengthening, whereby conservative Texas voters would vote Democratic for state offices but Republican for president. Those conservatives were more numerous and more closely aligned with the Republican Party. To be sure, the fact that some Democratic voters and leaders supported the Republican presidential candidate did not mean that candidate would always carry Texas. As the Who Are Texans? graphic shows, the fortunes of Republican presidential candidates fluctuated between 1944 and 2020. Nevertheless, presidential Republicanism would persist in Texas and other southern states until Republicans began to win state and local races in the 1990s and beyond.

Still, in state elections from 1874 to 1994 the Democratic Party was overwhelmingly dominant despite pockets of Republican strength. Traditionally, in the post–Civil War era, the "German counties" in the Texas Hill Country, which were settled by German immigrants, showed Republican leanings. Dallas County, whose voters were influenced by a powerful group of conservative businesspeople and a conservative newspaper, the *Dallas Morning News*, also showed early Republican strength, electing a very conservative Republican member of Congress in the 1950s.

During this era, the Democratic Party was an umbrella party that held a variety of groups and interests. Both liberals and conservatives belonged to the party, as did members of labor unions, businesspeople, farmers, and city dwellers. Often, liberals and conservatives battled for control of the party and its offices, but what little political organization existed tended to be based on personal ties and the popularity of individual candidates. Until about the 1940s, politics inside the Texas Democratic Party was often chaotic and confused, with relatively few significant ideological divisions. Democrats were for the most part conservative during this time period.

By about the mid-1940s, however, a split occurred between liberals and conservatives in the Democratic Party. New Deal economic policies and civil rights measures divided the party, and liberals and conservatives battled in the Democratic primaries.

Shivercrat movement a movement led by the Texas governor Allan Shivers during the 1950s in which conservative Democrats in Texas supported Republican candidate Dwight Eisenhower for the presidency because many of those conservative Democrats believed that the national Democratic Party had become too liberal

presidential Republicanism a voting pattern in which conservatives vote Democratic for state offices but Republican for president

Though Democrats dominated Texas politics for decades, presidential Republicanism grew when Democrats supported Republican presidential candidate Dwight Eisenhower, who ran for president in 1952 and 1956. Here, Eisenhower is seen campaigning in Lubbock.

Until the mid-1970s, the victor in these primary squabbles would then go on to win the general election fairly easily. However, by the late 1970s the winner of the Democratic primary had to face a significant conservative challenge from a Republican in the general election.[7]

The Era of Conservative Democrats

The Democrats who controlled Texas politics between Reconstruction and the mid-twentieth century were conservative on fiscal and racial issues and exerted a powerful influence in the region as well as in Congress. This may seem hard to fathom in today's political environment, wherein Democrats are liberal on these issues and Republicans conservative. But the Republican Party was started as an antislavery party and long remained identified with this legacy, whereas conservative Democrats in the early to mid-twentieth century were not particularly favorable to policies that would make it easier for African Americans to vote or participate in civic life in an equal manner.

In the many contests between conservative and liberal Democrats within Texas when the Democratic Party was the only game in town, the conservatives usually won because of the sheer fact that there were more of them in the state. However, some liberal leaders did emerge within the party, such as U.S. senator Ralph Yarborough, and to some extent, President Lyndon B. Johnson. They both held progressive views—unlike many of their White Texas counterparts. U.S. senator Lloyd Bentsen, Jr., became the vice-presidential candidate for Michael Dukakis in 1988 but was unable to win the state for his running mate. Instead, Republican George H. W. Bush, who had moved to Texas from Connecticut, won the state and the presidency. By then the national conservative wave that began with the election of Ronald Reagan as president in 1980 had reached Texas, and from that point on, the Democratic Party in the state shrank to become the minority party.

The Growth of the Republican Party

Over the last fifty years, one of the most important developments in Texas politics has been the growth of the Republican Party (see Figure 4.2). This growth can be seen along three interrelated dimensions: in terms of those who identify with the party, those who vote for Republican candidates in primaries and general elections, and those Republicans who have been elected to office.

In the 1950s more than 60 percent of Texans identified with the Democratic Party and fewer than 10 percent identified as Republicans. The remainder considered themselves independents. The 1970s saw a decline in Democratic affiliation and an increase in Republican affiliation, a pattern that accelerated during the 1980s and continued through the end of the century.[8] In October 2020, a *Texas Tribune* and University of Texas poll reported that 41 percent of Texans identified as Democratic or leaning

SOCIAL RESPONSIBILITY: GET INVOLVED

- Consider how electoral decisions could be made if candidates were not identified by party membership. Would it be more or less difficult for individuals to discover the candidates' views on the issues? Would fund-raising be more or less difficult?

- Would you be more or less inclined to participate in politics if politicians did not identify with particular parties? Why?

FIGURE 4.2

Party Composition of the Texas Delegation to the U.S. House of Representatives, 1845–2021

NOTE: Third-party data are not included.

SOURCE: Texas Politics Project at the University of Texas at Austin.

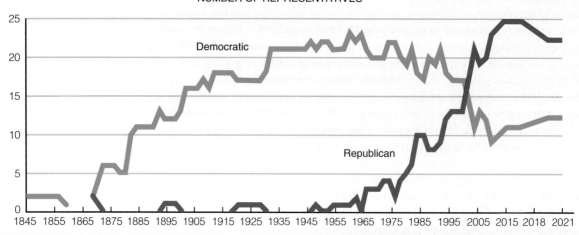

NUMBER OF REPRESENTATIVES

Democratic and 47 percent identified as Republican or leaning Republican. There is, however, clearly a difference between poll responses and election results. When one considers competition between the two parties in terms of actual voters in primaries or general elections, a different story emerges. By this measure, Texas is still a Republican state, but Democrats have been making significant gains since 2014.

In the first quarter of the twentieth century, from 1903 to 1927, Republicans never held more than one seat in the Texas Senate or more than two seats in the Texas House. For the next quarter-century, from 1927 to 1951, there were no Republicans at all in the legislature, until in 1950 a lone Republican was elected from Dallas to serve only one term in the House. It was another decade before Republicans were again elected to the legislature; this time two Republican members served in the House. Then in 1962, six Republicans were elected to the House from Dallas County and one from Midland County. By 1963 there were 10 Republicans in the House but still none in the Senate.[9]

As Table 4.1 shows, as late as 1974 there were very few Republican officeholders in the entire state of Texas. One of them was U.S. senator John Tower, and there were two Texas Republicans in the U.S. House of Representatives. No Republicans had been elected to state office in statewide elections. There were only 3 Republicans in the Texas Senate and only 16 in the Texas House.

Ronald Reagan's election as president in 1980 marked a significant change in how Texans began to vote in presidential and state elections. The Reagan era ushered in a period when conservative Democrats began to switch to the Republican Party in record numbers. This switch became more evident at the end of the George H. W. Bush presidency in the early 1990s, when Texas became a Republican state not only in presidential

TABLE 4.1

Republican Officeholders in Texas, 1974–2020

YEAR	U.S. SENATE	U.S. HOUSE	TEXAS SENATE	TEXAS HOUSE	OTHER STATEWIDE	TOTAL
1974	1	2	3	16	0	22
1980	1	5	7	35	1	49
1990	1	8	8	57	6	80
2000	2	13	16	72	27	130
2010	2	23	19	101	27	172
2012	2	24	19	95	27	167
2014	2	25	20	98	27	172
2016	2	25	20	94	27	168
2018	2	23	19	83	27	154
2020	2	23	18	83*	27	153

*As of November 2020, some races had not yet been called.

races but also in state races. In 2019 both U.S. senators from Texas and 23 of the 36 Texas members of the U.S. House of Representatives were Republican. In the state legislature, majorities of both the Senate (18 of the 31 members) and the House (83 of the 150 members) were Republican.

It was a record of remarkable Republican growth and Democratic decline. By 1999 every statewide elected official was Republican (and this remained true in 2020). That included the governor, lieutenant governor, attorney general, comptroller, land commissioner, agriculture commissioner, all three members of the Texas Railroad Commission, and all nine members of both the Texas Supreme Court and the Texas Court of Criminal Appeals. Only 20 years earlier, William Clements had been the first statewide official elected as a Republican since Reconstruction.

The Disappearance of Conservative Democrats

Conservative Democrats, also known as **Blue Dog Democrats**, are becoming an endangered species in Texas and in the rest of the South. Such Democrats never left the party they grew up in, but they have become marginalized in the national party because of their social conservatism. Many of these Democrats are opposed to abortion while supportive of gun rights, positions that put them at odds with the prevailing consensus in the Democratic Party. Some of the few conservative Democrats elected to Congress in recent years even refused to support Nancy Pelosi of San Francisco as their party leader because of their divergence from her more liberal views.

Blue Dog Democrats
another name for conservative Democrats, mostly from the South

Recent elections have continued the trend toward greater strength of Republicans in Texas. Some conservative Democrats—like Representative Henry Cuellar of Laredo, pictured here—continue to serve in Congress.

By 2012 all of the conservative Democrats elected to represent Texas in Congress had retired, switched parties, or lost re-election contests. For example, Chet Edwards, who represented Crawford, the home of former president George W. Bush, lost his bid for re-election in 2010 to Republican Bill Flores. Ralph Hall of Rockwall became a Republican in 2004 after spending many years as a conservative Democrat. He switched parties in order to have more influence in what was then Congress's majority party, although just two years later, the Democrats retook control of the U.S. House. In 2014, Hall decided to run for re-election at the age of 91 but lost in a runoff with Tea Party–backed candidate John Ratcliffe, who went on to win the seat.

The biggest losses for conservative Democrats came following the 2003 redistricting cycle, spearheaded by Tom DeLay. As House majority leader, DeLay wanted to take advantage of the new Republican majority in the state legislature to redraw the boundaries of the state's congressional districts, which he thought were too favorable to Democrats. Democrats had been in control of the State House in 2001, the year after the census when lines are always drawn. Republicans took control of the State House in the 2002 elections, and DeLay sensed an opportunity by organizing a dramatic though controversial redistricting session, which put many conservative Democrats from Texas at risk of losing their seats.

After this episode, two Democratic U.S. representatives, Charles Stenholm and Max Sandlin, lost their 2004 re-election bids to Republicans. Another Democrat, Jim Turner, decided not to seek re-election in his newly configured district in east Texas. Redistricting had left liberal Lloyd Doggett of Austin as the only White Democrat representing a majority White congressional district in Texas.

The pattern in Congress is also present at the state legislative level. Of the 55 Democrats in the Texas House of Representatives in 2013, only 11 were considered conservative in research conducted by Mark Jones of Rice University. This rating was relative to other Democrats, not Republicans; the most conservative Democrat in the Texas House is still more liberal than the most liberal Republican.[10]

In today's political environment, the influence of conservative Democrats and liberal Republicans is very limited. Both nationally and in Texas, conservatives are disproportionately members of the Republican Party and liberals of the Democratic Party.

Texas Party Politics Today

Analyze how ideological divisions and demographic change affect Texas political parties

Both Texas Democrats and Texas Republicans have factions within their party, and these factions emphasize different issues. For example, the Democratic Party in Texas has a large Latino base, which is very interested in the issue of immigration. The Republican Party has a strong and growing Tea Party contingent, which is making the party more antitax and fiscally conservative. Moreover, there are a shrinking number of truly independent voters who can swing elections. Often, both parties attempt to mobilize their own bases instead of trying to reach these swing voters. Political polarization has become more pronounced especially in the Texas legislature, meaning that in recent years, Democratic and Republican representatives have voted more often with their co-partisans. (In the recent legislative session, though, some major legislation passed in a bipartisan fashion.) In this section, we will examine some of these conflicts both between and within the major parties.

Party Unity and Disunity

All groups have opposing factions within them, and political parties are no exception. When a party becomes dominant in a state, these factional battles become particularly important because the stakes are higher for the factions of the dominant party.

As discussed earlier, when the Democratic Party dominated Texas politics, factional battles were common between liberals and conservatives in the party. These conflicts were especially notable during the 1950s, in the struggles between the pro-Eisenhower conservative Democrats, led by Allan Shivers, and the pro-Stevenson liberal and loyalist Democrats, led by Sam Rayburn, Lyndon Johnson, and Ralph Yarborough. Now that the Republican Party dominates the state, its factions have fought major battles for control as well. One faction is the religious right, which is especially concerned with issues such as abortion, prayer in public schools and at school events, the teaching of evolution in public schools, and the so-called bathroom bill, which would have made it state law to only use restrooms corresponding to the gender on one's birth certificate. The other major segment of the party is composed of economic conservatives, who are primarily concerned with reduced government spending and regulation. At the end of the day, however, both these factions usually end up supporting the Republican candidate in the general election.

In recent years, some Republicans, including two of the party's largest contributors in Texas, believed that some Republicans in the Texas House were insufficiently committed to conservative policies such as the bathroom bill and the sanctuary city ban and spent money to try to defeat them.[11] At least six Republican incumbents were aided by last-minute contributions from a political action committee that poured about $300,000 into their campaigns to help protect them from more conservative challengers. Nevertheless, two of the six were defeated in the primary and one had to win a runoff.[12] The 2014 primary battle between Dewhurst and Patrick shows that the ideological tensions in the Republican Party continue between what is essentially a conservative faction and an even more conservative faction, the latter identified with the Tea Party movement.

To maintain its political strength, the Republican Party has to keep these factional disputes within the party. For years, the Democratic Party battles between liberal and conservative wings were kept inside the party because there was no rival party to which one of the factions could go. Eventually the Republican Party emerged as a home where many conservative Democrats felt comfortable. Conceivably, the factional disputes in the Republican Party could lead one of the factions—the more moderate Republicans— to move to the Democratic Party.

The state legislative session in 2019 marked an important shift in the state Republican Party. Representative Dennis Bonnen (R-Angleton) became speaker and governed in a conciliatory fashion with bipartisan input on most major legislation. Governor Abbott and Lieutenant Governor Patrick also emphasized bread-and-butter issues such as property tax reform, increased school funding, raises for teachers, and relief for Hurricane Harvey victims. Absent in the 2019 legislative session was emphasis on divisive social issues such as abortion, sanctuary cities, and bathroom legislation. A small group of conservatives in the state House led by Representative Jonathan Stickland were not happy with the legislative session and believed that the new speaker abandoned conservative principles.

Urban, Rural, and Suburban Influences on Partisanship

As in the rest of the country, one of the major divides in Texas is rural versus urban. Today's large suburban populations must be added to this equation. Since World War II, the growth of suburban enclaves around major cities such as the Dallas–Fort Worth metroplex, Houston, and San Antonio has profoundly changed politics. Prior to the growth of suburbia, people lived either in cities or in rural areas. Rural residents were often cattle ranchers or farmers. As cattle raising and farming became more mechanized and large companies bought out local farmers, family farms and ranches became less profitable, and many rural residents relocated to cities to work in banks, oil companies, or other industries.

During the 1950s the federal government embarked on a major project to connect cities through an interstate highway system. One consequence of this system was that for those who wanted to escape urban congestion, it became easier to move to the outskirts of the city and travel by car to their jobs. While mass transit facilitated suburban commuting in other parts of the country, Texas taxpayers were unwilling to fund these infrastructure investments. Interstate highways also encouraged the process of "White

The Tea Party in Texas

With the election of many Tea Party–backed candidates and a more conservative turn in the Republican Party's positions on immigration, including the ban on sanctuary cities as well as increased border security, some have argued that the Republican Party has been taken over by the Tea Party. Do Texans think the Tea Party has too much influence, too little influence, or just the right amount? Where do you stand compared with other Texans? Given the data here, why do you think the Tea Party gained influence in the state in recent years?

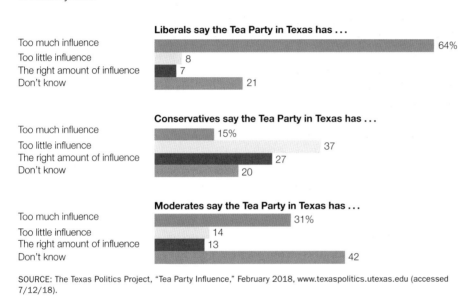

Liberals say the Tea Party in Texas has . . .

Too much influence	64%
Too little influence	8
The right amount of influence	7
Don't know	21

Conservatives say the Tea Party in Texas has . . .

Too much influence	15%
Too little influence	37
The right amount of influence	27
Don't know	20

Moderates say the Tea Party in Texas has . . .

Too much influence	31%
Too little influence	14
The right amount of influence	13
Don't know	42

SOURCE: The Texas Politics Project, "Tea Party Influence," February 2018, www.texaspolitics.utexas.edu (accessed 7/12/18).

flight," the mass exodus of more affluent Whites from urban to suburban areas, at least partly to avoid racial integration. This movement left urban areas with eroding tax bases and poorer populations, who often could not afford to purchase automobiles to commute between city and suburb.

The political result of this changing demographic is that cities have become more Democratic, even in Texas, where the urban strongholds of Austin, Dallas, El Paso, and Houston deliver the most Democratic votes in the state. Rural areas have remained solidly conservative and have become Republican, and suburban areas can best be described as hybrid areas with pockets of Republicans and Democrats, but an overall Republican majority. An important exception to these patterns is the Rio Grande Valley, which has large rural areas with Democratic dominance. However, voter turnout in the valley is substantially lower than in other parts of the state.

Voters also increasingly tend to settle in places with like-minded people; cities tend to attract more Democrats and suburban and rural areas more Republicans, reinforcing the political proclivities already established in such communities. A recent book, *Our Patchwork Nation,* by Dante Chinni and James Gimpel, explores this phenomenon nationwide, arguing that different communities have distinct political characteristics.[13]

The political shifts introduced by suburbanization are clearly seen in Dallas County over the last decade. In the early 1980s there had been a wholesale rush of incumbent Democratic judges in Dallas County into the Republican Party. Although varying explanations were given by the party switchers, perhaps the most honest and straightforward was by Judge Richard Mays: "My political philosophy about general things has nothing to do with me [*sic*] being a judge. . . . That's not the reason I'm switching parties. The reason I'm switching is that to be a judge in Dallas County you need to be a Republican." With Mays's switch in 1985, 32 of the 36 district judges in Dallas County were Republicans, though none had been Republicans before 1978.[14] By the late 1980s the only Democrat who could win a judicial race in Dallas County was Ron Chapman, who happened to share the name of the most popular disk jockey in the county. Only a few years later, all judges in Dallas County were Republican.[15]

As Dallas County became denser and the suburbs expanded to adjoining counties, Dallas transformed into a solidly Democratic county. This is illustrated by an almost overlooked judicial race in Dallas County in 2000. Only one article appeared in the *Dallas Morning News* about the puzzling results.[16] A three-term Republican judge, Bill Rhea, won re-election against a first-time Democratic candidate, Mary Ann Huey. On its own, that outcome was no surprise.[17]

What *was* remarkable about that district court race was that out of 560,558 votes cast, only 4,150 votes separated the two candidates. In other words, a three-term Republican judge with no scandal or other controversy surrounding his name won with only 50.3 percent of the vote.[18] Even more astounding, his opponent had run with no money, no political experience, and no support from the legal community. She ran in the same year that Texas governor George W. Bush was the presidential nominee, with no other Democratic judicial candidates on the ballot at the county level, and with little more than audacity on her side. It is no wonder that Judge Rhea commented, "I'm thrilled to be serving again and duly humbled by the vote count."

Judge Rhea's humbling experience was caused not by his judicial performance but rather by demographic changes. By 2000 the voters who had made up the former Republican base in Dallas County had begun moving to places such as Collin, Denton, and Rockwall counties. That suburban growth changed those traditionally Democratic counties into Republican ones but left Dallas itself with a larger African American and an even larger Latino population and returned it to the Democratic column that it left a little more than 30 years ago.

In the 2004 elections, George W. Bush carried Dallas County by fewer than 10,000 votes (50.72 percent), and the county elected Democrats as sheriff and four countywide elected judges. The 2006 elections were truly a watershed in the county's politics. A Democrat was elected county judge, a Democrat was elected district attorney, and all 42 Democrats who ran for county judgeships were elected. Democrats continued their sweep of countywide elections in 2008, 2010, 2012, 2016, and 2018.

In 2008, Harris County (containing Houston) also dramatically shifted to the Democratic column, electing a large number of Democrats to county office. However, the 2010 elections moved Harris back into the Republican column, and in 2012, it yielded a virtual tie between Obama and Republican presidential nominee Mitt Romney. In 2016, Hillary Clinton won Harris County by double digits, and Democrats swept the countywide races. In 2018, all countywide Republicans in Harris County were defeated by Democrats. In 2020, Harris County remained heavily Democratic as Joe Biden defeated Donald Trump 55.8 percent to 42.8 percent.

African Americans in Texas Political Parties

As noted earlier, about 12 percent of the Texas population is African American—roughly the same percentage as in the total U.S. population—and African Americans are concentrated in east Texas and in the major cities of Houston, Dallas, San Antonio, and Austin. In most elections, the vast majority of them cast their votes for Democrats. This is not unusual, as African Americans in other parts of the country are similarly loyal to the Democratic Party.

African Americans have been elected to represent Texas in Congress since Reconstruction. The first African American woman elected to Congress from Texas was Barbara Jordan, who played a major role in the investigation of Richard Nixon during the Watergate scandal. Her legacy remains strong among African Americans in Texas. In 2019, Texas was represented by six African Americans in the U.S. House: Republican Will Hurd of San Antonio and Democrats Eddie Bernice Johnson of Dallas, Al Green of Houston, Sheila Jackson Lee of Houston, Marc Veasey of Dallas, and Colin Allred of Richardson. In the state legislature as of 2019, 17 African Americans serve in the state House of Representatives and 2 serve in the state Senate.

The influence of African Americans in the Democratic Party in Texas is high not only because they tend to vote Democratic but because they tend to vote at higher rates than other ethnic groups. During the 2018 statewide elections, 45.8 percent of African Americans turned out to vote, versus 56.8 percent of Whites and only 25 percent of Latinos (see Table 4.2).

Sheila Jackson Lee has served as a representative for Houston since 1995. Here, she speaks at the funeral of George Floyd, a Houston native, who was killed by police in Minneapolis, Minnesota, in the spring of 2020.

TABLE 4.2

Turnout by Race: 2016 Presidential Year versus 2018 Statewide Election Year

	NUMBER OF REGISTERED VOTERS IN 2018 (IN MILLIONS)	TURNOUT OF REGISTERED VOTERS IN 2018 STATEWIDE ELECTION YEAR (%)	TURNOUT OF REGISTERED VOTERS IN 2016 PRESIDENTIAL YEAR (%)	DIFFERENCE BETWEEN 2016 AND 2018 (%)
White*	6.7	47.8%	56.8%	9%
African American	1.6	54.9	45.8	−9
Asian	0.4	30.4	26.3	−4
Latino	2.8	28.0	25.0	−3
Total	11.5	47.7	42.2	−6

*White does not include Whites who identify as Latino.
SOURCE: U.S. Census Bureau, "Voting and Registration in the Election of November 2018 and 2016—Detailed Tables."

This is not to say that all African Americans are Democrats. In 2015, Republican Will Hurd of San Antonio made history by becoming the first Black Republican elected from the state to Congress. Former railroad commissioner Michael Williams became the first Black Republican to be elected to the statewide post. The former Texas Supreme Court chief justice Wallace Jefferson is also an African American Republican and was elected by voters to his position. Other than Williams and Jefferson, only two other African Americans have been elected to statewide office since Reconstruction.

African Americans have been elected mayors of the three largest cities in Texas. Democrat Ron Kirk became Dallas's first African American mayor in 1995, and Democrat Lee Brown became Houston's first African American mayor in 1997. In 2002, Kirk ran for the U.S. Senate but lost to White Republican John Cornyn. In 2015, Houston elected its second African American mayor, Democrat Sylvester Turner. In 2014, African American independent Ivy Taylor was elected San Antonio's mayor, but subsequently lost her re-election to Independent Ron Nirenberg in 2017. In 2019, Dallas made history by electing its first African American mayor, Democrat Eric Johnson, who defeated Scott Griggs in June.

Latinos in Texas Political Parties

In the 2014 gubernatorial election, Republican Greg Abbott ran television ads in English and Spanish featuring his Latina mother-in-law's endorsement of his candidacy. Abbott's appeal to Latino voters in this way—if I am elected governor, Texas will have a Latina first lady—highlights at the very least the growing importance of this electorate.

Just 12 years prior to Abbott's election, Democrats had attempted to break the Republican lock on statewide offices by putting forward a "Dream Team" for the 2002 elections: a slate of nominees that aimed to mobilize voters of color to support the Democratic ticket while holding on to much of the party's traditional base of White voters.

Former secretary of Housing and Urban Development Julián Castro (right) and Congressperson Joaquin Castro of San Antonio (left) are two of a growing number of influential Latinos in the Democratic Party in Texas. Julián Castro ran a progressive campaign for the Democratic nomination for president in 2019 but suspended his campaign before primary elections began.

The team consisted of Tony Sanchez, a wealthy Latino businessman from Laredo who had been an appointee of Republican governor Rick Perry and had a record of not participating in many elections, running for governor alongside Ron Kirk for the U.S. Senate and John Sharp, a former state comptroller and White conservative Democrat, for lieutenant governor. The strategy failed dismally, as Sanchez lost to Perry (40 percent to 58 percent), Kirk lost to the Republican Cornyn (43 percent to 55 percent), and Sharp lost to the Republican Dewhurst (46 percent to 52 percent). Especially disappointing because Sanchez was the first Latino major-party nominee for governor, Latino voter turnout was only 32.8 percent. Sanchez had money and spent it with abandon, but he was a poor campaigner who could not even mobilize the Latino vote. Further, it appeared that negative campaigning, particularly directed at Sanchez, may have undercut support for the Democratic ticket among traditional White conservative voters.[19] The Democratic "Dream Team" became a nightmare.

Latinos have not fully realized their potential voting strength. Table 4.2 on p. 143 shows Latino voting population figures and turnout rates in comparison with those of other racial and ethnic groups in the state in 2018 (a statewide year) and 2016 (a presidential election year). This is an issue that we will explore in more depth in Chapter 5. For now, we should note that Latino voters have a significantly lower turnout rate than that of Whites and African Americans in both presidential years and statewide election years. Moreover, a large number of the Latinos living in Texas—perhaps around 2 million—are not citizens and thus not eligible to vote, even if they are documented.[20] Such facts will likely depress the electoral power of the Latino population in Texas in the short and medium terms. However, many of the children of these noncitizens were born in the United States and thus are themselves citizens eligible to vote. It would be surprising if being brought up and educated in the United States did not lead to higher turnout rates among younger Latinos in the future. The full impact of the Latino demographic surge on political parties may not be felt until the next generation comes of age.[21] Exit polls released just after the 2020 election indicated Latinos were 23 percent of the state electorate, a 1 percent increase from 2018.

Texan Julián Castro launched his bid for the Democratic nomination in 2019 hoping to build on his base of Latino support into the top tier of candidates. With well-known figures in the primary, Castro's challenge was to distinguish himself from the more than twenty candidates also hoping to gain traction in the primary for the opportunity to challenge Donald Trump in the general election. While Castro is not the first Latino to run for president, his candidacy marked an important milestone as he was among the first Texas Latinos to mount a credible campaign for president.

Political Parties and the Future of Texas

WE OFTEN THINK of conflict in politics as occurring between the Democratic and Republican parties, especially in government. While this is certainly true, conflict can also occur within political parties among different factions. These factions usually compromise, however, to support their candidates during the general election. Political parties therefore provide a structure through which candidates strive to win office.

One of the most striking developments in Texas politics over the past 20 to 25 years is that though one-party dominance persists, control of government has moved from near-total Democratic to near-total Republican control. This change was fueled by many factors, including the disappearance of conservative Democrats and the sorting of conservatives into the Republican Party and liberals into the Democratic Party. Like other southern states, Texas has long been very socially conservative and religious. As the Republican Party became the conservative party while Democrats became the liberal party, Texas has remained solidly conservative and therefore has become Republican. What would it take for Democrats to regain even some significant power in the state? There are three factors to watch as partisan politics in Texas evolves: divisions within the Republican Party, an influx of people from outside of Texas, and the effort put forth by the Democratic Party itself.

Divisions within the Republican Party could provide Democrats an opportunity to capitalize on what voters might perceive as dysfunction and extreme policies. If more Tea Party–backed Republicans are elected statewide and move further and further to the right, a centrist Democrat could possibly win a statewide race. Neighboring Louisiana elected a moderate-to-conservative Democrat as governor in 2015 and re-elected him in 2019 by capitalizing on the state Republican Party's move to the right and weak Republican candidates.

While Texas is becoming more racially and ethnically diverse and is now a majority-minority state (meaning that non-Hispanic Whites are less than half of the population), it is also seeing a major influx of White residents from other states. Many of these are conservatives attracted to the state's low taxes and light regulation policies. If these individuals vote at higher rates than others, then they will complicate efforts by the Democratic Party to make inroads.

Finally, the Democratic Party has to appeal to Texans by adopting policies that are not too far to the left. To some extent, Wendy Davis tried to do this on the issue of guns in her campaign for governor in 2014, but her reputation as a defender of abortion rights overshadowed her other policy positions, and she lost resoundingly to Greg Abbott. This failure to move the needle even slightly toward Democrats might give pause to Democratic donors nationally, who might instead choose to invest their resources in states that show more promise of "swinging" away from the Republicans. However, Beto O'Rourke's unabashedly progressive campaign for U.S. Senate against Senator Ted Cruz gave hope to many Democrats that the state was becoming more competitive. Was 2018 a fluke, given Cruz's unpopularity coupled with Trump's presidency and a dynamic, energetic O'Rourke? The 2020 election took on a decidedly different tone after the pandemic, which began in March 2020 and led to unprecedented job losses and economic depression. Campaign rallies, kissing babies, and shaking hands faded as Americans were concerned about the contagious novel coronavirus (COVID-19), which wreaked havoc on the world and led to the deaths of millions worldwide.

In early 2016 discussion about tapping former San Antonio mayor and former secretary of Housing and Urban Development Julián Castro as a possible running mate for Hillary Clinton led some to believe that this choice might mobilize Latino voters not only in Texas but nationwide. Even Castro's presence on the Democratic ticket, however, would probably not have moved Texas into the Democratic column in 2016. As Texas becomes more diverse, the Republican Party's lock on power is ebbing, especially in the state's urban and suburban areas. Rural areas have become more Republican, and urban areas have become more Democratic. The 2018 election led to Democratic gains in the Texas House and the loss of two suburban Republican incumbents in the U.S. House.

Clearly, a lot has to happen for Democratic power in Texas to increase, and while Beto O'Rourke did not win the Senate race, the very close margin indicates that Texas is moving slowly to a more competitive political environment statewide. The much closer margins in the statewide elections are evidence of this. We will see what the future holds.

Use 🐰 inQuizitive to help you study and master this material.

The Roles and Structure of Political Parties in Texas

> • Describe the main functions and structure of state party organizations (pp. 117–32)

In Texas, political parties serve as brand labels for voters to determine whom to vote for in elections that have little or no publicity. Texas political parties also have conventions and committees that help their members organize and mobilize in elections.

Key Terms

party platform (p. 117)
partisan polarization (p. 119)
political socialization (p. 119)
precinct (p. 124)
precinct chair (p. 124)
county executive committee (p. 124)
county chair (p. 124)
state chair and vice chair (p. 124)
state executive committee (p. 124)
precinct convention (p. 124)
county convention (p. 124)
state convention (p. 125)
Dixiecrats (p. 126)
La Raza Unida (p. 126)
"first past the post" (p. 128)
single-member district (p. 128)
proportional representation (p. 128)
Tea Party movement (p. 129)

Practice Quiz

1. Providing a label that helps voters identify those seeking office is an important function of
   a) the state.
   b) political parties.
   c) interest groups.
   d) regional and subregional governments.
   e) the president.

2. The process by which political parties become more distant from each other in terms of ideology is
   a) partisan convergence.
   b) partisan polarization.
   c) partisan conventions.
   d) partisan equilibrium.
   e) partisan deliverance.

3. All of the following groups constitute the Democratic Party base in Texas *except*
   a) business leaders.
   b) Latinos.
   c) African Americans.
   d) White liberals.
   e) urban residents.

4. Which group is the fastest growing in Texas?
   a) African Americans
   b) Latinos
   c) Asian Americans
   d) Native Americans
   e) All are growing equally

5. In the state of Texas, the highest level of temporary party organization is the
   a) state convention.
   b) state executive committee.
   c) governor's convention.
   d) civil executive committee.
   e) speaker's committee.

6. Which of the following third parties and movements had the most success in winning elections in post–World War II Texas?
   a) La Raza Unida
   b) the Dixiecrats
   c) the Green Party
   d) the Kinky Friedman movement
   e) the Constitution Party

Texas's History as a One-Party State

> • Trace the evolution of the party system in Texas (pp. 132–39)

Texas has traditionally been a one-party state, meaning that one party has been in control of state politics for a long time. In the post–Civil War period, the Democrats held power in the state, but since 1994 the Republicans have won every state-wide election and consequently dominate state politics.

Key Terms
Shivercrat movement (p. 134)
presidential Republicanism (p. 134)
Blue Dog Democrats (p. 137)

Practice Quiz
7. The Shivercrat movement was
    a) a group of conservative Democrats in Texas who supported Eisenhower for president.
    b) a group of liberal Democrats who supported equal rights for all Americans.
    c) a group of conservative Republicans who rejected the Obama administration.
    d) a group of liberal Republicans who rejected the Bush administration.
    e) a group of Libertarians.

8. In Texas, the Republican Party became the dominant party in
    a) the 1950s.
    b) the 1960s.
    c) the 1970s.
    d) the 1980s.
    e) the 1990s.

9. Blue Dog Democrats were
    a) northeastern Democrats with conservative views.
    b) southern Democrats with liberal views.
    c) southern Democrats with conservative views.
    d) northern Democrats with liberal views.
    e) western Democrats with liberal views.

10. *Presidential Republicanism* refers to which of the following?
    a) Texans voting for Republican local candidates
    b) Texans voting for Republican presidents and Democrats for state offices
    c) Texans voting for Republican presidents and Republicans for state offices
    d) Texans voting for Democratic local candidates
    e) Texans voting for third-party candidates at all levels

Texas Party Politics Today

> • Analyze how ideological divisions and demographic change affect Texas political parties (pp. 139–45)

Texas is a diverse state with divisions between north and south and east and west. Latinos currently constitute nearly 40 percent of the state's population and currently favor the Democratic Party, although their registration and turnout rates are lower than those of the other major demographic groups.

Practice Quiz
11. Which of the following is *not* true?
    a) Cities in Texas have become more Democratic.
    b) Cities in Texas are dominated by third parties.
    c) Rural areas of Texas are solidly Republican.
    d) Texas suburbs contain pockets of both Democrats and Republicans.
    e) Democrats dominate elections in Dallas County.

12. African Americans in Texas
    a) tend to cast their votes for Democrats.
    b) are a large part of the Republican base.
    c) vote mainly for independent candidates.
    d) constitute less than 10 percent of the population.
    e) split their votes evenly between the Democratic and Republican parties.

In 2020, Democrat Sri Preston Kulkarni ran to represent Texas's 22nd congressional district, which was long held by Republicans. Though he ultimately lost, the increasing presence of Democratic challengers in Republican strongholds is largely due to the changing demographics of the state, especially in its more populous areas.

Campaigns and Elections

WHY CAMPAIGNS AND ELECTIONS MATTER The outcomes of elections shape political life in Texas. In 2020, a presidential election year, voters nationwide focused heavily on the contest between President Trump and Democrat Joe Biden but also saw many competitive congressional races. In Texas, the U.S. Senate race between incumbent Republican John Cornyn and Democrat MJ Hegar was surprisingly competitive. After a runoff postponed to July due to the pandemic, Democrats chose MJ Hegar, an Air Force veteran with no elective office experience, over State Senator Royce West (D-Dallas). Hegar had lost a House race to Representative John Carter (R–Round Rock) in 2018. Hegar ran a campaign that sought to align herself with anti-Trump sentiment in the cities and suburbs. Although Hegar came up short and lost to Cornyn, it was another expensive campaign for Republicans after the tight race in 2018 between Cruz and O'Rourke. At the presidential level, Trump carried the state against Biden in the closest presidential race in modern Texas history.

Campaigns and elections for the House of Representatives were also noteworthy. In Fort Bend County, just southwest of Houston, lies the 22nd Congressional district, which has long been held by Republicans. Former House Majority Leader Tom DeLay represented this district when he was in Congress. In Sugar Land, the most populous city in the district, the population has changed considerably since DeLay's time. What was once a majority White suburb has transformed into one of the most diverse counties in the United States. Republican Pete Olson announced his retirement in 2019, leaving an open seat. Democrats once again nominated Sri Preston Kulkarni, a former diplomat who narrowly lost by 5 points to Olson in 2018. An Indian American, Kulkarni started from a base of the district's large Indian American population to mount a strong campaign. He was also able to raise a considerable amount of money. In the second quarter of 2020, he raised $950,000, the largest amount ever for that district, according to *The Hill*.

Republicans nominated Fort Bend County Sheriff Troy Nehls for the seat. He ran his campaign on his conservative record as sheriff and pointed to his public safety credentials. Nehls was bruised in the primary by his more conservative opponent, Kathaleen Wall, who outspent Nehls, attacked him with negative campaign ads, and tied herself to Trump by advocating for construction of the border wall.

Kulkarni campaigned as a mainstream Democrat by highlighting his commitments to comprehensive immigration reform and expanding access to affordable health care. Because this suburban district has a high median income and large college-educated population, along with considerable diversity, this race represents, in many ways, the future of Texas, and the extent to which Republicans in the Trump era can compete against Democrats, who in districts such as these oppose some of the policies coming from the Trump administration.

Even though Cornyn and Nehls won, both races presented challenges to the state's Republican Party based on President Trump's declining popularity in the state. Recall that in 2016, Trump only won Texas by 9 percentage points, while Mitt Romney won the state by 16 percentage points only four years earlier. While Trump was able to win Texas in 2020, many of the state's suburbs that had previously gone for Republican candidates have begun to elect Democrats, helping them keep control of the U.S. House of Representatives and narrow the margin of control for Republicans in the State House.

Why does it matter who is a U.S. senator or representative in the House? Congress makes our nation's laws, and it matters who we elect to represent us in Washington. In terms of size, the Texas delegation to Congress is second only to California, and federal dollars can only come back to the state through the efforts of our representatives in Washington. They also make sure that the policies we support are enacted at the national level. Elections to the city council, school board, state legislature, and governorship also make huge differences in our lives. Education funding, health care policy, taxes, and environmental policy all hang in the balance.

CHAPTER GOALS

- Describe the types of elections held in Texas and how they work (pp. 153–56)
- Explain how the rules for voting affect turnout among different groups of Texans (pp. 156–69)
- Present the main features of election campaigns in Texas (pp. 169–79)

Features of Elections in Texas

Describe the types of elections held in Texas and how they work

Elections are the most important vehicles by which the people express themselves in the democratic process in Texas. At the national level, elections are limited to the selection of the president and vice president (via the electoral college) and members of Congress. In Texas, however, voters select candidates for various offices in all three statewide branches of government (the legislature, executive, and judiciary) and in numerous local elections. There are a multitude of elections: primary elections, general elections, city elections, school board elections, special elections, elections for community college boards and the governing boards for many special districts, constitutional amendment elections, and bond elections for city, county, and state governments.

With so many different elections, it is difficult for voters to process all of the information and make choices. Voters often rely on mental shortcuts to make voting decisions. Partisanship is the shortcut, or what political scientists call a *cue*, used by most Texans. Other shortcuts could be race, gender, ethnicity, or other demographic characteristics when selecting candidates. With regard to decisions on bonds or amendments, voters can rely on endorsements by elected officials as well as on condensed summaries from newspapers or political parties.

Texans also vote on changes to the state constitution, which can alter public policy in the state. In theory, such elections are meant to enable the people to exercise some direct control over each branch. In practice, however, one-party dominance and low levels of voter participation have often told a different story, leaving the government exposed to special interests and big money.

Primary Elections

Primary elections are the first elections held in an **electoral cycle**. In Texas, primary elections are generally held on the second Tuesday in March of even-numbered years. Primary elections determine a political party's nominees for the general election. They are conducted by the party and funded jointly by the party and the state. Essentially, the party collects filing fees from those seeking its nomination and uses these funds to pay the costs of holding the primary election.

The Democratic and Republican parties both conduct primaries in nearly all of Texas's 254 counties. Within each county, voters cast ballots in precincts, with the number of precincts depending on the county's population. Less-populated counties such as Loving and Kenedy have as few as 6 precincts, whereas Harris County contains more than 1,000.

Those seeking their party's nomination file papers and pay a filing fee to their party. If several members of the same party are seeking the same office, such as governor, they compete against each other in the party's primary election, wherein one will be chosen to run in the general election. Winning the primary election requires an absolute majority: more votes than all opponents combined. If no candidate receives an absolute

primary election a ballot vote in which citizens select a party's nominee for the general election

electoral cycle the process in which candidates run for office beginning with campaigns for the party primary and ending with the general election, usually in November

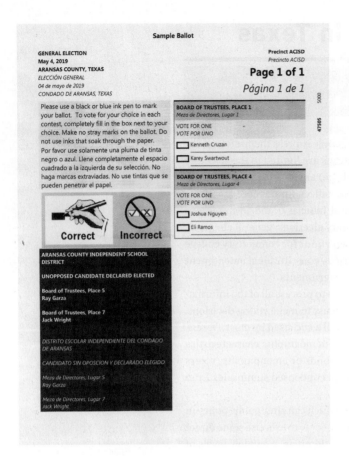

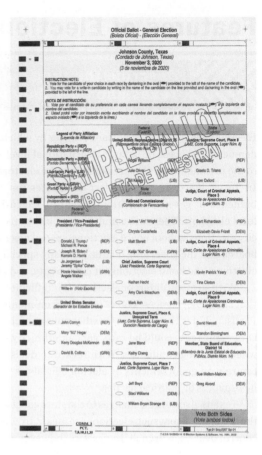

Texans vote in numerous elections each year. While November general elections ask Texans to vote for a variety of offices, many local elections only have candidates for a handful of positions on the ballot.

runoff primary a second primary election held between the two candidates who received the most votes in the first primary election if no candidate in that election received an absolute majority

open primary a primary election in which any registered voter can participate in the contest, regardless of party affiliation

closed primary a primary election in which only registered members of a particular political party can vote

majority, a **runoff primary** is held between the two candidates receiving the most votes. Voters who participate in the Republican Party primary cannot vote in a Democratic runoff; likewise, anyone who voted in the Democratic Party primary cannot vote in a Republican runoff. However, those who voted in neither the Democratic nor the Republican primary can vote in either the Republican or the Democratic runoff primary.

An **open primary** allows any registered voter to cast a ballot in either primary, but not both primaries. One can consider oneself a Republican and vote in the Democratic primary or can leave home intending to vote in the Democratic primary, change one's mind, and vote in the Republican primary.

The Texas Constitution and election laws call the Texas system a **closed primary** because one must declare one's party affiliation before voting, but in practice it is an open primary. Before receiving a primary ballot, the voter signs a roll sheet indicating eligibility to vote and pledging to support the party's candidates. By signing the roll sheet, the voter makes a declaration of party affiliation. However, because the affiliation is declared only a few moments prior to voting, the primary is closed only in the narrowest sense of the term. This declaration in no way legally binds a voter to support the party's candidates in future elections. Many other states have true closed primaries in that only voters who have registered as party members beforehand can vote in these elections.

General Elections

The **general election** to select members of Congress is held the first Tuesday following the first Monday in November of even-numbered years. The Democratic Party's nominee runs against the nominee of the Republican Party, and sometimes independent and minor-party candidates also appear on the general election ballot.

Major state officials (governor, lieutenant governor, comptroller of public accounts, attorney general, and so on) are elected in nonpresidential election years. This arrangement seeks to prevent presidential candidates from influencing the outcomes of Texas races. For example, it is possible that a popular Republican presidential candidate might draw more than the usual number of Republican votes, and an unusually large Republican presidential vote might swing the election for statewide candidates running under the Republican banner. Likewise, it prevents an uncommonly popular statewide candidate from influencing the presidential election. If statewide elections were held in presidential election years, a Democratic candidate for governor, for example, might influence Texas's presidential voting by increasing the number of votes for Democratic candidates in general.

Members of city councils, school boards, and other local government entities are also selected by general elections; however, these usually take place at a different time of year than the national and state elections. These elections are "nonpartisan," meaning the political parties of the candidates are not listed on the ballot. In many cases, this timing translates into very low voter turnout. For example, in the Houston municipal elections in November 2019, only 22.6 percent of the city's registered voters participated (versus 68 percent in the 2020 presidential election). Leaders in some parts of the state have proposed moving municipal elections to November to encourage a larger proportion of voters to participate.

In November 2019, Houston mayor Sylvester Turner won in a nonpartisan runoff election against Trump-endorsed Tony Buzbee. Since the race took place in a year without a national or statewide election, turnout was relatively low at 22.6 percent.

Special Elections

special election an election that is not held on a regularly scheduled basis; in Texas, a special election is called to fill a vacancy in office, to give approval for the state government to borrow money, or to ratify or reject amendments to the Texas Constitution

In Texas, **special elections** are used to fill vacancies in office, to give approval to borrow money, or to ratify or reject amendments to the Texas Constitution. The dates for special elections are specified by the Texas legislature. If a Texas state representative or senator resigns, the governor will call a special election to fill the vacancy.

Texas laws require voter approval before any governmental agency in Texas can assume long-term debt. If the local school district wants to borrow money to build a new high school and repair three elementary schools, for example, a special election must be held for voters to decide on the issue. The legislature proposes amendments to the Texas Constitution, and the voters in a special election then ratify or reject them.

Participation in Texas Elections

 Explain how the rules for voting affect turnout among different groups of Texans

When we think of political participation, we often think of voting. Signing petitions, protesting, and writing letters to newspapers and elected officials are also forms of political participation, but voting is the most basic and fundamental duty citizens have in a democracy. Here, we begin by examining the history of voting in the state and the regulations and procedures surrounding voting rights. Issues include who can vote, how easy it is to register to vote, and why so few Texans vote.

Who Can Vote?

"The franchise" refers to the act of voting or the right to vote. For much of the period of one-party Democratic control that began in the late nineteenth century, there were restrictions on the franchise.

Early Restrictions on the Franchise

Nineteenth Amendment ratified in 1920, amendment guaranteeing women the right to vote

suffrage the right to vote

Women were allowed to vote in primaries and party conventions in Texas in 1918 and obtained the right to vote in all elections as a result of the **Nineteenth Amendment** to the U.S. Constitution in 1920. However, some of the most influential politicians in the state were opposed to the franchise for women. Joseph Weldon Bailey, for example, who had been a Democratic leader in the U.S. House of Representatives and later the informal Democratic leader in the U.S. Senate, was a passionate opponent of women's **suffrage**, arguing that women could not vote because they could not perform the three basic duties of citizenship: jury service, *posse comitatus* service (citizens who are deputized to deal with an emergency), and military service. He believed that women's morals dictated their beliefs and women would force their beliefs on men. The result, he felt, would be prohibition of alcohol.[1] Tinie Wells, the wife of Jim Wells, perhaps the most influential south Texas political leader of his day, was also an important and influential spokesperson for the anti–women's suffrage movement.[2] Governor "Farmer Jim" Ferguson was another opponent of women's suffrage, but when he was impeached, his successor, William P. Hobby, proved a key supporter of women's right to vote. It was Governor Hobby who called the legislature into special session in 1919 to consider the Nineteenth Amendment. Thus, Texas became the ninth state and the first state in the South to ratify the women's suffrage amendment.[3]

In the early twentieth century, one restriction on voting was the **poll tax**. Enacted in 1902, it required people to pay a fee before an election in order to vote in it, supposedly to cover the costs of elections. The tax was usually between $1.50 and $1.75—a small sum today, but one that in the first third of the century could be one, two, or even more days' wages for a farm worker. Thus, it tended to disenfranchise poorer people.

The south Texas political bosses used the poll tax to great advantage. They would purchase large numbers of poll tax receipts and provide those receipts to their supporters who did not have the means to pay for the tax themselves. They depended on the bosses for jobs and other economic, legal, and political assistance and therefore would vote as the bosses wanted.

Although the poll tax was made illegal in federal elections in 1964 by the passage of the Twenty-Fourth Amendment to the U.S. Constitution, it remained legal in state elections in Texas until 1966.[4] And even after its elimination, Texas continued to require **early registration**—more than nine months before the general election—for voting. Early registration was required on a yearly basis, a requirement that effectively prevented itinerant workers from voting. Texas even prohibited anyone who was not a property owner from voting in revenue bond and tax elections. Texas also required an unusually long period of residency for voting. Voters had to have lived in the state for at least one year and the county for at least six months prior to voting. All of these provisions were voided by the courts in the 1970s because they unduly restricted the franchise.[5]

The most oppressive restriction on the franchise in Texas, however, was the **White primary**, which was designed to minimize the political strength of African American voters. In 1923 the Texas legislature flatly prohibited African Americans from voting in the Democratic primary. Since Texas was a one-party state at this time, the effect, of course, was to prevent African Americans from participating in the only "real" election contests. Texas was able to do this because of a 1921 U.S. Supreme Court decision, *Newberry v. United States*, which stated that the primary election was "in no real sense part of the manner of holding the [general] election."[6] This ruling cleared the way for southern states, including Texas, to exclude African Americans from voting in the primaries of either party. Over the next two decades, this practice came under scrutiny by federal courts numerous times; yet each time, the Texas legislature and state parties found a way to maintain the White primary and exclude African American voters.

The Supreme Court first struck down the Texas White primary law in 1927, finding that the legal ban on Black participation was a violation of the equal protection clause of the Fourteenth Amendment of the Constitution.[7] In response, the Texas legislature passed a law that authorized the state Democratic and Republican parties, through their executive committees, to determine the qualifications for voting in their primaries. That law, of course, allowed the parties to create White primaries. The legal argument behind it was that what a state could not do directly because of the Fourteenth Amendment, it could authorize political parties to do. However, in *Nixon v. Condon* (1932), the Supreme Court held that the party executive committees were acting as agents of the state and were thus in violation of the Fourteenth Amendment.[8] As a result, the Texas Democratic

poll tax a state-imposed tax on voters as a prerequisite for voting; poll taxes were rendered unconstitutional in national elections by the Twenty-Fourth Amendment, and in state elections by the Supreme Court in 1966

early registration the requirement that a voter register long before the general election; in effect in Texas until 1971

White primary primary election in which only White voters were eligible to participate

Participation in elections in Texas is low relative to that in other states. In the past, there were restrictions on the franchise. One such restriction that discouraged poor people from voting was the poll tax, which remained legal in Texas until 1966. Here, voters are asked to pay the poll tax and then vote against Pappy O'Daniel.

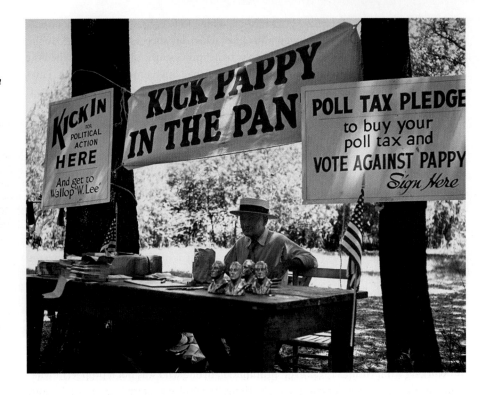

Party convention, acting on its own authority and without any state law, passed a resolution that confined party membership to White citizens. That case was also appealed to the U.S. Supreme Court, and in *Grovey v. Townsend* (1935), the Court held there was no violation of the Fourteenth Amendment. The Court said that the requirement of "equal protection under the law" applied only to "state action," not action by private groups. Since there was no state law authorizing the White primary, the Court believed there was no "state action," only discrimination by a private organization, the Democratic Party, which is not banned by the Fourteenth Amendment.[9] Thus, the Court upheld the White primary until 1944, when, in *Smith v. Allwright*, it decided that the operation of primary elections involved so much state activity and so much public responsibility that the White primary did involve unconstitutional state action.[10]

Even after the *Smith* decision, at least one Texas county held unofficial primaries by a Democratic political organization that excluded African Americans, the **Jaybird Party**. The winners in the Jaybird primary then entered the regular Democratic Party primary, in which they seldom had opposition and were never defeated for county office. In 1953, in *Terry v. Adams*, the U.S. Supreme Court finally ruled that the Jaybird primary was an integral, and effectively the only, part of the elective process in the county. Thus, the Fifteenth Amendment (which deals with the right to vote) was applicable, and the White "preprimary" primary of the Jaybird Party was ruled unconstitutional.[11]

What made the White primary restriction work for Democrats during this era was the fact that Texas was a one-party state, where elections were essentially decided in the Democratic primary. If Texas had had a competitive two-party system during this era, the state might have had a more difficult time imposing and maintaining such restric-

Jaybird Party after the White primary was ruled unconstitutional, this offshoot Democratic Party preselected candidates for the Democratic primary and prohibited African Americans from participating

tions on the franchise. In a competitive two-party system, to obtain and retain power, both parties have to search for ways to build and increase their base of support. In a one-party system, there is a greater incentive to restrict participation in the party in order to retain control over it. Losers in a battle for control of a one-party system essentially have no place to go. If they cannot maintain a place in the dominant party's councils, then they have no other avenue for expressing their political views.

Expanding the Franchise

As discussed above, in the early twentieth century, African Americans were not allowed to vote in the all-White Democratic primaries. They could later vote in the general election, but since the winner of the Democratic primary always won the general election, African Americans had essentially no influence in state politics. At least since the 1940s there has been a gradual expansion of the franchise in Texas. Much of that expansion was brought about by litigation in the federal courts, often by African American and Latino civil rights organizations. For example, the National Association for the Advancement of Colored People (NAACP) filed lawsuits throughout the 1960s and '70s challenging laws that restricted or otherwise stunted African American political advancement. The Mexican American Legal Defense and Education Fund (MALDEF) has been active since the 1970s in monitoring any changes in electoral laws that might have the effect of suppressing the votes of Latinos and other minorities, and it has challenged such changes—for instance, the voter identification bill adopted by Texas in 2011.

New federal laws also played an important role in the expansion of the franchise. The most important of these was the **Voting Rights Act of 1965**, which was applied to Texas as a result of amendments after 1975. President Lyndon B. Johnson signed this new law, initially aimed at ensuring that African Americans were not discriminated against at the polls, even though he knew it would damage his political popularity in the South.

The Voting Rights Act has had an important influence on elections in Texas. One provision of the law was to send federal examiners to southern states to register voters. In many southern states, including Texas, Blacks were systematically denied the ability to register to vote, much less attempt to vote. In Mississippi, only about 7 percent of Blacks had been registered to vote prior to 1965, but by 1967 more than 67 percent were registered. In Texas, just prior to the Voting Rights Act, approximately 35 percent of Blacks were registered to vote, but by 1971, the figure almost doubled to nearly 65 percent, according to the Southern Poverty Law Center. Section 2 of the Voting Rights Act involves a nationwide prohibition against the restriction of voting rights on the basis of race or ethnicity.

The Voting Rights Act has been renewed several times since 1965, and new provisions have been added. For example, bilingual ballots are now required in certain areas where more than 5 percent of voters speak a language other than English. In 2013, however, the Supreme Court ruled in *Shelby County v. Holder* that a key section of the Voting Rights Act was unconstitutional. This decision affects a provision requiring Texas to have any changes in its election districts or electoral procedures approved by the U.S. Department of Justice or a federal court in the District of Columbia before they go into effect. This provision was intended to make sure that the voting rights of minorities were not diminished.

Voting Rights Act of 1965 important legislation passed in order to ensure that African Americans would be guaranteed the right to vote. Renewed several times since 1965, the act also prevents the dilution of minority voting strength

The assurance of voting rights has been a key debate for decades. It exemplifies the tensions between federal and state government. Here, then–U.S. attorney general Eric Holder speaks in Houston about his opposition to Texas voter identification laws and his support of the Voting Rights Act of 1965.

Contracting the Vote? Critics of voter identification legislation passed in 2011 argue that it has made it more difficult for some people to vote in Texas. Over Democratic opposition, the Republican majority in the Texas legislature passed a law that requires a photo identification in order to vote. Republicans claimed that the requirement is necessary to prevent voter fraud. Democrats argued that evidence of such fraud is minimal and that the law will make it harder for low-income persons, students, and minorities (all of whom typically support Democrats) to vote.[12] The law specifies the acceptable forms of identification as a driver's license, an election identification certificate, a U.S. military ID, a U.S. citizenship certificate, a U.S. passport, and two items issued by the Texas Department of Public Safety: a personal ID card or a license to carry a concealed handgun.[13] A photo ID card issued by a college or university is not acceptable.

In 2015, however, a three-judge panel of a federal appeals court ruled that the Texas voter ID law violated the Voting Rights Act because it had a disparate impact on minority voters. Texas Republican leaders, such as Governor Abbott and Attorney General Paxton, have argued that Texas and other southern states should not be singled out for special scrutiny of their electoral practices and should be allowed to have a voter ID law without any approval process. They appealed the 2015 ruling to the full appellate court. Since other states have mounted similar legal challenges, the Supreme Court might ultimately decide on the constitutionality of voter ID laws. Even though the *Shelby* decision discussed earlier eliminated preclearance, Section 2 of the Voting Rights Act, which prohibits voter discrimination on the basis of race or ethnicity, is still in effect nationwide. This means that challenges to voter identification laws can be still brought. In the meantime, after a court order in 2016, Texas agreed that more forms of voter ID than its law authorized would be accepted at the polls (see Chapter 3). Citizen's Guide: Voter Identification Laws on p. 162 takes a closer look at this issue.

Qualifications to Vote Today Meeting the qualifications to register to vote in Texas is relatively easy today. A voter must be

1. eighteen years of age.
2. a U.S. citizen.
3. a resident of Texas for 30 days.
4. a resident of the county for 30 days.

To be eligible to vote, one must be a registered voter for 30 days preceding the election and a resident of the voting precinct on the day of the election. Two groups of citizens cannot vote even if they meet all the preceding qualifications: felons who have not completed their sentences and persons judged by a court to be mentally incompetent.

According to the Texas secretary of state, 79.4 percent of the state's voting-age population (15.8 million citizens) was registered to vote in 2018.[14] The **motor voter law**, a federal statute that requires states to allow individuals to register to vote when applying for or renewing driver's licenses, is one factor in increased registration. Public schools distribute voter registration cards as students turn 18, and most colleges and universities sponsor drives to encourage their students to register. Cooperative efforts between the secretary of state's office and corporations also increase the number of registered voters.

Following the November 2018 election, a Census Bureau survey of Texans found that registration rates among citizens varied across racial and ethnic lines. Latino eli-

motor voter law a national act, passed in 1993, that requires states to allow people to register to vote when applying for a driver's license

gible voters registered at a 50.8 percent rate, well below that of African Americans (63.4 percent) and non-Hispanic Whites (71.5 percent).[15]

Early Voting   In Texas, **early voting** is a procedure that allows people to vote not just in a 12-hour period on Election Day but also for two weeks prior to the election. The legislature has allowed early voting in an effort to increase participation by accommodating those who have trouble getting to the polls between 7 A.M. and 7 P.M. on Election Day. For most elections, early voting begins on the 17th day before Election Day and ends four days before it. Voting early is basically the same as voting on Election Day. A voter appears at one of the designated early voting polling places, presents appropriate identification, and receives and casts a ballot.

Since it was introduced in Texas in the late 1980s, early voting has at best only modestly increased voting participation, and predictions that Democrats would benefit from it did not hold true after Texas moved strongly into the Republican column. Republican candidates for the highest office on the ballot get a much larger proportion of early votes than do Democratic candidates. In 2020, for example, 51.7 percent of the early votes for president in Texas were cast for Donald Trump, compared with 48.2 percent for Joe Biden. On Election Day, voters in Texas preferred Donald Trump by a margin of 60.5 percent to Joe Biden's 39.4 percent. In terms of overall voting, nearly 86.8 percent of Texans voted during the early voting period, while only 13.2 percent of Texans voted on Election Day. Early voters voted slightly more Democratic than those on Election Day, but not enough to change the outcome in the presidential race (Figure 5.1).

Straight-Ticket Voting   When voting, Texans can press one button and vote for every Republican or Democrat on the ballot. Known as **straight-ticket voting**, Texans had increasingly resorted to just voting the party line in many elections. In the 2016 election, nearly 64 percent of Texans in the state's 10 largest counties voted

FIGURE 5.1

Early Voting and Overall Voting by Party in Texas

SOURCE: Texas Secretary of State.

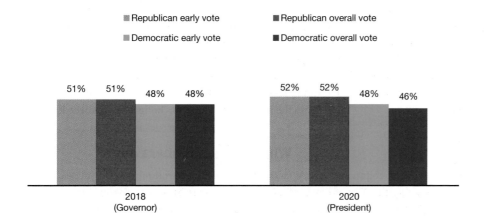

■ Republican early vote   ■ Republican overall vote
■ Democratic early vote   ■ Democratic overall vote

2018 (Governor): 51% 51% 48% 48%
2020 (President): 52% 52% 48% 46%

CITIZEN'S GUIDE

Voter Identification Laws

1 Why voter identification laws matter

According to the U.S. Constitution, states administer elections, not the federal government. This means that each state runs its elections differently. For example, Washington state voters cast their ballots by mail, rather than in person at the ballot box. States also set voter registration guidelines. In some states, you can show up to the polls on election day as an unregistered voter, automatically register, and vote in the election that day. In other states, such as Texas, voters must register in advance in order to vote. All of these differences suggest that who is a qualified, legitimate voter in any given election varies considerably by state, and in close elections, might change who wins and loses.

In 2011 the Texas legislature passed a law that requires all voters to produce photo identification when they present themselves to vote in an election. Prior to the law, Texans could present a voter registration certificate, which does not carry a photograph. Under the new law, not all forms of photo identification are considered valid for voting purposes. For example, state-issued concealed weapons permits are allowed, but student identification cards are not. A voter who shows up to the polls without appropriate photo identification may cast a provisional ballot but must return to the registrar's office with such identification within six days to make his or her vote count.

By the 2016 election, the Texas law had been softened somewhat by a federal court. Voters without an authorized identification were allowed to vote, but they had to sign an affidavit indicating they had a legitimate impediment to obtaining an approved identification card. The legislature passed a revised voter ID law in 2017 to address the concerns of the courts. It is still possible that a higher court will revisit Texas's law in future cases. In this citizen's guide, we will review how voter identification laws might impact elections in Texas, and what you need to do to make sure you are able to cast a vote.

2 What's the debate?

Supporters of stricter voter ID laws argue that requiring photo identification is necessary to ensure the integrity of the election system and assure Texans that their elections

are free from fraud. They claim that fraud is often undetected and difficult to prosecute; thus the absence of high rates of prosecution does not mean that voter fraud is a problem that should be ignored. The potential of penalties for breaking the law, they argue, will deter any attempts to commit fraud. Former governor Rick Perry noted that the law "makes sense" since people need to show photo identification to board airplanes and perform transactions with banks and other organizations.[a] Those in favor of the law also point to public opinion polls showing that the majority of Texans support the simple proposition that you must show photo identification to prove who you are in order to vote.

Opponents of the law claim that the measure is not really about preserving the integrity of the electoral system but is meant to minimize Democratic turnout in order to help the state Republican Party keep its hold on power. They argue that it puts an undue burden on populations who are less likely to possess photo identification (and who often vote for Democrats), such as elderly, disabled, minority, and poor voters, by making them go through additional steps to vote. Lubbock county commissioner Gilbert Flores noted that the bill's goal is to "weaken and deter the Hispanic vote."[b]

Texas's current voter ID law does provide for obtaining free photo identification from the state Department of Public Safety, but in some rural areas, opponents argue, the nearest DPS office is far away and not easily accessible. In addition, opponents suggest that the law is in essence a solution in search of a problem, pointing to research studies that show there is no real problem of voter fraud in Texas.

Legitimate arguments can be made for and against the legislation, but one thing is clear: Republicans strongly support it and Democrats have attempted to block it. This fact alone suggests that Republicans believe they will benefit from the law, while Democrats believe they will be harmed.

3 What do the numbers say?

In Wisconsin and North Carolina, federal judges agreed with challengers to those states' voter ID laws and declared them unconstitutional because of social science evidence suggesting that minorities were adversely affected by the new requirements. However, backers of the Texas law point to data showing that turnout in the November 2013 off-year election was nearly double that of previous off-year elections without the voter ID requirement, including in heavily Hispanic counties. This evidence suggests, they argue, that the law did not adversely affect minority turnout.

In terms of fraud, a small proportion of in-person voter fraud has been uncovered, as the data show. Out of the total number of ballots cast nationwide, 35 have been documented. In addition, MIT political scientist Charles Stewart has studied how voter identification laws might disproportionately affect certain voters.[c] He found that 9 percent of voters nationwide do not have driver's licenses, but if you differentiate by race, African Americans were more likely than other groups to not have driver's licenses and thus requisite photo identification to vote in certain states.

Confirmed Instances of Voter Fraud, 2000–14

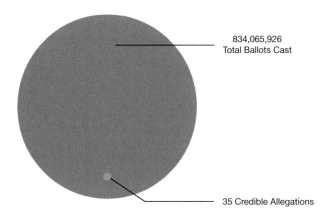

834,065,926
Total Ballots Cast

35 Credible Allegations

Percentage of Individuals without Driver's Licenses, 2013

Source: U.S. Elections Project.

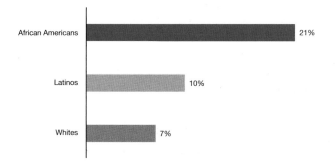

African Americans — 21%

Latinos — 10%

Whites — 7%

Communicating Effectively: What Do You Think?

● Do the arguments for the voter identification legislation outweigh the arguments against it?

● Why do you think a concealed weapons permit is an acceptable form of voter ID, but a school ID is not?

● Do you think a student ID should be accepted for voting? Write a brief letter to the editor of your school or local paper arguing your position.

WANT TO LEARN MORE?

To learn more about how elections are conducted in Texas, visit the Texas Secretary of State's website. There, you will find all the information you need to register to vote. The website will link you to your local county registrar, whom you can contact for more information on voting procedures in your county.

• www.sos.state.tx.us

• www.votetexas.gov

straight ticket.[16] State Republicans sought to eliminate straight-ticket voting in the 2017 legislative session mainly because Republican judges in some of the populous counties such as Harris were losing elections due to straight-ticket Democratic voting. For example, Lieutenant Governor Dan Patrick's son, a Harris county judge, lost his re-election bid and largely blamed straight-ticket Democratic voting for this loss. Governor Abbott signed the law, which began with the 2020 elections.

Redistricting: Where Do People Vote?

reapportionment process that takes place every 10 years to determine how many congressional seats each state will receive, depending on population shifts

Every 10 years, the U.S. Census is charged with counting how many people live in the United States. The process of **reapportionment** involves recalculating how many U.S. representatives each state is entitled to based on its new population. For example, Texas gained four new congressional seats following the 2010 Census because of the explosive population growth of the state. After the 2020 Census, Texas was poised to gain as many as three additional seats. (Since the House of Representatives is capped at 435 members, some states whose populations had increased more slowly during the previous 10 years, such as New York, lost some of their congressional seats.) In Texas, and many other states, the state legislature is tasked with drawing new congressional districts at least every 10 years to comply with the new overall number of seats allowed, as well as the principle of one person, one vote, a process called **redistricting**.

redistricting the process of redrawing election districts and redistributing legislative representatives in the Texas House, Texas Senate, and U.S. House; this process usually happens every 10 years to reflect shifts in population or in response to legal challenges in existing districts

Redistricting is always a blatantly political procedure in every state because the majority party uses it to retain power by creating as many friendly districts as it can. In 2011 the Republicans in charge of the Texas legislature attempted to draw as many Republican-voting districts as possible. (If Democrats had been in control, they would have tried to maximize their number of seats as well.) Complicating the Republicans' task was the fact that more than 67 percent of the population growth in Texas between 2000 and 2010 had been a result of Latino immigration and relatively high birthrates among both native-born and foreign-born Latinos. Given this, Latino leaders in the state wanted at least two of the new seats to be majority Latino. Most Latino-majority districts in Texas tend not to elect Republicans, however, putting the Republican-led legislature in a bind.

preclearance provision under Section 5 of the Voting Rights Act of 1965 that required any changes to election procedures or district lines to be approved by the U.S. Department of Justice or the U.S. District Court for the District of Columbia

Further complicating the situation were the terms by which Texas—until the 2013 U.S. Supreme Court decision in *Shelby County v. Holder*—had to comply with the Voting Rights Act. As noted earlier, a section of the act required that any changes to election procedures, including the drawing of new district lines, must go through the process of **preclearance** by federal authorities. Districts that have previously been created to help minorities win cannot be dismantled in order to benefit a particular political party. For the most part, it is the southern states of the old Confederacy that were subject to this provision. The preclearance requirement was but one example of the conflict between Texas and the federal government on a number of issues (see Chapter 3).[17]

In the 2011 redistricting round, several lawsuits were filed by different parties challenging the districts created by the Texas legislature, and the federal court stepped in. Ultimately, the legislature and the court created one new congressional district with a majority Latino population that stretched from Bexar County to Travis County along Interstate 35. The three other new districts were designed to elect Republicans, a goal accomplished by splitting Travis County, centered on Austin, into five congressional districts in order to dilute the Democratic vote. Since the majority of Travis County

Democrats are White, there are no protections under the law against diluting their vote. The U.S. representative for Austin, White Democrat Lloyd Doggett, was forced to run in the new Latino majority district, since the other four districts were majority Republican (Doggett still won re-election).

One possible way to reform redistricting would be to take the process away from politicians who have a vested interest in protecting their seats and their parties. Critics often say that redistricting by legislatures is the only time when politicians choose their voters and not the other way around. Some states, such as Arizona, have taken the responsibility away from the legislature by creating an independent redistricting commission. Such a commission, supporters argue, would create fairer districts in Texas as well. According to a 2018 *Texas Tribune* poll, 44 percent of respondents voiced support in principle for such a system, while 25 percent were opposed, and 31 percent were unsure.[18] Changing the system of redistricting would be politically challenging, however, because legislators of both parties greatly benefit from their ability to influence how district lines are drawn.

In the court case *Evenwel v. Abbott* (2015), plaintiffs sued the state of Texas claiming that using the total number of residents in each district as the basis for creating state legislative districts violated the principle of one person, one vote and the equal protection clause of the Fourteenth Amendment. Instead, they argued, the state should use registered or eligible voters to draw districts, because voters living in districts with high numbers of undocumented immigrants, children, or prisoners had their votes unconstitutionally diluted compared with those of voters in other districts. The Supreme Court ruled, however, that states were justified in using total population in drawing legislative districts.

How districts are drawn can also have an important effect on political outcomes at the local level. For example, in many cities, council members are elected at large rather than from separate geographical districts. How does this create a barrier to voting? Consider a city that has 10 city council seats and is 20 percent African American, 25 percent Latino, and 55 percent White. In at-large races, the White majority could theoretically capture all of the seats for White candidates. If the city had a single-member district system, however, because of segregated housing patterns at least 4 of the seats could well be won by minorities. Austin changed its at-large system of electing city council members in 2014, and the city saw an increase in the number of minority council members.

Turnout: Who Votes?

In the presidential election of 2020, according to the U.S. Elections Project, 66 percent of U.S. voting-eligible citizens voted.[19] An even fewer 61 percent of voting-eligible Texans exercised their right to vote. In fact, Texas historically ranked last in the nation in voter participation, but has inched up in the past several years. Figure 5.2 provides data on the abysmal turnout of registered voters in the various types of recent Texas elections. Considering the ease of registration and the ability to vote early, voter participation should be higher. Why do so few Texans vote? Several factors may contribute to the state's low participation rates:

1. low levels of educational attainment
2. low per capita income
3. high rate of poverty

4. location in the South
5. young population
6. lack of party competition
7. lack of media attention to substantive political issues
8. large numbers of undocumented residents and persons convicted of felonies

Education and income appear to be the two most important factors in determining whether someone votes, and the combination of the two is often referred to as *socioeconomic status* (SES). In Texas low levels of education and high levels of poverty are the strongest predictors of low voter participation. In addition, the average age of Texans is less than the national average, and since young people are less likely to vote, this factor may also contribute to Texas's low turnout rate. Although college students and other young adults were mobilized by President Obama's campaign in 2008, in general voter turnout among this demographic is low.

Texas was part of the Confederacy, and its level of participation is consistent with lower levels of voting in the South than in other parts of the United States. That said, Texas differs from most other southern states because of its large Latino population, many of whom are not registered to vote or are not citizens. Although registration rates and voting rates among Latinos will likely increase in coming years, for now they remain lower than those for Whites or African Americans.

There are other possible explanations for low voter participation in Texas. In keeping with the state's tradition of decentralized government, there are so many elections in Texas and so many candidates for office that voters simply feel overloaded. Note that as shown in Figure 5.2 (and discussed in Chapter 2), voter participation was much higher in the general election than in the special constitutional election. If there were fewer elections, the ballot might be longer, but voter turnout would likely be higher because more voters would be attracted to at least some races or issues on the ballot. Additionally, holding elections for state offices in nonpresidential election years decreases voter turnout because participation tends to be highest for presidential elections. A third problem

FIGURE 5.2

Turnout by Registered Voters in Texas Elections

SOURCE: Texas Secretary of State Elections Division.

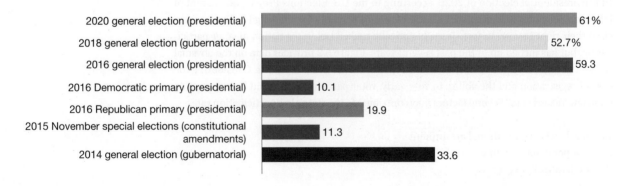

is that most elections in Texas involve very low-visibility offices. Few voters know much about these positions or the candidates for them, and this lack of knowledge naturally discourages voting. Efforts have been made in a number of states, most notably Washington, to increase voter knowledge by having the state provide biographical information about candidates to voters, but Texas makes little effort of this kind. Independent groups such as the League of Women Voters often provide voter guides, but only readers of newspapers or those who actively seek out such guides benefit from this information. Finally, some suggest that the voter identification law has reduced voter turnout even more.

Racial and Ethnic Variations in Voting and Participation While non-Hispanic Whites make up less than half the population of Texas, this does not mean that the majority of the state's voters are minorities. For example, in the November 2018 elections, Latinos composed only about 26 percent of the Texas electorate.[20]

WHAT DO TEXANS THINK?

Racial Bias in Voter ID Laws

After the passage of the state's voter identification law, some Texans argued that the election system was attempting to make it more difficult for racial and ethnic minorities to access the ballot box, the argument being that racial and ethnic minorities are less likely to have driver's licenses. Where do you stand relative to your fellow Texans?

"Based on what you know, do you think Texas's election system discriminates against racial and ethnic minorities?"

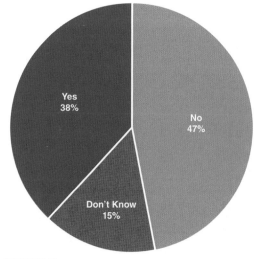

Yes
38%

No
47%

Don't Know
15%

SOURCE: *Texas Tribune*, October 2017.

As a result of a variety of factors, including the large undocumented population and the lower rate of voter turnout by Latino citizens, non-Hispanic Whites wield disproportionate influence in the state electorate. Because most Whites tend to vote for Republicans, the balance of power in most state elections currently tilts toward Republicans.

While the days of poll taxes are over, in contemporary Texas there are still barriers to voting such as reducing the number of polling places in certain areas, giving misleading information to voters, and intimidating voters by threatening employment or other economic retaliation. While such practices are becoming less frequent, there are still reports of them in every contested election.

The Importance of the Republican Primary

In this era of Republican dominance in the state, the Republican primary has become the key to determining the winner of a statewide election. As shown in Table 5.1, only 12.44 percent of registered voters and only 9.34 percent of the voting-age population in Texas voted in the Republican primary in 2020, but since the 1990s the winner of that

TABLE 5.1

Percentage of Registered Voters and Voting-Age Population Voting in the Republican Primaries

YEAR	REGISTERED VOTERS	PERCENTAGE OF REGISTERED VOTERS VOTING IN REPUBLICAN PRIMARIES	PERCENTAGE OF VOTING-AGE POPULATION VOTING IN REPUBLICAN PRIMARIES
2020	16,211,198	12.44%	9.34%
2018	15,249,541	10.16	7.79
2016	14,238,436	19.89	14.80
2014	13,601,324	9.98	7.18
2012	13,065,425	11.09	7.93
2010	13,023,358	11.40	8.00
2008	12,752,417	10.68	7.68
2006	12,722,671	5.15	3.94
2004	12,264,663	5.60	4.27
2002	12,218,164	5.09	4.01
2000	11,612,761	9.70	7.78

primary has gone on to win every statewide election. Of course, many of the Republican primaries for statewide offices are contested, and to be successful in winning office all that is needed is a majority of the vote in the primary.

Campaigns

Present the main features of election campaigns in Texas

The goal of the campaign is to attain sufficient support to win the primary election in March and then the general election in November. Some campaigns last a year or more; however, the more accepted practice is to limit the campaign to a few months before the election. For high-profile races such as governor, candidates often announce their intentions early in order to raise money. Candidates with more money are often taken more seriously by other campaign donors, as well as by the media, interest groups, and the national parties.

Candidates: Who Runs?

Candidates from all walks of life run for office in Texas. Business people, lawyers, stay-at-home mothers, teachers, retirees, and more have all run for office in Texas. The greater the prestige of the office, the more political experience candidates tend to have. Career paths for Texan officeholders usually begin with a run for a local office such as school board or city council. Many then decide to run for state representative, then state senator. Candidates for U.S. Congress usually have had prior political experience. For example, U.S. representative Randy Weber (R-Friendswood) previously served as a state representative.

Incumbents have the advantage in most races. Since there are no term limits in the Texas legislature, some members have served for many years. For example, Representative Tom Craddick (R-Midland) has served in the legislature for nearly 50 years. Challengers to incumbents rarely win, and many wait until a retirement to run for a seat.

Running as an Independent

It is unusual for a candidate to run for office in Texas as an independent. One reason is that there are substantial requirements for getting one's name on the ballot. Additionally, an independent candidate lacks the political support of party organizations and the advantage of having a party label on the ballot. Despite these obstacles, in 2006 two independent candidates ran for governor: musician and writer Kinky Friedman and former Austin mayor Carole Keeton Strayhorn, the state comptroller, who had been elected to that office as a Republican.

Both candidates were obviously hoping that an independent candidacy would attract the votes of Democrats who believed that a Democratic candidate for governor could not win in Texas. They also were hoping to get substantial votes from Republicans disaffected with the policies and performance of the Republican governor, Rick Perry. Strayhorn, in particular, seemed to have strong appeal to Democrats who usually contributed large sums to Democratic nominees. One study of her campaign contributions from July through December of 2005, for example, found that 52 percent of them were from people who had given exclusively or almost exclusively to Democrats over the previous five years.[21]

Each state decides its own requirements for getting on the ballot, and the process for independents to do so in Texas is relatively difficult. Friedman and Strayhorn, for example, had to meet the following requirements:

1. The candidates must obtain signatures on a petition from registered voters. The signatures must equal 1 percent of the total votes in the last governor's race. This meant that Friedman and Strayhorn each had to obtain 45,540 signatures.
2. The signatures must come from registered voters who did not participate in any political party primary election.
3. Signature collection cannot begin until the day after the last primary election. In 2018 this was June 21.
4. Voters may sign only one candidate's petition. If they sign both, only the first signature provided will count.[22]

The Democratic and Republican parties don't agree on much, but they do agree on keeping third-party competitors out. Making it difficult for independents to get their names on the ballot helps ensure that the two major parties will continue to dominate politics in the state well into the future. Elections may be open in Texas, but they work through the dominant political parties, helping to solidify their control over the political process and the major political offices in the state. The electoral performances of Friedman and Strayhorn also point to the difficulties of independent candidacy in that both of these candidates received only a small fraction of the overall vote.

Money

Campaigns involve attempts to reach the voters through print and electronic media, the mail, door-to-door campaigning, speeches to large and small groups, coffee hours, and telephone solicitation. Costs are enormous. In the 2018 gubernatorial race, Greg Abbott spent $46 million. There is no question, then, that money is important for candidate success in Texas. Candidates must continually raise funds by hosting events with donors, making phone calls to potential donors, and setting up websites that make it easy for ordinary citizens to contribute (see Table 5.2).

Candidates who run in Texas for federal office such as the U.S. Congress are subject to federal campaign finance laws, which are stricter than state laws and impose limits for campaign contributions. (Recently, though, the federal laws have been greatly weakened by U.S. Supreme Court decisions that have held that parts of those laws unconstitutionally restricted free speech.) Candidates for state offices are subject to state laws enacted in 1991 when the Texas Ethics Commission (TEC) was established. State candidates and lobbyists must file quarterly reports with the TEC detailing expenditures and contri-

TABLE 5.2

Money Raised by All Candidates in Texas, 2018

OFFICE	DEMOCRATIC ($)	REPUBLICAN ($)	THIRD-PARTY ($)
Governor	$2,067,292	$72,417,015	$37,299
Judicial	3,764,382	6,019,267	0
Other statewide	3,451,333	24,848,602	3,295
State House	13,400,562	36,567,487	103,612
State Senate	8,028,690	31,368,094	1,600

SOURCE: Calculated from Institute on Money in State Politics.

butions, but with the exception of judicial campaigns there are no limits to campaign contributions for state races. The state imposes a moratorium on contributions to state legislators just prior to the beginning of a legislative session.

Payments for media ads account for the greatest expense in most campaigns. In metropolitan areas, television, radio, and print advertising are very costly. Full-page ads in metropolitan newspapers can cost as much as $40,000. Candidates for metropolitan districts in the Texas House of Representatives and Texas Senate need to reach only a small portion of the area's population, but they are forced to purchase ads in media that go to hundreds of thousands of people not in their districts. In rural areas, any individual ad is relatively inexpensive. However, candidates must advertise in dozens of small newspapers and radio stations, and the costs add up.

Partisan affiliation matters a great deal when it comes to raising money. In the 2018 cycle, for all statewide offices, Republican campaign contributions have overwhelmed Democratic campaign contributions. According to an analysis by the *Texas Tribune*, in 2018 total contributions in state races were far greater for Republicans than for Democrats (see Table 5.3). The report estimates that 86 percent of the millions in contributions went to Republican candidates for state offices.[23] Because Republicans have been more likely to win statewide races, donors are more likely to donate to candidates who will hold positions of power.

Interest Groups

Interest groups (see Chapter 6) have recently become much more of a factor in state elections in Texas. For example, Empower Texans, a group backed by Michael Quinn Sullivan, spent millions of dollars in the 2016 Republican state legislative primaries to try to defeat backers of former speaker Joe Straus, whom they considered insufficiently conservative. While they were unable to unseat Straus himself in 2016, they were able to help oust some of his lieutenants, including state representative Debbie Riddle

TABLE 5.3

Campaign Contributions in Statewide Executive Offices: Texas General Elections, 2018

OFFICE	CANDIDATE	DOLLARS CONTRIBUTED	PERCENTAGE OF VOTE
Governor	Greg Abbott (R)	$72,412,015	55.8%
	Lupe Valdez (D)	1,253,688	42.5
Lieutenant governor	Dan Patrick (R)	25,749,140	51.3
	Mike Collier (D)	867,309	46.5
Agriculture commissioner	Sid Miller (R)	1,797,867	51.3
	Kim Olson (D)	386,223	46.4
Attorney general	Ken Paxton (R)	7,864,608	50.6
	Justin Nelson (D)	2,669,475	47.0
Comptroller	Glenn Hegar (R)	3,746,306	53.2
	Joi Chevalier (D)	59,282	43.4
Land commissioner	George P. Bush (R)	3,780,944	53.7
	Miguel Suazo (D)	93,955	43.1
Railroad commissioner	Christi Craddick (R)	5,471,872	53.2
	Roman McAllen (D)	22,298	43.9

SOURCE: Texas Ethics Commission Filings.

(R-Tomball). Straus announced his retirement from the legislature in 2017, thus paving the way for a conservative replacement in his legislative seat as well as the speakership.

Other interest groups have played important roles in shaping public policy in the state. For example, the Texas Association of Business and the Texas Public Policy Foundation have been very influential in advancing conservative legislation. These groups have helped sway Governor Abbott and other Republican officials to support laws that expand school vouchers, lower taxes, and reduce regulation in the state's economy. Because state legislators and other statewide officials are subject to only limited campaign regulations, the influence of interest groups in Texas politics will no doubt continue to grow.

Parties

In some places in the United States, political parties have a major role in the running of campaigns. That is not the case in Texas, where the candidates have the major responsibility for planning strategy, running their campaigns, and raising money. At times, party leaders will try to recruit individuals to run for office, especially if no candidates volunteer to seek an office or if the announced candidates appear to be weak ones. For the

Who Votes in Texas Statewide Elections?

Voter Turnout By Race, 2018

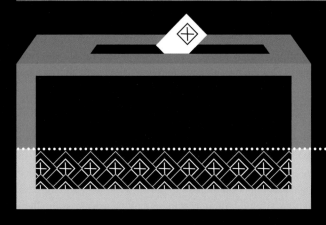

Texas Totals

Citizen Voting-Age Population
16,844,000

Total Voter Turnout*
42.2%

Texas is now a majority-minority state. This means that the nonwhite population exceeds the White population. However, this does not mean that the majority of the state's voters are nonwhite. It is still the case that the Latino population is underrepresented compared with their population on the state's voter rolls.

White Voter Turnout

● 10% voter turnout

Citizen Voting-Age Population
13,693,000

56.8%

Latino Voter Turnout

Citizen Voting-Age Population
4,878,000

25.0%

African American Voter Turnout

Citizen Voting-Age Population
2,198,000

45.8%

Asian Voter Turnout

Citizen Voting-Age Population
565,000

26.3%

* Percent of citizen voting-age population who voted in 2018.

SOURCE: Noncitizen data from U.S. Census Bureau, Current Population Survey.

QUANTITATIVE REASONING

- Some argue that people of color do not turn out to vote in Texas elections. Based on the data provided, is this true? How might you respond to such a statement?

- Based on the voter turnout data in the graph, what can you conclude about racial and ethnic differences in voter turnout?

most part, the benefit of the party to a candidate in Texas is that it provides the label under which the candidate runs. That "Democratic" or "Republican" label is important because many voters use the party label in casting their votes, especially for low-visibility races. The party also contains numerous activists whom the candidate can tap for campaign tasks such as manning phone banks, preparing mailings, and posting campaign ads. Additionally, the party does provide some direct support for the candidate, most commonly through campaigns to get out the vote for the party's candidates. Campaigning in Texas, however, is generally left up to the candidate, and in that effort the parties take a secondary role.

Incumbents hold a distinct advantage in election campaigns, insofar as officeholders have many ways to achieve name visibility. They can mail out news releases, send newsletters to their constituents, appear on television and radio talk shows, and give speeches to civic clubs. Newspaper coverage and local television news coverage of the politician also increase name recognition. Challengers have a more difficult time getting this crucial name visibility, although newer media outlets such as Facebook and Twitter can help both incumbents and challengers gain name recognition, especially among young people, often in less expensive ways.

The case of William R. Clements illustrates the importance of name recognition. In 1978, Clements was a political unknown until he spent thousands of dollars of his own fortune to publicize his name. He leased hundreds of billboards throughout the state. Each had a blue background with white letters proclaiming "CLEMENTS." In the print media, his early ads bore the simple message, "ELECT CLEMENTS." The unprecedented scale of this advertising effort made Clements's name better known among Texas voters, and this recognition, in turn, stimulated interest in his campaign's message. Clements won the race for governor, becoming the first Republican to hold that office in Texas since the end of Reconstruction.

Strategy

As important as name recognition is, even more important is that a campaign be well designed and well executed. A slipup in a well-funded campaign can generate controversy, as Greg Abbott discovered in his first campaign for governor. While Abbott has made efforts to appeal to the Latino vote, his campaign received criticism when in February 2014 he referred to law enforcement tactics in the border region as resembling "third world country practices that erode the social fabric of our communities." A journalist for the *Monitor*, a newspaper in the Rio Grande Valley, called on Abbott to apologize for his comments, but he refused, saying they were directed not at Latinos but rather at the lack of border security in south Texas. Abbott sought to repair his relationship with Latino voters by emphasizing his Latina wife as the imminent first Latina first lady of Texas. While this slipup did not cost him the election (he received 44 percent of the Latino vote—a healthy number for a Republican candidate), it still raised doubts in the minds of many Texan Latinos about the state's Republican Party and its relationship with the growing Latino vote.[24]

Candidates for statewide office in Texas routinely spend hundreds of thousands, if not millions, of dollars on their campaigns. Though much money goes to television advertising, candidates also spend time meeting voters one-on-one, as Republican attorney general candidate Ken Paxton does here at Joe Allen's Pit Bar-B-Que in Abilene.

How Did Texans Vote in 2020?

Race	Pop.%	🐴 = Biden	🐘 = Trump		

National

Race	Pop.%		Biden	Trump
White	67%		41%	58%
Black	13%		87%	12%
Latino	13%		65%	32%
Asian	4%		61%	34%
Other	4%		55%	41%

Texas

Race	Pop.%		Biden	Trump
White	60%		33%	66%
Black	12%		90%	9%
Latino	23%		58%	41%
Asian	3%		63%	30%
Other	2%		42%	56%

California

Race	Pop.%		Biden	Trump
White	47%		53%	45%
Black	9%		83%	14%
Latino	34%		77%	21%
Asian	5%		76%	23%
Other	5%		59%	37%

As expected, President Trump carried Texas on Election Day and won the state's 38 electoral votes. However, Joe Biden outperformed Hillary Clinton, as the margin of victory was much closer than in 2016. Racial divisions persisted between the parties, with Biden winning large majorities of African American, Latino, and Asian voters.

SOURCE: 2020 CNN exit poll data.

CRITICAL THINKING

- Looking at the data, how does the national vote compare to California and Texas?

- Why do you think Latinos were more supportive of Trump in Texas than they were nationally?

Public Opinion and Campaigns

Political candidates in Texas campaigns hire pollsters to conduct surveys of their constituents. They do this in order to get a sense of what their constituents think on important issues. By doing this, they can better serve them—they want to make sure they are voting in line with what their constituents want so that voters will choose to support them in future elections. Opponents to elected officials may hire pollsters (if they have adequate funds) to craft messages they think might sway voters to support them. Once polls are conducted, politicians target voters based on information such as where they live, their age, or other factors and contact them with specific messages they think will inspire them to vote. In close elections, tailoring a message to a significant voter group—suburban women with children, college-educated men, senior citizens, etc.—might make a difference.

Media

Campaigns in Texas are covered mostly by local and statewide media. One of the more thorough statewide media outlets covering Texas politics is the *Texas Tribune*, founded in 2009. Based in Austin, the *Tribune* is a one-stop shop for all aspects of Texas politics, including statistical data, campaign news, updates on legislation, and coverage of statewide issues.

Of course, the major city newspapers, including the *Houston Chronicle*, the *Dallas Morning News*, the *Fort Worth Star-Telegram*, the *San Antonio Express-News*, and the *Austin American Statesman*, cover state politics and campaigns extensively, especially local races in their respective readership areas (see Table 5.4). More important, they endorse candidates in primaries and general elections. These endorsements often carry important weight, especially in down-ballot races for local offices such as school board or city council, which do not attract significant attention from voters.

Television stations also play an important role in covering races by hosting programs and events aimed at informing the public about them. In Houston, Channel 2 KPRC hosts a weekly show called *Houston Newsmakers*. Hosted by Khambrel Marshall, this show often has political guests, hosts candidate debates, and informs the public on local political issues. Channel 13 KTRK in Houston hosts a public affairs show called *Viva Houston*, aimed at informing Latino viewers about local political issues. Local PBS stations in Houston, Dallas, and Austin also host programs with guests to help inform the public about local campaigns and elections.

Candidates promote their campaigns by running newspaper and television ads, meeting with newspaper editorial boards for endorsements, appearing on television shows, and any other means possible. Running a campaign can be expensive, and any opportunity for free airtime to increase name recognition can go a long way, especially in down-ballot races. In 2014 the Center for Public Integrity published a report indicating that nearly $39 million was spent by candidates and other organizations on political ads in Texas that year, a total second only to Pennsylvania.

TABLE 5.4

Texas's Top Five Daily Newspapers, 2019

Houston Chronicle
Dallas Morning News
Fort Worth Star-Telegram
San Antonio Express-News
Austin American Statesman

SOURCE: FullIntel, "The Top 10 Texas Daily Newspapers by Circulation," October 2019, www.fullintel.com (accessed 10/23/20).

Social Media Many, if not most, Texas candidates for all offices use Facebook and Twitter to push campaign messages, attack or defend themselves from opponents, and stay in touch with supporters and donors. While historically television was a very valuable tool for a Texas political candidate, modern-day candidates have increasingly relied on social media to get their messages out. Former Texas Supreme Court justice Don Willett (@JusticeWillett) was particularly active on Twitter, with over 110,000 followers. His tweets covered nearly every topic imaginable, with a particular emphasis on Texas themes. For example, one of his tweets in 2016 pictured freshly baked cornbread shaped like the state of Texas with the caption "when you are tired of cornbread shaped like Colorado or Wyoming."[25] His tweets captured the attention of another prolific tweeter, President Trump, who nominated him for the Fifth Circuit Court of Appeals in 2017.

Governor Abbott and other statewide leaders have relied on Facebook and Twitter to spread their messages and advertise with the public. Because officeholders do not have to pay for these messages, they are able to tout their accomplishments, policy proposals, and opinions about political situations more often. At times, however, elected officials can get in trouble if they tweet something that might be offensive. For example, during the 2016 presidential election, Agriculture Commissioner Sid Miller retweeted a tweet showing a poll in Pennsylvania substituting Hillary Clinton's name for an expletive. Miller apologized, blaming hackers and then a staff member for the tweet.[26]

Important Issues in Recent Texas Campaigns

The most high-profile race in 2020 was the contest between incumbent Republican senator John Cornyn and MJ Hegar. Hegar ran a grassroots campaign emphasizing opposition to President Trump's policies and offering an unabashedly progressive vision. She attempted to build on Beto O'Rourke's galvanization of young voters and criticized the Trump administration's policies on dealing with COVID-19. Cornyn fired back at Hegar, claiming she was too liberal for Texas. At the end of the day, campaigning in this race was limited due to the coronavirus pandemic, and Hegar ultimately came up short.

Gun rights continue to be a salient issue in Texas, especially given the increase in gun sales following the coronavirus pandemic, which began in March 2020. Texas has a concealed carry law allowing licensed individuals to carry concealed firearms throughout the state, with some exceptions such as bars. As of 2016, Texas also allows permit holders open carry of personal firearms in most public places, although individual businesses can choose not to allow it. Gun safety in schools was a major issue in May 2018, when a high school student in Santa Fe, Texas, just outside Houston, opened fire and killed 10 classmates. With schools closed during the pandemic, gun rights became more of a fundamental survival issue for many Texans who feared chaos due to possible

Immigration is a major issue in Texas elections, with Democrats and Republicans promoting starkly different plans for reform. Democrats tend to favor a path to citizenship for undocumented immigrants, while many Republicans emphasize stronger border security and stricter deportation measures.

shortages of food and other household items. Although Texas has traditionally not been open to gun control, Governor Abbott created a commission to study ways to improve school safety in the aftermath of the shooting. The National Rifle Association, the nation's leading pro-gun lobbying group, gave Abbott an A+ and Hegar an F on their gun control policies.

Immigration policy also became a very salient issue in all of the statewide races in 2020. The two senatorial candidates also sought to distinguish themselves on these issues. Cornyn called for more border security and a ban on sanctuary cities. Hegar, on the other hand, tied Cornyn to Trump and criticized his immigration policies. Republican candidates for all major elective offices pledged to enact strict border security measures and spend state resources on keeping illegal immigrants out of the state. This emphasis was a marked change from the 1990s, when then-governor George W. Bush appealed to the Latino vote in the state.

Tax policy also became a state campaign issue, especially the issue of property tax reform. In 2020, many property owners began to receive their property tax bills in March based on valuations from January 1. Many homeowners protested because the pandemic, which began in March 2020, led to high levels of unemployment, in addition to the price of oil, which slumped as well. With so many homeowners unable to pay their mortgages and property tax bills, some local officials called on the state to freeze property taxes at 2019 levels.

Since Texas does not have a state income tax, property taxes are somewhat higher than in other states. The state relies on property taxes to fund public education and on sales taxes for other state spending. Sales taxes in Texas average 8.25 percent on most items, with the exception of medicine and groceries, and increasing them disproportionately affects lower-income Texans, since a higher percentage of their income is spent on purchasing goods and services.

Though the issues above seem important ones, in recent statewide elections the distinguishing feature of the campaigns was actually the lack of emphasis on state issues.

Instead, Republicans did not pivot from the positions they held in the primary, continuing to stress issues such as immigration and support for President Trump. Likewise, Democratic candidates in Texas, in attempting to attract support from the Democratic base, ran hard against President Trump and his policies. In particular, congressional Democratic candidates ran issue ads on health care, promising to protect people with preexisting conditions and increase access to affordable health care. Although all statewide Republican candidates won their races, Democrats were heartened by the fact that the margins were some of the narrowest in recent memory.

One of the more interesting developments in 2020 in Texas was the deepening divide in voting patterns between urban/suburban areas and rural counties. Although cities have traditionally been more Democratic in Texas, the 2020 election witnessed growing shifts to Democrats in suburban areas, especially in Dallas and Houston. In the 7th congressional district, in the Houston suburbs, Democrat Lizzie Fletcher, who defeated longtime incumbent Republican John Culberson in 2018, was re-elected against an African American Republican Wesley Hunt. This was an important hold for Democrats, who capitalized on dissatisfaction with President Trump, especially among highly educated suburban White voters. Likewise, in the 32nd congressional district in the wealthy north Dallas suburbs, freshman African American Democrat Colin Allred was re-elected in a district largely populated by highly educated suburban White voters. In rural areas, Republican candidates fared well, thus intensifying the division in the state between strongly rural Republican areas and strongly Democratic urban areas. Meanwhile, suburban areas slowly shifted to Democrats.

After the 2018 elections, Republicans had kept control of both chambers of the state legislature, although Democrats picked up twelve seats in the state House—the largest shift in seats since 2010—and two seats in the state Senate. These seats largely came from suburban areas in Dallas and Houston, where incumbent Republicans representing suburban districts were swept away by higher Democratic support that was due to President Trump's unpopularity in these areas. While Democrats had hoped to build on these gains from 2018, they were unable to take control of the state House or defeat any congressional Republicans from Texas.

One thing is clear after the 2020 election, however: Texas is not as solidly Republican as it once was. Republican political consultant Bill Miller noted after the election results, "It's a new day in Texas politics. The old way of doing things, just focusing on the extreme elements of the base, consider that nostalgia. That day is gone."[27] Many of the statewide races were much closer than in previous years.

Another tension that emerged in 2020 was about how to deal with mail-in ballots given the ongoing coronavirus pandemic. Some local officials wanted to expand mail-in balloting to allow all voters this option. Republican leaders argued that possible fraud could ensue if too many voters beyond the elderly and those with disabilities, for example, were given this option. As such, mail-in ballots were limited in the 2020 election. Causing quite a bit of controversy, Governor Greg Abbott decreed that voters could drop off such ballots in only one location per county. Large counties such as Harris in Houston had only one drop-off box, leading to allegations that the governor was attempting to limit voter participation.

Campaigns, Elections, and the Future of Texas

ALTHOUGH REPUBLICANS have been winning statewide elections in Texas in recent years, the growing Latino population and increased diversification of the state may eventually change this pattern. Lupe Valdez had hoped to capitalize on these changing demographics in her bid for governor in 2018 but could not overcome countervailing winds against her candidacy, including the state's entrenched conservatism and Abbott's incumbency.

Campaigns—especially statewide campaigns—are very expensive in Texas, and gubernatorial campaigns can cost $40 million or more. For the most part, the candidates themselves must raise the money necessary to win an election. One effect of the high cost is that candidates are often wealthy individuals willing to use their own money in their campaigns. Such individuals, however, do not always prevail at the ballot box. Consider former lieutenant governor David Dewhurst, who invested millions of his own money in the Republican primary for a U.S. Senate seat in 2012 but suffered a bruising loss to Ted Cruz, leaving Dewhurst vulnerable in his bid for re-election as lieutenant governor two years later. Insurgent senator Dan Patrick challenged Dewhurst from the right in the primary and forced him into a runoff, which Patrick won easily.

Although Texas once tried to restrict the right to vote, primarily through poll taxes and White primaries, in recent years it has tried to expand the franchise through the motor voter law and through early voting. Yet voter participation in Texas is the lowest in the nation. Turnout in 2014 was only 33.4 percent of eligible voters, which was less than the turnout in 2010. Turnout in the 2016 presidential election was only 51.1 percent of eligible voters, up slightly from 49.6 percent in 2012. These low figures are probably due to the demographics of Texas voters and the state's political culture, but they may also reflect the scheduling of elections in Texas, the vast number of elections, and the large number of low-visibility candidates for office. The competitive Senate race in Texas led to an increase in turnout from 2016. Nearly 53 percent of registered voters cast ballots in the 2018 election. In 2020, turnout in Texas increased to 61 percent, a marked improvement that mirrored nationwide increases.

One of the biggest factors that could affect future Texas elections is the state's changing demographics. As we have discussed elsewhere in the text, the proportion of Latino voters in Texas is growing and that of White voters is shrinking. While not as strongly Democratic as African Americans, Latinos in Texas are more likely to identify as Democrats than Republicans. If this demographic trend continues, and if more Latinos register to vote and participate in state elections, Texas may once again become a competitive two-party state.

Use 🐰 INQUIZITIVE to help you study and master this material.

Features of Elections in Texas

- **Describe the types of elections held in Texas and how they work (pp. 153–56)**

Texas allows all registered voters the choice to vote in one party primary during an election season. Should a candidate not receive a majority of votes in a primary, a runoff is held to determine who the party nominee will be. The general election ultimately decides who is elected to office.

Key Terms

primary election (p. 153)
electoral cycle (p. 153)
runoff primary (p. 154)
open primary (p. 154)
closed primary (p. 154)
general election (p. 155)
special election (p. 156)

Practice Quiz

1. In a primary election,
 a) voters choose all local officials who will hold office in the following year.
 b) voters select federal officials for office.
 c) voters select their party's candidate for a general election.
 d) voters choose third-party candidates.
 e) voters cast ballots on proposed constitutional amendments.

2. Which of the following is *not* a type of election found in Texas?
 a) general
 b) primary
 c) distinguished
 d) special
 e) runoff primary

3. Officially, Texas has
 a) a joint primary.
 b) an extended primary.
 c) an open primary.
 d) a closed primary.
 e) a Jaybird primary.

4. The first Tuesday following the first Monday in November of even-numbered years is the day for which election?
 a) primary election
 b) runoff primary
 c) runoff for the general election
 d) secondary election
 e) general election

5. When are gubernatorial elections held?
 a) during presidential election years
 b) during odd-numbered years
 c) during even-numbered years that are not presidential election years
 d) every year
 e) every six months

Participation in Texas Elections

• **Explain how the rules for voting affect turnout among different groups of Texans (pp. 156–69)**

Participation in Texas elections varies by election. Turnout is lowest in party primaries, followed by elections when a presidential candidate is not on the ballot. Latinos and those of lower socioeconomic status are also less likely to vote in state elections.

Key Terms

Nineteenth Amendment (p. 156)
suffrage (p. 156)
poll tax (p. 157)
early registration (p. 157)
White primary (p. 157)
Jaybird Party (p. 158)
Voting Rights Act of 1965 (p. 159)
motor voter law (p. 160)
early voting (p. 161)
straight-ticket voting (p. 161)
reapportionment (p. 164)
redistricting (p. 164)
preclearance (p. 164)

Practice Quiz

6. Which of the following is true?
   a) Poll taxes are legal.
   b) Women acquired the right to vote in the original 1876 Texas Constitution.
   c) The poll tax restricted the participation of poor people in the general election.
   d) You do not have to be a resident of Texas to vote in Texas.
   e) Latinos vote at higher rates than African Americans.

7. Who has benefited the most from early voting?
   a) Republicans
   b) Democrats
   c) All parties have benefited equally
   d) Independents
   e) Greens

8. The procedure by which certain states, such as Texas, are required to obtain approval every time they make changes to districts is called
   a) redistricting.
   b) reapportionment.
   c) preclearance.
   d) external validation.
   e) judicial review.

9. The two most important factors in determining whether someone will vote are
   a) income and education.
   b) education and family history of voting.
   c) income and gender.
   d) party membership and gender.
   e) ethnicity and race.

10. In which of the following elections is voter turnout the highest?
   a) presidential elections
   b) gubernatorial general elections
   c) city elections
   d) runoff elections
   e) off-year congressional elections

Campaigns

- **Present the main features of election campaigns in Texas (pp. 169–79)**

Because of Texas's size, statewide campaigns can be expensive. There are several major media markets, which makes television advertising very expensive. Grassroots efforts to mobilize voters are also costly because of the large territory. This means wealthy candidates are often on the ballot.

Practice Quiz

11. The most costly item for most political campaigns is
  a) travel.
  b) security.
  c) fund-raising.
  d) media.
  e) food.

12. Who is the first Republican to become Texas governor since Reconstruction?
  a) William Clements
  b) Rick Perry
  c) George W. Bush
  d) Ann Richards
  e) Kinky Friedman

13. Which of the following was *not* a feature of the 2020 campaigns in Texas?
  a) Voter turnout increased over 2016.
  b) Enthusiasm increased across the state, with high rates of turnout.
  c) Senator John Cornyn was re-elected by a fairly wide margin.
  d) Support for Democratic candidates increased in urban and suburban areas.
  e) Republicans lost control of the state legislature.

14. Which of the following was true of the 2020 elections in Texas?
  a) Democrats won control of the state Senate.
  b) Republicans won all statewide races.
  c) Women voted for Republicans in record numbers.
  d) Latinos in Texas cities voted for Republicans in record numbers.
  e) Voters in rural areas shifted sharply toward the Democratic Party.

Dineen Majcher (right) was frustrated with the emphasis her daughter's school placed on standardized testing. She took action by helping to create an interest group and challenging Texas's education policies.

Interest Groups and Lobbying

WHY INTEREST GROUPS MATTER Dineen Majcher had had enough. A lawyer and mother of an incoming ninth grader in a prestigious Austin high school, she couldn't believe what she was hearing. Fifteen percent of her daughter's final grade in history would come from a new mandated statewide test, one that the teacher had never seen. This struck her as unfair and unreasonable. How could students prepare for such a test? Why 15 percent of the grade?

She went first to the principal to protest, but to no avail. This was after all a mandated state test, part of a 30-year effort by education reformers to bring testing and accountability to all elementary and secondary schools across the state. So Majcher raised the ante, getting the Austin School Board to request a waiver from the State Board of Education from the "15 percent rule." The request was denied. Raising the ante again, Majcher signed up to testify at legislative committee hearings that had been called for January 2012. During the hearings Majcher met others from across Texas who also were dissatisfied with the testing movement. Together these individuals established an interest group called Texans Advocating for Meaningful Student Assessment, or TAMSA. The group became known in the legislature as "Mothers Against Drunk Testing."

The goals of TAMSA were clearly articulated on its website: "to improve public education in Texas through the use of meaningful and effective student assessments that allow for more productive classroom instruction and more efficient use of public funds." On their face, these goals might seem to be relatively uncontroversial. In fact, however, they were questioning the philosophy of reform that had dominated education policy in the state for over thirty years.

TAMSA enabled people to join together and seek policy change in a number of ways: first, by providing like-minded individuals an organizational structure for discussing problems and offering solutions; second, by providing a vehicle for working with other organizations such as the Texas Association of School Administrators, who were also concerned with testing; third, by raising money to help pay for their efforts; and fourth, by educating the public and policy makers alike about the problems of testing across the elementary and secondary curriculum. TAMSA spearheaded the drive to change public policy regarding testing in the state. What had begun as a protest about unfair testing was morphing into an interest group with a clear political objective.

Since the early 1980s, testing had been seen as one of the best ways to ensure accountability by identifying schools that worked and those that didn't. Support for reform through testing and accountability came from a variety of sources inside and outside the legislature. Leading legislators from both parties, leaders at the Texas Education Agency, and business leaders all came to believe statewide testing was a key to higher performance. As governor, George W. Bush identified testing as a central part of his plan for educational reform in Texas and placed it at the heart of his No Child Left Behind initiatives as president. Key business interests, including the Texas Association of Business, supported expanded testing, seeing the tests as a way to ratchet up the quality of poorly performing schools across the state. Not surprisingly, the businesses involved in creating the tests also came to support expanded testing. As the debates over reform were proceeding in the legislature, the Pearson publishing company had a five-year contract with the state that was estimated to be worth $462 million. Testing itself had become big business with big interests seeking protection in the legislature.

Given the interests supporting testing and decades-old accountability initiatives, few thought at the beginning of the 2013 legislative session that change was in the wind. But it was. New legislators open to new ideas about reform were chairing the educational committees in both the House and the Senate. Entrenched interests in educational reform had lost their ability to control the agenda. On a paltry budget of under $100,000, drawing upon inexpensive social media and relying on the expertise of a few key members, TAMSA played a major role in getting the legislature to rethink what educational reform meant. In response to the efforts of TAMSA and other like-minded groups and individuals, the legislature dropped the number of end-of-year course exams from 15 to 5.

The story of Dineen Majcher and TAMSA highlights how interest groups matter in Texas politics. Interest groups provide support for existing policies in many areas of public policy, as well as for legislators in their electoral campaigns, and they help to articulate ideas from which policies can be crafted. In the case of TAMSA, interest groups have also challenged policies and advocated changes. Texas politics can be understood only with a clear understanding of the role that interest groups play in elections and in the legislative process.[1]

CHAPTERGOALS

- Define interest groups, and describe the major ways they try to influence Texas government (pp. 187–201)

- Describe the role of PACs in Texas elections (pp. 201–8)

- Explain how ordinary individuals can influence Texas government (pp. 208–10)

Interest Groups in the Political Process

It is probably true that all of us have political interests, goals, or objectives that can be achieved with governmental intervention. Many of us, however, will never act to achieve those goals. A few of us may speak privately to a legislator or other official. Some of us will join with others to try to convince the government to help us achieve our interests. When we do that, we have formed an **interest group**.

In Texas, as elsewhere, interest groups assume a variety of forms. A wide range of interests that are active in national, state, and local politics organize themselves into groups, including those concerned with business and labor (such as the real estate industry and the chemical workers' union), agriculture, the professions (such as law, medicine, and accounting), government affairs (such as state employees and cities), education (such as colleges and universities), and public interest causes (such as the environment). Interest groups can be established to serve the interests of a small number of people concerned with one particular interest, such as getting a road built in a county. They can also be established to serve the interests of a group of people with broader interests, such as those interested in reforming the school system by promoting vouchers, charter schools, home schooling, or better testing. A "peak association" is an interest group organized as an umbrella organization that seeks to coordinate the activities of member groups in a number of targeted areas.

interest group an organization established to influence the government's programs and policies

Resources and Strategies of Interest Groups

Political scientists have identified various resources that interest groups are able to mobilize in politics. First, interest groups have members. Groups can become influential because of whom they represent. The Texas Medical Association and the Texas Bar Association are excellent examples of groups representing influential people across Texas. Some people and industries clearly are more important to legislators than others. But numbers matter, too. In Texas, politicians who ignore the concerns of broad-based evangelical groups in discussions of abortion do so at their own peril. There are many evangelical Christians in Texas and their votes, especially for Republicans, are very much needed.

Second, interest groups have the ability to raise money. Clearly, it is advantageous to have access to a few deep-pocketed individuals when trying to raise money in support of a particular cause. But in the age of the internet, it is also useful for there to be large numbers of members who are willing to give, if only a little.

Third, interest groups possess information about their membership and about the problems that concern their membership. In recent years, interest groups have begun to mine large databases of people who might be interested in particular policies or issues. Such information can become a valuable resource for politicians seeking to raise money or to promote a particular policy objective. Interest groups also offer advice on the best ways to address the concerns of their membership. Interest groups clearly are motivated by their self-interest, and the positions they present to legislators reflect this interest. The first drafts of bills introduced into the Texas House or Senate often come from interest groups seeking to promote their own particular perspective.

The resources available to interest groups are the foundation upon which groups develop various strategies to promote their concerns. Among the strategies that we will explore in this chapter are (1) explicit political strategies such as grassroots organizing, get-out-the-vote and electioneering campaigns, and campaign financing; (2) legislative strategies such as lobbying and testifying before legislative committees; (3) public awareness strategies such as drafting policy reports, writing editorials, and conducting educational campaigns in various public forums; and (4) the judicial strategy of supporting litigation that challenges existing policies in court. As we will see, the strategies adopted by various interest groups largely depend on the resources available to them at the time.

Interest Groups and Democracy

The rights to associate with others and to petition government lie at the heart of the rights guaranteed by the U.S. and Texas constitutions. These constitutional rights have helped to make the United States and Texas into what political scientists call a "pluralistic society" where individuals organize into groups to serve common interests and compete with one another for power and influence. Pluralism provides multiple access points for interest groups to try to influence public policy. Interest groups can lobby city councils, state legislatures, school boards, and other governmental bodies. In *Federalist 10*, an essay written in defense of the U.S. Constitution in 1787, James Madison discussed how a large republic comprising many interests competing with one another in the political arena could work to protect individuals from the abusive power of any one powerful interest. Drawing upon Madison for inspiration, later pluralist writers in the twentieth century would argue that groups could check and balance one another in the political process, much like different branches of government checked and balanced one another in constitutional government. The problem with this approach, however, is that having a common interest is one thing. Organizing that common interest into an effective group that can act to promote that interest is quite something else.

Overcoming the Free Rider Problem
In his groundbreaking book *The Logic of Collective Action*, Mancur Olson analyzed a collective action problem that lies at the heart of interest-group politics. People have an interest in organizing into an interest group that effectively represents their interests in politics. But people also have an interest in getting someone else to pay for that group's organizational costs—so that in many groups people get the benefits of the group's activities despite the fact that others do the work. This is what political scientists call the **free rider problem**. If everyone acts as a free rider, everyone will be waiting for someone else

free rider problem the incentive to benefit from others' work without making a contribution, which leads individuals in a collective action situation to refuse to work together to do the work, and an organization will never form. To use an everyday example, free riders are people who show up to potluck dinners without contributing a dish and then proceed to benefit by consuming everyone else's dishes. Ironically, the larger the common interest, the more difficult it may be to overcome the free rider problem and create effective interest groups. According to Olson's theory, for example, a small number of insurance companies are more likely to form a powerful interest group to affect health care policy than are the millions of poor people who lack quality health care. Similarly, business interests are more likely to form a common front in politics than are consumers because it is easier for the business interests to overcome the costs of collective action, that is, the costs of acting together as an organized interest group.[2]

Interest groups engage in a number of activities to overcome the free rider problem. Sometimes, they offer people particular incentives to join a group. These selective benefits often cover a wide range of activities, from a subscription to a magazine, to access to special information on the internet, to invitations to special conferences, to special discounts. For example, AAA (the American Automobile Association), which advocates for road and vehicle safety, provides members with roadside assistance and travel discounts—strong incentives to join.

Interest groups also can provide people with what political scientists call solidary benefits, such as listing individuals' names as sponsors of an organization or offering free buttons, hats, or T-shirts that show their support for its activities. Such benefits, as well as the sense of belonging, strengthen the commitment an individual has to an interest group and help overcome the free rider problem.

Whose Interests Do Groups Represent? One of the most important lessons to be drawn from the logic of collective action is that some interests do not get represented easily in the political process. Upper-class business interests are more likely to be well represented than lower-class minority interests. A second lesson is that it is very difficult, even rare, for interest groups to emerge that protect the broad interests of large numbers of people or any vaguely defined public interest. Significantly, when such groups do emerge, as with the Prohibition (anti-alcohol) movement in the nineteenth and early twentieth centuries, or civil rights organizations in the 1950s and '60s, they can come to wield considerable power. Nevertheless, in the everyday politics in Texas as elsewhere, it is more likely for narrowly targeted interests to organize effectively in defense of their interests than it is for the public as a whole to organize. Even the above-mentioned "public interest groups" are not so much advancing the public good as a whole (whatever that may be) as advocating for the views that certain individuals have about the public good—such as increased awareness of climate change, or gun safety regulations.

Olson's theory of collective action provides an explanation of why it has often been claimed that business-oriented interest groups dominate the Texas legislature. Using campaign contributions, political pressure, and sometimes corruption, "the Lobby," as pro-business groups were called, was once purported to run Texas government. Some

---

PERSONAL RESPONSIBILITY: WHAT WOULD YOU DO?

- Do you think that business interests should have such a profound effect on Texas government and politics? Why or why not?

- Why do business interests have such a strong voice in Texas government and politics? If you were advising an environmental group on opposing business interests, what tactics would you suggest it take?

of the most influential business leaders of the state belonged to the "8F Crowd." At the Lamar Hotel in Houston, 8F was the number on a suite of rooms where George R. Brown held court. Brown was a founder of Brown & Root, one of the world's largest construction firms (and until 2007 part of the even larger Halliburton Company, and now independently operating together with Wink Engineering). He met regularly in 8F and elsewhere with other fabulously wealthy Texans such as Jesse Jones of Texas Commerce Bank and Tenneco, Gus Wortham of American General Insurance, and James Elkins of the Vinson & Elkins law firm and First City National Bank. These men socialized together and worked together to promote their political interests. For 40 years they were considered the kingmakers in Texas politics who determined much of the important policy of state government.[3] Indeed, the convention center in Houston is named after George R. Brown, and Jones and Wortham have their names attached to performing arts centers in downtown Houston.

The 8F Crowd was, of course, an interest group—an elite, wealthy, powerful, pro-business interest group. Although the 8F Crowd is long gone from the Texas political scene, much of what it did is still done in Texas politics by other interest groups, though no modern-day group is ascribed the influence that the 8F Crowd allegedly had.

Texas is known as a state that has long had powerful interest groups. During the Texas Constitutional Convention of 1875, an important role was played by the Grange, a powerful farmers' organization, of which many of the constitution's framers were members. As Chapter 2 indicated, the Constitution of 1876 reflected many of the values of Grange members. It was a document for rural Texas that was pro–small farmer and opposed to a powerful state government.

With the development of a strong oil and gas industry in Texas in the first half of the twentieth century, this industry in turn began playing an important role in state politics. The interests of major oil companies such as ExxonMobil, who have their headquarters in Texas and employ millions of the state's residents, are well represented in the state legislature. While the oil and gas industry remains very important, the state's economy has also become more diversified in recent years. Interest groups representing newer industries such as telecommunications and high-tech companies in the Austin area have also begun to influence legislation. For example, when the legislature in 2017 considered legislation to repeal city ordinances making background checks on Uber and Lyft drivers more stringent, both companies spent $2.3 million on lobbyists to help influence legislation. Their efforts were successful, as the legislature passed the new law.[4]

Interest Groups and Policy Makers

Interest groups want something from policy makers: policy that is beneficial for their groups. On the other hand, policy makers also benefit in a number of ways from developing relationships with interest groups. First, they gain information, insofar as interest groups can provide substantial expertise in areas that are their special concern. Additionally, interest groups can provide campaign funds to policy makers. In a state as large as Texas, with numerous media markets and with some party competition, considerable campaign funds are necessary to run and win elections. For example, in the 2020 senatorial race between John Cornyn and MJ Hegar, according to Ballotpedia, interest groups combined spent nearly $45 million.[5] An interest group can help raise money from its membership for a candidate sympathetic to the interest group's goals.

Interest groups can also work to supply votes to the policy maker. Besides assisting in mobilizing their own members, they can supply campaign workers to distribute campaign leaflets and to operate phone banks to get out the vote. Interest groups can also publicize issues through press conferences, press releases, publications, workshops, and hearings, and even by filing lawsuits. Finally, interest groups can engage in research and public education programs. It has become increasingly common for interest groups to run advertisements in the Texas media explaining why their particular approaches to a public policy problem would be more beneficial to Texans in general.

Newer companies associated with high-tech industries, including ride-sharing app Lyft, have begun to hire lobbyists to influence legislation in Texas.

Unlike a private citizen interested in and involved in politics, larger or better-funded interest groups have the advantages of time, money, expertise, and continuity. Although concerned individuals do have an impact on public policy in Texas, organized and well-funded interest groups have an advantage in affecting the policy process. It is difficult for a concerned citizen from McAllen to spend time in Austin developing relationships with policy makers and trying to convince them to support public policies compatible with the individual's goals. On the other hand, if that individual joins with like-minded people to create an organized interest group, the group may be more likely to achieve these policy goals. It might be possible to fund an office in Austin with a staff that could monitor events in state government on a daily basis and develop relationships with key policy makers.

Additionally, although some individuals in Texas do have the money to provide substantial campaign support to policy makers, even they can get more "bang for the buck" if they join with others in **bundling** their funds into a larger contribution from a group. The creation of an organized interest group also allows for the development of a staff, who can gain in-depth knowledge of an area of policy far greater than could be gained by most individuals working alone. Finally, an individual may be intensely concerned with an issue in one legislative session but find it difficult to sustain that interest over a period of many more sessions. The larger, better-funded, more successful organized interest groups have continuity. They are in Austin developing relationships with policy makers and presenting the views of the organization day in and day out, year in and year out. The result is that legislators and other policy makers can develop long-standing relationships with the interest groups and their representatives in Austin.

bundling the interest-group practice of combining campaign contributions from several sources into one larger contribution from the group, so as to increase the group's impact on the candidate

Consider the role of Raise Your Hand Texas, founded by Charles Butt of the H-E-B grocery store chain, located throughout Texas and parts of Northern Mexico. Raise Your Hand Texas is an interest group aimed at stopping school vouchers in Texas and promoting public education. In the 2013 legislative session, legislators were particularly influenced by the group. When Representative Ken King (R-Canadian) introduced a bill regarding education on the House floor, Representative Abel Herrero (D–Corpus Christi) asked his colleagues in the House whether Raise Your Hand Texas had taken a position on his bill.[6] At that point, one of them showed Herrero a text message showing that the group had supported the bill during the committee stage of the process. Herrero subsequently supported Raise Your Hand's position. This is but one example of how an interest group can have important influence over legislators.[7]

Types of Interest Groups and Lobbyists

lobbyist an individual employed by an interest group who tries to influence governmental decisions on behalf of that group

Interest groups strive to influence public opinion, make their views known to policy makers, and elect and support policy makers friendly to their points of view. To accomplish these goals, interest groups usually maintain **lobbyists** in Austin who try to gain access to policy makers and communicate their objectives to them.

There are several types of lobbyists. Some interest groups have full-time staffs in Austin whose members work as lobbyists. One form of interest group is, of course, a corporation, and companies often have government relations departments that lobby for the companies' interests; others hire law firms to do so. Lobbyists may be employed by an interest group to deal with one issue, or on a regular basis to deal with a range of issues. Some lobbyists represent only one client; others have large numbers of clients. Often industries in a particular field have broad interests that need representation. For example, an insurance company may have one specific interest it wishes to have represented. However, the insurance industry as a whole also has a wide range of issues that need representation, and thus it will form an industrywide interest group.

Interest groups may also represent professional groups. One of the most influential professional groups in Austin is the Texas Medical Association, which represents the interests of doctors. Other professional groups represent accountants, chiropractors, opticians, dentists, lawyers, and teachers.

That teachers are an important interest group suggests still another type of interest group—public-employee interest groups. Public school teachers may be the largest and most effective of these groups, but firefighters, police officers, and even justices of the peace and constables all are represented in Austin.

Some interest groups are formed with a single issue in mind, as the introduction to this chapter illustrates. For example, a group may be concerned about the regulation of abortion or school vouchers or tort reform or the environment. Other interest groups are concerned with multiple issues that affect their members. Public school teachers, for example, are concerned about job security, professional qualifications, health insurance, pensions, salaries, and other matters that affect the lives of teachers.

Civil rights groups such as the National Association for the Advancement of Colored People, the League of United Latin American Citizens, and the Mexican American Legal Defense and Education Fund are concerned about civil rights issues affecting the lives primarily of African Americans and Latinos. Not only do these groups often try to influence public opinion and the legislature but they have had notable success in representing their members' interests through litigation, especially in the federal courts. In the wake of George Floyd's death in May 2020, the Black Lives Matter movement gained considerable momentum nationwide through protests and influence in corporate America.

Other public interest groups promote consumer, environmental, and general public issues. Groups such as the Sierra Club focus on environmental interests, whereas Public Citizen and Common Cause work more broadly to promote more open government. These groups rarely have much funding, but they often can provide policy makers with information and expertise. In addition, they can mobilize their membership to support or oppose bills, and they can publicize matters that are important to their goals.

In recent years, the American Legislative Exchange Council (ALEC), a conservative policy group, has had a significant influence in Texas politics. ALEC provides funding and legislative assistance to conservative state legislators across the country. ALEC assists legislators by writing bills and pushing for their enactment all across the country.

This organization has been accused by some liberal groups in Texas of having excessive influence. For example, Progress Texas compared the language in ALEC's documents proposing "model bills" with actual legislation before the Texas legislature and found in many cases word-for-word copies, indicating the extent of the organization's influence.[8]

Getting Access to Policy Makers

In order to communicate the goals of their interest groups to policy makers, lobbyists must first gain access to those policy makers. Such access, of course, imposes on the time of legislators, so lobbyists often spend significant sums entertaining them. That entertainment is one of the most criticized aspects of lobbying. But from the lobbyists' perspective, entertainment is an important tool for reaching policy makers and putting them in a congenial frame of mind. Entertainment by lobbyists can involve expensive dinners, golf, and other items and activities. For example, lobbyists for Texas Utilities (TXU) bought a $300 saddle for one state representative and a $200 bench for another, and treated a state senator to a trip to the Masters golf tournament, where they picked up the dinner tab as well. One House member received a gun as a gift, another received a jacket, and several got "deer-processing" costs paid for by TXU.[9] When former representative Lon Burnam (D–Fort Worth) proposed legislation to regulate consumer versions of "stun guns," the lobbyist for TASER International as a joke gave Burnam a gift of a pink "stun gun" valued at more than $150.[10] In 2018, Senator Ted Cruz attended three Houston Rockets basketball games using tickets valued at $12,000 gifted to him by Robert Marling, the CEO of Woodforest National Bank. While these tickets did not violate Senate rules, they nevertheless drew media scrutiny.[11]

In the 2017 legislative session, lobbyists representing local governments in Texas spent more than $41 million lobbying the legislature, which amounted to 11 percent of the total spent on lobbying that year.[12] Texas lawmakers receive only $600 per month plus $190 a day when on legislative business, but they are permitted to use campaign contributions for expenses associated with holding office. This policy allows interest groups to fund lavish benefits for them. For example, Senator John Whitmire (D-Houston) used his contributions to fund a car lease for a BMW totaling over $100,000 over ten years. In addition, he has spent nearly $300,000 in sports tickets for his hometown

Senator John Whitmire (D-Houston) is well known for spending campaign contributions from interest groups on expenses that are not strictly campaign related. Republican senator Ted Cruz was criticized for accepting tickets to three Houston Rockets games in 2018 from a bank CEO, though the gift wasn't prohibited by Senate rules.

Andrea McWilliams is one of Texas's highest-paid and most successful lobbyists.

Houston Astros, Rockets, and Texans and classified the expenditures as "constituent entertainment."[13]

The Texas Ethics Commission keeps a list of registered lobbyists as well as of their clients. In 2018 there were 1,927 registered lobbyists in Texas.[14] However, because of the loose nature of Texas reporting laws, it is unclear what these lobbyists were paid. The Texas Ethics Commission also collects information on how much lobbying firms spend to influence Texas lawmakers. In 2019, this sum reached an astonishing $5,125,603.97, and this is just the amount that was reported.[15] Despite a new law requiring public disclosure of lobbying expenditures, most local governments have not disclosed publicly how much money they spent lobbying the legislature in the 2019 session.

Sometimes lobbyists have long-standing personal ties to policy makers, and those bonds can be invaluable to the lobbyists' clients. When lobbyist Andrea McWilliams celebrated her 40th birthday in California's wine country, six Texas lawmakers traveled to California for the party, including the chair of the House Appropriations Committee and the chair of the Senate Public Education Committee. In McWilliams's case, her personal ties to these lawmakers were probably strengthened by the fact that she and her clients had contributed more than $206,000 to their campaigns over the previous several years.[16] In the 2019 legislative session, McWilliams was one of the highest-paid lobbyists, with the largest number of clients and the largest revenue—$3.8 million.[17] *Texas Monthly* listed her among the most powerful Texans, and a friend described her as a "consigliere to the powerful and political."[18]

Access to policy makers may also be gained by building support for an issue among their constituents. For example, interest groups might contact constituents to encourage them to write or call legislators about a bill and offer their opinions. Essentially, the interest group tries to mobilize interested voters to become involved in the political process on behalf of the group's goals.

Registered Lobbyists: How Does Texas Compare?

While we often associate lobbyists with Washington, DC, the reality is that lobbyists are active at all levels of policy making. Some states, such as Texas, are larger and more populated, so it stands to reason that more lobbyists are active in those states and have a higher degree of impact on businesses and labor. The chart below compares Texas with five other states in terms of the number of registered lobbyists per 100,000 people who are actively persuading government officials.

Number of Lobbyists in Selected States

● Registered lobbyists   ● Lobbyists per 100,000 people

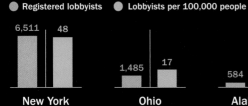

New York	**Ohio**	**Alabama**	**Florida**	**California**	**Texas**
6,511 / 48	1,485 / 17	584 / 16	2,124 / 14	2,179 / 8	1,540 / 8
13,620,990	8,832,187	3,666,511	15,333,067	18,377,841	25,782,389
Voting eligible pop.	Voting eligible pop.	Voting eligible pop.	Voting eligible pop.	Voting eligible pop.	Voting eligible pop.

Lobbyists per Capita, Nationwide

Lobbyists per 100,000 people   ● < 15   ● 15–24.9   ● 25–34.9   ● 35–44.9   ● > 45

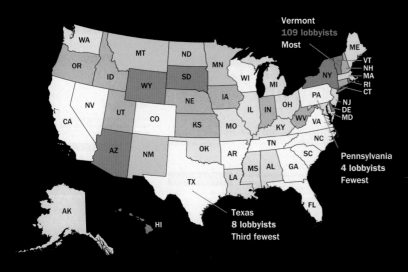

Vermont
109 lobbyists
Most

Pennsylvania
4 lobbyists
Fewest

Texas
8 lobbyists
Third fewest

NOTE: Data for registered lobbyists in Nevada are from 2016.

SOURCES: Population data from www.electproject.org/2018g; lobbyist data from www.followthemoney.org (accessed 10/20/20).

CRITICAL THINKING

- How does Texas compare with other states regarding the total number of lobbyists and the number of lobbyists per capita? Do you think Texas has too many, too few, or just the right number of lobbyists?

- Looking at the map, what can you conclude about the most populated states and the number of lobbyists per capita? Which states go against the norm? Why might this be?

Lobbying and Government's "Revolving Door" One important way of gaining access to those in government is to employ former officials as lobbyists. A lobbyist who is a former legislator often has friends in the legislature and can use that friendship to gain access. Additionally, a former legislator often is in an exceptionally good position to understand the personal relationships and informal power centers that must be involved in accomplishing a legislative objective. As a result, some of the best-paid lobbyists in Austin are former Texas state officials, who often are also former legislators.

In recent years, it has not been uncommon for former legislators to register as lobbyists. What they have in common is, as a writer for the *Texas Tribune* put it, knowledge of "how to pass bills, to kill them, whom to talk to, which clerks are friendly, whose birthdays are coming up—all inside stuff that makes the government machine whir."[19] Other especially valuable lobbyists have been former committee clerks for major committees and chiefs of staff of members who were on major committees.[20] In the 2017 legislative session, lobbyists included five recently retired lawmakers with a total of 31 lobbying contracts, allowing them to generate a total of $1.7 million in fees.[21] In 2013 former senator Tommy Williams of the Woodlands, who was chairman of the Senate Budget Committee, took a $300,000 per year job with the Texas A&M system after he left office. While he is not officially a "lobbyist," one of his duties is to advocate for Texas A&M in Austin. One gets a sense of the value of these ex-legislators-turned-lobbyists from the explanation Representative Jim Pitts gave for sponsoring an amendment pushed by an AT&T lobbyist and former legislator, Pat Heggerty. The amendment would have forced the state to pay for rerouting phone lines for road projects, and Pitts said, "I was just trying to help Pat out."[22] (The amendment failed to pass the House.) In 2019, the Texas Senate passed a bill requiring legislators to wait two years before retiring to become a paid lobbyist. The bill never made it to the governor's desk.

It is not only former legislators who can move on to successful lobbying careers. During the fourteen-year governorship of Rick Perry, dozens of his aides either left the

Empower Texans is a powerful political action committee that provides money to candidates, sometimes from undisclosed donors.

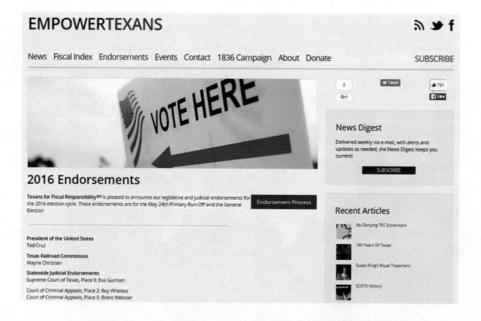

administration to become lobbyists or joined the administration after having been lobbyists. Some moved back and forth from administration to lobbying in a revolving door fashion.[23] In September 2017, for example, critics questioned the hiring of former lobbyist Luis Saenz as Governor Abbott's new chief of staff.

One former-legislator-turned-lobbyist reversed course and went back into the legislature. Todd Hunter had served in the legislature from 1989 to 1997. An active lobbyist as late as 2007, he was elected to the Texas House in 2008.[24] Jerry Patterson, former Texas land commissioner, was a state senator, became a lobbyist, and was able to move to his statewide office with little criticism of his role as a lobbyist. He then ran unsuccessfully for lieutenant governor in 2014 and most recently lost to George P. Bush in the 2018 primary for the Republican land commissioner nomination. However, David Sibley, a state senator who became a lobbyist and then tried to regain his old position, caught tremendous political flak for this decision and, to a considerable degree, lost the Republican primary because of it.[25] The issue of lobbying by former officials and their staffs is a significant one, as there is concern that policy decisions may be made with an eye toward future lucrative lobbying jobs.

Texas has only weak laws dealing with lobbying by former government officials. A former member of the governing body or a former executive head of a regulatory agency cannot lobby the agency for two years after leaving office. Senior employees or former officers of Texas regulatory agencies cannot ever lobby a governmental entity on matters they were involved in when employed by the government. However, there are no legal restrictions on lobbying by a former governor, former lieutenant governor, former legislator, or former aides to these officials.[26] In the 2015 and 2017 legislative sessions, Governor Abbott pledged action on ethics reform to address the problem of former legislators lobbying. Senator Van Taylor (R-Plano) introduced a bill that would impose a two-year limit before an outgoing legislator could lobby his or her former colleagues. The bill passed the Senate and a similar one passed the House, but Abbott vetoed the resulting legislation, claiming that it was not meaningful and included too many loopholes, including a provision to allow legislators to avoid reporting requirements by listing their assets and financial information under their spouse's name.[27]

What Lobbyists Do with Access

The public perception of lobbying may be that interested groups bring bags of money to members of the legislature in exchange for their votes on important bills. While lobbyists have no doubt showered legislators with gifts, sports tickets, and fancy meals, the reality is much more complex and far less underhanded. Once lobbyists obtain access to policy makers, they provide information that may be useful. For example, they may explain how a bill benefits a legislator's district, or how it benefits the state, or how it is perceived as being unfair. Because the staffs of Texas legislators are small, lobbyists perform useful functions by explaining what numerous bills are intended to do. They may even write bills to be introduced by friendly legislators or write amendments to bills. Almost certainly, if a bill affects the interests of a lobbyist's client and reaches a point in the legislative process where hearings are held on it, the lobbyist will arrange for testimony to be given at the hearing explaining the interest group's viewpoint on the proposed legislation.

Lobbying Reform

1 Why lobbying reform matters

Lobbyists come from different backgrounds. Most are lawyers, and many have not held elected office. However, in Austin, as in Washington, D.C., the number of former legislators taking high-paying jobs lobbying their former colleagues has grown substantially in recent years. In fact, this practice is becoming so common that the term *revolving door* has emerged to describe it. Many citizens have voiced concerns that former legislators are profiting from their time in public service and using their experience to benefit narrow (largely business) interests, rather than the public as a whole.

In the past two legislative sessions, legislators have proposed lobbying reform in order to address the issue of the revolving door. Representative Donna Howard (D-Austin) has proposed that former legislators should have to wait a period of time after their legislative service before they lobby. At the same time, Governor Greg Abbott has campaigned on broad ethics reform, including efforts to limit lobbying by former legislators. Nevertheless, a proposal to enact a two-session "cooling off" period before former legislators could lobby failed in the 2017 legislative session.

2 What's the debate?

It is not surprising that interest groups such as corporations or labor unions would want to hire former legislators as lobbyists. Former legislators have cultivated relationships with their colleagues as well as with staff members; therefore, they can easily arrange meetings for their clients with important government leaders. Lobbying firms see former legislators as strong investments because of their ability to influence legislation. Former legislators defend taking lobbying jobs by claiming that they have a right to make a living. Texas legislators point out that they make only $7,200 per year and that their experience should not go to waste once they leave office. Former legislators say they are uniquely suited to advise their clients because of their expertise in legislative politics. They also say they are employed not only to influence current legislators but also to educate them about the concerns of the lobbyists' cli-

Lobbying reforms have been proposed many times in the Texas legislature, but most measures have failed. Many lobbyists in Texas are former legislators.

ents, who are the legislators' constituents as well.[a] As long as reporting requirements exist so that the public knows whom they are lobbying for, they argue, then there are no ethical issues with this practice. Former legislator and current lobbyist Cliff Johnson defends his experience by suggesting, "You have to hire somebody to get through the administrative minefield."[b] Lobbying firms will naturally gravitate toward hiring individuals who know the legislative process and so are able to best represent them.

On the other hand, opponents of the revolving door claim that this practice is unethical and should be curtailed because legislators are public servants who should not personally profit from their time in office. Senator Jane Nelson (R–Flower Mound) expressed her opposition to the revolving door in this way: "It just doesn't feel right. I don't want people questioning: Is she filing that bill because she hopes to cash in on that at some point in the future? I would rather be boiled in oil."[c]

3 What do the numbers say?

According to the Center for Public Integrity, a nonpartisan investigative group, in 2015, Texas was ranked 39th among the states on government integrity. In particular, the state received a grade of F in legislative accountability and lobbying disclosure (measures that rank states according to how detailed and frequent reports need to be submitted and monitored by legislative leaders). Texas also received a D– in its ethics enforcement agencies, a measure that ranks states according to the ability of each state's enforcement agencies to monitor and sanction legislators found in violation of state laws. The only positive aspect from this report was an A for the budget process, which in Texas is considered transparent and well established. In a survey of 1,000 investigative and politics reporters conducted by political scientists, Texas was revealed among the nine states to be perceived as the most corrupt. No doubt these perceptions indicate that Texans are concerned about the corruption in state government.[d] In a June 2019 poll, 15 percent of Texans surveyed ranked corruption as the most important problem, ranking second only to immigration.[e]

State Rankings for Integrity

C	C–	D+	D	D–	F
AK	CA	HI	TN	GA	OK
	CT	RI	VA	UT	LA
		OH	WV	ID	OR
		AL	NC	MO	KS
		WA	NJ	MN	ME
		KY	WI	IN	PA
		NE	MT	FL	NV
		IA	AZ	NY	SD
		MA	MD	AR	DE
		CO		MS	WY
		IL		NH	MI
				NM	
				SC	
				ND	
				VT	
				TX	

Source: Public Integrity, 2018.

Communicating Effectively: What Do You Think?

● Do you agree or disagree that former legislators lobbying their former colleagues is unethical? Why?

● Should Texas enact laws to limit the ability of former legislators to lobby? If so, what specific provisions should be enacted and why?

WANT TO LEARN MORE?

If you want to learn more about who lobbies in Texas, and how much money is being spent on lobbying, consult the Texas Ethics Commission website:

- https://www.ethics.state.tx.us/

Go to this website to learn about who is donating to your state representative and state senator:

- app.influencetexas.com

Lobbyists do not limit their activities to the legislative process, however. Rules proposed by the bureaucracy or the courts can also affect the interests of lobbyists' clients. Lobbyists will testify at hearings on rules and try to provide information to administrators in face-to-face meetings as well.

Corruption There is always a concern that lobbyists may corrupt policy makers by bribing them in order to accomplish the interest groups' objectives. Early in the twentieth century, Sam Rayburn, later a famed U.S. representative and Speaker of the House, served in the Texas House of Representatives for six years. At that time, he was especially concerned with corruption and refused to accept free meals and entertainment from lobbyists. He called some of his fellow legislators "steak men." By that he meant that the legislators would sell their votes on a bill for a steak dinner at the Driskill Hotel in Austin. "Steak men" (and women) may still exist in Texas politics, but for the most part, lobbyists provide information, campaign contributions, and political support (or opposition) rather than bribes.

Still, some lobbying activities do seem ethically questionable. In 1989, "Bo" Pilgrim, a large poultry producer, distributed $10,000 checks to state senators in the capitol while he was lobbying them on workers' compensation reform. Perhaps even more troubling, some senators accepted the checks until media attention forced them to reconsider. Yet this practice of offering $10,000 while asking for a senator's vote on a specific bill was not illegal under state law. A year later, the Speaker of the Texas House of Representatives, "Gib" Lewis, got in trouble for his close relationship with a law firm that specialized in collecting delinquent taxes for local governments. In 1991, Lewis was indicted for receipt of an illegal gift from the firm. Ultimately, he plea bargained and received a minor penalty. The result of these scandals was legislation that created a state ethics commission. The legislation imposed additional lobbying reporting requirements and restrictions on speaking fees that interest groups paid legislators and pleasure trips that lobbyists provided. By no means was the law a major regulation of or restriction on lobbying practices, but it did impose some limits.

WHAT DO TEXANS THINK?

Corruption in State and Federal Government

When interest groups have too much power in Austin, Texans can come to see this as political corruption. If interest groups get their way over the needs of everyday Texans, then some may see this as corruption. Are Texans more approving of their state government or the federal government?

	TEXAS STATE GOVERNMENT (%)	FEDERAL GOVERNMENT (%)
Favorable	48%	24%
Unfavorable	29	53
Don't Know/Neutral	22	23

SOURCE: *Texas Tribune* poll, June 2019.

Who Represents Ordinary Texans?

Another problem with lobbying was well described by Craig McDonald, the director of a public interest lobby: "Legislators are rubbing shoulders with . . . lobbyists, almost all of whom hustle for business interests. While corporate interests dominate our legislative process, there is virtually no counterbalancing lobby to represent ordinary Texans. Nowhere on the list of Texas's biggest lobby spenders will you find a single group dedicated to the interests of consumers, the environment or human services. No wonder these citizen interests repeatedly get steamrolled in Austin."[28]

The Who Are Texans? graphic on p. 205 looks at campaign contributions to Texas legislators. Although the categories are very broad, it is clear that business interests dominate in Texas government. Of course, many issues considered by Texas government pit one business interest against another, and sometimes a business or professional organization may find itself aligned with consumer interests. For example, the Texas Trial Lawyers Association, an organization of plaintiffs' lawyers in Texas, frequently does so. Many of the clients of these lawyers are consumers who sue large businesses, and the interests of the lawyers and such clients are especially close since the lawyers are paid on a contingent fee basis, which means they don't receive payment unless their clients do.

It is also the case that lobbying is not all there is to the representation of interests in Austin. Interest groups without money may still mobilize their members in order to accomplish their objectives, or they may influence public opinion. Still, there is no question that money does help in politics. In this battle of mostly business interests, there may not be an objective voice, or at least a voice for the public interest, that reaches the ears of legislators.

How Interest Groups Impact Elections

Describe the role of PACs in Texas elections

Although lobbyists for interest groups try to gain access to government officials and inform them of the legislative desires of their clients, interest groups are not simply information channels. They also promote the political interests of elected officials who support their viewpoints and oppose the interests of those who do not. One major way of doing so is by making campaign contributions. An interest group may encourage individual members to make contributions to candidates, or it may collect funds from members and "bundle" those funds as a donation from the interest group. With the second option, the interest group creates a **political action committee (PAC)** to make the contribution.

There are numerous reasons for forming a PAC. A candidate is more likely to notice a substantial contribution from a PAC than many small contributions from individual members of an interest group. Additionally, the lobbyist who delivers a substantial PAC check to a candidate can more likely gain political access than can a lobbyist who simply

political action committee (PAC) a private group that raises and distributes funds for use in election campaigns

asks interest-group members to mail individual checks. The PAC becomes a way for the interest group to send a message to the candidate that its members care strongly enough about its agenda that they are prepared to back those goals with money. In some cases, a PAC can even serve as an intermediary to provide money to candidates that the interest group's members might not want to support publicly.

issue advocacy independent spending by individuals or interest groups on a campaign issue but not directly tied to a particular candidate

Instead of or in addition to giving money directly to the candidate, a PAC may engage in **issue advocacy** that might at times support the candidate but is independent of the candidate's control. The candidate need not report these independent expenditures on contribution disclosure statements. PACs may also spend money to support an issue rather than a specific candidate or to support such activities as "get out the vote" campaigns. In 2020 there were just over 2,000 active PACs in Texas that cumulatively spent just over $297 million. ActBlue Texas, a PAC aimed at electing Democrats, raised the most (nearly $23 million) to help candidates who supported its preferred policies.[29]

Campaign contributions can be, to a considerable degree, classified in terms of the economic interests represented by the contributors. The Who Are Texans? graphic on p. 205 shows that the largest contributor to candidates for the Texas legislature in 2019 was the finance, insurance, and real estate sector. This sector is a major part of the Texas economy and is subject to significant state regulation, characteristics that also apply to general business, energy and natural resources, construction, and health care. Compared with business, political parties, agriculture, and even candidates providing funds to their own campaigns, labor represents only a small amount of campaign spending.

Getting Out the Vote

Getting out the vote on Election Day is an important and difficult task. Both the Republican and the Democratic parties spend much time and money making sure that their voters get to the polls and vote for their candidates. In recent years, get-out-the-vote (GOTV) efforts by both parties have involved mining large databases to identify people who are likely to vote for their candidates, then calling these people on the phone, communicating with them through social media, and visiting them at home. Battleground Texas was a PAC launched in 2013 by the Democratic Party to identify potential Democratic voters, make them familiar with Democratic positions and candidates, and get them to vote. While it did not yield results in the 2014 elections and faded in influence, Beto O'Rourke established Powered by People, a PAC that spent $3.2 million in the 2020 elections to help elect Democrats in Texas. Similar efforts have been made by the Republican Party in recent years, particularly those identifying with the Tea Party movement.

GOTV initiatives also can be an important part of interest-group activity. The most successful GOTV campaign run by an interest group was that conducted in 1988 by the Texas Medical Association, which sought to elect its slate of candidates to the Texas Supreme Court. Physicians were encouraged to contribute money to TEXPAC, the medical association PAC, as well as to make individual contributions to certain candidates. Additionally, they were given slate cards with recommended candidates, literature endorsing these candidates, and even expensively produced videos. They were asked to encourage not only their families and friends but also their patients to vote for the candidates. Of the five candidates TEXPAC supported, four won. The effort by the medical association was remarkable for its fund-raising success and for its reaching and mobilizing the grass roots.[30] More recently, the Texas Organizing Project, a progressive group, has been quite successful in mobilizing voters at the local level to prevent schools from closing, revitalizing neighborhoods impacted by Hurricane Harvey, and pressuring the Environmental Protection Agency to impose fines on chemical plants in neighborhoods.

Most efforts by interest groups, however, are far less sophisticated. Generally, interest-group PACs simply provide resources for the candidates to get out the vote. In the 2010 primary campaign, Texans for Lawsuit Reform, which has had spectacular successes in forwarding its agenda over the past 15 years, suffered a remarkable failure. Although it contributed $602,290 to 28 candidates, 53 percent of this money was spent on 4 incumbent candidates who lost their primaries, and another 28 percent went to 3 candidates—2 of them incumbents—who were forced into runoff elections. Obviously, Texans for Lawsuit Reform thought these candidates were important for achieving its agenda, but it seemed questionable for an interest group to pump huge amounts of money into the campaigns of incumbent candidates who do not have the political strength to win even in their party's primary. And the high degree of financial support for candidates can be hurtful to the candidate. In one of these races, the winning candidate's main issue was that the defeated incumbent had received money from an organization known for giving huge sums to Republican candidates. This contribution, the winner claimed, was proof that the incumbent Democrat was not a real Democrat but a Republican with a Democratic label.[31]

Nevertheless, Texans for Lawsuit Reform has remained active, and between 2011 and 2019 contributed nearly $25 million dollars to over 375 different campaigns in Texas.[32] In more recent elections, Texans for Lawsuit Reform has focused on supporting incumbents, rather than seeking to oust legislators. It was successful in defending Sarah Davis of Houston, a moderate Republican who was challenged by a more conservative Republican in the 2018 primary.[33]

Defeating Opponents

Generally, incumbents have a huge advantage over challengers in elections. Since they are officeholders already, they usually have greater name recognition than challengers, and it is easy for them to get publicity by holding town hall meetings, announcing the relocation of new businesses to the district, or simply attending community events. Additionally, they usually have an established network of supporters who helped them get into office.

Because of the incumbency advantage, it is far safer for interest groups to try to work with incumbents than challengers. Campaign contributions, for example, overwhelmingly go to incumbents (see Figure 6.1). In the 2020 campaign for the Texas legislature, candidates raised more than $92 million.[34] The total amounts contributed to some incumbent legislators are spectacularly large. Former Speaker of the House Joe Straus, for example, received $8,429,380 in contributions in 2015—no doubt in recognition that he was in a position to advance or hinder much legislation. In the Texas Senate in 2017, Senator Kel Seliger (R-Amarillo) faced a challenge from another Republican who lost to him in 2013 by only five percentage points. Seliger's $1.7 million proved to be enough to fend off a challenge from former Midland mayor Mike Canon, whose campaign war chest was only $89,000.[35]

FIGURE 6.1

Contributions to Incumbents and Challengers for the Texas Legislature, 2020

SOURCE: National Institute on Money in State Politics.

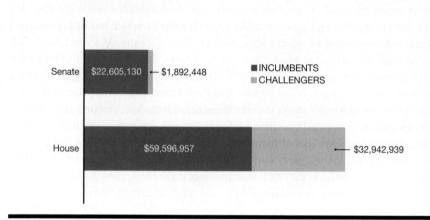

Of course, sometimes an interest group does not want to help a candidate or even pressure a candidate; it wants to defeat that candidate. Trying to do so can be a risky strategy, however, because if the candidate wins, then the interest group will be faced with a public official not only unsympathetic to its policy goals but also displeased with the interest group for its opposition. When that happens, the interest group will often "get well" or "get on the late train"—that is, make a substantial political contribution to the winning candidate whom it formerly opposed. Often, winning candidates have significant campaign debts after a grueling election battle, and they appreciate the late contributions of former enemies seeking to make amends.

Although "late-train" contributions may improve the relationship between officials and interest groups, usually candidates reserve a special loyalty for those supporters who backed them early. Without support at the very beginning of a campaign, it is hard for a candidate to build an organization and get the support necessary to make a decent campaign start. That is why early supporters are so valuable, and why the best lobbyists start early in trying to develop relationships with candidates and with new legislators. One national PAC, EMILY's List, is funded by women and provides early campaign contributions to female candidates. EMILY stands for Early Money Is Like Yeast, and yeast helps raise the dough—early money helps raise even more money. Legislators remember who was with them at the beginning of their political careers—and this memory can be immensely beneficial to the lobby that cultivated that early relationship.[36]

Sometimes PACs give to both candidates as a way to avoid alienating either one, though the possibility remains that such dual giving will wind up alienating both. At other times, interest groups simply don't care if they alienate a candidate. An extraordinary battle occurred in the 2012 Republican primary when Texans for Lawsuit Reform backed railroad commissioner Elizabeth Ames Jones in her challenge to Republican state senator Jeff Wentworth. Wentworth had served nearly five years in the Texas House before being elected to the state senate in 1992. He appeared to be well established and

Which Interest Groups Contribute the Most?

Contributions to Texas Legislature Candidates, 2018

 = $250,000

 Contributions to Democrats

 Contributions to Republicans

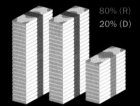 80% (R) 20% (D)

Finance, insurance, and real estate
$13,642,912

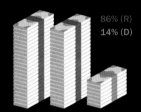 86% (R) 14% (D)

Ideology/single issue
$12,410,282

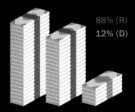 88% (R) 12% (D)

General business
$11,243,798

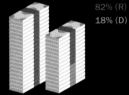 82% (R) 18% (D)

Energy and natural resources
$8,678,750

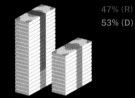 47% (R) 53% (D)

Lawyers and lobbyists
$7,759,489

 71% (R) 29% (D)

Health
$6,043,002

78% (R) 22% (D)

Construction
$3,427,898

 36% (R) 64% (D)

Labor
$3,146,973

 78% (R) 22% (D)

Agriculture
$2,713,084

 75% (R) 25% (D)

Communications and electronics
$2,141,378

 74% (R) 26% (D)

Transportation
$1,560,328

 68% (R) 32% (D)

Defense
$252,954

Interest groups try to achieve favorable policies not only by lobbying members of the Texas legislature directly but also by influencing who becomes a member of the legislature in the first place by donating to the election campaigns of favored candidates. The chart below breaks down contributions from employees of different industries by party in 2018.

QUANTITATIVE REASONING

- Which group contributes the highest percentage of contributions to Democrats? Republicans? Why might these groups provide strong support to a particular party?

- Which group provides the lowest total dollar amount to candidates of either political party? Why do you think this group provides less than other groups?

SOURCE: National Institute on State Money in Politics Industry Influence, followthemoney.org (accessed 10/25/20).

unbeatable, and an early poll showed him with a large lead. But although Wentworth had supported 21 of 23 bills designated by Texans for Lawsuit Reform as "major" legislation, he angered the interest group by criticizing a 2003 constitutional amendment that limited the amounts patients could receive in medical malpractice suits. While Wentworth was defeated, it was not by Jones, but by Donna Campbell, who had Tea Party backing. Nevertheless, Wentworth blamed his defeat on the "mammoth $2 million–plus negative campaign launched against me by Texans for Lawsuit Reform."[37] The defeat no doubt sent a message to Republican lawmakers that they had better not cross this particular interest group.

When an interest group is convinced that it cannot work with a public official toward its policy goals, it may undertake an all-out effort to defeat that official. Spending money by no means guarantees success, however. Dr. James Leininger is one of the biggest contributors to Republican candidates in Texas. In the 2006 election cycle, he gave over $5 million to Republican candidates in Texas, through both individual contributions and gifts to PACs that then made contributions. Leininger and some of the PACs he supports are strong supporters of school vouchers, and much of this money backed challengers to Republican incumbents unfavorable to vouchers. But the effort was unsuccessful, and the result, according to Texans for Public Justice, was a legislature "even less receptive to vouchers than its predecessor."[38]

A U.S. Supreme Court decision in 2009, *Citizens United v. Federal Election Commission*, allowed political contributors to create organizations supporting and/or opposing candidates without having to disclose their donors. These new funding structures in which donors do not have to be reported are known as sources of **dark money**.[39] For example, Empower Texans, the conservative nonprofit, spent about $290,000 on mailers, about $40,000 on internet ads, and about $18,000 on robo-calls. Another nonprofit that does not have to report donors is the Texas Organizing Project, which spent about $234,000 mostly supporting then–Harris County sheriff Adrian Garcia and 14 other local candidates. In the November 2018 elections, Empower Texans spent $4 million supporting Republican candidates for office in legislative races. In all, the group endorsed 42 candidates statewide. Only fourteen emerged victorious after the votes were counted. The group's heavy funds were not enough to counteract Democratic strength, especially in suburban areas around Austin, Dallas, and Houston. In 2020, the group endorsed only 18 candidates statewide, as the group was criticized for one of its staff mocking Governor Abbott for being in a wheelchair.

In January 2018 the Texas Association of Business came under fire for funding its political action committee with money from these unknown sources. While the organization claims the money was only used for administrative expenses, critics have called for the Texas Ethics Commission to investigate and determine if proper procedures were followed.[40]

Interest-group capture occurs when an interest group has such influence over an agency of government that it is said that the agency primarily serves the objectives of the interest group. Interest groups representing particular industries can develop long-term relationships in a number of ways with the agencies that regulate the industries they represent. For example, interest groups can donate money to the election or re-election of agency officials who must seek election to their office. Subject to certain ethics rules, industries can also hire former agency officials to work for them as lobbyists. The closer the connection between the agency and the industry, the more complete is the capture.

Such interest-group capture may have occurred with the Texas Railroad Commission, which has the primary responsibility for regulating the state's oil and natural gas

dark money political contributions whose donors are not legally required to be disclosed

interest-group capture process by which a government agency comes to serve the objectives of the interests that the agency is supposed to regulate

The Texas Railroad Commission regulates Texas's oil and gas drilling. Some say that this commission has been captured by those special interests, which sometimes advocates controversial procedures such as fracking.

industry, pipelines, and coal and uranium surface-mining operations. The commission is run by three statewide elected officials who serve staggered six-year terms. Although one unsuccessful candidate included railroad safety in his campaign platform, the Railroad Commission's name is long outdated, and the commission today has nothing to do with railroads.[41]

In 2010, Public Citizen, a consumer advocacy group, published a highly critical report on the commission, in which it said "political spending is out of control, well over half of campaign donations coming from the very industries the commission is supposed to regulate. Real or perceived, this creates a conflict of interest. Railroad commissioner is seen as a springboard to higher elected office in the state, giving influence-peddlers more incentive to curry favor and sitting commissioners to amass campaign war chests. . . . Campaign donations coming from regulated industries present a very real problem, inserting the probability that regulatory decisions are made in favor of large donors rather than the public's interest."[42]

A Public Citizen report pointed out that by 2010, 80 percent of donations to incumbent commissioners were from the industries they regulated, up from 45 percent in 2001, and that there had been nearly a tenfold increase in donations. Additionally, the size of individual donations had increased—in 2000, 80 percent of donations were $1,000 or more; in 2010, 92 percent were.[43] In the 2012 election an incumbent, Barry Smitherman, received $5,144,683 in campaign contributions, of which the oil and gas industry contributed the most among business/industrial interest groups. In a race for an open seat, Christi Craddick won with $2,850,158 in contributions. Again, contributions were led by the oil and gas industry.[44]

In the 2016 Republican primary for seats on the Railroad Commission, three candidates proposed banning donations from people or organizations that have business before the commission. These three candidates, however, raised very little funds for their campaigns and lost their primaries.[45]

The staff of the Sunset Advisory Commission prepared a report in 2012 that attempted to deal with some of the concerns that the Texas Railroad Commission had been captured by the oil and gas industry. Among other things, the report recommended that the commission's name be changed to realistically reflect its contemporary duties: the Texas Energy Resources Commission. It also recommended that solicitation and receipt of campaign contributions by commissioners or candidates seeking the office be limited to an 18-month period around the election rather than throughout the six-year term of office. It recommended that commissioners be banned from knowingly accepting contributions from those with contested cases before the commission, and that they be required to resign their office if they become candidates for another elected office. Further, it recommended that independent hearing examiners be used in contested cases involving oil and gas.[46] These reform proposals failed in the 2013 legislature[47] and in 2017, Governor Abbott signed a bill reauthorizing the commission for another 12 years, despite criticisms that reforms suggested by the Sunset Commission were not implemented.[48]

Individuals as Lobbyists

 Explain how ordinary individuals can influence Texas government

Although interest groups clearly have an advantage in influencing the legislative process, sometimes ordinary individuals can have a remarkable impact on public policy. As we saw at the beginning of the chapter in the case of Dineen Majcher and school testing, a persistent individual with a well-reasoned argument can make a difference. Another

Occasionally, ordinary individuals can have a direct influence on policy. Tyrus Burks (right) lobbied the legislature to require landlords to buy and install visual smoke alarms for hearing-impaired tenants who requested them.

example involves Tyrus Burks, who lost his wife and two children in a late-night electrical fire in West Dallas. Burks did not awaken in time to save them because he is deaf and did not hear the audible smoke alarm. Texas's state property code required the installation of audible smoke alarms but not visual alarms. In 2009, Burks became an advocate for a bill that would require property managers to buy visual smoke alarms if hearing-impaired tenants requested them and to install the alarms in visible locations such as bedrooms. Supported by state senator Royce West, the Sephra Burks Law, named for Tyrus's wife, who was also deaf, went into effect at the start of 2010. Tyrus Burks was an active lobbyist for the bill and gave legislative testimony in support of it.

Burks's efforts benefited from the support of the Texas Apartment Association, a major interest group representing apartment property interests, who backed the bill. Burks's story was tragic, and his argument was compelling. It would have been difficult for opposition to emerge against such a proposal. Still, his efforts resulted in a major victory for the deaf, who are protected by such a law requiring visual smoke alarms in only three other states and the District of Columbia.[49] Burks's achievement demonstrates that individuals can, at least sometimes, be successful lobbyists.

The problem is that relatively few Texans are engaged in their neighborhood, in their community, or in politics, and thus much lobbying is left to organized interest groups with professional lobbyists. Table 6.1 provides a number of measures of civic engagement, and all show Texas considerably lower than the national average on these measures. Texas is near the bottom of the nation in terms of measures of social connectedness that would lead to civic involvement, such as discussing politics with friends or family, group involvement, frequent communication with friends and family, and even trust in all or most of the people in the neighborhood. Nor, in comparison with other Americans, are Texans involved in volunteer activity or charitable donations. They tend not to contact or visit their public officials, vote, or register to vote. With such low levels of civic engagement, individual effects on the Texas political process are likely to be low.[50]

TABLE 6.1

Measures of Texas Civic Health

	PERCENTAGE OF TEXANS AGREEING (%)	NATIONAL AVERAGE (%)	RANKING OF TEXAS AMONG THE STATES
Discuss politics with friends or family a few times a week or more	23%	27%	50
Trust all or most people in the neighborhood	48	56	45
Donate $25 or more to charitable or religious organizations	46	52	40
Volunteer activity	23	25	39
Registered to vote	68	76	44
Voting	55	61	47

SOURCE: Regina Lawrence, Deborah Wise, and Emily Einsohn, *Texas Civic Health Index* (Austin: Annette Strauss Institute for Civic Life, 2018).

Interestingly, while in one survey 52 percent of Texans claimed they were very interested in politics and public affairs and 37 percent said they were somewhat interested, Texas has the lowest proportion of actual voters of any state. Texans give all sorts of reasons for not voting, the most common being that they are too busy or that work conflicts with voting and the next most common being that they either are not interested or believe their vote does not matter.[51] Of course, the low level of voting participation means that organized interest groups fill the void in political activity and can wield vast influence in the state's political process.

Interest Groups and the Future of Texas

THOUGH NO SINGLE INTEREST group or coalition of interest groups dominates Texas politics, by far most lobbyists represent business interests, and the bulk of PAC money comes from them as well. Often, of course, businesses are pitted against one another in the political process. Also, public interest, civil rights, consumer, and environmental groups may still succeed by mobilizing public opinion and influencing the media. However, only a few interest groups offer alternatives to business perspectives on policy issues. Less frequently, ordinary individuals are able to influence public policy. Although they tend to be at a disadvantage in terms of money and other resources, dedicated individuals with a compelling argument sometimes succeed in lobbying for specific legislation. This is especially true when they are pursuing goals that do not put them in conflict with well-organized and well-funded interest groups.

The influence of interest groups in Texas shows no signs of diminishing. As long as federal and state law allows donations and the creation of PACs and other groups, we will see the strong influence of interest groups not only in Austin but also in Washington. Texas is a pro-business state, and the Texas Association of Business will continue to be a dominant interest group representing the concerns of corporations and entrepreneurs in Austin.

At times, however, business interests might conflict with those of other groups. We have seen this on the issue of immigration. Business leaders have often welcomed more immigrants because of the low-cost labor they provide. While the state is limited in what it can do to curtail immigration, the election and re-election of Lieutenant Governor Dan Patrick and his emphasis on curtailing immigration might pose a counternarrative to business interest groups. As Texas becomes more diverse and more immigrants settle in the state, the response by different interest groups will be something to watch.

Use 🐰 INQUIZITIVE to help you study and master this material.

Interest Groups in the Political Process

- **Define interest groups, and describe the major ways they try to influence Texas government (pp. 187–201)**

Interest groups in Texas are organizations of interested citizens who band together to influence public policy. Lobbyists are hired to cultivate relationships with legislators and convince them of their clients' interests. The goal of lobbyists is to gain access to policy makers to persuade them to support the positions of the interest group.

Key Terms
interest group (p. 187)
free rider problem (p. 188)
bundling (p. 191)
lobbyist (p. 192)

Practice Quiz
1. The "8F Crowd"
   a) was a group of legislators who failed the eighth grade.
   b) was a group of extremely wealthy Texans who met in Suite 8F of the Lamar Hotel in Houston and controlled Texas politics for 40 years.
   c) were 25 legislators who boycotted the eighth session of the legislature in order to prevent the legislators from taking any action because it lacked a quorum.
   d) was made up of eight lobbyists who were close friends of the governor.
   e) were the eight most powerful officials in the state who met in Suite F of the Austin State Office Building.

2. Interest groups provide public officials with all the following *except*
   a) information.
   b) money.
   c) media coverage.
   d) votes.
   e) committee assignments.

3. The goals of interest groups include all *except*
   a) electing people to office in order to support the groups' goals.
   b) influencing those who control government.
   c) educating the public and members about issues of importance to the group.
   d) providing campaign funds for favored candidates.
   e) maintaining a heterogeneous membership.

4. Interest groups have an advantage over individuals in influencing policy because interest groups usually have
   a) more time to influence officials.
   b) greater expertise than individuals.
   c) more money to influence elections.
   d) more staff.
   e) all of the above

5. When interest groups combine small contributions from many sources to form one large contribution, it is called
   a) bundling.
   b) compacting.
   c) cracking.
   d) polling.
   e) packing.

6. The most important thing interest groups need to be effective is
   a) the support of a majority of Texans.
   b) office space in Austin.
   c) a variety of issues on which to lobby.
   d) a large, paid staff.
   e) access to politicians.

7. Trial lawyers are which type of interest group?
   a) professional group
   b) public employee group
   c) single-issue group
   d) consumer group
   e) business group

8. Interest groups often hire former legislators as lobbyists to
  a) gain greater access to current legislators.
  b) benefit from the policy expertise of former legislators.
  c) benefit from the personal "insider" knowledge of the former legislator.
  d) all of the above
  e) none of the above

9. Lobbyists are
  a) all corrupt.
  b) all unethical.
  c) important sources of information for legislators.
  d) harmful to the democratic process.
  e) never retired legislators.

How Interest Groups Impact Elections

- **Describe the role of PACs in Texas elections (pp. 201–8)**

Political action committees (PACs) are private groups that raise and distribute funds for election campaigns. Interest groups play a major role in getting out the vote. Interest-group money can play a major role in defeating as well as electing candidates.

Key Terms
political action committee (PAC) (p. 201)
issue advocacy (p. 202)
dark money (p. 206)
interest-group capture (p. 206)

Practice Quiz
10. In Texas, the most powerful interest groups represent which interests?
  a) consumer
  b) civil rights
  c) business
  d) owners of oil wells
  e) public employee

11. PACs are used to
  a) stir the public's interest in politics.
  b) raise money from individuals, which is then bundled and given to candidates.
  c) create media campaigns to influence the course of government.
  d) create grassroots campaigns.
  e) all of the above

12. One of the most important grassroots tactics of interest groups is
  a) to gain support from all the mayors of towns in a district.
  b) to get out the vote.
  c) to form political alliances with executive and legislative leaders.
  d) to lobby the judicial branch of national and state government.
  e) to interpret the needs of their members.

13. *Dark money* refers to
  a) money that is illegally donated to politicians for their re-election.
  b) money that cannot be used to pay typical campaign expenditures.
  c) vouchers that candidates can use to fund their campaigns.
  d) donated money that does not have to be reported by a campaign.
  e) money that is printed on special dark green paper specifically formulated for campaigns.

14. *Interest group capture* refers to the idea that
  a) interest groups are controlled by politicians.
  b) through long-term relationships, government interests come to serve the objectives of an interest group.
  c) politicians work for the public good by controlling special interests.
  d) labor unions are controlled by business.
  e) business interests are captured by labor unions.

Individuals as Lobbyists

• **Explain how ordinary individuals can influence Texas government (pp. 208–10)**

Citizens can lobby their legislators by calling, writing, or visiting their offices. Industries and well-financed interests can afford professional lobbyists to try to influence legislation, but legislators will listen to individual citizens, especially if they join together in large numbers.

Practice Quiz

15. Individuals have the best chance to influence public policy when they
   a) are not opposed by organized interest groups.
   b) are polite.
   c) entertain legislators.
   d) vote.
   e) live in Austin.

16. On the measures of civic health, Texas
   a) ranks higher than most other states.
   b) ranks lower than most other states.
   c) ranks about the same as other states.
   d) is stronger than average on some measures and weaker than average on others.
   e) ranks highly when it comes to Texans contacting elected officials, compared with other states.

Erin Zwiener was one of the 12 Democrats to capture seats from Republicans in the Texas House of Representatives in the 2018 elections. What effect will a slimmer Republican majority have on legislating in the Texas House?

The Legislature

WHY THE TEXAS LEGISLATURE MATTERS During the 2018 elections, Texas voters made history by electing the largest number of women to the state legislature ever. Women now constitute 24 percent of the state legislature, lower than their percentage of the population but steadily increasing nonetheless. This increase mirrors trends in the U.S. Congress, with the highest number of women ever serving in the U.S. House of Representatives in 2019–20. Interestingly, while there are more women members than ever, Texas has seen a decrease in the number of Republican women serving in the state House. In 2002, there were 19 Republican women in the Texas House; today there are 6. The increase in female members of the House is clearly on the Democratic side. And this increase was one of the keys to the Democrats chipping away at the Republican majority in the Texas state House. In 2018, Democrats captured 12 seats. A resurgent Democratic Party and more female members may reshape the state House for years to come.

One of these Democratic freshmen is Representative Erin Zwiener of Driftwood, Texas. Representative Zwiener ran for an open seat in Hays County, outside Austin, which had been represented by Jason Isaac, a Republican who unsuccessfully ran for Congress. Zwiener was a first-time candidate and author of a children's book who had moved to Driftwood from New Mexico in 2016. After winning the Democratic primary, Zwiener went on to narrowly defeat Republican Ken Strange in an election during which she was pregnant and gave birth to her child during the campaign. Zwiener was also the founding member of the newly composed state House LGBTQ Caucus.

Why is this story about Representative Zwiener important? In many ways, the Texas legislature reflects the state of Texas and, more broadly, the country. As Texas—like the United States overall—has become more diverse, candidates representing the changing nature of Texas have begun to run for office and win. Indeed, the literature on women in politics shows that when women run, they win. The challenge is to get women to run for elective office, including the state legislature. Zwiener is an example of what can happen when a strong female candidate runs for the right office at the right time.

The Texas legislature has become more representative of the state. As the state has become more diverse and less solidly Republican, one of the first political institutions to begin to reflect this is the state House (because of its frequent elections). This diversity means that fierce political debates and disagreements remain, as they do throughout the state and the country. For example, Republicans have internal divisions between moderates and more conservative members.

What the Texas legislature does makes an important difference in the lives of everyone in Texas. As the state becomes more divided into different political factions, it is all the more important for Texans to know how the legislature works in order to elect representatives who will serve their interests and work to enact policies that reflect their vision for a safe and prosperous Texas. How will these new members like Representative Zwiener adapt and respond to the customs and structure of the legislature? How will women legislators fight for issues they care about given their increased numbers? How will a new generation of leaders try to break through partisanship to enact their agendas? What will greater Democratic strength mean for how the legislature operates and what policies it enacts?

CHAPTER GOALS

- Describe the organization and basic rules of the legislature (pp. 217–21)
- Explain representation and the politics of redistricting (pp. 222–25)
- Outline the legislative and nonlegislative powers of the legislature (pp. 225–29)
- Trace the process through which law is made in Texas (pp. 229–40)
- Analyze how party leadership and partisanship affect power in the legislature (pp. 241–47)

Structure of the Texas Legislature

Describe the organization and basic rules of the legislature

The Texas state legislature is the most important representative institution in the state, and the Texas Constitution spells out in Article 3 precisely how the legislature is to be organized. The U.S. Constitution guarantees that every state will have a republican form of government, and the Texas Constitution complies with this by establishing a bicameral legislature modeled on the U.S. Congress. As such, members share many of the duties and responsibilities that are taken up at the national level by members of the U.S. Congress. Like members of the U.S. Congress, the members of the Texas House and Senate are responsible for bringing the interests and concerns of their constituencies directly into the democratic political processes. But the important constitutional and institutional differences between the U.S. Congress and the Texas state legislature must also be taken into account to understand the role that the legislature plays in democracy in Texas.

Bicameralism

Like the U.S. Congress and all the states except Nebraska, Texas has a **bicameral** legislature, with two chambers: the Texas House of Representatives and the Texas Senate. The legislature's 150 House members and 31 senators meet in regular session for 140 days every odd-numbered year. Senators serve four-year terms, and House members serve for two years. Each represents a single-member district. A Texas state senator now represents more people than does a member of the U.S. House of Representatives. Elections are held in November of even-numbered years, and senators and House members take office in January of odd-numbered years.

bicameral having a legislative assembly composed of two chambers or houses

Bicameralism creates interesting dynamics in a legislature. For one thing, it means that before a law is passed, it will be voted on by two deliberative bodies representing different constituencies. If a bill cannot be killed in one house, it can be killed or modified in the other body. Bicameralism is meant to make sure that no one chamber takes complete control of the lawmaking process. House and Senate leaders must come to agreement if they want legislation to pass. With the legislature comprising Texans from all corners of the state, these representatives will make sure that legislation benefits or does not harm their districts. While bicameralism necessarily leads to more compromise, one drawback is that it might lead to situations in which major issues are not adequately or swiftly addressed. This is also a problem in Texas because of the 140-day session every other year.

One distinctive aspect of bicameralism in Texas is that the author of a bill in one house that is then amended in the other body has the option of accepting or rejecting the amendment. If the author accepts the amendment, the bill moves forward; if the author rejects it, the bill is killed.

Bicameralism also allows a member of one body of the legislature to retaliate against a member of either body for not cooperating on desired legislation. For example, a "local and consent" calendar in the House is usually reserved for uncontroversial bills or bills limited to a localized problem. In order for a bill from that calendar to be passed, there has to be no objection to it from any member of the House. That requirement provides a perfect opportunity for members to retaliate against other members for perceived slights.[1]

Sessions of the Legislature

Not all state legislatures meet for the same time periods. Some meet every year, like the U.S. Congress. Texas's legislature generally meets every other year unless the governor calls it to meet between regular sessions.

Regular Sessions

regular session the 140-day period, occurring only in odd-numbered years, during which the Texas legislature meets to consider and pass bills

biennial occurring every two years

The Texas Constitution specifies that **regular sessions** of the Texas legislature be held for 140 days in odd-numbered years. The **biennial** legislative sessions have their origin in the nineteenth-century idea that legislative service is a part-time job and the belief that short, biennial sessions would limit the power of the legislature. For a few years, legislators were encouraged to end their work early by being paid for only 120 days of service.

Thousands of bills and resolutions are introduced into the legislature during a regular session, and the 140-day limitation places a considerable restriction on legislators' ability to deal with this workload. In the 2019 regular legislative session, for example, 7,324 bills were introduced and 1,429 passed. The governor vetoed 56 of the bills passed by the legislature.[2] Hundreds of bills pass in the last hours of a legislative session, most with little or no debate. More die in the end-of-session crush of business because there isn't time to consider them.

Special Sessions

special session a legislative session called by the governor that addresses an agenda set by him or her and that lasts no longer than 30 days

If the legislature does not finish its business by the end of the regular session or if problems requiring legislation arise between regular sessions, the governor may call a **special session**. Special sessions last no more than 30 days, but there is no limit to the number of special sessions a governor can call, and the governor sets their agenda. Texas has averaged one special session per year since 1876. Although years may go by with no special session, in some years there may be three or four.

The ability to call a special session and set its agenda provides the governor with control over which issues are discussed and what bills are passed (see Chapter 8). In many instances, the governor, the Speaker of the Texas House, the lieutenant governor, and various committee chairs will meet to decide what will be done to solve the problem at hand. Once the leaders address the issue and develop solutions, the governor calls the special session.

Once the special session begins, the governor can open it to different issues. At times, the governor bargains for a legislator's vote in return for adding to the special session agenda an issue of importance to that legislator. In 2003, Governor Rick Perry called three special sessions of the legislature to address congressional redistricting. In 2004 a fourth special session was called to address school finance. In 2005 two more special sessions addressed school finance. There was also a special session in 2006, 2009, and 2011. In 2013 two special sessions were called to deal with Texas abortion laws, and in 2017 one special session was called by Governor Abbott to deal with the "bathroom bill" as well as 19 other issues selected by the governor.

The Texas House of Representatives meets every other year for about 140 days in Austin, Texas.

Between legislative sessions, members serve on interim committees that may require a few days of their time each month. Legislators are also frequently called on to present programs to schools, colleges, and civic clubs. They supervise the staff of their district offices and address the needs of their constituents. Special sessions, interim committee meetings, speeches, and constituent services require long hours with little remuneration. Many members devote more than 40 hours a week to legislative business in addition to maintaining their full-time jobs.

In the twenty-first century, Texas is a modern state with more than 80 percent of its population living in metropolitan areas. Population growth continues at a rapid rate, and the state's economic output exceeds that of many nations. Using part-time legislators serving biennial 140-day sessions may not work well anymore in allowing the legislature to respond quickly and effectively to problems that arise in such a large and complex state.

Legislative Staff The legislature would not be able to function without legislative staff. Each legislator employs staff to assist them with carrying out their duties of representing their constituents. In addition to staff, hundreds of interns also descend upon Austin every legislative session to help legislators and their staff complete their business. When legislators are fund-raising or representing their constituents at home, staffers take care of helping constituents with their concerns, responding to emails and letters, and making sure that state agencies are serving the public. According to the National Council of State Legislators, Texas employed 2,359 staff members in 2015. This places Texas among the states with the most staff, with New York employing slightly more (2,865) the same year. Legislative staff are essential to making sure the legislature functions in session and out of session as well. They work behind the scenes serving their legislator, and in turn, the citizens of Texas.

How Much Do Legislators Get Paid?

Legislators in Texas cannot expect to live on their legislative salaries alone. In keeping with the Texas constitutional tradition of a low-cost, part-time legislature, Texas legislators receive a salary of only $7,200 per year. Legislators also receive a payment of $221 a day when the legislature is in session. When the legislature is not in session, legislators may claim up to 12 days per month of **per diem** pay if they are in Austin on official business, or 16 days if they are committee chairs. The legislators themselves determine what qualifies as official business, and it is common to pay expenses from officeholder expense accounts and to pocket the per diem so that it becomes a salary supplement. Legislative retirement pensions are very generous. The pension is tied to district judges' salaries, which are $140,000 a year. That salary is multiplied by the years of service of the legislator times 2.3 percent. A legislator who has served 10 years thus would qualify for a pension of $32,200 per year, and one who has served 20 years for a pension of $64,400 per year. Lawmakers are eligible for pensions with at least 8 years of service. With 8 years of service, the lawmaker can start collecting a pension at age 60. With 10 years of service, a lawmaker can start collecting at age 50.[3]

Originally, per diem rates were set by the Texas Constitution, and a constitutional amendment was necessary to change this restriction. In 1991, Texans adopted an amendment allowing the Texas Ethics Commission to propose changes in legislative salaries, which then require voter approval. At the start of each regular session, the Ethics Commission sets the legislative per diem. In 2019 the commission authorized a per diem increase to $221.

per diem daily payment to a public official engaged in state business

Representation in the Texas Legislature

There are 150 Texas House districts and 31 Texas Senate districts. One senator or one member of the House represents each district, a system called representation by **single-member districts**. Districts must be roughly equal in population. House districts each contain just over 168,000 people, while Senate districts contain just over 811,000. Some districts are geographically small, like House district 137, which is one of 29 districts in Harris County in the Houston metropolitan area. Some districts are large, like Senate district 19, which covers 35,000 square miles and parts of 17 counties in West Texas.

Table 7.1 lists the constitutional requirements for becoming a member of the Texas legislature, which are minimal. These requirements are in keeping with the political philosophy of those who wrote the Constitution of 1876. They believed holding public office required little or no formal training and should be open to most citizens.

In Texas, the legislature tends to be whiter, more male, Protestant, college educated, and affluent than the overall population. Most legislators also have a professional or business occupation. This profile does not mean that others cannot be elected to the state legislature, but it does indicate that individuals with most of these characteristics have a distinct advantage. Members of the legislature must have jobs that allow them the flexibility to campaign for office and to work in the legislature for 140 days every other year, as well as in special legislative sessions and meetings of committees when the legislature is not in session. About one-third of the members of the legislature are attorneys. The legal profession is one of the few careers that both pays well and offers the flexibility

single-member district a district in which one official is elected rather than multiple officials

TABLE 7.1

Constitutional Requirements to be a Member of the Texas Legislature

	AGE	CITIZENSHIP STATUS	RESIDENCY IN THE STATE (YEARS)	RESIDENCY IN THE DISTRICT (YEARS)
TEXAS SENATE	26	U.S. Citizen	5	1
TEXAS HOUSE OF REPRESENTATIVES	21	U.S. Citizen	2	1

a legislator needs. Lawyers who serve in the legislature may even gain increased legal business either from interests with legislative concerns or because of the enhanced visibility of a lawyer-legislator.[4]

Legislators have the power to get things done for or in the name of **constituents**. Efforts on behalf of constituents may involve legislative activity, such as introducing a bill or voting on a resolution. Often, however, these efforts involve nonlegislative activity, such as arranging an appointment for a constituent with a government agency that regulates some aspect of the constituent's life, writing a letter of recommendation for a constituent, or giving a speech to a civic group in the legislator's district. These kinds of nonlegislative activities are called **constituent service**. Legislative staff are essential for providing effective and responsive constituent service.

constituent a person who is represented by an elected official

When the legislature is not in session, representatives are still actively involved in promoting their agendas. Representatives use social media such as Facebook, Twitter, and Instagram to communicate to their constituents and support policies they believe in. Unlike members of Congress, however, Texas legislators have to simultaneously make a living and continue to represent their constituents if they hope to be re-elected.

constituent service nonlegislative activities legislators perform to assist people living in their districts, including writing letters of recommendation, giving speeches to civic groups, or working to solve a problem for someone in their community

Who Are Texans: Who Are the Members of the Texas Legislature? shows the proportions of minorities and women serving in the legislature. Although those numbers have increased over the years, they are not in proportion to the shares of these groups in the Texas population. Civil rights laws have increased voting by minorities by providing protection for political districts where minorities form the majority of the population. The 2013 U.S. Supreme Court decision overturning part of the Voting Rights Act has led to reduced legal protection for such districts, since the 2021 redistricting process in Texas is not subject to preclearance by the Department of Justice. Thus, more minority officeholders have been elected and, as the Latino population in Texas increases, additional Latino and Latina legislators are likely to be elected. Women of all races and ethnicities have also had an increased role in politics, especially since the 1970s, as evidenced by the sharp increase in the number of female legislators elected in 2018 and 2020.

Republicans control both houses of the Texas legislature. In 2020 there were 13 Democrats and 18 Republicans in the Texas Senate and 67 Democrats and 83 Republicans in the Texas House of Representatives.

Redistricting

redistricting the process of redrawing election districts and redistributing legislative representatives in the Texas House, Texas Senate, and U.S. House; this usually happens every 10 years to reflect shifts in population or in response to legal challenges in existing districts

one-person, one-vote principle the principle that all districts should have roughly equal populations

The Texas legislature is divided into single-member districts, and the makeup of the population in each district—such as how many Republicans or Latinos or wealthy people it includes—has a profound effect on who wins that seat in the legislature. Because of the stakes involved, one of the most controversial and partisan issues in Texas politics is **redistricting**—the redrawing of district lines for the Texas House, the Texas Senate, and the U.S. House of Representatives, which must be done at least every 10 years, after the federal census.

Each of the newly drawn districts for the Texas House must now contain an almost equal number of people, as must each of those for the Texas Senate. That requirement guarantees that each person's vote counts the same whether the vote is cast in Houston, Big Lake, El Paso, Presidio, Brownsville, or Commerce. For much of the first half of the twentieth century, Texas and other states failed to draw new boundaries for their legislative districts, and even when Texas finally did so, it was not done willingly. Not until the U.S. Supreme Court's decisions in *Baker v. Carr* (1962) and *Reynolds v. Sims* (1964), compelling the legislature to draw new districts, were boundaries drawn that represented the population fairly.[5] These and subsequent decisions meant that Texas had to draw legislative districts of roughly equal populations—a concept known as the **one-person, one-vote principle**. This principle was eventually challenged in a Supreme Court case emanating from Texas (*Evenwel v. Abbott*) in which two Texas residents sued, claiming that districts should be drawn based on registered or eligible voters rather than total population, the standard used by the state. The plaintiffs argued that their votes were unfairly diluted because they lived in a state legislative district with a smaller proportion of nonvoting residents, compared with districts containing many prisoners, felons, and/or immigrants ineligible to vote. The Court disagreed, siding with the state's argument that the historical practice of using total population to draw legislative districts was consistent with the Constitution.

Congressional redistricting is also a responsibility of the legislature. Once the U.S. Census prescribes how many seats each state is entitled to in the U.S. House of Representatives, the Texas legislature divides Texas into the appropriate number of congressional districts. According to the 1964 Supreme Court case *Wesberry v. Sanders*, each state's U.S. House districts must be roughly equal in population.[6] Depending on how the districts are drawn, the representation of the two political parties in the U.S. House can be significantly changed. Indeed, redistricting can so change the division of the parties that control of the House can be affected. Thus, maneuvering over redistricting is highly partisan.

If the legislature fails to redistrict at the first regular session after the census, the task falls to the Legislative Redistricting Board (LRB). The LRB has five members: the lieutenant governor, the Speaker of the House, the attorney general, the commissioner of the General Land Office, and the comptroller of public

In 2006 the U.S. Supreme Court upheld most of the new boundaries drawn in Republicans' controversial redistricting but found that some of the redrawn districts failed to protect minority voting rights. Here, former governor Perry displays the new redistricting map. The new map drawn by Republicans after the 2010 census again went to federal courts.

Who Are the Members of the Texas Legislature?

The Texas legislature is designed to be a representative body, which looks and sounds like the state as a whole. How well does the legislature represent Texas? In many ways, the legislature does not look like Texas. The state is evenly split between men and women, while the legislature is three-quarters male. While the state has no ethnic majority in its population, more than two-thirds of Texas legislators are White. Perhaps the biggest differences, though, relate to socioeconomic status. Over half of the members of the legislature hold graduate degrees, while only 9 percent of the population does.

Gender

	Texas pop.	Texas House	Texas Senate
Female	50%	21%	29%
Male	50%	79%	71%

Race

	Texas pop.	Texas House	Texas Senate
White	43%	64%	70%
African American	13%	13%	7%
Latino	39%	21%	23%
Asian	5%	2%	0%

Education*

	Texas pop.	Texas House	Texas Senate
< HS diploma	19%	0%	0%
High school grad.	48%	7%	3%
Associate's degree	17%	3%	0%
Bachelor's degree	7%	53%	39%
Graduate degree	9%	37%	58%

Occupation*

- Business
- Attorney
- Community service
- Health care
- Education
- Other

Texas House

- 35%
- 30%
- 5%
- 25%
- 4%
- 1%

Texas Senate

- 39%
- 23%
- 13%
- 23%
- 3%

* Education and occupation data are from the 2015 session of the Texas legislature.

Key

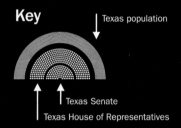

Texas population

Texas Senate

Texas House of Representatives

SOURCES: For Texas legislature, numbers calculated by author based on data from the Directory of Elected Officials of the Texas Tribune, www.texastribune.org/directory. State demographic data calculated from the U.S. Census Bureau American Community Survey, www.census.gov (accessed 11/10/18).

QUANTITATIVE REASONING

- How much do you think the racial, gender, and socio-economic makeup of the Texas legislature matters to the type of laws that the legislature passes? If the legislature had more people of color, more women, or more middle-class members, would it pass different policies?

- Why do you think that members of the Texas legislature come from the more educated, higher socioeconomic groups? Does the structure of the Texas legislature encourage or discourage people from particular occupations to run?

accounts. When the legislature adjourns without redistricting, the LRB convenes. The LRB must meet within 90 days of legislative adjournment and complete its responsibilities within another 60 days.

Texas redistricting plans must comply with the federal Voting Rights Act, although the U.S. Supreme Court has recently weakened that law. A federal court can temporarily redraw district lines if a redistricting violates this law by disadvantaging minority voters.

Power and Partisanship in the Redistricting Battle

Republican control of the Texas House and Senate beginning in 2002 heralded more than simply a shift to unified party control of the legislature. With the partisan shift came a significant decline in the harmonious, bipartisan spirit that had largely governed the Texas legislature.

This new partisan tension in the legislature rose to a fever pitch in 2003 when Republicans, with the support of their U.S. Congress majority leader, Tom DeLay, sought to alter the Texas congressional districts for partisan advantage. The Republican goal was to increase Republican representation in the Texas congressional delegation and, in so doing, help ensure a continuing Republican majority in the U.S. House of Representatives. The Republican effort was unconventional in that it occurred in midcycle—that is, it was the second redistricting after the 2000 census. As a rule, redistricting occurs only once after each decennial census, although there is no legal requirement that this be the case.

The Republican congressional redistricting plan was not enacted without political turmoil, however. At the end of 2003, 51 Democrats from the state legislature walked out and left the state, where the Texas state police did not have jurisdiction to bring them back to the state capitol. Eventually, the legislature redrew lines but not without resistance from Democrats.

Most notable about the 2004 redistricting was that seven incumbent congressional Democrats were targeted for defeat. For the most part, Republicans were successful in reshaping the partisan composition of the Texas delegation to the U.S. House of Representatives. However, the 2006 election led to Democratic control of the U.S. House and to a Texas congressional delegation with vastly weakened power in Washington because of the loss of key Democrats in the redistricting.[7]

The 2010 census led to another round of redistricting for the Texas legislature and the U.S. House of Representatives. The overwhelmingly Republican legislature designed a redistricting plan strongly favorable to Republicans, but the plan ran afoul of a federal court, which held that it violated minority voting rights. The court ordered a redistricting plan that was more favorable to Democrats. Redistricting has seemingly become a perpetual issue before the Texas legislature, which in 2013 again voted on redistricting for the Texas House, the Texas Senate, and Texas's U.S. congressional districts. The legislature basically accepted the districting done by the federal courts prior to the 2012 elections, although there were legal challenges to the Texas House and the congressional district lines on the grounds that insufficient recognition of minority interests was given in developing the 2012 districts.[8] In June 2018 the U.S. Supreme Court ruled in a

5–4 decision that Texas did not demonstrate intentional discrimination when drawing most legislative districts in 2013. The Court did rule, however, that Texas impermissibly used race as the predominant factor in the creation of one district in the Fort Worth area, and that district would have to be redrawn. The decision did not affect the Court's previous ruling in *Shelby County, Alabama v. Holder* (2013), which effectively eliminated the requirement that Texas had to have its new district lines approved by the Department of Justice. Future courts, however, can and most probably will revisit the drawing of legislative districts in Texas to ensure compliance with federal laws.

Powers of the Legislature

 Outline the legislative and nonlegislative powers of the legislature

The Texas legislature sets public policy by passing bills, but it also supervises the state bureaucracy through the budgetary process and the Sunset Act, an act that provides for the review and, when deemed appropriate, the termination of state agencies. This supervision is achieved using both legislative and nonlegislative powers. Legislative powers consist of passing bills and resolutions. Nonlegislative powers are those functions falling outside the lawmaking function.

Legislative Powers

Bills   Revenue bills must begin in the House of Representatives. All other bills may start in either the House or the Senate. For decades, a **bill** would be introduced in either the House or the Senate and work its way through the legislative process in that chamber before being considered by the other one. A bill introduced in the Senate would have to be passed by the Senate prior to going to the House. Today, it is customary for a bill to be introduced in the House and the same bill, a companion bill, to be introduced in the Senate at the same time. This simultaneous consideration of bills saves time in the legislature.

bill a proposed law that has been sponsored by a member of the legislature and submitted to the clerk of the House or Senate

There are three classifications of bills in the Texas legislature: (1) local bills, (2) special bills, and (3) general bills. **Local bills** affect only units of local government such as a city, a county, special districts, or more than one city in a county. A local bill, for example, might allow a county to create a sports authority such as the Harris County agency overseeing NRG Park or to establish a community college. **Special bills** give individuals or corporations an exemption from state law, and are less common than local bills. The Texas Constitution prohibits special bills for most purposes, since they can invite legal challenges. **General bills** apply to all people and/or property in the state. General bills define criminal behavior; establish standards for divorce, child custody, or bankruptcy; and address other matters affecting people and property throughout the state.

local bill a bill affecting only units of local government, such as a city, county, or special district

special bill a bill that gives an individual or a corporation a special exemption from state law

general bill a bill that applies to all people and/or property in the state

Legislators often introduce bills and sponsor them in order to signal to their constituents that they are working for them and championing issues on their behalf. Claiming

CITIZEN'S GUIDE

Your Role in the Legislature

1 Why getting to know your legislator matters

Every Texan is represented in the state legislature by a state representative and a state senator. These representatives are elected by constituents in legislative districts. State House districts are smaller than state Senate districts, so people from two different state House districts can be represented by the same state senator. It is important that you, as a Texan, know who your legislators are and how what they do affects you. By making your opinions known to your legislators, you can make a difference. In this citizen's guide, we hope to provide you with the information you need to determine why knowing and connecting with your legislators are important and give you a roadmap to get involved.

2 What can you do?

With so much attention to national politics, we often forget that state and local governments have a profound impact on our everyday lives. Decisions about the highways we drive on, the funding that state colleges and universities receive from the state, health care for the state's poor, and elementary and secondary education, just to name a few, are made in Austin by state legislators. As good citizens, then, let's take a few moments to consider the different ways we can try to influence what our state legislators do.

The first thing to do is identify who represents you and what they stand for. You can find who your state legislators are by going to **https://wrm.capitol.texas.gov/home** and entering your address. These days, every legislator has a website, Facebook profile, Instagram feed, or Twitter handle. By following your legislators or exploring their websites, you can usually find out what issues they prioritize and how they have voted on key bills. If they are approaching an election, they may highlight their successes in order to ask for your vote in the next election. Local newspapers and television stations will also report on the legislator's activities, but sometimes this only happens when they do something controversial or, worse yet, unethical.

If a legislator represents you, you are part of that legislator's constituency. If your beliefs align with your legislator's, he or she needs your support and vote to continue in his or her office. If you support what your legislator is doing, take the time to write or email letting the legislator know this. Often, this type of communication can also spur the legislator to more actively fight for an issue if the legislator believes many people in his or her district are passionate about something. If you oppose something the legislator is doing, you have even more reason to write or email your legislator so he or she knows you are watching and will hold him or her accountable in the next election. You may even inspire the legislator to take your opinion into account when the legislator makes his or her next vote on the issue you highlighted in your letter.

3 What do the numbers say?

We know that participation is fairly low in Texas, but how often do Texans participate by voting and engaging with their elected officials? According to a report by the Moody College of Communication at the University of Texas at Austin, only 25 percent of Texans reported having signed a petition.[a] Only 14 percent reported contacting a politician. Even fewer (11 percent) reported donating to a political candidate.

One of the key factors that explains this type of political participation is educational status. Twenty-six percent of individuals with bachelor degrees or higher contacted an elected official at least once a year. However, only 3 percent of individuals with less than a high school diploma contacted an elected official at least once. While these numbers are depressing, the only way to change these statistics is to become active and participate. Participation starts with voting regularly, but it doesn't end there. It involves the kind of active engagement described above. By contacting your legislator, you will stand out as one of the few concerned citizens who take the time to get involved.

Contact an Elected Official at Least Once a Year by Educational Level in Texas

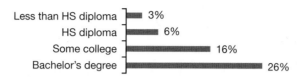

Less than HS diploma	3%
HS diploma	6%
Some college	16%
Bachelor's degree	26%

Frequently Talks about Politics by Educational Level in Texas

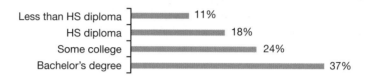

Less than HS diploma	11%
HS diploma	18%
Some college	24%
Bachelor's degree	37%

Other Forms of Political Participation in Texas

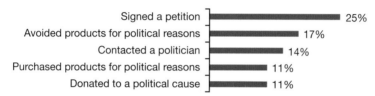

Signed a petition	25%
Avoided products for political reasons	17%
Contacted a politician	14%
Purchased products for political reasons	11%
Donated to a political cause	11%

Communicating Effectively: What Do You Think?

- Why do you think so few people sign petitions, contact their representatives, or donate to political candidates?

- Why do you think educational attainment matters so much for political engagement?

- If you had to come up with a public relations campaign to encourage people to contact their representatives and participate, what would it look like and how would it be designed?

WANT TO LEARN MORE?

It is important for you to get engaged in what happens at the Texas state legislature. You should take the time to find out who your legislators are, research their background, and contact them if you need assistance or want to express your views on public policy. To find out who your state representative and state senator are, check out this website:

- Project Vote Smart
  Votesmart.org

State senator Judith Zaffirini (D-Laredo) is an active sponsor of bills in the legislature.

resolution an expression of opinion on an issue by a legislative body

concurrent resolution a resolution that is of interest to both chambers of the legislature and must pass both the House and Senate and generally be signed by the governor

joint resolution a resolution, commonly a proposed amendment to the Texas Constitution or ratification of an amendment to the U.S. Constitution, that must pass both the House and Senate but that does not require the governor's signature

simple resolution a resolution that concerns only the Texas House or Senate, such as the adoption of a rule or the appointment of an employee, and that does not require the governor's signature

credit for these activities can help representatives get re-elected. There are a few standouts in the legislature in terms of high numbers of bill sponsorships. In the 2019 regular session of the legislature, for example, Senator Judith Zaffirini (D-Laredo) sponsored the most (486 bills). In the House, Representative Ryan Guillen (D–Rio Grande City) sponsored the most (466 bills).[9]

Resolutions There are three types of **resolutions** in the Texas legislature: (1) concurrent resolutions, (2) joint resolutions, and (3) simple resolutions. **Concurrent resolutions** must pass both the House and Senate, and they require the governor's signature. These resolutions involve issues of interest to both chambers. They may request information from a state agency or call on Congress for some action. In the 2019 legislative session, Senate Concurrent Resolution 10, for example, expressed opposition to the enactment or enforcement in Texas of a law that automatically suspends the driver's license of an individual who is convicted of any drug-related offense.

Joint resolutions require passage in both the House and Senate but do not require the governor's signature. The most common use of joint resolutions is to propose amendments to the Texas Constitution or to ratify amendments to the U.S. Constitution. Resolutions that propose amendments to the Texas Constitution require a two-thirds vote of the membership of both houses of the state legislature. Ratification of amendments to the U.S. Constitution requires a majority vote in both the Texas House and Senate.

Simple resolutions concern only the Texas House or the Senate, and they do not require the governor's signature. They are used to adopt rules, to request opinions from the attorney general, to appoint employees to office in the House or Senate, or to honor outstanding achievements by Texas residents. For example, in 2019, Senate resolution 535 by all Republican state senators expressed the sense of the Senate that there is a crisis at the U.S.-Mexico border and urging Congress to pass a budget that funds border security. That same year, HR 2126 by Representative Four Price (R-Amarillo) commemorates Christmas Day on December 25, 2019.

Resolutions of honor or recognition are acted on without debate and without requiring members to read the resolution. Such resolutions are mostly symbolic acts that are designed to promote goodwill with voters. However, at times they can go terribly wrong. A Fort Worth doctor was twice honored by the Texas House of Representatives as the "doctor of the day." It was then reported, to the embarrassment of the House and the legislators who introduced him to the House, that the doctor was a registered sex offender who had been convicted of having a sexual relationship with a 17-year-old female patient.[10]

Nonlegislative Powers

In addition to the power to serve constituents as described above, nonlegislative powers include electoral powers, investigative powers, directive and supervisory powers, and judicial powers. The functions of these powers fall outside the scope of passing bills and resolutions; however, the passage of legislation may be necessary to exercise these powers.

Electoral powers of the legislature consist of formally counting returns in the elections for governor and lieutenant governor. This task is accomplished during a joint session of the legislature when it is organized for the regular session.

Investigative powers can be exercised by the House of Representatives, by the Senate, or jointly by both bodies. The legislature can undertake to investigate problems facing the state, the integrity of a state agency, or almost anything else it wishes. A special investigative committee is established by a simple resolution creating the committee, establishing its jurisdiction, and explaining the need for the investigation. If the special committee is formed in the House, the Speaker appoints the members of the committee. The lieutenant governor appoints members for special committees in the Senate. The Speaker and the lieutenant governor share appointments for a joint investigation.

Directive and supervisory powers enable the legislature to have considerable control over the executive branch of government. Through the passage of the state budget, the legislature determines the size of the appropriation each state agency has to spend for the next two years. The amount of money an agency has determines how well it can carry out its goals and objectives. A review of each agency of state government takes place every 12 years.

Judicial powers include the ability of the House to impeach members of the executive and judicial branches of state government. On **impeachment**, a trial takes place in the Senate. A majority vote of the House is required to bring charges, and a two-thirds vote of senators attending is necessary to convict an individual of the impeachment charges. Unlike the U.S. Constitution, the Texas Constitution does not explicitly define what constitutes an impeachable offense. This determination will be made by the House and Senate in the impeachment process itself.[11] Impeachment is rare in Texas. Governor Jim Ferguson was impeached in 1917, and a state judge was impeached in 1975.[12]

Each body can compel attendance of its members at regular and special sessions. More than once, Texas Rangers have handcuffed absent members and brought them to the legislature. On rare occasions, a chamber punishes nonmembers who disrupt legislative proceedings by imprisoning them for up to 48 hours. Finally, the House and Senate both judge the qualifications of members and can expel a member for cause. For example, either chamber can decide whether to seat members, but this has not been done since the Reconstruction era since it would require overturning the will of the voters in a district.

electoral power the legislature's mandated role in counting returns in the elections for governor and lieutenant governor

investigative power the power, exercised by the House, the Senate, or both chambers jointly, to investigate problems facing the state

directive and supervisory power the legislature's power over the executive branch; for example, the legislature determines the size of appropriations for state agencies

judicial power the power of the House to impeach and of the Senate to convict members of the executive and judicial branches of state government

impeachment according to the Texas Constitution, the formal charge by the House of Representatives that leads to a trial in the Senate and possibly to the removal of a state official

How a Bill Becomes a Law in Texas

 Trace the process through which law is made in Texas

Anyone can write a bill, but only members of the legislature can introduce a bill. Bills may be written by members of the executive branch, by lobbyists, by constituents, or by local governmental entities. Legislators may also write bills, often with the help of legislative staff expert in drafting legislation. Revenue bills must start in the House of

Representatives. Other bills can start in either the House or Senate. Figure 7.1 shows the flow of a bill from the time it is introduced in the Texas House of Representatives to its final passage and submission to the governor. A bill introduced in the Senate would follow the same procedure in reverse. This figure may suggest that the process of how a bill becomes law is long, detailed, and cumbersome. However, when the process is distilled to its basic parts, there are only six steps. For a bill that starts in the House these steps are (1) **introduction**, (2) **referral**, (3) **consideration by standing committee**, and (4) **floor action**. Steps (1) through (4) are repeated in the Senate. Step (5) is action by a **conference committee** and approval by both houses, and finally, step (6) is action by the governor.

Introduction

A legislator introduces a bill by placing copies of it with the clerk of the House. In the Senate, the secretary of the Senate receives the bill. The clerk or secretary numbers the bill and enrolls it by recording its number, title, caption, and sponsor in a ledger. Similar information is entered into a computer.

Rules of the legislature require that the bill be read on three separate occasions. After enrollment, the bill is read for the first time by its number, title, and caption.

Referral

After undergoing first reading, the bill is assigned to a **standing committee** by the Speaker. In the Senate, the lieutenant governor assigns it to a committee. Since committees in the Texas legislature have overlapping jurisdictions, the Speaker and lieutenant governor can assign a bill to either a friendly committee or an unfriendly one. The committee to which a bill is assigned can determine whether the bill survives or dies in committee.

Committee Action

Every bill introduced in the Texas legislature is assigned to a committee, and the vast majority of bills die in committee. The chair of the committee kills most by **pigeonholing**, meaning that the chair sets the bill aside and never brings it before the committee.

Standing committees are considered the "workhorses" of the legislature (see Table 7.2). If the bill does not die in committee, it most likely is amended. Few bills leave the committee in the same form as they arrived. Changes are made to make the bill more acceptable to the entire legislature or to meet the political desires of the leadership or members of the committee. Parts of several bills can also be combined to form a single bill. Hearings can take place to allow experts and the public to educate committee members on the good and bad points of the bill. In the Senate, all bills reported by the committee must have a public hearing.

introduction the first step in the legislative process, during which a member of the legislature drafts a bill and files a copy of it with the clerk of the House or secretary of the Senate

referral the second step in the legislative process, during which a bill is assigned to the appropriate standing committee by the Speaker (for House bills) or the lieutenant governor (for Senate bills)

consideration by standing committee the third step in the legislative process, during which a bill is killed, amended, or heard by a standing committee

floor action the fourth step in the legislative process, during which a bill referred by a standing committee is scheduled for floor debate by the Calendars Committee

conference committee a joint committee created to work out a compromise on House and Senate versions of a piece of legislation

standing committee a permanent committee with the power to propose and write legislation that covers a particular subject, such as finance or agriculture

pigeonholing a step in the legislative process during which a bill is killed by the chair of the standing committee to which it was referred, as a result of his or her setting the bill aside and not bringing it before the committee

TABLE 7.2

Standing Committees of the Texas Senate and House (86th Legislature), 2019

SENATE STANDING COMMITTEES	HOUSE STANDING COMMITTEES	
Administration	Agriculture & Livestock	International Relations & Economic Development
Agriculture	Appropriations	Investments & Financial Services
Business & Commerce	Business & Industry	Judiciary & Civil Jurisprudence
Criminal Justice	Calendars	Land & Resource Management
Education	Corrections	Licensing & Administrative Procedures
Finance	County Affairs	Local & Consent Calendars
Health & Human Services	Criminal Jurisprudence	Natural Resources
Higher Education	Culture, Recreation & Tourism	Pensions, Investments & Financial Services
Intergovernmental Relations	Defense & Veterans' Affairs	Public Education
Natural Resources & Economic Development	Elections	Public Health
Nominations	Energy Resources	Redistricting
Property Tax	Environmental Regulation	Resolutions Calendars
State Affairs	General Investigating	Special Purpose Districts
Transportation	Higher Education	State Affairs
Veteran Affairs & Border Security	Homeland Security & Public Safety	Transportation
Water & Rural Affairs	House Administration	Urban Affairs
	Human Services	Ways & Means
	Insurance	

Floor Action

In the House, bills referred by a standing committee go next to the Calendars Committee, which, after consulting the Speaker, schedules bills for debate. The Speaker determines the length of debate in the House. Customarily, each member is allowed 10 minutes of debate. Early in the session when the agenda is not crowded, debate may last longer. Later in the session when there is a crush of legislative business, debate will be more limited. Some bills will be voted on without debate; however, important or controversial bills are usually allocated adequate time.

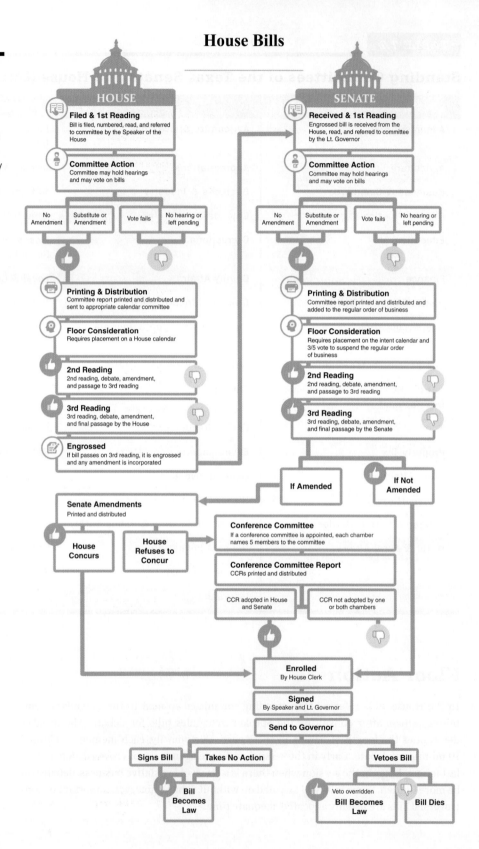

FIGURE 7.1

How a Bill Becomes a Law in Texas

Passing legislation in Texas is a complicated process. There are many points along the way where a bill can die.

House Bills

HOUSE

Filed & 1st Reading
Bill is filed, numbered, read, and referred to committee by the Speaker of the House

Committee Action
Committee may hold hearings and may vote on bills

No Amendment | Substitute or Amendment | Vote fails | No hearing or left pending

Printing & Distribution
Committee report printed and distributed and sent to appropriate calendar committee

Floor Consideration
Requires placement on a House calendar

2nd Reading
2nd reading, debate, amendment, and passage to 3rd reading

3rd Reading
3rd reading, debate, amendment, and final passage by the House

Engrossed
If bill passes on 3rd reading, it is engrossed and any amendment is incorporated

SENATE

Received & 1st Reading
Engrossed bill is received from the House, read, and referred to committee by the Lt. Governor

Committee Action
Committee may hold hearings and may vote on bills

No Amendment | Substitute or Amendment | Vote fails | No hearing or left pending

Printing & Distribution
Committee report printed and distributed and added to the regular order of business

Floor Consideration
Requires placement on the intent calendar and 3/5 vote to suspend the regular order of business

2nd Reading
2nd reading, debate, amendment, and passage to 3rd reading

3rd Reading
3rd reading, debate, amendment, and final passage by the Senate

If Amended | **If Not Amended**

Senate Amendments
Printed and distributed

House Concurs | **House Refuses to Concur**

Conference Committee
If a conference committee is appointed, each chamber names 5 members to the committee

Conference Committee Report
CCRs printed and distributed

CCR adopted in House and Senate | CCR not adopted by one or both chambers

Enrolled
By House Clerk

Signed
By Speaker and Lt. Governor

Send to Governor

Signs Bill | **Takes No Action** | **Vetoes Bill**

Bill Becomes Law

Veto overridden
Bill Becomes Law | **Bill Dies**

Senate Bills

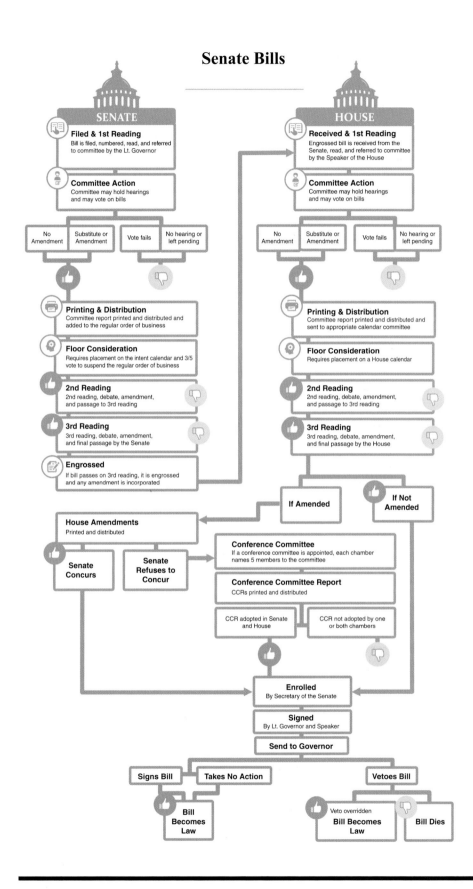

filibuster a tactic used by members of the Senate to try to prevent action on legislation they oppose by continuously holding the floor and speaking until the majority backs down

Debate in the Senate is unlimited, which means it is possible for a senator to **filibuster**. A filibuster occurs when a senator talks for a lengthy period of time in an effort to kill a bill or to obtain amendments or other compromises. There are certain rules that apply to the filibuster in the Texas Senate that are quite different from those in the U.S. Senate. There is no eating or drinking during a filibuster. Senators must stand at their desks and may not lean, sit, or use their desk or chair in any way. Remarks must be confined to the issue under consideration. Finally, one must speak in an audible voice.

Once given the floor, senators have unlimited time to speak as long as they follow Senate rules, and it requires a vote of three-fifths of the Senate to end a filibuster. Since World War II, there have been more than 100 filibusters. The longest was in 1977 by Senator Bill Meier, who spoke for 43 hours. Given the time constraints under which the Texas legislature operates, even the threat of a filibuster may be sufficient to kill or force changes in a bill. In 2013 Senator Wendy Davis became famous nationwide for her nearly 24-hour filibuster against a bill requiring sonograms for women who wanted abortions. She went on to win the 2014 Democratic gubernatorial nomination but lost the general election to Republican Greg Abbott.

Another tactic used in both the House and the Senate to prevent or delay passage of a bill is called "chubbing." Here, one or more members debate bills at length to slow down the legislative process. Like the filibuster, this is a particularly effective tactic as the legislative session draws to a close.

Sponsors of a bill are expected to gather sufficient votes to pass it. In fact, before the Calendars Committee schedules the bill for floor debate, sponsors often assure the committee that they have enough votes for it to pass.

WHAT DO TEXANS THINK?

Approval of the Legislature

Voters across the country think very poorly of the performance of the U.S. Congress. At the same time, members of the Congress are re-elected at very high rates. Voters hate Congress but love their own member of Congress. What about the performance of the Texas legislature? Nearly 30 percent of Texans disapprove of the legislature. For Congress, it is even worse: 58 percent of Texans disapprove of Congress and 21 percent approve. Why do you think the Texas legislature has a higher overall approval rating than Congress among Texans?

DO YOU APPROVE OR DISAPPROVE OF THE TEXAS LEGISLATURE'S JOB PERFORMANCE?	
Approve strongly	8%
Approve somewhat	30
Neither approve nor disapprove	22
Disapprove somewhat	16
Disapprove strongly	13
Don't know	11

DO YOU APPROVE OR DISAPPROVE OF THE U.S. CONGRESS'S JOB PERFORMANCE?	
Approve strongly	7%
Approve somewhat	14
Neither approve nor disapprove	18
Disapprove somewhat	23
Disapprove strongly	35
Don't know	4

SOURCE: *Texas Tribune* UT Poll, June 2019 for Texas legislature and October 2019 for Congress.

Often, the governor, lieutenant governor, and Speaker of the House must be coordinated in proposing and approving legislation. Here, Lieutenant Governor Dan Patrick, Governor Greg Abbott, and former speaker Dennis Bonnen discuss tax reform in Texas during the 2019 legislative session.

The Senate has limited time to consider bills, so the order of bills is important. The "regular order of business" is that bills are considered in the order they come out of committee. However, on highly salient issues, the Senate can suspend the rule and fast-track consideration of a bill. In the past, this rule could only be suspended if two-thirds of the Senate agreed. This made it difficult to pass controversial legislation because it meant that essentially two-thirds of the Senate would have to agree in order for a bill to proceed. Recently this has meant that Democrats (the minority party) could essentially block legislation they did not approve of. Lieutenant Governor Patrick changed this rule when he became lieutenant governor in 2015. Now a simple majority has to approve suspending the rule, thereby speeding legislation to the Senate floor.

Conference Committee

Bills must pass the House and Senate in exactly the same form. If their versions of the bill are different in any way, it is sent to a conference committee. Conference committees have 10 members: 5 members from the House appointed by the Speaker, and 5 members from the Senate appointed by the lieutenant governor. Senate rules require that the latter group must include 2 members of the standing committee that considered the bill. Unless specifically instructed, the conference committee cannot change parts of the bill that are the same in both the House and the Senate versions. Changes are made and compromises reached only on parts that differ.

Once a compromise is reached, the report of the conference committee goes to the House and Senate. It can be debated in each chamber but cannot be changed. It must be either accepted or rejected as is. If either chamber fails to approve the report, the bill is dead. Although it is possible for the conference committee to try a second time to reach a compromise, it is unusual for conference committees to do so.

Before a law is passed in Texas, it is voted on by the two chambers of the legislature—the House and the Senate. Raising one finger means "yes" and raising two fingers means "no."

veto according to the Texas Constitution, the governor's power to turn down legislation; can be overridden by a two-thirds vote of both the House and Senate

post-adjournment veto a veto of a bill that occurs after the legislature adjourns, thus preventing the legislature from overriding it

line-item veto the power of the executive to veto specific provisions (lines) of an appropriations bill passed by the legislature

If the report is accepted in both chambers of the legislature, a final copy of the bill is prepared. The Speaker of the House, the clerk of the House, the president of the Senate (lieutenant governor), and the secretary of the Senate sign the bill. Signatures of the Speaker and lieutenant governor are required by Article 3, Section 38, of the Texas Constitution. The next stop is the governor's desk.

The Governor

It is the governor's responsibility to sign or **veto** legislation. During the first 130 days of a regular session, the governor has 10 days from the time a bill arrives on his or her desk to sign or veto the legislation. If the governor neither signs nor vetoes the bill in the 10 days, it becomes law without the governor's signature. In the last 10 days of a session, the governor has 20 days from the time the bill arrives on his or her desk to sign or veto the legislation. Again, if the governor does neither, it becomes law without the governor's signature. The U.S. president may sometimes kill a bill without signing it through what is called a "pocket veto." The Texas governor does not have this power.

The governor's veto can be overridden by a two-thirds vote of both the House and the Senate. Anytime the governor vetoes a bill, he or she attaches a message explaining why it was vetoed. It is then returned to the chamber that originated the bill. If the presiding officer chooses to allow a vote to override the veto, a vote is scheduled. Only two vetoes have been overridden in more than 70 years.

Many bills, including almost all important or controversial ones, arrive on the governor's desk in the last few days of a session. If the governor wants to veto a bill that comes to him or her from day 131 to day 140, the governor simply waits to do so until the legislature has adjourned, after which the veto cannot be overridden. Vetoing legislation after legislative adjournment is called a **post-adjournment veto**, or a strong veto, since the legislature has no opportunity to overturn it. The post-adjournment veto provides the governor with an excellent bargaining tool, since he or she can threaten a veto unless changes are made in a bill. Since George W. Bush's first term as governor in 1995, on average governors have vetoed 42 bills per year, Governor Rick Perry setting the all-time record of 82 vetoes in 2001.

The governor also has a **line-item veto** that allows him or her to sign a bill but draw lines through specific items, deleting them from the bill. Except for the items that the governor has deleted, the bill becomes law. In Texas, the line-item veto applies only to the state's omnibus appropriations bill. Governor Abbott used the line-item veto in 2017 to cut $120 million from the state budget. Some of these cuts included funding to impoverished areas of south Texas known as colonias, as well as funding of environmental programs and a program meant to assist poor Texans in repairing their vehicles if the vehicles failed emissions tests.[13]

Other Ways in Which the Governor Influences Legislation

Message power is the governor's ability to communicate with the legislature. Early in each session, the governor delivers a State of the State message that is similar to the president's

How Representative Is the Texas Legislature Compared with Other States?

	Texas	California	Florida	New York	Ohio
Gender	Female 20% · · · Male 80%	Female 23% · · · Male 77%	Female 26% · · · Male 74%	Female 28% · · · Male 72%	Female 22% · · · Male 78%
Race	Latino 24% · · · African American 10%	Latino 23% · · · African American 8%	Latino 16% · · · African American 16%	Latino 8% · · · African American 15%	Latino 3% · · · African American 14%
Education level*	H.S. diploma 2%; Bachelor's degree 39%; Graduate degree 54%	H.S. diploma 0%; Bachelor's degree 44%; Graduate degree 44%	H.S. diploma 4%; Bachelor's degree 33%; Graduate degree 51%	H.S. diploma 2%; Bachelor's degree 27%; Graduate degree 58%	H.S. diploma 3%; Bachelor's degree 41%; Graduate degree 44%

The Texas legislature is predominately White and male, even though the state population has become more diverse. The Latino and African American populations in Texas combine to form nearly half of the state's residents, although this is not reflected in the legislature. How does Texas compare with other states on the representation of women, minorities, and educational attainment?

CRITICAL THINKING

- How does Texas compare with the other states in the chart regarding the racial and ethnic composition of the legislature? What might explain any differences?

- How representative are the five legislatures presented in terms of educational level? How is Texas similar to or different from the other states in this regard?

* Education level data is from 2016.

SOURCE: National Conference of State Legislators, www.ncsl.org/research/about-state-legislatures (accessed 11/20/18).

State of the Union message. In this address, the governor puts forth a vision for Texas and what legislation will accomplish that vision. In addition, if the governor chooses to submit an executive budget, a letter stating why this budget should be adopted accompanies it. The budget and this letter reveal the governor's priorities for the upcoming legislative session.

Periodically, the governor will visit with legislators to gain their vote on a bill. A personal visit can be persuasive, but increasingly, it is members of the governor's paid staff who are sent on these legislative visits. Like lobbyists for corporations and interest groups, the governor's representatives use their skills to encourage passage of bills the governor favors and to kill bills the governor opposes. However, there is a problem with this practice. The Texas Constitution forbids use of tax dollars to influence the legislature, and the governor's staff is, of course, paid through tax dollars. The governor's representatives avoid this ban by claiming they are simply providing needed information to the legislators.

Additional Players in the Legislative Process

In addition to the legislators and the governor, there are others involved in the lawmaking process. One official, the comptroller of public accounts, has direct involvement in the legislative process, while other players are involved indirectly.

The Comptroller of Public Accounts
The comptroller of public accounts issues revenue estimates to inform the legislature of the amount of money it can spend in the next two years. Texas's operating budgets must balance because the Texas Constitution forbids borrowing money to conduct the daily operations of government. The estimate provided by the comptroller sets the limit on state spending. If the legislature wants to spend more than the comptroller estimates, it must enhance revenue—that is, increase taxes and fees.

The comptroller's estimates can be political in nature. The comptroller can provide a low revenue estimate and tell the legislature that the estimate will remain low until it passes bills the comptroller wants. On passage of those bills, the comptroller can revise the estimate to increase the spending limit and allow the legislature to complete its business.

The Media
The media can determine issues of legislative importance by the selection of stories they cover. If they cover more stories on crime, criminal justice issues will move toward the top of the legislature's agenda. A media focus on corporate fraud, rising homeowners' insurance rates, alcohol-related traffic deaths, or poor performance by Texas public school students will increase legislative attention to these issues.

In mid-2019, the media expressed great interest in the new Speaker Dennis Bonnen and incendiary comments he made while meeting with Michael Quinn Sullivan, a lobbyist for Empower Texans, a conservative interest group in the state. Sullivan secretly recorded his conversation with Bonnen and then released the tape to news outlets, which eventually led to Bonnen's decision to not seek re-election and resign as Speaker at the end of his term due to his negative comments about some of his colleagues.

The media can influence the legislative agenda through the stories that they cover. Accordingly, legislators try to attract media attention that will support their positions. Here, former speaker Dennis Bonnen strikes the gavel to begin the 86th Texas Legislative Session.

The media also inform the public about the issues the legislature is considering and about the job it is doing during the session. Stories portraying the legislature as modern, efficient, and hardworking provide the public with a positive image of the legislature, whereas stories about legislators sleeping at their desks or killing legislation on technicalities provide a negative image.

Legislators also use social media such as Twitter, Facebook, and Instagram to communicate their messages. They advertise their positions and take credit for sponsoring bills. Followers on Twitter or fans on Facebook can then retweet or share legislators' concerns, which in turn helps them set an image for their constituents. While some legislators do their own tweeting or postings, others allow their staffs to update the legislators' social media profiles. As with other forms of communication, though, legislators must be careful not to make mistakes. When state senator Dan Patrick was running for lieutenant governor in 2014, he accidentally tweeted "MARRIAGE= ONE MAN & ONE MAN," shocking supporters who had assumed he was for traditional marriage. Although he quickly deleted the tweet and updated it to "MARRIAGE= ONE MAN & ONE WOMAN," media outlets reported this blunder.

The Courts Federal and state courts influence the legislative agenda because the ability to rule acts of the legislature and actions of state agencies unconstitutional gives courts significant power over issues the legislature addresses. In recent years, subjects of the courts' scrutiny have included the Texas prison system, the state's treatment of patients in state mental hospitals, the funding of public education, and equality of funding for colleges and universities in south Texas. To a remarkable

The public and interest groups may also influence the legislature. During a special session in which the legislature dealt with tax reduction, these Houston-area real estate agents and others demonstrated in favor of property tax relief.

degree, state and federal courts have issued decisions that have forced the Texas legislature to act in areas it would have preferred to avoid—largely because action required a significant expenditure of money.

Lobbyists and Interest Groups During a regular session, roughly 1,800 individuals register as lobbyists and attempt to influence the legislature. As we saw in Chapter 6, a lobbyist's job is to convince legislators to support the interest the lobbyist represents. Lobbyists want legislators' votes on bills. And at the least, they desire access to legislators.

Interest groups in Texas have been actively involved in supporting legislation as well as stopping legislation they do not support. The Texas Association of Business is a very active interest group lobbying legislators to support its agenda of lower taxes and fewer regulations. Its leader, Jeff Moseley, is one of the most influential power brokers in Austin. Other interest groups, such as the Texas Alliance for Life, have been very successful in passing abortion restrictions in the Texas legislature in recent years. Its leader, Joe Pojman, has been a powerful presence lobbying legislators and most recently has led the effort to defund Planned Parenthood from the state budget. Many more interest groups employ lobbyists to influence and educate legislators in Austin as well as in Washington, D.C.

The Public Individuals can influence legislators, who are evaluated at each election. If the people believe their elected officials are representing them well, legislators are re-elected. Legislators who fail to live up to expectations might not be re-elected.

The public can serve as lobbyists. Letters, emails, or telephone calls urging representatives or senators to vote a certain way constitute a lobbying effort. In many instances, the public will write to legislators when the media publicize a particular issue, or an interest group will make it easier for members to write to their legislators. Members of the public can also write legislation but must convince at least one legislator to sponsor it and introduce it for consideration by the legislature.

Some legislators also commission public opinion polls, especially right before an election. While most of the time the purpose is to find out where legislators stand in their districts, some polls ascertain how the public feels on important issues facing the district. The legislator can then choose to emphasize certain issues in the election. If, for example, the legislator does not personally place a high priority on a particular issue such as immigration but polls show a majority of his constituents do, then he may well choose to emphasize this issue in his campaign.

Power and Partisanship in the Legislature

Analyze how party leadership and partisanship affect power in the legislature

Among the most powerful political figures in Texas are the leaders of the House and Senate. They play a key role in structuring the committees of the legislature, setting the state's political agenda, and passing or defeating bills.

Leadership

The **Speaker** of the Texas House of Representatives and the lieutenant governor are two of the most powerful political figures in the state. Republican representative Dade Phelan (R-Beaumont) is the Speaker of the House. Dan Patrick, who in 2014 was first elected **lieutenant governor**, leads the Senate. The Texas House and Senate endow both officials with considerable control over the legislative process. It is fair to say that both of them can usually kill legislation they oppose, and often they have the power to pass legislation they support.

Members of the House elect the Speaker at the beginning of the regular session. At the same time, the members also adopt rules that give the Speaker institutional powers sufficient to control the work of the House. Speakers usually are the dominant figures in the House and wield vast power.

Speaker the chief presiding officer of the House of Representatives; the Speaker is the most important party and House leader, and can influence the legislative agenda, the fate of individual pieces of legislation, and members' positions within the House

lieutenant governor a statewide elected official who is the presiding officer of the Senate; the lieutenant governor is one of the most important officials in state government and has significant control over legislation in the state Senate; the second-highest elected official in the state and president of the state Senate

Dan Patrick has served as lieutenant governor since 2015. In this role, his main responsibility is to preside over the Senate.

One of the most interesting developments in modern times in the Texas legislature was the turmoil surrounding the 2009–17 speakership of Republican Joe Straus. Straus represented the moderate wing of the Republican Party and became Speaker because of moderate Republicans and Democrats coming together to elect him. As Speaker, he worked fairly well with Lieutenant Governor David Dewhurst during his first term, but when the more conservative Dan Patrick was elected lieutenant governor, tensions arose between the two on a variety of issues, especially the sanctuary cities and bathroom bills in 2017. While some more conservative Republicans tried to challenge Straus during his speakership, he retained his seat until announcing his retirement in 2017.

The lieutenant governor is elected statewide to a four-year term. His or her major responsibility is to serve as president of the Senate and to preside over it. Unlike the Speaker, who is a member of the chamber he presides over, the lieutenant governor is not a member of the Senate and may vote only to break a tie.

At the start of each regular session, senators adopt rules that the Senate will follow for the next two years. Article 22 of the Senate Rules requires a vote of two-thirds of the members present to suspend any rule of the Senate unless the rules specify a different majority. The rules also establish the office of president pro tempore of the Senate, who is a member elected by the Senate to perform the duties of the lieutenant governor in his or her absence or disability. These rules also give the lieutenant governor enormous control of the work of the Senate. Among those powers granted to the lieutenant governor under the rules are

- the power to decide all questions about rules on the Senate floor (subject to appeal from members)
- the power to recognize members on the floor (determines who gets to speak)
- the power to break a tie on a particular vote
- the power to refer bills to committees
- the power to appoint members to standing committees, subcommittees, special committees, and conference committees

Centralizing Power: Sources of the Leadership's Power

The operation of the Texas legislature is significantly different from that of the U.S. Congress. In the U.S. Congress, the leader of the president's party in the House or the Senate often works closely with the president and White House staff. Additionally, the level of partisanship is high. Committee appointments are made in such a way that the majority party controls every committee, and chairs of those committees are always members of the majority party. Each house of Congress has majority party leadership and minority party leadership. Such divisions are not as rigid in the Texas legislature, where it is usual for members of the minority party to chair some committees. Selecting someone from the other party to chair a committee would never happen in the U.S. Congress today.

The Texas legislature is not organized along party lines the way the U.S. Congress is. Leadership and power have become centralized in the Speaker and lieutenant governor. Committee assignments and committee chair appointments cross party lines so that in the Texas House, for example, where the majority party is now Republican, a Democrat may chair an important committee and successfully sponsor important legislation. The bipartisan appointment of committee chairs, however, may be a declining tradition. With the retirement of Joe Straus and Dennis Bonnen's short-lived speakership and their respective coalition of Democrats and moderate Republicans, it remains to be seen whether this bipartisan tradition of sharing committee chairs will continue.

Besides the selection of committee chairs, other factors may also come to undermine the state legislature's tradition of nonpartisan politics. Because most of the powers of the Speaker and of the lieutenant governor are granted by the rules that each chamber's membership votes on at the beginning of the legislative session, these powers could potentially be greatly reduced if the members of the legislature so chose. One could, for example, imagine a future Republican Senate that would reduce the powers of the lieutenant governor over the Texas Senate if a Democrat were elected lieutenant governor.

Increasing partisanship led to abandonment of the two-thirds rule for several bills in the Senate in recent years. The redistricting bill in 2003 would have been impossible to pass without this rule change, which allowed passage by simple majority vote. In the 2009 special session of the legislature, the Republican majority in the Texas Senate passed a highly partisan bill that required voters to show identification, an action possible only because the two-thirds rule is not used in special sessions.[14] In 2011 the Texas Senate again abandoned the two-thirds rule, which paved the way for the voter identification bill to become law.

As the Texas Senate has become more partisan, it is not surprising that Lieutenant Governor Patrick was able to successfully change Senate rules to abolish the two-thirds rule altogether in 2015. Republicans did not want to rely on having to lure a single Democratic senator in order to pass their legislation.

The structure of the Texas legislature and the lack of formal lines of gubernatorial authority there are very important in centralizing power in the hands of the Speaker and the lieutenant governor. However, these officials have other important sources of power as well. One of those powers—especially important in the Texas House—is the power of **recognition**. In the House, the Speaker controls legislative debate, including who speaks and how long debate will last. On occasion, the Speaker ignores or skips a member seeking recognition to speak. Lack of recognition is a signal to other members of the House that this individual has fallen from the Speaker's good graces, and the ability to pick and choose among those desiring to speak on the House floor allows the Speaker to structure the debate and to affect the outcome of legislation. The Senate rule allowing unlimited debate decreases the lieutenant governor's power in this area.

recognition the power to control floor debate by recognizing who can speak before the House and the Senate

As mentioned earlier, the Senate has a rule that for votes to be taken on bills, the bills must be taken in order. Given the vast powers of the lieutenant governor, on issues that are important to him, he can usually control the votes of at least one-third of the membership. Thus, if a bill is opposed by the lieutenant governor, he or she can frequently prevent it from being taken out of order for consideration.

Appointment Power
One of the most important duties and sources of power for the Speaker and the lieutenant governor is the power to assign members to standing committees and to appoint chairs of those committees. The committees on which legislators serve are important

PERSONAL RESPONSIBILITY: WHAT WOULD YOU DO?

- Who are the most important leaders in the Texas legislature? What are their powers?

- If you were the Speaker or the lieutenant governor, would you appoint committee chairs from the opposite party? Why or why not? What would be the likely consequences of your decision?

both to individual members and to the presiding officer. For members, assignments to powerful committees increase their prestige in the legislature. Committee assignment also affects how well constituents are represented.

As mentioned earlier, party affiliation and seniority are of only moderate importance in committee assignments. The most important factor is the members' relationships with the presiding officer. To maintain control over the legislature, the Speaker and lieutenant governor use their committee assignment powers to appoint members who are loyal to them and who support their legislative agendas. When chairs and vice chairs of important committees are appointed, usually only the most loyal friends and allies of the Speaker and lieutenant governor are chosen. Speaker Straus stated that one issue important to him when appointing chairs and members of committees was to ensure that the committees "reflect the geographic and demographic diversity of Texas."[15]

At the beginning of every legislative session, members of the House are asked to submit a list of committees on which they would like to serve. The Speaker then assigns committee memberships with consideration given to the members' seniority, their leadership skills, and their interest in particular issues. Chairs and other leadership positions are often given to more senior members with leadership skills and interests in the areas over which their committee has jurisdiction.[16] Straus, a Republican, was initially elected Speaker with Democratic votes in a successful challenge to the leadership of his predecessor, a more conservative speaker. As Table 7.3 shows, former Speaker Straus named Democrats as chairs of standing committees of the House roughly in proportion to their numbers in the House. Of course, some committees are more important than others, but in a purely partisan legislative body, no Democrats would be appointed chair of a committee by a Republican speaker. Dennis Bonnen continued Straus's tradition of naming Democrats as chairs of standing committees during his short term as Speaker.

Unlike the House, the appointment of committee chairs in the Senate has become more partisan, not less, especially during Dan Patrick's tenure as Senate president. In 2013, 7 of the 18 standing committee chairs in the Senate were Democrats, and 13 of the 37 standing committee chairs in the House were Democrats. Nevertheless, like Straus (as Table 7.3 shows), then-Lieutenant Governor Dewhurst maintained a practice of appointing Democrats to chair Senate standing committees roughly in proportion to the number of Democrats overall in the Texas Senate. Since Dan Patrick's election as lieutenant governor, his appointments to Senate committees have all been Republicans.

Not only do the Speaker and the lieutenant governor have vast committee assignment powers, but committees in the Texas legislature also have overlapping jurisdiction. Although each bill must be assigned to a committee, there is more than one committee to which it can be assigned. Since the Speaker and the lieutenant governor assign bills to committees in their respective chambers, they use the bill assignment power to influence the fate of the bill. They can, for example, assign bills they oppose to committees they believe hostile to the bill and those they support to committees they believe will favor the bill.

Since bills must pass the House and Senate in exactly the same form, the Speaker and the lieutenant governor can exercise still another important influence on policy through their power to appoint conference committees. As we have seen, if any differences exist in a bill passed by both the House and the Senate, the bill goes to a conference committee that works out the differences in the House and Senate versions. By appointing the conference committee members, the Speaker and lieutenant governor can affect the language and even the fate of the bill.

TABLE 7.3

Partisanship of Committee Chair Appointments

HOUSE

	2011		2013		2015		2017		2019	
Speaker	Straus		Straus		Straus		Straus		Bonnen	
	DEM.	REP.	DEM.	REP.	DEM.	REP.	DEM.	REP.	DEM.	REP.
Standing committees	11	25	13	24	13	25	13	25	12	22
Select committees	0	3	1	3	1	4	1	3	2	4
Joint committee	0	1	0	1	0	3	0	7	0	3
Democratic House committee chairs (%)	28%		33%		22%		29%		33%	
Democrats in House (%)	33%		37%		34%		37%		45%	

SENATE

	2011		2013*		2015		2017		2019	
Lieutenant governor	Dewhurst		Dewhurst		Patrick		Patrick		Patrick	
	DEM.	REP.	DEM.	REP.	DEM.	REP.	DEM.	REP.	DEM.	REP.
Standing committees	7	12	7	11	2	12	2	12	2	14
Select committees	1	1	0	2	0	4	0	4	0	3
Democratic Senate committee chairs (%)	38%		35%		11%		11%		11%	
Democrats in Senate	39%		37%		35%		35%		39%	

*As a result of the death of a Democratic senator, there were only 30 senators during this session.
SOURCES: Legislative Reference Library and *Texas Tribune*.

Partisan Voting in the Texas Legislature

Between 1876 and 1980, the Democratic Party controlled both houses of the Texas legislature. The last 30 years of the twentieth century saw the growth of the Republican Party in both the House and the Senate, culminating in the Republican seizure of power in both houses in 2004. As conservative Republicans replaced conservative Democrats, particularly from rural and suburban districts, more traditional ideological splits appeared along partisan lines. When Representative Straus initially gained the speakership in 2011 with liberal Democratic and moderate Republican votes, some observers felt that the partisan rhetoric might become muted. As more conservative Republicans were elected

FIGURE 7.2

Ideological Differences in the Texas House of Representatives

Ideological differences between state legislators have grown in recent years. This graphic illustrates how ideology scores of Texas legislators have diverged over time.

SOURCE: Boris Shor and Nolan McCarty, "Aggregate State Legislator Shor-McCarty Ideology Data, May 2016 update," Harvard Dataverse, V1.

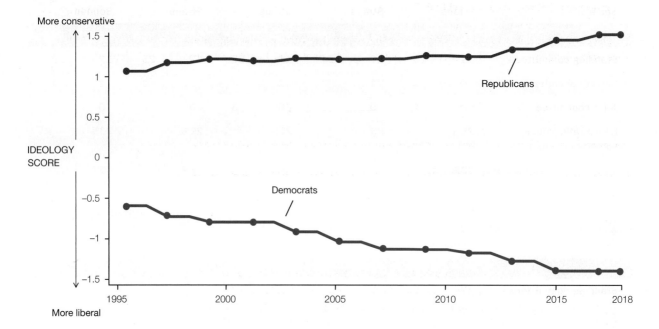

in his second term and moderate Republicans either retired or were defeated, however, partisan divisions appeared with a vengeance. Ideological differences between Democrats and Republicans now play a major role in legislative politics (see Figure 7.2).

It is possible to show the increasing gulf between Democrats and Republicans by using roll-call votes cast by members of the Texas House over time. If one categorizes the votes along the dimension of liberalism–conservatism such that a score of –1.00 is extreme liberal and a score of 1.00 is extreme conservative, the average score of Republicans in the Texas House in 1973 was 0.44. The average score for Democrats was 0.01. In contrast, in 2009 the average Republican score was 0.67, a significant movement toward increased conservatism. Meanwhile, the Democrats in the Texas House became increasingly liberal. In 2009 the Democratic score was –0.34.

Another indication of the partisan gap between Democrats and Republicans in the Texas House is that in 1973, 37 percent of Democratic House members were more conservative than the most liberal Republican in the House. Since 1999 there has been no Democrat in the House who has been more conservative than the most liberal Republican.[17] In a recent study of the 2015 Texas House, political scientist Mark Jones found that every Democrat was more liberal than any Republican.[18] Jones found the same pattern in the Texas Senate.[19] The ideological gap between Democrats and Republicans makes it harder to find common ground across party lines and produce a policy consensus. In that sense, the Texas legislature is becoming more like the U.S. Congress. As sociologist Paul Starr has pointed out regarding Congress,

> Traditionally, political parties in the United States have been broad coalitions that overlapped each other ideologically. The Republicans had included liberals . . . and the Democrats had included conservatives. But by 2009, the ideological alignment of the parties was nearly complete. . . . The growing ideological divergence between the two parties made cooperation between them more difficult.[20]

The pattern Starr saw in the U.S. Congress is now seen in the Texas legislature. With it we are seeing the end of the cooperation between Democrats and Republicans in Austin.

The Legislature and the Future of Texas

THE TEXAS LEGISLATURE has become more and more like the U.S. Congress in terms of political polarization and partisan division. Democrats have chipped away at the Republican margin in the state House, giving their party hope that they may one day retake control. Today, the legislature is still controlled by Republicans, who are themselves internally divided between establishment and Tea Party factions. In November 2017, establishment Republican Speaker Joe Straus (R–San Antonio) shocked the Texas political world by announcing he would not seek re-election to the House. His retirement delighted some conservative Republicans in the House such as Matt Rinaldi, who called Straus a "terrible Speaker . . . almost totalitarian. He silenced the voices of the majority in the House."[21] To the chagrin of the more conservative members, Representative Dennis Bonnen, R-Angleton, assembled a bipartisan coalition to become speaker in 2019, but his speakership was cut short due to the release of a recording of him making disparaging comments about many of his colleagues. A Tea Party speaker would have heralded a more conservative direction in the House as well as the elimination of the little bipartisanship that exists there, in the form of some Democratic committee chairs and some cooperation that Straus and Bonnen had to employ with Democrats who helped elect them.

The end of the two-thirds rule in the Texas Senate also heralds a new era of partisanship. The rule required members of both parties to work together to pass legislation. Now that only a majority is needed, partisanship and rancor among Texas senators will probably increase.

The Texas legislature seems in some ways an archaic institution. Unless there are special sessions, it meets only once every two years, and it is a part-time body with very limited compensation for its members. The structure of the legislature has survived since the 1876 Constitution, however, and there seems little likelihood that it will soon change. Especially notable regarding the legislature is the vast power held by the Speaker and the lieutenant governor. The 1876 Constitution showed its distrust of a powerful governor, and the result is that in Texas the governor must share political influence with two other major figures over whom the governor exerts no formal control. Still, the discontent exhibited by conservative Republicans against Speakers Straus and Bonnen reminds us that it is perilous for the Speaker to try to exert so much power that he becomes subject to rebuke from a constituency whose views he ultimately must reflect—the views of a majority of the members of the Texas House. With Straus's retirement, a new era in the Texas House was poised to begin under Speaker Bonnen, who in many respects led a legislative session that was remarkably successful, passing legislation to raise teacher salaries, increase education funding, and fund infrastructure after Hurricane Harvey. His resignation left the state House in political limbo in 2019 after the legislative session, with no clear successor in sight at the time. Democrats took advantage of this disarray by fielding more candidates to run in 2020 hoping to flip the House back in time for the all-important redistricting cycle in 2021. However, Republicans maintained control with more or less the same margin and quickly coalesced around Representative Dade Phelan of Beaumont to lead as Speaker in 2021.

Use ⛄ INQUIZITIVE to help you study and master this material.

Structure of the Texas Legislature

- **Describe the organization and basic rules of the legislature (pp. 217–21)**

The Texas legislature is bicameral. The leader of the House is the Speaker, and the lieutenant governor presides over the Texas Senate. Although the typical member of the legislature is White and male, women and minorities have increased their representation in recent years. Representatives use social media and other forms of communication to stay in touch with people in their districts.

Key Terms
bicameral (p. 217)
regular session (p. 218)
biennial (p. 218)
special session (p. 218)
per diem (p. 220)
single-member district (p. 220)
constituent (p. 221)
constituent service (p. 221)

Practice Quiz
1. There are ___ members of the Texas Senate, and state senators serve a ___-year term.
   a) 31/4
   b) 100/6
   c) 150/2
   d) 300/6
   e) 435/2

2. Texas House members differ from Texas Senate members because
   a) House members represent smaller districts and are subject to more frequent elections.
   b) House members represent people, and senators represent counties.
   c) House members are elected from single-member districts and senators from multimember districts.
   d) House members have term limits, and senators do not have term limits.
   e) House members must live in the state for 10 years before standing for election, and senators do not have a residency requirement.

3. The Texas legislature meets in regular session
   a) 90 days every year.
   b) 180 days every year.
   c) 140 days each odd-numbered year and 60 days each even-numbered year.
   d) 140 days each odd-numbered year.
   e) 180 days each even-numbered year.

4. The agenda for a special session of the Texas legislature is set by the
   a) lieutenant governor and the Speaker of the House.
   b) governor.
   c) Texas Supreme Court.
   d) chair of the joint committee on special sessions.
   e) agenda-setting committee.

Redistricting

- **Explain representation and the politics of redistricting (pp. 222–25)**

One of the most partisan activities of the legislature involves redrawing of district lines for the Texas House of Representatives and the Texas Senate. New districts must be drawn at least every 10 years to reflect changes in the population of the state. This process of redistricting provides the opportunities for the dominant political party to create districts for their partisan advantage. While there are some legal and constitutional restrictions on redistricting, generally as long as the districts reflect equal populations and racial or ethnic minorities are not disadvantaged, legislators have great freedom in drawing district boundaries.

Key Terms

redistricting (p. 222)
one-person, one-vote principle (p. 222)

Practice Quiz

5. An important issue for the legislature at least every 10 years is
   a) adopting a budget.
   b) deciding the order of succession to the office of governor.
   c) impeaching the lieutenant governor.
   d) redistricting.
   e) electing the president.

6. Legislative districts in Texas
   a) are created by a nonpartisan commission.
   b) are designed to benefit partisan interests.
   c) are voted on in a special election.
   d) are created in a cooperative effort between the two parties.
   e) are designed by the Center for Legislative Districts every 10 years.

Powers of the Legislature

- Outline the legislative and nonlegislative powers of the legislature (pp. 225–29)

The Texas legislature passes bills and resolutions and supervises the state bureaucracy through the budgetary process and sunset legislation.

Key Terms

bill (p. 225)
local bill (p. 225)
special bill (p. 225)
general bill (p. 225)
resolution (p. 228)
concurrent resolution (p. 228)
joint resolution (p. 228)
simple resolution (p. 228)
electoral power (p. 229)
investigative power (p. 229)
directive and supervisory power (p. 229)
judicial power (p. 229)
impeachment (p. 229)

Practice Quiz

7. The Texas legislature does not pass this type of bill or resolution:
   a) local bill.
   b) special bill.
   c) joint resolution.
   d) concurrent resolution.
   e) holiday resolution.

8. Texas legislators do not
   a) provide assistance to constituents.
   b) investigate wrongdoing by federal agencies.
   c) investigate wrongdoing in state agencies.
   d) pass bills and resolutions.
   e) count election returns for governor and lieutenant governor.

How a Bill Becomes a Law in Texas

- Trace the process through which law is made in Texas (pp. 229–40)

The process of a how a bill becomes a law is similar to that at the federal level. A key difference is the governor's use of the line-item veto by which the governor can eliminate individual appropriations or line items in the state budget. Additionally, the lieutenant governor and the Speaker of the Texas House have exceptionally strong powers. The committee system plays a major role in shaping the legislative process.

Key Terms

introduction (p. 230)
referral (p. 230)
consideration by standing committee (p. 230)
floor action (p. 230)
conference committee (p. 230)
standing committee (p. 230)

pigeonholing (p. 230)
filibuster (p. 234)
veto (p. 236)
post-adjournment veto (p. 236)
line-item veto (p. 236)

Practice Quiz

9. If a bill fails to pass the Texas House and Texas Senate in exactly the same form, the bill
   a) dies.
   b) is returned to the standing committee in the House or Senate that originally considered the bill.
   c) is sent to a conference committee.
   d) is sent to the governor, who decides which version of the bill will be signed.
   e) becomes a law.

10. The ___ provides the governor a powerful tool with which to bargain with the legislature.
   a) ability to introduce five bills in a regular session
   b) post-adjournment veto
   c) pocket veto
   d) message power
   e) initiative

11. Which state official, in large part, determines the total amount of money the legislature may appropriate?
   a) governor
   b) lieutenant governor
   c) treasurer
   d) comptroller of public accounts
   e) attorney general

Power and Partisanship in the Legislature

- **Analyze how party leadership and partisanship affect power in the legislature (pp. 241–47)**

The Speaker of the House and the lieutenant governor are the most important actors in the legislature. Together they help to centralize power in the legislature, and they facilitate or prevent the passage of legislation. The legislature has become increasingly partisan.

Key Terms
Speaker (p. 241)
lieutenant governor (p. 241)
recognition (p. 243)

Practice Quiz

12. The two most powerful political figures in the Texas legislature are the
   a) governor and the lieutenant governor.
   b) governor and the attorney general.
   c) Speaker of the House and the governor.
   d) Speaker of the House and the lieutenant governor.
   e) chairs of the finance committee in each house.

13. The Speaker of the Texas House is chosen
   a) in a statewide election.
   b) in a party-line vote by members of the Texas House.
   c) by a majority of the members of the House, whether Democrat or Republican.
   d) by seniority in the House.
   e) by lot.

14. The lieutenant governor is the presiding officer of
   a) the Texas Senate.
   b) the governor's cabinet.
   c) the Texas legislature.
   d) the Legislative Conference committees.
   e) the treasury.

15. The chairs of the Texas House committees are
   a) of the same party as the Speaker.
   b) selected on the basis of seniority.
   c) chosen because of their experience.
   d) both Democrats and Republicans.
   e) independents.

16. The ability of the lieutenant governor and the Speaker of the House to control the final outcome of legislation comes from their power to
   a) appoint members of conference committees.
   b) refuse to approve the work of standing committees.
   c) exercise the legislative line-item veto.
   d) change up to three lines in any bill.
   e) control floor debate.

17. In recent years, the Texas legislature has
   a) become more partisan.
   b) become less partisan.
   c) become more experienced in lawmaking.
   d) been more inclined to let the governor make policy.
   e) been more respectful of county officials.

In 2019, Governor Greg Abbott named longtime adviser David Whitley as Texas's secretary of state. After Whitley uncovered what he believed to be a voter fraud scandal, which was proven otherwise, his confirmation was blocked by Democrats in the Texas Senate.

The Executive Branch

WHY THE EXECUTIVE BRANCH MATTERS Texas has multiple centers of power in its executive branch, each with its own independent power base. Some of these positions, like the governor, are highly visible, and others, like the land commissioner, are obscure. The multiple executive offices reflect the concern of the framers of Texas's 1876 Constitution that power should be dispersed among a number of executive officials. Reflecting this goal, all but one executive official in Texas is elected. The only exception is the secretary of state, who is appointed by the governor with the consent of two-thirds of the state Senate. Generally, the position is an uncontroversial one where the secretary of state is a "glorified keeper of certain state records." However, Governor Abbott's appointment of his close friend and former staffer David Whitley showed that even the Texas secretary of state has considerable power, and when that power is used incompetently, the result is a political fiasco.

After Whitley took office but prior to his being confirmed by the state Senate, Whitley's staff issued a press release that questioned the citizenship of 95,000 Texas voters. Whitley proceeded to turn over a list of these people to Texas attorney general Ken Paxton, who has the authority to prosecute illegal voting as felonies. It initially appeared to be a major political coup. After Whitley's press release, President Trump tweeted about the number of illegal votes in Texas and added, "Voter fraud is rampant." Ken Paxton tweeted a "Voter Fraud Alert," and Governor Abbott thanked Paxton and Whitley "for uncovering and investigating this illegal voter registration." It appeared that Whitley had uncovered the most pervasive voter fraud in the nation. Quickly, however, reality set in.

Whitley's list of 95,000 voters was obtained by merging voter registration records with Texas Department of Public Safety records that showed people had used documentation such as green cards or work visas to obtain drivers' licenses or state ID cards. Use of such documentation indicated that the applicants were not citizens. However, licenses do not have to be renewed for several years, and Texans are not required to notify the Department of Public Safety when they become naturalized citizens. Many of the people on Whitley's list could have been noncitizens when they applied for drivers' licenses and then became naturalized citizens and legally voted. There was still another problem with the data: the secretary of state's office included in its list people who had submitted their voting registration applications at Department of Public

Safety offices where they had been confirmed as citizens. In Harris County, that meant that 60 percent of the voters on the list should not have been.[1]

Civil rights groups and the Mexican American Legislative Caucus questioned whether the secretary of state knew that naturalized citizens were on the list and asserted that this was an effort at voter suppression. The League of United Latin American Citizens sued, claiming Whitley was trying to intimidate registered voters. It was not long before Whitley's actions faced challenges in three federal lawsuits and one federal judge halted the citizenship review of people on Whitley's list amid concerns that naturalized citizens were being targeted. To end the lawsuits, the secretary of state agreed to stop the citizenship review of voters, and Texans were left owing $450,000 in costs and attorney fees to the naturalized citizens and civil rights groups who had sued.[2]

Whitley's confirmation became a highly partisan issue in the state Senate, where Democrats opposed Whitley and Republicans supported him. Abbott made every effort to get his friend confirmed, even calling several Democrats in the Senate individually to his office to try to change their votes. The day before the end of the legislative session, the Senate Republican Caucus chair, Paul Bettencourt (Houston), asked Democratic senator José Rodríguez (El Paso) if Whitley's confirmation could receive a vote with no questions or speeches. Rodriguez replied that the Democrats had pages of questions and would delay for hours, effectively killing bills that needed votes at the end of the session. It was clear Whitley would not be confirmed, and he resigned as secretary of state.[3]

Abbott let the Democrats know that their opposition to Whitley had angered him. Minutes before the session ended, Abbott notified the Senate that he had vetoed four uncontroversial bills that had bipartisan support but which were promoted by several of the Democrats who had opposed Whitley.[4]

As it turned out, things worked out for Whitley. Abbott hired him in a staff position at a salary of $205,000 a year (more than the secretary of state's salary)[5] for a job that did not require senate confirmation. From that position, Whitley moved on to a position in lobbying.

Whitley's tenure as secretary of state tells us that even a Texas executive office in which duties are mostly routine administrative tasks has responsibilities that have far-reaching consequences. An error, even by a relatively obscure officer, can do harm to Texans, lead to major and expensive litigation, cause the officer to lose his job, and bring embarrassment to the governor.

CHAPTERGOALS

- Describe the powers of the Texas governor and the limits of the governor's power (pp. 255–71)
- Identify the other elected officials who make up Texas's plural executive (pp. 271–80)
- Explain the roles played by boards, commissions, and regulatory agencies (pp. 280–88)

The Governor

Describe the powers of the Texas governor and the limits of the governor's power

At the national level, the president represents and is responsible to the American people as a whole. The president is the spokesperson for the government and the people in national and international affairs. Throughout the twentieth century, various presidents expanded the powers granted them by the U.S. Constitution into what some commentators call the "imperial presidency." The governorship in Texas is not nearly as powerful. In fact, executive power in Texas is divided among a number of separately elected officials, all of whom are elected by and responsible to the people as a whole. This plural executive has important implications for political life in the Lone Star State.

Texas scores below average on a scale that compares the institutional power of its governor with that of governors in other states. In a study by political scientist Margaret Ferguson, Texas tied with one other state for a ranking of 41st among the states in the overall institutional powers of the governor.[6] The *2019 Book of the States* examined the formal powers of the office of governors throughout the United States and noted that the Texas governor, unlike governors of 27 states, has to share responsibility with others for budget making. The Texas governor, as do governors in 34 other states, has the **line-item veto** for the amounts in appropriations bills. Unlike in 23 other states, Texas governors do not have the power to line-item veto the language of appropriations bills. Texas governors do have considerable power to have their vetoes upheld by the legislature, since a supermajority of two-thirds of each house is required to override a veto. But Texas is one of only 15 states where the governor cannot reorganize government without approval of the legislature.

To understand the restrictions placed on the office, it is necessary to remember that the Constitution of 1876 was a reaction to the Reconstruction government that existed in Texas following the Civil War. During Reconstruction, the governor was very powerful, and many Texans regarded state government as oppressive and corrupt. When a new constitution was drafted at the end of the Reconstruction era, Texans did their best to ensure that no state official had extensive power. The Texas Constitution of 1876 placed strict limits on the governor's ability to control the people appointed to office and almost eliminated the possibility that appointees to office could be removed. Power was further fragmented among other officeholders. Each of these officeholders is elected and has separate and distinct responsibilities. Members of major state boards, such as the Railroad Commission and the State Board of Education, are also elected and are largely outside the control of the governor.

Former state representative Brian McCall argues that Texas governors can be quite powerful in spite of the weaknesses of the office that are inherent in the Texas Constitution. He points out that governors can realize many of their goals if they are flexible, have a vision of what they want to accomplish, and are willing to motivate others to achieve that vision and work cooperatively with the legislature. McCall notes that when former governor Allan Shivers was asked about the weak governorship of Texas, he responded, "I never thought it was weak. I had all the power I needed."[7]

line-item veto the power of the executive to veto specific provisions (lines) of an appropriations bill passed by the legislature

George W. Bush was governor of Texas from 1995 until he was elected president of the United States in 2000. Here, Bush is seen campaigning for re-election as governor in 1998. Like Rick Perry, Bush was able to achieve a number of his political goals as governor, despite the limited powers of the office.

McCall, in stressing that capable individuals could parlay the Texas governorship into a position of power, noted that only the governor has the power to call special sessions of the legislature. The governor can pardon criminals and can permit fugitives to be extradited to other states. The governor appoints people to state governing boards and commissions. Only the governor can declare martial law. Only the governor can veto acts or specific appropriations passed by the legislature. Through the traditional State of the State address delivered at the beginning of every legislative session, the governor can outline his or her priorities for the state and convince others of the importance of those priorities. Finally, the governor can be a major persuasive force in mobilizing interest groups, editorial boards of newspapers, and other opinion leaders to support his or her agenda.

Not all governors have the personal skills to turn the office into a powerful one. However, McCall argues that modern governors such as John Connally, Ann Richards, and George Bush have had the persuasive skills that have enabled them to achieve major political objectives in spite of the constitutional limitations on the powers of the office.[8]

Qualifications

Only three formal constitutional qualifications are required to become governor of Texas. Article 4 of the Texas Constitution requires the governor to (1) be at least 30 years of age, (2) be a U.S. citizen, and (3) have lived in Texas for five years immediately before election. Texas governors have tended to be male, White, conservative, Protestant, middle-aged, and either personally wealthy or with access to wealth, and they have had considerable prior political experience. Although women compose more than 50 percent of the population of the United States and Texas, only two women—Miriam Ferguson (1925–27, 1933–35) and Ann Richards (1991–95)—have served as governor of Texas.

Elected or Appointed Executive Officials?

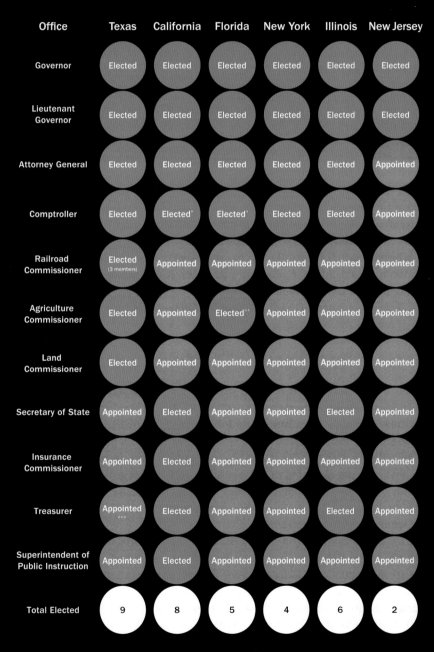

Office	Texas	California	Florida	New York	Illinois	New Jersey
Governor	Elected	Elected	Elected	Elected	Elected	Elected
Lieutenant Governor	Elected	Elected	Elected	Elected	Elected	Elected
Attorney General	Elected	Elected	Elected	Elected	Elected	Appointed
Comptroller	Elected	Elected*	Elected*	Elected	Elected	Appointed
Railroad Commissioner	Elected (3 members)	Appointed	Appointed	Appointed	Appointed	Appointed
Agriculture Commissioner	Elected	Appointed	Elected**	Appointed	Appointed	Appointed
Land Commissioner	Elected	Appointed	Appointed	Appointed	Appointed	Appointed
Secretary of State	Appointed	Elected	Appointed	Appointed	Elected	Appointed
Insurance Commissioner	Appointed	Elected	Appointed	Appointed	Appointed	Appointed
Treasurer	Appointed***	Elected	Appointed	Appointed	Elected	Appointed
Superintendent of Public Instruction	Appointed	Elected	Appointed	Appointed	Appointed	Appointed
Total Elected	9	8	5	4	6	2

Texas elects on a statewide basis a large number of officials who have at least some executive responsibilities. Along with many other states, the large number of statewide elected officials reflects Texas's desire to have a plural executive and to lessen the power of the governor. Most states also elect their lieutenant governor, attorney general (the chief legal officer of the state), and comptroller (the chief financial officer). After those offices, however, there are considerable differences among the executive officers who are appointed and elected.

* In California, the position is called controller, and in Florida, it is chief financial officer.
** In Florida, the position is commissioner of agriculture and consumer services.
*** In Texas, the office of State Treasurer was abolished in 1996.

SOURCE: Calculated from data presented at Ballotpedia.org.

CRITICAL THINKING

- Is there greater accountability to the voters in states with few statewide elected officials such as New Jersey or many such as Texas? Do you think it makes a difference that Texas has an appointed rather than an elected insurance commissioner and superintendent of public instruction?

- Why does Texas have offices such as Railroad Commission of Texas and General Land Office that are unknown in other states?

Rick Perry's (right) 14-year tenure as Texas's governor was the longest in the state's history. Greg Abbott has served as governor since 2015.

Access to money is important because a campaign for the Texas governorship can cost tens of millions of dollars. The 2010 gubernatorial campaign set a record, costing about $91 million when all primary and general election candidates are considered. Sam Kinch, a former editor of *Texas Weekly*, has suggested that prior political experience is an important consideration in selecting a governor. Kinch maintained that although experience may not mean that someone will be a better governor, it does mean he or she is more likely to know how to handle the pressures of the office.[9]

Election and Term of Office

Before 1974, Texas governors served two-year terms, and most were elected to a maximum of two consecutive two-year terms. As Table 8.1 shows, there have been exceptions, such as Coke Stevenson, Price Daniel, and John Connally, who each served for six years, and Allan Shivers, who served for eight years. In 1972, Texas voters adopted a constitutional amendment changing the governor's term to four years. In 1974, Dolph Briscoe was the first governor elected to a four-year term of office. George W. Bush was the first elected for two consecutive four-year terms, although he was elected president before completing the second. His successor, Rick Perry, served from 2000 through 2014, the longest tenure for a Texas governor.

William Clements's victory over John Hill in the gubernatorial campaign of 1978 was the first time since Reconstruction that a Republican won the office. George W. Bush was the second Republican elected governor, in 1994, and his two successors have been Republican as well.

Gubernatorial elections are held in off-years (years in which a president is not elected) to minimize the effect of presidential elections on the selection of the Texas governor. The Texas legislature, controlled at the time by Democrats, designed the off-year system to eliminate the possibility that a popular Republican presidential candi-

TABLE 8.1

Governors of Texas and Their Terms of Office since 1874

Richard Coke	1874–76*	Miriam Ferguson	1933–35
Richard B. Hubbard	1876–79	James V. Allred	1935–39
Oran M. Roberts	1879–83	W. Lee O'Daniel	1939–41*
John Ireland	1883–87	Coke Stevenson	1941–47
Lawrence S. Ross	1887–91	Beauford H. Jester	1947–49**
James S. Hogg	1891–95	Allan Shivers	1949–57
Charles A. Culberson	1895–99	Price Daniel	1957–63
Joseph D. Sayers	1899–1903	John Connally	1963–69
S. W. T. Lanham	1903–07	Preston Smith	1969–73
Thomas M. Campbell	1907–11	Dolph Briscoe	1973–79†
Oscar B. Colquitt	1911–15	William Clements	1979–83
James E. Ferguson	1915–17***	Mark White	1983–87
William P. Hobby	1917–21	William Clements	1987–91
Pat M. Neff	1921–25	Ann Richards	1991–95
Miriam Ferguson	1925–27	George W. Bush	1995–2000††
Dan Moody	1927–31	Rick Perry	2000–2015
Ross Sterling	1931–33	Greg Abbott	2015–

*Resigned to become U.S. senator.
**Died in office.
***Impeached.
†Term changed to four years with the 1974 general election.
††Resigned to become president of the United States.
SOURCE: Texas Legislative Reference Library.

date would bring votes to a Republican candidate for governor. Likewise, party leaders wanted to negate the chances of an unpopular Democratic presidential candidate costing a Democratic gubernatorial candidate votes. Unfortunately, because of this timing, voter turnout in gubernatorial contests is even lower than it is in presidential years.

Campaigns

Just as with campaigns for president, Texas gubernatorial campaigns have become lengthy. For Greg Abbott's second election in November 2018, he announced in July 2017 that he would run for governor, and even before that he was amassing campaign funds. Successful candidates must win their party's primary election in March. They then

Public debates give Texans the chance to see gubernatorial candidates face off over key campaign issues. In September 2018, Lupe Valdez and Greg Abbott held their first debate in Austin.

continue campaigning until the November general election. Successful candidates spend thousands of hours and millions of dollars campaigning. The money goes for staff salaries, travel, opinion polls, telephone banks, direct mailings, and advertisements in print, television, radio, and digital media.

By the time Abbott announced his campaign for re-election, he already had a campaign treasury of $40 million. In contrast, Democrats had a difficult time fielding a serious candidate against Abbott, who looked unbeatable. Finally, on December 6, 2017, Dallas County sheriff Lupe Valdez announced her candidacy. Valdez was one of most visible Democratic candidates, but by modern Texas gubernatorial standards she had a very late start in fund-raising and in the campaign. Abbott was reelected in 2018, winning by 13.3 percent over Valdez.

Removal of a Governor

impeachment the formal charge by the House of Representatives that leads to a trial in the Senate and the possible removal of a state official

In Texas, the only constitutional method of removing a governor from office is by **impeachment** and conviction. "To impeach" means to accuse or to indict, and impeachment is similar to a true bill (indictment) by a grand jury. The Texas Constitution notes that the governor may be impeached, but it does not give any grounds for impeachment. Possible justifications for impeachment are failure to perform the duties of governor, gross incompetence, and official misconduct.

The impeachment process in Texas is similar to the process for impeaching a president. Impeachment begins in the Texas House of Representatives. A majority vote of the House is required to impeach or to bring charges. If the House votes for impeachment, the trial takes place in the Texas Senate. One or more members of the House prosecute

Who Elected Governor Greg Abbott in 2018?

Greg Abbott's support was widespread across the state. He had decisive support in nonborder rural counties. His greatest weakness was in border counties and the state's most urban counties.

2018 Election Results, by County

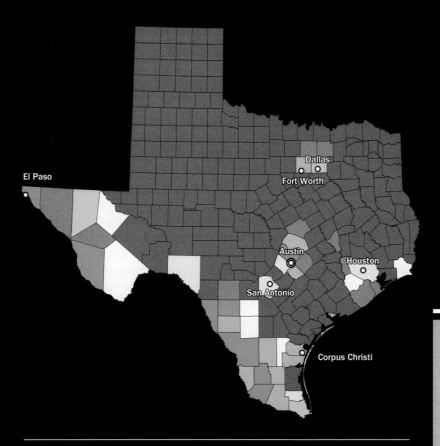

Margin of victory

- \> 30%
- 20–29%
- 10–19%
- 0.1–9%

Greg Abbott (R)

- \> 30%
- 20–29%
- 10–19%
- 0.1–9%

Lupe Valdez (D)

Vote Share

🐘 = Greg Abbott   🐴 = Lupe Valdez

Urban and suburban	46% / 54%
Rural and small town	77% / 23%

SOURCE: Office of the Secretary of State, "2018 Election Night Returns," www.sos.state.tx.us (accessed 11/8/18).

QUANTITATIVE REASONING

- Lupe Valdez's strengths were in the counties along the Mexican border and in urban counties; Abbott was strongest in rural Texas, counties with smaller cities, and suburban counties. What do you think caused the differences in support for Valdez and Abbott?

- Given the election results, which parts of the state are likely to benefit the most form Governor Abbott's policies?

the case, and the chief justice of the supreme court of Texas presides over the trial. A two-thirds vote of the senators present and voting is necessary to convict. If convicted, the governor is removed from office and disqualified from holding any other state office.

Governor James Ferguson was the only Texas governor to be impeached and convicted. He had sought to remove several members of the faculty at the University of Texas at Austin whom he opposed and, when he failed to remove them, he vetoed practically the entire University of Texas legislative appropriation. After these actions led to broader investigations into Ferguson's conduct as governor, the Texas House voted 21 articles of impeachment against him, and the Texas Senate convicted him on 10 articles. Three charges were related to his actions regarding the University of Texas, five to misapplication of funds, one to his failure to enforce banking laws, and one to his secret receipt of $156,500 in cash. After impeachment, Jim Ferguson could no longer run for governor, but his wife, Miriam, ran with the slogan, "Two governors for the price of one." She served two terms as governor—from 1925 to 1927 and from 1933 to 1935.

Succession

The Texas Constitution provides for the lieutenant governor to become governor if the office becomes vacant through impeachment and conviction, death, resignation, or the governor's absence from the state.

In December 2000 a succession occurred when Governor George W. Bush became president-elect of the United States and resigned as governor. Lieutenant Governor Rick Perry immediately took the oath to become governor of Texas. The only time a Texas governor died in office was when Governor Beauford Jester suffered a fatal heart attack on July 11, 1949. Lieutenant Governor Allan Shivers became governor and, like Perry, was able to win later election to that office.

Should the governor leave the bounds of the state, the lieutenant governor becomes acting governor. If the governor is impeached, the lieutenant governor serves as acting governor before and during the trial. While serving as acting governor, the lieutenant governor earns the governor's daily salary, which is far better than the $26 earned as lieutenant governor. (However, a governor who is absent from the state still earns the same daily salary.)

Compensation

The governor's salary is set by the legislature. Texas pays its governor $150,000 annually. In addition to this salary, the governor receives use of an official mansion near the capitol grounds. The governor also receives use of a vehicle and a state-owned aircraft and the services of a personal staff.

Staff

The governor's staff consists of nearly 300 people organized into several divisions. The Executive Office, headed by the chief of staff, has overall responsibility for staff management and has primary contact with the governor. Governor Abbott's chief of staff is

Luis Saenz. Under Saenz's supervision are staff offices that deal with such matters as scheduling for the governor, political matters relating to the first lady, appointments to offices, legislative matters, budget, policy, and constituent communications.[10]

The staff keeps the governor informed about issues and problems facing the state, and it may suggest courses of action. In addition, during a four-year term, a governor makes about 3,000 appointments to various state posts. Since it is impossible for a governor to be acquainted personally with each appointee, some of the staff find qualified individuals for each post and recommend them to the governor. Other staff members track legislation. They talk with legislators, especially key people such as committee chairs, and let the governor know when his or her personal touch might make a difference in the outcome of legislation. For each bill that passes the legislature, a staff member prepares a summary with a recommendation that the governor sign or veto the bill.

Recent governors have used their staffs to make themselves more accessible to the public. Governor Abbott, like his immediate predecessors, encourages this accessibility through the Office of Constituent Communications, which reviews and responds to all communications to the governor.

Executive Powers of the Governor

Appointment Power To a substantial degree, the governor runs the state by appointing persons to supervisory positions over the state bureaucracy. To a great extent, Texas government is run through many boards and commissions, and the governor's power of **appointment** is the most significant executive power. Altogether, the governor makes appointments to over 400 multimember state boards or single-member commissioners that direct the operation of a broad array of state agencies (see Table 8.2). These agencies may be as obscure as the Texas Funeral Service Commission or the State Preservation Board or as well-known as the Public Utility Commission of Texas or the Texas Department of Human Services, but each is important to its constituents. Governor Perry's long tenure allowed him to appoint every board member or commissioner who made policy for state agencies, and through these appointments he was able to exert significant control throughout state government.

The power of appointment enables the governor to exercise the power of **patronage**—rewarding supporters by appointing them to office. An April 2016 report found that roughly a quarter of Governor Abbott's appointees were campaign contributors. That was consistent with the proportion of appointees by Governor Perry who were campaign contributors.[11] Another report in May 2017 found that 71 of the nearly 800 appointees of Governor Abbott had donated a combined total of $8.6 million to Governor Abbott's campaign account since 2013. Top donors received appointments to university boards of regents, to the Higher Education Coordinating Board, and to the Texas Parks and Wildlife Department.[12] Most of these offices pay no salary or small salaries, but they do offer supporters some prestige. The governor can also use the appointment power to repay political favors by appointing friends and associates of legislators to office as well as to garner political IOUs from other politicians.

Most important, a governor can use the appointment power to influence agency policy. Of course, large donors generally share the same views as the governor, so their appointment can also be a way to influence agency policy in the direction sought by the

appointment the power of the chief executive, whether the president of the United States or the governor of a state, to appoint persons to office

patronage the resources available to higher officials, usually opportunities to make political appointments to offices and to confer grants, licenses, or special favors to supporters

TABLE 8.2

The Governor's Appointment Power

The following are examples of some of the entities in Texas, in just four policy areas, where the governor has the power to appoint members. This power can provide the governor with significant influence over policy in these areas.

WATER

Angelina and Neches River Authority, Upper, Lower, and Central Colorado River Authority, Brazos River Authority, Canadian River Compact Commissioner, Board of Pilot Commissioners for Galveston County Ports, Guadalupe-Blanco River Authority, Upper Guadalupe River Authority, Gulf of Mexico Fishery Management Council, Gulf States Marine Fisheries Commission, Lavaca-Navidad River Authority, Nueces River Authority, Red River Authority and Red River Compact Commission, Sabine River Authority and Sabine River Compact Commission, San Antonio River Authority, San Jacinto River Authority, Trinity River Authority, Sulphur River Basin Authority, Western States Water Council, Evergreen Underground Water Conservation District, Drought Preparedness Council

HEALTH

Aging and Disability Services Council, Texas Council on Alzheimer's Disease and Related Disorders, Texas Council on Autism and Pervasive Developmental Disorders, Chronic Kidney Disease Task Force, Texas Council for Developmental Disabilities, Health Professions Council, Oversight Committee of the Cancer Prevention and Research Institute, Council on Cardiovascular Disease and Stroke, Sickle Cell Disease Advisory Committee

LAW ENFORCEMENT

Automobile Burglary and Theft Prevention Authority, Border Security Council, Task Force to Reduce Child Abuse and Neglect, Crime Stoppers Council, Crime Victims' Institute Advisory Council, Texas Board of Criminal Justice, Homeland Security Council, Commission on Jail Standards, Juvenile Justice Advisory Board, Juvenile Probation Commission, Commission on Law Enforcement Officer Standards and Education

PROFESSIONAL LICENSING

Texas Optometry Board, Board of Orthotics and Prosthetics, Board of Nursing, Board of Occupational Therapy Examiners, Board for the Licensure of Professional Medical Physicists, Medical Board, Board of Examiners of Marriage and Family Therapists, Board of Examiners in the Fitting and Dispensing of Hearing Instruments, Board of Podiatric Medical Examiners, Physician Assistant Board, Board of Plumbing Examiners, Board of Physical Therapy Examiners, Board of Pharmacy, Board of Veterinary Medical Examiners, Appraiser Licensing and Certification Board, Board of Architectural Examiners, Board of Chiropractic Examiners, Board of Dental Examiners, State Board of Examiners of Dietitians, State Board for Educator Certification

governor. Sometimes a governor needs to appoint people who are highly competent at solving agency problems whether or not they were large donors. When Abbott talked Chris Traylor out of retirement to chair the Health and Human Services Commission, it was clear that Abbott needed the widely respected Traylor, a former deputy executive commissioner, to lead the troubled commission out of its difficulties involving questionable contracts.[13] To a great degree, the effectiveness of a governor's appointees will determine the governor's success in office.

In some cases, the governor shares appointment power with others. For example, the State Commission on Judicial Conduct, which regulates the ethics and behavior of Texas judges, is governed by a 13-member board. Six of the members, appointed by the Texas Supreme Court, are judges representing various court levels. Two members, appointed by the state bar, are lawyers but non-judges. The governor appoints five citizen members. Some of the entities to which the governor makes appointments are advisory as opposed to policy-making. For example, the governor appoints the three-member Firefighters' Star of Texas Award Advisory Committee, which considers an award for firefighters killed or seriously injured in the line of duty.

Other entities are both advisory and appointed by several different officers. For example, the Oilfield Cleanup Fund Advisory Committee has 10 members. One member is appointed by the lieutenant governor, one by the presiding officer of the Texas House of Representatives committee with primary jurisdiction over energy resources, one by the lieutenant governor from the academic field of geology or economics, one by the Speaker of the Texas House from the field of geology or economics, one by the governor, and one each by the executive officers (or the officers' designees) of the Texas Oil and Gas Association, the Texas Independent Producers and Royalty Owners Association, the Panhandle Producers and Royalty Owners Association, the Permian Basin Producers Association, and the Alliance of Energy Producers. This committee meets with the Railroad Commission about oilfield cleanup issues and reports to the governor, the lieutenant governor, and the Speaker about any problems in the administration of oilfield cleanup funds and about any recommendations for legislation dealing with oilfield cleanup. Oilfield cleanup is not a top priority for most Texans, but it is a vital issue for oil producers and royalty owners. The governor has an appointive role in a number of these rather obscure advisory entities that provide input to state government for specialized issues, including the Nursing Facility Administrators Advisory Committee, the Advisory Committee to the Texas Board of Criminal Justice on Offenders with Medical or Mental Impairments, and the Governor's Advisory Council on Physical Fitness.

The governor also makes appointments to many commissions that have major policy impact. For example, the governor appoints all members to the governing boards of

Josh McGee was a controversial Abbott appointee to chair the State Pension Review Board, since he had been outspoken in his criticism of governmental pensions.

Texas public universities. Additionally, the governor appoints all of the nine members to the Texas Higher Education Coordinating Board, which oversees all public postsecondary education in the state, including determining when public colleges and universities start or continue offering degrees and what core class requirements all students in state colleges or universities must take. Other major agencies for which the governor appoints the leadership are the Parks and Wildlife Commission and the Alcoholic Beverage Commission. Many of the other bodies over which the governor has supervision through the appointment process deal with water (its conservation, use, control, and navigation), health and aging, law enforcement, and professional licensing.

The Senate's Role in Gubernatorial Appointments
The governor appoints people to office, but the Texas Senate must confirm them. However, because the Senate may not be in session for almost two years after an appointment, the appointee takes office immediately and does not wait for Senate confirmation. Nevertheless, the governor cannot ignore how he or she thinks the Senate will react to appointees.

An important limitation on the power of the governor to appoint people to office is the informal requirement that the appointee's state senator must approve. This practice is known as **senatorial courtesy** and applies regardless of the party affiliation of the governor, senator, or appointee. Usually, if the appointee's senator concurs in the appointment, the remainder of the Senate will agree. However, if the appointee's senator opposes the appointment, the remainder of the Senate will also oppose it.

The process for removing an appointee is also complicated. The approval of two-thirds of the Texas Senate is required for a governor to remove one of his or her appointees who refuses to resign. Along with the practice of senatorial courtesy, this complex procedure for the termination of members of boards and commissions can be a significant limitation on the governor's power to influence the policies of state agencies. Chairs of boards, however, serve at the pleasure of the governor and so can easily be removed if they do something that displeases him or her.

Budgetary Power
Officially, the governor is Texas's chief budget officer. As such, governors submit an **executive budget** to the legislature. This budget suggests a plan for revenue and expenditure for Texas, but more important, it indicates the governor's priorities for the state in the next biennium.

In 1949, in an effort to gain more control over the state's budget, the legislature established the Legislative Budget Board (LBB), which is responsible for preparing a **legislative budget**. Thus, two budgets are prepared and submitted to the legislature: an executive budget by the governor and a legislative budget by the LBB. As a creation of the legislature, the LBB's budget proposal receives more consideration by the House and Senate than the governor's recommendations. In 1989, Governor Clements recognized the futility of submitting an executive budget and simply endorsed the recommendations of the LBB. Ann Richards followed Clements's precedent, but Governor Bush took a more active role in budget preparation, and Governor Perry was very involved in dealing with the state's 2011 budgetary shortfall. Governor Abbott also has shown involvement in budgetary policy making.

The governor has some control over the final appropriations bill through the use of the line-item veto. It is possible for the governor to refuse to spend appropriated money or to transfer money from one agency to another if there are unusual circumstances. However, the governor usually must have the approval of the LBB. There is one excep-

senatorial courtesy in Texas, the practice whereby the governor seeks the indication that the senator from the candidate's home district supports the nomination

executive budget the state budget prepared and submitted by the governor to the legislature, which indicates the governor's spending priorities. The executive budget is overshadowed in terms of importance by the legislative budget

legislative budget the state budget that is prepared and submitted by the Legislative Budget Board (LBB) and that is fully considered by the House and Senate

tion to the constraint on gubernatorial power to transfer funds. The governor can declare an emergency and bypass the other legislative members of the LBB. In 2020, Governor Abbott declared an emergency due to COVID-19 and authorized use of all of the state's available resources necessary to cope with the crisis.

Military and Police Power The governor is commander in chief of the state's National Guard units when they are not under presidential orders. These units are headed by the adjutant general, who is appointed by the governor. The governor can declare martial law, which suspends most civil authority and imposes military rule over an area to protect lives and property. Martial law can be declared in the event of a riot, a flood, a hurricane, a tornado, or another disaster.

In Texas, law enforcement and police power are primarily a local responsibility, and the governor has few responsibilities in this area. The governor appoints, with Senate approval, the three-member Public Safety Commission, which directs the work of the Department of Public Safety (DPS). The DPS is responsible for highway traffic enforcement (highway patrol), drivers' licensing, motor vehicle inspection, truck weighing stations, and the Texas Rangers (an elite, highly trained force of about 150 officers with 58 support staff). When circumstances warrant, the governor can assume command of the Rangers. If there is evidence of ongoing violence or corruption, the governor can use informal powers, the prestige of the governor's office, and appeals to the media to compel appropriate action from local law enforcement officials.

In 2015, in what must be the most bizarre use of the governor's military power in modern times, Governor Abbott directed the Texas State Guard to monitor a U.S. military exercise code-named Jade Helm 15. Prodded by conspiracy theories hatched by talk radio hosts, people became convinced the exercise meant a federal takeover of Texas or at least the imposition of martial law and the confiscation of Texans' guns. Abbott received hundreds of letters and emails from people who demanded action from the

The Texas National Guard is instrumental in providing relief and assistance during state emergencies. In 2015, Governor Abbott mysteriously instructed the Texas State Guard to participate in the military exercise Jade Helm, which sparked suspicions and conspiracy theories across Texas and the nation.

governor. The effect of Abbott's order, however, was a strong political backlash from those who thought he disrespected the military and embarrassed himself and the state. Michael Hayden, a former CIA and NSA director, has stated that a Russian misinformation campaign also encouraged the Jade Helm 15 hysteria and that hysteria, coupled with Abbott's response, persuaded the Russians to begin a misinformation campaign in the 2016 elections.[14]

In the wake of protests over the death of George Floyd, a Black man killed in Minneapolis police custody, Governor Abbott activated more than 1,000 members of the Texas National Guard as well as sending state troopers to assist local police departments. He also authorized federal law enforcement officers to perform the duties of state peace officers.

Legislative Powers of the Governor

The governor's legislative powers include message power, the power of the veto, and the authority to call special sessions and set their agendas. If a governor uses these powers effectively, he or she can have considerable control over the state's legislative business.

Message Power Any communication between the governor and the legislature is part of the message power. Early in each regular session, the governor delivers a State of the State message. In this speech to a joint session of the legislature, the governor explains his or her plan for the state in the coming two years. The address, which may propose specific programs or simply set general goals, is covered by most news media and is often broadcast on public television and radio stations, analyzed on blogs, and discussed on social media.

If the governor submits an executive budget, he or she may address the legislature on the important items in the proposed plan of spending and revenue. At the very least, the budget proposal is forwarded to the legislature with a letter briefly explaining it.

Lobbying by governors is another part of the message power. Governors try to pass or defeat bills important to them. For example, in his 2019 State of the State address, Governor Abbott stressed the need to pay teachers more and emphasized the importance of improving school safety. He called for improvements in the provision of mental health services and criticized the growth of property taxes, which he wanted to be restrained. In light of Hurricane Harvey, Abbott called for improvements in disaster response. He wanted a crackdown on criminal gangs as well as human trafficking. He stressed the need to protect the victims of human trafficking as well as ensuring justice for survivors of rape and sexual assault by funding forensic testing of rape kits. Finally, Abbott asked for greater support for veterans.[15]

veto the governor's power to turn down legislation; can be overridden by a two-thirds vote of both the House and Senate

Veto Power Governors of Texas can sign or **veto** legislation, but in most cases they sign it. In his first three legislative sessions, Greg Abbott vetoed 153 bills. Many of the vetoes are of bills that are not of widespread significance. For example, Abbott vetoed a resolution that designated the bowie knife as the official state knife of Texas.[16] Overall Abbott has exercised his veto power in only about 3 percent of the cases in which a bill was presented to the governor for signature.[17] In modern times, vetoes are simply not overridden by the legislature. The state's Legislative Reference Library found that from 1876 to 2013 there had been only 26 legislative overrides of vetoes, and 10 of those occurred in 1941 during the administration of Governor W. Lee (Pappy) O'Daniel. No veto override has occurred since 1979.[18] A veto of a bill after the legislature adjourns is called a **post-adjournment veto** (or strong veto). This veto cannot be overridden, because the legislature that passed the vetoed bill no longer exists.

Texas governors also possess the line-item veto, the ability to veto individual parts of an appropriations bill. To exercise this power, the governor signs the bill but strikes particular lines in it. Items struck from the bill do not become law, but the remainder of the appropriations bill does.

The line-item veto allows the governor considerable control over appropriations to state agencies, and this power can be used to reduce state expenditures or to punish agencies or programs disfavored by the governor.[19] It is one important power of the Texas governor that is not available to the president of the United States. The U.S. Supreme Court has held that a presidential line-item veto violates the principle of separation of powers in the U.S. Constitution.

In the 2017 legislative session, Abbott used the line-item veto to cut about $120 million from the $217 billion two-year state budget. Claiming that the budget already included other funding sources for those living in colonias, Abbott vetoed $860,000 in aid to Texans living there. He cut funding for a legislative law clinic at the University of Texas Law School, for state education employees who study dual-credit programs, and for "safety education" at the Texas Department of Public Safety. Using the attorney general's opinion, which expanded his veto powers by allowing the governor to veto directives to state agencies that were included in the budget but did not actually make an appropriation, Abbott line-item vetoed a number of environmental bills such as $87 million for the Low-Income Vehicle Repair Assistance Program, which he claimed had done little to improve air quality. He also cut $6 million for air quality planning at the Texas Commission on Environmental Quality and $2 million for a study of brackish groundwater.[20] In 2019 Abbott signed the roughly $250 billion state budget with no line-item vetoes.[21]

Special Sessions As we saw in Chapter 7, the governor has the power to call special sessions of the Texas legislature, which may last for no more than 30 days and may consider only those items placed on the agenda by the governor. **Special sessions** are called to address critical problems as defined by the governor. Their nature allows the legislature to focus attention on specific issues.

From 1989 through 2019 the legislature met in 23 special sessions. Among other topics, these sessions considered the complicated and divisive issues of reform of workers' compensation laws, public school finance, reapportionment, and voter identification. The sessions ranged from 30 days to 2 days, with 6 of the sessions occurring in 1989–90 and 5 from 2005 through 2011. In 2013, 3 special sessions were called, 2 lasting 30 days and 1 lasting 7 days.

Judicial Powers of the Governor

Texas elects all of its appellate and district court judges, but when vacancies occur because of the death, resignation, or retirement of judges or because of the creation of new courts, the governor is responsible for appointing people to fill these vacancies. The governor also fills vacancies (before an election) in the office of district attorney. Once

post-adjournment veto a veto of a bill that occurs after the legislature adjourns, thus preventing the legislature from overriding it

special session a legislative session called by the governor that addresses an agenda set by him or her and that lasts no longer than 30 days

Governor Abbott's Job Approval

A June 2020 public opinion poll shows 49 percent of Texas voters approve of Abbott as governor. He has very low approval from Democrats, and 41 percent of independents approve of Abbott. However, Abbott is very strong among Republicans. Given these numbers, do you think he stands a chance of being defeated in a Republican primary? Could he be defeated in a general election?

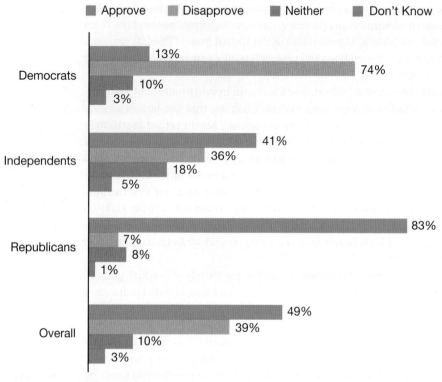

■ Approve ■ Disapprove ■ Neither ■ Don't Know

Democrats
- 13%
- 74%
- 10%
- 3%

Independents
- 41%
- 36%
- 18%
- 5%

Republicans
- 83%
- 7%
- 8%
- 1%

Overall
- 49%
- 39%
- 10%
- 3%

SOURCE: UT/*Texas Tribune* poll.
Note: Data may not add up to 100 percent due to rounding.

appointed to office, judges tend to remain in office. Through this power to appoint judges, the governor has considerable influence over the Texas judicial system.

The governor has limited powers to issue clemencies for people convicted of crimes. Clemency normally includes the power to issue pardons, grant paroles, and issue reprieves. The governor's power in this area is severely limited, however, because of abuses by previous governors. Pardons can be granted only on the recommendation of the Board of Pardons and Paroles. Governors have the ability to grant each person condemned to death one 30-day reprieve. Additional reprieves and any other act of clemency must be recommended by the Board of Pardons and Paroles.

In 2017–20, Governor Abbott issued only 21 total pardons, most for relatively minor offenses. The most surprising act of clemency by Governor Abbott was his 2018 decision to spare Thomas Whitaker from the death penalty. Whitaker had planned the murder of his family with his roommate in order to collect inheritance money. His mother and brother died, and his father was wounded. After the Board of Pardons and Paroles unanimously recommended clemency for Whitaker, Abbott reduced his sentence to life imprisonment less than one hour before Whitaker was scheduled to be executed. There were a number of reasons Abbott, who has presented himself as a law-and-order official, granted clemency to Whitaker. One was that the roommate, who was the person who actually fired the weapon, had received a life sentence; another was that Whitaker waived any right to parole; and Whitaker's father had begged that his son be spared.[22]

The Plural Executive

Identify the other elected officials who make up Texas's plural executive

When Texans drafted a constitution in 1876, they chose to limit executive power and disperse it through several elected officials called the **plural executive**. Texans elect six of the seven people who make up the plural executive: the governor, lieutenant governor, attorney general, comptroller of public accounts, commissioner of the General Land Office, and commissioner of agriculture (see Table 8.3). The governor appoints the seventh person, the secretary of state, as we saw in the story of David Whitley at the beginning of the chapter. With the exception of the commissioner of agriculture, whose office

plural executive an executive branch in which power is fragmented because the election of statewide officeholders is independent of the election of the governor

TABLE 8.3

Elected Officials in Texas with Executive Responsibilities

SINGLE-ELECTED EXECUTIVES	
Governor	Greg Abbott (R)
Lieutenant governor	Dan Patrick (R)
Attorney general	Ken Paxton (R)
Commissioner of the General Land Office	George P. Bush (R)
Agriculture commissioner	Sid Miller (R)
Comptroller	Glenn Hegar (R)
MULTI-MEMBER ELECTED EXECUTIVES	
Railroad Commission (3 members)	
State Board of Education (15 members)	
APPOINTED EXECUTIVES	
Secretary of state	Ruth R. Hughs (R)

is created by statute, these offices are established by Article 4, Section 1, of the Texas Constitution. Except for the lieutenant governor, who receives the same salary as a legislator, salaries of members of the plural executive are set by the legislature.

The Railroad Commission of Texas and the State Board of Education also assume considerable executive authority in the state, although these offices are not formally part of the executive branch established under Article 4 of the Texas Constitution. Instead they were created by the legislature under statutory law authority. This statutory law origin is important because the constitution allows the legislature to decide in both cases how large the commission or board will be, whether its members will be appointed or elected, and how long their terms of office will be. If the legislature wanted to change the way that the Railroad Commission or the Board of Education is selected, all it would have to do is pass a new law. To change the other executive offices' term or authority would demand a constitutional amendment. The ultimate result of all these constitutional nuances is vast fragmentation of responsibility for public policy in the state.

Elections for offices in the plural executive are partisan, and each member of the plural executive may choose to operate independently of the others. At times, the members may be in competition with each other, often because of conflicting personal ambitions. That situation occurred when John Hill was attorney general and sought to take the governorship from Dolph Briscoe, and when Mark White was attorney general and sought the governorship from Bill Clements. Because of the difficulty of defeating incumbents, however, it is far more likely that members of the plural executive will wait for a vacancy in a more prestigious office before seeking that office.

One can get a sense of the importance of the various positions in the plural executive by looking at the campaign contributions received by winning candidates for these offices (Table 8.4). Two things are especially notable about these figures. One is the enormous amounts of money that are contributed to candidates. The Republican candidate for land commissioner, George P. Bush, had over $4.35 million in contributions, a large sum for a rather uncompetitive race for this office. George P. Bush is the son of former

TABLE 8.4

Campaign Contributions in 2018 for Statewide Elective Offices

OFFICE	WINNING CANDIDATE	CONTRIBUTIONS TO WINNER ($)	LOSING CANDIDATE	CONTRIBUTIONS TO LOSER ($)
Governor	Greg Abbott (R)	$78,182,840	Lupe Valdez (D)	$2,043,080
Lieutenant governor	Dan Patrick (R)	31,023,592	Mike Collier (D)	1,535,606
Attorney general	Ken Paxton (R)	12,164,809	Justin Nelson (D)	6,576,343
Comptroller	Glenn Hegar (R)	4,623,450	Joi Chevalier (D)	71,104
Agriculture commissioner	Sid Miller (R)	2,089,413	Kim Olson (D)	479,737
Land commissioner	George P. Bush (R)	4,355,562	Miguel Suazo (D)	225,452
Railroad commissioner*	Christi Craddick (R)	6,138,045	Roman McAllen (D)	39,738

*There was an election for one position on the three-member Railroad Commission.
SOURCE: National Institute on Money in State Politics.

Florida governor and 2016 presidential candidate Jeb Bush, nephew of former president George W. Bush, and grandson of former president George H. W. Bush and is viewed as an up-and-coming Republican star. His family ties may explain Bush's success at fundraising, but it is clear that large sums were given to all the Republican candidates for these offices.

The other thing that stands out about Table 8.4 is how lopsided the contributions are in favor of the Republican candidates. One explanation may be that all the Republican candidates were incumbents and incumbents usually have a fund-raising advantage. Part of the reason for the large sums contributed to Republican candidates may be that some faced primary opposition. That, for example, was the case with the race for land commissioner, in which George P. Bush was opposed by the previous land commissioner, Jerry Patterson. For years, Republican candidates for statewide office have done exceedingly well against Democrats, which probably explains a large part of their fund-raising advantage. The electoral performance of Democrats in the 2018 statewide elections was the best in years, and so the Republican fund-raising advantage over Democrats may decline.

Lieutenant Governor

The **lieutenant governor** has executive responsibilities, such as serving as acting governor when the governor is out of state and succeeding a governor who resigns, is incapacitated, or is impeached. The real power of the office of lieutenant governor, however, is derived from its place in the legislative process.

lieutenant governor the second-highest elected official in the state and president of the state Senate

In 2014, Texans elected conservative state senator Dan Patrick to the powerful position of lieutenant governor. Here, Patrick presides over a session in the Senate that took up a bill to restrict access to abortions.

According to the Texas Constitution, the lieutenant governor is the "Constitutional President of the Senate" and has the right to debate and vote on all issues when the Senate sits as a "Committee of the Whole." The Texas Constitution also grants the lieutenant governor the power to cast a deciding vote in the Senate when there is a tie. Like the Speaker of the House, the lieutenant governor signs all bills and resolutions. The constitution names the lieutenant governor to the Legislative Redistricting Board, a five-member committee that apportions the state into senatorial and house districts if the legislature fails to do so following a census. Other powers of the lieutenant governor are derived from various statutes passed by the legislature. For example, the lieutenant governor is chair of the Legislative Budget Board and a member of a number of other boards and committees, including the Legislative Audit Committee, the Legislative Education Board, the Cash Management Committee, and the Bond Review Board.

The Texas Constitution grants the Senate the power to make its own rules, and traditionally the Senate has granted significant power to the lieutenant governor. The Senate rules empower the lieutenant governor to decide all parliamentary questions and to use discretion in following Senate procedural rules. The lieutenant governor is also empowered to set up standing and special committees and to appoint committee members and chairs. The Senate rules, and not just the Texas Constitution, make the lieutenant governor one of the most powerful political leaders in the state. New Senate rules passed by a future Senate could, of course, substantially alter the power possessed by the lieutenant governor.

Political Style of Lieutenant Governors In 2014 and 2018, Texas elected and re-elected Tea Party–backed conservative Republican Dan Patrick as lieutenant governor. Patrick was a Houston AM radio talk show host, and he parlayed his talk show skills and his audience support into a state senate seat in 2006. In 2013 he was chosen as one of the worst Texas legislators by *Texas Monthly*, which claimed he was a bully and an ideologue who treated the committee he chaired, the Education Committee, as if it were part of his radio show. He lectured other legislators, interrupted witnesses, and assumed that those who disagreed with his bills did not understand them. The only opinion that mattered to him, *Texas Monthly* claimed, was Patrick's.[23] Still, he ran (and won) an extraordinary race for lieutenant governor against three Republicans in the primary and against state senator Leticia Van De Putte, a very capable Democratic opponent in the general election.

Patrick's political agenda reflected his Tea Party/religious right support, which represents a different political faction and a different political orientation from the business-oriented agenda of previous lieutenant governors. Patrick changed the rules of the state Senate to make it easier for votes to be taken on bills opposed by the Democratic minority, and he sought to lessen the power of Democrats over committees by exercising his power to appoint committee chairs. He sought to restrict abortion as much as possible, to control the border, and to promote gun rights. In the 2017 legislative session, Patrick continued to promote gun rights and religious liberty, to prevent public funds from being used to process union dues, and to weaken the influence of the federal Environmental Protection Agency.[24] One key issue for him was support for the "bathroom bill," which required persons to use the bathroom, showers, and locker rooms of public schools and other state and local buildings that matched the sex specified on their birth certificate as opposed to their gender identity. Much of his agenda in the 2017 session was stymied by Speaker Joe Straus, who represented the traditional, moderate-conservative, pro-business wing of the Republican Party.

Patrick's margin of victory in the 2018 lieutenant governor's race dropped dramatically from 2014, going from 58 percent of the vote to 51 percent. Patrick blamed straight-ticket voting for his declining victory margin—although straight ticket voting also existed when he ran in 2014.[25] Possibly as a result of this narrower margin, the 2019 legislative session saw far less attention to matters such as "bathroom bills" and much more attention to the economic issues that directly affect Texans such as high property taxes and school finance.

Attorney General

The **attorney general** is elected to a four-year term and acts as the chief lawyer for the state of Texas. Currently, the Texas attorney general oversees the work of more than 700 lawyers.

attorney general elected state official who serves as the state's chief civil lawyer

The attorney general is, in effect, head of Texas's civil law firm. The office is concerned primarily with civil matters. When a lawsuit is filed against the state or by the state, the attorney general's office manages the legal activities surrounding that lawsuit. When a state agency needs legal representation, the office usually represents the agency. In any lawsuit to which Texas is a party, the attorney general's office has full responsibility to resolve the case and can litigate, compromise, settle, or choose not to continue the litigation.

One of the more important powers of the office comes from the opinion process. Any agency of state or local government can ask for an advisory opinion on the legality of an action. The office will rule on the question, and the ruling generally has the force of law unless overturned by a court or the legislature.

The office has little responsibility in criminal law but may appoint a special prosecutor if a local district attorney asks for assistance. This can happen when there is a potential conflict of interest—for example, if the district attorney is a friend of or works with a local official who is under criminal investigation. In one case, lawyers from the Attorney General's office prosecuted a state district judge in Collin County on bribery charges. (That judge was ultimately vindicated on appeal.) Generally, criminal cases in Texas are prosecuted by district or county attorneys elected in each county. The county is usually responsible for the costs of the trial and for all appeals in state court. If a criminal case is appealed to the federal courts, the attorney general's office assumes responsibility.

Probably the most controversial and criticized aspect of the work of the office is child support collection. Almost one-half of its 4,000 employees are involved in collecting child support. However, this program is the subject of intense criticism because much child support remains uncollected.

In 2014 and 2018 Ken Paxton was elected and re-elected attorney general. Paxton had served in the Texas House from 2002 to 2012 and then was elected to the Texas Senate. He was elected as attorney general with the support of the Tea Party in 2014 when the former attorney general, Greg Abbott, ran for and was elected governor. Taking a page from Abbott's political playbook as attorney general, Paxton emphasized suing the federal government. His biography on the attorney general's website notes, "In his first year in office, General Paxton hit the ground running, filing eight lawsuits against the federal government to protect Texas sovereignty on environmental issues, health care, religious freedom and immigration."[26] Though Texas attorneys general had battled in the past with the federal government over integration and offshore oil ownership, Abbott and Paxton appear to have been the most litigious of Texas attorneys general when it comes to suits against the federal government.

A cloud has remained over Paxton during his years as attorney general because he has been charged with two first degree felonies involving securities fraud and one third degree felony involving failure to register as a securities agent. He has pled not guilty to these charges, but his trial has been delayed for five years. Most recently, employees in his office have accused him of bribery and abuse of office because of his unilateral appointment of a special prosecutor to investigate charges of law enforcement improprieties during an investigation of a wealthy developer and campaign contributor.

Commissioner of the General Land Office

land commissioner elected state official who is the manager of most publicly owned lands

The General Land Office (GLO) is the oldest state agency in Texas. Historically, the head of the agency, the **land commissioner**, gave away land. Today, the GLO is the manager for most publicly owned lands in Texas. Texas owns, or has mineral rights in, 13 million acres of land in the state, plus all submerged lands up to 10.35 miles into the Gulf of Mexico. All but 28 of Texas's 254 counties contain some of these public lands.

The GLO also awards rights for grazing and oil and gas exploration on this land. Thousands of producing oil and gas wells on state-owned land are managed by the GLO, and a significant portion of royalties on oil and natural gas produced by these wells goes to the state's Permanent School Fund and Permanent University Fund. These responsibilities make the office of land commissioner quite influential.

The commissioner also manages the Veterans' Land Program, through which the state makes low-cost loans to Texas veterans. The program includes loans for land, housing, and home improvements. In addition, the GLO was recently given authority over some environmental matters. The land commissioner is responsible for environmental quality on public lands and waters, especially along the Texas coast. All of Texas's Gulf Coast beaches are publicly owned and under the jurisdiction of the GLO.

George P. Bush was elected commissioner of the GLO in 2014 and was re-elected in 2018 with 53.7 percent of the vote. Bush is generally believed to have sought the position as a stepping-stone to higher political office. However, he has taken an active and aggressive role in running and changing the GLO. He terminated two top-level GLO officials, and a third has resigned. In the wake of critical reports from the state auditor that found problems with the GLO's

The General Land Office is influential in large part because it awards oil and gas exploration rights for publicly owned lands. Here, Land Commissioner George P. Bush speaks in front of the Alamo, which is now under GLO supervision.

contracting process and internal audits that found numerous other problems, Bush undertook a complete restructuring of the organization.

Bush's major problem, however, was related not to his management of the organization, but to the Alamo. In the wake of fiscal problems with the Alamo and deterioration of the structure, Bush took over the Alamo from the Daughters of the Republic of Texas, its longtime managers. Litigation ensued between the GLO and the Daughters of the Republic of Texas. That was followed by opposition to redesign part of the facility. Conspiracy theorists objected when UNESCO gave the San Antonio missions, including the Alamo, a World Heritage designation. They claimed that Bush was allowing the United Nations to take over the Alamo. There was also opposition to the way Bush was handling state funding for Alamo improvements, the assertion being there was insufficient transparency in the use of these funds. Bush has further been criticized by his opponents for what was claimed to be his agency's inadequate response to Hurricane Harvey. He has also been criticized for receiving campaign contributions from those doing business with the GLO.

Agriculture Commissioner

The **agriculture commissioner** is primarily responsible for enforcing agricultural laws. These include administration of animal quarantine laws, inspection of food, and enforcement of disease- and pest-control programs. Enforcement of the state's laws helps to ensure that Texas's farm products are of high quality and disease free.

Farming and ranching are big business in Texas. Although many small family farms still exist in the state, large corporate farms increasingly dominate Texas agriculture. These large agribusinesses are greatly affected by the decisions of the commissioner, which can increase or decrease the costs of production. Changes in production costs affect the profit margins of these agribusinesses and ultimately the price consumers pay for food products.

The current agriculture commissioner, Sid Miller, was first elected in 2014 and quickly became an attention-getter within state government. He ran into trouble with the state legislature for his intense lobbying of them in behalf of his agency, for his extravagant proposal to renovate his office, for $413,700 in bonuses given to 146 of his employees, and for employing an ex-felon at the agency. Though he did not face criminal charges, he came under criminal investigation for using state funds to travel to a rodeo and to obtain an injection for pain treatment.

Publicity seems to be a primary goal of Miller's administration. For his first official act as commissioner, he held a press conference in which he granted full amnesty to cupcakes. He said he wished to reassure Texans that it was legal to bring cupcakes and other sweets to school and that he would protect that right. He then took a large bite of a cupcake and said, "Let them eat cake." He also sent a cupcake to each member of the House and Senate. Subsequently, Miller's search for publicity has continued. He has threatened to slap anyone who wishes him "Happy Holidays" rather than "Merry Christmas"; has advocated dropping nuclear bombs on "the Muslim world"; and has spoken in favor of deep fryers and soda machines in public schools. During the 2016 presidential election campaign, Miller referred to Hillary Clinton with a vulgar term, then deleted the tweet and blamed it on an overzealous staff member. Miller has been criticized for

agriculture commissioner elected state official who is primarily responsible for enforcing agricultural laws

Commissioner of Agriculture Sid Miller bites into a cupcake at a press conference where he granted full amnesty to cupcakes in order to assure Texans it was legal to bring sweets to school.

the numerous false and misleading stories that he has posted on social media, which he has defended by saying, "I'm not a news source."[27] Though Miller had two Republican challengers when he ran for re-election in 2018, he won the primary rather easily and won 51.3 percent of the vote in the general election.

Comptroller of Public Accounts

comptroller elected state official who directs the collection of taxes and other revenues and estimates revenues for the budgeting process

The **comptroller** is a powerful state official because he or she directs the collection of tax and nontax revenues and issues an estimate of anticipated state revenues before each legislative session. The taxes collected by the comptroller include the general sales tax, severance tax on natural resources, business franchise tax, motor fuels tax, most occupational taxes, and many minor taxes.

Although collecting billions in revenue is important and more visible, estimating revenues provides the comptroller with more power. These estimates, issued monthly during legislative sessions, are vital to the appropriations process because the legislature is prohibited from spending more than the comptroller estimates will be available. Final passage of any appropriations bill is contingent on the comptroller's certifying that revenues will be available to cover the monies spent in the appropriation. If the comptroller is unable to certify that monies are available to pay for the appropriation, the legislature must reduce the appropriation or increase revenues. More than just an auditor, accountant, and tax collector, the comptroller is a key figure in the appropriations process.

In 1996 the office of state treasurer was eliminated, and the comptroller assumed the duties of that office. Since then, the comptroller has been the official custodian of state funds, responsible for the safety of the state's money and for investing that money. To ensure the safety of Texas's money, funds are deposited only in financial institutions designated by the State Depository Board as eligible to receive state monies. Deposits are required to earn as much money as possible. The more money earned as interest on deposits, the fewer tax dollars are needed.

Glenn Hegar was first elected comptroller in 2014. While facing Democratic opposition in 2018, Hegar ran unopposed in the Republican primary and was re-elected in 2018 with 53.2 percent of the vote. Hegar faced the unenviable task of estimating the effect and duration of the dramatic decline in oil prices and the effects of the coronavirus pandemic on tax revenues and on the Texas economy in general. Inaccurate estimates could force unnecessary budget cuts or bring about tax increases.

Secretary of State

Strangely, given Texas's fragmentation of power, the governor does appoint the Texas **secretary of state**, even though this office is an elective one in most other states. Though much of the work is collecting information and keeping records, the secretary of state is an important officer with many responsibilities, and, as the story of David Whitley in the introduction to this chapter shows, a secretary of state's actions can generate intense political controversy.

As Texas's chief election official, the secretary of state conducts voter registration drives. His or her office works with organizations such as the League of Women Voters to increase the number of registered voters. The secretary of state's office also collects election-night returns from county judges and county clerks and makes the results available to the media. This service provides media and voters with a convenient method of receiving the latest official election returns in Texas.

secretary of state state official, appointed by the governor, whose primary responsibility is administering elections

The Plural Executive and the Governor

The plural executive dilutes the ability of the governor to control state government. The governor appoints the secretary of state but has no control over other members of the plural executive. All its members are elected independently, and they do not run as a team. The other elected members do not answer to the governor, and they do not serve as a cabinet. They tend to operate their offices as independent entities, and they jealously guard their turf. The plural executive can make state government appear as if it is going in several different directions at once. This is especially true when members of the plural executive are political rivals. For example, it is widely rumored that Land Commissioner George P. Bush is eyeing another statewide office, most likely lieutenant governor. Whether Dan Patrick will leave that office to open the position for Bush without a fight remains to be seen.

Boards, Commissions, and Regulatory Agencies

 Explain the roles played by boards, commissions, and regulatory agencies

bureaucracy the complex structure of offices, tasks, rules, and principles of organization that are employed by all large-scale institutions to coordinate the work of their personnel

The state **bureaucracy** in Texas has numerous state boards, commissions, councils, and committees as well as major agencies within the plural executive that have administrative or advisory functions. In addition to the governmental bodies under the direct control of the single executives who are part of the elected plural executive, there are also bodies (1) run by multimember boards appointed by the governor and confirmed by the Senate; (2) run by single executives appointed by the governor and confirmed by the Senate; (3) run by boards appointed by several members of the plural executive or even by legislative officers, and confirmed by the Senate; and (4) run by multimember boards elected by the people. Overall, the state bureaucracy employed 328,396 people in 2019[28] compared with 324,369 in 2018.[29]

Appointment power coupled with long tenure gives a governor strong influence over the state bureaucracy. Governor Perry's lengthy service gave him enormous influence throughout state government, as he is the only Texas governor in modern history to have made every appointment in state government that a governor can make—and he also made numerous appointments to vacancies in office such as the Texas appellate courts and scores of district judgeships. The result, according to former state representative and author Brian McCall, is that "in this regard, [Perry] is by far the most powerful governor in Texas history. No governor has been able to do what he has done."[30] Perry placed many of his closest advisers in key positions, which spread not only his personal influence but also his personal political philosophy of a pro-business state government.

Multimember Appointed Boards

As we have discussed, most boards and commissions in Texas are headed by members appointed by the governor and confirmed by the Senate. Some commissioners are appointed by a variety of other people, including the lieutenant governor, the Speaker of the House, or leaders of professional organizations such as the state bar or state medical association. Multimember commissions with heads appointed by the governor include obscure agencies such as the Bandera County River Authority, the State Seed and Plant Board, the Caddo Lake Compact Commission, and the Texas Funeral Service Commission. Better-known agencies include the Texas Alcoholic Beverage Commission, the Parks

The Parks and Wildlife Department is an agency in the Texas executive branch and is led by a board appointed by the governor. The department manages natural resources and fishing, hunting, and outdoor recreation in the state. Here, a researcher collects notes on fish caught in Matagorda Bay, Texas.

and Wildlife Department, the Texas Youth Commission, and the Texas Department of Corrections. Except in the case of a major controversy, such as the sexual abuse scandal that embroiled the Texas Youth Commission in 2007, these agencies work in anonymity, although several of them have a direct effect on the lives of Texans.

Appointed Single Executives

The Texas Department of Insurance is run by one commissioner appointed by the governor for a two-year term and confirmed by the Senate. The purpose of the Department of Insurance is to regulate the insurance market in Texas, a complicated task that affects most Texans.

Although insurance companies advocate less regulation, consumer groups argue that the insurance commissioner has inadequate powers to deal with insurance companies. Indeed, it is doubtful that the commissioner has sufficient power to force an uncooperative insurer to comply with his or her decisions. The commissioner is also faced with the seemingly intractable problem of keeping rates low and coverage available in hurricane- and flood-prone areas to which more and more people are moving.

Multimember Elected Boards

Members of two state agencies are elected by the voters: the Railroad Commission of Texas and the State Board of Education. The Railroad Commission has 3 members elected statewide to six-year terms of office. One of the 3 members is elected every two years. The Board of Education is a 15-member board elected to four-year terms from single-member districts.

Plural versus Single Executive

1 Why does the number of executive officers matter?

Throughout this chapter, we have described Texas's plural executive. Texas has a number of executive officers who are elected and have major responsibilities in running state government. This diffusion of responsibility within state government is not limited to Texas. Most states have a plural executive to some degree where several elected officials have executive responsibilities. Among the more common elected offices in the states other than governor are attorney general in 43 states; secretary of state in 37 states; treasurer in 34 states; auditor in 22 states. Nine states have a comptroller and 9 have a commissioner of agriculture.[a]

Some states, New Jersey being the classic example, instead have single executives. The New Jersey governor appoints all state officials except the lieutenant governor, who also is elected statewide. State constitutions setting up single executive systems adopted a view that favored an elected governor who appointed the heads of departments and a cabinet so that state administrators were directly responsible to the governor.[b]

2 What's the debate?

Supporters of a plural executive worry about an all-powerful governor. That was certainly the concern of the authors of Texas's 1876 Constitution who wanted to be certain that no governor of Texas would ever again have the power of Governor E. J. Davis. Having a plural executive prevents any governor from becoming too powerful. At the same time, plural executives make sure that government is closer to the people. Officials with responsibilities in a specific issue area are likely to be more responsive to the voters affected by their jurisdiction than a governor would be who had a general responsibility for every issue in the state.

In contrast, supporters of a single executive believe that centralized control of government ensures there will be efficient government, since decisions and actions are cen-

Some members of the plural executive include (beginning second from the left) Lieutenant Governor Dan Patrick, Agriculture Commissioner Sid Miller, Land Commissioner George P. Bush, Comptroller Glenn Hegar, and Attorney General Ken Paxton.

tralized with no competing power bases from other elected officials. Additionally, a single executive has a broad political agenda, which prevents parts of the executive branch from serving the narrow concerns of particular interest groups rather than of the state as a whole.

3 What do the numbers say?

In a study of the institutional powers of all state governors, Professor Margaret Ferguson created six categories measuring the power of the governor and then an overall category. Each category is measured on a 5-point scale with a score of 5 representing the greatest power and a score of 0 representing the least. The table below presents the rankings for the institutional power of the Texas governor compared with other large urban states as well as the average scores for all states' governors.

In which categories does the Texas governor have the greatest institutional power? Compared with other large states, does the Texas governor appear to have sufficient power to effectively lead the state government?

The Institutional Powers of State Governors

STATE	SEPARATELY ELECTED OFFICIALS	TENURE POTENTIAL	APPOINTMENT POWER	BUDGET POWER	VETO POWER	PARTY CONTROL	OVERALL SCORE
Alaska*	5	4	3.7	5	2	4	3.94
New York	4	5	3.2	2	5	2	3.53
Illinois	3	5	2.8	2	5	2	3.31
Florida	3	4	2.3	2	2.5	4	2.97
Texas	2	5	1.7	2	2.5	4	2.86
California	1.5	4	2.5	4	2.5	2	2.75
Oregon**	2	4	2.3	2	2.5	2	2.47
All States	2.96	4.14	2.76	3.42	2.83	3.29	3.23

*Highest possible score.
**Lowest possible score.
Source: Margaret Ferguson, "Governors and the Executive Branch," in *Politics in the American States: A Comparative Analysis*, ed. Virginia Gray, Russell L. Hanson, and Thad Kousser (Thousand Oaks, CA: CQ Press, 2018), 251–53.

Communicating Effectively: What Do You Think?

- Are there particular powers of the Texas governor that make the office unusually weak or strong?

- Would you increase, decrease, or keep the powers of the Texas governor at the current level? Why?

- Should the Texas governor have the same powers as governors in other large urban states?

WANT TO LEARN MORE?

Power in state executive offices is central to understanding the functioning of state governments. Several organizations provide information on leadership of state governments and the problems and policies associated with governing states.

- The Center on the American Governor
  governors.rutgers.edu

- National Governors Association
  www.nga.org

- The Council of State Governments
  www.csg.org

Railroad Commission of Texas (RRC) At one time, the Railroad Commission of Texas (RRC) was one of the most powerful state agencies in the nation. It not only regulated intrastate railroads, trucks, and bus transportation but also supervised the oil and natural gas industry in Texas. For most of the RRC's existence, in fact, regulation of the oil and gas industry was its primary focus.

During the RRC's heyday when Texas was a major oil producer, the commission limited production in order to conserve oil and to maintain prices. Consequently, the RRC was one of the most economically significant governmental bodies on the national and international stage. As oil production shifted to the Middle East, the RRC became the model for OPEC, the Organization of Petroleum Exporting Countries, which also seeks to limit oil production to maintain prices. At one time, members of the Texas RRC wielded such vast economic power that they were among the state's most influential politicians.

Today, while the RRC is a shadow of its former self, renewed energy production in Texas as a result of fracking and horizontal drilling appears to be increasing its importance. In 2020, a Democrat, Chrysta Castañeda, ran a campaign against her Republican opponent, Jim Wright, an oil and gas businessperson who had paid fines for violating environmental rules. She ran on a pro-environmental regulation platform and received $2.6 million in campaign financing from Michael Bloomberg. Wright won an overwhelming victory in the race.

State Board of Education (SBOE) The State Board of Education (SBOE) sets policy for public education (pre-kindergarten to 12th-grade programs supported by the state government) in Texas. The education bureaucracy that enforces the SBOE's rules and regulations is called the Texas Education Agency (TEA). Together these two bodies control public education in Texas by determining licensing requirements for public school teachers, setting minimum high school graduation criteria for recommended or advanced curriculums, establishing standards for accreditation of public schools, and selecting public school textbooks.

The commissioner of education is appointed by the governor from a list of candidates submitted by the SBOE. He or she is administrative head of the TEA and serves as adviser to the SBOE. The commissioner of education is at the apex of the public education bureaucracy in Texas.

The SBOE is composed of 15 members. The board is elected from single-member districts, and both Democrats and Republicans can be elected to it. Also, SBOE district lines are drawn in such a way that it is rare for a seat on the board to flip from one party to the other. In 2018, there were seven seats up for election. Democrats won four of the seats on the board and Republicans won three. In 2020, there were eight seats on the board up for election with Democrats winning two and Republicans winning six. SBOE incumbents of both parties are generally able to win re-election with little in campaign contributions compared with those for other elected executive offices—probably because SBOE offices are low visibility and each board member's district is one-fifteenth the size of the entire state.

Although tensions on the SBOE have lessened recently, the board was once an ideological battleground. In 2009, for example, one such battle led the board to review how evolution was taught in public schools. In a partial defeat for religious conservatives, no longer are teachers required to teach the "strengths and weaknesses" of evolution, although they are encouraged to teach "all sides."

The State Board of Education sets policy for public education, from pre-kindergarten through 12th grade. In 2018, the board approved the inclusion of Mexican-American studies classes as elective courses in public school curriculums.

Other battles have broken out over other aspects of educational policy. For example, in late 2015 a Facebook posting that went viral brought the SBOE process for reviewing textbooks to widespread attention and led to a major effort to change it. Roni Dean-Burren, the mother of a 9th grader, posted what her son's geography text said about the Atlantic slave trade between the 1500s and 1800s: that it "brought millions of workers from Africa to the southern United States to work on agricultural plantations." One might conclude from this language that the enslaved people were voluntary paid plantation employees, and the publisher quickly apologized and promised to correct the terminology.

The larger issue was whether the process for reviewing textbooks was adequate. The existing process had led to numerous ideological struggles within the board over proper treatment of religion, the Civil War, and even climate change. Under that process, the board relies on citizen panels to review texts, with the panel members nominated by board members. Others can also review the texts and testify during SBOE meetings about their objections to language or ideas in the texts. In the aftermath of the outcry over the use of "workers" rather than "slaves," one SBOE member proposed letting university experts fact-check textbooks. That motion failed by an 8–7 vote. However, another motion passed unanimously: in the future, review panels should have at least a majority of people "with sufficient content expertise and experience" to make judgments about textbooks. Whether this new policy reduces the ideological battles and factual errors in texts remains to be seen.[31]

Making Agencies Accountable

In a democracy, elected officials are ultimately responsible to the voters. Appointed officials are indirectly accountable to the people through the elected officials who appoint them. Both are responsible to legislatures that determine responsibilities and appropriate money to carry out those responsibilities. In Texas, the plural executive is responsible to the legislature for its biennial funding and to the voters for re-election. The myriad state agencies look to the legislature for funding, and once every 12 years they must justify their existence to the **Sunset Advisory Commission (SAC)**.

The 12-member SAC has 5 members from the Texas Senate and 1 public member appointed by the lieutenant governor, plus 5 members from the Texas House and 1 public member appointed by the Speaker of the Texas House. It was created in 1977 by the Sunset Review Act, which established specific criteria to be considered in evaluating the continuing need for an agency. One of several laws enacted in the mid-1970s to bring more openness and accountability to Texas government, the Sunset process establishes a date on which an agency is abolished unless the legislature passes a bill for the agency to continue in operation.

During its Sunset review, an agency must document its efficiency, the extent to which it meets legislative mandates, and its promptness and effectiveness in handling complaints, and it must establish the continuing need for its services. The review process is lengthy, lasting almost two years.

After a thorough study of an agency, the SAC recommends one of three actions to the legislature: (1) the agency continues as is, with no change in its organization or functions; (2) the agency continues but with changes (reorganization, a new focus for the agency, or merger with other agencies); or (3) the agency is abolished. If option 1 or 2 is recommended, specific action by the legislature is required to re-create the agency in its existing form or with some or all of the changes recommended by the SAC. If the legislature agrees the agency should be abolished (option 3), no action is necessary. It will expire at the Sunset deadline and the agency is no more.

Each state agency has been through the Sunset process. The legislature has allowed the sun to set on more than 37 agencies or programs, and 46 others have been merged with existing bodies. Since its beginning the legislature has accepted 80 percent of recommendations of the SAC, which the agency claims to have saved Texas taxpayers $981 million.[32]

The Executive in the Age of COVID-19

In spite of the institutional weaknesses of the Texas governor, the COVID-19 crisis has shown that in a disaster the governor can wield great power. With the onset of the pandemic, Governor Abbott issued several executive orders under authority of the Texas Disaster Act. In the early stages of the crisis, he limited the size of gatherings and closed schools, bars, and restaurants. He prohibited nonessential surgeries and medical procedures and established an advisory group on reopening the economy. Abbott required air travelers from New York, New Jersey, Connecticut, and New Orleans and road travelers from Louisiana to self-quarantine. He opposed judges and district attorneys in the largest counties by forbidding no-money bonds for suspects accused of violent crimes or previously convicted of violent crimes, thus stopping the release of some inmates from jails that were COVID-19 hotspots. He postponed some elections. He then issued several orders providing for a gradual re-opening of the economy.[33] Indeed, the exercise of emergency powers by Governor Abbott has been remarkable and has led major figures in the Texas Republican Party such as the party chairman, Allen West, state senator Bob Hall, and Agriculture Commissioner Sid Miller to openly oppose Abbott's assumption of powers without legislative approval.

In the early stages of the pandemic, Abbott deferred to local officials regarding stay-at-home orders. Within a brief period, however, it became clear the governor was not supportive of some of the actions of officials in urban (and Democratic) areas of the state and his orders preempted several decisions of local officials. Abbott's orders reopening businesses overrode all local orders regarding business closures and, while Abbott recommended wearing masks, he overrode local orders that required masks to be worn.[34]

The refusal of a Dallas salon owner, Shelley Luther, to keep her business closed and her subsequent jailing generated enormous publicity. With that publicity came an outpouring of support for the salon owner from Republicans. That led Abbott to announce that he was modifying his stay-at-home order, eliminating jail time for Texans who violated the order, and making that elimination of jail time retroactive. Abbott coupled these actions with criticism of the judge who sentenced Luther. It was clear Abbott was responding to his political base at that point rather than to the demands of the virus. As the state's economy began a partial reopening, the number of COVID-19 cases and the number of deaths dramatically increased. The expansion of the disease forced Abbott to respond. He encouraged the use of masks and allowed local governments to impose mask requirements. Most significantly, with the increased infections and deaths, Abbott backtracked. He closed bars, and the number of persons allowed to dine in restaurants was reduced from 75 percent capacity to 50 percent. More recently, Abbott allowed some business openings with county official approval, expanded the early voting period, and prevented more than one ballot drop-off location per county.

Salon owner Shelley Luther was arrested in 2020 after refusing to close her business during the coronavirus pandemic. After outrage grew over her arrest, Governor Abbott loosened the stay-at-home order. Here, she gives an emotional statement upon her release from jail.

While the greatest failure of the executive branch during the COVID-19 crisis was the overly rapid effort to reopen the state's economy, a close second would be the poor performance of the Texas Workforce Commission, which is the state agency responsible for the management of the unemployment insurance program. The commission is governed by three commissioners who are appointed by the governor. One of the commissioners represents employers, one labor, and one the public. The response of the commission to rapid and widespread unemployment that was brought about largely by the pandemic can only be described as slow, chaotic, and inefficient. Perhaps the failure of the commission to respond to burgeoning unemployment may be excused by the speed and the enormity of the state's economic decline, although that excuse probably is not satisfactory to people who were out of work, in need, and not adequately served by the commission. At this point it remains unclear if there will be political consequences for the commission's failed response to the unemployment crisis.

The Executive Branch and the Future of Texas

THE FEAR OF A STRONG EXECUTIVE who could ignore the wishes of either the legislature or the people, as was the case during Reconstruction in Texas, led in 1876 to a constitution that created a plural executive. The governor is the chief executive officer in the state, elected directly by the popular vote of all the people of Texas. People turn to the governor for leadership and direction during times of crisis, but the power of the Texas governor is limited. Many key executive officials, including the lieutenant governor, the attorney general, the comptroller, and the land commissioner, are, like the governor, elected directly by the people. These members of the plural executive, along with other popularly elected statewide boards and commissions, possess power and authority that under other constitutional arrangements the governor might possess.

Following in the footsteps of an exceptionally powerful Texas governor, Greg Abbott initially seemed to be moving to the right in the Texas Republican Party. However, in the 2019 legislative session, his focus was primarily on property taxes, school finance, and the state budget, and he avoided the "hot button" issues so popular with the far right in the Republican Party, such as the "bathroom bill." It may well be the case that Abbott's political future will be determined by COVID-19. Will it continue its devastating effect on Texans and the state's economy, and, if it does, will Texans hold Abbott responsible for an insufficient response? Alternatively, will Abbott's broad use of emergency powers without legislative approval lead to a reaction against his leadership? Abbott currently is in a peculiar political dilemma: on the one hand, he is being criticized for not doing enough to deal with the pandemic; on the other, he is being attacked for what his critics call his dictatorial control.

Land Commissioner George P. Bush was heavily criticized for some of his campaign contributions and for his operation of the General Land Office. What once seemed like a bright political future has dimmed somewhat, although there are predictions he will attempt to move on to other statewide offices. Agriculture Commissioner Sid Miller is the political publicity hound of the group, although his antics have spawned considerable political opposition. Lieutenant Governor Dan Patrick pushed hard to become the leader of the right wing in state politics, although, like Governor Abbott, he backtracked in the 2019 legislative session to have more focus on economic issues. Comptroller Glenn Hegar has been simply trying to cope with the massive economic effects of Texas's growth that are coupled with the dramatic decline in oil prices and the devastating economic effects of the pandemic. Attorney General Ken Paxton has been trying to survive his indictments while filing suits to have provisions such as Deferred Action for Childhood Arrivals (DACA) and the Affordable Care Act declared unconstitutional. Paxton's political survival skills are noteworthy, since in spite of his legal troubles, he had no opposition in the Republican primary. The mix of these competing roles, ambitions, and personal goals is what makes the plural executive of Texas so tumultuous. Nevertheless, one has to wonder how enmeshed in scandal Paxton can become before he faces negative reaction from either the courts, other political leaders in the state, or the electorate.

The Democrats' strong showing in the 2018 elections and demographic changes in the state have provided some support for the view that the Democratic Party is on the cusp of coming back into power in state politics. The margins of victory for Republican statewide candidates were relatively low in 2018, and in some cases, such as the attorney general's race, margin of victory was very low. It remains to be seen whether the new energy in the Democratic Party will continue and will increase in later elections. At least in the near future, the Republican Party remains in firm control of state-level politics. Still, the differences in the values, abilities, ambitions, and goals of these members of the plural executive will provide the fodder for the policies and controversies of the future.

STUDY GUIDE

Use ⚙ INQUIZITIVE to help you study and master this material.

The Governor

- **Describe the powers of the Texas governor and the limits of the governor's power (pp. 255–71)**

Although the Texas governor is considered weak compared with governors of many other states, the governor still has appointment, budgetary, military, and police powers. Among his legislative powers are message and veto powers and the ability to call special sessions of the legislature.

Key Terms

line-item veto (p. 255)
impeachment (p. 260)
appointment (p. 263)
patronage (p. 263)
senatorial courtesy (p. 266)
executive budget (p. 266)
legislative budget (p. 266)
veto (p. 268)
post-adjournment veto (p. 269)
special session (p. 269)

Practice Quiz

1. Which of the following is *not* necessary to become governor of Texas?
  a) A governor must be at least 30 years of age.
  b) A governor must have lived in Texas for at least five years.
  c) A governor must be a U.S. citizen.
  d) A governor must be a lawyer.
  e) A governor must have substantial campaign funding.

2. The election for governor of Texas is held in an off-year in order to
  a) increase voter participation in elections in odd-numbered years.

  b) influence the presidential vote in Texas.
  c) decrease the likelihood of voter fraud.
  d) give governors an opportunity to campaign for presidential candidates.
  e) prevent the presidential vote in Texas from influencing the election of state officials.

3. The constitutional method of removing the governor is
  a) *quo warranto* proceedings.
  b) *ex post facto* removal.
  c) a vote of no confidence.
  d) impeachment.
  e) impeachment and conviction.

4. The governor's most effective power in controlling the executive branch of state government is the power
  a) of the veto.
  b) of appointment.
  c) of removal.
  d) of judicial review.
  e) to create a state budget.

5. The governor's veto is absolute when it is a
  a) line-item veto.
  b) special veto.
  c) budgetary veto.
  d) post-adjournment veto.
  e) select veto.

6. The governor can grant
  a) pardons.
  b) suspended sentences.
  c) probation.
  d) retrials.
  e) parole.

The Plural Executive

Unlike the president of the United States, the governor of Texas does not appoint a cabinet. Voters in Texas elect the lieutenant governor and other major statewide offices in separate elections. This disperses power within the executive branch, which means that executive officers must compromise not only with the legislature but also within the executive branch.

Key Terms

plural executive (p. 271)
lieutenant governor (p. 273)
attorney general (p. 275)
land commissioner (p. 276)
agriculture commissioner (p. 277)
comptroller (p. 278)
secretary of state (p. 279)

Practice Quiz

7. Which member of the plural executive is appointed?
   a) secretary of state
   b) land commissioner
   c) lieutenant governor
   d) comptroller of public accounts
   e) attorney general

8. The attorney general is
   a) part of the governor's cabinet.
   b) elected independently of the governor.
   c) appointed by the Texas Supreme Court.
   d) the governor's lawyer.
   e) chosen by the State Bar of Texas.

9. The land commissioner
   a) records all property deeds.
   b) administers state land.
   c) surveys property in Texas.
   d) is appointed by the state Senate.
   e) administers Big Bend National Park.

10. Members of the plural executive are accountable to the
   a) Sunset Advisory Commission.
   b) voters.
   c) constitution.
   d) state supreme court.
   e) Travis County district attorney.

Boards, Commissions, and Regulatory Agencies

• **Explain the roles played by boards, commissions, and regulatory agencies (pp. 280–88)**

The governor has the power to appoint people to commissions, councils, committees, and regulatory agencies. Such institutions have important powers to interpret state regulations and make a difference in the lives of everyday Texans.

Key Terms
bureaucracy (p. 280)
Sunset Advisory Commission (SAC) (p. 286)

Practice Quiz

11. The Texas Department of Insurance
   a) has limited power to regulate insurance rates.
   b) collects the penalties for not buying health insurance under Obamacare.
   c) sells insurance for mold coverage.
   d) is run by a five-member elected board.
   e) All of the above are features of the Texas Department of Insurance.

12. The Railroad Commission of Texas
   a) is responsible for the safety of the state's railroads.
   b) issues bonds to support the state's transportation needs.
   c) regulates oil and gas production in Texas.
   d) approves mergers of railroads.
   e) is the most powerful agency in the state.

13. The State Board of Education
   a) has a major role in determining the books used in Texas public schools.
   b) is appointed by the legislature.
   c) reviews applications to state colleges and universities.
   d) is responsible for school property tax rates.
   e) governs local boards of education.

14. Which agency investigates the performance of state agencies and recommends whether an agency should be abolished, continued as is, or continued with changes?
   a) Legislative Budget Board
   b) Legislative Research Bureau
   c) Texas Research League
   d) Public Utility Commission
   e) Sunset Advisory Commission

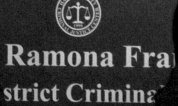

The 2018 elections led to victory for Democratic candidates in all contested Harris County judicial races and the two courts of appeal based in Houston. One effect of the election was that 19 Harris County judges, including Judge Ramona Franklin, pictured here, are now African American women, a dramatic increase in the diversity of the Texas judiciary.

The Judiciary

WHY THE JUDICIARY MATTERS Texas judges have always been overwhelmingly White males. A sign of change occurred in the 2018 elections when Harris County elected 17 additional African American female judges, bringing the total to 19 since there were already 2 on the bench. The 19 judges called themselves the "Harris County Black Girl Magic," and they represented a record number of African American female judges.

The success of these candidates was due in large part to three factors. First, after winning their respective primaries, they worked as a group to mobilize Democratic voters in the general election. Second, they ran as Democrats with a popular candidate at the top of the ticket. Although Beto O'Rourke, the Democratic nominee for the Senate seat held by Ted Cruz, lost the race, he carried Harris County by 17 percent.[1] The third factor explaining the success of the African American judges was the prevalence of straight-ticket voting in Harris County (where by marking the ballot for Democrat or Republican, votes are cast for all candidates of that party). Professors Stefan Haag and William Young noted that straight-ticket voting for Democratic Party candidates was higher where there were urban voters, Latina and Latino voters, African American voters, and elderly voters. Overall in Harris County in 2018, 77.2 percent of the total vote was straight-ticket with the Democrats having a substantial advantage—55.3 percent of the straight-ticket votes were cast for Democrats and 44 percent were cast for Republicans. In looking at the five Harris County precincts with the largest percentage of African Americans, 82.6 percent of the total votes cast in those five precincts were straight-ticket with 98.1 percent cast for Democrats and 1.7 percent for Republicans. In the five Harris County precincts with the largest percentage of Latino voters, 78.1 percent of the ballots cast were straight-ticket with 82.7 percent cast for Democrats and 16.5 percent cast for Republicans. The result of the 2018 balloting in Harris County was that Democrats won every district court contest.[2]

One consequence of the election of these African American judges in Harris County is that the judiciary will more closely mirror the population of the county. A majority of people in Harris County are people of color; 20 percent of the population is African American and over 43 percent is Latino.[3] These elections also reflect how strongly Harris County voters voted for Democrats in general. And the same pattern was true in most of the major urban counties in Texas. Bexar County, for example, voted for O'Rourke by a majority of nearly 60 percent; Dallas County by about 66 percent; El Paso County by 74 percent; Travis County by 74 percent; and even Tarrant County, which had been a Republican stronghold, by 49.9 percent to Cruz's 49.2 percent.[4]

"Harris County Black Girl Magic" is not just a phenomenon in Harris County; the number of people of color in the large urban counties has increased, as has the number of Democratic voters. As we have seen, Texas Democratic voters are far more likely to be African American or Latino than are Republican voters. This means that as the Democratic Party makes advances in the large urban counties, there are likely to be more African American and Latino officeholders who have the same race or ethnicity as their constituents.

Or does it? One move that might have undercut the change in the judiciary in the large urban counties was a law passed by the Texas legislature in 2017 that eliminated straight-ticket voting in the 2020 elections and beyond. Although all candidates had a party label, voters had to vote individually for candidates rather than voting once simply for all candidates with the preferred party label.

Supporters of the law claimed that it would encourage voters to cast informed ballots rather than simply voting for every candidate with a Democratic or Republican party label. Opponents believed the law was simply designed to discourage Democratic votes.[5] However, the 2020 judicial elections suggest that the elimination of straight-ticket voting did not offer any advantage to Republican judges running in Texas's pro-Biden urban areas. All Republican judicial candidates were defeated in races for district courts in Harris, Bexar, Travis, and Dallas counties as well as Republican judicial candidates running for courts of appeal in those counties.

CHAPTERGOALS

- Explain the legal process and the differences between criminal and civil law (pp. 297–300)
- Describe how the Texas court system is organized (pp. 301–7)
- Evaluate the process for selecting judges in Texas (pp. 307–21)
- Understand the key issues facing the Texas court system today (pp. 321–26)

The Legal Process

The Texas legal system can be thought of as divided into civil law and criminal law. Just as the Texas Supreme Court hears civil cases and the Texas Court of Criminal Appeals hears criminal cases, it is useful to think of the law as divided into these parts. **Civil law** involves a dispute, usually between private individuals, over relationships, obligations, and responsibility. Though there are exceptions with a violation of the civil law, the remedy is often for the offending party to pay compensation to the injured party.

In contrast, **criminal law** involves the violation of concepts of right and wrong as defined by criminal statutes. In criminal law, the state accuses individuals of violations, and if found guilty the violator is subject to punishment. In some cases, that punishment may involve loss of liberty or even loss of life.

civil law a branch of law that deals with disputes, usually between private individuals over relationships, obligations, and responsibility

criminal law the branch of law that regulates the conduct of individuals, defines crimes, and specifies punishment for criminal acts

Civil Law

In civil law, an aggrieved person will usually obtain a lawyer and file a petition that details the **complaint** against the person accused of causing the harm. The petition is filed with the clerk of court, who issues a citation against the defendant. The defendant will usually file an **answer** explaining why the allegations are not valid. Depending on the issue, the amounts of money that may be awarded as damages, and the probability of success, the aggrieved person may be able to obtain the services of a lawyer on a contingent fee basis. This means that the lawyer will not charge the individual if the case is lost but will obtain a portion of the damages awarded if the case is won. It is not unusual for such **contingent fee** arrangements to involve one-third or more of the damages awarded plus expenses. Lawyers who handle cases on contingent fee agreements often handle personal-injury cases and are known as trial lawyers. Traditionally, these lawyers will contribute money to judicial candidates who are sympathetic to plaintiffs. They make money only if they win, so they have a strong economic interest in supporting judicial candidates who are sympathetic to plaintiffs and to the awarding of large damages.

The person being sued either will usually hire an attorney on his or her own or, if insured, will be represented by an attorney paid for by the insurance company. Fee arrangements vary for civil defense lawyers, but often they are paid by the hour, in which case they get paid whether they win or lose. Their economic incentives to contribute money to judicial campaigns may be different from the incentives trial lawyers have, but civil defense lawyers do contribute large sums to judicial campaigns in order to elect judges who support their views on **tort** law.

The court to which a civil case is taken depends on the type of case and the amount of money involved. (See the next section on Court Structure.) Most commonly, a civil case will be settled, meaning the dispute is resolved without going to court. Settlements may, however, occur during trial, sometimes immediately before a jury renders its decision. If a case is not settled and goes to trial, it may be heard either by a judge or,

complaint the presentation of a grievance by the plaintiff in a civil case

answer the presentation of a defendant's defense against an allegation in a civil case

contingent fee a fee paid to the lawyer in a civil case that is contingent on winning the case

tort a civil wrong that causes harm to another; it is remedied by awarding economic damages to the injured party

if requested by either side, by a jury. Juries at the district court level consist of 12 jurors, whereas juries in lower-level courts consist of 6 jurors. Civil jury verdicts do not have to be unanimous in Texas; five-sixths of the jurors are sufficient for a verdict. The burden of proof is on the plaintiff. The standard of proof that the plaintiff must meet is **preponderance of the evidence**, meaning that the plaintiff must show that it is more likely than not that the defendant is the cause of the harm suffered by the plaintiff.

preponderance of the evidence the standard of proof in a civil jury case, by which the plaintiff must show that the defendant is more likely than not the cause of the harm suffered by the plaintiff

Civil cases may involve tiny amounts of damages or they may involve billions of dollars and have the potential of breaking huge corporations, such as happened in the 1980s when Pennzoil successfully sued Texaco in a dispute over the takeover of the Getty Oil Company.[6]

Civil case verdicts may, of course, be appealed. Appeals are usually from the trial court to the intermediate court of appeal and perhaps further to the state supreme court. Given the cost of appeals and the delay involved, it is not unusual for some settlement to be reached after the verdict but before the case goes through the appellate process. For example, a plaintiff might agree to settle for much less than the verdict in the case to avoid the expense and delay of further appeals.

Litigating a civil case is time consuming and expensive. As a result, in Texas and other states, it is increasingly common to try to negotiate a settlement through mediation or arbitration. With arbitration, the parties to the dispute agree to present their case to a decision maker and to be bound by the decision. With mediation, the parties to the dispute try to reach a compromise resolution of the problem without going to trial. Mediation is especially popular in civil disputes because the parties to the dispute are reaching the agreement and are not forced into a particular decision as they would be with arbitration. Mediation is also a very flexible process for resolving disputes where resolutions of disputes are contractual agreements between the opposing parties. To resolve the dispute, they may agree to any legal remedy. One of the most unusual such remedies occurred a number of years ago when Southwest Airlines and Stevens Aviation had a dispute over which company could use the slogan "Plane Smart." The two sides initially agreed to decide the issue by having an arm-wrestling match between Southwest's and Stevens Aviation's company chairmen. Lawyers later worked out another agreement, but the company chairmen went ahead and held their arm-wrestling event.

In addition to civil cases that involve tort law, a major civil law issue involves family law. The most common family law cases deal with divorce, adoption, child support, and child custody cases. Some of the larger urban counties have specialized courts that only deal with family law issues.

probate the supervision of the estates of deceased persons

Another major civil law matter involves **probate**. Texas has specialized probate courts in urban areas, although in more rural parts of Texas other county courts handle these matters. Probate courts deal with wills of deceased persons, challenges to those wills, and the distribution of the estates of persons who have died without wills. They also handle guardianship cases for those who are incompetent to handle their own affairs.

Criminal Law

felony a serious criminal offense, punishable by a prison sentence or a fine; a capital felony is possibly punishable by death

misdemeanor a minor criminal offense, usually punishable by a fine or a jail sentence

In criminal cases, the state alleges a violation of a criminal law and is represented in court by a prosecutor. They prosecute serious crimes which are felonies and lesser offenses which are misdemeanors. **Felonies** can result in a prison sentence and the most serious felonies are capital cases, which can result in the death penalty. **Misdemeanors** can result in a jail sentence. Although prosecutors handle juvenile justice cases, juvenile cases are treated differently from cases involving adult crime. Some larger Texas counties even have specialized juvenile courts to deal with juvenile offenders. In dealing with juvenile offenders, there is greater emphasis on treatment and rehabilitation than exists with adult offenders.

Some prosecutors have lengthy careers as prosecutors and have vast trial experience. These long-career prosecutors will often handle the most difficult and complex cases. However, because the pay of prosecutors is often much lower than that of private lawyers who do litigation in the private sector, it is common for prosecutors to be quite young and inexperienced. Once they gain trial experience, prosecutors commonly move into the private sector.

Defendants may hire criminal defense attorneys, who usually charge a flat fee to handle the case. Criminal defense lawyers do not work on a contingent fee basis. Since most criminal defendants are found guilty, criminal defense lawyers often prefer to obtain as much of their fee as possible in advance of the verdict.

Some parts of Texas have public defender offices where salaried lawyers provide at least some criminal defense services for low-income persons in a county. Bexar County has established the first public defender office for indigent criminal appeals. Travis County has a public defender office representing only poor people with mental impairments.[7] In west Texas, a public defender office represents indigents in capital cases.[8]

In Texas, poor criminal defendants are more commonly represented by lawyers appointed by the judge. Usually, the government-paid fees for court-appointed lawyers are less than would be paid to lawyers of nonindigent defendants. Thus, some lawyers are reluctant to fulfill court appointments; others may not put the time and energy into a court-appointed case that they would if they were privately paid; others take court appointments because they have a limited number of paying clients; and still others take court appointments to gain experience.

Despite the challenges facing indigent defendants, a small number of lawyers have reaped huge payments from counties for representing them. One lawyer in Collin County received $460,000 in 2018 for representing indigents, which was more than double the fees charged by any other court-appointed lawyer in the county.[9] In Harris County 86 lawyers who serve as appointed counsel have indigent defense caseloads far larger than the recommended maximum felony caseload of 77 to 174 cases. One of those attorneys, who has a caseload of 583, has made $1.54 million handling indigent cases over the past five years.[10]

With felonies, prior to the trial there will be an indictment by a grand jury. In Texas a grand jury consists of 12 persons and two alternates who sit for two to six months. Depending on the county, a grand jury may meet only once or twice a year, or it may meet several times a week. Until recently, most Texas grand jurors were chosen by a commissioner system. A district judge would appoint several grand jury commissioners, who then selected 15 to 20 citizens of the county. The first 12 who were qualified became the **grand jury**.[11] This "pick-a-pal" system led to older, White, and affluent grand jurors. Also, the *Houston Chronicle* found that under this system Harris County grand jurors were collaborating with prosecutors in trying to affirm the prosecutors' versions of events.[12] New legislation now requires that grand juries be selected randomly from a pool of qualified citizens. Interestingly, under the new system Harris County grand jurors have indicted police officers, something that had not happened in a decade under the "pick-a-pal" system.

grand jury jury that determines whether sufficient evidence is available to justify a trial; grand juries do not rule on the accused's guilt or innocence

Other grand jury reform proposals were proposed, but never approved. These failed reforms include a proposal that prosecutors show grand jurors evidence that might help a suspect's case; that suspects' attorneys be present during questioning; that suspects be notified when they are under investigation and receive evidence that does not identify victims or witnesses if they ask for it; and that prevent prosecutors from going to another grand jury if the initial one declines to indict (unless there is new evidence).[13] In short, the prosecution still has a huge advantage over the defense in a grand jury, but grand juries representing a cross section of the community are more willing to indict police officers and seem to be more independent of prosecutors.

Grand juries can inquire into any criminal matter but usually spend most of their time on felony crimes. They work in secret and rely heavily on the information provided by the prosecutor, though in some rare cases grand juries will work quite independently of the prosecutor. If nine of the grand jurors decide a trial is warranted, they will indict a suspect. An **indictment** is also known as a "true bill." On the other hand, sometimes a grand jury does not believe a trial is warranted. In those cases, the grand jury issues a "no bill" decision.

Although a suspect has the right to trial by jury, he or she may waive that right and undergo a **bench trial** before the judge only. Most commonly, the suspect will engage in a plea bargain. With plea bargaining, a suspect agrees to plead guilty in exchange for a lighter sentence than might be imposed if the suspect were found guilty at trial. Approximately 97 percent of criminal convictions in Texas are the result of **plea bargains**.[14] If the suspect does choose trial by jury, felony juries will have 12 members; misdemeanor juries will have 6 members. There must be a unanimous verdict of guilty or not guilty. If the jurors are not unanimous, the result is a hung jury and a mistrial is declared. The prosecutor may then choose to retry the suspect.

In addition to the requirement of unanimity in jury decisions, another important difference between civil and criminal cases is the standard of proof. In criminal cases, rather than the standard of preponderance of the evidence, the standard is **beyond a reasonable doubt**. This means that the prosecutor must prove the charges against the defendant, and they must be proven to a very high standard.

If a guilty verdict is returned, there will be a separate hearing on the sentence, which in Texas is sometimes also determined by the jury. At the sentencing hearing, factors such as prior record and background will be considered, even though these factors could not be considered at the trial portion of the proceeding.

Of course, a criminal defendant may also appeal a verdict. Usually, appeals are by a convicted defendant who alleges that an error in the trial may have affected the case's outcome. Criminal defendants will appeal their convictions to an intermediate appeals court and perhaps further to the Texas Court of Criminal Appeals. In capital cases, however, the appeal will be directly to the Texas Court of Criminal Appeals.

indictment a written statement issued by a grand jury that charges a suspect with a crime and states that a trial is warranted

bench trial a trial held without a jury and before only a judge

plea bargain negotiated agreement in a criminal case in which a defendant agrees to plead guilty in return for the state's agreement to reduce the severity of the criminal charge or prison sentence the defendant is facing

beyond a reasonable doubt the legal standard in criminal cases that requires the prosecution to prove guilt beyond a reasonable doubt

Court Structure

Describe how the Texas court system is organized

Texas has a large and complex court structure consisting of multiple courts with over-lapping jurisdiction (see Figure 9.1). Additionally, some courts have specialized jurisdiction, whereas others have broad authority to handle a variety of cases. Table 9.1 provides information on characteristics of the Texas courts regarding their jurisdiction and the tenure and salaries of judges on those courts.

At the highest level for civil cases is the **Texas Supreme Court**. This court hears civil cases for which it is the final court of appeal at the state level. The only requirements for being a Texas Supreme Court justice are that one must be a citizen of the United States and of Texas, be at least 35 years of age and under 74 years, and have been either a practicing lawyer or judge for at least 10 years. The **Texas Court of Criminal Appeals** is the highest appeals court in the state for criminal cases. Perhaps the most important role of the Court of Criminal Appeals is its jurisdiction over automatic appeals in death penalty cases.

Texas Supreme Court the highest civil court in Texas; consists of nine justices and has final state appellate authority over civil cases

Texas Court of Criminal Appeals the highest criminal court in Texas; consists of nine justices and has final state appellate authority over criminal cases

FIGURE 9.1

The Structure of the Texas Court System

SOURCE: Texas Office of Court Administration.

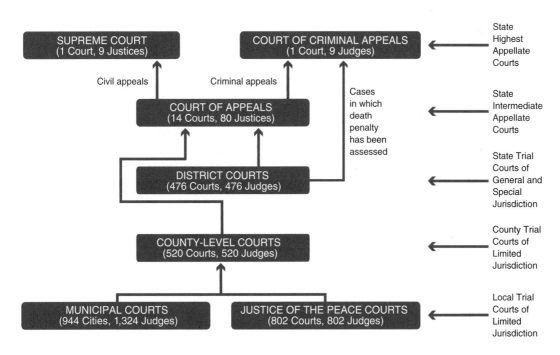

TABLE 9.1

Texas Courts

COURT	JURISDICTION	NUMBER OF JUDGES	TERM OF OFFICE	SALARY
Supreme Court	Civil cases	9	6 years	$168,000 plus $2,500 more for chief justice
Court of Criminal Appeals	Criminal cases	9	6 years	$168,000 plus $2,500 more for presiding judge
Courts of appeal	General	80 judges on 14 courts of appeal	6 years	$154,000, which can be supplemented by additional funds and longevity pay. There is $2,500 additional for each chief justice of the 14 courts.
District courts	General, but may be specialized often into civil and criminal	476 judges	4 years	$140,000, which may be supplemented by up to $18,000 in county funds along with longevity pay
Constitutional county courts	Civil actions less than $10,000; probate; misdemeanors; some appeals from lower courts. In larger counties, exclusively an administrative rather than judicial position	254	4 years	Varies
County-courts-at-law	General (usually limited to $200,000 in civil cases). 18 of the courts limited to probate, guardianship, and mental health issues	266	4 years	Varies
Justice of the peace	Civil actions under $10,000; small claims; fine only misdemeanors; magistrate functions	802	4 years	Varies
Municipal judges	Fine-only misdemeanors; municipal ordinances; limited civil matters; magistrate functions	1,324 judges in 944 cities	Varies; often 2 years	Varies

SOURCE: Texas Office of Court Administration.

FIGURE 9.2

Map of the Courts of Appeal

SOURCE: Texas Office of Court Administration.

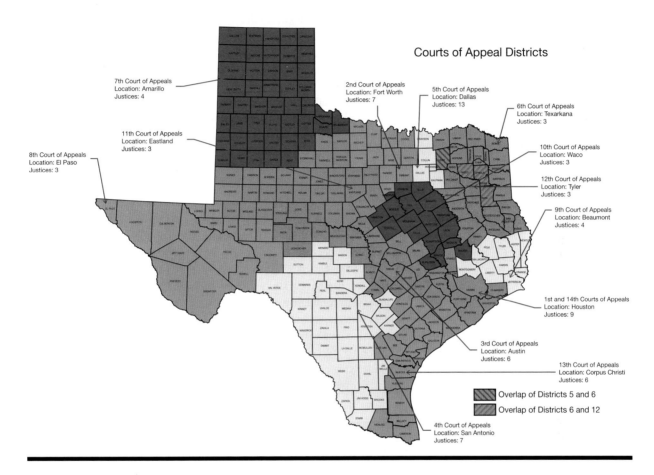

Courts of Appeal Districts

7th Court of Appeals
Location: Amarillo
Justices: 4

11th Court of Appeals
Location: Eastland
Justices: 3

8th Court of Appeals
Location: El Paso
Justices: 3

2nd Court of Appeals
Location: Fort Worth
Justices: 7

5th Court of Appeals
Location: Dallas
Justices: 13

6th Court of Appeals
Location: Texarkana
Justices: 3

10th Court of Appeals
Location: Waco
Justices: 3

12th Court of Appeals
Location: Tyler
Justices: 3

9th Court of Appeals
Location: Beaumont
Justices: 4

1st and 14th Courts of Appeals
Location: Houston
Justices: 9

3rd Court of Appeals
Location: Austin
Justices: 6

13th Court of Appeals
Location: Corpus Christi
Justices: 6

Overlap of Districts 5 and 6

Overlap of Districts 6 and 12

4th Court of Appeals
Location: San Antonio
Justices: 7

Both the Texas Supreme Court and the Court of Criminal Appeals have appellate jurisdiction. This means that they have the authority to review the decisions of lower courts to determine whether legal principles and court procedures were followed correctly. They also have the power to order that a case be retried if mistakes were made. Texas has 14 other appellate courts, which Figure 9.2 shows are located in various parts of the state, and which have both criminal and civil jurisdiction. These **courts of appeal** are intermediate appellate courts that hear appeals from the trial courts. Usually, before the Texas Supreme Court or the Court of Criminal Appeals hears a case, the initial appeal has been heard by one of the courts of appeal. Although occasionally every judge on a court of appeal will hear a case, most appeals at this level are heard by panels of three judges. The requirements for a court of appeal justice are the same as those for justices of the higher courts.

The major trial courts in Texas are the **district courts**. Each county has at least one district court, although in rural parts of the state several counties may be served by one district court. Urban counties have many district courts. Harris County (Houston),

courts of appeal the 14 intermediate-level appellate courts that hear appeals from district and county courts to determine whether the decisions of these lower courts followed legal principles and court procedures correctly

district courts the major trial courts in Texas, which usually have general jurisdiction over a broad range of civil and criminal cases

for example, has 60 district courts, and Dallas County has 39. District courts usually have general jurisdiction, meaning that they hear a broad range of civil and criminal cases that include felonies, divorces, land disputes, election contests, and civil lawsuits. However, in urban counties, some district courts with specialized jurisdiction hear only civil, criminal, juvenile, or family law matters.

Texas policy makers have recognized that there are many offenders who continually recycle through the system. As a result, some courts are **specialty courts** that address particular crimes or serve particular populations. Rather than punishing offenders, these courts focus on rehabilitation and attempt to address the underlying causes of repetitive offenses.

A common type of specialty court in Texas is veterans' courts. When a brain injury or mental issue from military service in a combat zone has affected a veteran, a veterans' court (which like other specialty courts is part of a district court dealing with criminal cases) can hear any criminal case in which a veteran is charged. The idea behind this court is to develop an individualized treatment plan for the veteran. Another specialized court focuses on encouraging prostitutes to leave that life by moving into residential counseling and later outpatient treatment. Counseling, education, and job training are also provided by the court.

By far the most common of specialty courts are drug courts, where regular monitoring of drug offenders occurs—far more intensive monitoring than in traditional probation—and where the courts work to stop offenders' pattern of drug abuse. Drug courts have been more intensively studied than other specialty courts, and it has been found that offenders who complete a drug court's program have far lower rates of recidivism than offenders who do not complete or who do not participate in a program.[15] There are also DWI courts that deal with cases involving offenders who abuse alcohol and drive. Rather than imprisoning DWI offenders, the idea is to try to rehabilitate the offenders by focusing on the underlying alcohol problem. Successful completion of a specialty court's program will result in dismissal of the charges against the offender.

specialty courts usually part of district courts and focusing on trying to resolve the underlying problems such as mental health, alcohol and drug abuse, and prostitution that lead to recurring criminal behavior

The Texas Supreme Court is the highest civil court in Texas. The court consists of nine justices. In the fall of 2020, Justice Paul Green retired, and Rebeca Huddle was appointed in his place.

Texas is unusual in having the office of **county judge** in each of its 254 counties. This official presides over the county commissioners' court and thus has responsibilities for administration of county government. In the early stages of the pandemic, several county judges acted quickly to respond to the crisis. Dallas County Judge Clay Jenkins took the lead, relying on his emergency powers to issue orders that limited the size of gatherings, closed bars and restaurants, and then imposed a shelter-in-place order. In rural parts of the state, the county judge also presides over a **county court**, which has jurisdiction over both criminal and civil cases and may also hear appeals from municipal courts or from justice of the peace courts. County judges combine political-administrative functions with some judicial functions. However, in the more populated counties, statutory county-courts-at-law, as well as statutory probate courts, have eliminated most and sometimes all of the county judges' judicial duties.

County court judges receive about $25,000 in extra compensation if they sign a one-page declaration at the start of every year in which they promise that 40 percent of their work will involve court cases. This extra compensation program for county judges has been in existence for over 20 years.

In a 2016 investigation by the *Austin American-Statesman*, it was found that this extra compensation amounted to nearly a 50 percent pay increase in some of the rural counties and that 219 of the 254 county judges claimed the extra money, even though it appeared many of them did not actually spend 40 percent of their time on court cases. The Kent County judge, for example, only handled about a half dozen court cases in 2015, although he received the extra pay. The county auditor in Austin County refused to pay the county judge the extra money because the auditor claimed the judge had performed negligible judicial functions. Some county judges took cases from statutory county-court-at-law judges so that they would have a judicial caseload and be able to obtain the extra money.[16] In spite of the apparent abuse of this extra pay arrangement, nothing has been done by the state to increase supervision of the county judges' judicial work or to audit their activities.

Since the **statutory county-courts-at-law** were created by statute, often at widely different times, the jurisdiction of these courts varies significantly. Usually, they hear appeals from justices of the peace and from municipal courts as well as having civil and criminal jurisdiction. However, some of the county-courts-at-law have specialized jurisdiction; most commonly these are in the most urban counties, where some of the courts have only civil jurisdiction and others only criminal jurisdiction.

In the most urban areas of the state, the legislature has created **statutory probate courts**. These courts are highly specialized, as their primary activity involves matters relating to the disposition of property of deceased persons. They may also deal with guardianship of people unable to handle their own affairs and with commitments of people to mental institutions. In other parts of the state, depending on the statute, probate matters may be heard by the county court, the county-court-at-law, or the district court.

Each county in Texas has between one and eight justice of the peace precincts, depending on population. Within each precinct are **justice of the peace courts** which primarily hear class C misdemeanors, which are less serious crimes usually involving traffic offenses. They also have jurisdiction over minor civil matters, functioning as small claims courts. These suits can be handled informally, as the rules governing suits may not be "so complex that a reasonable person without legal training would have difficulty understanding or applying the rules."[17] Justices of the peace may issue search and arrest warrants.

county judge the person in each of Texas's 254 counties who presides over the county commissioners' court, with responsibility for the administration of county government; some county judges carry out judicial responsibilities

county courts the courts that exist in some counties and that are presided over by county judges

statutory county-courts-at-law courts that tend to hear less serious criminal cases than those heard by district courts; they usually hear civil cases that involve smaller economic claims than are heard by district courts

statutory probate courts specialized courts whose jurisdiction is limited to probate and guardianship matters

justice of the peace courts local trial courts with limited jurisdiction over small claims and very minor criminal misdemeanors

The Texas Court of Criminal Appeals is the highest court in the state for criminal cases. Like the Texas Supreme Court, it has nine justices (pictured here as of 2020).

Justices of the peace mostly handle traffic misdemeanors. Of the 2.6 million cases added to justice of the peace caseloads in the 2019 fiscal year, 66 percent were traffic cases. In contrast, 24 percent of the justice of the peace caseloads involved civil cases.[18]

Justices of the peace have faced considerable criticism in recent years. Professor Barbara Kirby found that between 2008 and 2014, 28 to 62 percent of the disciplinary actions imposed on judges for inappropriate or unethical behavior by the State Commission on Judicial Conduct were on justices of the peace. Kirby found that between December 2002 and April 2015, 50 Texas judges had been suspended from their duties by the commission—one of the most severe punishments imposed. Of those 50 judges, 21 were justices of the peace and 19 of those justices did not have a law degree. One of the most common sanctions imposed on justices of the peace by the commission is a requirement that they undergo additional education because, the commission explained, "Legal and procedural issues are often complex, so it is not surprising that some judges, particularly non-lawyer judges, take judicial action that may exceed their authority or that is contrary to procedural rules."[19]

Only about 10 percent of the justices of the peace in Texas are lawyers, and the justices' lack of legal credentials has led to considerable debate in the state.[20] The office has existed in Texas since 1837, even before statehood. In the days of the frontier, justices of the peace provided legal authority where no other existed. The initial idea was that a justice of the peace would be a respected person in the community who was chosen for ability, judgment, and integrity. Today, as former Texas state bar president W. Frank Newton has pointed out, "in almost every large metropolitan area, there are some JPs [justices of the peace] who do virtually nothing and sort of get lost in the shuffle. People don't tend to get all excited about JP elections. Most people don't know what a JP does. JP is not a very prestigious job."[21]

Municipal courts have been created by the legislature in each of the incorporated cities of the state. Municipal courts have jurisdiction over violations of city **ordinances** and, concurrent with justice of the peace courts, have jurisdiction over class C misdemeanors, for which the punishment for conviction is a fine. Municipal judges may issue search and arrest warrants, but they have only limited civil jurisdiction. Municipal courts, like justice of the peace courts, function primarily as traffic courts. During fiscal year 2019, about 5,000,000 cases were filed in municipal courts, and 72 percent were traffic cases.[22]

municipal courts local trial courts with limited jurisdiction over violations of city ordinances and very minor criminal misdemeanors

ordinance a regulation enacted by a city government in each of Texas's incorporated cities and towns

Judicial Politics

 Evaluate the process for selecting judges in Texas

Like the federal courts, the state and local courts in Texas are responsible for securing liberty and equality under the law. However, the democratic mechanisms put into place in Texas to select judges and hold them accountable for their actions are quite different from those at the national level. Federal judges are appointed by the president and confirmed by the Senate. They have lifetime appointments. This means that federal judges, subject to good behavior in office, are free from the ebb and flow of democratic politics. They do not have to cater to public opinion and are empowered to interpret the law as they see fit, without fear of reprisal at the polls. In Texas, however, judges are elected. Although they may initially be appointed, sooner or later they are accountable to the voters. Election of judges brings not only the people but also interest groups into the selection and retention of judges. The influence of special interest money in judicial campaigns raises important questions about the relationship between the rule of law and the nature of democratic politics.

Initial Appointment of Judges by the Governor

Because the governor appoints district and appellate judges to the bench to fill vacancies prior to an election or to fill judgeships on new courts, a substantial percentage of judges initially get on the bench through appointment. Although some governors have been criticized for the relatively small number of people of color they appointed, gubernatorial appointment of judges has generated little additional controversy.[23] As of September 2019 about 36 percent of appellate judges and about 27 percent of district judges initially got on the bench through appointment.[24] However, the controversial issue in Texas judicial politics deals with how the remaining judges obtained their seats and how all judges must retain their seats if they wish to remain in office. That controversy involves the partisan election of judges in Texas.

Judicial Elections Become Highly Partisan

Until 1978 the selection of judges in partisan elections did not create much concern. Texas was an overwhelmingly Democratic state, and judges were elected as Democrats. The only real competition occurred in the Democratic primary, and with the political advantage of incumbency, judges were rarely defeated even in the primary. Competition in judicial races occurred in those relatively rare cases where there was an open seat in which no incumbent sought office. One journalist aptly described the judicial elections of that era in this way:

> Justices' names seldom appeared in the press and were known only to the legal community. Most justices had been judges in the lower courts; a few had served in the Legislature. At election time, sitting justices almost never drew opposition. Some justices resigned before the end of their terms, enabling their replacements to be named by the governor and to run as incumbents. In the event that an open seat was actually contested, the decisive factor in the race was the state bar poll, which was the key to newspaper endorsements and the support of courthouse politicians.[25]

Beginning in 1978, however, changes began to occur in Texas judicial politics. That year, William Clements, the first Republican governor since Reconstruction, was elected. The governor has the power to appoint judges to the district and higher courts when new courts have been created or when a judicial vacancy occurs as a result of death, resignation, or retirement. Unlike the previous Democratic governors, who appointed members of the Democratic Party, Clements began appointing Republicans. With that advantage

Is justice for sale in Texas? Because statewide judicial races are expensive, candidates for judgeships have been forced to raise considerable amounts of money. This, in turn, has led to criticism that judicial decisions are, in effect, being bought.

of incumbency and with the increasing popularity of the Republican Party label, some of the Republican judges began to win re-election.

Helped by the popularity of Ronald Reagan in Texas, other Republicans began seeking judicial offices and winning. Thus, by the early 1980s, in statewide elections and in several counties in Texas, competition began to appear in judicial races. With that competition, incumbent judges began to be defeated. Sensing the growth of Republican strength, a number of Democratic judges changed to a Republican Party affiliation. At the same time, judicial elections became more expensive because judicial candidates needed money to run meaningful and competitive campaigns. In particular, campaigns that used television advertising became very expensive because of high media costs.

Judicial candidates needed money because judicial races tend to have low-visibility campaigns in which voters are unaware of the candidates. Money was needed to give judicial candidates some degree of name visibility to voters. However, in general, Texas voters do not give much money to judicial campaigns. Instead, it is lawyers and interest groups who tend to be donors in judicial races. Thus, by the early 1980s, there was a new and expensive competitiveness in Texas judicial politics that in turn fed a demand for reforms in the way Texas judges were selected.

Proposed Reforms of the Texas Judiciary

There have been numerous efforts to reform the Texas judiciary. In general, reformers are concerned with (1) changing the system for selecting judges, (2) judicial campaign finance, (3) increasing representation of people of color on the bench, and (4) restructuring the judiciary to make it more rational and efficient.

Changing the System for Selecting Judges The reform movement focused on changing the method by which judges are selected has been concerned with the low visibility of judicial races in Texas. Voters are rarely aware of the qualifications and abilities of judicial candidates and, as a result, rely on party labels when electing judges. At other times, reformers claim, voters rely on the attractiveness of judicial candidates' names in voting, since they lack other knowledge of the candidates. Still another problem pointed out by these reformers is that in urban counties there are so many candidates on the ballot that it is impossible for voters to make informed decisions about each one.

In some states, judges are elected in nonpartisan elections, in which judicial candidates run for office without a party label; in some other states, judges are appointed by the executive; and in a couple of states, the legislature selects judges. By far the most frequently proposed reform nationwide, however, has been to switch to **merit selection** of judges. Under this system, a blue-ribbon commission solicits interest in a vacant judicial seat and screens possible candidates for that seat. The commission then recommends to the governor three to five persons who it believes are highly qualified for the

merit selection a judicial reform under which judges would be nominated by a blue-ribbon committee, then be appointed by the governor and, after a brief period in office, run in a retention election

Judicial Elections and Straight-Ticket Voting

1 Why partisan judicial elections matter

Judges in Texas are chosen in partisan elections to ensure that judges are accountable to the people. Yet, in order to make judges accountable to the electorate, voters must know what attitudes and values judicial candidates have. If voters are blindly casting their ballots, it is impossible for them to hold judges accountable for their behavior and for their decisions and, of course, those decisions can have an important impact on Texans. It is important to a community, for example, to know whether a judge is lenient in sentencing habitual drunk drivers. It is also important to know if judges require high bail for certain crimes or whether appellate judges are skeptical of the size of jury awards. There may be a few cases of broad societal interest, but there are many more routine cases that have an effect on society and where Texas voters may wish to elect judges who reflect their values.

The problem is that judicial elections are down-ballot—toward the bottom of the ballot under the more high-profile races for candidates such as senator or governor. And judicial campaigns are low-information campaigns. Judicial candidates do not raise enough campaign contributions to reach out to voters and express their views. Additionally, judicial candidates ethically cannot make political campaign promises like executive or legislative candidates. It would, for example, be improper for a judicial candidate to promise rulings against insurance companies or promise imprisonment for all persons charged with drunk driving. The role of a judge is to hear both sides of an issue and reach a decision based on law. Thus, what a judge can promise is more limited than what candidates for nonjudicial offices can say.

2 What's the debate?

Both political parties recognize that Texas judges are "nearly anonymous people in charge of the third branch of state government" and that Texas voters "have only the vaguest idea of who they are."[a] Republicans have passed legislation to address the problem of the uninformed voter in judicial races by eliminating straight-ticket voting in the 2020 elections and afterward. Chief Justice Nathan Hecht, a Republican, has stated that in 2018, when hundreds of incumbent

The large number of judicial elections makes it difficult for voters to be informed about each candidate. Most voters make their decision based on party identification and name recognition.

judges were voted out of office, the state judiciary "lost seven centuries of judicial experience at a single stroke."[b] The reason, of course, was the partisan election of judges combined with straight-ticket Democratic voting in large urban areas driven by the U.S. Senate candidacy of Beto O'Rourke.

The sponsor of the legislation banning straight-ticket voting was Republican representative Ron Simmons, who insisted that the bill was not partisan. He argued that the bill "would help all Texans" and that by requiring voters to vote for each individual candidate, the result would be educated voters casting knowledgeable ballots.[c] The Democrats insisted that the bill was partisan and was designed to reduce the chances that Democrats would win down-ballot races. They argued that it would make it more difficult for African American and Latino voters who often vote straight tickets. They further argued that it would make voting harder for the sick and disabled who would have to wade through lengthy ballots, and that it would lower turnout because voting would take longer, leading to greater delays at the polls.

3 What do the numbers say?

Two-thirds of the voters in the 48 largest counties cast straight-ticket ballots and half of the 2018 vote came from seven urban counties—Bexar, Collin, Dallas, Denton, Har-

Number of Judicial Races on 2018 Ballot in Urban Counties in Texas

COUNTY	STATEWIDE CONTESTED JUDICIAL RACES	COURT OF APPEALS CONTESTED RACES	DISTRICT JUDGE CONTESTED RACES	COUNTY-LEVEL CONTESTED JUDICIAL RACES	TOTAL
Bexar	4	5	9	15	33
Dallas	4	8	3	0	15
Harris	4	10	36	23	73
Tarrant	4	3	2	0	9
Travis	4	4	0	0	8
Nueces	4	4	2	1	11

SOURCE: Compiled from data on Ballotpedia.org.

ris, Tarrant, and Travis counties. In those counties, Democrats got 55.2 percent of the straight-ticket vote and Republicans got 44.1 percent.

In 2020 voters in counties that supported the Democratic presidential nominee, such as Harris, Dallas, Travis, and Bexar counties, elected only Democratic judges. Counties that supported the Republican presidential nominee generally elected Republican judges. Even without straight-ticket voting, voters are casting their ballots mainly with the party label as a guide to their decision making.

Communicating Effectively: What Do You Think?

- Is it a problem that most voters don't look beyond the judicial candidates' party label when voting in judicial elections? Why or why not?

- Is the removal of the straight-ticket vote a way to weaken Democrats' efforts to win judicial seats, or is it a way to ensure that voters will be knowledgeable when they vote for candidates? Does the 2020 election suggest that the ban on straight-ticket voting was meaningless?

- If the large number of judicial candidates on the ballot is a problem, what solution would you propose?

WANT TO LEARN MORE?

Several organizations provide material on the issues involving state judiciaries and on the various problems of and systems of judicial selection in the states.

- Brennan Center for Justice
  brennancenter.org

- National Center for State Courts
  ncsc.org

- American Bar Association
  americanbar.org

position, and the governor appoints one of those recommended to the vacancy, subject to state senate confirmation. After serving for about one year, the appointed judge runs in a **retention election** where he or she has no opponent but voters decide if they wish to retain the judge in office. Thereafter, the judge would continue to run for re-election in a retention election. The result of adopting merit selection, in the view of its advocates, is a far greater likelihood that judges will be highly competent and will have little need to depend on lawyers and interest groups for funding to remain in office. Retention elections can be expensive campaigns, but in general they are very low-budget.

Reformers advocate this plan because they believe voters lack sufficient knowledge of judicial candidates and rely too heavily on the party label in casting their ballots. Part of the reason for that lack of voter knowledge of judicial candidates is the sheer number of those candidates in urban counties in Texas. With 73 contested judicial races in Harris County at the countywide level and higher in 2018 and 23 contested judicial races in 2020, it is hard to imagine how voters can be informed. As a result, they vote for the party rather than for the best-qualified person. In 2016, for example, 65 percent of Harris County voters cast a straight-ticket ballot, which meant that they voted the party label rather than for the individual candidate. **Straight-ticket voting** can sweep experienced judges out of office solely because of their party affiliation. However, the 2020 elections indicated that voters cast their ballots for judges based on party affiliation even absent the ability to vote a straight ticket. When Harris County juvenile judge Glenn Devlin was defeated, he released almost all defendants who appeared before him the day after the election, only asking the defendants whether they intended to kill anyone before he released them. Seven juveniles were released including four facing aggravated robbery charges. Judge Devlin explained that in light of the election he believed that was what the voters wanted. While it seems doubtful that voters wanted juveniles charged with violent crimes to be released, it was the case that Republican judges running for re-election lost solely because of their political party affiliation.[26]

In the absence of voter awareness of judicial candidates, reformers are also concerned that voters will rely on irrelevant factors such as the perceived attractiveness of a candidate's name when they vote for judges. In 2008 there was heavy voting for Democrats in Harris County because of the popularity of presidential candidate Barack Obama. So many voters voted straight Democratic that all but four Republican judges were voted out of office. Interestingly, the four Republican judges who survived were all challenged by Democrats with more unusual names. As a result, the incumbent Republican judge Sharon McCally was able to defeat the Democratic challenger Ashish Mahendru; Mark Kent Ellis defeated Mekisha Murray; Patricia Kerrigan defeated Andres Pereira; and Joseph Halbach defeated Goodwille Pierre.[27]

An example of voter confusion over names occurred in the 2016 Republican primary race for a Place 5 (appellate courts have multiple members, and judicial candidates run for specific seats or places on those courts) on the Court of Criminal Appeals. No incumbent was running for re-election, and there were four candidates, including one with stellar credentials: Sid Harle had been a criminal defense attorney, a Bexar County prosecutor, and a longtime trial judge who had presided over more capital murder cases than any other judge in Texas, and he was a former chair of the State Commission on Judicial Conduct. His three opponents had no judicial experience, and one had civil rather than criminal law experience. Yet Harle finished fourth in the race with only about 18.5 percent of the vote. The candidate with the highest percentage of votes had limited criminal trial and appellate experience over an 18-year career and did not run an active campaign.

Justice Brett Busby
@BrettBusby

Many can't pay rent due to the pandemic, and I and my #SCOTX colleagues are responding with a new order. It ensures evictions from housing covered by the CARES Act are delayed until 7/25. Texans must have safe places to stay to defeat this virus; this order will help us do that!

Justice Brett Busby, who sits on the Texas Supreme Court, posted a misleading campaign advertisement during the coronavirus pandemic asserting that the court had extended eviction deadlines for renters. However, this deadline was already federally mandated by the CARES Act.

He ran not as Richard Walker, but used his middle name, Scott, on the ballot—and "Scott Walker" happened to be the name of the then highly visible Republican governor of Wisconsin.[28] Walker later overwhelmingly won the Republican runoff primary and won in the general election.

While reformers are passionate about structural changes to how judges are selected in Texas, restructuring the system would be a major change, and such changes are always difficult to initiate. A major change might upset voters, who like being able to vote for judges, and it would surely upset political parties, which like having large numbers of judicial candidates running under their party label. It might also upset lawyers accustomed to the traditional ways of selecting judges and even judges who have benefited from the present system.

In looking at the experience of other states, it seems clear that each state has developed a judicial selection system to reflect its own political objectives. While systems of judicial selections can roughly be classified as merit selection, partisan election, nonpartisan election, gubernatorial appointment, and selection by the legislature, states have great variations in selection systems within these broad categories. Illinois, for example, has partisan election of judges for their initial terms and then retention elections for subsequent elections. Missouri has merit selection for some courts and partisan election for others. New Mexico has merit selection for initial selection of judges, but in the next general election, the judge must run in a partisan election. The winning candidate serves the remainder of the term, at which time the judge runs in a retention election for another term. To be retained, the judge must receive at least a 57 percent affirmative vote. If the judge is not retained, the nominating commission presents another list of judicial candidates to the governor, who then appoints a new judge. Governors appoint judges in California, but a commission has the power to veto their appointment. When it comes to the details, there are almost as many ways to select judges as there are states. (See Texas and the Nation on p. 315.)

The defeat of a large number of Republican incumbent judges in 2018 led to the appointment of a commission to study judicial reform and possibly recommend a change in how Texas selects judges. Any change in the judicial selection system that is proposed by the commission, however, is certain to be interpreted by Democrats as a partisan effort to protect Republicans in Texas's urban areas.

Judicial Campaign Finance Of special concern to reformers has been the role of money in judicial campaigns, insofar as campaign funds are seen as creating problems for the integrity of the judicial branch and for the appearance of fairness in judicial decision making. Contributions for judicial races in Texas can sometimes amount to several hundred thousand dollars, especially for hotly contested district court or appellate court races. In general, however, the most expensive races are for the Texas Supreme Court.

When Texas Supreme Court races are contested between Democratic and Republican candidates, a candidate can raise well over $1 million. However, hard-fought races are now rare, as these statewide elections have moved into the Republican column. Because these are statewide races and because this court sets the tone of tort law (civil lawsuits over harm to another) throughout the state, a great deal of money is needed and a great deal can be raised (see Table 9.2). One million dollars may seem like a small sum for a statewide race in Texas considering that in his 2018 campaign for governor, Greg Abbott alone raised over $78 million and that even the winning candidate for railroad commissioner, Christi Craddick, raised over $6 million.[29] Unlike other elected officials, however, judicial candidates are supposed to be neutral decision makers not reflecting the

TABLE 9.2

State Supreme Court Elections in 2017–18 with More Than $1,000,000 in Contributions

STATE	SYSTEM OF SELECTION	SEATS UP FOR ELECTION	TOTAL CONTRIBUTIONS
Pennsylvania	Partisan	3	$2,632,612
North Carolina[1]	Nonpartisan	1	$2,025,130
West Virginia[2]	Nonpartisan	2	$1,333,126
Alabama	Partisan	5	$6,442,218
Wisconsin (2016)	Nonpartisan	2	$2,862,776
Michigan[3]	Nonpartisan	2	$2,995,893
Texas	Partisan	3	$2,643,362
Nevada	Nonpartisan	3	$1,718,111
Ohio[3]	Nonpartisan	2	$1,618,007
Georgia	Nonpartisan	5	$1,065,691

[1]North Carolina changed to partisan judicial elections in December 2016.
[2]West Virginia changed to nonpartisan judicial elections in April 2015.
[3]Michigan and Ohio have partisan primaries, but nonpartisan general elections for judges.

SOURCE: FollowTheMoney.org.

Comparing How Texas Selects Its Judges to the Rest of the Country

Method of Initial Selection for State's Highest Court Judges

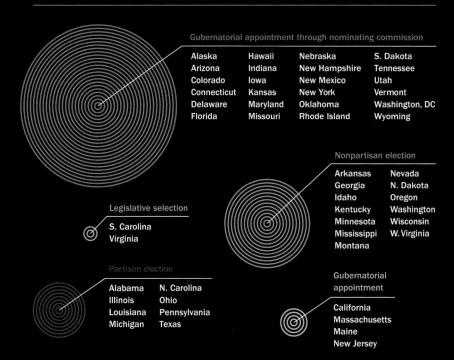

Gubernatorial appointment through nominating commission

Alaska	Hawaii	Nebraska	S. Dakota
Arizona	Indiana	New Hampshire	Tennessee
Colorado	Iowa	New Mexico	Utah
Connecticut	Kansas	New York	Vermont
Delaware	Maryland	Oklahoma	Washington, DC
Florida	Missouri	Rhode Island	Wyoming

Nonpartisan election

Arkansas	Nevada
Georgia	N. Dakota
Idaho	Oregon
Kentucky	Washington
Minnesota	Wisconsin
Mississippi	W. Virginia
Montana	

Legislative selection

S. Carolina
Virginia

Partisan election

Alabama	N. Carolina
Illinois	Ohio
Louisiana	Pennsylvania
Michigan	Texas

Gubernatorial appointment

California
Massachusetts
Maine
New Jersey

Texas is one of eight states that choose their state judges through partisan elections. Voters generally decide for whom to vote based on party affiliation. With so many offices on the ballot, it is simply easier for voters to use their party affiliation as a shortcut. Not all states select judges this way. Most states employ a merit selection method through nominating commissions that make recommendations to the governor. Other states have judges selected by the governor without nominating commissions. Thirteen states elect their judges in nonpartisan elections, meaning that the role of political parties in judicial elections is minimized. The state legislature chooses judges in the remaining two states.

Judicial Selection Methods: A Regional View

- Gubernatorial appointment through nominating commission
- Gubernatorial appointment
- Partisan election
- Nonpartisan election
- Legislative selection

SOURCES: American Judicature Society, Judicial Selection in the States, www.judicial selection.us/and IAALS, the Institute for the Advancement of the American Legal System at the University of Denver published in "Selection and Retention of State Judges," *Texas Bar Journal* (February 2016): 92–97.

CRITICAL THINKING

- What are the advantages of nonpartisan elections to select judges? Which method of selection do you think is the best and why?

- Are there regional patterns in how judges are selected? If so, why do you think that is?

values of particular interests in the state. Yet winning Texas Supreme Court candidates overwhelmingly get their contributions from the oil and gas industry, lawyers, lobbyists, and the finance sector.

As Texas's statewide judicial elections have become less competitive, the amounts contributed to supreme court candidates have dropped precipitously. In 1988, when Texas Supreme Court races were still competitive between Democrats and Republicans, total contributions for supreme court candidates came to over $11.4 million, with one candidate alone receiving over $2 million in contributions.[30] By 2014 far less money was contributed to or needed by Republican candidates, since they faced no serious threat from Democratic opponents. To the extent that there is any real battle for a position on the Texas Supreme Court, it is now within the Republican primary, though in 2018 all three of the incumbent Republican justices were unopposed in the primary and easily won re-election in the general election. In 2020 as well, the four Republicans had no primary opposition and readily won in the general election.

While the statewide elections for Texas Supreme Court and the lesser-funded Texas Court of Criminal Appeals have been uncompetitive, the 2018 elections for the intermediate appellate courts that are centered in the state's most urban counties were highly competitive. Judges on these courts are even less known than statewide elected judges, but they wield considerable power. Of the cases appealed to these courts, overall the courts of appeal reverse 30 percent of trial court decisions.[31]

Table 9.3 shows the highly competitive nature of the urban courts of appeal in the 2018 election. In the seven courts of appeal in the table, 19 incumbent Republican judges were defeated and Democrats won every race except for an open seat on the 2nd Court of Appeals in Fort Worth. Some of the campaigns received a great deal of money, such as

TABLE 9.3

Electoral Competition on the Courts of Appeal, 2018

COURT OF APPEAL	NUMBER OF CONTESTED SEATS	NUMBER OF DEMOCRATS WHO WON	REPUBLICAN INCUMBENTS DEFEATED	AVERAGE DEMOCRATIC CAMPAIGN CONTRIBUTIONS	AVERAGE REPUBLICAN CAMPAIGN CONTRIBUTIONS
1st Court—Houston	5	5	4	$77,944	$959,048
2nd Court—Fort Worth	1	0	0	$8,769	$45,491
3rd Court—Austin	4	4	4	$120,929	$1,903,511
4th Court—San Antonio	5	5	1	$322,513	$205,972
5th Court—Dallas	8	8	5	$118,633	$109,124
13th Court—Corpus Christi	4	4	0	$192,184	$102,719
14th Court—Houston	5	5	5	$44,969	$193,836

SOURCE: FollowTheMoney.org.

Republicans on the 3rd Court of Appeals in Austin, and some candidates received little money, such as the Democrat who ran for the open seat on the 2nd Court of Appeals in Fort Worth. The 2020 elections showed a similar pattern where Democratic Court of Appeals candidates defeated all the Republican judicial candidates on the 1st, 3rd, 4th, 5th, and 14th courts of appeal.

In contrast to efforts to change Texas from partisan election to merit selection, judicial campaign finance reform has seen success in the form of the **Judicial Campaign Fairness Act**. Texas is the only state with a campaign finance regulation of this type. Among the most important aspects of compliance with the act are campaign contribution limitations. For example, statewide judicial candidates must limit themselves to contributions of no more than $5,000 from any individual in any election. Additionally, statewide candidates can receive no more than $30,000 per election from any law firm. Although the amounts of money that can be donated are still quite high, there has been a significant reduction from contribution amounts in the 1980s when, prior to the act, some donors would give candidates $25,000, $50,000, and even more. These contribution limitations are imposed by law; however, judicial candidates may also voluntarily agree to campaign expenditure limitations specified in the law—for example, a $2 million expenditure limit for statewide judicial candidates and a $500,000 limit for candidates for courts of appeal in areas larger than one million persons.[32]

Judicial Campaign Fairness Act a judicial reform that places limits on judicial campaign contributions

Increasing Representation of People of Color on the Bench

Another group of reformers has been interested in increasing the numbers of African Americans and Latinas and Latinos on the bench. In 1985, Professor Paul Brest wrote, "Judges are far from a representative cross-section of American society. They are overwhelmingly Anglo, male, well educated, and upper or upper middle class. They are also members of the legal profession. . . . Women, Blacks, and Hispanics are only the groups most notoriously under-represented on the judiciary."[33] What Brest wrote in 1985 is still true in Texas and throughout the nation. Although African Americans and Hispanics together make up about 50 percent of the Texas population, relatively few Texas judges belong to these groups.

The lack of diversity on the bench creates significant problems for the legitimacy of the courts and for the proper functioning of those courts within a diverse population. Professor Sherrilyn Ifill has argued that diversity among judges is necessary for impartiality in judicial decision making, public confidence in the court system, and the perception that society as a whole is represented on the bench. Ifill wrote, "First, the creation of a racially diverse bench can introduce traditionally excluded perspectives and values into judicial decision making. The interplay of diverse views and perspectives can enrich judicial decision making. . . . Second, racial diversity on the bench also encourages judicial impartiality, by ensuring that a single set of values or views do not dominate judicial decision making."[34]

Although women do not make up 50 percent of the Texas judiciary as they do of the population, there is a higher proportion of women in the Texas judiciary than of people of color. In Texas, the first woman to serve as a state judge was Sarah Hughes, who was appointed in 1935

PERSONAL RESPONSIBILITY: WHAT WOULD YOU DO?

- Few people of color hold judicial office in Texas. Although African Americans and Latinos make up about 50 percent of the Texas population, relatively few Texas judges belong to these groups. Offer at least three suggestions, including alternative election methods, to increase the number of people of color holding judicial office in Texas.

In 2009, Rick Perry appointed Eva Guzman (left)—the first Latina woman to serve on the Texas Supreme Court—to fill a vacancy on the court. Guzman was elected to a full term in the 2010 election and re-elected in 2016. In 2018, Lina Hidalgo (right) was elected as the first Latina and the first female Harris County Judge.

and served as a district judge until 1961, when she was appointed to the federal bench. Famous for a number of her decisions, including one that forced Dallas County to build a new jail, she is probably best known as the judge who swore in Lyndon Johnson as president after the assassination of John F. Kennedy. By September 2019, 46 percent of appellate judges in Texas were women, and 37 percent of district judges were women. In contrast, only 3 percent of appellate judges and 10 percent of district judges are African American, and only 18 percent of appellate judges and 19 percent of district judges are Latino.[35]

Different interpretations have been offered for the low numbers of people of color on the bench. The lack of racial and ethnic diversity among the judiciary is a nationwide problem. Civil rights groups in several states with elective judiciaries, including Texas, have argued that judicial districts that are countywide or larger are dominated by Whites who vote against judicial candidates of color. These groups have argued that for people of color to get elected as judges, there must be smaller judicial districts where voters of color make up the majority of the population. One problem with dividing judicial districts into areas smaller than counties, however, is that Latino and African American organizations have been unable to agree on the appropriate method of creating smaller districts. Both groups have sought to divide counties in different ways to reflect their group's respective interests. Additionally, the business community in Texas has been opposed to smaller judicial districts out of fear that they will lead to the election of judges whose largely minority constituencies might be hostile and favor individual plaintiffs in lawsuits against businesses.

An alternative perspective is that candidates of color in Texas, like voters of color, tend to be Democrats at a time when Republicans still dominate judicial races. Thus, people of color do not get elected to judicial office because they run as Democrats. If the reason for the lack of people of color on the bench is that they run as Democrats rather than as Republicans, there should be an increase in representation of people of color if Democrats continue to be elected to the bench as occurred in 2018 with "Harris County Black Girl Magic." Still another argument is that there are few judges of color because there are few lawyers of color and, with the exception of county judges and justices of the peace, judges in Texas must be lawyers. Only 6 percent of lawyers in Texas are African American and only 10 percent are Latino.[36]

Who Are Texas's Judges?

—By race   ● White   ● African American   ● Latino   ● Other

—By gender   ● Male   ● Female

Trial Courts

Trial courts include district courts, county courts at law, and probate courts

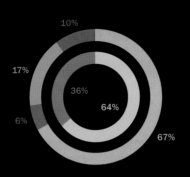

10%
17%
36% 64%
6%
67%

Appellate Courts

Appellate courts include the state Supreme Court, courts of appeal, and Court of Criminal Appeals

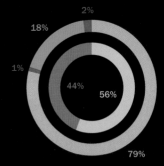

2%
18%
1%
44% 56%
79%

Texas Lawyers

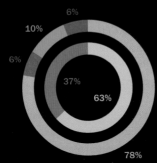

6%
10%
6%
37% 63%
78%

Texas Population

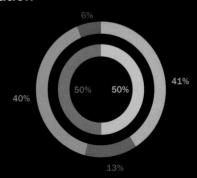

6%
40% 41%
50% 50%
13%

Although the proportion of women, Latino, and African American judges is roughly representative of the proportion of women, Latino, and African American lawyers, the composition of the Texas judiciary is very unrepresentative of the Texas population as a whole. Should there be a rough proportionality between the racial/ethnic/gender composition of the judiciary and Texas as a whole?

QUANTITATIVE REASONING

- Are there more or fewer minority judges in Texas than minorities in the state population overall? (Texas is 13 percent African American and 40 percent Latino.)

- What are some of the factors that might lead to an increase in the representation of minorities in the state's courts?

SOURCES: Texas Office of Court Administration, Profile of Appellate and Trial Judges as of September 1, 2020; State Bar of Texas, "State Bar of Texas Membership: Attorney Statistical Profile (2019–2020)"; U.S. Census "Quickfacts," July 1, 2019.

Favorability toward the Courts and Criminal Justice System by Race/Ethnicity

A University of Texas/*Texas Tribune* poll of 1,200 registered Texas voters asked their favorability toward the courts and the criminal justice system. Thirty-nine percent of White Texans had favorable attitudes, but only 24 percent of African Americans had favorable attitudes. What do you think explains the disparity in favorability ratings toward the courts and criminal justice system between White and African American Texans?

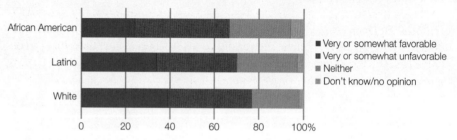

SOURCE: University of Texas/*Texas Tribune* poll, June 2019. Survey was conducted May 31–June 9, 2019 of 1,200 registered voters in Texas.

Restructuring the Texas Judiciary to Make It More Rational and Efficient Texas judges may be elected, but they do not represent an electorate in the way legislators or county commissioners do. As a result, their districts are not subject to redistricting according to the one person–one vote standards used in redistricting legislative bodies. The result is that Texas judicial districts are a hodgepodge of jurisdictions. Things have not changed much since a 1993 report that criticized the structure of the Texas courts:

> The framers of our current Constitution deliberately designed a system to "localize justice," establishing a multiplicity of largely autonomous conveniently located courts across the state. With the passage of time, the organization of the courts has become more, not less, cumbersome. A case may frequently be eligible for filing in more than one court, either because of overlapping geographical boundaries or overlapping subject matter jurisdiction. Courts with the same name may have different responsibilities and similar places may have quite dissimilar court structures.[37]

As a state bar commission pointed out, the idea behind having justice of the peace courts, statutory county courts, constitutional county courts, and district courts was that each level of court was supposed to have its own jurisdiction that was to be consistent across each court at that level. That consistency has not come about; instead, these courts have developed into a "patchwork array."[38]

One illustration of this cumbersome court structure can be found in the district court structure in Anderson County in east Texas. There are four district courts in Anderson

County. One of those courts also has jurisdiction in Henderson and Houston counties; one also has jurisdiction in Freestone, Leon, and Limestone counties; one has jurisdiction only in Houston County; and the fourth also has jurisdiction in Cherokee County.

The appellate courts in Texas are also plagued by a cumbersome structure, especially in the ten counties in the Houston area. These 10 counties are served by two courts of appeal—the 1st and the 14th Courts of Appeal—that have overlapping jurisdictions, and cases are randomly assigned between them. The result is that at times the two courts render opposing decisions in cases that rely on the same facts, so that there is no precedent that lower courts and lawyers in the 10-county area can rely on. The effect of this situation is a lack of certainty and predictability, which one justice described as "practicing law on a guess and a gamble."[39]

These structural problems in the Texas judicial system are primarily a concern of the Texas legal community. While reforms have addressed some of the problems in the design of the Texas court system, such as the passage of a law in 2011 that allows justice of the peace courts to handle small claims with less formal rules of procedure, changes are rare and piecemeal rather than comprehensive.

Issues in the Texas Court System Today

Understand the key issues facing the Texas court system today

The Texas court system today faces many challenges. These range from the level of experience judges have, to how the court system is financed, to the regulation of lawyers, and the disciplining of judges guilty of misconduct.

Having Experienced Judges and Funding the Courts

Texas Supreme Court chief justice Nathan Hecht has expressed concern over the defeat of judges in the 2018 election and the loss of decades of judicial experience. In his view, the system of judicial selection in Texas needs to be changed. However, in the absence of change in the system of selection, at the minimum Hecht has argued that it is necessary to have experienced judges on the bench. That is accomplished in two ways: (1) have age and experience requirements in order to become a judge and (2) provide sufficient salaries to judges to encourage them to stay on the bench. Currently, for example, a county-court-at-law judge only has to be 25 years old—an age where it is impossible to have gained much legal experience. District judges are only required to have four years of legal experience, a limited background in the law when one considers that district judges hear major criminal and civil cases. Additionally, though the salaries of judges are large compared with those of Texans as a whole, they are not compared with the salaries of experienced private attorneys. Chief Justice Hecht has noted that when inflation is controlled, Texas judges are paid less than they were in 1991. Low salaries for experienced judges compared with what they could make in the private sector discourage them from continuing in judicial positions.[40]

Finally, much of the funding for Texas courts comes from counties where those judges hear cases. As Texas grows, the demands placed on the courts increase, but the growth of Texas places demands on all aspects of government. It is difficult for the Texas courts to compete for funds when Texans are demanding better highways, quality education, good police protection, and lower taxes. One of the great issues facing the Texas judiciary is how to get sufficient funding to handle increased caseloads brought about by the dramatic growth of the state.

Civil Cases and Tort Reform

Figure 9.3 shows the numbers of civil cases disposed of by the appellate courts and the trial courts in 2018–19. The Texas county court system and especially the district courts are handling huge caseloads. The most important type of civil cases, because of the large amounts of money involved, is tort law—cases in which one person has been harmed by the actions of another. For example, medical malpractice cases are a common type of tort case.

FIGURE 9.3

Civil Cases Disposed of by Texas Courts, September 1, 2018–August 31, 2019

*Excludes civil cases related to criminal matters and family law cases.

SOURCE: Texas Office of Court Administration, "2019 Annual Statistical Report."

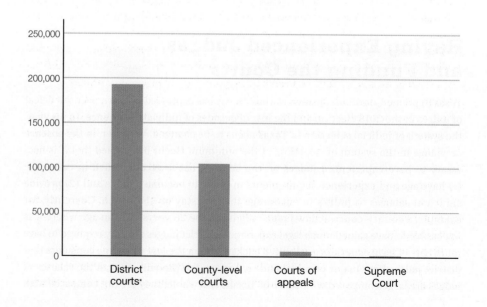

In the early to mid-1980s, the Texas Supreme Court tended to be sympathetic to the plaintiffs' positions in tort cases. That is, the court tended to support the side in a case that was suing businesses, professionals, and insurance companies. However, in 1988 more justices began to be elected who favored the defendants in civil lawsuits. One reason for this change was that in 1988 Republican justices began to be elected, and they were more conservative than many of the previous justices, who were Democrats. Interest groups that were harmed by the pro-plaintiff tendencies of the court began to organize, raise and spend money, and elect justices more sympathetic to their perspective. Today the Texas Supreme Court is quite favorable to defendants in civil cases, in part because it is now an all-Republican and conservative court. Additionally, during Governor Perry's administration a number of laws were passed, most notably involving medical malpractice lawsuits, that make it much harder for the plaintiff to prevail over the defendant in a lawsuit.[41] If the 2018 and 2020 elections signal future Democratic judicial successes, it would seem likely that Texans will again see changes in interpretations of tort law toward a more pro-plaintiff position.

The Regulation of the Legal Profession

Lawyers occupy a crucial role in the legal process. Constitutional county court judges and justices of the peace do not have to be lawyers, but all other judges must be "learned in the law," a term found in the Texas Constitution whose meaning has come to require a law degree. In order to practice law, one must be a licensed lawyer, and in order to be licensed in Texas, it is generally necessary to complete a Juris Doctor (JD) degree at a law school accredited by the American Bar Association. Usually this degree takes three years beyond the bachelor's degree if the law student attends full-time. After completing law school, a prospective lawyer must take the state bar exam. After passing the Texas state bar, one may be sworn in as a lawyer in Texas. Texas has an integrated bar, which means that all licensed lawyers in the state must join and pay dues to the State Bar of Texas. That agency, which is under the administrative control of the Texas Supreme Court, offers a variety of services to lawyers such as insurance plans, a journal, and professional meetings. Since lawyers must undergo continuing education, the state bar authorizes continuing education credit for a number of educational programs.

The State Bar of Texas is unusual in that it is not only a professional organization of lawyers but also an agency of government that is charged with enforcing ethical standards for the profession. Lawyers can be disciplined for a variety of infractions, ranging from serious criminal behavior, to failing to keep a client informed of the status of a legal matter, to failing to promptly pay out funds from a legal settlement. The state bar may also enforce rules against illegal efforts to generate litigation. In 2018–2019 the state bar exercised its enforcement power by disbarring 14 Texas lawyers, obtaining the resignations from legal practice of 17, suspending the legal practice of 152, publicly reprimanding 32, and privately reprimanding 124. The bar also offers what is known as the grievance referral program, where lawyers with problems such as substance abuse or mental health issues will be referred for assistance in dealing with those problems rather than face more severe sanctions.[42]

Illegal generation of litigation is commonly known as barratry, and the state legislature has become so concerned about lawyers' inappropriately generating legal business that in 2011 it passed new legislation that allows for a penalty of up to $10,000 and

The State Bar of Texas web page shows the variety of activities of the state bar. Every lawyer licensed to practice in Texas must be a member of the State Bar of Texas.

the recovery of attorney's fees. The goal of the legislation was to prevent what is commonly known as "ambulance chasing," which appears to remain a problem in spite of long-standing state bar rules against it. Some of the horror stories of barratry include people being solicited to sign contracts with lawyers for lawsuits at home, in hospitals, and even during funerals. At times the relatives of accident victims have been offered large payments to sign a contract with a particular lawyer to file a lawsuit.[43]

In order for the state bar to discipline a lawyer, a finding of wrongdoing is, of course, required. When a lawyer is charged with criminal offenses, he or she can practice until a court finds they are guilty of a crime. This can lead to bizarre situations. For example, Rayan Ganesh graduated from South Texas College of Law and was licensed in 2012. In July 2016 he was arrested on two counts of indecency with a child. In February 2017 he was indicted on seven counts of barratry. Ganesh continued practicing law, and a local television channel reported that he was representing 650 clients, an astounding number in light of the fact that a typical criminal defense lawyer in private practice has a caseload of 50–100 clients. Ganesh was finally convicted in April 2018 of two counts of felony indecency with a child by exposure and sentenced to imprisonment. Between his arrest and his conviction, a reporter found him recruiting clients in the Dallas County courthouse. Despite Ganesh's serious legal problems, the state bar was unable to prevent him from practicing law until he was found guilty.[44]

Judicial Conduct

The State Commission on Judicial Conduct was created by a constitutional amendment in 1965 and charged with investigating allegations of judicial misconduct and disability and with disciplining judges. The 13 members of the commission serve six-year terms and are unpaid. The commission is an unusual hybrid agency in that two attorney members are appointed by the state bar and six judicial members are appointed by the Texas Supreme Court. There are also five citizen members, who can be neither lawyers nor judges and are appointed by the governor. The state Senate confirms the commission members.

In a rare dispute with the commission, Governor Abbott removed two members he appointed to the commission when, nine months after their appointment, it was time for senate confirmation. The problem was that a McLennan County justice of the peace and the justice's staff were giving all same-sex couples who wished to be married a document stating, "I'm sorry, but Judge Hensley has a sincerely held religious belief as a Christian, and will not be able to perform any same sex wedding." The judge did perform opposite sex weddings. A list of local persons who would officiate at same-sex weddings was provided. That led the judge to be given a public warning by the commission. Abbott rebuked his appointees for their actions by withdrawing their appointments.[45] The justice of the peace has sued over the disciplinary action and, in still another rare action, Attorney General Ken Paxton has refused to defend the commission in the lawsuit.[46]

In dealing with disciplinary issues involving Texas judges, the commission relies on complaints from the public, from attorneys, and from members of the judiciary. In 2019 the commission disposed of 1,694 cases. A common complaint is that the person disagrees with the judge's decision, but of course this is not a violation of the Code of Judicial Conduct, the ethical code promulgated by the Texas Supreme Court that is enforced by the commission.

The commission's decision making is done behind closed doors and thus lacks openness and transparency. Still, other than impeachment by the legislature or criminal prosecution of judges—both rare and extreme measures—the commission is the only mechanism for regulating ethical and legal conduct of Texas judges.[47]

In 2019 the commission imposed 80 sanctions on judges. In 4 other cases, judges chose to resign rather than be sanctioned. The commission can recommend public censure or removal of a judge or the judge's involuntary retirement to a review tribunal composed of the chief justice of Texas and six appellate judges. The tribunal's decision can be appealed by the affected judge to the Texas Supreme Court. No such case occurred in 2019. Other decisions of the commission can be appealed to a court of review consisting of three appellate judges. In 2019, there were three appeals to a court of review.[48]

Many of the disciplinary actions of the commission involve private sanctions of the judge. In 2019, 23 sanctions were of a private nature and consisted of the commission providing a private admonition, warning, or reprimand (admonitions are less severe sanctions than warnings, which are less severe than reprimands). Often with private or public sanctions, judges are required to seek additional legal education. Forty-six disciplinary actions involved public sanctions, which are much more embarrassing to the judge and can be used in opposition to the judge in future campaigns for office.

A sanction in 2015 received considerable media attention. It was against Justice Nora Longoria of the 13th Court of Appeals, who had been stopped by McAllen police for speeding. It became clear that she had been drinking, and she was emotional and uncooperative with the police. Among other things, she demanded to see the police supervisor, and she told the police she was a judge. She was charged with DWI. At trial she pled no contest to the speeding charge and was fined $500, and the DWI charge was dismissed. However, McAllen police released dashcam footage of the stop, which portrayed Justice Longoria very negatively, and it became a popular item on social media. The commission provided a public admonition to Justice Longoria.[49]

The most widely publicized disciplinary case against a judge in recent years was against the presiding judge of the Texas Court of

Justice Nora Longoria of the 13th Court of Appeals received a public admonition from the State Commission on Judicial Conduct due to her behavior during a traffic stop by McAllen police.

Criminal Appeals, Sharon Keller. In 2007, Judge Keller refused to keep the clerk's office at the court open beyond 5 P.M. to receive an appeal from death-row inmate Michael Richard. As a result, Richard was executed later that evening. Although Keller received a public warning from the State Commission on Judicial Conduct, she was successful in her litigation against the discipline by arguing that a warning cannot be a penalty following a formal proceeding against a judge.[50] Re-elected to another six-year term in 2012 with 55.49 percent of the vote and in 2018 with 52.2 percent of the vote, Keller remains the presiding judge of the court.

The Courts and Coronavirus

In the early stages of the coronavirus pandemic, the Texas Supreme Court issued orders that debtors' bank accounts could not be frozen and that debtors' funds could not be seized by creditors. The court also issued an order that delayed eviction proceedings unless the tenant posed an imminent threat or was engaged in criminal activity. Additionally, substantial delays were recommended for in-person hearings and jury trials. If in-person hearings were held, it was recommended that there be social distancing and that masks should be worn. Courts started using remote conferencing for hearings such as plea and bond hearings.

Trials were substantially delayed along with some hearings and some people charged with crimes remained jailed due to delays. Most importantly, however, the pandemic cast the Texas Supreme Court into political controversy to a degree not seen in years. In 2020, four incumbent Republican justices were up for re-election and they were targeted by Democrats as a result of several decisions the court made during the pandemic. In the face of 1.9 million unemployed Texans, the court decided that evictions and debt collections could begin again in late May. Then, a number of district judges sued, challenging Governor Abbott's order banning the release of inmates from county jails if the inmates were accused of violent crimes or had previously been convicted of violent crimes, unless they paid money bail. The reason for the suit was to remove inmates from jails that were COVID-19 hotspots. The Texas Supreme Court ruled that the judges lacked standing to bring the suit—that is, they had not suffered an injury that justified the suit.

In still another controversial decision, the court ordered the release of Shelley Luther from the Dallas County jail where she had been sentenced for violating a court order to comply with Governor Abbott's business closure directive. Luther, who had opened her beauty salon in violation of the directive, received tremendous publicity and support for her actions, especially among leading Republican political figures and the Republican rank and file.

By far the court's most controversial decision during the pandemic was its ruling on mail-in voting, which developed into a major partisan issue. The court held that fear of contracting COVID-19 at the polling place was not by itself a disability that would allow a voter to vote by mail. This issue split Democrats, who supported voting by mail, and Republicans, from President Trump on down, who opposed the expansion of voting by mail, claiming it would lead to voter fraud.[51] Finally, the pandemic reduced the chances that there would be successful judicial reform legislation in the next legislative session since the legislature would have to focus on revenue and budgeting concerns brought on by the impact of the COVID-19 crisis.

The Judiciary and the Future of Texas

TEXAS ELECTS its judges in partisan judicial elections. For many years, when the Democratic Party was dominant, Texas judicial elections were low-budget, noncompetitive events. However, with the growth of the Republican Party, they became highly political, and large amounts of money have been raised for judicial candidates, especially in Texas Supreme Court races. Because the Texas Supreme Court sets the tone of tort law in the state, often these races pitted candidates backed by business interests against those backed by plaintiffs' lawyers. Statewide judicial elections have calmed down in recent years as the Democratic Party has weakened, and statewide judicial elections have become less competitive. However, some courts of appeal races and judicial races in urban counties have become much more competitive.

Because voters often don't know much about judicial candidates, they often decide on the basis of the candidate's party affiliation or name appeal. This tendency has caused problems, and numerous efforts have been undertaken to change the way judges are selected in Texas. There have been efforts to change to merit selection. Groups representing people of color have pushed to reduce the size of judicial districts in order to increase the election of judges of color. However, no major change has so far been successful. No majority coalition can agree on appropriate changes in the judicial selection system, and significant opposition to change comes from groups such as political parties. Additionally, Texans seem satisfied with the current system of selection and seem to prefer to elect their judges.

The only change affecting judicial elections to date has been the Judicial Campaign Fairness Act, which provides limitations on campaign contributions to judicial candidates. Additionally, a recent change in Texas law banned straight-ticket voting in 2020, although the elimination of straight-ticket voting did not have a dramatic effect on judicial elections in 2020. Recent injustices in the Texas criminal system that are discussed in Chapter 13 do raise questions about how the system can be improved. One might speculate that a criminal justice system in which both judges and prosecutors are elected creates political pressures to gain convictions at all costs.

Because the Texas court system affects the liberty and especially the pocketbooks of Texans, it will continue to be an area of concern and controversy. And the most controversial area of Texas justice will continue to be the process by which judges are selected. Nevertheless, efforts to change the state's judicial system have been going on for decades with no result. Perhaps the newly appointed commission to examine judicial selection in Texas will come up with a recommendation that will change the way judges are selected. The Republican leadership of Texas has certainly become concerned about the influx of Democratic judges as a result of the 2018 and 2020 elections, and they seem more supportive of changes in the system. However, even relatively minor changes in the judiciary, such as redistricting trial courts, seem to be a low priority in Texas. If there are any reforms, they are likely to be minor ones where, for the most part, the judiciary will continue "as is" with overlapping jurisdictions and a mishmash of courts.

STUDY GUIDE

Use 🐰 INQUIZITIVE to help you study and master this material.

The Legal Process

- **Explain the legal process and the differences between criminal and civil law (pp. 297–300)**

Civil law is dramatically different from criminal law, with the burden of proof relying on different standards. Plaintiffs are the initiators of legal actions in civil cases. Defendants in civil cases respond to accusations made against them. Civil cases may lead to trial or dismissal by a judge. They may also be resolved by a settlement between the parties. The state is a prosecutor in a criminal case, and the accused individual is the defendant. Criminal cases can result in a trial, a dismissal, or a plea bargain.

Key Terms
civil law (p. 297)
criminal law (p. 297)
complaint (p. 297)
answer (p. 297)
contingent fee (p. 297)
tort (p. 297)
preponderance of the evidence (p. 298)
probate (p. 298)

felony (p. 298)
misdemeanor (p. 298)
grand jury (p. 299)
indictment (p. 300)
bench trial (p. 300)
plea bargain (p. 300)
beyond a reasonable doubt (p. 300)

Practice Quiz
1. Grand juries
   a) determine the guilt of defendants.
   b) decide whether a trial of an accused is warranted.
   c) agree to plea bargains.
   d) recommend that defendants undergo bench trials.
   e) hear appeals of convictions.

2. On conviction, the criminal's punishment is determined
   a) by the grand jury.
   b) in a separate hearing by the jury or judge that determined the person's guilt.
   c) by the prosecuting attorney.
   d) by the prosecuting and defense attorneys.
   e) by the Texas Court of Criminal Appeals.

Court Structure

- **Describe how the Texas court system is organized (pp. 301–7)**

The appellate court system in Texas is divided into civil and criminal tracks with the Texas Supreme Court being the highest state-level court for civil cases and the Texas Criminal Court of Appeals being the highest for criminal cases. Texas has an intermediate appellate court system and trial courts that range from district courts for the most important criminal and civil cases, to county courts for less important criminal and civil cases, to justices of the peace and municipal courts for settling the lowest level of conflicts.

Key Terms
Texas Supreme Court (p. 301)
Texas Court of Criminal Appeals (p. 301)
courts of appeal (p. 303)
district courts (p. 303)
specialty courts (p. 304)
county judge (p. 305)
county courts (p. 305)
statutory county-courts-at-law (p. 305)
statutory probate courts (p. 305)
justice of the peace courts (p. 305)
municipal courts (p. 307)
ordinance (p. 307)

Practice Quiz

3. The highest criminal court in the state of Texas is the
   a) Texas Supreme Court.
   b) Texas Court of Appeals.
   c) Texas Court of Criminal Appeals.
   d) county court.
   e) district court.

4. The trial courts for felonies in Texas are the
   a) courts of appeal.
   b) justice of the peace courts.
   c) district courts.
   d) municipal courts.
   e) county courts.

5. Which of the following positions in the judiciary are filled primarily by non-lawyers?
   a) Texas Supreme Court justices
   b) district judges
   c) justices of the peace
   d) Texas Criminal Court of Appeals justices
   e) probate judges

Judicial Politics

- **Evaluate the process for selecting judges in Texas (pp. 307–21)**

Partisan elections make judges accountable to voters, but critics claim that unqualified judges are elected solely because of their party labels. These critics advocate alternatives for choosing judges such as merit selection. People of color are not proportionately represented, possibly in part because most judges are elected from large districts that are nonminority.

Key Terms

merit selection (p. 309)
retention election (p. 312)
straight-ticket voting (p. 312)
Judicial Campaign Fairness Act (p. 317)

Practice Quiz

6. Candidates for judicial office in Texas
   a) are chosen through a merit-selection process.
   b) run in nonpartisan elections.
   c) are chosen by the Texas Senate.
   d) have lifetime tenure like federal judges.
   e) run in partisan judicial elections.

7. Texas's movement from being a Democratic to a Republican state led to
   a) defeats of large numbers of incumbent judges.
   b) party switching by incumbent judges.
   c) large campaign contributions to judges.
   d) election of more Republican judges.
   e) all of the above

8. In Texas, which event marked the rise of the Republican Party and partisan judicial elections?
   a) the election of President Ronald Reagan
   b) the impeachment of William Jefferson Clinton
   c) the appointment of Tom Phillips as chief justice of the United States
   d) the election of Bill Clements as governor of Texas
   e) the Shivercrat movement

9. Judicial elections have become highly competitive
   a) in urban areas in Texas.
   b) at the Texas Court of Criminal Appeals.
   c) in West Texas.
   d) at the Texas Supreme Court.
   d) in the counties bordering Louisiana.

10. Which of the following sets campaign contribution limits for judicial candidates in Texas?
   a) Judicial Campaign Fairness Act
   b) Judicial Campaign Law
   c) Equal Justice Act
   d) Code of Judicial Conduct
   e) Federal Rules of Civil Procedure

11. Which of the following groups has the largest number of judges?
   a) African Americans
   b) American Indians
   c) Asian Americans
   d) Latinos
   e) women

Issues in the Texas Court System Today

> • **Understand the key issues facing the Texas court system today (pp. 321–26)**

Texas courts make decisions affecting Texans on a variety of issues, including the ultimate penalty of death and tort cases such as medical malpractice.

Practice Quiz

12. Philosophically, in the past few years, Texas courts became
   a) more pro-defendant in civil cases.
   b) more liberal.
   c) more pro-defendant in criminal cases.
   d) more conservative.
   e) hostile to tort reform.

13. All lawyers who regularly practice in Texas
   a) must be members of the State Bar of Texas.
   b) must have graduated from a Texas law school.
   c) must appear in court at least twice a year.
   d) must volunteer to sit on grand juries.
   e) do not need any additional training once they have a law license.

14. The State Commission on Judicial Conduct
   a) screens judicial candidates to determine if they are qualified to be judges.
   b) offers continuing education courses for judges.
   c) investigates complaints of ethical violations by judges.
   d) recommends trial judges for promotion to appellate courts.
   e) makes rules governing the conduct of judges.

Hurricane Harvey drove people from their homes and inflicted damage throughout Houston and the surrounding areas. Local government played a critical, controversial role in the response, as it did during the coronavirus pandemic.

Local Government

WHY LOCAL GOVERNMENT MATTERS Ordinarily, Texans give local government little attention as long as the trash is picked up and the potholes are repaired. Two recent emergencies, however, show the great importance of local government to the well-being of Texans.

One crisis involved Hurricane Harvey which made landfall on August 25, 2017, as a Category 4 hurricane near Rockport, Texas. The storm moved around southern Texas for days, in the process dropping more than twenty trillion gallons of rain across Texas and Louisiana—enough water to supply New York City's water needs for over five decades. Some estimated that $97 billion in property was destroyed and other loss estimates were even higher. By September 1, 2017, the Texas Division of Emergency Management estimated 185,149 houses were damaged or destroyed and 364,000 persons had registered for FEMA assistance. At that time, 42,399 persons were in shelters and FEMA had already distributed 1,900,000 meals in Texas. Houston, the largest city in Texas and the fourth-largest city in the United States with a population of 2.3 million, was flooded. At Cedar Bayou, on the outskirts of Houston, 51.88 inches of rain were recorded in just under five days. This was a new record for the heaviest rainfall in the continental United States.

During the flooding, local government was inundated by rescue calls. There were cries for help from people flooded in their homes, cars, businesses, hospitals, and nursing homes. But somehow Houston and the surrounding area managed with a relatively small loss of life, given the overwhelming nature of the flooding. One estimate was that 107 persons died in the United States as a result of Harvey; in 2005 over 1,800 people died as a result of Hurricane Katrina. The combined governmental response coupled with the volunteer work of private citizens meant the response to Harvey was generally viewed favorably. A poll of 1,200 registered Texas voters in February 2018 found that 61 percent of Texans approved of the local government response to Harvey and only 11 percent disapproved.[1]

Houston's mayor Sylvester Turner was criticized for not ordering an evacuation of Houston; Governor Abbott had said that if he were living in the area he would leave and head north. However, Turner and other local officials insisted it was best to stay put rather than evacuate, and most people did not leave. In 2005, Hurricane Rita headed toward Houston and 3.7 million people left the Houston area. That evacuation was a disaster. Interstate 45 turned into a one-hundred-mile parking lot; cars ran out of fuel; no gasoline was available along the interstate. Dozens of people died in accidents, in a bus fire, and of heat stroke. Hurricane

Rita changed course and Houston was not severely hit. The evacuation was far more harmful than the storm. It is likely that Turner's decision not to evacuate Houston in 2017 was the correct one.

The second crisis that showed the importance of local government in Texas was the coronavirus pandemic of 2020. As with Hurricane Harvey, it was local government that occupied the front lines in the effort to protect public well-being. One of the state's leaders in responding to the pandemic was County Judge Clay Jenkins of Dallas County, who had previously had experience with outbreaks of the West Nile and Ebola viruses. Over the opposition of other officials in the county, Jenkins worked to limit bars and restaurants to takeout and delivery in Dallas County. He also worked with other county judges to implore Governor Abbott to close schools and restrict operation of bars and restaurants on a statewide basis. The next day Abbott closed schools, banned dine-in service, and limited gatherings to 10 people. When Abbott did not issue a statewide shelter-in-place order, Jenkins did so for Dallas County, which was followed quickly by Bexar, Travis, and Harris and then by other counties and some cities. Such actions to control COVID-19 were taken by county judges and some mayors under their powers under the Texas Disaster Act of 1975, which recognized that local officials needed extraordinary powers to deal with crisis situations in their communities. The actions of local officials to limit Texans' exposure to the coronavirus no doubt prevented many infections and saved numerous lives.

Local government is important to Texans. It was a local governmental decision, likely a wise one, that prevented the evacuation of the Houston area. Local government played a major role in the rescue operations caused by the flooding disaster and it had a major role in feeding and sheltering the victims of Harvey. Likewise, it was local government that first acted to limit social contacts which would have exacerbated the coronavirus contagion. As noted in the introduction to Chapter 1, it was the action of local officials that prevented widespread contagion when they canceled the South by Southwest festival in early March 2020. It was also local government that was directly involved in planning for the need for expanded hospital services to deal with COVID-19 illnesses. Local government does not get the same level of media attention that state and national government receive, but crises such as Hurricane Harvey and the COVID-19 pandemic emphasize the vast importance of local government to our lives.

CHAPTERGOALS

- Explain the importance, role, and structure of county government in Texas (pp. 335–42)

- Describe the major characteristics of city government in Texas (pp. 343–57)

- Examine the role of special purpose districts in Texas government (pp. 357–63)

- Examine the financial issues facing local government (pp. 364–67)

County Government in Texas

Explain the importance, role, and structure of county government in Texas

Local government institutions play a major role in Texas. There are more than 5,147 general-purpose local governments, an average of about 20 per county,[2] which provide water, electricity, and sewer services as well as police protection and public education.

All but two states have governmental units known as counties (or parishes), but Texas has 254 counties, more than any other state.[3] County government in Texas is primarily a way of governing rural areas. Because Texas is so vast, with huge areas that are sparsely populated, county government remains an important aspect of local government. As was discussed in Chapter 2, however, the Texas Constitution places numerous restrictions on government, and many of those are restrictions on counties. Indeed, in Texas, counties have very constricted governmental powers. Because they lack much of the power of self-government, they often function primarily as an administrative arm of the state government.

What Are the Functions of County Government?

The main functions of Texas county government are construction and maintenance of county roads and bridges, law enforcement, dispute resolution, record-keeping, and administration of social services. Like most other aspects of county government in Texas, these five primary functions are performed with great variation among the counties.

County road and bridge construction and maintenance have traditionally been such important functions of county government that the county commissioners' court—those elected officials in charge of county government—are often called "road commissioners." County commissioners maintain more than one-half of the roads in the state,[4] including roughly 134,000 miles of rural roadways and 17,000 rural bridges. Maintenance of these roads and bridges is a major cost for county government.[5] For example, a 20-foot-wide asphalt road for lightweight traffic costs a county $45,000 per mile to resurface; a road of the same width for heavy trucks costs about $100,000 per mile.[6] Although a 1947 law allowed counties to place their road system under the authority of a county engineer, in most counties roads and bridges remain one of the most important responsibilities of the commissioners.

Law enforcement, another important responsibility of county government, is undertaken by **constables** and by the sheriff. The sheriff is the chief law-enforcement officer within county government. In rural counties with few city police departments, the sheriff may be the major law-enforcement official in the county. In addition to law enforcement and the provision of deputies for the district and county courts, sheriffs are responsible for the county jail and the safety of prisoners. In many counties, operating a county jail is an expensive and major undertaking. On March 1, 2020, for example, Harris County was guarding and supervising over 9,000 inmates in its county jail, and Dallas

constable precinct-level county official involved with serving legal papers, serving as bailiff in justice of the peace courts, and, in some counties, enforcing the law

County had 5,900. On the other hand, 23 counties had no jails. Overall, there were 68,000 inmates in Texas county jails.[7]

Although the law-enforcement budget must be approved by the county commissioners, sheriffs often have considerable influence in county government and develop their own law-enforcement styles.

Traditionally in Texas, the office of constable has been an elective office with limited duties. Constables have served civil court papers and provided bailiffs for justices of the peace. However, some constables have transformed their offices into full-fledged police departments. Some constables' offices have traffic enforcement roles; some enforce truancy laws; and some have even formed heavily armed, tactical units that patrol high-crime areas. Since constables are elected officials, they are not subject to much oversight by other public officials, and they tend to function as law enforcement fiefdoms in larger counties in Texas.

County attorneys and **district attorneys** also perform a law-enforcement role by prosecuting criminal cases. Usually, the district attorneys prosecute the more serious criminal cases in the district courts, whereas the county attorneys prosecute the lesser criminal cases in the county courts. In more urban counties, the offices of county attorney and district attorney may be combined into one office that is usually called the office of criminal district attorney.

Record-keeping is another important function of county government. **County clerks** keep vital statistics for the county, issue marriage licenses and birth and death certificates, and maintain records for the commissioners' court and the county courts. Most important, the county clerk is responsible for records relating to property transactions. Sometimes the county clerk also maintains election and voting records. If there is a **district clerk**, he or she maintains records for the district courts, though in small counties this office is combined with the office of the county clerk. Tax records are maintained by the **county tax assessor-collector**, who in many counties also collects taxes, though in the smaller counties the sheriff often performs this job. Although in many counties constitutional amendments have eliminated the office of county treasurer, in those where the office still exists, the treasurer is responsible for receiving and spending county funds. The **county auditor** now does much of the former work of the county treasurer. There are now 200 county auditors in Texas, who are appointed by the county's district judges. Not only do they audit the county's funds, but in large counties they will also often prepare the county budget for the commissioners' court.

Counties also have an important role in dispute resolution through their court systems. Civil law is a way to resolve disputes between people, and the justice of the peace court and the county and district courts deal with large numbers of civil disputes as well as criminal matters. County and district attorneys may also represent the interests of the county or state in disputes that involve governmental interests.

Finally, counties may perform a social service function. The services provided vary from county to county, but the most important ones involve providing emergency welfare assistance, which may include food, housing, rental assistance, or shelter. Larger counties have health departments to work on the prevention and control of communicable diseases. Some counties operate mental health services, and some provide parks, airports, fire protection, and sanitation facilities. One of the most important social services provided by counties is indigent health care.

county attorney county official who prosecutes lesser criminal cases in the county court

district attorney public official who prosecutes the more serious criminal cases in the district court

county clerk public official who is the main record-keeper of the county

district clerk public official who is the main record-keeper of district court documents

county tax assessor-collector public official who maintains the county tax records and collects the taxes owed to the county

county auditor public official, appointed by the district judges, who receives and disburses county funds; in large counties, this official also prepares the county budget

Numerous County Offices: Checks and Balances or Built-In Problems?

As with the state government, county government in Texas involves many elected governmental officials. Some argue that the large number of public officials at the county level is desirable because it creates a strong system of checks and balances, allowing no one official to dominate county government.[8] However, that system of checks and balances comes at a high price, in the form of problems in coordination of governmental activity, much as at the state level.

One of the most important bodies of county elected officials is the **county commissioners' court**, which is the main governing unit in the county. Although the commissioners' court is not a judicial body, it may have gotten its name from the Republic of Texas Constitution (1836–45), in which the county governing unit consisted of the chief justice of the county court and the justices of the peace within the county.[9]

The current structure of the county commissioners' court, shown in Figure 10.1, consists of a **county judge** and four commissioners. The county judge is elected countywide and serves for four years. He or she presides over the meetings of the commissioners' court and has administrative powers as well as judicial powers in rural counties. In those counties, the county judge hears minor criminal cases and handles some civil matters such as probate (the process by which legal title to property transfers from someone who has died to that person's legal heirs and beneficiaries). In larger, more urban counties, the county judge is an administrator only, with the former judicial duties of the office usually performed by probate judges or county-court-at-law judges.

county commissioners' court the main governing body of each county; has the authority to set the county tax rate and budget

county judge the person in each of Texas's 254 counties who presides over the constitutional county court and county commissioners' court, with responsibility for the administration of county government; some county judges also carry out judicial responsibilities

FIGURE 10.1

The County Commissioners' Court

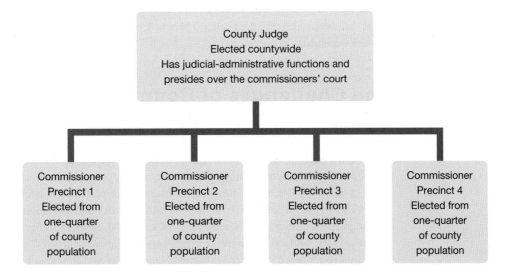

county commissioner
government official (four
per county) on the county
commissioners' court whose
main duty is the construction and
maintenance of roads and bridges

Each commissioners' court also has four **county commissioners**, each of whom is elected from a precinct that encompasses roughly one-fourth of the population of the county. The main responsibility of county commissioners is the construction and maintenance of county roads and bridges. That aspect of a commissioner's work is, of course, very important to rural residents; it can be politically controversial and has sometimes been tinged with corruption.[10]

The commissioners' court also sets the county tax rate and the county budget. Related to its taxing and budgeting powers is its power to make contracts and pay bills. Other than road and bridge expenditures, perhaps the most important expenditure of most county commissioners' courts is building and maintaining county jails. Health care for people in poverty can be a significant cost for counties as well, along with, in some cases, fire protection and sanitation. Some counties also have costs associated with maintaining libraries and hospitals and providing emergency welfare measures, such as those brought on by natural disasters or fires. The commissioners' court can appoint certain county officials, and it can hire personnel as well as fill vacancies in county offices. It also administers elections in the county.

The numerous elected officials in Texas counties each have an independent power base. It seems nearly inevitable that tensions would develop between the budgetary powers of the commissioners' courts and the needs and desires of other elected county officials. Such disputes among county officials can be mundane, as was the battle between Titus County commissioners and the county attorney over whether the commission could ban the county attorney's dog from the courthouse.[11] The disputes can also be far more serious and acrimonious, such as the litigation between the Galveston County commissioners and district court judge Lonnie Cox over the commissioners' firing of the county court administrator. After winding its way through the state courts, the Texas Supreme Court held that Judge Cox lacked the constitutional and statutory authority to compel the county commissioners to reinstate a county judicial employee at a specific salary. District court judges could not legislate from the bench nor could they replace the decisions of a legislative body of government. The bitter controversy between the county commissioners and the judge cost taxpayers over $1 million.[12]

As Table 10.1 shows, other officeholders are elected at the county level and still others at the precinct level of the county. There is some variation in the numbers of officeholders, depending on the county.

The Challenges of County Government

Are Some Counties Too Small? Texas is a large, diverse state with great variation among its counties. There is great variation in the numbers of government officials, the duties of officials, and the services provided by the different county governments. Brewster County has a population of only 9,203, but it covers a territory of 6,193 square miles, about the size of Connecticut and Rhode Island combined. Rockwall County, in contrast, has only 149 square miles and a population of 87,809. Although Harris County has a population of 4,441,370, Loving County has a population of only 86, yet Loving County covers a huge land area—nearly 677 square miles.[13]

A small population may create a sense of community and closeness to local government, but it can place a huge strain on county resources when unusual events occur, such as an expensive murder trial or a natural disaster. For example, after suffering from

TABLE 10.1

Countywide and Precinct-Level Elected Officials

COUNTYWIDE OFFICIALS	PRECINCT-LEVEL OFFICIALS
County judge	County commissioners
Possibly county-court-at-law judges, possibly probate judges, and district judges	Justices of the peace
County and district attorney or criminal district attorney	Constables
Sheriff	
County and district clerk or district clerk	
Possibly county treasurer	
Tax assessor-collector	
Possibly county surveyor	

flooding and a bad economy, Presidio County, with a population of less than 7,000, ran out of money to pay its bills. Several county phone lines were disconnected for lack of payment, and the county had to cut its budget by 30 percent and raise taxes in order to continue functioning.[14]

Polk County in east Texas (population of about 46,000) estimated that it had unanticipated costs of $200,000 when the U.S. Supreme Court overturned the sentence of Johnny Paul Penry, who had been convicted in the stabbing death of a woman in 1979, and sent the case back for another trial. Even with $100,000 in aid from the state to help pay the bill, the costs of this one trial represented a tremendous burden.[15] An even more severe situation faced tiny Franklin County (population 10,600) in 2007, when it needed to come up with a minimum of $250,000 for a murder trial.[16] Since capital murder cases were so rare in the county, the commissioners had no money at all budgeted for such a purpose. As in Presidio County, for small counties such as Polk and Franklin, expenses like these require either major cuts in other budget items or tax increases or both.

Very small counties in the Big Bend area of Texas are discovering that they cannot afford to prosecute the drug violations that are too small for the federal government to prosecute. In counties that have Border Patrol checkpoints, relatively minor drug cases have been prosecuted at the county level, although the federal government has provided some aid for funding these prosecutions. But Hudspeth County (population 3,300) has discovered that for every $1 it gets for handling federal border crimes and seized assets, it costs the county $2 to detain, process, and prosecute the offenders. The cost has gotten so substantial that the county has chosen to no longer prosecute the federal drug cases sent to it. Brooks County (population 7,200) had previously stopped taking the federal drug cases from its Border Patrol checkpoint because the county found the costs too great, and Kenedy County (population 400) has recently made the same decision. Part of the problem is that the federal government has reimbursed local authorities only for

The county commissioners' court is the main governing unit at the county level, with control over the county budget and projects such as road construction. Here, Travis County commissioner Brigid Shea presents a water conservation program to the community that would save the county millions of gallons of drinking water per year.

prosecution costs and not for detention costs. For small-population counties, that policy imposed too great a financial burden, since detention is the most expensive item in the county budget.[17]

Counties exist as they do for a variety of reasons. The original goal of making county seats easily accessible by horseback is, of course, no longer pertinent. Other reasons are political. For example, wealthy landowners may have urged the legislature to create counties so that they could control county government and hence the amount of property taxes they might pay. In modern times, there is arguably no practical reason for Texas to have so many counties. Even moderate-size counties by Texas standards may be too small to function adequately in unusual situations. It would take a state constitutional amendment to merge counties so that many of them would have a sufficient population to function efficiently and a sufficient tax base to deliver services adequately. But the issue of county mergers is not one that is on the political agenda. It would likely be controversial because of residents' traditional loyalties to a county, because county officeholders would fear losing their jobs, and because voters might feel they would lose control over county government since a vote in a populous county is less influential than one in a small county.

Accountability of County Officials County officials are made accountable to the public through elections. Generally, every four years the voters get a chance to review county officials and make a judgment about their competence, efficiency, ability, and fitness to hold office for another four years. One question is whether having elections every four years is a sufficient mechanism to ensure the accountability of officials. In cases of inefficiency or incompetence, the only alternative to elections

for the removal of county officials is a rarely used and generally unsuccessful judicial proceeding against an official believed incapable of performing duties.

One example of the problems of accountability of county officials involved Susan Hawk, the district attorney of Dallas County. A political superstar, Hawk had been a highly successful assistant district attorney in the county beginning at the age of 24. At 32, she was elected a state district judge, and in 2014 she resigned from the bench to run against incumbent Democrat Craig Watkins for district attorney. Hawk was the only Republican who won a countywide race in Dallas County that year. As the newly elected district attorney, Hawk was responsible for running an office with 260 assistant district attorneys and 190 support staff.

Even during her campaign, however, she began to have problems due to severe depression and an addiction to prescription pain medications. She became suicidal and paranoid and went into a rehabilitation facility, claiming she was going to have back surgery. After she became district attorney, her paranoia continued, and she became manic and forgetful, sometimes making impulsive decisions. She fired top assistant district attorneys, including people who were close associates. By the summer of 2015, she was again suicidal and was planning her resignation when she obtained treatment. After Hawk fired a lawyer who oversaw the budget of the D.A.'s office, the lawyer claimed Hawk had repeatedly tried to misuse public funds. A removal suit was filed against Hawk, but in early 2016 it was dismissed.[18] Hawk's mental health problems were not under control, however, and she was frequently in treatment. Finally, in September 2016 she resigned, waiting just long enough to prevent an election for her replacement, who in Democratic Dallas County would most likely have been a Democrat. In December 2016, Governor Abbott appointed Republican Faith Johnson as Dallas County's first Black female district attorney. Johnson lost her re-election bid to John Creuzot in the November 2018 election.[19]

David Wilson (right) misled voters in his campaign for Houston Community College trustee by mischaracterizing himself and his endorsements to appeal to African American voters. His actions are one example of many that cause some to question how to hold locally elected officials accountable.

The descent of Susan Hawk into depression, drug abuse, and paranoia is a tragedy, but in the process of trying to gain self-control, Hawk damaged the careers of several employees in the district attorney's office and introduced considerable confusion and chaos into the office. Her story may be the most dramatic, but numerous other examples raise concerns about possible lack of accountability on the part of local governmental officials. Dallas County commissioner John Wiley Price faced an 11-count indictment from the U.S. attorney on corruption charges; he was alleged to have received $950,000 in payments in money, cars, and land. Following a contentious and lengthy investigation and trial, Price was found not guilty on 7 of the 11 charges for bribery and fraud in April 2017. Federal prosecutors decided not to retry the tax fraud charges in May 2017. But questions about Price's actions continued to be raised in the media as late as October 2017.[20] Houston Community College trustee Dave Wilson won his office with a questionable campaign that wrongly suggested to his heavily African American constituents that he was Black. Wilson is White, but his campaign leaflets did not show his picture, instead featuring pictures of African Americans that were taken off the internet and shown beside the request, "Please vote for our friend and neighbor Dave Wilson." One leaflet said Wilson was endorsed by Ron Wilson—who it turns out was his cousin in Iowa rather than the African American former state representative who most voters would have assumed was meant.[21]

Local officials are supposed to be closest to the electorate, and therefore voters are supposed to be more aware of their strengths and flaws. But is this actually the case? Do voters have sufficient awareness of local officials when they elect them, and are future elections a sufficient control over the behavior of those officials once they are in office?

City Government in Texas

Describe the major characteristics of city government in Texas

Politics at the local level is often politics at its most basic. Unlike in presidential elections, in which the issues may well involve questions of war and peace, or state elections, which may involve issues such as whether a state should have an income tax, in local elections the most pressing issue may well be potholes in the city streets. Although pothole repair may not seem high in the hierarchy of political concerns, it is exactly such an issue that most directly and routinely affects most people's lives, and thus it becomes a prime issue for discussion among candidates. As mundane as such concerns are, these are the fundamental issues in most local elections because they reflect the needs and expectations that residents have of local government.

General-Law versus Home-Rule Cities

In 2018 there were 1,214 incorporated municipalities in Texas, ranging in size from 18 in Los Ybanez to over 2.3 million in Houston (see Table 10.2). Like county governments, municipal governments are creations of the state of Texas. In the early years of the Republic of Texas, the Texas Congress was responsible for enacting laws that incorporated cities. Article XI, Section 4 of the 1876 Constitution provided for the incorporation of "general law" cities under 10,000 people, but was lowered to 5,000 in 1909.[22] The number of urban areas grew in the state in the late nineteenth and early twentieth centuries, making the management of local affairs a growing burden on the state legislature. In 1912 the legislature passed the Home-Rule Charter Amendment to the constitution that enabled cities of more than 5,000 inhabitants to adopt charters providing some degree of local self-government. Today there are 345 incorporated cities with more than 5,000 residents operating under home-rule provisions and an additional 871 operating under general law. Table 10.2 lists the 10 largest of these. In contrast, California has only 121 home-rule cities and Illinois has only 209.[23]

The difference between a general-law city and a home-rule city is crucial not only because of the size of the city but because of the way in which self-government in the locality operates. Cities and towns of fewer than 5,000 people are chartered by general statute, as was the case for all cities and towns prior to the 1912 home-rule amendments. Under the so-called Dillon Rule doctrine, "general-law" cities and towns may act or organize themselves only as explicitly permitted by statutory law passed by the state legislature.[24] The constitution also limits what they can do. For example, general-law cities may levy, assess, and collect taxes as authorized by statute. But the constitution sets a maximum property tax rate of $1.50 per $100 valuation, compared with $2.50 per $100 valuation for home-rule cities.

Home-rule cities, on the other hand, work under a charter passed by the citizens. The **home-rule charter** essentially lays down the rules under which a city will operate.[25] The general principle for home-rule cities is that cities exercise power under the charter unless

home-rule charter the rules under which a city operates; local governments have considerable independent governing power under these charters

TABLE 10.2

Texas's Largest Home-Rule Cities

NAME	2019 POPULATION ESTIMATES	FORM OF GOVERNMENT	FIRST CHARTER	PRESENT FORM ADOPTED
Houston	2,320,268	Mayor-council	1905	1994
San Antonio	1,547,253	Council-manager	1914	1951
Dallas	1,343,573	Council-manager	1889	1907
Austin	978,908	Council-manager	1919	1994
Fort Worth	909,585	Council-manager	1924	1985
El Paso	681,728	Council-manager	1873	2004
Arlington	398,854	Council-manager	1920	1990
Corpus Christi	326,586	Council-manager	1926	1993
Plano	287,677	Council-manager	1961	1993
Laredo	262,491	Council-manager	1848	1911

SOURCES: Compiled from *Texas Almanac 2006–2007* (Dallas: *Dallas Morning News*, 2006), 340–64; *Texas Almanac 2008–2009* (Dallas: *Dallas Morning News*, 2008), 8; Texas State Data Center; www.citypopulation.de; City Charter of the City of Laredo as Amended (2010); City of El Paso website; U.S. Census Bureau, "Quick Facts," July 1, 2019.

the state constitution or the legislature through law says otherwise. The state legislature may "preempt" a particular policy passed by local governments when it perceives that the policy is not in the interest of the state. Preemption has become an increasingly important issue in Texas and the nation over the past few years.[26] See the Citizen's Guide to this chapter.

Home-rule charters provide for the form of government that operates in the city and specify the number of members serving on the city's governing body. They also may grant the governing body the power to annex land adjacent to the city as well as to set property tax rates up to $2.50 per $100 valuation. Home-rule cities are also constitutionally authorized to borrow money in ways not available to smaller municipal entities. Home-rule charters must be consistent with the state constitution and any other relevant statutory provisions. For example, the state has mandated that most city elections take place on a date provided by the Texas Election Code. City elections must be conducted under the general guidelines set by the state. Nevertheless, home rule in Texas traditionally has delegated enormous power to local city governments. According to a report by the Advisory Commission on Intergovernmental Relations, the Texas Constitution allows cities more "home rule" than does any other state.[27]

Preemption and Home-Rule While home-rule cities have substantial power to act independently of state control, the city of Denton discovered that there are limits on local control when home rule comes into conflict with the oil industry and

Favorability toward Local Government

There is a widespread belief that government closer to the people is the most desirable. In one poll, favorability toward local government was far higher than unfavorable ratings among urban, suburban, and rural Texans. But many Texans said they were neither favorable nor unfavorable. Why? What could local officials do to change these numbers?

	VERY FAVORABLE	SOMEWHAT FAVORABLE	NEITHER	SOMEWHAT UNFAVORABLE	VERY UNFAVORABLE	DON'T KNOW/ NO OPINION
All Texans	14%	33%	25%	15%	9%	4%
Urban	16	31	24	16	9	4
Suburban	12	35	26	13	10	4
Rural	15	33	23	18	9	3

SOURCE: University of Texas/*Texas Tribune* poll of 1,200 registered voters in Texas between February 3 and February 10, 2017. Margin of error +/− 2.83 percent.

state government. In 2014, Denton was the home of 277 gas wells. Concerned about the effects of the fracking drilling technique used for gas production, nearly 59 percent of the voters in Denton passed an ordinance on November 11, 2014, banning further fracking in the city. Immediately the petroleum industry sued the city over the ban, and the industry was joined in opposition by the Texas General Land Office. In May 2015 the legislature passed HB 40 preempting the fracking ban. By June 2015, Denton's city council was forced to repeal the ban. In the brief lifetime of the Denton anti-fracking law, the city spent over $800,000 trying to defend the ordinance and oil interests meanwhile spent over $1.0 million challenging it.[28]

The 2015 fight over Denton's anti-fracking ordinances was only the first round in an intense debate that broke out early during the next legislative session over the wisdom of numerous city ordinances. Proclaiming that we are not the "United States of municipalities," Governor Abbott led the charge on a variety of initiatives to **preempt** or set aside local ordinances. Among proposed preemption initiatives were bills banning sanctuary cities in Texas and ending local regulation of ride-hailing services that originally drove Uber and Lyft out of Austin. Another bill that provided tax credit to offset local tree removal fees was vetoed by Abbott as not going far enough. (Abbott himself had experienced this inconvenience when he tried to remove trees on his property in Austin.) The special session of the legislature in the summer of 2017 was dominated by a host of preemption issues. Two popular preemption bills passed: a new bill limiting local regulations of tree removal and a second bill restricting the annexation powers of local government. Others were more controversial and failed to pass including

preemption the legislature's power to overrule ordinances or actions of local home-rule cities

- a bill requiring transgender people to use the bathroom according to the sex on their birth certificate.
- a bill limiting the growth of local property taxes.

- a bill capping local government spending.
- a bill speeding up local permit processes.
- a bill preventing local rule changes midway through local construction projects.
- a bill preempting local restrictions on mobile devices in cars.
- a bill prohibiting local governments from sending money to Planned Parenthood.[29]

Preemption controversies covering a wide range of issues continued during the 2019 legislative session. One estimate identified 62 bills filed during the 2019 session that sought to strike down a variety of local ordinances, including ordinances in San Antonio, Austin, and Dallas to provide paid sick time to all city employees.[30] The ordinances are now being litigated in state and federal court and likely will get serious pushback in the 2021 legislative session.

Another bill, HB 2840, passed the legislature in 2019, creating new rules making it easier for the public to speak out at local government meetings. In the past, many local governments had a "Persons to Be Heard" segment where interested individuals could speak up about an issue under consideration at certain well-defined points in time. Unfortunately, many local governments did not provide for any citizen input or limited the input to the beginning or end of a meeting. Under new rules, people can speak out at the beginning of a local government meeting, at the end, or before a vote on every listed item. As Dave Lieber, a consumer watchdog columnist for the *Dallas Morning News*, noted, "HB 2840 is a license to speak up, talk more, get involved and be a better watchdog."[31]

The most important piece of preemption in 2019 took place under the auspices of property tax reform when the state legislature constrained the ability of local governments to raise property taxes without going to the voters for their approval (see Chapter 11).

What was driving this debate over preemption and local self-government? There were many factors, but one stands out: the growing partisanship in the state legislature fueled by an aggressive conservative wing of the Republican Party. As noted in earlier chapters, the Democratic Party now dominates many of the large urban areas in the state, but an increasingly conservative Republican Party now controls most suburban, exurban, and rural parts of the state as well as the executive and state legislature. By expanding state preemption activity, the Republican Party effectively sought to impose its social conservative and free market ideology throughout the state, particularly into urban enclaves controlled by Democrats.[32]

Local Government and the Coronavirus

Mayors and county judges are of particular importance in responding to the coronavirus at the local level. These offices are given substantial regulatory authority under the Texas Disaster Act, although the decisions of these officials can be overridden by the governor. In the early stages of the pandemic, Governor Abbott deferred to the decisions of mayors and county judges. One reason was that the coronavirus was not affecting the entire state; rather, it was mostly in urban and suburban areas, although there were cases in rural areas especially where prisons and meat processing facilities were located. As a result, it seemed reasonable to have local officials deal with the local effects of the pandemic.

However, the emphasis on local responses to the pandemic led to a patchwork of regulations. Some cities, for example, had regulations that were stricter than the counties in which they were located. Additionally, some cities crossed county lines and were subject to differing local regulations. Early in the pandemic, tensions developed among local officials as to what the appropriate response should be or how economic concerns should be balanced against public health concerns. How strict should shelter-in-place policies be in a particular locale? How long should local businesses be closed down to prevent the spread of the virus? When and how should these businesses be allowed to reopen? Who should be responsible for making these decisions? County commissioners in various parts of the state believed they were not sufficiently consulted by county judges and demanded a role in the decision-making process. Urban counties had stricter regulations than neighboring suburban counties, which led to claims that contagion was being transported into the cities from suburban dwellers.

As the pandemic settled into the state, pressures built to loosen the restrictions because of the economic damage done by stay-in-place regulations. Republican state officials developed views on the response to the coronavirus that diverged from those of Democratic officials in the cities and urban counties. Pressures among Republican state officials to preempt local public health initiatives increased in the late spring as demands to reopen the economy built.

In early May 2020, Governor Abbott started taking a more active role in imposing directives, which often conflicted with and superseded local regulations. Attorney General Paxton sent warning letters in mid-May to city officials in Austin, Dallas, and San Antonio and to county officials in Travis, Dallas, and Bexar counties that said they were not in compliance with Governor Abbott's directives. Paxton also wrote that Dallas County could not ban law offices from opening, that masking requirements were invalid, that Austin's requirement of remote worship services with a 10-person-to-a-room limit was not allowed, and that local shelter-in-place orders could not be enforced. Abbott banned releasing county jail inmates without money bail if they had been arrested for a violent crime or had previously been convicted of one. Perhaps the oddest repudiation of local action by state officials occurred when Governor Abbott, Lieutenant Governor Patrick, and Attorney General Paxton criticized a Democratic district judge in Dallas for jailing a salon owner, Shelley Luther, who had refused to comply with Abbott's business closure directive.

In an October 2020 order, Abbott again showed deference to county officials when he issued an order that allowed bars to reopen to 50 percent capacity if that reopening was approved by county judges. That decision suggested Abbott may be inclined to return to his initial position of allowing local regulatory decision making during the pandemic.

In the long run, the biggest impact of the pandemic on local government is likely to be financial. The pandemic has led to widespread unemployment and reduced revenues for cities from everything from sales taxes to tourism. Those losses of revenue have already led to layoffs of local government employees and a reduction of government services, and more layoffs and reductions are expected.

State Preemption of Local Laws

1 Why state preemption of local laws matters

As Texas's cities have grown, conflicts have emerged between cities and the state. Cities have passed laws that respond to local concerns that have increasingly come in conflict with state policy goals. Since cities are under the authority of the state, the state legislature has responded with laws that prevent local governments from legislating in these controversial issue areas. This city-state tension is important because people in cities might be strongly supportive of policies that legislators in rural and suburban areas might not want. Should the views of voters and legislators statewide trump those of voters and legislators in urban areas with specific needs?

In Texas, this municipal legislation is often passed by Democratic urban areas that are contrary to the Republican state government and so there is an underlying element of partisanship in the state's preemption of local legislation. This is reflected in Governor Greg Abbott's desire "to reduce, restrict and prohibit local regulations."[a] And the bitterness over local legislation conflicting with state goals is seen in the recorded conversation between Texas House Speaker Dennis Bonnen, then–House GOP chair Dustin Burrows, and political activist Michael Sullivan. Burrows told Sullivan, "We hate cities and counties." Speaker Bonnen added, "Any mayor, county judge that was dumbass enough to come meet with me, I told them with great clarity, my goal is for this to be the worst session in the history of the Legislature for cities and counties." To that, Burrows added, "I hope the next session's even worse."[b]

2 What's the debate?

Supporters of local legislation free from state preemption take the position that government closest to the people is best. Local government is in a better position to understand the needs of the community than is state government and, therefore, should be allowed to legislate in the interests of that community. In contrast, supporters of state preemption believe that local interests may act in ways that are contrary to the interests of the state as a whole and when that happens, the state should stop legislation that

In 2014, voters in Denton, Texas, decided to ban fracking in the county, but state law preempted this local law.

it believes is contrary to the overall interests of the state. In short, local governments are agents of the state and not institutions that are free to choose their own legislative agenda without reference to that of the state as a whole.

3 What do the numbers say?

The table shows that over the past several years a number of states have passed legislation that has preempted local laws in a variety of issue areas.

Texas has been very active as a preemption state. In the 2019 legislative session, 62 preemption bills were filed in Austin.[c] Not all of them passed, but several did that were significant limitations on the powers of local government: the state banned the use of red light cameras; it banned local governments from charging fees to telecommunications companies for their use of public rights of way; and, in what was probably the biggest hit to city budgets, it limited the ability of cities to increase property tax revenues more than 3.5 percent without holding a voter approval election known as a roll-back election.[d] One preemption bill that did not pass but was considered important by the Speaker of the Texas House and one that he would give high priority in the next legislative session would prevent taxpayer funds being used to lobby the legislature.[e]

PREEMPTION ISSUE	NUMBER OF STATES
Minimum Wage Laws	25
Paid Sick Days Laws	23
Regulation of Ride Sharing Networks	44
Regulation of Guns or Ammunition	43
Municipal Broadband Networks	20
Control Over 5G Technology	23
Plastic Bag Bans	15
Rent Control	31
Sanctuary Policies	11
Regulation of E-Cigarettes	10
Predictable Work Scheduling Laws	9
Fair Hiring Laws	5
Soda Taxes	4

Source: Kim Haddow, Anthony Gad, & Katy Fleury, "The Growing Shadow of State Interference," Local Solutions Support Center, 2019.

Communicating Effectively: What Do You Think?

● Should cities be allowed to legislate without preemption by the state?

● If the state does preempt local legislation, is there any reason for local governments to exist?

● Would states continue to preempt local legislation if state legislatures and local governments shared the same political party control?

WANT TO LEARN MORE?

The following are sources of additional information on the issue of preemption.

- National League of Cities
  www.nlc.org

- National Conference of State Legislatures
  www.ncsl.org

- CityLab
  www.citylab.com

Forms of Government in Texas Cities

mayor-council form of government a form of city government in which the mayor is the chief executive and the city council is the legislative body; in the *strong mayor–council* variation, the mayor's powers enable him or her to control executive departments and the agenda of the city council; in the *weak mayor–council* variation, the mayor's power is more limited

at-large election an election in which officials are selected by voters of the entire geographical area, rather than from smaller districts within that area

single-member district an electorate that elects only one representative for each district

commissioner form of government a form of city government in which the city is run by a small group of elected commissioners who act in both legislative and executive capacities

council-manager form of government a form of city government in which public policies are developed by the city council and executive and administrative functions are assigned to a professional city manager

Texas home-rule cities have had three major forms of city government: the mayor-council form, the commissioner form, and the council-manager form. The **mayor-council form of government** is the oldest. It consists of an elected mayor and city council. The mayor is usually elected from the city in an **at-large election**. The council may be elected either at large or from a group of **single-member districts**, or a mixture of the two. In the mayor-council form of government, the mayor is the chief executive officer of the city. He or she presides over council meetings and has a variety of appointment powers. The city council, meanwhile, serves as the legislative body in the city, passing local laws and watching over the executive departments.

There have been both strong mayor–council systems and weak ones, depending on the powers given to the mayor by the city charter or state statute. In the *strong mayor–council* variation, various executive powers, such as appointment and removal powers for boards and departments as well as veto powers, are concentrated in the office of mayor. These powers enable the mayor to establish effective control over various executive departments in the city and to control the legislative agenda of the city council. In the *weak mayor–council* variation, these executive powers are much more limited, fragmenting power between the mayor and other elected or appointed officials. Strong-mayor systems reflect a perspective that having a strong executive in charge of city government makes it operate more efficiently. In contrast, weak-mayor systems diffuse power, with city council members retaining a great deal of power. Advocates of the latter say this system gives a greater voice to the various constituencies represented by the members.[33]

The mayor-council form of government is the dominant form of government in most general-law cities, although it is considerably less popular among home-rule cities. According to a 2017 survey by the *Texas Almanac*, about 48 percent of Texas municipalities had mayors but not city managers or city administrators.[34]

A second form of city government is the **commissioner form of government**. Under this system, the city is run by a small commission, composed of between five and seven members generally elected at large. The commission acts in both a legislative and an executive capacity. As a group, commissioners enact laws for the city. At the same time, each commissioner is in charge of one of the executive departments. One commissioner is also designated as the mayor to preside at meetings.

The commission plan, which came to be known as the "Texas Idea," reflected a desire to bring to city government good business practices that would somehow escape the squabbles and inefficiency of traditional local government found in the mayor-council form. It was believed that commissioners with direct responsibility for operation of various departments would bring professional management to government.[35] At its peak in 1918 the commission form was used by approximately 500 cities across the country including 75 cities in Texas. Following World War I, the number of commission-form cities decreased. By 2000 no city in Texas had a pure commission form of government, although 26 still claimed to have some variation of it.[36]

Essentially the "Texas Idea" led to the third form of city government found in Texas, the **council-manager form of government**. A city manager replaced the commissioners because a single manager provided the professional management of city government without the squabbles and jurisdictional disputes that naturally occurred with the multiple managers of the various departments in the commission system.[37] As originally envisioned, a city council elected in at-large elections was to be the policy-making body. Council members generally received little or no pay and were intended to be publicly motivated citizens interested in serving the public good, rather than professional politicians. A mayor was selected from among the council members. The city manager was to be a professional public manager who served as the chief executive and administrative official in the city. As in the commissioner form of government, the goal of the council-manager form was twofold: to free local government from the seamier side of politics and to bring administrative expertise to local government. Today, almost 52 percent of the 1,216 incorporated Texas municipalities have some form of city manager government.[38] Across the United States, it has become the most popular form of government for cities of over 10,000 residents.[39]

Today, council-manager systems vary across the state in a number of ways. The desire for professional administration of local government remains high. Most city managers have graduate degrees and are paid high salaries like executive officers in the private sector. But a desire for more political accountability through traditional democratic processes has introduced some changes. The growing ethnic and racial diversity of some Texas cities has forced many political leaders to question the wisdom of freeing local government too much from democratic controls. In most cities, mayors now are elected at large from the population as a whole, rather than from among the council. Many cities also elect council members from single-member districts rather than at large. Many see at-large elections as undercutting representation of people of color by diluting minority votes. Only when Dallas moved from an at-large council to one elected from single-member districts in 1991 did people of color come to play a major role in the decision-making processes of city government. But most cities and towns under the council-manager system continue to view local political offices as part-time jobs. Mayoral and council salaries remain low (although a few cities, such as Austin, offer considerably higher salaries). The demand for more democratic accountability in local government will likely continue to lead to more changes in the council-manager system of government across Texas. Balancing professional efficiency in city government with democratic political processes will continue to be a problem as Texas's metropolitan areas grow and diversify in the twenty-first century.

Tales of Five Cities

Houston Houston is the largest city in Texas. It has over 2.2 million people and a strong mayor–council form of government. There are 18 elected officials in the city serving concurrent four-year terms, including a mayor, a controller, and 16 council members. The mayor serves as the chief executive. Much of the mayor's power stems from the authority to appoint department heads and members of advisory boards, subject to council approval. The mayor also presides over the city council and has voting privileges on it. The 16-member council is a legislative body composed of 5 at-large seats and 11 single-member district seats.

Unlike in most other cities, the controller in Houston is an elected official.[40] The controller is the city's chief financial officer. Besides investing city funds, conducting internal audits of city departments, and operating the city's financial management system, the controller is also responsible for certifying the availability of funds for city council

Pictured here are the mayors of Texas's two largest cities. Sylvester Turner (left) is the current mayor of Houston. Prior to being elected mayor in the closest mayoral election in Houston history, he served in the Texas State House from 1989 to 2016. Ron Nirenberg (right) became mayor of San Antonio on June 21, 2017, after defeating the incumbent mayor Ivy Taylor in a runoff. Previously he had served two terms on the San Antonio City Council.

initiatives. In the end, the office of the controller is both a professional and a political position. Not surprisingly, the controller often comes into conflict with the mayor and the council over important policy issues.

Although local politics in Houston is nominally nonpartisan, in recent years it has taken on a partisan flavor. Houston's current mayor is Sylvester Turner, a well-known Democrat who had previously served in the Texas legislature for 26 years and had major responsibilities for the state's budget while in that position. Turner had unsuccessfully sought the mayor's office in 1991 and in 2003 but won in 2015 and was reelected in 2019. He is the second African American to serve as Houston's mayor.

San Antonio San Antonio, which has overtaken Dallas as the second-largest city in Texas, has a council-manager form of government. The council is composed of 10 members elected from single-member districts on a nonpartisan basis plus the mayor, who is the 11th member of the council and is selected at large. All members of the council serve for two-year terms. Until an election in 2015 that amended the city charter, the mayor's salary was a paltry $4,040 per year, and other council members were paid $20 per meeting, not to exceed $1,040 per year. Recognizing that service as an elected official in San Antonio had become a full-time job, voters raised salaries for council members to $45,722 a year and $61,725 for the mayor, currently Ron Nirenberg. This charter amendment was approved by 54.8 percent of those voting. Council members are subject to recall if 10 percent of the qualified voters in a district sign a petition of recall and a recall election is successful. The city charter also provides for initiatives and referendums that emerge from the voters.

The city manager in San Antonio serves at the pleasure of the council as the chief executive and administrative official in the city. He or she has wide-ranging appointment and removal authority over officers and employees in all city departments. The current city manager, Erik Walsh, supervises a budget of $2.9 billion and 12,000 employees. Indicative of the city manager's central role in running the city is his salary, which in 2019 was $312,000.

Dallas   Dallas also operates under a council-manager form of government. Until the late twentieth century, city politics had been dominated for years by the White business community. At-large nonpartisan elections tended to elect a council that was relatively united in its understanding of the problems facing the city and its vision of where the city should go. In the late 1980s and early 1990s, however, a bitter struggle over rewriting the city charter divided the city along racial lines.

The new charter, which went into effect in 1991, called for a 14-member council elected from single-member districts and a mayor elected at large. Members are limited to serving four two-year terms consecutively. Under the new charter, membership on the council was transformed as a significant number of African American and Latino members were elected.

As in other council-manager systems, the power of the mayor in Dallas is weak. The mayor—currently Eric Johnson—presides over council meetings, creates council committees, and appoints members, chairs, and co-chairs. In many ways, however, the mayor is only first among equals on the council. The council as a whole is the legislative body for the city, approving budgets, determining the tax rate, and appointing key public officials, including the city manager, city attorney, city auditor, city secretary, municipal court judges, and various citizen boards and commissions. The city manager serves at the will of the council and is removable by a two-thirds vote of the members. As in San Antonio, the city manager's powers in Dallas are vast. As the chief administrative officer, the city manager has the power to appoint and remove all heads of departments and subordinate officers and employees in the city, subject to civil service provisions.

Despite the ideal of removing the city manager from the pressures of political life in Dallas, recent city managers have found themselves forced to accommodate the reality

Dallas mayor Eric Johnson, elected in 2019, like other mayors in council-manager city governments has relatively little power. Here, he answers questions at a coronavirus briefing.

Austin's mayor, Democrat Steve Adler, speaks at a celebration of same-sex marriage rights at a church in Austin.

of an increasingly politicized city council. The political pressures emerging from Dallas's single-member district council may ultimately compel the city to reexamine the wisdom of retaining a council-manager system. As Dallas learned in the 1990s, efficient government and democratic governance are not as easy to balance as advocates of the council-manager system once thought.

Austin Austin, the 11th most populous city in the United States and the 4th most populous city in Texas, is the seat of Travis County and the capital of the state. In the November 2012 elections, Austinites adopted by more than a 60 percent margin a plan to change the method for selecting members of the city council. Under the old system, a mayor and a 6-member city council were all elected citywide. A city manager served as chief administrative officer of the city. Austin continues to have a city manager; however, since 2014 only the mayor is elected citywide. The 10 city council members are elected from single-member districts. (Until this change, Austin was the largest city in the United States whose city council did not include at least some members elected from geographic districts.)[41]

Over the previous 40 years, Austin voters had rejected district plans six times. In 2014, however, there was a strong grassroots movement favoring the 10-district plan, with support from a broad coalition of groups such as the Travis County Republican Party and Latino groups. One important reason for the success of the proposal was that it appeared on the November ballot, when there was a larger and more diverse group of voters than in the prior six elections. The proposal required that the districts be drawn by a commission of citizens chosen through an application process overseen by the city auditor. The first elections under the new system were in 2014.[42] Among the effects of the replacement of at-large districts with single-member districts was increased representation of people of color on the council. In 2020, the mayor of Austin was White as were 6 city council members. One African American and 3 Latinos held the remaining seats on the 10-member city council.

El Paso El Paso, located in the far western part of the state, has a distinctive culture from its sister cities to the east. Home to over 679,000 people, El Paso is on the border with Mexico, which makes the city a center for international trade. The military is also important to the El Paso economy because of the presence of Fort Bliss. El Paso's ethnic composition is quite different from the state's other largest cities or the state as a whole. Only 3.8 percent of the city's population was African American—far smaller than the proportion of African Americans statewide. However, 80.9 percent of the city's population is Latino, far larger than the overall proportion of Latinos in Texas.

The mayor of El Paso, Dee Margo, speaks at a press conference after the shooting at a Walmart in August 2019.

Until 2004, El Paso worked under a charter that provided for a strong mayor and eight district representatives who ran on a slate every two years.[43] Local politics was highly partisan and dominated by the Democratic Party. Turnover was high among all leadership positions. Between 1989 and 2004, El Paso had seven mayors. Because the mayor appointed the chief administrative officer in the city, there were frequent turnovers in the

Who Governs Texas's Cities?

Racial and Ethnic Composition of Texas's Major Cities and Their City Councils

● White ● African American ● Latino ● Other

Houston

City pop. — 24.6% · 22.5% · 44.8% · 8.1%
Council — 50% · 37.5% · 12.5%

Houston has an African American mayor. Houston has a 16-member city council with five members elected at large. Four of the five at-large members are White and one is African American.

San Antonio

City pop. — 24.8% · 6.9% · 64.2% · 4.1%
Council — 20% · 10% · 70%

San Antonio has an Asian mayor. The 10 city council members are elected from single-member districts.

Dallas

City pop. — 29% · 24.3% · 41.7% · 5%
Council — 50% · 21% · 29%

Dallas has an African American mayor. The 14 city council members are elected from single-member districts.

Austin

City pop. — 48.3% · 7.8% · 34.3% · 9.6%
Council — 60% · 10% · 30%

Austin has a White mayor. The 10 city council members are elected from single-member districts.

El Paso

City pop. — 13.2% · 3.8% · 80.9% · 2.1%
Council — 25% · 12.5% · 62.5%

El Paso has a White mayor. The eight city council members are elected from single-member districts.

Representation is an important issue at all levels of government. Who's in power can have a profound impact on what policies are enacted. A snapshot of representation at the municipal level raises critical questions: Can a community be properly represented when its elected officials do not reflect the racial and ethnic characteristics of the community? For example, does it make a difference that the Dallas city council is 29 percent Latino while the Dallas population is 41.7 percent Latino? Whom are the elected officials representing? Is it the population as a whole or the people who vote?

QUANTITATIVE REASONING

- Of these major Texas cities, which city council best reflects the racial/ethnic composition of its population? Which council diverges most from its city's racial/ethnic composition?

- Do you think it is important that the city councils do reflect the racial/ethnic composition of their communities? Why or why not?

SOURCE: U.S. Census, QuickFacts, July 1, 2019; data on city councils are from 2020, taken from each city's website.

Poverty and unemployment continue to plague El Paso. The city government is trying to attract more jobs by developing the downtown area.

professional staff. Many felt that the process of city government had become too politicized and lacked professionalism and accountability. While there was much sentiment for charter reform in the community as a whole and among groups such as the blue-ribbon City Charter's Citizen Advisory Committee, there was no clear advocate for changing the charter.

This changed in 2003 when Joe Wardy challenged and then beat the incumbent mayor on a platform that included charter revision. Along with four other council members who ran on a platform supporting charter change, Wardy was responsible for opening a public dialogue that educated the citizenry and key political leaders in the community. There was no organized opposition to the reform proposal. Some raised concerns about the accountability of an unpopular or ineffective city manager. But these were put to rest for the most part by the proposed revisions that enabled the council to remove a city manager with the support of five council members with the mayor's approval or six without the mayor's approval.

The charter revisions moving from a strong-mayor form of government to a nonpartisan council-manager form were approved by the voters in February 2004. Turnout was low at 8 percent, although this was typical for local elections in El Paso. Under the new charter, the city manager would report directly to the mayor and city council. Elections would be nonpartisan, and city council members would serve four-year, staggered terms.

El Paso was the largest of 24 municipalities in the United States to adopt a manager-council form of government between 1998 and 2004. During the same period, 19 other cities in the United States rejected adopting a manager-council form of government, and 14 abandoned manager-council government for a strong-mayor system. Among the large cities that adopted a strong-mayor form were Oakland, California, and Miami, Florida.

Clearly there is considerable disagreement across the United States as to the best form of local government. Different political, economic, and cultural circumstances can lead cities to go in different directions. But in Texas, the dominant form of local government continues to be the manager-council form, with Houston as the sole holdout for the strong-mayor system.

Special Purpose Districts

 Examine the role of special purpose districts in Texas government

A **special purpose district** is a unit of local government that performs a single service in a limited geographic area. Special purpose districts can solve problems that cut across different units of government. Special purpose districts can be created to serve an entire county, part of a county, all of two or more counties, or parts of two or more counties. Nationwide, the number of special purpose districts has increased by 400 percent since the middle of the twentieth century.[44] In Texas, the number increased from 491 in 1952 to 2,600 in 2012. In addition, there were 1,079 independent school districts, which are also classified as special purpose districts.[45]

Special purpose districts can be created to do almost anything that is legal. Some are formed to provide hospital care, others to furnish pure water to communities, still others to provide mosquito control, navigation, flood control, sanitation, drainage, fire protection, ambulance services, and law enforcement. They can take in large amounts of tax monies to accomplish their purposes.

special purpose district a unit of local government that performs a single service, such as education or sanitation, within a limited geographic area

Types of Special Purpose Districts

There are two types of special purpose districts in Texas. The first is the **school district**, which consists of independent school districts in the state. These districts offer public education from pre-kindergarten through 12th grade. Almost all school districts offer the full range of elementary and secondary education; however, some small, rural districts provide education only through the 8th grade, the 6th grade, or the 4th grade. Those with limited offerings contract with nearby districts to complete the education of their students.

The second classification of special purpose districts is the **nonschool special district**. Everything except the school districts is included in this category. Municipal utility districts, economic development corporations, hospital districts, and fire-prevention districts are the most common examples.

In addition to county taxes a property owner in Upshur County, Texas, will pay taxes to two special purpose districts—the Union Grove Independent School District and the Emergency Services District No. 1 (fire protection). A property owner in Hopkins County will pay to the Sulphur Springs Independent School District and to the Hopkins County Hospital District. A property owner in Collin County will pay taxes to the Plano Independent School District and to the Collin College District. One property owner in Houston pays taxes to the Houston Independent School District, the Harris County Department of Education, the Harris County Flood Control District, the Port of Houston

school district a specific type of special district that provides public education in a designated area

nonschool special district any special district other than a school district; examples include municipal utility districts (MUDs) and hospital districts

Authority, the Harris County Hospital District, the Lone Star College System, Emergency Service District No. 13 (fire protection), and Emergency Service District No. 11 (EMS).

School Districts

Every square inch of land in Texas is part of a school district, and the state contains 1,265 school districts. Some school districts in east and west Texas cover an entire county. In metropolitan counties, there may be a dozen or more school districts. Each is governed by an elected board of trustees composed of five to nine members. The board employs a superintendent to oversee the daily operation of the school district. On the recommendation of the superintendent, the trustees

- set overall policy for the school district.
- adopt the budget for the school district.
- set the tax rate for the school district. (The maximum rate is $1.04 for each $100 of the assessed property value unless voters approve a higher rate.)
- select textbooks for classroom use.
- hire principals, faculty, and support staff.
- set the school calendar.
- determine salaries and benefits for employees.

Educating millions of students is a daunting task. By localizing public education, the state places much of the burden on the local school districts but also allows local residents to participate in governing them. Unfortunately, few people vote in the elections to select members of the board of trustees. Even fewer individuals attend meetings of the school board.

Nonschool Special Purpose Districts

Nonschool special purpose districts include a vast number of types. Larger counties tend to have many different special purpose districts. Dallas County, for example, has 13 nonschool special purpose districts. Harris County is the record holder for special purpose districts in Texas, with nearly 500 nonschool special purpose districts.[46] Some of the most common types are as follows.

municipal utility district (MUD) a special district that offers services such as electricity, water, sewage, and sanitation outside the city limits

Municipal Utility Districts
Municipal utility districts (MUDs) offer electricity, water, sewer, and sanitation services outside the city limits. These governments might offer all utility services or only one or two, depending on the needs of the special district. Though MUDs are located throughout Texas, the vast majority are found in the Houston metropolitan area.

MUDs can be a financial blessing for developers. Entrepreneurs who build new housing outside city limits must furnish utilities to these homes, but few developers can afford to do this over a long period of time.

Banks and finance companies, legislators, and land developers maintain a warm and snug relationship with each other. Banks and finance companies willingly lend developers millions of dollars to establish residential subdivisions, build new homes, and run

How Extensive Are Texas's Local Governments?

Number of Local Governments in Each State, 2017

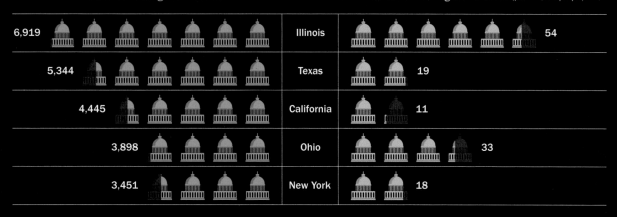

		Number of local governments		Number of local governments (per 100,000 people)	
6,919			Illinois		54
5,344			Texas		19
4,445			California		11
3,898			Ohio		33
3,451			New York		18

	Total local govts.	Per 100K people		Total local govts.	Per 100K people		Total local govts.	Per 100K people		Total local govts.	Per 100K people		Total local govts.	Per 100K people
IL	6,919	54	WI	3,097	54	AR	1,542	51	NC	971	9	UT	620	20
TX	5,344	19	MI	2,864	29	OR	1,511	36	MS	970	32	NH	542	40
PA	4,831	38	ND	2,665	353	GA	1,381	13	TN	907	14	VA	518	6
CA	4,445	11	IN	2,639	40	NJ	1,339	15	MA	859	13	LA	517	11
OH	3,898	33	NE	2,539	132	KY	1,323	30	ME	835	63	MD	345	6
KS	3,793	130	IA	1,942	62	MT	1,227	116	WY	795	137	DE	335	35
MO	3,769	62	SD	1,917	219	AL	1,196	25	VT	730	117	NV	190	6
MN	3,644	65	WA	1,901	26	ID	1,171	68	AZ	659	9	AK	180	24
NY	3,451	18	OK	1,831	47	NM	1,014	49	WV	652	36	RI	130	12
CO	3,142	56	FL	1,713	8	SC	972	13	CT	626	18	HI	22	2

Local governments include county governments, school board districts, special districts, and municipal utility districts. One would expect that Texas's political culture would lead it to have fewer local governments than other states with traditions of more governmental involvement. Is this the case?

NOTE: Different sources provide different numbers of local governments, but Texas does have somewhat more than 4,800 local governments.

SOURCES: Governing, "2017 Census of Government-Organizations"; "Local Governments by States," April 25, 2019 (accessed 6/17/2020).

CRITICAL THINKING

- What are some of the characteristics of states with large numbers of local governments?

- Does the picture change when we factor in population? Which states have larger numbers of local governments per capita? What might explain these differences?

water and sewer services to these houses. When a few houses are sold, the developer asks the residents to establish a MUD. Enabling the legislation is seldom a problem because of the close relationship between developers and local legislators.

Once the MUD is up and running, the board of directors sets a tax rate and determines how much to charge residents for its services. One of its first activities is to borrow money by issuing bonds (interest-bearing financial instruments that are sold in financial markets to fund government projects). The bond proceeds are used to purchase the utilities from the developer, often at a premium. Using the proceeds from the sale of the utilities, the developer is able to repay loans. By establishing the MUD, residents agree to pay a property tax to retire the bonded indebtedness. In addition to the property tax, residents pay a monthly fee for the water, sewer, and sanitation services.

Community College Districts Community college districts are classified as nonschool special purpose districts because the public education they offer is not from pre-kindergarten through 12th grade but postsecondary academic and vocational programs. Community colleges are governed by an elected board of regents. Residents of the district pay a property tax to the district and in return pay lower tuition. The board employs a president or chancellor, who operates the college on a daily basis. The regents set policy on the recommendation of the president or chancellor. Among the regents' responsibilities are to

- set overall policy for the district.
- set the tax rate.
- set the cost of tuition and fees.
- build new buildings and repair older ones.
- hire teachers, counselors, administrators, and nonprofessional staff.
- set the school calendar.
- determine salaries and benefits for employees.

Hospital, Emergency Services, and Flood Control Districts A number of counties have hospital districts, some of which are designed to serve the poor and uninsured and supplement the costs of indigent medical care through taxes imposed by the hospital district. Emergency services districts provide fire and ambulance services to areas not served otherwise. The districts can be of varying size— Harris County has more than 30 emergency services districts, though most counties in Texas contain only 1 or 2 such districts.[47] Flood control districts are established to solve a multicounty problem, since flooding is seldom confined to a single county.

Creating, Governing, and Paying for a Special Purpose District
Special purpose districts are created by voters of the area to be served. Creating a special purpose district requires

- a petition signed by the residents of the area to be served, requesting the legislature to authorize a special election to create a special district.
- enabling legislation in the form of a law that authorizes such an election.
- approval by a majority of those voting in the special election.

Most special purpose districts are governed by boards elected by the voters of the district. Each board is the policy-making group for its district. The directors set the tax rate and establish rules and policy for the operation of the district, which often employs an individual to run it on a day-to-day basis.

Property taxes are the primary source of revenue for special purpose districts. This was not always the case. In 1949 school districts received 80 percent of their income from the state, and the school district furnished 20 percent, primarily from property taxes. Today, property taxes constitute as much as 90 percent of revenues for some districts. The second-largest source of income is **user fees**, raised from providing goods and services. Water districts, for example, sell water, sewer, and sometimes sanitation services. State and federal aid furnish the remainder of special district funding. Property tax rates and user fees are set by governing boards.

property tax a tax based on an assessment of the value of one's property, which is used to fund the services provided by local governments, such as education

user fee a fee paid for public goods and services, such as water or sewage service

Problems with Special Purpose Districts

Hidden Governments

Everyone in Texas lives in at least one special purpose district, their school district. Most people live in several, have the opportunity to vote for people to represent them on the governing board of each district, and pay property taxes to these agencies of government. Yet few people are aware these agencies exist, thus their reputation as **hidden governments**.

hidden government a term that refers to special purpose districts of which many citizens are unaware

Special purpose districts provide needed services in specific geographic areas, where existing governments may lack authority to provide the service or funds to finance the project. In theory, special purpose districts are an example of democracy at work. They are created by a vote of the residents of the area to be served, and their governing boards are elected by the voters. Board meetings, at which decisions on policy, taxing, and fees are made, are open for attendance by any interested residents. However, fewer than 10 percent of eligible voters cast ballots in special purpose district elections, and fewer than 1 percent of district residents ever attend a board meeting.

Abuses of Power

There is a potential for abuse in the creation of special purpose districts. Many of them were originally authorized by the Texas legislature to develop the economies of poor, rural counties. More recently, however, developers of large tracts of land began creating these districts to place the burden of developing the property's infrastructure on future owners of the property. In order to comply with the law, all the developers must do is create the district and hold an election in which at least one short-term resident must vote. These short-term residents then approve bonds in the millions of dollars that must be paid for with the taxation of future homes and property owners. In the 1980s this kind of special purpose district creation in Harris County led to defaults on bond issues after a housing bust.

In 2001 a major investigation of special purpose districts created by developers in Dallas found unusual and questionable practices. Some developers drew district boundaries to exclude existing residents of an area. The developers then moved people into rent-free mobile homes within these boundaries shortly before the special district election, in which these newly established "residents" were the only ones eligible to vote. After approving large bond sales for the construction of roads, water lines, and sewers, the voters for the new district would often move away. Future homeowners in the area

The creation of special purpose districts by real estate developers has sometimes been controversial. Recent investigations have charged developers with abusing the process in order to circumvent inconvenient laws and to give the developers greater control over taxes and other government functions in the district.

were then expected to pay for the bonds with property taxes on their homes. The investigation found that sometimes a single voter—and always fewer than 10 voters—approved the bonded indebtedness that helped the developers create an infrastructure for their properties. In the Lantana subdivision near Flower Mound, for example, a family of three voted to authorize $277 million in bond sales by two water districts. That bond proposition rivals the biggest bond proposals by the city of Dallas.[48] Similar schemes have been especially prevalent in Travis, Harris, and Denton counties.

One danger is that development will not proceed as planned in the areas covered by these special purpose districts, which can lead to exceptionally high charges to existing homeowners to cover the debt or bankruptcy of the special purpose districts. In this case, the holders of the bonds lose all or part of their investment. One such outcome occurred in the Grimes County Municipal Utility District No. 1, which defaulted on its $1.86 million in water and sewer revenue bonds. The district could not hope to make payments on the bonds when it ended up providing services to only three customers.[49]

The pervasiveness of special purpose districts is shown by one study of Texas special purpose districts that addresses water issues. The study found that about 1,000 MUDs were engaged in supplying water, 48 special purpose districts existed to deal with water drainage issues, and 66 special purpose districts existed solely to supply fresh water. Others had the following purposes: 91 to conserve groundwater, 25 to provide for irrigation, 46 to improve levees, 42 to manage municipal water, 26 to deal with navigation, and 31 to deal with rivers. Finally, 55 special utility districts dealt with general water issues, 221 were water control and improvement districts, and 18 were water improvement districts. Of course, this hodgepodge of special purpose districts dealing with all aspects of water makes a coherent approach to statewide water policy virtually impossible.[50]

PERSONAL RESPONSIBILITY: WHAT WOULD YOU DO?

- Why are there so many special purpose districts in Texas? Do you feel cities and counties should do the jobs that special purpose districts do? Why don't they?

- Do you think cities and counties should more closely monitor the activities of special purpose districts? Who do you think should be in charge of that oversight?

Councils of Government (COGs)

The Regional Planning Act of 1965 initially provided for the creation of regional **councils of government (COGs)** to promote coordination and planning across all local governments in a particular region. Councils of government are not special purpose districts, as they do not tax or impose user fees. Still, they play an important role at the regional level in providing planning and coordination across numerous local government boundaries. Major water, airport, or highway projects, among others, involve many local governments, and councils are necessary to work across these many local entities.

There are 24 regional councils in Texas today (Figure 10.2), each with its own bylaws or articles of agreement. At least two-thirds of the governing body of a regional council must consist of local elected officials of cities and counties, but it may also include citizen members and representatives of other groups.

The basic responsibilities of regional councils include planning for the economic development of an area, helping local governments carry out regional projects, contracting with local governments to provide certain services, and reviewing applications for state and federal financial assistance. Originally, COGs focused considerable attention on meeting federal mandates for water and sewer provision, open space, and housing planning. More recently, activities have focused on comprehensive planning and service delivery in such policy areas as aging, employment and training, criminal justice, economic development, environmental quality, and transportation.[51]

council of government (COG)
a regional planning board composed of local elected officials and some private citizens from the region

---

FIGURE 10.2

Regional Councils of Government in Texas

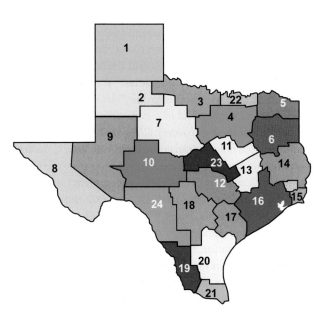

Region Name	Number
Alamo Area Council of Governments	18
Ark-Tex Council of Governments	5
Brazos Valley Council of Governments	13
Capital Area Council of Governments	12
Central Texas Council of Governments	23
Coastal Bend Council of Governments	20
Concho Valley Council of Governments	10
Deep East Texas Council of Governments	14
East Texas Council of Governments	6
Golden Crescent Regional Planning Commission	17
Heart of Texas Council of Governments	11
Houston-Galveston Area Council	16
Lower Rio Grande Valley Development Council	21
Middle Rio Grande Development Council	24
Nortex Regional Planning Commission	3
North Central Texas Council of Governments	4
Panhandle Regional Planning Commission	1
Permian Basin Regional Planning Commission	9
Rio Grande Council of Governments	8
South East Texas Regional Planning Commission	15
South Plains Association of Governments	2
South Texas Development Council	19
Texoma Council of Governments	22
West Central Texas Council of Governments	7

Financial Issues Facing Local Government

Examine the financial issues facing local government

As noted earlier, there are many different forms of local government in Texas, including county governments, municipal governments, school districts, and nonschool special purpose districts. These governments manage money through special financial mechanisms that rely on their ability to tax. Two of these mechanisms, capital appreciation bonds and local government pensions, raise important opportunities and problems for local government.

Capital Appreciation Bonds

capital appreciation bond (CAB) a long-term, high-interest-paying bond that pays off both principal and interest in one lump sum when the bond reaches maturity

A **capital appreciation bond (CAB)** is a method by which local governments—almost always school districts—borrow money. Its main use is by school districts to raise revenue for development in times of rapid population growth.[52] Local governments often sell bonds to obtain funds for projects, but unlike traditional government-issued bonds, capital appreciation bonds do not make periodic interest payments to bondholders over the course of the bond; instead, the local government promises to pay back the initial investment in the bond and all accrued interest when the bond reaches maturity. The bond is sold for an amount that is far less than the lump sum payment the local government has to make when the bond matures. Essentially, this type of bond is a way for local government to get money now for a promise to pay back much more money in one lump sum far into the future. This bond's main use is to avoid a state law passed in 1991 commonly called "the 50-cent test." This law required governments to show that their bonds could be repaid with a tax rate no more than 50 cents per $100 of the assessed property value at the time the bond was issued. If a government was near the 50-cent limit, a capital appreciation bond can avoid the impact of "the 50-cent test" since no payments of any kind are required on the bond until the bond becomes due years into the future.

This type of bond has been causing a great deal of controversy, especially in California, Texas, and Michigan. But despite the controversy, CABs are becoming more and more common in Texas. According to the nonpartisan group California Watch, "in Texas, 590 districts and other government entities have issued these bonds over the past six years—more than any other state."[53] Combined, Texas's local governments issued more than $2.3 billion in CABs in over 700 separate issuances between 2007 and 2011—debts that will eventually cost more than $20 billion to repay.[54] The per capita debt of Texas's state government ranks 45th in the nation. However, when local debt is taken into consideration, it jumps to 15th highest in the nation.[55]

CABs are extremely long-term bonds. In many cases they do not have to be paid by the local government until 40 years after they are issued.[56] During this entire time period, the issuer does not have to pay a dime to investors—meaning that local government officials can promise new education facilities to voters without raising current taxes.[57] CABs also tend to pay high interest to bond investors.

The dilemma of entities that use these bonds is well illustrated by the Forney Independent School District in Kaufman County. Forney is east of Dallas and is now one of the 10 fastest-growing cities in the state. In the past fifteen years its population has more than tripled and its school district's enrollment has risen by 330 percent. If increased indebtedness would cause a rapidly growing school district to run afoul of "the 50-cent test," a school district like the Forney ISD can issue capital appreciation bonds and build now while paying much later. Of course, issuing such bonds must be done with caution to avoid causing exceptional indebtedness for the school district in the future. By the end of fiscal 2014, the Forney ISD had issued 4 of the 20 most expensive capital appreciation bonds in the state. Forney ISD received $30 million in immediate funding, but the district will have to pay more than $208 million in 30–40 years when the bonds reach maturity.[58]

Michigan was so concerned about the dangers of this form of bond for future generations that it banned its use and California imposed severe restrictions on issuing these bonds when the media reported that the San Diego–area Poway Unified School District had issued $105 million in capital appreciation bonds that would ultimately cost the district almost $1 billion.[59] In 2015, the Texas legislature considered a number of bills related to capital appreciation bonds, but only one passed. This bill prohibited local governments (including school districts) from issuing CABs for terms longer than 20 years and from refunding CABs to extend their maturity dates. CAB debt was also limited to 25 percent of the outstanding bond debt of the local governmental entity. CABs may be the only way that school districts can obtain the funding to pay for rapid growth, but the incautious use of them could have dire long-term consequences for local government finances.[60]

Local Government Pensions

Another area of concern with local government involves the cost and financial health of pension plans. Several municipal bankruptcies throughout the United States in 2012 brought attention to the instability of a number of state and local public pension plans.[61]

Pension shortfalls became a major issue in Texas in 2016. Texas has 81 different local governmental pension plans that cover nearly 184,000 persons and that have net assets of over $28 billion. Unfortunately, not all these pension plans have sufficient funds to meet their obligations to pay retirees.

A report by Moody's released in late November 2016 found that Dallas and Houston had two of the largest unfunded liabilities of local governments in the United States. Dallas ranked second in the nation (behind Chicago) with a liability 549 percent of annual operating revenues, while Houston ranked fourth with a 414 percent liability of operating revenues. The problems did not stop there. Austin ranked 9th, and San Antonio ranked 12th with liabilities as a percentage of annual operating revenues of 267 percent and 188 percent, respectively.[62]

Houston's city workers have three major pension systems—the Houston Police Officers' Pension System, the Houston Firefighters' Relief and Retirement Fund, and the Houston Municipal Employees Pension System. Houston expected its contributions to pensions to rise to 17.1 percent of all city expenditures by 2017.[63] The city's pension costs in 2015 for the Firefighters' Relief and Retirement Fund were 34 percent of the fire department's annual payroll.[64] Bill King, while running for mayor of Houston in the 2015 election, claimed that if the problem with city employee pensions was not fixed, "it's game over" for city finances.[65]

Probably the most extreme example in Texas of a failing pension system was the Dallas Police and Fire Pension System. Its problems were so severe that Dallas has imposed immediate and drastic reforms to the system. Reforms were necessary because of overly generous benefits and remarkably poor management, which put pension benefits for Dallas police officers and firefighters at risk. According to one accounting of the fund, it had $3 billion in assets and $8 billion in liabilities and without changes would have been broke in 15 years. One reason is that pensioners in the fund got an automatic 4 percent annual cost-of-living increase. Given low inflation and the fund's low returns on investments, such an increase is not sustainable.

deferred retirement option plan (DROP) retirement plan in which local government employees who are eligible to retire have their retirement benefits deposited in an account in which the benefits draw interest until actual retirement. Some of these plans pay high interest and cost-of-living adjustments and may be coupled with very early retirement ages

Another problem was the **deferred retirement option plan (DROP)**. Dallas police and firefighter base salaries are low in comparison to those of Fort Worth and neighboring suburbs, and since police and firefighters can retire after 20 years of service, the DROP plan was created in 1993 to discourage them from leaving employment after only two decades. Under the plan, if a 20-year veteran chose to stop contributing to the pension plan and entered DROP, it was as if the police officer or firefighter had retired, but that person could continue working. Instead of being paid out to the person, his or her pension checks would be deposited in a DROP account paying between 8 and 10 percent interest.

Still another problem with the Dallas system was that fund managers appeared to have tried to maximize returns by investing in speculative real estate deals, such as paying $34 million for some Arizona desert land that later sold for $7.5 million. Managers also overvalued real estate and made rosy assumptions, such as 8.5 percent yearly returns on investment, which did not ultimately come to pass.

Taxpayers in Dallas already contributed $100 million per year to the pension fund. It would have been difficult to get them to contribute much more, although the alternative had to be pension reductions for police and firefighters. In the meantime, the credit rating for Dallas bonds had been reduced, in part because of concerns about the problems with the police and firefighter pension fund. A lower credit rating for bonds issued by a governmental entity means that the entity has to pay a higher interest rate to borrowers.[66]

The Dallas pension problems were so severe that in the November 2016 election, 69 percent of Dallas voters approved changes that should reduce the pension's liabilities by $2.15 billion over the next 30 years. Voters usually tend to be uninterested in and unaware of problems associated with government employee pension plans, but the effects on a government's financial stability and tax system can be enormous.

Bailing out the pension plans of Houston and Dallas was a major issue confronting the 2017 legislative session. Separate bills were passed during the session addressing the specific problems confronting each city's plan. In general, though, the solutions were the same: there were reductions in future pension accruals for workers and retirees and provisions were made for the plans to receive additional contributions from their respective cities. Financial benchmarks were also laid down for future years that would have to be met or there would be more benefit cuts. The Dallas bill also banned lump sum withdrawals under the DROP program.

All in all, the actions of the legislature brought some stability to the pension plans of Houston and Dallas and helped to protect the credit rating of each city, at least in the medium term. However, the current solutions to local government pension problems may be only temporary. For example, Fort Worth calculated its pension shortfall at $1.6 billion by assuming a future return on its pension investments would be 7.5 percent. However, Moody's, a major investment service, calculated the Fort Worth pension shortfall at $3.6 billion assuming a 4 percent return on pension investments.[67] Nor have all pension problems been addressed. Retirees receive other benefits as part of their retirement besides money; most significantly they receive health care benefits. Overall, Texas has about $89 billion in unfunded liability for retiree health care costs. Unless something is done to address that cost, the state will again face a major problem with retiree funding.[68]

Future Pension Policy Pensions have a huge effect on state, county, and local governments. And for some local governments, employee pensions have already become unmanageable. Some pension administrators have recognized that their plans were no longer economically viable and have instituted significant plan changes.

One example of significant pension plan changes has come in El Paso, which has increased the standard age of retirement for city employees, increased the years of service required to receive a pension, and changed the formula for calculating pension amounts to be less favorable to the employee. As an example, prior to the pension changes, assume an employee chose to retire at age 60 with 25 years and 5 months of service with the city and that the employee's final wages were $2,000 per month. That employee's pension would be $1,270.85 per month. Under the new plan, that employee would receive $1,143.76, or $127.09 a month less, a 10 percent reduction.[69] For that employee, this no doubt seems a drastic cut in retirement pay, but such changes make pension systems viable.

The complex financial issues involved in providing pensions to local government workers may seem tiresome to try to understand. But they cut to the core of the problems facing government officials in the early twenty-first century. If local governments in Texas are to thrive in the coming decades, they must not be burdened with debts that cannot be paid.

Local Government and the Future of Texas

IN MANY WAYS, local government affects the average citizen's life much more than either the federal or the state government. Local government generally works well in Texas in providing basic services. It picks up the trash, provides water, provides fire and police protection, and maintains local roads. However, in some ways local government may not be functioning as well as we might hope.

As Texas has become more diverse and as Latinos and African Americans have gained political power, there is a greater demand for democratic responsiveness from local government. That demand is most clearly seen in the movement away from at-large city councils and toward single-member city council districts. But is local government sufficiently responsive? Special purpose districts have been described as "hidden governments," suggesting a real lack of democratic accountability for their actions. It is unclear that there is sufficient democratic accountability even for high-level county officials such as district attorneys. As Texas looks to the future, the issue of expanding democratic accountability in local government looms as increasingly important.

The most immediate issue involving local government has arisen out of the coronavirus crisis. Initially, local governments provided the response to the pandemic, although tensions rapidly developed among those governments over the patchwork of policies that different counties and cities designed. That was quickly followed by tensions between state officials, most notably the governor and attorney general, and local governments. As the pandemic raged in the state, the governor began preempting local actions. Adding to this rather chaotic approach to the coronavirus, the governor subsequently loosened some of his initial restrictions on local government efforts. Left remaining from the pandemic response is the question of balancing state and local interests when making public health decisions. The pandemic has also created tremendous financial problems for local governments that have already led to budgetary cuts, and more reductions seem likely. Closed businesses and stay-at-home orders mean less sales tax revenue, a mainstay of local budgets. There is lost revenue from the declines in air travel, tourism, and conventions as well. The longer the pandemic, the more will be the revenue losses and the subsequent decline in local government services.

One issue, currently far from the minds of Texas policy makers, is the way local government is structured in Texas. Should real estate developers support a handful of persons in a special district to incur millions in debt for that district and for future residents of that district? In terms of county governments, does Texas need 254 counties? Many of these counties are too small to deal with important concerns such as supporting the costs of a capital punishment trial. Though consolidation of governments in Texas and greater regulation of special purpose districts are matters that are not currently on the state's political agenda, demands for a more transparent and efficient government should lead to consideration of such issues.

Finally, there are potential financial disasters facing local governments in their pension systems and in their methods of borrowing money. These problems must be dealt with in the near future to avoid financial calamity at the local level in the next few decades. Many employee pension plans are currently costing local governments more and more of their resources while the ability of those funds to pay future pensions is becoming less likely. For Texas's urban centers, the crisis in local pension funds will become increasingly apparent and, as time goes by, harder to resolve. Most likely, this crisis cannot be resolved only with a tax increase. It will require pension reductions and ultimately a rethinking of how local employees receive support in retirement.

STUDY GUIDE

Use **INQUIZITIVE** to help you study and master this material.

County Government in Texas

- **Explain the importance, role, and structure of county government in Texas (pp. 335–42)**

There are more counties in Texas than in any other state. County governance in Texas affects the lives of everyday Texans in ways ranging from hospital care to trash pickup.

Key Terms

constable (p. 335)
county attorney (p. 336)
district attorney (p. 336)
county clerk (p. 336)
district clerk (p. 336)
county tax assessor-collector (p. 336)
county auditor (p. 336)
county commissioners' court (p. 337)
county judge (p. 337)
county commissioner (p. 338)

Practice Quiz

1. Which of the following is *not* a type of local government found in Texas?
   a) city
   b) council of government
   c) county
   d) special district
   e) municipal

2. The basic governing body of a county is known as
   a) a council of government.
   b) a county council.
   c) a city-manager government.
   d) a county commissioners' court.
   e) a county governing committee.

3. How many counties are there in Texas?
   a) 25
   b) 56
   c) 110
   d) 254
   e) 500

4. All county commissioners' precincts must be equal in population according to
   a) Article 1 of the Texas Constitution.
   b) the Civil Rights Act of 1964.
   c) the Voting Rights Act of 1975.
   d) *Avery v. Midland County*.
   e) *Marbury v. Madison*.

5. A county judge
   a) only hears appellate cases from JP courts.
   b) is an appointive position from the governor.
   c) presides over the constitutional county court and the county commissioners' court.
   d) implements all the decisions of the Supreme Court affecting the county.
   e) judges juvenile cases.

6. Which county officials are responsible for the jail and the safety of the prisoners?
   a) sheriff
   b) county council
   c) county commissioners' court
   d) council of mayors
   e) city manager

City Government in Texas

• **Describe the major characteristics of city government in Texas (pp. 343–57)**

Municipalities in Texas vary in terms of how they are governed. Some cities have strong mayors who run the city, while other cities have weak mayors where the day-to-day running of the city is delegated to city managers. Mayors and city councils often decide issues that directly affect the lives of everyday people.

Key Terms
home-rule charter (p. 343)
preemption (p. 345)
mayor-council form of government (p. 350)
at-large election (p. 350)
single-member district (p. 350)
commissioner form of government (p. 350)
council-manager form of government (p. 350)

Practice Quiz

7. To adopt a home-rule charter, a city must have a minimum population of
   a) 201.
   b) 5,000.
   c) 10,000.
   d) 50,000.
   e) There is no minimum.

8. The two legal classifications of Texas cities are
   a) local and regional.
   b) general law and home rule.
   c) tax and nontax.
   d) charter and noncharter.
   e) big and small.

9. The form of city government that allows the mayor to establish control over most of the city's government is called the
   a) commissioner form of city government.
   b) council-manager form of city government.
   c) council of government form of city government.
   d) strong mayor–council form of city government.
   e) none of the above

10. A city controller
   a) works directly for the governor.
   b) controls and manages the election in a city.
   c) is a city's chief elected official who presides over the city council.
   d) is independent of all political control in a small statutory city.
   e) is a city's chief financial officer.

11. Cities that have home rule
   a) make ordinances and regulations without interference by the state.
   b) have considerable freedom to make ordinances and regulations, but the state legislature can preempt their actions.
   c) have rules that prevent homes from being taxed.
   d) are allowed great leeway by the state legislature because they are heavily Republican.
   e) are concentrated in west Texas.

Special Purpose Districts

• **Examine the role of special purpose districts in Texas government (pp. 357–63)**

Special purpose districts often span different cities and counties. They are tasked with operating such things as school districts or water utility districts. They have the authority to levy property taxes to fund the operation of services essential to the lives of many residents.

Key Terms
special purpose district (p. 357)
school district (p. 357)
nonschool special district (p. 357)
municipal utility district (MUD) (p. 358)
property tax (p. 361)
user fee (p. 361)
hidden government (p. 361)
council of government (COG) (p. 363)

Practice Quiz

12. Which local government provides a single service not provided by any other local government?

a) special district

b) council of government

c) police district

d) city

e) county

13. What are the two types of special purpose districts found in Texas?

a) school and nonschool

b) home rule and general law

c) tax and nontax

d) statutory and constitutional

e) none of the above

14. A special purpose district

a) must be limited to under 150,000 people.

b) covers the entire state to provide a particular service.

c) is a unit of local government that performs a special service in a limited geographic area.

d) temporarily combines two congressional districts.

e) none of the above

15. A MUD

a) serves the needs of developers.

b) is generally opposed by banks and real estate developers as being too expensive.

c) provides ambulance service inside a city's geographic limits.

d) delegates the setting of tax rates in a particular geographic area to the state legislature.

e) provides funding for special purpose districts.

16. Comprehensive planning and service delivery in a specific geographic area are the function of a

a) special district.

b) council of government.

c) city.

d) county.

e) town.

Financial Issues Facing Local Government

- **Examine the financial issues facing local government (pp. 364–67)**

Local government in Texas is facing a looming financial crisis as a result of widespread issuance of capital appreciation bonds, which allow funds to be raised in the present while interest and payments on the principal are paid far into the future, and the liabilities imposed on local government by generous retirement plans for governmental employees.

Key Terms

capital appreciation bond (CAB) (p. 364)

deferred retirement option plan (DROP) (p. 366)

Practice Quiz

17. Capital appreciation bonds

a) are long-term bonds on which local governments pay back principal and interest on a yearly basis.

b) are short-term bonds on which local governments borrow money for emergencies.

c) are bonds on which interest is paid quarterly by local governments but the principal is not paid back for 40 years.

d) are bonds on which principal and interest are not paid back until the end of a lengthy term while local governments can use the borrowed money immediately.

e) create such long-term financial risks that they are illegal in Texas.

18. Some governmental employee retirement plans in Texas

a) impose huge financial liabilities on government.

b) need to be increased to support needy retired employees.

c) have not kept up with inflation.

d) will soon be merged into the Social Security retirement program.

e) are so minimal that it is hard to recruit employees at the local level.

The way the state raises and spends money affects many aspects of life in Texas, including tuition and fees at public colleges and universities.

Public Finance

WHY PUBLIC FINANCE MATTERS For college students, the state budget might appear to be pretty far removed from everyday life and things such as attending class, preparing for an exam, or getting everything in order for a timely graduation. But like it or not, the budgetary decisions made by legislators every two years affect students where they matter most: in the pocketbook.

This became clear in 2003, when state political leaders found themselves staring at a $10 billion shortfall in the upcoming budget period. Mandated by the state constitution to maintain a balanced budget, they needed to find new ways to close the budget gap without raising taxes. One method was to cut higher education funding and to make up the difference by allowing universities to gain more control over the tuition and fees charged to students.

Prior to 2003, tuition and fee rates for state universities had been set by the state legislature, and in Texas they tended to be low when compared with tuition and fees in other states.[1] After 2003, the situation changed as universities began raising tuition and fees to meet revenue shortfalls. Tuition and fees doubled in Texas between 2003 and 2018. At the same time, state spending on higher education declined by 26 percent (in inflation-adjusted dollars).[2] For the 2019–20 fiscal year, the average tuition and fees for attending a public university in Texas had risen to $9,502 for an in-state student to slightly above the national average.[3] And, as students know all too well, tuition and fees are not the only expenses that they face as undergraduates. According to a study by the Texas Higher Education Coordinating Board, total costs for attending a four-year college or university were $24,798, including $1,244 for books and supplies, $9,560 for room and board, $2,220 for transportation, and $2,272 for other expenses.[4] Not surprisingly, student loan debt skyrocketed in the second decade of the 21st century as students tried to finance their college education. A study by the *Houston Chronicle* found that 56 percent of students from Texas colleges graduated with a student loan debt of $28,565 in 2018.[5]

During regular sessions of the state legislature, universities and colleges now line up to present a new round of tuition and fee increases to fund necessary expenses. In response, lawmakers find themselves in a bind. On one hand, they want to support higher education in Texas. They particularly want to support those higher educational institutions in their districts that serve as economic engines to local development. On the other hand, they don't want to put added burdens on their constituents who want a higher education degree.

Spiraling student debt coupled with higher tuition and fees is making it difficult for Texans to attend college. Many state leaders believe that college spending is out of control. If universities cannot hold the line on costs, then perhaps the legislature should limit increases in tuition and fees. For the most part, however, university administrations across the state tend to support continued deregulation, arguing that each university or university system is better equipped to make decisions about tuition and fees than the legislature.[6]

There was talk in early 2020 that the next legislative session would address the problem of rising tuition and fees and funding higher education. The economic crisis brought on by the coronavirus in Texas in the spring of 2020 likely silenced such wishful thinking. Sharply declining tax revenues from sales tax, oil and natural gas production, and other smaller state taxes beginning in March 2020 compelled the comptroller and other legislative leaders to rethink the state budget and to warn state universities that cuts were likely coming. Hiring freezes went into effect across higher education in Texas throughout the spring 2020 semester. Severe budgetary cuts in 2020 and 2021 could put additional pressure on universities and colleges to reduce drastically current expenditures and begin another round of increased tuition and fees.

The debate over higher education tuition and fees is one example of how matters of public finance lie at the heart of Texas government. Passing a balanced budget is the most important task presented to the state legislature during its regular session every two years. Priorities must be identified and money must be allocated across a wide range of governmental activities through a variety of financial mechanisms. Difficult decisions must be made about how to fund governmental activities through increased taxes and fees. Understanding public policy demands a mastery of public finance. That is the subject of this chapter.

CHAPTERGOALS

- Explain the purpose of the state budget and what is typically included (pp. 375–77)

- Describe the general pattern of state spending in Texas and where state revenue comes from (pp. 377–87)

- Describe how the money in the budget is organized into specific funds (pp. 387–90)

- Outline the constitutional provisions that affect how the state budget is made (pp. 390–94)

- Identify the steps, players, and political tensions in making the state budget (pp. 394–401)

What Is the Budget?

Explain the purpose of the state budget and what is typically included

The Texas Constitution mandates that the legislature operate within a "balanced budget." On its face, this idea is straightforward: a balanced budget would exist whenever the projected income from tax revenues is equal to or exceeds the projected expenditure. But there are actually a number of different ways to talk about the funds that constitute the "budget." General tax revenue flows into the state's coffers from a variety of sources for different purposes. One way is to divide them into the following five broad and overlapping categories.[7]

- **General Revenue Funds** includes the nondedicated portion of the General Revenue Fund, which is the state's primary operating fund. It also includes three large educational funds (the Available School Fund, the State Instructional Materials Fund, and the Foundation School Fund). Appropriations from General Revenue Funds totaled $124.48 billion for the 2020–21 biennium.

- **General Revenue–Dedicated Funds** is a subset of the General Revenue Fund and includes over 200 funds dedicated to specific purposes, such as the State Parks Account and the college operating accounts (which hold tuition funds). Generally speaking, the legislature can appropriate money from these accounts only for their dedicated purposes. The balances in this budget are used to certify that the constitutional pay-as-you-go limits (discussed below) are being met. Appropriations from the General Revenue–Dedicated Funds amounted to $6.17 billion for the 2020–21 biennium.

- **Federal Funds** includes all grants, payments, and reimbursements received from the federal government by state agencies and institutions, including those from the Medicaid program, Title 1 Grants to Local Educational Agencies, transportation grants, and the Children's Health Insurance Program. Almost $86.5 billion was appropriated from Federal Funds for the 2020–21 biennium.

- **Other Funds** consists of all other funds flowing into the state treasury that are not included in the other methods of financing. These include, among others, the State Highway Fund, the Texas Mobility Fund, the Property Tax Relief Fund, and the Economic Stabilization Fund. For the 2020–21 biennium, $37.4 billion was appropriated from Other Funds.

- **All Funds** is the aggregate of all these ways of financing government and refers to all revenue that goes through agencies, including federal and state programs.

Some important things must be noted about this complicated system of public financing through these various budgets. First, the state budget involves huge amounts of money (see Table 11.1). Second, much of this money lies outside the direct control of

General Revenue Funds a nondedicated revenue account that functions as the state's primary operating fund

General Revenue–Dedicated Funds budget composed of funds for dedicated revenues that target money for specific purposes

Federal Funds includes all grants, payments, and reimbursements received from the federal government by state agencies and institutions

Other Funds consists of all other funds flowing into the state treasury that are not included in other state budgets; this includes the Texas Highway Fund, various trust funds operated by the state, and certain revenues held for local higher education accounts

All Funds the aggregate of all these ways of financing government; refers to revenue that goes through agencies, including federal and state programs

TABLE 11.1

Summary of All Funds State Budget Allocation by Biennium (in billions of dollars)

ALL FUNCTIONS	EXPENDED/BUDGETED 2018–19	APPROPRIATED 2020–21	PERCENTAGE CHANGE*
Article I: General Government	$7.8	$7.5	−4.2%
Article II: Health and Human Services	$83.8	$84.3	0.6%
Article III: Agencies of Education	$82.2	$95.9	16.6%
Public Education	$61.3	$70.4	14.8%
Higher Education	$20.9	$25.5	21.9%
Article IV: The Judiciary	$0.9	$0.9	8.8%
Article V: Public Safety and Criminal Justice	$18.9	$12.5	−33.4%
Article VI: Natural Resources	$8.5	$9.0	6.3%
Article VII: Business and Economic Development	$36.7	$37.1	0.9%
Article VIII: Regulatory	$0.7	$0.7	4.3%
Article IX: General Provisions	0	0	N/A
Article X: The Legislature	$0.4	$0.4	0.2%
Total, all articles	$239.8	$248.3	3.6%

*Percentage change calculated by actual numbers before rounding off.
SOURCE: Texas Legislative Budget Board, *Fiscal Size-Up: 2020–21 Biennium* (May 2020), p. 2.

the legislature. Trust funds and other dedicated funds exist for particular purposes and are hard to manipulate for other budgetary purposes. As a result, legislators seeking to balance the budget are often left with relatively few places to cut expenditures. Given its large share of the General Revenue Funds budget, education is often at the top of the list. Third, federal expenditures have a very important role in shaping the overall direction of the state budget. The bulk of federal expenditures is in two areas: health and human services, and education. Strings are often attached to these monies: if legislators want federal dollars, they must spend state dollars first. Figure 11.1 highlights the increasingly important role that federal dollars have played in spending patterns in Texas. Expenditures from the All Funds budget (which takes into account federal spending) have continued to grow steadily since 2008. The pressure to maximize federal dollars flowing into Texas is one legislative goal. But legislators also desire to minimize state spending and not raise taxes.

FIGURE 11.1

Trends in State Government Expenditures

*Appropriated.

SOURCE: Texas Legislative Budget Board, *Fiscal Size-Up: 2020–21 Biennium* (May 2020), p. 28.

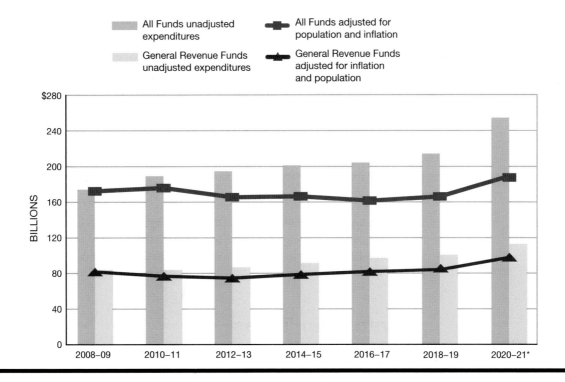

Spending and Revenue in Texas

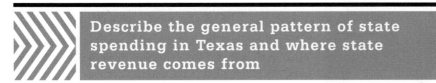

Describe the general pattern of state spending in Texas and where state revenue comes from

Texas has a reputation of being a "low service, low tax" state that seeks to maintain a favorable environment for business. In this section, we will look at the general pattern of state spending in Texas, as well as taxes and other sources of revenue in the state.

Trends in State Spending

For the most part, Texas's reputation as a low-spending state is accurate. In the aggregate, Texas spends less than other states. A 2019 Kaiser Foundation Study found that among the 50 states, Texas state expenditures per capita was $3,925, well below the national average of $5,976.[8]

Evaluating state expenditures over the past decade and trying to identify overall trends is complicated (see Figure 11.1). We must distinguish between state expenditures controlled by the legislature (General Revenue Funds) and All Funds expenditures (which include spending from the federal government that passes through the state). In addition, to get a clear picture of state expenditures over time demands, we must take into account two complicating factors: inflation rates and an expanding population.

In unadjusted dollars (that is, not taking into account inflation or population increases), state spending (General Revenue Funds) in Texas rose from $86.0 billion in the 2012–13 biennium to $118.3 billion in the 2020–21 biennium. However, in real per capita dollars (that is, controlling for inflation and population increases), state spending actually increased by 9.6 percent.[9]

When considering state and federal spending in Texas together (see All Funds in Figure 11.1), the story is different. Unadjusted spending for all funds (state and federal) in Texas rose from around $190.6 billion in 2012–13 to over $248.0 billion in 2020–21. In real per capita dollars, spending over the same period only increased by 6.9 percent. Considerable federal money continues to flow into Texas in the third decade of the twenty-first century.[10]

Revenue in Texas

After the legislature passes the biennial state budget, the state comptroller certifies the budget, confirming that it is within current revenue estimates for the period. Here, state comptroller Glenn Hegar certifies the 2020–21 budget.

Spending is only part of Texas's "low service, low tax" reputation. The taxes that fund government are the other dimension. It is difficult to compare the state tax burden Texans face with that of citizens in other states. There are a variety of taxes that individuals can pay to state governments, including state income taxes, general state sales taxes, specific state sales taxes, local sales taxes, and property taxes. Moreover, some kinds of taxes can be lower in one state than another but be offset by higher local taxes.

According to a WalletHub 2019 study, Texas ranked 33rd among the 50 states with a tax burden of 8.18 percent, meaning that 8.18 percent on one's personal income went to state and local taxes in Texas.[11] (See Texas and the Nation on p. 379.)

Texas is one of seven states that does not have a personal income tax. (Two other states, Tennessee and New Hampshire, only tax income from dividends and interest.) On the other hand, Texas has a sales tax of 6.25 percent, the 13th highest in the nation. Combined general state and local sales taxes in the state can reach 8.25 percent. As we will see later in this chapter, a variety of specific sales taxes also raise revenue to fund government, including ones on cigarettes, alcohol, and gasoline.

Do Democratic or Republican States Pay More Taxes?

Tax burden is a measure used to calculate the proportion of total personal income that people pay toward state and local taxes. The tax burden varies across states based on property taxes, individual income taxes, and sales and excise taxes. While Texas does not have a personal income tax, it has other important taxes that raise the tax burden. Interestingly, states that tend to vote Democratic in presidential elections tend to have a higher tax burden when compared with those that tend to vote Republican.

State and Local Tax Burden versus 2016 Election Results

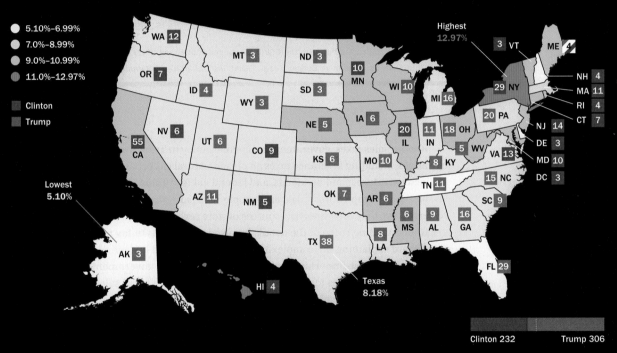

- 5.10%–6.99%
- 7.0%–8.99%
- 9.0%–10.99%
- 11.0%–12.97%

Clinton
Trump

Highest 12.97%

Lowest 5.10%

Texas 8.18%

Clinton 232   Trump 306

Partisanship and State and Local Taxes

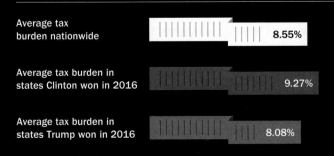

Average tax burden nationwide	8.55%
Average tax burden in states Clinton won in 2016	9.27%
Average tax burden in states Trump won in 2016	8.08%

SOURCE: Allen McCann, "Tax Burden by State," WalletHub, April 2, 2019, https://wallethub.com/edu/states-with-highest-lowest-tax-burden/20494/ (accessed 6/17/2020).

CRITICAL THINKING

- Texas has no state income tax. Why is its overall state and local tax burden not lower, in relation to other states?

- If the average Trump and Clinton states were part of the state and local tax burden rankings, what would their rankings be? What do you think accounts for the divergence in those states' approach to state and local taxes?

TABLE 11.2

State Revenue by Source, 2018–19 and 2020–21 Bienniums (in billions of dollars)

REVENUE	2018–19	2020–21	PERCENTAGE CHANGE
Tax collections	$115.0	$124.0	7.8%
Federal receipts	$81.5	$87.9	7.8%
Licenses, fees, fines, and penalties	$13.0	$13.3	2.1%
Interest and investment income	$4.4	$4.4	1.6%
Lottery	$4.7	$4.6	−2.3%
Land income	$4.3	$4.6	7.7%
Other revenue sources	$25.2	$20.8	−17.3%
Total, net revenue	$248.1	$259.7	4.7%

*Estimated. Calculated prior to the COVID-19 pandemic in spring 2020.

SOURCE: Texas Legislative Budget Board, *Fiscal Size-Up: 2020–21 Biennium* (May 2020), p. 35.

Besides sales taxes, government and public policy in Texas are funded from a variety of sources, including severance taxes on oil and natural gas produced in the state, licensing income, interest and dividends, and federal aid (see Table 11.2). Many of these taxes are based on complex formulas, and people often are unaware they are paying them. Nevertheless, they are important sources of state revenue.

Understanding some of the details involved with the state tax revenues goes a long way toward explaining the complexity of public finance and budgeting in Texas (see Figure 11.2). The most important single tax financing Texas government is the sales tax. Today, the general sales tax in Texas is 6.25 percent of the retail sales price of tangible personal property and selected services. Together, county, city, and metropolitan transit authorities are allowed to impose up to an additional 2 percent sales tax. For example, in Dallas as in many other urban areas of the state, the total sales tax is 8.25 percent (6.25 percent state sales tax and 2.0 percent for the Dallas Area Rapid Transit system).

The oil severance tax (incurred when oil is removed from the ground within a taxing jurisdiction) is 4.6 percent of the market value of a barrel of oil produced in the state. (There is also an oil regulation tax of three-sixteenths of one cent per barrel of oil produced in Texas.) The tax revenue from oil production fluctuates with the price of oil and the volume of oil produced in Texas. The fluctuation of the price of oil in Texas and throughout the world in 2020 bodes ill for stability in the oil industry. This could have serious implications for revenues generated during the 2020–21 biennium.

There also is a 7.5 percent tax on the market value of all natural gas produced in the state. As with the oil tax, the tax raised from natural gas depends on the price and the amount produced. Revenues from natural gas have fluctuated considerably over time.

Who Pays the Most State Taxes in Texas?

Taxes as a Percentage of Income in Texas, 2018*

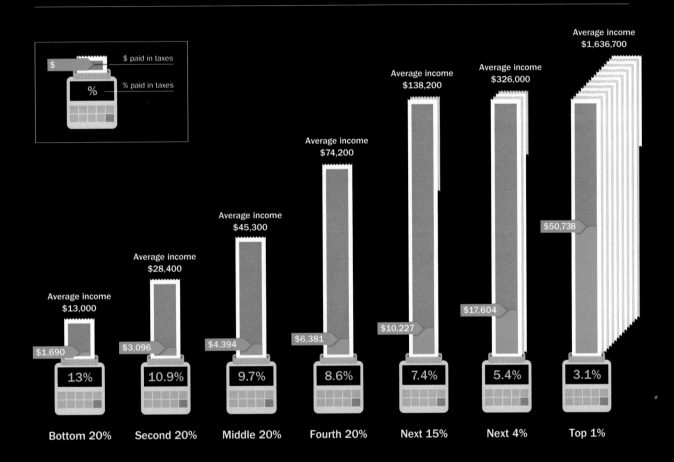

$ — $ paid in taxes
% — % paid in taxes

Average income $13,000
$1,690
13%
Bottom 20%

Average income $28,400
$3,096
10.9%
Second 20%

Average income $45,300
$4,394
9.7%
Middle 20%

Average income $74,200
$6,381
8.6%
Fourth 20%

Average income $138,200
$10,227
7.4%
Next 15%

Average income $326,000
$17,604
5.4%
Next 4%

Average income $1,636,700
$50,738
3.1%
Top 1%

Texas has no state income tax, which does keep overall individual tax rates down. However, this means that the state's revenues rely heavily on sales and property taxes. These taxes are regressive—those with lower incomes pay a higher share of their income in taxes; those with higher incomes pay a lower share of their income in taxes.

* Based on family income for non-elderly taxpayers.

SOURCE: Institute for Taxation and Economic Policy, www.itep.org (accessed 6/17/20).

QUANTITATIVE REASONING

- Which group pays the highest percentage of its income in taxes in Texas?

- How would the proportions paid in taxes change across all incomes if a progressive state income tax was instituted?

Another major tax in Texas is the motor fuels tax. Currently this tax is 20 cents per gallon of gasoline and diesel fuel. There is a 15-cents-per-gallon tax on liquefied gas. The revenues flowing from the motor fuels tax are "dedicated," meaning that they can be used only for purposes specified by the legislature. About three-quarters of these monies are appropriated to the Texas Department of Transportation and the Texas Department of Public Safety and are dedicated to the construction, maintenance, and policing of public roads. Most of the remaining one-quarter of the revenues are dedicated to public education.

A 6.25 percent tax is charged on the sales price of all motor vehicles in the state. There is also a 10 percent tax on all rental vehicles up to 30 days and 6.25 percent thereafter. Newly manufactured homes are taxed at 5 percent of 65 percent of the sale price.

The so-called franchise tax is imposed on all corporations in Texas for the privilege of doing business in the state. The franchise tax is a complicated (and controversial) tax on businesses based upon earnings. The comptroller's office projects that this tax

FIGURE 11.2

State Tax Revenue Sources, 2020–21 Biennium

*Percentages calculated based on constitutionally and statutorily dedicated tax revenues and appropriations in the 2020–21 General Appropriations Act, as modified by other legislation.

SOURCE: Texas Legislative Budget Board, *Fiscal Size-Up: 2020–21 Biennium* (May 2020), p. 35.

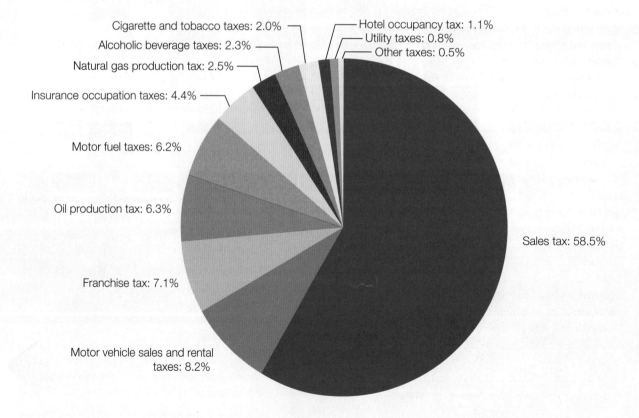

Cigarette and tobacco taxes: 2.0%
Alcoholic beverage taxes: 2.3%
Natural gas production tax: 2.5%
Insurance occupation taxes: 4.4%
Motor fuel taxes: 6.2%
Oil production tax: 6.3%
Franchise tax: 7.1%
Motor vehicle sales and rental taxes: 8.2%
Hotel occupancy tax: 1.1%
Utility taxes: 0.8%
Other taxes: 0.5%
Sales tax: 58.5%

will generate $8.8 billion in the 2020–21 biennium (see Table 11.3).[12]

Other Smaller State Revenue Sources The remainder of state revenues flow in from a variety of other smaller taxes. These include taxes on cigarettes and tobacco, alcohol beverage sales, on insurance premiums, on utilities, on hotels and motels, and other sundry business activities.

The Question of the Income Tax in Texas

There have been occasional calls for the institution of a state income tax in Texas. Unlike sales and use taxes, which are applied equally to everyone whatever their income, income taxes can be made **progressive**. With a progressive income tax (like the federal income tax), people with lower income pay a lower tax rate than people with higher income. Progressive income taxes thus place a higher tax burden on the rich than on the poor. Most taxes in Texas are **regressive**, meaning people with a lower income pay taxes at a higher rate than those with higher incomes (see the Citizen's Guide on p. 384).

Few Texas politicians, however, have been willing to support an income tax, the absence of which has always been one of the state's most attractive features to business. It was not until the late 1980s that the first serious attempt to put a state income tax in place was undertaken. Responding to mounting budgetary pressures, the retiring lieutenant governor, Bill Hobby, came out in favor of an income tax in 1989. Bob Bullock, Hobby's successor, announced in 1991 that he would actively campaign for an income tax. A blue-ribbon panel chaired by former governor John Connally was charged with looking into new revenue sources for the state. The committee ended up recommending to the legislature both a corporate and a personal income tax, but not without generating an enormous amount of controversy.[13]

Connally himself opposed the income-tax recommendations, as did Governor Ann Richards. By the 1993 legislative session, Bullock was backing off. He proposed a constitutional amendment requiring voter approval of any personal income tax and specifying that the revenue from it be used to support public education. The amendment quickly passed the legislature and was overwhelmingly approved by voters.

As noted in the Citizen's Guide to Chapter 2, the state legislature passed and the voters approved in 2019 another constitutional amendment related to an income tax, making it even more difficult to institute an income tax in Texas. In the future, a constitutional amendment overturning the constitutional ban on an income tax would have to be passed first, and then a new statute would have to be put into place establishing an income tax. Neither action appears likely in the foreseeable future.

Gas prices have fluctuated widely in recent years. The state of Texas collects a tax of 20 cents per gallon on motor fuels. The federal government collects an additional 18.4 cents per gallon, but Texas still pay less tax for gasoline than residents of many other states. During the coronavirus pandemic, gas prices plummeted even further in Texas.

progressive tax type of tax wherein the tax burden falls more heavily on upper-income individuals

regressive tax type of tax wherein the tax burden falls more heavily on lower-income individuals

SOCIAL RESPONSIBILITY: GET INVOLVED

- Do you think sales and use taxes are a fair way for the state to generate revenue? Why or why not?

- If you were writing a letter to the editor on behalf of a group advocating for poor Texans, how would you argue that the state change tax policy to help your supporters?

The Texas Tax System

1 Why Texas's tax system matters

States generally rely upon three types of taxes for funding governmental services: personal income taxes, consumption taxes, and property taxes. Income taxes generally take a certain percentage of one's income. A tax is considered *progressive* when the tax rates rise as income rises. For example, a poor person might pay a 10 percent tax on each additional dollar of income while a rich person might pay significantly more. Consumption taxes such as sales taxes are flat rates added to the price of the commodity or service being purchased. The tax is collected by the seller at the time of purchase and then sent to the state taxing agency. The higher the value or the commodity or service, the higher the tax paid. And since everyone who consumes the commodity or service pays the same percentage in taxes, these taxes can be seen as *regressive*—lower-income people pay a higher percentage of their income in consumption taxes than wealthy people. Property taxes take a certain percentage of the value of the property. The more valuable the property, the higher the tax. Property taxes are considered "somewhat regressive" because poor homeowners pay a higher percentage of their income in property taxes than do wealthy homeowners.

In Texas, three features define the overall tax system used to fund state government. First, there is neither a flat income tax nor a (progressive) graduated income tax in Texas. Second, the state relies heavily on (regressive) sales and use taxes. Third, local government, particularly local public school systems, rely heavily on property taxes for funding their operation. Property taxes on individuals and businesses are generally considered somewhat regressive.

A 2018 study conducted by the Institute on Taxation and Economic Policy found that Texas had the second most unfair tax system in the nation. The study estimated that in Texas people with incomes in the bottom 20 percent paid 13.1 percent of their income in state and local taxes, while those with incomes in the upper 1 percent paid only 3.1 percent of their income.[a]

There have been occasional calls for the institution of a graduated state income tax in Texas. Supporters argue not only that the income tax is a more reliable source of revenue for the state but also that it can be made fairer. Unlike sales and use taxes, which are applied equally to everyone whatever their income, income taxes can be made progressive—that is, people with lower income pay a lower tax rate than people with higher income. Progressive income taxes thus place a higher tax burden on the rich than on the poor.

2 What's the debate?

Many commentators have complained that the tax system in Texas is unfair because it is too regressive.[b] Lying in the background in the debate between regressive and progressive taxes are two important ideas about public finance: first, there is the idea that income equality in a democratic society is good and income *in*equality is bad. Regressive tax systems that promote inequality thus are bad and unfair in that they promote inequality, while progressive tax systems are good in that they promote equality. Second, there is the idea that the tax system should be used to promote equality and fairness through the establishment of a more progressive tax system.

Some people reject the idea that progressive taxes are fairer than regressive taxes. Some conservatives say tax rates should be the same across all income levels. They argue that the goal of a tax system should be to provide an efficient way of funding state government activities, not make the world fairer. And many conservative Republicans in Texas view taxes as being just bad in and of themselves. Above all else, they feel that taxes must be minimized for all income classes in Texas.

3 What do the numbers say?

Are states like Texas that rely on sales taxes and property taxes more "inequitable" than states that rely on income taxes? Is the sales tax regressive in Texas? Do people in poverty in Texas pay a greater percentage of their incomes on taxes than those living in more progressive states? There is considerable variation across states regarding the types of taxes put into place to fund state government. There is also considerable variation regarding the tax burdens these taxes put upon different income groups.

Sales Tax, Income Tax, and Inequality across States

States vary in the total taxes people must pay. Income taxes and sales taxes are important factors in determining tax burdens and how progressive or regressive a state tax system may be.

RANK	STATE	LOWEST 20%	TOP 1%	TAXES AS A SHARE OF FAMILY INCOME	
				STATE SALES TAXES	STATE INCOME TAXES
#1	Washington	17.80%	3.00%	6.50%	None
#2	Texas	13.10%	3.10%	6.25%*	None
#3	Florida	12.70%	2.30%	6.00%	None
#4	South Dakota	11.20%	2.50%	4.50%	None
#5	Nevada	10.20%	1.90%	8.375	None
					INCOME TAX RANGE
#51	California	10.50%	12.40%	7.25%	1–12.3%
#50	District of Columbia	6.30%	9.50%	6.00%	4–8.9%
#49	Vermont	8.70%	10.40%	6.00%	3.55–9.4%
#48	Delaware	5.50%	6.50%	0%	2.2–6.6%
#47	Minnesota	8.70%	10.10%	6.88%	5.3–9.85%

*An additional 2% may be added for local mass transit systems.
SOURCE: Carl Davis et al., *Who Pays? A Distributional Analysis of the Tax Systems in All 50 States*, 6th ed. (Washington, DC: Institute on Taxation and Economic Policy, January 2018).

Communicating Effectively: What Do You Think?

- Do you believe that "tax fairness" is best viewed through the ideas of progressive and regressive taxes?
- Is it the job of the tax system to promote equality across income groups?
- What are the pros and cons to instituting an income tax in Texas?
- Would an income tax make the tax system in Texas more equitable?

WANT TO LEARN MORE?

- Carl Davis et al., *Who Pays? A Distributional Analysis of the Tax Systems in All 50 States*, 6th ed. (Washington, DC: Institute on Taxation and Economic Policy, January 2018).

- Tax Foundation
  taxfoundation.org

- Internal Revenue Service, "Understanding Taxes"
  https://apps.irs.gov/

- *Investopedia*, "The Difference between Regressive, Proportional, and Progressive Taxes"
  https://www.investopedia.com/

Other State Revenue

matching funds federal monies going to a state based on state spending for a program

The largest source of revenue for Texas is the federal government. Historically, Texas spends relatively little, compared with other states, for jointly funded state-federal programs. As a result, federal grants and **matching funds** (federal monies going to a state based on the state's spending for a program) also have been relatively low. For the 2020–21 biennium, federal funds accounted for $87.9 billion, about 33.8 percent of the total state revenue, up 7.8 percent from the previous biennium. Much of the increase in these federal funds in recent years can be attributed to Medicaid, a state-federal program providing funds to finance health care delivery to the poor.[14]

In addition to taxes and federal monies, Texas has a number of other revenue sources, including licenses, fees and fines, sales of goods and services provided by the state, and

TABLE 11.3

Tax Collections Biennial Comparison by Source, 2018–19 and 2020–21 (in billions of dollars)

	2018–19	2020–21*	PERCENTAGE CHANGE**
Sales tax	$66.0	$72.5	9.9%
Oil production taxes	7.3	7.8	7.7
Natural gas production tax	3.1	3.07	−1.6
Motor fuels tax	7.4	7.8	3.4
Motor vehicle sales and rental taxes	10.0	10.2	2.1
Franchise tax	7.9	8.8	11.8
Cigarette and tobacco taxes	2.7	2.5	−7.6
Alcoholic beverages taxes	2.7	2.9	9.4
Insurance occupation taxes	5.1	5.5	7.4
Utility taxes	0.9	0.96	3.8
Hotel occupancy tax	1.2	1.35	9.3
Inheritance tax	0	0	0
Other taxes	0.4	0.5	17.1
Total tax collections	$98.1	$107.1	9.2%

*Estimated.
**Biennial change and percentage change have been calculated on actual amounts before rounding in all tables and graphics in this chapter. Totals may not sum as a result of rounding.

SOURCE: Texas Legislative Budget Board, *Fiscal Size-Up: 2018–19 Biennium* (September 2018), p. 31.

land income. In recent years, two other sources have had a major impact on the state budget. A state lottery was approved by the state legislature and the voters in 1991. Although voters endorsed the lottery overwhelmingly, some argue that using gambling as a source of state revenues unfairly takes money from people who can least afford it by fooling them into thinking that they too can strike it rich if only they have a little luck. Large numbers of people from all social classes continue to play the lottery. In fiscal year 2019 lottery ticket sales totaled $6.3 billion. Of those sales, $4.1 billion was paid to players and $335.8 million was paid to retailers for commissions, bonuses, and incentives. In addition, $1.5 billion was transferred to the Foundation School Fund and $19.2 million to the Texas Veterans Commission, and $70.9 million of unclaimed prizes was transferred to the state.[15]

A second major source of nontax revenue is a result of the settlement the state reached with tobacco companies in 1998 over false and misleading statements about the safety of tobacco products. Under the settlement, Texas was to receive over $17.3 billion over the next 25 years and an additional $580 million every year thereafter from the tobacco industry. The Texas comptroller's office projects that Texas tobacco settlement receipts will total $884.2 million in 2020–21. This drop is the result of a projected decline in cigarette sales.[16]

State Funds

 Describe how the money in the budget is organized into specific funds

Money comes into state coffers from a variety of sources and is dispersed to a wide range of activities. But this money doesn't flow into and out of just one pot. There are, in fact, 400 funds in the state treasury whose monies are directed to a wide variety of functions. Understanding how money flows into and out of these funds lies at the heart of mastering the state budget. We examine some of the most important funds here.

As previously mentioned, the *General Revenue Fund*s consists of two parts: nondedicated General Revenue and General Revenue–Dedicated accounts. The nondedicated revenue is the state's primary operating fund and the place where most state taxes and fees flow. Expenditures may be made directly from the nondedicated funds and may be transferred to other special funds or accounts for allocation.

The **Permanent School Fund (PSF)** was created in 1854 with a $2 million appropriation by the legislature to fund primary and secondary schools. The Constitution of 1876, along with subsequent acts, stipulated that certain lands and sales from them would constitute the PSF. The second-largest educational endowment in the country, the PSF is managed primarily by the state board of education. The fund distributes money to school districts across the state on the basis of attendance and guarantees bonds issued by local school boards, enabling them to borrow money at lower interest rates. The value of this fund fluctuated throughout the turbulent first decade of the twenty-first century. At the end of fiscal year 2019, the fund balance had recovered to $46.5 billion. The fund provided $1.2 million to help fund public education in 2019.[17]

Permanent School Fund (PSF) fund created in 1854 that provides monies for primary and secondary schools

The **Available School Fund (ASF)** is a dedicated fund established by the constitution for the support of public education in the state. The ASF is funded through distributions of the Permanent School Fund and 25 percent of the state's motor fuels tax revenue. The ASF also provides funds for another fund, the Instructional Materials Fund, which funds state purchases of instructional materials. Revenue flowing into the ASF for the 2020–21 biennium from the motor fuels tax and PSF together is projected to be $5.3 billion.

The **State Highway Fund** comes from a variety of sources, including motor vehicle registration fees, the federal highway fund, and the sales tax on motor lubricants. A significant portion of the motor fuels tax is initially deposited in the General Revenue Fund and then allocated to the State Highway Fund. The purposes of the State Highway Fund are constructing, maintaining, and policing roadways in Texas and acquiring rights of way for them. Constitutional amendments in 2014 and 2015 provide for diverting billions of dollars into this fund from the Economic Stabilization Fund (discussed below) and state sales and use taxes. The comptroller's office estimates that $28.9 billion will flow into the State Highway Fund for the 2020–21 biennium.[18]

The **Economic Stabilization Fund (ESF)**, commonly known as the Rainy Day Fund, was established through constitutional amendment in 1988 to provide relief during times of financial distress. The fund is generated by a formula involving the base year of 1987. If collections from oil and gas taxes in any year exceed the 1987 amount, 75 percent of the excess is transferred to the fund. Half of any "unencumbered" general revenue—that is, revenue not already targeted for a specific purpose—also goes into the fund. The legislature has the authority to contribute additional funds but never has.

Under certain extraordinary circumstances, ESF monies can be appropriated with a three-fifths vote of members of both houses of the legislature. These circumstances include when a budget deficit develops in a biennium or when the comptroller estimates that revenue will decline from one biennium to the next. Money can also be appropriated from this fund for other purposes at any time with the support of two-thirds of members present in both houses.

Few thought that large sums would accumulate in the fund. The first transfer of funds from oil and gas tax revenues, $18.5 million, took place in 1990, and the ESF account balance remained below $100 million until 2001, when more than $700 million was transferred into the account. In 2003 the ESF was depleted to help solve the impending $10 billion budget shortfall. That year and in 2005 the legislature appropriated ESF monies to a variety of agencies, including the Teacher Retirement System, various health and human service agencies, the governor's office, and the Texas Education Agency.

Rising tax revenues from oil and gas production in the first decade of the twenty-first century flooded the ESF with cash. In 2014 and 2015 constitutional amendments transferred rainy day funds to water and transportation initiatives in the state. The fund is expected to generate $3.6 billion in revenues and expend $4.4 billion in payouts in the 2020–21 biennium. A $9.4 billion balance is projected at the end of the 2020–21 biennium, although these numbers are likely far too optimistic in light of the economic downturn accompanying the coronavirus pandemic of 2020 (see Table 11.4). This fund contains more cash than similar funds in any other state. Only Alaska, also awash in oil and gas revenues, had a fund whose size approached that of its Texas counterpart. The debate over whether or how to use the Rainy Day Fund to close a budget shortfall was a major issue during the 2011 and 2013 legislative sessions and likely will be so again whenever the economy falters and the state revenues decline.[19]

TABLE 11.4

Economic Stabilization Fund History, Fiscal Years 2002 to 2019 (in billions of dollars)

BIENNIUM	REVENUES	EXPENDITURES	ENDING BALANCE
2002–03	$0.8	$0.4	$0.4
2004–05	1.0	1.5	−0.1
2006–07	2.5	1.2	1.2
2008–09	5.5	0.1	6.7
2010–11	1.5	3.2	5.0
2012–13	3.0	1.9	6.2
2014–15	4.3	2.0	8.5
2016–17	1.8	0.0	10.3
2018–19	2.5	2.7	10.1
2020–21*	3.6	4.4	9.4

*Projected estimates before coronavirus pandemic.
NOTE: These are reported figures. Columns and rows may not add because of rounding.

SOURCE: Comptroller of Public Accounts, 2015 Certification Revenue Estimate. See also Texas Legislative Budget Board, *Fiscal Size-Up: 2020–21 Biennium* (May 2020), p. 45.

To appreciate the importance of the operations of Texas's 400 funds and the complexity that they introduce into the budgetary process, one need only look at a few funds lying at the heart of higher education. Specific legislative goals are met through the creation of these funds and the allocation and reallocation of money to and from them. Some funds, such as the Permanent University Fund or the Higher Education Fund, were established to channel money directly to certain institutions of higher education. Others, like the National Research University Fund, are intended to encourage universities to behave in certain ways and to achieve a specific set of legislative objectives.

The **Permanent University Fund (PUF)** contributes to the support of most institutions in the University of Texas (UT) and Texas A&M University systems. Originally established in 1876 by a land grant of 1 million acres, the fund now contains approximately 2.1 million acres in 24 west Texas counties. Under the state constitution, all income from surface leases of this land goes into the Available University Fund (AUF), a fund set up to distribute PUF monies. Income from mineral leases and proceeds from the sale of PUF lands go into PUF and are invested. In 1999 an amendment to the constitution authorized the UT Board of Regents to channel investment income into the AUF. Two-thirds of the monies going to AUF go to the UT system; one-third goes to the Texas A&M system. The estimated market value of the PUF in March 2020 was a little under $22 billion.[20]

The **Higher Education Fund (HEF)** was established by a constitutional amendment for universities that did not have access to PUF monies. It is funded through the General

Permanent University Fund (PUF) fund established in 1876 and funded from the proceeds from land owned by the state; monies go to various universities in the University of Texas (UT) and Texas A&M systems

Higher Education Fund (HEF) state higher education fund for universities not having access to PUF monies

Revenue Fund. Appropriations for the HEF are projected to be $787.5 million for the 2020–21 biennium. An advisory committee made up of member institutions provides input to the Texas Higher Education Coordinating Board, which in turn makes recommendations to the legislature for budgetary allocation to each school out of the HEF.

The **National Research University Fund (NRUF)** was established through a 2009 constitutional amendment to provide a source of funding for universities seeking to achieve national prominence as research institutions. Under the amendment, money was transferred from the HEF to the NRUF. UT Austin and Texas A&M are already considered national research institutions and therefore do not qualify for this fund. Eligibility criteria and distribution rules were established in 2011 by the legislature. An institution must be identified as an emerging research university by the Higher Education Coordinating Board and must spend at least $45 million per year in specifically defined types of research. In addition, universities must meet at least four of the following criteria to qualify: (1) maintain an endowment of at least $400 million in the two preceding academic years; (2) produce 200 Ph.D. degrees during the previous two years; (3) have a freshman class of high academic achievement; (4) be designated as a member of the Association of Research Libraries, have a Phi Beta Kappa chapter, or be a member of Phi Kappa Phi; (5) have a certain number of tenured faculty who have demonstrated excellence by winning a Nobel Prize or other prestigious fellowships, or have been elected to one of the National Academies; and (6) have a demonstrable excellence in graduate education. In 2018 the value of the fund was almost $738 million.[21]

In 2011 seven universities were designated as emerging research universities, each of which could have access to these funds if certain criteria were met. They were Texas Tech University, the University of Texas at Arlington, the University of Texas at Dallas, the University of Texas at El Paso, the University of Texas at San Antonio, the University of Houston, and the University of North Texas. In 2012, Texas Tech and the University of Houston were identified by the Coordinating Board as being eligible to receive some of these NRUF monies subject to meeting a state audit. The University of Texas at Dallas also became eligible for NRUF funds. Appropriations from the fund are estimated to total $50.2 million for the 2020–21 biennium.[22]

The Texas Constitution and the Budget

 Outline the constitutional provisions that affect how the state budget is made

A number of constitutional factors affect the way the budget is made in Texas. Probably the biggest constraint on the budgetary process has to do with time limits. As noted in Figure 11.3, the legislature is compelled to write a two-year, or biennial, budget because of the constitutional provision that the legislature may meet in regular session only once every two years. One of the effects of this restricted time frame is to force government agencies to project their budgetary needs well in advance of any clear understanding of the particular problems they may be facing during the biennium. In addition, the

Texas Biennial Budget Cycle

SOURCE: Senate Research Center, *Budget 101: A Guide to the Budget Process in Texas* (January 2011), p. 5.

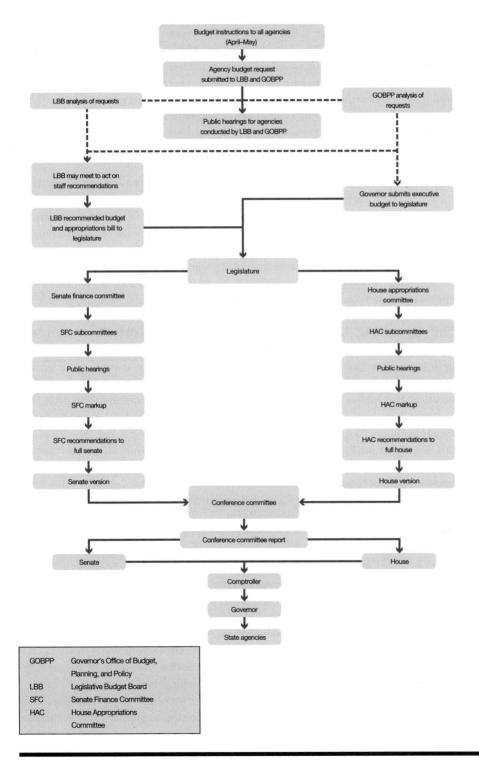

legislature can meet for only 140 days in regular session. This seriously limits the amount of time that the legislature can spend analyzing the budget or developing innovative responses to pressing matters of public importance.

Another important factor is that a large portion of the biennial budget is dedicated for special purposes by federal law or by the Texas Constitution or state statute. These dedicated funds include federal monies earmarked for financing health care for the poor (Medicaid), as well as state funds for highways, education, teachers' retirement, and numerous other purposes. The purpose of dedicated funds is not difficult to understand. Supporters of particular programs want to create a stable revenue source for them. But in protecting their own programs, supporters encourage other interests to do likewise, with the result that the legislature loses control of a large portion of the budget.

Finally, a number of specific constitutional provisions constrain the legislature's control of the budget.[23] Two of these—the pay-as-you-go limit and the spending limit—limit the appropriations process in very specific ways.

The Pay-as-You-Go Limit
Article 3, Section 49a (pay-as-you-go limit), of the Texas Constitution requires the state to maintain a balanced budget. Under this provision, the General Revenue Fund budget is not allowed to exceed the projected available revenue. All bills that get as far as **appropriations** in the legislative process must be sent to the comptroller of public accounts so that the comptroller can certify the bills are within available budget limit projections. One of the most important consequences of the pay-as-you-go limit is to put the comptroller at the heart of the budget process.[24]

The Spending Limit, or the Limit on the Growth of Certain Appropriations
Article 8, Section 22, of the Texas Constitution, which was passed in 1978, specifies that the growth in appropriations cannot be more than the growth of the state's economy, not counting dedicated spending as specified in the state constitution. This means that when the state's economy shrinks, appropriations also have to shrink. The Legislative Budget Board (LBB) is responsible for determining what the proper financial figures are to meet this mandate. Under Texas law, the LBB makes this determination by dividing the estimated total state personal income for the next biennium by the estimated total state personal income for the current biennium. The board may adopt "a more comprehensive definition of the rate of growth" if the alternative definition is approved by a special committee composed of the governor, the Speaker of the House, and the comptroller.[25]

One might think that there would be times that the LBB would be reluctant to perform its constitutional duties. Adopting particularly dismal projections derived from the growth formula hardly makes one popular politically. But there are checks in place to make sure that the projections are made and the limit on growth is delivered in a timely fashion to the legislature. Under law, the LBB is prohibited from distributing the budget or the appropriations bill to either the legislature or the governor until this limit on the rate of growth of appropriations has been adopted. If the LBB fails to adopt a growth limit (and a spending limit), the rate of growth in the state's economy is treated as if it were zero. State revenues not dedicated by the Texas Constitution to particular functions must remain at the same level as in the previous biennium.

For 2020–21 these two spending limits worked in the following way: the comptroller calculated the available revenue to be $2.9 billion, above appropriations after some technical adjustments. Meanwhile, the LBB calculated that the spending limit was $105.8 billion, $3.4 billion above the biennial appropriations. Both constitutional provisions were thus met.[26]

Along with the pay-as-you-go limit and the spending limit, three other constitutional provisions affect the budgeting process.

The Welfare Spending Limit Article 3, Section 51a, provides that the amount of money the state pays for assistance to or on behalf of needy dependent children and their caretakers shall not exceed 1 percent of the state budget in any biennium. This article sets a constitutional limit on the amount of money that the state may pay out to welfare beneficiaries under the Temporary Assistance for Needy Families program (TANF). As defined by the Texas Human Resources Code, the 2020–21 biennial budget was $248.3 billion, creating a welfare spending limit of around $2.5 billion. State funds appropriated for TANF, however, were only $86.5 million, far below the 1 percent limit. State expenditures on Medicaid are not included in this spending limit.[27]

Limitation on Debt Payable from the General Revenue Fund The state constitution also limits the amount of debt the state can incur. Essentially, Texas state debt payments cannot be more than 5 percent of state revenue. One of the

WHAT DO TEXANS THINK?

Is State Government Careful or Careless with Tax Dollars?

The Texas Constitution puts limits on how money can be spent by the state legislature. The budgetary process forces legislators to pass a balanced budget and to make up for unexpected deficits in the previous budgetary cycle. Overall, more Texans believe that state government is careful with tax dollars (44 percent) than believe it is mostly careless (37 percent). But there are sharp differences between Republicans and Democrats on this issue. Why do you think that such a high percentage of Democrats (56 percent) believe that state government is mostly careless with people's tax dollars? Why do you think that such a high percentage of Republicans (66 percent) believe that state government is mostly careful with people's tax dollars?

	DEMOCRATS	INDEPENDENTS	REPUBLICANS	ALL TEXANS
Mostly careful with people's tax dollars	23%	40%	66%	44%
Mostly careless with people's tax dollars	56	40	20	37
Don't know	21	21	14	18

SOURCE: University of Texas/*Texas Tribune* Poll, Texas Politics Project, texaspolitics.utexas.edu/set/state-government-careful-or-careless-tax-dollars-october-2017#party-id, October 2017. Margin of error is +/− 2.83%.

consequences of this constitutional debt limit is that compared with other states (as well as with the federal government), the Texas debt burden is relatively low. A 2015 Tax Foundation study calculated that Texas's per capita debt burden was $1,509, as contrasted with $6,935 in New York, $4,997 in Illinois, and $4,944 in California. Texas's per capita state debt was ranked 45th out of the 50 states.[28]

Budget-Execution Authority Under a constitutional amendment passed in 1985, the legislature was empowered to establish rules for the expenditure of funds by state agencies. Today the rules provide that between legislative sessions, the governor or the LBB may propose (1) that an agency stop spending money appropriated to it in the budget, (2) that money be transferred from one agency to another, or (3) that the purpose for an appropriation to a particular agency be changed. If the governor proposes the changes, the LBB must approve or amend the proposal. If the LBB proposes the changes, the governor must approve or amend the proposal.

The Budgetary Process

 Identify the steps, players, and political tensions in making the state budget

In theory, Texas has a "dual-budget" system. This means that responsibility for preparing an initial draft of the budget is shared by the governor through the Governor's Office of Budget, Planning, and Policy (GOBPP) and the legislature through the LBB. In practice, the budget is primarily the responsibility of the legislature.

The GOBPP is responsible for advising the governor regarding fiscal matters. It prepares the governor's budget recommendations for the legislature, monitors state appropriations and operations, provides analysis on fiscal and economic matters, coordinates federal programs in the state, and assists in the operations of various regional and state planning councils.

Before 1949 there was little coordination in public budgeting. Financial procedures varied, and state agencies were funded by individual appropriations. In 1949 a law was enacted to establish the 10-member LBB, whose primary job would be to recommend appropriations for all agencies of state government. The board is chaired by the lieutenant governor. The vice chair is the Speaker of the House. Other members include the chairs of the House Appropriations Committee, the House Committee on Ways and Means, the Senate Finance Committee, and the Senate State Affairs Committee. Two additional members from the Senate and the House are chosen by the lieutenant governor and the Speaker, respectively.

The LBB appoints a budget director, who brings together budgeting requests from the various state agencies and prepares appropriations bills for them. The LBB is also responsible for evaluating agency programs and developing estimates of the probable costs of implementing legislation introduced in a legislative session. The LBB's draft budget, not the governor's, is the basis for final legislation. Table 11.5 summarizes the duties of key players in the budgetary process.

TABLE 11.5

Key Players in the Budgetary Process

THE LEGISLATIVE BUDGET BOARD (LBB)

1. Adopts a constitutional spending limit

2. Prepares a general appropriations bill

3. Prepares agency performance reports

4. Guides, reviews, and finalizes agency strategic plans

5. Prepares fiscal notes regarding costs and impacts of proposed legislation

6. Engages in "budget execution actions" in conjunction with the governor by transferring money from one assigned purpose to another purpose or to another agency

THE GOVERNOR AND THE GOVERNOR'S OFFICE OF BUDGET, PLANNING, AND POLICY (GOBPP)

1. Develop a strategic plan for the state

2. Help to develop agency Legislative Appropriation Requests (LARs)

3. Hold LAR hearings, often in conjunction with the legislature

4. Deliver a governor's appropriations budget and a general appropriations bill at the beginning of the legislative session

5. Exercise a line-item veto after an appropriations bill is passed by the legislature

6. Engage in "budget execution actions" in conjunction with the LBB by transferring money from one assigned purpose to another purpose or to another agency

THE COMPTROLLER OF PUBLIC ACCOUNTS

1. Submits a statement regarding the estimated anticipated revenues for the coming biennium

2. Certifies that an appropriations bill is in balance with projected state revenues

3. Collects state taxes

4. Tracks 600+ separate revenue and spending funds and makes sure that agencies stay within their budgets

Estimation and Planning

The budgetary process involves two stages. In the first stage, the LBB develops a draft budget based on requests supplied by state agencies. This draft budget follows a series of steps. First, each agency develops a strategic plan, which includes (1) a mission statement, (2) a statement about the goals of the agency, (3) a discussion of the population served by the agency, (4) an explanation of the means that will be used to achieve the goals, and (5) an identification of the measures to be used to assess the agency's success in meeting these goals. This information provides the basis for LBB funding recommendations for each agency. In the spring or early summer prior to the legislative session, the LBB sends out detailed Legislative Appropriation Request (LAR) instructions to the agencies. The LBB and the GOBPP then hold hearings with each agency where the agency's strategic plan and LAR are discussed. LARs become the starting point for the appropriations bill that is prepared by the LBB. *Legislative Budget Estimates* is a publication of the LBB that contains information on the proposed appropriations bill, including expenditures for previous bienniums and proposed expenditures for the next biennium.[29]

While the draft budgets are being prepared, the comptroller's office prepares the Biennial Revenue Estimate (BRE), a detailed forecast of the total revenue that the state is expected to take in over the next biennium. The Texas Constitution requires that the BRE contain "an itemized estimate of the anticipated revenue . . . to be credited during the succeeding biennium." The BRE includes other information to assist legislators in the budget process, including (1) statements about the anticipated revenue from different sources, (2) an analysis of the economic outlook facing Texas and the nation, and (3) a detailed accounting of the funds in the state treasury. Through this forecast, the comptroller effectively sets a ceiling on what the state legislature may spend. Although the legislature can override the comptroller's estimates with a four-fifths vote of each house, this has never happened. The BRE is updated by the comptroller when economic conditions change significantly, or special sessions of the legislature are called.

The difficulty of making accurate projections about tax revenue over the next biennium has been a concern in recent years. A study conducted by the comptroller's office in 2015 highlighted how frequently actual tax revenues undershot or overshot its projections. Interestingly, the study found that over the past 40 years overestimations of tax revenue were a result of an unexpected recession or a "precipitous" decline in energy prices. Underestimations were associated with soaring energy prices, the implementation of new technologies in the oil and gas industry (such as fracking), and boom periods in the economy that led to higher employment rates and an expansion of the housing market. One thing was clear from the study: making accurate predictions about tax collections over a two-year period is difficult, if not impossible.[30]

Two events threatened to disrupt the estimate and planning stage of the budgetary process for the 2021 legislative session. First, in late 2019 Lieutenant Governor Patrick began to publicly attack the Legislative Budget Board, claiming that the LBB had assumed too much control over the budgetary process through its control over information. Over the last two sessions, Patrick had grown dissatisfied with the LBB, viewing it as anything but a nonpartisan information-gathering organization.

According to critics, since becoming lieutenant governor, Patrick has tried to undermine the LBB. Veteran employees have left the LBB and many vacant positions have not been filled. Between 2015 and 2019 the size of the LBB fell from 146 to 108 employees. The executive director position was empty for over a year, when a new director was appointed who was much more in tune with Patrick's conservative agenda. When critics accused Patrick of allowing the LBB to fall apart, Patrick replied that his critics were "absolutely right. . . . As co-chair of the LBB, I have worked to eliminate the influence of the liberal bureaucrats who are running the LBB when I got there so we can move forward protecting taxpayer dollars."[31]

The second event threatening to disturb the estimate and planning stage of the budgetary process was the coronavirus pandemic and the resulting economic crisis. Due to shelter-in-place orders that were designed to slow the spread of the virus, unemployment skyrocketed in Texas, approaching depression-era levels in some communities.

In turn, sales tax revenues along with other tax revenue streams plummeted. The state budget was in peril as the coronavirus spread. By the early summer, no one knew how much revenue would flow into state coffers for the remainder of the 2020–21 biennium. Earlier projections were no longer useful. Things were made even worse by the collapse of the oil industry worldwide in the early spring of 2020, which drove prices down below $20 a barrel. As the price of oil fell, so did Texas's severance tax revenues. By the summer, state agencies were being told to hold the line on spending and hiring and to be ready for impending cuts or even "clawbacks" (giving budgeted money back to the state) demanded by the state.[32]

The old rules for estimating and planning a budget may not hold true during the 2021 legislative session. Some commentators thought a special session might need to be held before the end of 2020 to address the budget crisis, although that was unlikely. On May 13, 2020, Republican senator Jane Nelson, the head of the Senate Finance Committee, announced that "zero-based budgeting" would be put into effect for the next legislative session. Unlike an incremental approach, where agency budgets are largely based on previous biennium expenditures (taking into account increases in population and inflation), zero-based budgeting demands that agencies justify their expenditures starting from scratch. Conservatives have long argued that zero-based budgeting would help hold down wasteful spending in an expanding government.[33] Liberals have rejected this claim out of hand. But the budget crisis brought on by the coronavirus coupled to an attack on the LBB by Lieutenant Governor Patrick may provide conservatives with an opportunity to change the way that legislators estimate and plan the budget for the next biennium.

The Legislative Process

The second stage of the budget process involves the legislative process. By the seventh day of each regular session, appropriations bills are submitted by the LBB to the House Appropriations Committee and the Senate Finance Committee. Traditionally, the bills are introduced to these committees by their respective chairs, although any member may do so. The bills then work their way through the committee system of each house separately and are subject to hearings, debates, and revisions. This process of drafting the bill is referred to as a "markup." Final versions of the budget are prepared by the House Appropriations Committee and the Senate Finance Committee. Each house then votes on the bill. Differences between the two versions of the bill are reconciled in a conference committee.

The conference committee is composed of representatives from the Senate and the House. Senate members are selected by the lieutenant governor or the president pro tempore of the Senate. The senator sponsoring the bill, traditionally the chair of the Senate Finance Committee, appoints the chair of the Senate conferees. At least two members from the Senate Finance Committee must sit on the conference committee. The Speaker of the House appoints all conferees from the House as well as the chair of the House conferees. Traditionally, Senate and House representatives alternate each session in chairing the conference committee.

Specific rules govern how disagreements between the Senate and House versions of the appropriations bills are to be handled.[34]

The Legislative Budget Board is a key player in the budgeting process in Texas. Here, the Texas House Appropriations Committee hears from Ursula Parks, former director of the LBB.

- Items that appear in both versions of the bill must be included in the final conference committee report.
- Items that appear in both versions of the bill with identical amounts allocated to them may not be changed by the committee.
- Items that appear in both versions of the bill with differing amounts allocated to them cannot be eliminated. The committee has the discretion to fund these items at a level not larger than the larger allocation or smaller than the smaller allocation.
- Items that appear in one version of the bill but not the other can be included or eliminated from the final bill subject to the discretion of the committee. However, no more money may be allocated to that item than is found in the original version of the bill.
- Items found in neither version of the bill may not be included in the final conference report. However, the conference committee has the discretion to propose the appropriation of money for bills that already have been passed by the legislature.

While constraining the discretionary authority of the committee to a degree, these rules still leave considerable room for political maneuvering. Membership on this important committee is a highly prized commodity. Once the bill passes the conference committee, it is returned to both houses for final passage.

Under Article 3, Section 49a, of the Texas Constitution, the comptroller has the formal authority to "certify" the budget. This means that the comptroller confirms that the comptroller's office has analyzed the budget and concluded that it is within the current revenue estimates. For all intents and purposes, the budget is being declared balanced. If the general appropriations bill is not certified by the comptroller, it is returned to the house in which it originated. The legislature normally must then either decrease expenditures or raise revenues to make up the difference. According to provisions set out in Article 3, Section 49a, under conditions of "imperative public necessity" the legislature may with a four-fifths vote in each house decide to spend in excess of anticipated revenue.

After certification, the budget moves on to the governor, who can sign, not sign, or veto the entire bill or exercise the line-item veto. With the line-item veto, in particular, the governor has the power to unravel some of the compromises that legislators may have forged to get the bill through the committee system. The line-item veto also potentially gives the governor enormous power to limit expenditures in certain targeted areas. Of course, line-item vetoes exercised too vigorously in one session can come back to haunt the governor's legislative agenda in the next session.

The appropriations bill takes effect on September 1 in odd-numbered years. All agencies are bound by it. Monitoring agency compliance with the budget is the job of the LBB and the **state auditor's office**. The governor and the LBB have the authority to execute the budget, which includes the power to shift funds between agency programs or between agencies if necessary when the legislature is not in session. This power to execute the budget is an important one. It has been a tool used by the governor and the LBB to cope with unanticipated shortfalls in the budget by ordering state agencies to cut their expenditures in the middle of a biennium.

As noted in Chapter 8, the governor is also able to move funds from one account to another without permission of the LBB if he or she declares an emergency. Such a situation has only occurred once—in the summer of 2014—when Governor Perry declared an emergency and transferred funds to pay for the deployment of National Guard troops along the border with Mexico to cope with illegal immigration into Texas.

state auditor's office develops independent audits of state agencies, including institutions of higher education; these audits are used to evaluate agencies

The Challenge of Budgeting in Texas

Unlike the federal government, the Texas state government cannot approve a budget deficit and must pass a balanced budget every two years. The budgetary process is a complicated process full of uncertainty. Projecting expenditures in programs such as Medicaid, public education, and higher education is difficult. Predicting future tax revenues is even more problematic. An unexpected recession or bust in oil prices can drive revenues down significantly, throwing the projected state budget into a deficit that must be resolved before it can be passed. And the reverse can be true: an unexpected economic boom or surge in oil prices can drive up revenues unexpectedly, creating an unexpected surplus. Not surprisingly, the specifics of the politics surrounding budget surpluses in Texas in the twenty-first century can be quite different from those involving deficits. Comparing the situations facing the legislature in 2015 when there was a projected surplus with 2017 when there was a projected deficit is useful.

Confronting a Budget Surplus   The 2015 state legislature began its session with a revenue estimate that far exceeded expected expenditures. A budget surplus was brought on by the comptroller having underestimated revenues flowing into state coffers for the 2014–15 biennium by $11.3 billion. This was the worst estimate in 40 years of budgeting.[35] Special interest groups and think tanks debated the costs and benefits of managing the surplus either by cutting taxes or by creating new programs or expanding old ones. But in the Republican-dominated state legislature there was never any doubt of the course of action to be pursued. Taxes were going to be cut. The only real issues were what taxes to cut and by how much.

The budgetary surplus also made possible some new programs. During the regular session, the legislature established small programs related to education, including a High-Quality Prekindergarten Grant Program for public and charter schools. The largest new initiative centered on a constitutional amendment to address transportation needs by transferring state sales tax and motor vehicle sales tax revenues from the General Revenue Fund to the State Highway Fund. This amendment was approved by the voters in November 2017 and began adding money to the State Highway Fund in 2018.[36]

Confronting a Budget Deficit The state legislature faced a very different budget scenario in 2017 when an ever-widening deficit was projected. Part of the problem lay in the legislature's responses to the surpluses in the 2015 session just discussed. The oil and gas fracking boom had led to a massive tax infusion into the state coffers. But this began to slow down in 2016 as prices dropped and production fell. Less severance tax revenue than had been originally projected was coming into the state. In addition, the rededicated sales tax revenues to the newly created transportation fund removed an estimated $5 billion from the General Revenue Fund. In January 2017, Comptroller Glenn Hegar estimated that the biennial revenue would be $3 billion less than in the previous session. Creative solutions had to be found to address both the revenue and the expenditure sides of the budget.

After considerable controversy as to how to raise revenues, the House and Senate reached a compromise: get $1.8 billion in onetime revenue by delaying the sales tax transfer, and withdraw $989 million from the Rainy Day Fund, but only for capital and nonrecurring items. An additional $668 million became available through another bookkeeping trick: Comptroller Hegar allowed a number of dedicated accounts with the general revenue to be available for certifications through a funds consolidation bill. Hegar also made available another $500 million for spending certification by speeding up the sales of state-owned financial assets.

On the expenditure side, $1.3 billion in cuts were put into place in the 2018–19 budget compared with the 2016–17 budget. Public education was cut by $600 million, health and human services by $100 million, and public safety by $200 million. Additional miscellaneous programs were cut to the tune of $600 million. Higher education received a paltry increase of $200 million across the state, and state health insurance was increased by $400 million. Cuts were particularly controversial in public education, where maintaining current levels of funding would have cost an additional $4 billion in state expenditures. Significantly, the final state Medicaid appropriation did not fund for medical inflation or an increased demand for Medicaid services. And more ominously, caseload growth was funded only through the first year of the biennium. A supplemental appropriation of up to $2 billion could be needed to fund Medicaid in 2019.

Essentially, legislators had met the formal challenges of the deficit—passing a balanced budget certified by the comptroller—but only by pushing some financial decisions into the future, where they would still need to be confronted. The Texas Taxpayers and Research Association calculated there was a potential budgetary shortfall for the next biennium of up to $7.9 billion. The $2 billion Medicaid shortfall could be addressed by reworking or eliminating Obamacare. But that still left the structural gap brought on by the bookkeeping tricks and the use of the Rainy Day Fund to balance the budget during the 2017 session. Clearly more revenue was needed from somewhere. But where?

Lurking in the background in the debate over the deficit in 2017 was the belief that buying time might be a good thing for responsible public finance. After all, a return to $80 a barrel oil prices would lead to a surge in oil production that, in turn, would fill the state's coffers with oil severance taxes. For tax-weary Republican Party leaders or their supporters in the state, raising revenues through increased oil and natural gas production was not as controversial as raising sales taxes or property taxes on individuals.[37]

The Budget Process Today

The politics of budgetary surpluses and deficits in Texas today are contentious but predictable. First, as long as conservative Republicans are in power, cutting taxes will always be high on the agenda as will minimizing tax increases. Expanding social welfare or educational programs will not likely take priority even during times of surplus, and cuts are always high on the agenda during deficit times. Moreover, those programs that are expanded or added, such as transportation, will likely address the needs of the business community or the economy as a whole.

Second, not all tax cuts or tax increases are the same. Different interests are served by different tax cuts or increases. Sales tax cuts create different winners and losers than do franchise tax cuts. Property tax cuts can benefit the taxpayer but adversely affect the schools that rely on those taxes. Hence, while property tax cuts may seem to have universal support, they may nevertheless not be popular in expanding suburban communities trying to raise money to build new schools to educate a rapidly expanding population. Third, grappling with a budgetary surplus or deficit is complicated not only because of the politics surrounding the budgetary process but also because of the difficulty in projecting a budget on both the revenue side and the expenditure side two years into the future. Individuals have trouble estimating their income and spending two years into the future. Given the complexity of the budgetary process, why should the legislature be expected to do much better? Passing a meaningful balanced budget is hard work, involving many compromises and sacrifices. It is the hardest and most important work that the legislature engages in during every regular session.

Public Finance and the Future of Texas

PUBLIC FINANCE will continue to be a troubling issue for political leaders in Texas. Texas's economy is tied inextricably to the booms and busts of the U.S. economy as well as the world economy. A declining economy can cut back on consumer spending, which affects the sales tax revenue. Falling housing prices can adversely affect property tax revenue. Falling prices for oil and natural gas can cut into severance tax revenues and the revenue flowing into the Rainy Day

Fund. But the reverse is also true: an expanding international and domestic economy and rising wages can lead to steady increases in sales tax revenue. Higher oil and natural gas prices can drive up severance tax income on oil and natural gas production, leading to additional growth in the Rainy Day Fund. Such are the rules that govern public finance in Texas in the early twenty-first century.

State budgetary policy ultimately depends on the successful implementation of a national economic policy that works. As was noted in Chapter 1, Texas is no longer, and maybe never was, an island apart from national and international economic trends. Going in to 2020, Texas Republicans were confident about the direction of the national economy under the Trump administration. Similarly, Texas Republicans viewed the budgetary and policy initiatives put into place under their leadership to be enlightened and pro-growth, freed from the tax and spend policies of the Democratic Party. Tax revenues were increasing and the budget was balanced, leaving room for tax cuts. And then the coronavirus changed everything.

By the summer of 2020, no one knew how bad the Texas economy and state budget ultimately would be hit by the coronavirus and the efforts by state and local officials to bring the contagion under control. Many local political leaders continued to argue for strong shelter-in-place orders in April and May as a response to the pandemic. Others, like Governor Abbott, offered a more moderate approach to stemming the disease, suggesting that after a short period of shelter-in-place, the economy must be opened up carefully again. But there were some political leaders, like Lieutenant Governor Patrick, who believed the response to the outbreak worse than the disease. Destroying the Texas economy and the state budget was too high a price to pay for containing the spread of the virus. Patrick argued that the economy was being crushed and that "there are more important things than living. And that's saving this country for my grandchildren and saving this country for all of us."[38]

Four factors will continue to define public finance in Texas over the next biennium. First, economic conditions will determine how much revenue is flowing into state coffers. Going into the 2021 legislation, the economic crisis brought on by the coronavirus will likely dominate discussion of state public finance. Second, there will be increased demands from the federal government for paying for expanded federal initiatives in health care (see Chapter 12). Third, increased population will lead to increased demands on state agencies for services ranging from health care to roads, to water, and to public education. All other things being equal, a larger population demands more from government, and that costs money. Fourth, there is a growing antigovernment feeling among portions of the population in Texas that state government is too big already. For Tea Partiers and other conservative Republicans, "No new taxes" is a successful mantra for winning office. Whether it will be a successful one for legislating and leading is another question.

Use 🐰 INQUIZITIVE to help you study and master this material.

What Is the Budget?

- Explain the purpose of the state budget and what is typically included (pp. 375–77)

Texas is required to operate within a balanced budget. The budget can be considered in light of five revenue streams: the General Revenue Funds, the General Revenue–Dedicated Funds, Federal Funds, Other Funds, and All Funds.

Key Terms
General Revenue Funds (p. 375)
General Revenue–Dedicated Funds (p. 375)
Federal Funds (p. 375)
Other Funds (p. 375)
All Funds (p. 375)

Practice Quiz

1. The Texas Constitution requires that the Texas budget be
    a) balanced.
    b) approved by the governor's cabinet.
    c) funded only from sales taxes.
    d) approved by the governor, the legislature, and the state treasurer.
    e) funded only from federal grants.

2. Federal expenditures primarily affect the state budget in which two areas?
    a) energy and law enforcement
    b) health and human services and education
    c) business development and highways
    d) interstate highways and airports
    e) Medicare and transportation

Spending and Revenue in Texas

- Describe the general pattern of state spending in Texas and where state revenue comes from (pp. 377–87)

Texas spends less than the national average in a variety of policy areas, including education and highway spending. Although Texas does not have an income tax, it has one of the highest sales taxes in the nation. However, the per capita revenue from those sales taxes is among the lowest in the nation. Property taxes in Texas are among the highest in the nation. Among other important state taxes are the natural gas production tax and the oil production and regulation tax. Although a controversial issue in the past, a state income tax has little support either in the legislature or in the population as a whole.

Key Terms
progressive tax (p. 383)
regressive tax (p. 383)
matching funds (p. 386)

Practice Quiz

3. Texas has the reputation for being
    a) a low-service, low-tax state.
    b) a high-service, high-tax state.
    c) a low-service, high-tax state.
    d) a high-service, low-tax state.
    e) an average-service, average-tax state.

4. One major revenue source for Texas is the sales tax, which is
    a) 8.25 percent for state government and 2.25 percent for local government.
    b) 4.25 percent for state government and 2 percent for local government.
    c) 6.25 percent for state government and 2 percent for local government.
    d) 5 percent for state government and 1.25 percent for local government.
    e) none of the above

5. A Texas personal income tax
   a) used to exist but was repealed because of new taxes on oil production.
   b) would have to be approved by the voters, and the revenues from it would have to support public education.
   c) would have to be passed through a constitutional amendment.
   d) could only be imposed on incomes greater than $250,000 per year.
   e) would be unlikely to raise much revenue.

State Funds

> • Describe how the money in the budget is organized into specific funds (pp. 387–90)

Money flows into and out of a variety of over 400 different funds controlled by the state. Among the most important are the General Revenue Fund, the Permanent School Fund, the State Highway Fund, and the Economic Stabilization Fund (the Rainy Day Fund). The existence of these funds makes budgeting a complicated process.

Key Terms
Permanent School Fund (PSF) (p. 387)
Available School Fund (ASF) (p. 388)
State Highway Fund (p. 388)
Economic Stabilization Fund (ESF) (p. 388)
Permanent University Fund (PUF) (p. 389)
Higher Education Fund (HEF) (p. 389)
National Research University Fund (NRUF) (p. 390)

Practice Quiz
6. The Rainy Day Fund
   a) provides funds for flood victims.
   b) was designed to provide funding for the state during times of financial distress.
   c) contains only a small amount of state funds.
   d) is used to promote oil and gas development.
   e) can only be spent by the Texas comptroller.

7. The National Research University Fund
   a) pays for university-level research at all state universities.
   b) provides the funding for the University of Texas at Austin.
   c) funds Texas universities seeking national prominence as research institutions.
   d) only provides funds to universities with Nobel Prize winners.
   e) will not provide funds if more than 20 percent of students fail to graduate in four years.

The Texas Constitution and the Budget

> • Outline the constitutional provisions that affect how the state budget is made (pp. 390–94)

There are many constitutional restrictions on the budget, including the requirement of a biennial budget, a pay-as-you-go limit, a limit on the growth of some appropriations, a welfare spending limit, limitation on debt payable from the General Revenue Fund, and rules on the spending of funds by state agencies. These restrictions play important roles in shaping the budget policy-making process.

Key Terms
Article 3, Section 49a (pay-as-you-go limit) (p. 392)
appropriations (p. 392)

Practice Quiz
8. Which of the following is *not* a constitutional constraint on the budgetary process in Texas?
   a) the annual budget
   b) a welfare spending limit
   c) a pay-as-you-go limit
   d) a limitation on the debt payable from the General Revenue Fund
   e) All are constitutional limits.

9. What is meant by "the budget-execution authority"?
   a) the power to execute the laws of the land
   b) the legislature's power to establish rules for the expenditure of funds by state agencies
   c) the governor's power to veto the budget
   d) the LBB's power to create the budget for the judiciary in Texas
   e) none of the above

The Budgetary Process

> • Identify the steps, players, and political tensions in making the state budget (pp. 394–401)

In theory, Texas has a dual-budget system with budgeting shared by the governor and the legislature. In reality, the budget is the responsibility of the legislature. There are a series of steps that the budget must go through to be passed by the legislature. Among the most important is the requirement that the Texas comptroller certify the budget as being balanced. At the beginning of the budgetary process the legislature can be faced with projected surpluses or projected deficits that call for very different responses. In recent sessions, budgetary politics has been dominated by the Republican Party's desire to lower taxes and, when necessary, cut program spending.

Key Terms
state auditor's office (p. 399)

Practice Quiz
10. Who is the chief planning officer of the state of Texas?
   a) the lieutenant governor
   b) the Speaker of the House
   c) the comptroller
   d) the governor
   e) the state treasurer

11. The principal job of the Legislative Budget Board is
   a) to keep track of the expenses of the executive.
   b) to monitor the operations of the House.
   c) to raise taxes.
   d) to recommend appropriations for all agencies of state government.
   e) to conduct audits of state expenditures.

12. A budgetary surplus is best defined as
   a) a budgetary situation wherein the comptroller believes that taxes are too high.
   b) a budgetary situation wherein projected revenues exceed projected expenditures.
   c) a budgetary situation wherein projected revenues are less than projected expenditures.
   d) a budgetary situation wherein the governor discovers that more money is available for the state to spend than the legislature initially thought.
   e) a budgetary situation wherein the federal government provides emergency funds to address a problem in Texas.

13. What is one of the recent projected deficits that dominated budgetary politics during the 2017 session of the legislature?
   a) declining oil prices
   b) declining demand for Medicaid services
   c) increased sales tax receipts
   d) decline in the Rainy Day Fund
   e) the comptroller getting rid of accounting tricks to balance the budget

Child Protective Services in Texas plays a major role in ensuring the well-being of many children. However, the program has come under scrutiny in recent years due to underfunding, overburdened caseworkers, and thus poor outcomes for the children under the government's charge. Here, the CPS program director hugs a child before he is adopted by his grandparents.

Public Policy

WHY PUBLIC POLICY MATTERS One of the most important responsibilities of the state is protecting those who can't protect themselves. In Texas, this massive task falls to the 13,000 employees of the Texas Department of Family and Protective Services (DFPS). One of the most sensitive programs run by DFPS is Child Protective Services (CPS). CPS's job is to investigate cases of child neglect or abuse and, when necessary, remove a child from parents' custody and place the child in a relative's home or in a foster home. One might think that CPS would be a relatively small issue, the province of policy wonks and interested family members. But by the 2017 session of the legislature, CPS had become one of the top concerns of the governor and the legislative leaders.[1] Why and how this happened says much about why public policy matters.

Advocates for children in Texas have long bemoaned the underfunding of CPS. The state employs too few caseworkers to watch over the foster care program, and turnover is too high. In 2004, DFPS calculated that a caseload of 25 clients per worker would theoretically allow caseworkers to have meaningful contact with all children in their charge. In reality, the actual caseload per worker was around 34. The state made disturbingly little effort to look at the workload of caseworkers or evaluate the effects of the high average caseloads or caseworker turnover on the children themselves.

In 2011 a New York–based advocacy group brought a class-action suit on behalf of all children in long-term care in Texas. In a 260-page ruling, U.S. District Judge Janis Jack of Corpus Christi found that "excessive caseloads and overburdened caseworkers cause an unreasonable risk of harm" to foster children.[2] The court found that almost 3,000 children considered to be at risk each day were either seen by caseworkers outside of the required 24-hour period following a report of possible abuse or not seen at all. Things were so bad that the judge concluded the state had violated a "substantive due process right" under the Fourteenth Amendment of the U.S. Constitution that foster children had to be free from "an unreasonable risk of harm caused by the state."[3] The court ordered DFPS to implement reforms that protected children and directed the agency to hire enough caseworkers to ensure that caseloads were manageable.

The court ruling, in addition to the $40 million deficit that CPS faced in 2017, placed CPS reform high on Governor Abbott's legislative agenda for the 2017 session. Lieutenant Governor Patrick and House Speaker Straus called upon DFPS Commissioner Hank Whitman to immediately develop a plan to hire and train more caseworkers. They also called upon the agency to "create a culture of accountability."[4] As a result, four major bills were passed during the regular session that addressed the child protective service crisis.

If one of the goals of this legislation was to get the court out of the business of reforming child welfare, the legislature failed. In January 2018, Judge Jack ruled that CPS would remain under the "watchful eye" of a court-appointed special master. Years of inaction by Texas officials led the judge to argue that the officials could not be trusted to act in the best interests of children under the care of the state. Texas, represented by Attorney General Paxton, appealed the ruling on the grounds that unelected judges should not be allowed to assume control of state institutions.[5] A second federal court ordered a temporary stay of Jack's final ruling and asked for more information about the case.[6] An appeals court later upheld the judge's rulings allowing for the appointment of two monitors to oversee that Texas was actually following the new rules.

Child Protective Services was a back-burner issue for most of the 2019 legislative session. But it came to the forefront again in November 2019 when Judge Jack found the state in contempt of court for failing to comply with her earlier orders. Judge Jack was direct and forceful in criticism of state officials: "I can no longer find (the Texas Department of Family and Protective Services) to be credible in any way. . . . It's shameful. . . . You cannot be relied upon for anything. Period."[7] The conflict between Judge Jack and the state intensified in late February 2020 when Judge Jack opened an investigation of the death of a 14-year-old girl in state custody who died from a blood clot.

Whatever the final outcome of the conflict between Judge Jack and state officials, one thing is clear: the state will no longer be allowed to ignore the needs of children in its charge, and changes are coming to the structure and operations of CPS. The responses of the legislature to the court's findings and rulings will redefine the duties and obligations that the state has to some of its most vulnerable members. The failures of Child Protective Services to protect its wards, and the legislative and judicial responses to the CPS crisis, demonstrate vividly why public policy matters to Texans in the twenty-first century.

CHAPTER GOALS

- Describe the key steps and concepts in the policy-making process (pp. 409–11)

- Describe the major issues that have shaped education policy in Texas (pp. 412–24)

- Describe the state's role in addressing poverty and how it is affected by national policies (pp. 424–30)

- Explain why Medicaid in particular and health care policy in general have been so controversial in Texas (pp. 431–40)

The Policy-Making Process

Describe the key steps and concepts in the policy-making process

In broadest terms, public policy refers to the outputs of governmental institutions. More narrowly, public policy can be defined as the expressed goals of a governmental body backed by incentives or sanctions.[8] Public policies can be found in laws passed by legislative bodies as well as in the rules, regulations, and orders from properly authorized public agencies. The incentives or sanctions can include a wide range of strategies, from subsidies that reward individuals for acting in a certain way to monetary or criminal penalties that punish people for engaging in particular actions.

One way that political scientists have approached the study of public policy is by focusing attention upon the different stages of the policy-making process: the political and administrative process through which governmental goals are identified, formulated, articulated into law, and evaluated.[9] Analyzing stages of the policy-making process does not mean that public policy is made in a simple linear way. The real world of policy making is, in fact, much messier; stages in the process may overlap or even collapse into one another. Nevertheless, the idea that there are stages of the policy-making process has proven to be a useful analytical framework for understanding the various factors that go into the making of public policy.

Problem Identification

The first stage is problem identification. Here, society at large and actors in the political system develop an understanding of how we must think about and address a particular problem. Roger Cobb and Charles Elder refer to this set of ideas as a "systemic agenda" where an issue is "commonly perceived by members of the political community as meriting public attention and as involving matters within the legitimate jurisdiction of existing governmental authority."[10] This systemic agenda is used by citizens and policy makers to understand the nature of public problems and to shape and direct the way policy makers will develop public policy aimed at them. For example, if we view the problem of poverty as fundamentally one of limited income, we might conclude that the best solution is increasing welfare payments to the poor. However, if we consider the problem to be behavior that causes people to be poor, such as unwillingness to work or poor job skills, we might conclude that policies directed toward encouraging work or subsidizing education are better courses of action. In the problem identification stage, our ideology—that is, our ideas, concepts, and visions about the way society works—plays a major role in defining public-policy making.

Policy Formulation

Policy formulation is the second stage of the policy-making process. Here, the more general ideas that the public and lawmakers have about social and political problems are clarified, and strategies for dealing with these specifically defined problems are developed. Policy formulation involves the detailed procedures that guide the passage of legislation and the development of administrative rules and regulations. Setting the agenda on what problems will be discussed, how these problems will be understood, and what concrete measures will be taken to address them lies at the heart of all policy formulation.

Implementation   The third stage in the policy-making process is implementation. At this stage, the goals of public policy along with the incentives or sanctions to support them are put into effect by a particular government agency. Identifying the appropriate agency to implement a program is crucial at this stage. Similarly, budgetary policy plays a major role in the implementation stage and can determine the success or failure of a particular public policy. A well-formulated public policy can be dashed by poorly executed or poorly funded implementation.

Evaluation   The fourth stage of the policy-making process is evaluation. At a certain point all public policies must be evaluated for their effectiveness. In the best of all possible worlds, evaluation procedures would assess the stated goals of a particular policy against the actual outcomes of the implemented policy. Good evaluation would lead to a rethinking of the policy in light of the problem being addressed and the solutions formulated to address it. Similarly, good evaluation could lead to a rethinking of the strategies being used and the resources being committed to implementing the policy. Closing the loop between problem identification and program evaluation is one of the most difficult problems facing policy makers.

Some political scientists identify policy legitimation as another stage in the policy-making process. Legitimation—the establishment and recognition in the political community of the legality and constitutionality of a particular policy initiative—is probably better understood not as a separate stage but as something that takes place throughout the entire policy-making process. Legitimation can include a wide range of activities: open discussions of a problem in the press, committee investigations and oversight investigations, following the appropriate rules for passing a bill in the legislature or making a rule in an administrative agency, and judicial review of the policy. Establishing the legitimacy of a public policy throughout the various stages of the policy-making process is an essential part of any democratic political system.

Rationality in Policy Making

An often-stated goal of policy makers is to make public policy more rational and more efficient. **Rationality**, in this regard, generally refers to the idea that we have clearly identified the goals that we wish to achieve and have formulated and implemented policies that address these problems in an efficient manner. Efficiency refers to the idea that policy should maximize the outputs of government with a minimum commitment of resources. Given this commitment to rationality in policy making, people are often surprised by how irrational and inefficient public policy can seem in a democracy. Part of the problem lies in the fact that the policy-making process is highly complex. Writing reports, holding committee hearings, and passing legislation often involve political compromises that muddy the waters of policy making. Vagueness in the problem identification stage along with compromises made among competing parties in the policy formulation stage can work against the development of rational and efficient solutions to problems.

Additional factors tend to work against rationality and efficiency in the making of public policy. The first is the fact that governments tend to work incrementally. Neither legislators nor government agencies begin their work on a particular problem from

rationality the idea in public-policy making that we have clearly identified goals and that we seek to achieve these goals in an optimal or efficient manner

As shown here, education policy involves the four key stages in the policy-making process. Clockwise from top left: A policy issue such as school funding is identified. Politicians create policies to address the issue. Elected officials pass legislation to address the problem. Educational professionals implement policy changes (for example, adding more computers in classrooms). Finally, policies are evaluated and changes are considered. Here, the Texas education commissioner Mike Morath visits a middle school classroom in Dallas.

scratch every year. Year in and year out, there is a general agreement among policy makers on the nature of a public problem and on how it should be addressed. Programs, policies, and budgets tend to grow incrementally from one policy cycle to another.

A second factor is that policy makers and other politically active individuals may not behave strictly rationally or efficiently. The economist Herbert Simon has argued that individual rationality is limited by a number of factors, including the expense of getting information about a problem, the cognitive limitations of the human mind, and the time constraints that all individuals face in making a decision.[11] Rather than seeking to rationally understand everything that is involved in a particular policy problem or optimize every action taken to address this problem, policy makers may simply seek to reach a decision that is satisfactory rather than optimal. This can lead to less-than-rational and less-than-efficient public policy.

To appreciate the process and politics of policy making in Texas, we will turn to a discussion of three policy areas shaping Texas's political life: education, welfare, and health care.

Education Policy

Describe the major issues that have shaped education policy in Texas

Education policy is complex. There is no one education "problem" that has been identified to drive education policy, nor is there just one formulated solution to this problem. Education policy in Texas involves a large number of overlapping problems, each of which has spawned a variety of solutions.

Education is big business in Texas. For the 2020–21 biennium, a projected $49.7 billion in state General Revenue monies went to public education. Local property taxes are projected to contribute $67.0 billion in revenue to local school districts. The federal government contributed an estimated $10.4 billion to fund a variety of education-related programs, including Child Nutrition Grants, No Child Left Behind Grants, disabilities funding, and other formula grants.[12]

There are 1,023 regular school districts in Texas, with over 8,096 public schools as of 2018. More than 5.4 million students were enrolled in public schools in Texas in 2019, second only to California. The student-teacher ratio of 15.1 students per teacher compares favorably with the national average of 16.0. But the average expenditure of $9,375 per student is far below the national average of $12,201. Texas ranked 41st in per capita student expenditure in 2020–21.[13]

Along with the regular school districts there are over 707 open-enrollment charter school campuses serving 296,323 students as of 2016–17. Although funded with public monies, charter schools have been set up as an alternative to traditional public schools, often because the public schools have failed to meet the needs of certain groups of students. Charter schools are in many ways more flexible than public schools, but they must meet the standards set by the state for public schools.[14]

There are many challenges facing educational policy in Texas, but a few stand out. First, there is the low level of public spending per pupil. Second, the demographics are not only increasingly people of color but also increasingly disadvantaged. Of all students, 18.2 percent had "limited English proficiency," 60.6 percent were considered "economically disadvantaged" (meaning they were poor), and 50.1 percent were considered "at risk" (meaning that given their circumstances, they were more likely to fail academically). Not surprisingly, these demographic characteristics often lead to lower performance on national and state tests. Third, Texas students have high dropout rates,[15] particularly among Latinos and African Americans, which affect state and federal efforts to address the problem of poverty. To understand how policy makers are dealing with these challenges, we must look deeper into the making of educational policy since the founding of the state.

The Roots of Education Policy in Texas

Through the first half of the twentieth century, public education was largely a local affair. Schools were funded by local taxes, and decisions such as what to teach and how long the school year would be were made at the local level. Many school systems were chronically

TABLE 12.1

Public Schools in Texas: A Snapshot

Total students	5.4 million
STUDENT DEMOGRAPHICS	
African American	12.6%
Asian	4.4%
Latino	52.4%
White	27.9%
Other	2.7%
At-risk students	50.8%
Economically disadvantaged	58.7%
Limited English proficiency	19.7%
Drop Out Rates all students	1.90%
TEACHER DEMOGRAPHICS	
Total full-time equivalents	358,450
African American	10.5%
Asian	1.7%
Latino	27.7%
White	58.4%
AVERAGE TEACHER SALARIES	
Base average	$54,122
Beginner	$47,218
1–5 years	$50,408
6–10 years	$52,786
11–20 years	$56,041
20+ years	$62,039
SCHOOL FACTS	
Number of school districts and charters	1,200
Number of schools	8,766
Student-teacher ratio	15 to 1
National student-teacher ratio	16 to 1
Charter school campuses	707
PUBLIC SCHOOL STAFF	
Administrators	29,437
Support staff (counselors, librarians, nurses)	70,570
Aides and auxiliary staff	256,192

Source: https://schools.texastribune.org/states/tx/.

Texas has a large and complicated public school system fraught with nearly constant public-policy battles, including that over the level of funding for public schools.

Gilmer-Aikin Laws education reform legislation passed in 1949 that supplemented local funding of education with public monies, raised teachers' salaries, mandated a minimum length for the school year, and provided for more state supervision of public education

short of funds, facing such problems as a shortage of supplies and textbooks, inadequate facilities, and poorly trained teachers. In 1949 the state legislature tried to address some of these problems by passing the **Gilmer-Aikin Laws**, under which school districts were consolidated into 2,900 administrative units, state equalization funding was provided to supplement local taxes, teachers' salaries were raised, and a minimum school year of 175 teaching days was established. In addition, the laws established the Texas Education Agency (TEA), originally known as the State Department of Education, to supervise public education in the state.

The Gilmer-Aikin Laws also established the elected 21-member State Board of Education as the policy-making body for public education, selecting budgets, establishing regulations for school accreditation, executing contracts for the purchase of textbooks, and investing in the Permanent School Fund. The board also has the power to appoint a commissioner of education, subject to confirmation by the Texas Senate, who serves a four-year term as the chief executive officer for the TEA. The TEA is responsible for setting standards for public schools and for handling federal funds related to public education. For the next 70 years, educational policy in the state would work through the overall institutional framework established by the Gilmer-Aikin Laws.[16]

Three specific challenges have played major roles in Texas educational policy over the last 50 years: desegregation, equity in funding, and the search for educational excellence. Each has its own set of policy formulations, implementation procedures, and evaluative processes.

Desegregation

Few problems have troubled educational policy in Texas, and given rise to such controversial policy formulations or implementations, as much as desegregation.

Segregation of the races was provided for under the Texas Constitution of 1876 and upheld by the U.S. Supreme Court in *Plessy v. Ferguson* (1896) through the now-infamous "separate but equal" doctrine. In Texas, as elsewhere across the South, segregated schools may have been separate, but they were far from equal. In the 1920s and '30s, for example, Texas spent an average of one-third less per student on the education of African American students than on White students.[17]

The U.S. Supreme Court overturned *Plessy v. Ferguson* in the 1954 case *Brown v. Board of Education*, ruling that state-imposed segregation in schools violated the **equal protection clause** of the Fourteenth Amendment. School districts were ordered to desegregate their school systems "with all deliberate speed." In Texas the San Antonio school district became one of the first in the nation to comply with the order, but other districts in the state, such as Houston's, were much slower.

The desegregation of public schools was hampered by political opposition at both the local and state levels. In 1957 the Texas legislature passed laws encouraging school districts to resist federally ordered desegregation, although then-governor Price Daniel, Sr., chose to ignore them.[18] By the late 1960s legally segregated schools were largely a thing of the past. Nevertheless, de facto segregation remains a problem, particularly in urban areas with large minority populations. As in many other urban areas across the country, many middle- and upper-income Whites in Texas abandoned urban public school systems for suburban public schools or private schools.

equal protection clause provision in the Fourteenth Amendment of the U.S. Constitution guaranteeing citizens the "equal protection of the laws"; this clause has been the basis for the civil rights of African Americans, women, and other groups

Equity in Funding

In addition to *Brown v. Board of Education*, two later court cases have played a major role in shaping education policy and politics in Texas over the last 50 years: *San Antonio v. Rodríguez* and *Edgewood ISD v. Kirby*. These cases forced policy makers to look at the funding problems of education in a new light and to formulate new solutions to address these problems.

San Antonio v. Rodríguez

San Antonio v. Rodríguez was a landmark case involving the constitutionality of using property taxes to fund public schools.[19] Lawyers for eight children in the poor Edgewood independent school district (ISD) in the San Antonio area argued that the system of financing public schools based on local property taxes was unfair. The Edgewood school district had one of the highest property tax rates in the country, but it could raise only $37 per pupil. Meanwhile the neighboring school district of Alamo Heights was able to raise $413 per pupil with a much lower property tax rate. The reason was that the value of the property subject to taxation in Alamo Heights far exceeded that in Edgewood.

In 1971 a federal district court ruled that the Texas school finance system was unconstitutional under the equal protection clause of the Fourteenth Amendment to the U.S. Constitution. However, on appeal to the U.S. Supreme Court, the decision was overturned. In 1973 the Court ruled 5–4 that the clause did not require states such as Texas to subsidize poorer school districts.

Edgewood ISD v. Kirby

The second landmark case involving the financing of public schools was *Edgewood ISD v. Kirby*. Unlike *Rodríguez*, *Edgewood* considered whether the system of funding public schools through local property taxes fulfilled the Texas State Constitution's provisions on education. Much of the litigation over the next few years would center on Article 7, Section 1, of the 1876 Constitution, which read:

A general diffusion of knowledge being essential to the preservation of the liberties and rights of the people, it shall be the duty of the Legislature of the State to establish and make suitable provision for the support and maintenance of an efficient system of free public schools.

A key constitutional issue would be exactly what constituted a "general diffusion of knowledge" and an "efficient system of free public schools."

On behalf of the Edgewood ISD, the Mexican American Legal Defense and Education Fund sued William Kirby, the state commissioner of education, in 1984. Initially, only 8 school districts were represented in the case. By the time the case was finally decided, however, 67 other districts had joined the original plaintiffs. The plaintiffs argued that the state's reliance on local property taxes to fund public education discriminated against poor children by denying them equal opportunities in education. One month after the original case was filed, the legislature passed a modest reform measure that increased state aid to poor districts. In 1985, however, the plaintiffs filed an amended lawsuit arguing that the legislature's action was far from satisfactory.

A state district judge ruled in favor of the plaintiffs, a decision that was reversed by the state appeals court. But in 1989, in a 9–0 decision, the Texas Supreme Court held that the funding system was, indeed, in violation of the state constitution. The court held that education was a fundamental right under the Texas Constitution and that the "glaring disparities" between rich and poor schools violated the efficiency clause of the constitution. Although it did not demand "absolute equality" in per pupil spending, the court did require a standard of "substantially equal access to similar revenues per pupil at similar levels of tax effort."[20] It ordered the legislature to implement an equitable system by the 1990–91 school year.

The ruling touched off a political firestorm that swept through Texas politics throughout the 1990s and into the first two decades of the twenty-first century. Over the years, various courts held various funding provisions for public education to be unconstitutional, and the legislature responded with various fixes, one of which was dubbed the "Robin Hood" plan because it transferred funds from rich to poor districts.

The back-and-forth wrangling over funding public education came to a head in 2013 when state district judge John Dietz ruled that the state had violated the constitution by underfunding schools during the 2011 session,[21] but his ruling was not the last say in the matter. On May 13, 2016, the Texas Supreme Court overruled Judge Dietz's decision and declared the existing funding system to be constitutional. Acknowledging that the system was "Byzantine," "undeniably imperfect," and open to improvement, the all-Republican court held, with no dissents, that it met the minimum constitutional provisions for the "general diffusion of knowledge." Further, the court stated that its job was not to second-guess the legislature when it came to the best funding of public education.[22]

The importance of this decision to public education policy cannot be stressed enough. It had two immediate effects. First, state courts were taken out of the policy-making process regarding financing public education for the first time since the original *Edgewood* decision in 1989. Second, the debate over equity and financing public education was pushed firmly into the legislative budgetary process.

The New Debate over Funding Public Education Giving the legislature primary responsibility to resolve funding questions has not been without its challenges. There are essentially two sources that fund public education in the state:

Who Attends Public School in Texas?

Two factors have played a role in shaping the demographics of the children attending Texas urban public schools since *Brown v. Board of Education*. First, the state has become more diverse, with a growing Latino presence in large urban areas. Second, while African American attendance has remained steady, White attendance has not. In major cities like Houston and Dallas, Whites have moved to suburban school districts, leaving the largest urban school districts to serve populations of color, particularly Latinos. While Texas schools are legally desegregated, there is de facto segregation in public education across much of the state.

Demographics of Selected Houston-Area School Districts, 2017–18

District	White	African American	Latino	Other	Total students
1. Aldine	2.2%	22.7%	72.9%	2.2%	67,234
2. Alief	4.0%	29.0%	52.4%	14.6%	46,223
3. Channelview	7.4%	11.3%	78.4%	2.9%	9,643
4. Cypress–Fairbanks	24.8%	18.2%	44.3%	12.7%	116,138
5. Friendswood	70.2%	1.8%	17.6%	10.4%	6,047
6. Houston	8.8%	24.0%	61.7%	5.5%	213,528
7. Huffman	73.9%	2.3%	21.8%	2.0%	3,517
8. Spring	7.9%	39.9%	45.6%	6.6%	36,079

Percentage of White Students in Houston-Area School Districts

Under 5.0%   5.1–10.0%   10.1–25.0%   25.1–50.0%   Above 50.0%

Public School Enrollment by Race versus Texas State Population, 2017–18

Latino

Enrollment
52.4%

State population
39.6%

African American

Enrollment
12.6%

State population
12.8%

White

Enrollment
27.8%

State population
41.5%

Other

Enrollment
7.2%

State population
6.0%

SOURCES: Schools.texastribune.org/districts; Texas Education Agency, Enrollment Trends, tea.texas.gov.

QUANTITATIVE REASONING

- Drawing on the data and the map, develop an argument that, despite *Brown v. Board of Education*, public schools in Texas are still segregated.

- What factors might account for this segregation? Should policy makers be concerned about de facto segregation of public school districts? What should policy makers do?

general revenue funding from the state and funding from local property taxes. During the 2017 legislative session, legislators cut $600 million from general revenue funding of public education in the face of a looming budget deficit. This cut came on top of the legislature's refusal to spend an additional $4 billion to keep funding levels per student equal to those of the previous biennium. Legislators expected that increases in local property taxes of up to 7 percent per year would bridge the state spending shortfall. This shift from state to local funding of public education reflected a long-term trend. In 2008 the state covered 48.5 percent of the cost of public education. By 2019, state support had dropped to 38 percent.[23]

The shifting burden of public school funding from state general revenues to local property taxes, in turn, sparked a new controversy: bringing rising property taxes under control. Lieutenant Governor Patrick and Governor Abbott both came out in favor of legislation that would preempt local governments from raising taxes significantly without the support of a referendum vote (see Chapter 10). A special finance commission was set up to hold hearings around the state and delivered a report on the problems of funding public education before the next legislative session in 2019.

Funding public education and property tax reform were the two most important issues to come before the state legislature during the 2019 regular session. One hundred and twenty bills related to education issues passed during the 2019 session, including $6 billion in new funding and about $5 billion in property tax relief.[24]

Educational Excellence and Accountability in Texas

Whereas the debate over equity in public education was touched off by litigation, a different set of factors has driven the debate over the quality of education in the state and how best to promote educational excellence. The beginning of the debate in Texas over these issues was actually part of a larger national debate over the state of education in the United States.[25] A 1983 report by the National Commission on Excellence in Education, *A Nation at Risk*, identified a number of crises in the nation's educational system. Test scores were declining, and functional illiteracy was on the rise. Students were simply not equipped with the intellectual skills required in the modern world. If steps were not taken soon to reform education in the United States, the report argued, the nation was at risk of falling behind in the rapidly changing world of international competition.[26]

Educational reform was put on the state agenda in 1983 when the legislature established the Select Committee on Public Education (SCOPE),[27] which was intended both to figure out how to fund pay raises for teachers and to evaluate the entire system of public education in the state. In the end, SCOPE presented 140 recommendations for reform in its final report on April 19, 1984. Among the most controversial was "No Pass, No Play," under which students who failed to earn a passing grade of 70 could not participate in any extracurricular activities for the next six-week grading period. But "No Pass, No Play" was only the tip of the iceberg. Other proposals created new standards for students' attendance and performance; annual school performance reports and tighter accreditation standards, with schools that did not meet the standards losing state funds; a longer school year—extended from 175 to 180 days; and a professional career ladder

One means of encouraging educational excellence has been to allow students to transfer from low-performing to high-performing schools. Charter schools are promoting competition among the schools and allowing parents more choices.

for teachers that tied pay raises to performance.[28] In July 1984 many of the reform proposals were put into place in a 266-page education reform bill, along with the necessary accompanying tax increases.

A second round in the debate over excellence and accountability in the public school system opened during the 1995 legislative session. There was strong business and bipartisan support for reforms that supported increased accountability through testing. But there were some important differences from the SCOPE reforms in the reform package finally signed by Republican governor George W. Bush. The SCOPE reforms had generally centralized control over education policy in the state. The Bush reforms, in contrast, gave more discretion to local school districts to achieve the educational goals the state was mandating. Some of them were symbolic. The controversial "No Pass, No Play" rule was relaxed, cutting the period of nonparticipation from six to three weeks and lifting a ban on practicing while on scholastic probation. But other changes were more substantive. Local control of public schools was increased by limiting the power of the TEA. Local voters were empowered to adopt home charters that could free their school districts from many state requirements. The 1995 reforms also enabled students under certain circumstances to transfer from low-performing schools to high-performing schools in their districts, thus promoting competition among schools by holding them accountable for the performance of their students.[29]

One of the most controversial aspects of the reform movement was the development of statewide assessment standards. "Testing," as assessment came to be known, was first instituted in 1986 with the Texas Educational Assessment of Minimal Skills (TEAMS) exams, which sought to certify that students from all districts met certain minimum academic expectations. Students had to pass TEAMS to be eligible to receive a high school diploma. Two subsequent testing initiatives were ultimately replaced by the State of Texas Assessments of Academic Readiness (STAAR), 15 end-of-course exams across

Efforts to improve the quality of the Texas public school education and student outcomes have taken different forms over the years. Statewide testing and methods of school evaluation have met with backlash from teachers and legislators alike. However, schools continue to innovate to achieve better outcomes for students, like using special desks (pictured here) to keep children active while learning.

the curriculum for grades 9 through 12 beginning in 2011. The idea was to have passing standards increased with subsequent administrations of the exam. Schools would be held accountable for their student performances. In the process, it was hoped that public education in Texas would ratchet upward in quality.

Unfortunately, high-minded expectations were dashed as failure rates stayed stubbornly high. In 2012 the TEA reported that passing rates on five of the STAAR end-of-course exams ranged from 87 percent in biology to 55 percent in English writing. Although failing students were allowed to retake the test, fears began to mount about the impact that failure rates would have on retention and graduation rates. In addition, a storm brewed up out of the classrooms as teachers and administrators complained about the growing need to teach to the tests.[30]

Support among business and political elites for an expanded, intensified set of tests to reform public education collapsed during the 2013 legislative session. As we discussed in the introduction to Chapter 6, new groups with different interests emerged to challenge the consensus around accountability and testing that had driven educational reform policy for 25 years. Under House bill 5, the state legislature cut the number of required end-of-course tests from 15 to 5. The idea of testing to promote academic excellence was not abandoned completely, but it no longer held center stage for reformers. As state senator Dan Patrick, the chair of the Senate Public Education Committee, noted, "By the elimination of 15 [tests] to 5 . . . that could save 40 or more days of testing, give teachers more time to teach, be innovative and creative."[31]

In 2015 the state legislature moved toward an accountability system that would evaluate schools on an A–F scale, replacing the old pass/fail system. Many educators rejected the scale, arguing that it relied too much on the standardized tests that were still being given, rather than how schools were improving. In 2017 the legislature tried again and finally passed a compromise bill on the last day of the session that proposed to evaluate schools on three dimensions: student achievement, student progress, and a "closing the gaps" measure. Elementary and middle schools would focus on the results of standardized state exams while high schools would look at graduation rates and the rates of students taking advanced courses. No one was completely satisfied with the final results, and many interest groups were upset that they were not able to weigh in on the final version of the compromise bill. Most interested parties expected that the issue of accountability and testing would come up again in the next legislative session.[32]

Education Policy in a New Era

One might have hoped that the educational reforms of the past 30 years would have ushered in an era of rising educational attainment in Texas in the twenty-first century. This has not happened. New problems identified by policy makers in recent years have led to new initiatives to overhaul education in the state. Despite the efforts of policy makers, teachers' salaries and overall state and local spending on public education have remained low compared with those in other states, as have graduation rates. In 2017 the average SAT scores in Texas were 515 in reading and 507 in math, compared with a national average of 531 in reading and 528 in math.[33] Although the dropout rate in grades 7 through 12 has been declining since the 1990s, it has remained high among people of color.

For a few years at the turn of the century, scores on standardized tests improved across the state, leading many to think that developing new assessment tests would succeed in holding teachers and schools more accountable. But with the implementation of the more rigorous STAAR assessments, overall student performance stayed flat or fell on various tests. More disturbingly, there appeared to be a growing "achievement gap" as people of color and at-risk students failed at higher rates than Whites in consecutive iterations of the tests.[34]

Vouchers and Charter Schools The perceived failure of reform efforts based on testing and accountability led some to advocate new ideas in public education. One new idea—actually an old idea from the early 1960s—being offered by conservatives, particularly in the Tea Party wing of the Republican Party, is vouchers. The basic idea of vouchers is simple: increase competition in the school system by letting funding follow the students. If a public school doesn't work, let parents and students opt out of it and take their funding with them.[35] Among the recurring criticisms of voucher-based reform is that middle- and upper-middle-income students will leave poorer students behind in poorly funded public schools.

An alternative to vouchers has been available to some in Texas through open-enrollment charter schools. Like vouchers, the idea of charter schools is to make more options available to parents and students, particularly in places where schools are underperforming. As part of a larger 1995 reform package, the legislature authorized the establishment of charter schools that would have increased flexibility to deliver education to student populations with special needs. Working under their own charters and granted the freedom to manage their own schools, charter schools operate under the TEA and receive their own accountability ranking based on test scores. While they receive state monies, as of 2019 they do not receive local tax revenue or, in most cases, funding for facilities. Charter schools are able to receive privately raised funds.

The criticisms of charter schools resemble, in some ways, the criticisms of vouchers. Opponents fear that charter schools will drain money from public schools. While serving the needs of their specially identified student bodies, some suggest that they will distract attention away from the needs of other, possibly more needy groups. In addition, there is some concern that charter schools will not be able to meet the challenges of educating youth any better than traditional public schools.[36]

Increased Funding A third alternative to current education policy is rather simple: spend more money, a lot more money. Here, the idea is that Texas schools fail because they are woefully underfunded. Salaries of teachers are too low, and state regulations on the curriculum and classroom are too great. Get the best teachers in the

Does the state spend too much, too little, or about right on primary and secondary education?

How much state money should be spent on elementary and secondary education? How are education spending priorities to be balanced against other budgetary priorities such as health care or higher education? When addressing these questions, legislators often look to public opinion for guidance. As the following figure shows, Republicans think differently from Democrats when it comes to evaluating whether the state spends too much, too little, or the right amount on primary or secondary schools. Given these data, do you think the legislature will spend more on education in the future?

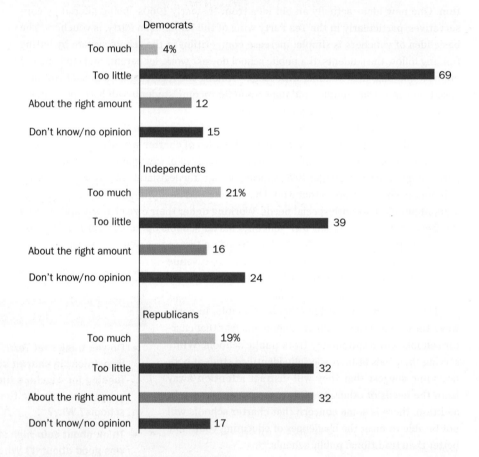

SOURCE: University of Texas/*Texas Tribune* Poll, The Texas Project at the University of Texas at Austin, February 14, 2020, p. 241.

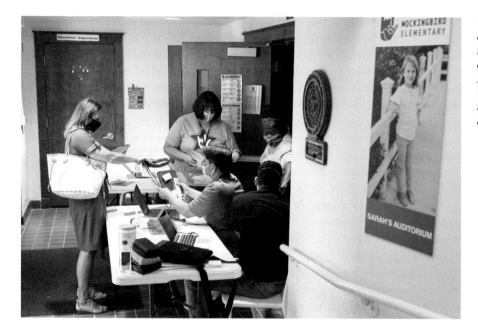

Virtual education during the coronavirus pandemic revealed inequalities in Texas public education. Here, Mockingbird Elementary School in Dallas, Texas, distributes equipment to families to facilitate remote learning.

classroom, some argue, and the problem of public education will be able to right itself. Vouchers and charter schools are seen as threats to this alternative.

Interestingly, the public appears to be in favor of increased expenditures going to public education, but it splits along partisan lines. A poll conducted by the University of Texas in 2017 found that 71 percent of Texans believed that increasing pay to teachers would be an extremely effective or somewhat effective way of improving public education in Texas, including 91 percent of Democrats and 58 percent of Republicans. Even 41 percent of self-identified Tea Partyers agreed. But when respondents were asked if increasing overall funding would be effective, a different story emerged. Eighty-two percent of Democrats agreed that increased overall funding would improve public education, but only 50 percent of Republicans did. One of the problems facing policy makers in the future will be formulating reform proposals amid a divided electorate.[37]

Public Education and the Coronavirus Pandemic

In the spring of 2020 the coronavirus pandemic disrupted public education in Texas. Not since 1919 had the country or state experienced such a rapidly spreading contagion, one that threatened to overwhelm the health care delivery system in Texas. The public schools were seen to be incubators for the virus and local and state officials felt that some actions had to be taken to contain the growing threat. On March 19, 2020, Governor Abbott issued an executive order that temporarily closed schools—along with restaurants, gyms, and bars—across the state until April 3.[38] The shutdown was then extended until May 4 and then to the end of the school year. STAAR testing was canceled for the 2019–20 academic year. School districts scrambled to find ways to complete the academic year by offering academic work online. Curriculums and assessment had to be reconceived and prepared for delivery. Teachers and students had to learn how to use new software such as Zoom, Teams, Webex, and Skype and then how to deliver the classes over the internet.

Virtual education exacerbated many of the inequalities found in Texas's public school system. Middle-class and wealthier students often had access to computers and internet service at home, though many poorer students did not. But even these wealthier students found themselves competing for computer and internet time with their parents, many of whom had to work while sheltering at home. Efforts were made by school districts to get less well-off students access to computers and internet hotspots so they could access online classes, but these efforts were far from being successful. Public officials welcomed the end of the school year in May and began to wonder what the future held in store.

Throughout the late spring and early summer, a variety of plans for opening the public schools in the fall were being brought forward, ranging from remaining fully virtual to staggering student attendance throughout the school week to opening schools completely. Decisions about how schools would operate in the 2020–21 academic year likely would take place at the school district level but could easily be affected by statewide or countywide public health orders. Most experts agreed that the key component of any reopening would be student safety. Barring an effective vaccine, this meant that reopening would have to take place under conditions of social distancing where students maintained a safe distance from one another, and effective testing and tracing of students who came down with the disease. These are difficult conditions to meet in a school environment. One thing was clear: the challenges facing public education would be difficult until the coronavirus was brought under control.

Welfare Policy

Describe the state's role in addressing poverty and how it is affected by national policies

Another long-term policy issue in Texas has been how to provide for the basic needs of poor people in the state. This issue raises fundamental questions about the state's role in helping people in poverty and the extent to which national policies determine the state's response to the needs of the poor. Welfare policy is a clear example of how changes in problem identification and formulation can lead to an overhaul in policy implementation and evaluation.

Poverty in Texas

Poverty has never been an easy topic to talk about in Texas. The idea that some individuals have trouble taking care of themselves or meeting the basic needs of their families seems to fly in the face of Texas's individualistic culture. In light of the booming Texas economy through much of the twenty-first century, many policy makers seem to have hoped that the poverty problem would go away. It hasn't.

Policy makers define "poverty" in very specific terms: it is the condition under which individuals or families do not have the resources to meet their basic needs, including food, shelter, health care, transportation, and clothing. The U.S. Department of Health and Human Services' "poverty index" calculates the consumption requirements of families based on their size and composition. The poverty index is adjusted every year to account for the rate of inflation. Although there is considerable controversy as to whether it adequately measures the minimal needs of a family, the poverty index is the generally accepted standard against which poverty is measured.

Though poverty in Texas afflicts many different social groups, Latinos currently make up the majority of Texans living below the poverty line. The border counties in Texas are by far the poorest in the state.

In 2019, 13.6 percent of Texans (over 3.8 million people) lived below the poverty line. The five counties of more than 10,000 residents with the highest percentage of people living in poverty were along the border: Willacy County (35.0 percent), Starr County (33.2 percent), Zavala County (32.0 percent), Cameron County (27.9 percent), Hidalgo County (30.0 percent), and Zapata County (28.4 percent). The counties with the lowest were three in the Dallas–Fort Worth area, Rockwall County (5.1 percent), Collin County (6.4 percent), and Denton County (7.3 percent); one north of Austin, Williamson County (6.4 percent); and two north of San Antonio, Kendall County (7.5 percent) and Comal County (7.1 percent). In addition, in 2019, a total of 3.9 million people (approximately 13.4 percent of all residents of Texas) were enrolled in Medicaid, the federally financed, state-operated program providing medical services to low-income people, and over 3.4 million people participated in the nation's most important anti-hunger program, the Supplemental Nutritional Assistance Program (SNAP). Poverty remains one of the most intractable problems facing the state.[39]

In 2020 the federal poverty guideline was $12,760 a year for one person and $4,480 a year for each additional person in the family. In 2019 the U.S. Census Bureau calculated that 13.6 percent of Texans lived in poverty, 12th worst in the nation among the states.[40] A study conducted by the Henry J. Kaiser Family Foundation in 2019 found that over 18.7 percent of Latinos, 18.4 percent of African Americans, and 7.9 percent of Whites in Texas are poor. Of those over the age of 65 in Texas, 10.5 percent are poor compared with 9.2 percent in the nation as a whole. Poverty among children under age 18 is much higher in Texas (19 percent) than in the United States as a whole (16.6 percent).[41]

Texas uses federal poverty guidelines to determine eligibility for a variety of social programs. For example, a family of three is eligible for reduced-price school meals if the family is at no more than 185 percent of the poverty level. A family of three is eligible for free school meals and food stamps (the Supplemental Nutritional Assistance Program or SNAP) if the family is at no more than 130 percent of the poverty level.

The Texas Health and Human Services Commission (HHS)—which since 2003 has overseen the Department of Family and Protective Services, the Department of Assistive and Rehabilitative Services, the Department of Aging and Disability Services, and the Department of State Health Services—is responsible for coordinating, determining eligibility for, and administering the major welfare and antipoverty programs in Texas (see Table 12.2). These programs include Temporary Assistance for Needy Families (TANF), a welfare program for families with dependent children; Medicaid; SNAP; and other programs to address family violence, provide disaster relief, and settle refugees. The appropriated budget for HHS programs in the 2020–21 biennium was $76.7 billion, with an

TABLE 12.2

Agency Budgets for the 2020–21 Biennium, All Funds

Health and Human Services Commission	$76.7 billion
Department of Family and Protective Services	$4.42 billion
Department of State Health Services	$1.7 billion
TOTAL	$82.8 billion

SOURCE: Texas Legislative Budget Board, *Fiscal Size-Up: 2020–21 Biennium* (May 2020), p. 162.

additional $4.4 billion allocated to the Department of Family and Protective Services (see the introduction to this chapter for a discussion of DFPS) and $1.7 billion allocated to the Department of Health Services. HHS agencies employ almost 41,000 state workers at more than 1,000 locations.[42]

Poverty is a complicated policy issue in Texas. There are more than 200 programs administered by HHS that are aimed at different problems related to poverty. We will now focus attention on two of the most important of these initiatives: welfare, in this section, and health care financing, in the following section. Understanding how these programs evolved over time and the reforms that have been put into place over the past 20 years will shed considerable light on public-policy making in the state.

New Deal President Franklin Delano Roosevelt's 1930s programs to stimulate the national economy and provide relief to victims of the Great Depression

Medicaid a federal and state program financing medical services to low-income people

Welfare in Texas, 1935–1996

The origins of modern welfare policy lie in President Franklin Delano Roosevelt's **New Deal**.[43] Prior to the 1930s welfare was considered a state and local responsibility. The Great Depression overwhelmed many state and local welfare arrangements, however, causing the federal government to expand its role in addressing the needs of the poor and the unemployed. The Social Security Act of 1935 transformed the way in which welfare policy was implemented in the United States. States administered and determined the benefit levels for a series of welfare programs, but in exchange for federal assistance in funding, the programs had to meet certain minimum federal guidelines.

The Department of Public Welfare was established in Texas in 1939 to run the state's various public assistance programs.[44] Its name would eventually be changed to the Department of Health and Human Services in 2003, reflecting a shift in policy makers' desire to think of the agency less as a welfare provider and more as a service agency to people in poverty.

In the 1960s new federal programs aimed at poverty proliferated.[45] In 1965, Congress established **Medicaid**, a state-federal program to finance health care for the poor. President Lyndon Johnson's "War on Poverty" also expanded the number of social service programs available to the poor. Increasingly, it was argued, the solution to alleviating

The Texas Department of Public Welfare was established in 1939 during the New Deal. This photo shows farmers receiving support from the government at the time.

poverty was through expanded federal control over welfare programs. In 1972 a new federal program called **Supplemental Security Income (SSI)** replaced earlier state-federal antipoverty programs for the elderly, the blind, and the permanently disabled. Between 1967 and 1973 participation rates and expenditures for welfare in Texas exploded. The number of children on the nation's major welfare program, **Aid to Families with Dependent Children (AFDC)**, more than quadrupled, from 80,000 to 325,000, while the number of families on AFDC more than quintupled, from 23,000 to 120,000. Rates leveled off in the late 1970s but began to push upward again in the 1980s.

The Idea of Dependency and Welfare Reform in the 1990s

By the mid-1980s a new critique of welfare programs had begun to emerge, which led to a new understanding of what the problem of poverty was and how solutions might be developed to address it. At its heart lay the idea that the well-intentioned policies of the 1960s had backfired and created a dysfunctional underclass of people dependent on welfare. Programs such as AFDC may have helped people financially in the short run, but in the long run, some argued, they had robbed people of the character traits and moral values that would enable them to succeed in a market economy.[46] These critics believed that the skyrocketing rate of children born to poor, unwed mothers was in part the result of a perverse set of incentives created by welfare programs. Under the existing welfare system, at least to a point, the more children one had, the higher one's welfare payment. Because some states, including Texas, did not provide welfare to families with fathers in the home, fathers were actually being encouraged to abandon their families so that the families might qualify for welfare. According to critics, the poor didn't need a permanent source of income from the state; they needed encouragement and proper incentives to become independent workers.

Growing discontent over welfare policy across the country encouraged many states, including Texas, to seek waivers from federal regulations so that they might experiment with reform.[47] Welfare became an issue during the 1994 state elections. The winner of that year's governor's race, Republican George W. Bush, echoed conservative critics of the welfare system, arguing that it was robbing people of their independence. Among the changes he called for were

- strengthening child support procedures and penalties
- imposing a two-year limit on benefits for recipients able to work
- requiring individuals receiving welfare to accept a state-sponsored job if after two years they were unable to find work
- creating new child-care and job-training programs
- requiring unwed mothers to live with their parents or grandparents
- moving family support systems from the state to the local level

Data released by the comptroller, John Sharp, a Democrat, lent support to Bush's contention that there were serious problems with the existing system of welfare in Texas. Over one-quarter of all welfare recipients in 1993 were "long-term" recipients who had remained on the rolls for five years or more. The publication of *A Partnership for*

Supplemental Security Income (SSI) a national welfare program passed in 1972 that provides assistance to low-income elderly or disabled individuals; replaced the federal-state programs that had offered assistance to the blind, the permanently and totally disabled, and the aged

Aid to Families with Dependent Children (AFDC) a federally and state-financed program for children living with parents or relatives who fell below state standards of need; replaced in 1996 by TANF

In 2019 over 3.4 million Texans participated in the food stamps program (now called SNAP), which allows low-income people to buy groceries with a special debit card. SNAP benefits are paid by the federal government, but the state and federal governments share administrative costs.

Independence: Welfare Reform in Texas by the comptroller's office helped to set the legislative agenda for the debate over welfare policy. The report documented how welfare often failed to help those most in need and how it encouraged those already on it to become dependent on government largesse. Among the report's 100 proposals were many of the reforms that had been implemented by conservative reformers in other states.

A bipartisan legislative coalition ultimately supported major welfare reform in Texas. On May 26, 1995, the vote on House bill 1863 was 128 to 9 in the House and 30 to 1 in the Senate. The law provided a number of "carrot and stick" incentives that sought to mold the character of welfare recipients in positive ways and wean them off welfare. Among the carrots were expanded education and job-training programs, as well as pilot studies involving transitional child care and medical benefits. Among the sticks were a limitation on benefits to 36 months, alimony for ex-spouses in poverty who couldn't support themselves, and a five-year ban on reapplying for benefits once they ran out. To implement the state reforms, Texas secured a waiver that freed the state from various federal regulations regarding welfare programs. In granting the waivers to Texas and other states, President Bill Clinton's administration hoped to stimulate innovative reforms that might be duplicated elsewhere.

Texas was ahead of the welfare reform curve in 1995. In 1996, Clinton signed into law the most important reform in federal welfare policy since the New Deal. The Personal Responsibility and Work Opportunity Reconciliation Act essentially rethought the assumptions that had guided the expansion of welfare programs for 60 years. Under the legislation, AFDC, JOBS (a work-related training program), and the Emergency Assistance Program were combined into one block grant titled **Temporary Assistance for Needy Families (TANF)**. As with the welfare reforms instituted in Texas and other states, the primary purpose of TANF was to make families self-sufficient by ending the cycle of dependency on government benefits. States were given great flexibility in setting benefit levels, eligibility requirements, and other program details.

Today in Texas, TANF provides temporary financial assistance to single-parent and two-parent families in which one or both parents are unemployed or have a disability.[48] (The program also provides a onetime $1,000 payment to individuals in certain crisis situations.) To qualify for TANF, a recipient's income must be less than $188 a month for a family of three (one parent and two dependent children). People participating in TANF receive a monthly assistance payment based on the size of their family. They cannot receive this assistance for more than 60 months, but they are also eligible for Medicaid benefits, SNAP, and child day-care services. Unless legally exempt, recipients are also required to participate in an employment services program, attend parenting skills classes, get vaccines for their children, make sure their children go to school, and agree not to abuse drugs or alcohol.

The maximum monthly grant available to a household of three under TANF is low, only $303 a month for a home with one parent. For the 2020–2021 biennium, TANF expenditures were projected to be $96.3 million, including $86.5 million from General Revenue Funds and the remainder from the federal government. This expenditure has been dropping significantly since 1995 due to decreasing caseloads brought on by welfare reform at the national level.[49]

Temporary Assistance for Needy Families (TANF) a welfare program passed in 1996 to provide temporary assistance to families with needy children; replacing the AFDC program, TANF sought to make poor families self-sufficient and to give states greater flexibility in setting benefit levels, eligibility requirements, and other program details

Evaluating Welfare Reforms

Texas is now into its third decade of welfare policy as reformed by the state and federal government in the 1990s. The success of the welfare reforms in Texas has been evaluated along a number of dimensions, two of which stand out.

Judged by changes in the number of people on welfare, the reforms appear to be a success. The average monthly number of people on welfare in Texas rose from a little more than 500,000 in 1989 to a peak of more than 750,000 in 1994, then began to fall after the 1995 reforms. The decline in the number of people on welfare continued over the next decade, falling to approximately 156,000 people in 2006 and to approximately 40,000 in early 2020. Of these recipients, 86 percent are children.[50]

Judged by a second measure—the number of people moving from welfare to work— the results of the 1995 reforms have been more mixed. Studies over the past decade have found that the caseload for TANF has fallen and that the workforce in Texas has grown as the Great Recession has faded from memory. Fewer individuals are relying on TANF for their income. Poverty measures have also fallen in Texas, as the percentage of those in Texas living in poverty fell to 13.6 percent. Jobs have generally seemed to be available for people willing and able to work.

But some statistics trouble policy makers as they evaluate the success of the welfare reforms. In 2019 Texas's overall poverty rate of 13.6 percent and the percentage of children under the age of 18 in poverty (19 percent) were both high by national standards.[51] Though the welfare reforms instituted in the 1990s and reaffirmed over the next 20 years may have curtailed welfare expenditures to poor people, this simply means that fewer people in poverty are getting cash assistance. In 1995–96, 43 percent of poor families in Texas received TANF funds, compared with 68 percent nationwide. In 2015–16, the numbers had dropped to 4 percent in Texas and 23 percent nationwide. One study found that of the 619,400 families living in poverty in Texas and 282,400 families living in deep poverty in Texas, only 26,400 received TANF in 2015–16.[52] Little has happened since 2017 to change these figures.

Public spending on monetary assistance programs such as TANF has declined sharply over the last 20 years as the number of people enrolled in the program has declined. At the same time, however, funding for non-cash assistance programs has more than tripled during the same time period and is now over $700 million in Texas. As welfare rolls and expenditures have declined, Texas has used the federal block grant funds allocated to it to fund antipoverty initiatives to cover a wide range of other programs, including Child Protective Services, the program we discussed in the introduction to this chapter. Other block grant monies have gone to early childhood intervention services and mental health state hospitals. In the 2018–19 budget, $3 million of this block grant money will go to abortion alternative programs, and $4 million a year will go to the Texas Education Agency for "school improvement and support programs." The welfare reforms of the 1990s have not eliminated poverty by making people in poverty more independent. But the reforms have clearly redirected the way in which Texas addresses the needs of poor people in the state, away from cash assistance and toward social services.[53]

Welfare and the Coronavirus The coronavirus pandemic may be changing how Texans perceive and experience poverty and how the state may be responding to it in the future.

Although he had issued an executive order closing public schools in mid-March, Governor Abbott had resisted issuing a shelter-in-place policy throughout the state. He encouraged local officials to institute more restrictive policies if they deemed it appropriate to prevent the spread of the disease in their communities. In late March local county judges from many of the larger counties such as Dallas, Harris, Travis, and Bexar counties did precisely that, ordering shelter-in-place policies for their communities.[54] The orders had a devastating impact on local economies. Anything not deemed an "essential business" to the economy ground to a halt. Unemployment rates exploded. Between March and April 2020, over 1.8 million Texans applied for unemployment insurance, more than had applied in all of 2019. The unemployment rate rose from 3.5 percent in February 2020 to 4.7 percent in March and showed no signs of letting up in May. The collapse in the price of oil in the spring only made matters worse, as the oil industry started cutting back on employment for reasons unrelated to the pandemic.

Unemployment affected all income classes, but poor people, who had little savings to begin with, were hit hardest. Food became scarce for many people, including students participating in free-lunch programs at public schools. Many schools continued to provide food to poor students, even though they were closed for classes. In March 2020 the number of people applying for the SNAP program doubled from the previous year, from 114,008 applications in 2019 to 230,809 in 2020. Long lines formed outside food banks that distributed free food to those in need.[55] For many of the less well off, it looked like the beginnings of a new depression, and the existing welfare system was struggling to address the needs of people in poverty in a satisfactory manner.

State leaders such as the governor and the lieutenant governor began calling for policies that would open up the economy almost as soon as it was closed. Getting people back to work would put money in people's pockets and food on their tables. There was a danger that opening the economy could spark a second wave of coronavirus infections throughout Texas, but this had to be balanced against the pressing needs of people needing wages and food. If the economy was not jump-started relatively soon, in late 2020 or early 2021, policy makers likely would have to rethink the entire thrust of welfare policy in the state.

Medicaid and Health Care Policy

Explain why Medicaid in particular and health care policy in general have been so controversial in Texas

Health insurance is a major policy problem facing Texas. People get health insurance from a variety of sources, including employer-provided policies, individually purchased policies, Medicare (a federal program for the elderly), and Medicaid (a state-federal program for poor people). In 2018 an estimated 17.7 percent of Texans were uninsured, the highest percentage of any state and much higher than the 10 percent figure for the U.S. population as a whole. Figure 12.1 shows the breakdown of this uninsured population by age group and race/ethnicity. Approximately 855,800 children under age 18 (18 percent) were without insurance, far above the national average of 14 percent.[56]

Medicaid

Other than health insurance programs established for state employees, Texas's principal policy initiative regarding health care and health insurance is Medicaid, a program closely linked to poverty programs. Medicaid, which provides for the health care of poor

---

FIGURE 12.1

Texas's Uninsured Population by Age and Race/Ethnicity (Estimated)

SOURCES: Texas Health and Human Services Commission, *Texas Medicaid and CHIP Reference Guide*, 12th ed. (February 2018); Henry J. Kaiser Family Foundation, kff.org.

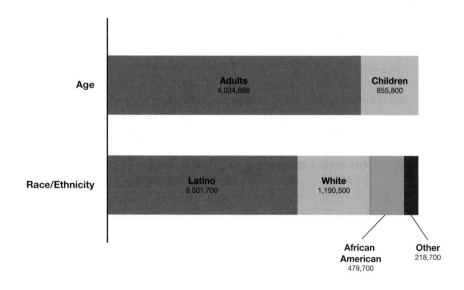

people, particularly poor children, is an especially costly program for the state. The case-load for Medicaid has exploded in recent years, pushed up by the Great Recession and the coronavirus pandemic. For the 2020–21 biennium, $61.5 billion in federal and state funds has been appropriated for the Medicaid program in Texas. Of these funds, $37.9 billion is from the federal government sources, while the remaining $23.6 billion is from state sources. There is an important caveat to these appropriations in that they do not include "full funding for anticipated increases due to medical inflation, higher utilization, or increased acuity." As in recent biennium budgets, the legislature decided to under-fund the Medicaid program for the 2020-21 biennium for now, waiting for a supplemental appropriation in 2023 to make up the difference.[57]

Medicaid is a joint state-federal program established under the Social Security Amendments of 1965 as Title XIX of the Social Security Act. This act requires that Texas and other states follow certain principles and meet certain standards if they are to receive federal money to help fund the program. First, Medicaid services must be available on a statewide basis. Second, the same level of service must be available to all clients throughout the state. Children are entitled to a broader range of services than adults. Third, participants must be allowed to use any health care provider who meets program standards. (Providers, of course, must be willing to accept Medicaid recipients.) Fourth, the amount, duration, and scope of medical services must be "sufficiently reasonable." Exactly what kind and how much of these services are considered "sufficiently reasonable" is vague and often contested, and Medicaid reimbursement rates for providers tend to be much lower than those under conventional private insurance plans. While Texas may limit the services provided to adult clients, it may not arbitrarily deny services for specific conditions or illnesses.

Federal law also allows states to be granted waivers from these principles to create programs directed toward particular clients. In this approach, federal Medicaid policy mirrors the initiatives in welfare policy that give states more freedom of action in developing programs to serve clients.

Medicaid Participation Over the last five decades, Medicaid has grown from a narrowly defined program targeting low-income people on public assistance to a large, complex program serving a variety of special groups. In the late 1980s and early 1990s, Medicaid was expanded to include older adults not fully covered by Medicare, people with disabilities, and pregnant women. Individuals participating in TANF and SSI automatically qualify for Medicaid, as do others who meet these other criteria.

A variety of factors can affect an individual's eligibility to participate in Medicaid. For example, eligibility can change when a parent or caregiver has a change in income, when a child is born, or when a child reaches a certain age. For these reasons, there is significant fluctuation in Medicaid enrollment from month to month. Figure 12.2 shows participation today in Medicaid by gender, age, and race/ethnicity.

Administration and Financing of Medicaid in Texas In Texas, Medicaid is administered through the Texas Health and Human Services Commission. At the federal level, the Centers for Medicare and Medicaid in the Department of Health and Human Services monitor Texas's Medicaid program and establish basic services, delivery, quality, funding, and eligibility standards. Through Medicaid, Texas and the federal government together pay for a variety of health care services for a number of low-income populations, including physicians' bills, inpatient care in a hospital,

FIGURE 12.2

Texas Medicaid Recipients by Gender, Age, and Race/Ethnicity (Estimated)

NOTE: Total numbers fluctuate month by month based on total number of clients.

SOURCES: Texas Health and Human Services Commission, *Texas Medicaid and CHIP in Perspective (The "Pink Book")* (February 2015), chap. 5, pp. 5–14 to 5–15; Texas Health and Human Services Commission, *Texas Medicaid and Chip Reference Guide.*

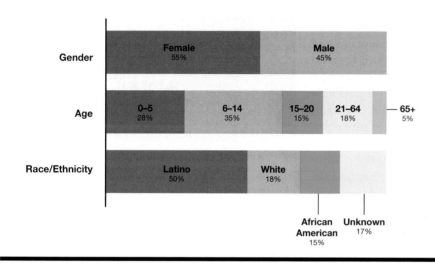

outpatient care, and pharmacy, lab, and X-ray services. Medicaid also provides for selected long-term and support services, including home- and community-based services for the disabled, home-health and personal care, and nursing services. There is no cap on Medicaid expenditures in Texas.

The federal portion of the financing for the program is determined every year by comparing average state per capita income to the average national per capita income. Lower-income states receive a larger share of federal assistance than higher-income states. Each state thus has its own FMAP (federal medical assistance percentage). In 2018 the FMAP for Texas was 58 percent, which means that 42 percent of all Medicaid expenditures were state funded.[58]

A program related to Medicaid is the Children's Health Insurance Program (CHIP), which provides coverage for children in families with incomes too high to qualify for Medicaid. Established in 1997 under Title XXI of the Social Security Act, CHIP is administered like Medicaid through the Centers for Medicare and Medicaid Services in the U.S. Department of Health and Human Services. Federal funds for CHIP are capped, and when a state's cap is reached, no more funds are available. As with Medicaid, there is a match rate based on the state's average per capita income. For Texas, the match rate in 2019 was 93.7 percent, meaning the state only funded 6.3 percent of the CHIP expenditure.

Medicaid and CHIP expenditures have become an increasing part of both the national and the state budgets. In 1996 the total Texas Medicaid budget (both federal and state dollars) was $8.2 billion. For the 2020–21 biennium, the total Medicaid budget in All

Abortion Policy in Texas

1 Why does abortion policy matter?

Abortion laws have been among the most contentious public policies in the United States for the past 50 years. At the heart of the policy debate is a fundamental disagreement over the moral, constitutional, and medical issues involved in abortion. Do women have the freedom to control the medical choices about their bodies? Do women have a constitutional right to terminate a pregnancy? Does the state have an interest in regulating and limiting abortion as a medical procedure? Do fetuses and unborn children have rights that should be protected by the state?

In 1973 the U.S. Supreme Court ruled in *Roe v. Wade* that a woman's right to privacy extended to her decision to have an abortion. This right was balanced, however, by the state's interest in safe and effective medical procedures. The balance has led to considerable controversy over nearly half a century as many state legislatures tried to limit the opportunities for women to have an abortion.

2 What's the debate?

Across the nation, the Republican Party has taken a strong stance against abortion, arguing that abortion should be outlawed. In recent years, Texas Republicans have targeted organizations like Planned Parenthood that provide abortion services around the state, making it increasingly difficult for women to get abortion services. Democrats, in contrast, have tended to support more comprehensive birth control services, including abortion.

Texas passed legislation in 2013 that would have limited the number of abortion clinics in Texas. These restrictions, requiring abortion facilities to be like surgical facilities and requiring doctors providing abortions to have admitting privileges at a nearby hospital, were invalidated by the U.S. Supreme Court in 2016. In the decision *Whole Woman's Health v. Hellerstedt*, the Court reaffirmed a woman's right to abortion services without facing an undue burden imposed by the state. Although there have been other restrictions on abortion passed by the Texas legislature that have wound their way through the court process, *Whole Woman's Health* was upheld by the U.S. Supreme Court in the summer of 2020.

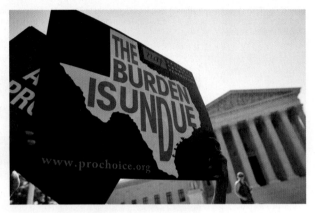

High-profile Supreme Court cases regarding abortion policy often draw protesters to the steps of the Court.

In defending the law, Texas emphasized that the law was designed to improve the standard of care for abortion patients and to improve the health and safety of women obtaining abortions. With passage of the law, Texas argued that there would still be 12 abortion clinics (one of those near El Paso in Santa Teresa, NM) and that 83 percent of women of reproductive age would live within 150 miles of at least 1 of the clinics. By requiring abortion clinics to meet the standards of surgical facilities, 9 clinics had to close, although Texas argued that was the cost of improved health care for women. Additionally, requiring doctors who performed abortions to have admitting privileges at a nearby hospital would reduce communication errors and time delays if women who underwent abortions developed complications. The state noted that 210 women in Texas annually had to be hospitalized after an abortion and this law protected their health and safety.[a]

Opponents of the law argued that abortions were very safe and the law was a burden on women's access to abortion procedures. They noted that abortions were far safer than colonoscopies with a mortality rate of 0.007 percent or liposuction with a mortality rate of 0.02 percent.[b]

Abortions are still legal in Texas. Undue burdens cannot be placed upon women seeking an abortion. But what does that mean? Women have a constitutional right to privacy that prohibits the wholesale outlawing of abortion services. The legislature can continue to demand minimum health and safety standards from abortion providers. But what does that mean concretely after the *Whole Woman's Health* decision? Can legislators regulate abortion providers out of existence in Texas by making it too expensive or by cutting organizations like Planned Parenthood off from state monies? Is it true that abortions are unsafe and need expanded regulations to protect women?

3 What do the numbers say?

At the heart of the current controversy over abortion in Texas is the Republican contention that the state must reduce access to abortion in the interest of public health because abortions are dangerous medical procedures and must meet stricter regulatory guidelines. But what do the numbers say? How safe is an abortion procedure in Texas today without stringent new rules and regulations? Here we present data provided in a brief provided to the U.S. Supreme Court by the American College of Obstetricians and Gynecologists in the case *Whole Woman's Health v. Hellerstedt*.

The Health Risks of Abortion

Total number of abortions in Texas (2001–13)	993,844
Total number of deaths of women in Texas from abortion (2001–13)	5
Risk of death of women in Texas from abortion	0.0005%
Risk of death of women from abortion nationwide	0.00073%
Rate of complications during abortions in Texas	0.05%
Percentage of abortions performed in clinics or doctors' offices in Texas	83%
Percentage of abortions performed in non-hospital settings nationwide	95%

SOURCE: Brief, amicus curiae of the American College of Obstetricians and Gynecologists, *Whole Woman's Health v. Hellerstedt*.

Communicating Effectively: What Do You Think?

- Do the data persuade you that requiring abortion clinics to meet the standards of surgical facilities is needed or that requiring doctors who perform abortions to have admitting privileges at nearby hospitals would improve women's health?

- Do you think that the legislation requiring abortion clinics to meet the standards of surgical facilities or that requiring doctors who perform abortions to have admitting privileges at nearby hospitals is a measure to improve health, or is it a restriction on abortion access masquerading as a health measure? Why?

- Does the information provided by the American College of Obstetricians and Gynecologists make any difference in the debate about the regulation of abortions? Is this an issue of values and politics rather than an issue that can be decided by social data?

WANT TO LEARN MORE?

There are dozens of resources and organizations on all sides of the abortion debate. Among the most prominent are

- National Right to Life
  www.nrlc.org

- American Civil Liberties Union
  www.aclu.org/issues/reproductive-freedom/abortion

- NARAL Pro-Choice America
  www.prochoiceamerica.org

Funds was $61.5 billion, 24.8 percent of the state budget. CHIP appropriations were $2.0 billion in the All Funds budget for 2020–21.

Broader Health Care Issues in Texas

Medicaid policy is embedded in a larger national discussion over health care in America and the proper way to fund it. Numerous controversies divide the public and politicians at all levels of government. Is health care fundamentally a private or a public issue? How can exploding health care costs, including the costs of private insurance such as Blue Cross Blue Shield or public insurance such as Medicare and Medicaid, be brought under control? Should individuals be compelled to purchase health care insurance? If so, how much and what kind of insurance? Who should pay for individuals who cannot afford to pay for private insurance themselves? What is the proper role for the state and federal governments in the delivery of health care across the nation?

As in other state-federal programs, federal money for Medicaid is accompanied by federal rules and regulations with which the state must comply to maintain this funding. This sometimes breeds tremendous political controversy between the state of Texas and the federal government.

Cost is the single most important issue confronting policy makers regarding Medicaid in Texas. Now encompassing more than 29 percent of state expenditures, Medicaid in Texas threatens to overwhelm the budget. In the spring of 2012, Texas comptroller Susan Combs began referring to Medicaid as "The Big Red," the program that was going to push an otherwise healthy state budget into the red. She claimed that by 2023 "Big Red is going to be over a third of state spending."[59] Medicaid expenditures, many mandated by the federal government, would begin to crowd out other forms of spending from the state budget.

Policy makers are forever looking for ways to make the program less costly. Two strategies have predominated over the past 20 years: first, to bring more efficiency into the program, and second, to institute cost controls and cutbacks to providers. Both efforts have had limited success, and at the same time have sparked concern over the quality of care being offered to Medicaid participants across the state. As cost containment efforts intensify, Texas policy makers inside and outside the legislature will be compelled to increase their monitoring of the delivery of the program.

Health care remains a controversial issue in Texas. While Texas holds as the state with the highest rate of uninsured individuals, many have used the Affordable Care Act to sign up for health care.

The Affordable Care Act

In March 2010, Congress passed two bills, the Patient Protection and Affordable Care Act and the Health Care and Education Reconciliation Act of 2010, which together became known as the Affordable Care Act (ACA), often referred to as Obamacare. The passage of the ACA transformed the debate over health care policy in the United States. Passed on a party line vote by Congress, the legislation required individuals not covered by existing plans to purchase health insurance or pay a penalty. The provision was eliminated beginning in 2019. Along with this "individual mandate," as the mandatory coverage came to be called, the act also increased coverage for preexisting conditions and expanded medical insurance to an estimated 30 million people at the time.[60]

What Are the Trade-Offs in Texas Public Policy?

The contemporary Texas government tends to pass conservative policies (lower taxes and lower levels of social services). The maps below allow us to look at the relationship between overall tax burden and the percent of uninsured people in the state. Texas collects the eighteenth-lowest share of taxes of any state. But when government lacks revenue, it cannot spend money to address social problems, such as providing health insurance to those who cannot afford it.

Overall Tax Burden by State

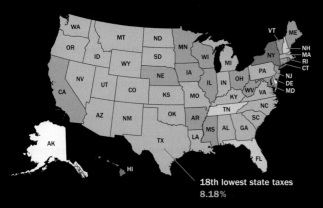

18th lowest state taxes
8.18%

5.1% ● ● ● ● ● 13.0%

Percentage without Health Insurance

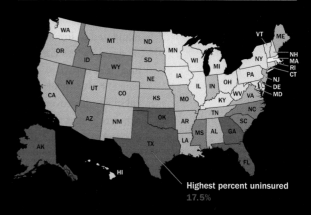

Highest percent uninsured
17.5%

2.8% ● ● ● ● ● 17.5%

State Taxes Compared with Percent Uninsured

	Low tax rank	Uninsured rank		Low tax rank	Uninsured rank		Low tax rank	Uninsured rank
Alaska	1	4	Texas	18	1	Wisconsin	35	40
Delaware	2	38	Washington	19	34	West Virginia	36	33
Tennessee	3	13	Indiana	20	23	Nebraska	37	22
Florida	4	5	Oregon	21	31	Maryland	38	36
New Hampshire	5	37	Nevada	22	8	Ohio	39	35
Oklahoma	6	2	Arizona	23	12	California	40	30
Montana	7	21	Utah	24	16	Iowa	41	45
Alabama	8	14	North Carolina	25	10	Illinois	42	32
South Dakota	9	15	Michigan	26	44	Connecticut	43	43
Wyoming	10	7	Louisiana	27	24	New Jersey	44	27
South Carolina	11	9	Pennsylvania	28	41	Rhode Island	45	46
Idaho	12	11	New Mexico	29	17	Minnesota	46	47
Virginia	13	19	Kansas	30	20	Vermont	47	48
North Dakota	14	29	Kentucky	31	42	Maine	48	25
Missouri	15	18	Massachusetts	32	50	Hawaii	49	49
Georgia	16	3	Mississippi	33	6	New York	50	39
Colorado	17	28	Arkansas	34	26			

SOURCES: Annual Results 2019, https://www.americashealthrankings.org/; Adam McCann, "Tax Burden by State 2019," WalletHub, https://wallethub.com/ (accessed 6/17/2020).

CRITICAL THINKING

- What appears to be the relationship between state taxes and insurance rates in a state?

- If Obamacare is fully implemented, will the numbers of uninsured change? Why or why not?

When fully implemented, the ACA was expected to bring significant change to the health insurance market in Texas as well as to Texas's Medicaid program.[61] Initial estimates in 2012 projected that under the ACA insurance coverage in Texas would rise to 91 percent, with almost 40 percent of the remaining uninsured being undocumented persons. The expansion of Medicaid in Texas would be funded through a complicated set of subsidies based on family income. For the first three years of the expansion (2014–16), the federal government would cover all costs for newly eligible participants in Medicaid and CHIP. Thereafter, the percentage would slowly decline, committing Texas to a larger portion of the funding. The long-term effect of the ACA for Texas would be a budgetary one. Increased expenditures on Medicaid and health care in Texas are all but inevitable.

The ACA sparked a national controversy. A majority of the states (including Texas) and a number of private individuals and groups challenged the constitutionality of the act in court, focusing on the mandatory coverage provisions. For three days in March 2012 the U.S. Supreme Court held oral arguments on the case, *National Federation of Independent Business v. Sebelius*. A complicated decision was delivered by a divided Court on June 28, 2012. Four liberal justices believed that most features of the ACA were constitutional. Four conservative justices countered that they were not. Representing the decisive vote, Chief Justice Roberts rejected the idea that people could be mandated or forced to buy insurance under Congress's power to regulate commerce, but he nevertheless concluded that a tax penalizing people who did not get medical insurance met constitutional muster. Regarding the expansion of Medicaid, he supported a conservative position, arguing that states could not be bullied into expanding medical insurance coverage for lower-income segments of the population. Chief Justice Roberts wrote that for federalism to thrive, states had to have a meaningful and real choice as to whether or not they would participate in federally sponsored programs.

The complicated Court decision opened the door for a new round of political posturing around the health care issue in Texas. Governor Perry announced that Texas would refuse to participate in the expanded Medicaid program, giving up millions of federal dollars for not having to incur new financial responsibilities at the state level. The state legislature, supporting Governor Perry, has refused to expand Medicaid in Texas. An estimate by the Kaiser Family Foundation in 2014 concluded that over 1 million uninsured adults in Texas, 17 percent of the uninsured in the state, would not be brought under the ACA provisions to expand Medicaid because of Texas's actions (or inactions).[62] Perry also decided that the state would not go into the business of designing an insurance exchange in the state. Texas would let the federal government sell federally designed insurance policies in the state on its own.

Tax reform in 2017 under the Trump administration further muddied the waters surrounding provisions of the ACA. Originally, the ACA required individuals to prove that they were insured when they filed their federal income taxes or they would incur a tax penalty. As noted above, this provision was held constitutional by the U.S. Supreme Court, upholding the mandate as a tax, not interstate commerce, in *NFIB v. Sebelius*. However, the Trump-inspired 2017 tax reconciliation act removed the tax penalties while keeping the mandate beginning in 2019. This effectively undercut an important part of the ACA's initiatives to lower the number of uninsured people through tax penalties.

Although the ACA is still in effect, it is unclear what that will mean for lower-income Texans over the long run (see Figure 12.3). Health insurance coverage overall has increased in Texas since 2013. The percentage of uninsured in Texas dropped between 2013 and 2018 from 22.1 percent to 17.7 percent, though this is still the highest rate of uninsured

FIGURE 12.3

Where Do Texans Get Their Insurance? (2018)

SOURCE: Henry J. Kaiser Family Foundation, kff.org.

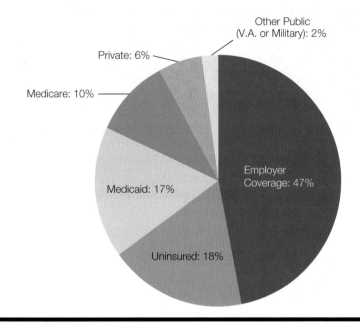

Other Public (V.A. or Military): 2%
Private: 6%
Medicare: 10%
Medicaid: 17%
Uninsured: 18%
Employer Coverage: 47%

in the nation.[63] Texas's refusal to participate in the optional state-federal expansion of Medicaid has effectively denied insurance coverage to many poor people.[64] And then there is the issue of undocumented workers in Texas, who compose a growing portion of uninsured individuals. Trump tax reforms have raised even more questions about the future of the ACA and health care in Texas. One thing is clear: few individuals are willing to argue that Texas has solved the problem of providing health care to poor people.

Medicaid and the Coronavirus Pandemic As in the areas of public education and welfare policy, the coronavirus posed new unexpected challenges to Medicaid and health care policy in Texas. The virus threatened to overwhelm Texas's public health care system across the state, as it had in New York City, if preventative measures were not taken early on to stem the outbreak. The shelter-in-place orders put into effect by county judges in large urban and suburban counties in March 2020 were aimed at "flattening the curve" (meaning holding down the exponential spread of the contagion) so that hospitals would not be overwhelmed by seriously ill patients.

Going into the summer, it appeared that this strategy was working, but not without steep costs. Routine medical services were seriously cut back as the health care community mobilized to face the pandemic. In the process, hospitals, private medical practices, and clinics started to hemorrhage money as they focused all their attention on seriously ill coronavirus patients. Rising rates of unemployment left many more people with no medical insurance at the very time that they needed it the most. Some funding assistance

Since the Affordable Care Act was signed into law, some Texans have advocated for the state to expand Medicaid coverage to offer health insurance to more low-income Texans. The coronavirus pandemic may bring this issue to the fore in the next legislative session as the state manages the public-health crisis.

came from the federal government in the early spring, notably funds in support of testing. But for the most part, the public health system limped along, hoping that the pandemic would recede on its own and life could get back to some new normal.

The COVID-19 outbreak exposed the fragile financial foundations upon which public health care in Texas rested. Decisions not to expand Medicaid as most other states had after the passage of the Affordable Care Act now left a growing portion of the population facing the pandemic on their own without medical insurance and, perhaps, without a job. The question of medical insurance and expanding Medicaid would likely be raised with renewed intensity in the next legislative session as policy makers tried to learn the lessons the pandemic had to teach.

Public Policy and the Future of Texas

IN THIS CHAPTER, we examined various aspects of social-policy making in Texas. We focused particular attention on the complex issues that have driven the various stages of the policy-making process in public education, welfare, and health care. Looking at these matters with a critical eye to the future demands that we pay attention to a number of key political questions: How are problems identified by policy makers and the public at large? What kinds of solutions are formulated to address these problems? Who benefits by a particular public policy? Who pays for the policy? What ideas are used to justify or legitimate a particular program? How are programs evaluated? How do particular public policies evolve and change over time to address new problems? How do they alter the relationship between individual citizens and the government that represents them in Austin?

In earlier chapters, we saw how the high-tech revolution transformed Texas's economy in the 1980s and '90s. We also traced how social and political changes have restructured the political party system in the state and increased the power of the Republican Party. In this chapter, we have seen how many of these shifts resulted in important changes in public policy in the twentieth and twenty-first centuries.

What will be the future of public policy in the areas of education, welfare, and health care? What issues will be seen as problems? What policies will be formulated to address these problems? How will those new policies be implemented, evaluated, and legitimated? Going into the fall of 2020 and the spring of 2021, policy makers' concerns in education, welfare, and health policy centered upon responding to the challenges of the coronavirus outbreak in Texas. Educating children in person and online lay at the heart of education policy. Getting basic food, income, and health care needs met for those people in poverty were also center stage. Once the pandemic is over, however, other long-term issues will surely return to prominence.

Funding and fairness issues in public education will be dominated by the legislature now that the courts have pulled out of the business of figuring out what was meant in the constitution by "efficiency." Charter schools likely will continue to expand, challenging the dominance of traditional public schools. Poverty policy will continue to take a backseat to other policy areas, as the state continues to find ways to reform welfare by ending dependency and by putting people back to work.

The wild card for the state may be health care policy. Will the state ever accept the expansion of Medicaid and insurance services provided under the Affordable Care Act? What will be done to address the continuing problem of the uninsured? What lessons has Texas learned from the coronavirus pandemic? Must the poor be allowed to fend for themselves, even those who are too young to do much fending? There is a chance that the state will punt on these issues, leaving segments of the poor and uninsured exposed.

STUDY GUIDE

Use 🐰 INQUIZITIVE to help you study and master this material.

The Policy-Making Process

- **Describe the key steps and concepts in the policy-making process (pp. 409–11)**

Public policies are the outputs of governmental institutions. There are a number of stages in the policy-making process. The first stage is problem identification, where society at large and political actors develop an understanding of a problem and how that problem can be addressed. The second stage in the process is policy formulation, where strategies for dealing with specifically defined problems are developed. The third stage is policy implementation, where the goals of public policy along with incentives or sanctions to support them are put into effect by a particular government agency. The fourth stage of the process is evaluation, where efforts are made to evaluate the effectiveness of a policy. Some political scientists argue that still another stage in the process is policy legitimation, where the legality and constitutionality of a particular policy initiative are determined.

Key Terms
rationality (p. 410)

Practice Quiz

1. Among the factors that work against rationality and efficiency in the making of public policies is that
   a) politicians are more interested in votes than in effective policies.
   b) administrators of policies often seek the easiest way of administering laws rather than the most efficient ways.
   c) governments work incrementally.
   d) rational and efficient policies are often difficult to legitimate to a broader public.
   e) all of the above

2. An example of policy legitimation is when
   a) the courts uphold the constitutionality of a law.
   b) the governor vetoes a particular bill.
   c) the governor appoints an official to run a bureaucracy.
   d) political scientists research the effectiveness of a law.
   e) the legislature does not repeal a law during the legislative session following its passage.

Education Policy

- **Describe the major issues that have shaped education policy in Texas (pp. 412–24)**

One of the most important functions of state government is providing and funding public education. Under the Gilmer-Aikin Laws, Texas extended its control over financing and administering public education through local school districts. As in many southern states, segregation of public schools was a major problem that was not dealt with until federal courts forced Texas to desegregate in the 1950s and '60s. Equity in the funding of public education remains a major issue in Texas. State courts continue to play an important role in addressing the equity issue. Concerns over excellence and accountability in public education persist today.

Key Terms
Gilmer-Aikin Laws (p. 414)
equal protection clause (p. 415)

Practice Quiz
3. The Gilmer-Aikin Laws
   a) regulate schools in the Gilmer-Aikin ISD.
   b) were major educational reforms passed in 1949.
   c) established an office of elected state superinten-dent of public instruction.
   d) allowed for homeschooling of children.
   e) required that money raised from the poll tax be spent on public education.

4. State courts tried to address the issue of equity in the funding of public schools
   a) in the case of *Edgewood ISD v. Kirby*.
   b) in the case of *Brown v. Board of Education*.
   c) in the case of *San Antonio v. Rodríguez*.
   d) by appointing Ross Perot to recommend changes to the property tax in Texas.
   e) by abolishing the office of the State Board of Education.

5. Among the reforms in public education in Texas to improve the quality of education was
   a) "No Pass, No Play."
   b) "No Play, No Pass."
   c) a shorter school year.
   d) more flexible standards for accrediting schools.
   e) tying teacher pay raises to student grades.

Welfare Policy

- **Describe the state's role in addressing poverty and how it is affected by national policies (pp. 424–30)**

Texas has large numbers of people living in poverty who have received governmental assistance since the New Deal when the Social Security Act of 1935 was passed. Texas's most important welfare program was AFDC. President Lyndon Johnson's War on Poverty expanded social welfare programs for the poor in the 1960s. But compared with those in other states, welfare benefits remained low in Texas. Concerns over the problem of welfare dependency led to major reforms at the national level in 1996 when AFDC was replaced with TANF. Since these reforms, welfare rolls have declined, although poverty has remained a chronic problem among a significant portion of the Texas population.

Key Terms
New Deal (p. 426)
Medicaid (p. 426)
Supplemental Security Income (SSI) (p. 427)
Aid to Families with Dependent Children (AFDC) (p. 427)
Temporary Assistance for Needy Families (TANF) (p. 428)

Practice Quiz

6. Poverty among those over age 65 and those under age 18 in Texas
   a) is almost nonexistent because of the welfare reforms of the 1990s.
   b) is at a level above the national average.
   c) is at a level below the national average.
   d) was largely eliminated by the Social Security Act of 1935.
   e) was largely eliminated by Lyndon Johnson's War on Poverty.

7. The welfare reforms of the 1990s
   a) resulted from a belief that the welfare policies of the 1960s had failed.
   b) led to a 36-month limitation on welfare benefits in Texas.
   c) led to a five-year ban on reapplying for benefits once benefits ran out.
   d) expanded education and job-training programs.
   e) all of the above

8. Two presidents who had major roles in welfare policy are
   a) Franklin Delano Roosevelt and Lyndon B. Johnson.
   b) Dwight Eisenhower and Herbert Hoover.
   c) Harry Truman and John F. Kennedy.
   d) Woodrow Wilson and Franklin Delano Roosevelt.
   e) Lyndon B. Johnson and George H. W. Bush.

Medicaid and Health Care Policy

- **Explain why Medicaid in particular and health care policy in general have been so controversial in Texas (pp. 431–40)**

One major welfare program that has become increasingly costly is Medicaid, a state-federal program that finances health care for the poor. Reforms instituted under the Obama administration have significantly expanded health care coverage for the poor. Texas, however, is not participating in that expansion. The rising cost of Medicaid is seen by many conservatives to be a growing threat to the financial integrity of the state's budget.

Practice Quiz

9. Which of the following statements is *true* about Medicaid in Texas?
- **a)** Medicaid is a program that was part of the New Deal.
- **b)** Texas policy makers make all the major decisions regarding the principles and standards directing Medicaid in Texas. There is no federal oversight.
- **c)** Texas can apply for a waiver with the federal government, enabling it to create programs directed toward particular clients.
- **d)** Medicaid employs doctors and nurses as members of the Department of Health and Human Services hired to provide medical care to the poor.
- **e)** Medicaid is funded entirely by the state.

10. The Affordable Care Act
- **a)** was part of the War on Poverty.
- **b)** merged Medicare and Medicaid into a single program.
- **c)** will increase health insurance coverage to millions of Texans.
- **d)** was declared unconstitutional by the Texas Supreme Court.
- **e)** originated in the Texas legislature.

The death of five police officers at an otherwise peaceful Black Lives Matter protest demonstrated the tense relationship that exists between law enforcement and the African American community. Here, members of the Dallas Police Department honor one of the five officers killed in the ambush.

Crime, Corrections, and Public Safety

WHY POLICIES AROUND CRIME, CORRECTIONS, AND PUBLIC SAFETY MATTER On July 7, 2016, there was a peaceful march of about 800 people through downtown Dallas. The march was one of several throughout the country that were held to protest recent police shootings of African American men in Baton Rouge and in a Minneapolis suburb. About 100 police officers were on hand to monitor the march.

The marchers were chanting "Hands up, don't shoot!," which was a chant that had been used by protestors since the shooting death of Michael Brown in Ferguson, Missouri, in 2014.

Suddenly, shots rang out. There was so much gunfire that police initially believed there were multiple snipers. The protestors scattered and shouted, "Go, go, go . . . run, run, run! Someone's shot!" Massive confusion erupted. A total of 12 police officers returned fire in a fast-moving series of gun battles that took place over several blocks. Three people were arrested who ultimately were determined to have nothing to do with the shooting. Instead, the shooter was a heavily armed single sniper who was cornered in a garage at El Centro Community College. Negotiations with the sniper and exchanges of gunfire with him went on for hours. Finally, police killed him by detonating explosives near him that had been carried there by a robot.

The sniper told a hostage negotiator that he was upset about the Black Lives Matter movement and the recent police shootings of Black men. He had claimed that "the end is coming" and that bombs were planted throughout the area. That claim was false, but a search of his home led to the discovery of bomb-making material, ballistic vests, and additional rifles and ammunition along with a journal of combat tactics.

Five police officers died. Seven officers and two civilians were wounded. It was the deadliest day for law enforcement since September 11, 2001. More law enforcement officers have died in the line of duty in Texas than in any other state since 1980.

The horrific shootings in Dallas underscore the dangerousness of police work and the fact that at any moment a situation can flare into a life-threatening situation. Then–Dallas police chief David Brown commented shortly after the killings, "All I know is that this must stop, this divisiveness between our police and our citizens."[1]

The peaceful demonstration from which the police killings emerged was over a fundamental issue in policing in Texas and throughout the country—one that was highlighted further by the 2020 killing of George Floyd at the hands of Minneapolis police officers (discussed later). How do police who must ➤

enforce laws and who must frequently deal with lawbreakers, as well as with citizens who are often in very tension-filled situations, maintain a positive relationship with the communities they police while providing for their own personal safety?

Policing, however, is only part of the criminal justice process in Texas. It is within the criminal justice process that the power of the state is greatest. Criminal law can take away an individual's liberty and even life. Texas has long been the poster child for its harshness in criminal punishment. No state executes more prisoners than Texas, and no state has a larger correctional population than Texas.[2] In this chapter, we will look both at the basics of the criminal justice system and at recent issues related to criminal justice in Texas.

CHAPTER GOALS

- Describe the characteristics of policing in Texas and analyze the controversies surrounding it (pp. 449–54)

- Identify the major classifications of crime under Texas law and the types of punishments that may be imposed (pp. 454–57)

- Outline the procedural steps that occur after a person is arrested (pp. 457–65)

- Describe prisons and corrections policy in Texas (pp. 465–76)

- Explain why Texas's criminal justice system is controversial and how it is being reformed (pp. 476–80)

Policing in Texas

Describe the characteristics of policing in Texas and analyze the controversies surrounding it

Law enforcement officers have the power of arrest and the power to use force in the conduct of their duties. It is an awesome responsibility that is carried out by a multiplicity of police organizations such as the Texas Department of Public Safety, city police departments, sheriff's departments, constables' offices, independent school district police departments, and college police departments.

Police Departments

The size of police departments in Texas ranges from about 5,200 in the Houston Police Department to tiny one-officer departments.[3] The small town of Anton, Texas, population 1,200, has one such department—a single police officer who, in case of trouble, has as his nearest backup the Hockley County Sheriff's Office, which is 25 miles away. There are 25 city police departments in Texas with only one officer, and 25 police departments have closed in the Panhandle and South Plains since 2000 because of the costs of operating a police department. Those towns without a police department rely on assistance from county sheriff's departments.[4]

One of the biggest problems facing police departments is their response time to calls for assistance. The Dallas Police Department, in particular, has faced criticism for slow response times. The Dallas Police Department has a four-category system for responding to calls. Priority 1 is a response to an emergency call, and the average time of these in 2019 was 7.81 minutes. Priority 4 is a response to a noncritical call, and the average time of these in 2019 was 67.97 minutes. One reason for the slow response times is that over six years the size of the department has dropped from 3,700 officers to 3,150 in 2020.[5]

A problem with the recruitment and retention of police officers in large urban departments is that nearby suburban departments pay much more, which encourages officers to move to higher-paying positions in areas where policing demands are likely to be less than in more populated urban areas. Starting pay for a Dallas police officer is $44,659 a year. In nearby Plano, it is $63,757. At the same time, it is difficult for very small police departments to have the tax base sufficient to support a police department. Often, small departments offer such a meager salary that officers are encouraged to move elsewhere. In 2017 the Kent County Sheriff's Department, with three full-time officers including the sheriff, advertised for a patrol deputy with a starting salary of $35,000.[6]

Small-town police officers do have advantages over urban officers, however. One major advantage is that they know the communities they serve. The single officer in Anton, Texas, for example, has lived in the town for 32 years and knows almost everyone. When people in Anton call the police, they rarely call the dispatch office, but instead call the officer's cell phone.[7] In contrast, officers in Texas's urban areas are unlikely to have much of a personal relationship with the communities in which they patrol. Diversity training is now required of police officers, and some departments pay a bonus for officers who speak languages common in the community, such as Spanish. Nevertheless, urban police are rarely the friendly neighbor that officers in small towns and rural counties in Texas are.

Texas Commission on Law Enforcement

The major state regulatory agency that develops and enforces law enforcement standards is the Texas Commission on Law Enforcement. It was established in 1965, though it was not until two years later that it received any state funding. Initially a small agency with only a director and a staff of three, it has grown substantially—as has its responsibility in **licensing** those in law enforcement. Beginning in 1969, the commission was responsible for certifying all peace officers—law enforcement officers such as police, sheriffs, constables, and highway patrol—with the exception of those who were elected officers under the Texas Constitution. Those duties were expanded in 1979 to the certification of county jailers and in 1989 to the certification of those in telecommunications. In 1997 the commission's duties were again expanded to Texas private prison jailers who are responsible for federal prisoners or for prisoners from other states. Once the commission licenses these persons, it requires that they undergo continuing education. The commission revokes licenses if standards are not met, and it also monitors police training academies.

The commission is governed by nine commissioners who are appointed by the governor and confirmed by the Senate. They are chosen for six-year terms, and terms expire for three members every two years. Commissioners are selected from three categories. Three are chief administrators of law enforcement agencies such as sheriffs, constables, or chiefs of police; three must be licensed by the commission, and two of those must be peace officers in nonsupervisory positions; and three must be private citizens.[8]

licensing (of law enforcement officials) in order to be a Texas peace officer, one must meet the requirements imposed by the Texas Commission on Law Enforcement, the regulatory body for peace officers and certain other officers in the state

Controversies Surrounding Policing in Texas

Police have not only the power of arrest but also the power to use reasonable force in doing so. It is the **use of force** by police that is the most controversial issue involving police in Texas and the nation. Rarely, however, does the use of force result in major consequences to police. The *Texas Tribune* examined 656 police shootings in the largest cities in Texas between 2010 and 2015. Thirty-eight percent of these shootings were fatal, and 41 percent of those shot were African American. Of these 656 shootings, 25 officers were subject to disciplinary action and 10 were terminated as police officers. Seven were indicted for criminal charges, though none of those were charged with murder, and none were convicted.[9]

More recently, six police officers have been charged with murder, and three have been tried and convicted. One, Ken Johnson, was with the Farmers Branch Police Department and was off duty and in plain clothes when he chased two teenagers he saw breaking into his vehicle. After a short vehicle chase in which he rammed their vehicle off the road, he quickly began shooting at the teens. He fired 16 times, killing one and wounding the

use of force peace officers may use reasonable force to effect an arrest or to protect themselves or others

other. The officer claimed he saw one of the teens reach down after the crash and pull a weapon. A box cutter was found in the vehicle, but it was a tool used in the dead teen's work. No gun was found.[10] Johnson was found guilty of murder and aggravated assault and sentenced to 10 years in prison on the murder charge and 10 years' probation for the aggravated assault.

Another officer, Roy Oliver, was with the Balch Springs Police Department. He killed a 15-year-old high school freshman who, with his friends, was driving away from a party that police had been called to investigate. Oliver opened fire on the vehicle with an AR-15 rifle. The department initially defended the officer, claiming that the driver of the car had attempted to back over the officer. Video of the incident, however, showed the car was moving away from the officer.[11] Oliver was found guilty of murder and sentenced to 15 years in prison and a $10,000 fine.

The third and most publicized case was the conviction of Dallas police officer Amber Guyger, who was sentenced to prison for 10 years for the murder of Botham Jean, who was watching television in his apartment when Guyger entered the apartment and shot him in the mistaken belief that he was an intruder in her apartment.

Prior to the conviction of Ken Johnson, the Farmers Branch officer, the last time a police officer was convicted of murder was 1973. In that case, Dallas police officer Darrell Cain held a gun to the head of a 12-year-old boy and, on the second pull of the trigger, killed him while the boy was handcuffed inside a patrol car. Although Cain claimed the shooting was an accident, he was convicted and sentenced to five years, and he served half of that time.[12]

Ken Johnson, a Farmers Branch police officer, was the first police officer in Texas to be charged with murder since 1973. After shooting two teenage boys while off duty, killing one and injuring the other, he was sentenced to 10 years in prison.

Police shootings generally do not go to trial. One example of such a shooting occurred in 2016 in Beckville after a Texas Department of Public Safety (DPS) trooper attempted to pull over a 23-year-old for speeding. Rather than stopping, a vehicle chase ensued, followed by a foot chase. The trooper drew his gun and repeatedly shouted for the 23-year-old to stop and put his hands up. Instead, the suspect continued running until he tripped and fell. The trooper claimed he believed the young man had a gun and shot him in the back five times because he failed to show his hands. The young man was unarmed, and the trooper at the time had no reason to suspect the young man of any crime other than speeding. The Texas Rangers investigated the shooting and reported to the grand jury information about previous traffic tickets and a drug charge that were unknown to the trooper at the time of the shooting. The grand jury refused to return an indictment.[13]

It is, of course, difficult to second-guess a police officer who must make a split-second decision about whether to fire a weapon. If a suspect makes a sudden movement, the officer must act quickly, and in some cases the suspect's actions are later determined to be unrelated to use of a weapon against an officer. Still, police use of force has become a major issue in Texas, in part because of a concern that police use of force may be indicative of racial bias. Between September 2015 and May 2017, 302 officer-involved shootings occurred in Texas. Fifty-three of the persons involved were unarmed, and 22 were African Americans.[14]

One potential remedy for concerns over the appropriateness of police use of force is the increased use of video cameras in police vehicles and on police officers. It was video of the incident involving the Balch Springs police officer, for example, that showed,

Favorability toward Police

Republicans have more favorable attitudes toward the police than Democrats and independents. Why would that partisan difference exist? Whites and Latinos have more favorable attitudes toward the police than do African Americans. Why do you think there are racial differences in attitudes toward the police?

	VERY/SOMEWHAT FAVORABLE	NEITHER FAVORABLE NOR UNFAVORABLE	VERY/SOMEWHAT UNFAVORABLE	DON'T KNOW/ NO OPINION
All	55%	13%	30%	3%
Democrat	27	19	53	2
Republican	84	7	8	1
Independent	44	19	29	8
White	64	9	25	1
African American	30	22	44	4
Latino	46	17	33	4

SOURCE: University of Texas/*Texas Tribune* poll of 1,200 registered voters in Texas between June 19 and June 29, 2020. Margin of error is +/− 2.89 percent.

contrary to the initial explanation that the department gave for the shooting, that the car was not going toward the police officer but away from him. Beginning in September 2017, a law went into effect requiring police departments to report officer-involved shootings to the state and imposing a substantial financial penalty if the department does not do so. Amazingly, there was no accurate central repository for information on officer-involved shootings, and some police departments were unwilling to report that information. The new legislation should offer a better sense of the extent of officer-involved shootings in the state along with the causes of these shootings.

One concern has been the potential for bias in the investigation of officer-involved shootings. A hint of such investigation bias occurred in the Beckville shooting when the Texas Ranger report to the grand jury mentioned the shooting victim's traffic record and drug charge, although the DPS trooper did not have knowledge of this record when the shooting occurred. While no such proposal is currently being considered, an independent investigation body solely focused on the examination of officer-involved shootings might provide a remedy for concerns about bias in the investigation of these shootings.

The Sandra Bland Case The Sandra Bland case is probably the most highly publicized case that involved questionable police practices in Texas unrelated to officer-involved shootings. In 2015, Bland returned from Naperville, Illinois, to her alma mater, Prairie View A&M, to start a new job working with the university's alumni association. A DPS trooper stopped Bland for failing to signal a lane change. The encounter escalated when Bland refused a request to extinguish her cigarette and the trooper threatened to use a Taser on her. The trooper claimed Bland was combative and uncooperative and that he removed her from her car to conduct a safer traffic investigation. He then arrested her for assaulting a public servant. She was taken to the Waller County jail, where she remained because she was unable to pay the $500 bail. After being in the jail for three days, Bland was found dead in her cell. A medical examiner ruled the death a suicide. While an investigation of her death led to no criminal charges at the jail, the trooper was indicted for perjury and was terminated from his position. Later, an agreement was made between prosecutors and the trooper that led to the perjury charge being dropped in exchange for the trooper never again seeking a law enforcement position. DPS claimed the trooper had violated its courtesy policy, had prolonged the stop beyond the time reasonably necessary, and had failed to follow procedure for interviewing traffic violators. The key question was, of course, how a simple traffic stop could possibly escalate into a death in a county jail. Bland was African American, and there were questions about whether her race played a role in her treatment. Additionally, there were questions about how frequently simple police stops unnecessarily escalated, particularly in the absence of police dashboard camera video coverage.[15]

In 2016, Bland's family agreed to a settlement in a civil suit in which they would be paid $100,000 by the Department of Public Safety and $1.8 million by Waller County. Additionally, the county agreed to provide emergency nurses on all shifts at the jail, use electronic sensors to ensure timely cell checks, and seek state funds for jail improvements. However, in 2017 the proposed **Sandra Bland Act** was largely gutted in the legislature because of opposition by police groups. The bill would have required officers to acquire signatures or recorded consent before they conducted a search and would have prevented jailing persons for offenses in which the maximum punishment was a fine.

Sandra Bland Act legislation in response to the arrest and jailing of Sandra Bland, who died in jail; the law requires independent investigation of jail deaths and alternatives to jailing those with mental or substance abuse problems

Sandra Bland was stopped for a minor traffic violation that escalated and led to her being jailed. Bland subsequently died in the county jail, which led to a national outcry. In response to national attention over Sandra Bland's case, major political figures such as Lieutenant Governor Dan Patrick spoke to the press about her death.

The law that did pass does, however, mandate diversion of persons with mental health or substance abuse problems to treatment and does require an independent agency to investigate jail deaths.[16]

The Death of George Floyd It was not the death of a Texan in police custody, however, that led to the most recent widespread outcry in both Texas and the nation over police brutality. It was the killing of George Floyd in May 2020 by a Minneapolis, Minnesota, police officer, who held Floyd down during arrest by placing a knee on Floyd's neck. Bystanders, some of whom warned the other police standing by that Floyd was in distress, videotaped Floyd and the police behavior. Video of the police action (and inaction) and Floyd's death was widely publicized and led to multiday demonstrations against police brutality. Large demonstrations occurred in Dallas, Austin, and Houston, but there were some demonstrations even in smaller Texas cities such as McKinney, Paris, and Sulphur Springs.

There was some violence associated with some of the demonstrations, some arrests, some injuries, and one death. What was clear from the response to George Floyd's death, however, was outrage over what happened to him and a desire that police violence be curtailed. The effect of the demonstrations on statewide policing policy is uncertain at this point. However, several Texas cities have now banned choke holds. Houston is requiring the police to use conflict de-escalation techniques and has limited no-knock warrants (warrants that allow police officers to enter a residence without knocking or announcing themselves first). Dallas is now requiring police officers to intervene when another officer engages in unnecessary violence. Austin has banned the use of rubber bullets, beanbag munitions, tear gas, and pepper spray, and is reducing the police budget. How long-standing and widespread the movement to reform police practices will be remains to be seen.

Categorizing Crime in Texas

Identify the major classifications of crime under Texas law and the types of punishments that may be imposed

Crimes, of course, are classified by legislation into different levels of seriousness, and punishments vary according to the seriousness of the crime. In the Texas criminal justice system, crimes are classified as felonies or misdemeanors. Table 13.1 shows the punishment range for the various classifications of crime in Texas.

Felonies and Misdemeanors

felony a serious criminal offense, punishable by a prison sentence or a fine; a capital felony is punishable by death or a life sentence

A **felony** is a serious criminal offense that subjects a convicted person to a fine of up to $10,000 and/or prison punishment ranging from six months to the death penalty. The right to vote, to have a gun, or to have certain occupational licenses can also be taken

TABLE 13.1

Classification of Crimes

FELONY CRIMES	EXAMPLES	PENALTIES*
Capital murder	Killing a peace officer or firefighter in the line of duty, killing a small child, murder for hire, death occurring during the commission of certain crimes	Death or life without parole
First degree	Aggravated (using a weapon) assault on a public servant, aggravated kidnapping, aggravated sexual assault, arson of a habitation	5 to 99 years in state prison or life; fine up to $10,000
Second degree	Arson, bigamy, bribery, robbery, sexual assault, manslaughter, possession of 50 to 2,000 pounds of marijuana	2 to 20 years in state prison; fine up to $10,000
Third degree	Stalking conviction, third driving while intoxicated (DWI) charge, third offense of violation of a protective order	2 to 10 years in state prison; fine up to $10,000
State jail	Burglary of a building, DWI with a child as a passenger, forgery of a check, possession of less than one gram of a controlled substance	180 days to 2 years in a state jail; fine up to $10,000

MISDEMEANOR CRIMES	EXAMPLES	PENALTIES*
Class A	Burglary of a vehicle, second DWI offense, public lewdness, possession of two to four ounces of marijuana	No more than 1 year in county jail; fine up to $4,000
Class B	Prostitution, terrorist threats, first DWI charge, criminal trespass, possession of two ounces or less of marijuana	No more than 180 days in county jail; fine up to $2,000
Class C	Public intoxication, disorderly conduct, minor's possession of alcohol	Fine up to $500

*In many cases, probation is a possible substitute for serving jail or prison time. If jail or prison time is imposed, it is possible to obtain parole or early release.

SOURCES: "Texas Criminal Laws & Penalties," Texas Criminal Defense Lawyer; Fred Dahr, "Crimes and Punishment in Texas State Court," texasdefenselaw.com.

away, although in Texas voting rights for felons are restored after the sentence has been fully discharged. There are degrees of felonies, with more severe sentences attached to higher degrees. The most serious felony is capital murder, for which the penalty can be death or life imprisonment without parole.

Misdemeanors are less serious crimes, for which the penalty is a fine of $4,000 or less and/or a sentence of up to one year in the county jail. The right to vote, to possess a weapon, or to have some occupational licenses is not lost as a result of a misdemeanor conviction. There are three classes of misdemeanors, again with more severe sentences attached to more serious crimes (see Table 13.1).

misdemeanor a minor criminal offense usually punishable by a small fine and/or short jail sentence

Punishing Crime

probation punishment where an offender is not imprisoned but remains in the community under specified rules and under the supervision of a probation officer

In some cases, especially if it is the defendant's first conviction, the judge may allow **probation** or community supervision rather than a jail or prison sentence. Probation is a suspension of the jail or prison sentence with the understanding that the defendant will meet certain requirements imposed by the court. These usually include reporting to a probation officer on a regular basis, holding a steady job, paying fines or restitution, and abstaining from alcohol or drug use. Generally, community supervision can run up to 2 years for misdemeanors and up to 10 years for felonies, although if a probationer complies with the rules, it is possible to obtain early release from probation after serving one-third of the term.[17]

Violation of probation requirements can result in being sent to jail or prison to serve out the sentence behind bars. Often, prosecutors know that people with lengthy probation sentences will find it difficult to comply with all of the requirements. So, in cases where they believe it will be difficult to get a conviction, they might agree to a plea bargain allowing community supervision for a long period. They expect that the defendant will violate probation and spend time in jail or prison.

parole the conditional release of an offender who has served some prison time, under specified rules and under the supervision of a parole officer

People who are sentenced to prison may be released on **parole** after a period of time behind bars. The decision to grant parole is made by the Texas Board of Pardons and Paroles, composed of a chair and six members who serve six-year staggered terms. Besides determining grants of parole, conditions of parole, and revocation of parole, the board makes recommendations to the governor about sentences and clemency. In order for the governor to alter a prisoner's sentence or grant clemency, a majority of the board must support the change.

People serving time for capital crimes are not eligible for parole, and generally those convicted of other violent crimes must serve at least half their sentence before being considered for parole. People convicted of nonviolent crimes must serve at least one-fourth of their sentences or 15 years, whichever is less, before being considered. The Board of Pardons and Paroles uses a complex formula that considers such factors as the offender's prior record, previous parole violations, employment history, prison disciplinary record, the severity of the current offense, the age of the offender, educational or vocational opportunities taken during confinement, and whether the offender is a gang member. If a prisoner is granted parole, he or she must comply with the requirements imposed or, like probation violators, he or she can be sent to prison for the remainder of the sentence.[18] In the 2018 fiscal year, over 6,500 persons had their parole revoked and were returned to prison, and over 21,600 persons successfully completed parole and were discharged.[19]

There are also sentencing enhancements—certain circumstances, such as previous convictions—that increase the classification of or penalties for the crime. For example, a DWI (Driving While Intoxicated) offense is a class B misdemeanor, but a second DWI is a class A misdemeanor, and a third DWI is a third degree felony. That means, of course, that a second or third DWI conviction will result in more serious penalties than will the first DWI offense.

"three strikes" provision a law that allows persons convicted of three felonies (or in some cases two felonies) to be sentenced to life imprisonment

Texas enhances sentences for repeat felony offenders as well. If a person convicted of a third degree felony has a prior felony conviction, that person is sentenced for a second degree felony. Similarly, a second degree felony is punished as a first degree felony if the person had a prior felony conviction. A person convicted of a third felony can be sentenced to life imprisonment based on a **"three strikes" provision** in the penal code, and in some cases, such as sexual assault cases, two felony convictions are sufficient for life imprisonment.

The Criminal Justice Process

 Outline the procedural steps that occur after a person is arrested

Several procedural steps occur after a person is arrested and before guilt or innocence is determined. In Texas, as in most other states, this process may take months or even years. The major steps are listed below.

Arraignment and Posting Bail

Generally, when a person is arrested for a felony or misdemeanor and jailed rather than ticketed, he or she will be arraigned before a judge. At the arraignment, the charges will be explained to the accused, and he or she will be reminded of their due process rights—such as the right to remain silent and the right to an attorney.

After being charged, a defendant may be offered the chance to be released from jail on bail until the trial, and the amount of bail is generally set at the arraignment. **Bail** is money paid to the state to ensure a defendant's future appearance in court. Usually, if the defendant does not show up for trial, the bail is forfeited. If the defendant appears as required, the bail money is returned. Often, bail is more than the accused can pay, and so he or she will arrange with a bail bondsman to pay the bail in exchange for a nonrefundable payment that is often 10 percent of the amount, or higher. Even a defendant who cannot provide bail or pay a bondsman to do so can possibly be released on personal recognizance, which is a personal promise to appear. This possibility is most likely if the accused has ties in the community such as a family or employment and does not have a criminal record. If an accused cannot provide bail or be released without bail, he or she usually will be held in jail until the trial.

Recently, a federal court declared the operation of the money bail system in Harris County for indigent misdemeanor arrestees to be unconstitutional. The court found that keeping poor misdemeanor defendants in jail had detrimental effects on their employment, made it more likely that they would be found guilty than persons released on bail, and encouraged those indigents who were jailed to plead guilty. Also, there seemed no good reason to jail indigent misdemeanor defendants. The court found that there was not a significant difference in failure to appear for trial between those who provided money for bail and those who were released without bail. A three-judge appellate panel ruled that the Harris County bail system was indeed unconstitutional. Dallas County has also been sued over its bail practices and, as with Harris County, is having to change its bail practices. The decision has enormous implications statewide and throughout the nation. A likely effect is that misdemeanor arrestees will often be released on personal recognizance rather than being required to pay bail.[20]

bail payment of money to the state as an assurance that an accused person who is released from jail pending trial will appear for trial; if the accused does not appear, the bail is forfeited

Bail Reform in Texas

1 Why bail reform matters

There are a lot of people in jail in Texas. Many of those people are accused of misdemeanors and simply there awaiting trial. The Harris County jail is the third largest in the United States and roughly 70,000 misdemeanors are processed each year in Harris County.[a] In his 2019 State of the Judiciary address, Texas Supreme Court chief justice Nathan Hecht said, "Twenty-five years ago, one third of the jail population was awaiting trial. Now the percentage is three-fourths. Most of those detained are non-violent, unlikely to re-offend, and posing no risk of flight. Many are held because they're too poor to make bail. Though presumed innocent and no risk to public safety, they remain in jail, losing jobs and families, and emerge more likely to re-offend." These inmates are a burden to their communities and, claimed Hecht, Texas taxpayers are paying $1 billion a year to keep people in jail who should be released.[b]

Frequently, a defendant does not have sufficient funds to pay the full amount of bail. Therefore, he or she will arrange with a bail bondsman to post the bail in exchange for a nonrefundable payment. Bail bondsmen oppose bail reform because they would suffer financial losses if defendants were released on their promise to return for trial.

2 What's the debate?

Bail reform was initiated by the three federal court decisions focused on the question of whether or not bail should be set for people awaiting trials for misdemeanors, without regard for their ability to pay. The first and most comprehensive decision was in Harris County.[c] Harris County detained over 40 percent of misdemeanor offenders until the disposition of their cases. The magistrates generally relied on an approved schedule of bail amounts ranging from $500 to $5,000—applying bail to persons charged with particular crimes after hearings generally lasting a minute. The ability to pay was generally not a factor in setting bail.

Reformers believe either that nonviolent indigents should be released on their personal recognizance—that is, their promise to return for trial—or that their ability to pay should be a factor in determining bail. Use of personal recognizance or risk assessment software that considers ability to pay, reformers argue, reduces jail costs, does not punish people for their poverty, poses no threat to the community, allows poor people to retain contact with their families, and allows people to continue working. Reformers also argue that, based on limited data, persons who were released on personal recognizance showed up for trial at the same rate as or higher than those paying for bonds. [d]

One of the most powerful interest groups opposed to bail reform are bail bond companies that for a fee—often 10 percent of the bail amount—will pay the bail of the incarcerated person. There are also advocates for victim's rights who are opposed to bail reform. They argue there is no reliable way to predict if people released from jail will flee or reoffend.[e] Without bail, they say, people will simply fail to appear in court. It is costly to deal with those persons who do not appear and there are cases where people who are released on their own recognizance wind up committing violent crimes.[f] It is better, reform opponents argue, to let elected and experienced judges determine conditions for release.

What do the numbers say?

Which group—those detained or those released—were convicted more often? Which group had to use court-appointed lawyers ("appointed counsel") rather than their own attorneys? Which group ultimately served longer sentences?

The Consequences of Those Charged with Misdemeanors Being Held in Jail versus Being Released Pending Trial

	OVERALL	HELD IN JAIL	RELEASED PENDING TRIAL
Convicted	68.3%	79.4%	55.7%
Pled guilty	65.6%	76.8%	52.8%
Sentenced to any jail time	58.7%	75%	40.2%
Sentence of jail days	17	25.4	7.4
Sentenced to probation	14.0%	6.2%	22.9%
Sentence of probation days	49.4	22.5	79.9
Requested appointed counsel	53.2%	71.3%	32.6%
Amount of bail	$2,225	$2,786	$1,624
Class A misdemeanor	30.7%	33.5%	27.4%
Total defendants	380,689	202,386	178,303

SOURCE: Paul Heaton, Sandra Mayson, and Megan Stevenson, "The Downstream Consequences of Misdemeanor Pretrial Detention," 69 *Stanford Law Review* 711 at 736 (2017).

Communicating Effectively: What Do You Think?

- Is reform of the bail system an important problem or should the current system be retained? Why?

- If you think the bail system should be changed, how would you do it?

- What additional data or evidence would you need in order to make the argument for your ideas as strong as possible?

WANT TO LEARN MORE?

The Texas legislature has focused on bail reform recently, and this has become an important issue nationwide. As you start to form your own opinions on this issue, several organizations provide more information on the costs and benefits of reform.

- Texas Criminal Justice Coalition www.texascjc.org

- The Marshall Project www.themarshallproject.org

- Texas Alliance for Safe Communities www.texasallianceforsafecommunities.org

Grand Jury Indictment

grand jury jury that determines whether sufficient evidence is available to justify a trial; grand juries do not rule on the accused's guilt or innocence

Although the procedure can vary, after arraignment a felony case will generally be presented to a **grand jury**—12 persons who will determine if there is sufficient evidence to hold the accused for trial. Grand juries do not find people guilty or not guilty but instead will vote a "true bill," meaning that they find probable cause that the accused has committed the crime, or a "no bill," meaning that they do not find probable cause. A person would, of course, be held for trial only if there is a "true bill." A grand jury indictment is far from conviction, as all a grand jury determines is the existence of probable cause, and usually the decision is based only on a presentation by the prosecutor. For a conviction in a trial, there must be a finding of guilt "beyond a reasonable doubt," which is a demanding standard of proof for a prosecutor. At a trial the defense is also heard. It has the opportunity to cross-examine witnesses and present its version of events. The major criticism of the grand jury is that it usually hears only what the prosecutor chooses to let it hear and that it serves as a "rubber stamp" for the prosecutor's decision.

On September 1, 2015, a major change occurred in the way grand juries are selected in Texas. Texas was the last state to use what was commonly called the "pick-a-pal" or "key man" system, in which a district judge appointed commissioners who chose persons to serve on grand juries. One problem with this system was that those who were chosen tended to be unrepresentative of the community. The new system selects 12 grand jurors and 4 alternates in a random selection process such as the one for trial juries.

Pretrial Hearings

After indictment for a felony, there will likely be a number of pretrial hearings in which the accused will formally plead guilty or not guilty, the trial is scheduled, and various motions may be presented, such as ones to move the trial or exclude certain evidence. These hearings vary in length but in most cases are quite brief. In a criminal trial, a common motion is one to exclude certain evidence on the grounds that it was illegally seized in violation of the Fourth Amendment to the U.S. Constitution. In these instances, the judge examines the facts of the seizure and determines whether the evidence was legally seized and therefore can be used at trial.

Plea Bargaining

plea bargain negotiated agreement in a criminal case in which a defendant agrees to plead guilty in return for the state's agreement to reduce the severity of the charge or prison sentence the defendant is facing

Although **plea bargaining** can occur during a trial and even after a finding of guilt but before sentencing, the prosecution and the defense will often discuss a punishment in exchange for a guilty plea and reach an agreement before the trial. The prosecutor's offer might involve reducing the charge, dropping some of the charges, or recommending a lighter sentence than the defendant might get at trial if found guilty.

Plea bargaining is one way that prosecutors maintain high conviction rates. But plea bargaining is not only necessary politically; it is also crucial in managing the limited resources of the prosecutor's office and the courts. Prosecuting a case that goes to trial after a defendant pleads not guilty can cost thousands and even hundreds of thousands of dollars. A trial also uses up the limited time employees have. If plea bargaining were suddenly abandoned in Texas, the criminal justice system would quickly come to a halt as a result of a massive overflow of trials. Defense lawyers often have an incentive to plea bargain as well. In many cases, they can generate more income by representing numerous defendants (who often have limited resources) in plea negotiations than by engaging in a few time-consuming trials. And plea bargains can benefit defendants, even innocent ones, in that they get an assured sentence that may be less than they would receive if they went to trial and were found guilty and then sentenced by either a judge or a jury.

The judge with jurisdiction over the case will almost always agree with a plea bargain made by the district attorney's office. For one thing, plea bargains reduce the crowded dockets of judges. Without a trial, the judge cannot be aware of the strengths and weaknesses of the state's case and so will generally recognize that the district attorney is in a far better position to determine the appropriate sentence.

Trial and Sentencing

If the case does go to trial, a defendant may choose to waive the right to a jury trial and instead have the judge determine guilt. Such cases include those where a judge is perceived as inclined to favor the defendant or where the crime is believed to be one that would inflame jurors' emotions against the defendant. A defendant may also have a jury trial but waive the right to sentencing by a jury, so that the judge determines the sentence if there is a guilty verdict. In Texas, felony juries are composed of 12 people, and misdemeanor juries are composed of 6. Decisions by criminal juries must be unanimous, and for both felonies and misdemeanors the standard of proof must be "beyond a reasonable doubt." If the jury's decision in either a felony or misdemeanor case is not unanimous, the case results in a mistrial, and the prosecutor must decide whether to retry the defendant.

If the defendant is acquitted (found not guilty), he or she is, of course, set free. If the defendant is found guilty, there will be a jail or prison sentence or probation and/or a fine. A defendant may appeal a guilty verdict by asking a higher court to reconsider the lower court's decision. Very minor criminal cases that are heard by municipal courts or by justice of the peace courts can be appealed to the county courts. More serious misdemeanors and felonies, however, are heard by county or district courts, and appeals from those courts go to one of the 14 courts of appeal in Texas. Any further appeal will be to the highest criminal court in Texas, the Texas Court of Criminal Appeals. Death penalty cases are appealed directly from trial courts to the Texas Court of Criminal Appeals. In rare events where a question of U.S. constitutional or statutory law is raised, it may also be possible to appeal to the federal courts.

Does the Criminal Justice System Create Criminals?

In some cases, the requirements of the Texas criminal justice system can be quite burdensome on individuals. For some people, complying with the rules of the process can be difficult and even financially impossible. One common crime in Texas, especially among younger offenders, is possession of less than two ounces of marijuana. Although a few Texas counties treat this crime as the equivalent of a traffic offense where the police officer tickets the offender, in other counties offenders will be taken to jail to be held until the bond hearing and until they can make bail. Although a recent federal court decision is in the process of changing bail requirements for misdemeanors in Harris County and potentially throughout Texas, for the time being in much of Texas, bail on such a charge would be $500, which means that either the full $500 will have to be posted with the county or a bail bondsman will have to be retained for roughly a $50 nonrefundable fee. After bail is posted, the defendant will eventually have to go to trial in a county-court-at-law. Some defendants hire an attorney, which may cost $1,000 to $3,000 for the entire process in this type of case; others may appear in court without an attorney. It would not be unusual for a first offense to result in at least a $500 fine plus court costs, a sentence of 30 hours of community service, a sentence of 15 hours in an approved drug education course, and nine months' probation during which the defendant would pay a fee for each visit to the probation officer and any drug testing required by the probation officer. After court costs, probation costs, and the fine, the offender will probably have spent about $1,000 to $1,200, plus legal fees.

While on probation, the offender will not be allowed to use drugs or alcohol and will be subject to testing. There will be a required visit with a drug counselor and regular trips to a probation officer. Travel will be restricted. If the offender is in compliance, he or she will probably get early release from probation. If not, probation could be full length and jail time is possible. Additionally, because this is a drug case, the offender's driver's license will be suspended for six months. If the offender must drive in order to get to and from work or to care for family matters, he or she must go to court and obtain an occupational driver's license. Filing this paperwork can easily cost nearly $300, not counting possible attorney's fees. In order to drive legally, the offender will also have to purchase an SR-22 automobile insurance policy for two years. This high-risk policy, in which the insurance company reports directly to the state that the offender has automobile insurance coverage, can cost twice as much as a regular policy.

Cite and release is a tactic to decrease the number of people who go to jail for having small amounts of marijuana, which costs localities time and money. This tactic, though legal since 2007, was rarely used by police departments in Texas, though as marijuana has been legalized in several states across the nation, its use has increased.

Thus, an arrest for possession of a marijuana cigarette can easily cost more than $5,000 to $7,000 overall in fines, court costs, insurance charges, probation fees, and attorney costs, not to mention time in jail after arrest and, if the marijuana was found in the offender's vehicle, towing and impoundment charges. Failure to comply with all probation requirements can lead to violation of probation and other criminal charges such as driving with a suspended license or driving without proper insurance. The structure of the criminal justice process even for minor crimes such as class B misdemeanors may deter future crimes because of the severity of punishment, but the cost and penalty structure also seem to encourage failure and further criminality by the offender.

Reform of Marijuana Laws There have recently been dramatic changes in marijuana law enforcement in Texas, however. In 2007 the Texas legislature gave police the option to cite and then release a person arrested for possession of less than four ounces of marijuana. The citation is much like a traffic ticket where the person would have to appear in court and would be subject to criminal punishment, but would not be arrested, booked, or put in jail until bail is paid. For years this option was rarely used by police departments, but recently several counties have begun to use "cite and release" since it saves police time and costs to local governments associated with keeping someone in jail. Increasingly there is also the view that jailing a person for small amounts of marijuana is an overly harsh punishment.

Still the most dramatic change in low-level marijuana law enforcement appears to have been unanticipated. In the 2019 legislative session, hemp was legalized in Texas. Most of the law focused on the production of hemp and agricultural regulations, but the law also narrowed the definition of marijuana to cannabis containing more than 0.3 percent tetrahydrocannabinol (THC). Anything less than 0.3 percent THC was legal hemp. The problem was that the public laboratories used by law enforcement could only test for the presence of THC, not for how much THC was present. As a result, prosecutors around the state began dropping hundreds of low-level marijuana cases. Some police departments have relied on private laboratories that have the equipment to measure the amount of THC, but it costs local governments hundreds of dollars per test to use these private laboratories. The effect of the hemp law on marijuana prosecutions has been remarkable, dropping the number of low-level marijuana cases filed by more than half.[21]

Crime and Texas District Attorneys

Ordinarily when we think of the criminal justice system, we think of the police who make arrests and the courts that adjudicate those cases. The most important actors in the Texas criminal justice system, however, are probably the prosecuting attorneys. Some counties have an elected **county attorney** whose office represents the state in misdemeanor criminal cases. The county attorney usually provides legal advice to the county commissioners as well, although generally the county attorney does not represent the county in civil cases. Counties with elected county attorneys also have elected **district attorneys**, who represent the state in felony cases. Some counties have merged the offices of county and district attorney into an office that represents the state in both misdemeanor and felony cases and is often called the office of the criminal district attorney.[22]

In urban counties in Texas, the office of the district attorney is huge, encompassing several hundred lawyers, investigators, and support staff. In 2020 the Harris County district attorney's office employed 329 prosecutors and a total of about 700 employees. In many rural counties, the district attorney's office includes only one or two lawyers. The head of every district attorney's office in Texas is an elected officer who runs under a party label for a four-year term. As the chief prosecuting officers of a county or district, district attorneys have traditionally campaigned as "tough on crime" and they brag about high conviction rates. It has generally been the case that if they appear to be too lenient or their conviction rates are too low, political opponents will emerge who will accuse them of not doing their job appropriately.

In the urban counties in Texas, however, a new type of district attorney has been emerging who places a greater emphasis on prosecuting violent crimes than on minor ones and who cultivates an image as a reformer. That new style has been especially notable in the larger urban counties where district attorneys often support programs to examine claims of actual innocence by persons convicted of crimes and who seek to

county attorney an elected official in some counties who prosecutes misdemeanor cases

district attorney public official who prosecutes the more serious criminal cases in the district court

One of the most colorful and widely publicized reform district attorneys in Texas is Mark Gonzalez of Nueces County, who campaigned against extreme sentencing and mass incarceration.

minimize jail or requiring money bail for persons accused of minor crimes. While the number of reform district attorneys is small, their jurisdictions are generally among the state's larger counties and so they have great influence on criminal justice prosecutions in the state.

The district attorney has prosecutorial discretion, which means the power to charge or not charge a person with a crime. Even when a case is presented before a grand jury to determine if a criminal indictment should be issued, the grand jury is dependent on the prosecutor to present the evidence that may lead to an indictment, and a prosecutor has great discretion in choosing both whether to go before a grand jury and whether to accept or not accept the decision of a particular grand jury.

Crime and Criminal Defense

Persons accused of crime may represent themselves or may retain a criminal defense lawyer to represent them. Since the famous Supreme Court case *Gideon v. Wainwright* (1963), persons too poor to hire a lawyer have had a constitutional right to have an attorney appointed to represent them in serious cases. As mentioned in Chapter 9, in Texas that representation is generally provided by **assigned counsel**—that is, the judge will appoint a lawyer to represent people who cannot afford one. However, in some counties in at least some types of cases, such people will be represented by a **public defender**, a lawyer who is paid a salary by the government to represent indigent defendants. With assigned counsel, usually judges appoint a private attorney on a case-by-case basis for a fee that varies according to the county and the legal service performed. One concern with this system is that the fee may be so small that the assigned attorneys do not do an adequate job in representing their clients. The issue of the quality of representation provided to indigents in Texas is an important one because large numbers of cases

assigned counsel private lawyers appointed by judges to provide legal representation for indigent defendants in serious criminal cases; the lawyer's fee is determined by and paid by the county

public defender salaried lawyer who is funded by the government or by grants who represents indigents in Texas in some counties or for some types of cases

are tried and substantial amounts of money are spent in providing this representation. Table 13.2 specifies the 2018 costs of indigent defense in the state and the numbers of cases involving poor people whose lawyers are paid by the state.

Some of the fees counties pay for assigned counsel seem remarkably inadequate. As examples, Bexar County pays appointed counsel $75 an hour for trial work involving a state jail felony, $100 an hour for a second degree felony, and $125 an hour for a first degree felony. Harris County pays $300 a day for trial work in a state jail felony, $400 a day for a second degree felony, and $500 a day for a first degree felony. The joint Jack and Wise County judicial district pays lawyers $400 for each half day of trial work for felonies and $250 for each half day of trial work for misdemeanors to a maximum of $1,000.[23]

Public defenders are far rarer in Texas than are assigned counsel. However, a statewide public defender program is available for capital cases and serves participating small and midsize counties. There are a small number of other public defender offices in Texas, and they are regional or countywide in scope. Some of those have specialized caseloads such as mentally ill defendants, rural areas, appeals, or juvenile defendants. The public defender program for capital cases has been evaluated by comparing it with assigned counsel in capital cases, and several interesting findings have emerged from the study. For one thing, in rural areas of the state, few lawyers are qualified to handle capital cases. In an area of Texas spanning over 80,000 square miles, for example, only 13 private lawyers are qualified for these cases. For such an area, death penalty specialists who are public defenders are particularly useful, and they also have the necessary support team that would be difficult to organize in the more rural and isolated parts of the state. For many smaller counties, the cost of death penalty cases is prohibitive—defense costs alone often exceed $100,000. Participating in a public defender program with death penalty specialists can greatly reduce costs for these counties. The public defenders were also more likely than assigned counsel to avoid a death penalty and to get better dispositions for their clients overall.[24] Death penalty work is very specialized and complex, but the success of public defender programs over assigned counsel in such cases suggests that an expansion of public defender programs in other areas may be beneficial to indigent defendants.

Crime, Corrections, and the Texas Prison System

 Describe prisons and corrections policy in Texas

It has long been claimed that Texas does things in a big way, and that is certainly true of its levels of crime and the way it deals with criminals. As of August 31, 2018, there were 145,019 offenders incarcerated in the state's prisons, state jails, and substance abuse facilities.[25] These numbers exclude those incarcerated in municipal and county facilities. The average cost per day for each bed in the state's correctional facilities was about $53. It costs about 26 times more to imprison someone than to place that person on probation and about 18 times more to keep him or her in prison than on parole.[26]

History of the Prison System

Shortly after Texas joined the Union, construction was authorized for a state penitentiary in Huntsville. The 225-cell facility opened in 1849. It confined prisoners in single cells at night and congregated them during the day to work in silence. From 1870 to 1883 the entire prison system was leased to private contractors who used the labor of inmates in exchange for providing maintenance and prisoner supervision. After 1883 convicts were leased to railroads, planters, and others who provided the prisoners with food and clothing and paid a stipend to the state. These leasing arrangements were abandoned in 1910 as a result of scandals and abuses of the system.[27]

Under the new state-run system, however, abuses continued. In 1924 an investigation found inadequate care and brutal treatment of prisoners as well as inefficient management. That investigation led to the creation of a state prison board, which supervised the work of a general prison manager. Still, abuses continued, and by the mid-1940s the Texas prison system was considered one of the worst in the nation. In 1974 the Joint Committee on Prison Reform submitted findings to the legislature that found serious fault with numerous aspects of the system's operation—from inmates' living and working conditions to their classification, and from medical care to staff training. Still, no significant reforms were made.[28]

The event that had the most dramatic effect on the system's operation in modern times was a federal court case, *Ruiz v. Estelle*.[29] Lawsuits filed by prisoners are nothing

David Ruiz (right) and other Texas prison inmates filed a class-action lawsuit demanding stronger rights for prisoners. The case resulted in changes in how Texas prisons operated.

Who Is in Prison in Texas?

Prison Population in Texas by Race, 2018

■ % of Texas population   ■ % of prison population

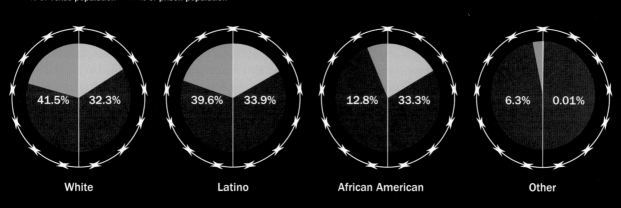

41.5% 32.3%	39.6% 33.9%	12.8% 33.3%	6.3% 0.01%
White	Latino	African American	Other

Death Row Population in Texas, 2020

■ % of Texas population   ■ % of death row population

White	Latino	African American	Other
41.5%	39.6%	12.8%	6.3%

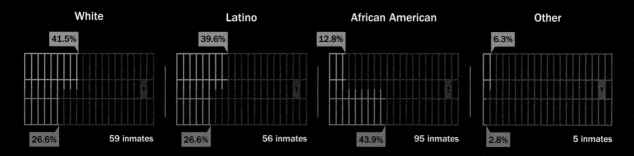

26.6% — 59 inmates	26.6% — 56 inmates	43.9% — 95 inmates	2.8% — 5 inmates

While Texas does not lead the nation in its incarceration rate, it is still the fifth highest in the United States. A disproportionately high number of African Americans are serving in the state's prisons compared with their percentage of the population of the state. Though only 12.8 percent of the state's population is African American, one-third of the prison population is.

SOURCES: U.S. Census, QuickFacts, July 1, 2019; Texas Department of Criminal Justice, Fiscal Year 2018 Statistical Report (February 2019); Texas Department of Criminal Justice, Death Row Information, January 31, 2020 (accessed 6/17/20).

QUANTITATIVE REASONING

- The Texas population is 39.6 percent Latino, 12.8 percent African American, and 41.5 percent White. According to the data shown here, how does the Texas prison population compare?

- What might explain the racial/ethnic makeup of the prison population in Texas?

new. During the tenure of W. J. Estelle, Jr., the prison director from 1973 to 1983 and the defendant in the *Ruiz* case, prisoners filed 19,696 cases in the federal courts in Texas, a caseload amounting to about 20 percent of the federal court docket in Texas during that period.[30] However, the *Ruiz* case was exceptional. A class-action suit on behalf of inmates that began in 1972, it focused on issues of crowding in the system, security and supervision, health care, discipline, and access to the courts. In 1980 a federal court concluded that inmates' constitutionally guaranteed rights had been violated. Texas joined several other states in having its prison system declared unconstitutional.

The result was the appointment by the court of a special master, a court officer, to oversee the system to eliminate constitutional violations such as overcrowding, improper supervision, and improper care of inmates. This massive reform had to be imposed by the federal courts because the state seemed unwilling or unable to reform its own prison system. Federal court supervision of the system ended in 2002.

For a long time, many in Texas government resisted federal court supervision of the prison system, arguing, for example, that the *Ruiz* decision amounted to judicial activism and interfered with the rights of the state. To reduce the overcrowding in state prisons to comply with *Ruiz*, the state encouraged the early release of prisoners, some of whom then committed more crimes. *Ruiz* did, however, help turn the criminal justice system into a major public policy issue in Texas.

The Prison System Today

The Texas prison system is operated by the Texas Department of Criminal Justice. This agency is run by a nine-member board appointed by the governor, and members serve staggered six-year terms. The board hires an executive director to lead the sprawling agency, and it is responsible for developing the rules and regulations that govern the entire state prison system.[31] Since 1993 the Department of Criminal Justice is responsible not only for the massive prison system in Texas, where convicted felons are incarcerated, but also for the much smaller state jail system. State jails are minimum security facilities, and they hold low-level drug and property crime offenders who are sentenced to serve 180 days to two years. Unlike county jails, no one in the state jail system is awaiting trial; they have all been convicted and are serving a sentence.[32]

The Department of Criminal Justice also runs a small program called Substance Abuse Felony Punishment Facilities (SAFPF), which provides assistance to offenders who need treatment for substance abuse problems. Offenders may be sentenced to this program by a judge, or the Board of Pardons and Paroles may require substance abuse services as a condition of parole. Typically, offenders receive a six-month in-prison treatment program, as much as three months of additional treatment in a residential treatment facility, six to nine months of outpatient treatment, and up to twelve months of support groups and supervision.[33]

In the wake of estimates in 2007 that Texas would need 17,000 new prison beds costing $1 billion by 2012, the Texas legislature increased the capacity of prison alternatives such as drug treatment and halfway homes, much cheaper alternatives to prison.[34] Until 2007, when the Texas legislature began to seriously address alternatives to imprisonment, the state government had significantly increased the incarceration of offenders by building more prisons, especially in the early 1990s. In 2011, however, for the first time in Texas history, the state actually closed a prison—the century-old Central Unit in

Sugar Land. After that, seven other prisons closed, making a total of eight prison closings in a six-year period.[35]

From 1976 to 1990 the rate of property crime in Texas rose 38 percent, and the rate of violent crime rose 113 percent. Since prison expansion in this period did not keep up with these increases, generous early-release policies were used to make room for newly convicted inmates. With prison expansion, however, early-release policies were reduced. In 1990, for example, 38,000 prisoners were given early release; in 1997, with a much larger prison population, only 28,000 were.[36] The steady lengthening of sentences is shown in Figure 13.1. In 1994 prisoners on average were released after serving one-third of their sentences. In 2018 prisoners were serving 61 percent of their sentences before being released. Inmates at state jails served on average 99.5 percent of their sentences.

As shown in Figure 13.2, the Texas prison population reached its peak in 2000 and then dropped off. In 1980, at the time of the *Ruiz* case, there were fewer than 30,000 inmates in the state. By the early 2000s, the number had jumped to over 150,000, then dropped to 134,152 by 2018.[37]

FIGURE 13.1

Percentage of Prison Sentence Served by Texas Inmates

SOURCES: Criminal Justice Policy Council, "Percentage of Prison Sentence Served for All Release Types, Fiscal Years 1994–2004"; Texas Department of Criminal Justice, Statistical Reports Fiscal Years 2006–2018.

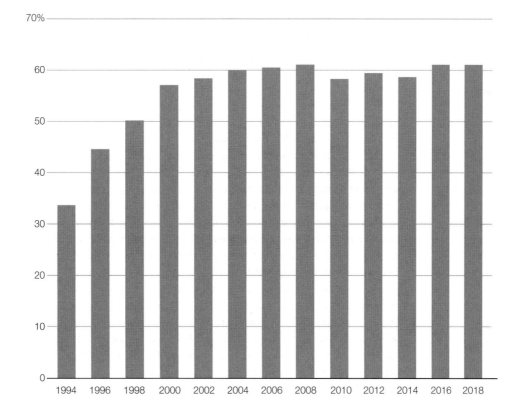

FIGURE 13.2

Texas Inmate Population, 1980–2018

SOURCES: Criminal Justice Policy Council, "Texas Department of Criminal Justice State Incarcerated Population, Fiscal Years 1988–2002"; Texas Department of Criminal Justice, Statistical Reports 2006–2018.

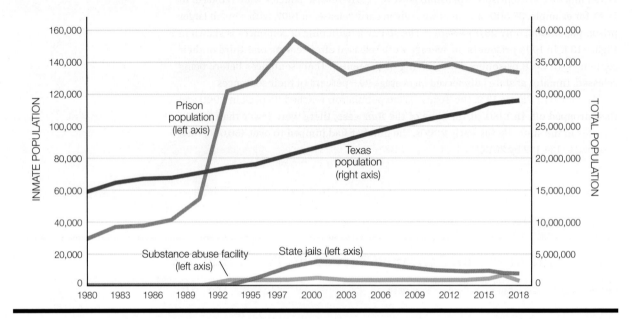

For much of the 1980s the rates of violent and property crime in Texas were especially high.[38] By the mid-1990s, however, those rates had dropped. While some observers argued that the drop was due to increased incarceration of offenders, there may also be other causes, such as demographic changes. Of course, changes in laws and treatment practices also affect the crime rate and the incarceration rate. Long sentences for habitual criminals, for example, are relatively new, as are long sentences for the use of a firearm in the commission of a crime.[39] The number of prison inmates per 100,000 citizens of the total population in Texas in 2018 was 549. Only five states, including Louisiana with an astounding incarceration rate of 695 per 100,000, beat the Texas per capita rate. (See the Texas and the Nation graphic.) Texas had 12.7 percent of the nation's total state prison population in 2018, and no other state had more inmates in its prison system than Texas.[40] Nevertheless, the state ranked high in crime rates. Texas ranks 15th among the states in violent crimes per 100,000 persons.[41] As Figure 13.3 shows, Texas imprisons mostly violent offenders. In 2018, 57 percent of Texas prison inmates had been convicted of violent offenses, 13 percent of property offenses, and 17 percent of drug offenses.[42]

It is especially difficult for felons to gain legitimate employment after their release—so much so that the federal government offers a large tax credit to employers who give jobs to people who have served a felony sentence. This difficulty makes it more likely that former prisoners will commit further crimes. Another problem is that the average sentence in a Texas prison is 18.5 years. After such a substantial time in prison, it

FIGURE 13.3

Prison Population by Offense, 2018

Note: Data may not add up to 100 percent due to rounding.

SOURCE: Texas Department of Criminal Justice, "Fiscal Year 2018 Statistical Report."

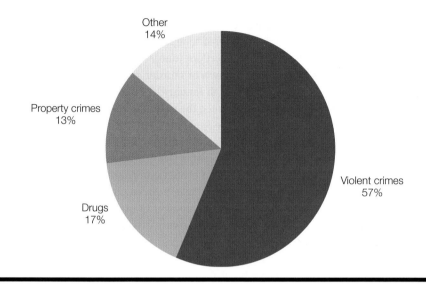

is hard to readjust to life in the free world, and support structures such as family members have often died or removed the inmate from their lives. Still another problem is that the average educational achievement of an inmate in Texas prisons is only 8.43 years.[43] Finally, frequent drug and alcohol addiction among felons makes employment difficult and encourages criminal behavior. The problem of addiction was recognized during Governor Ann Richards's administration. Drug and alcohol treatment efforts begun at that time have continued and expanded.

The Death Penalty

In 1835, when Texas was administered by Stephen F. Austin, the first death penalty was imposed on Joseph Clayton, who was hanged for murder. In those early years, hangings were public affairs where crowds would gather to watch the execution. It was not until 1923 that public executions were outlawed, hangings were changed to electrocution, and the state rather than the county became responsible for carrying out the sentence.

Electrocution was believed to be a more humane and civilized means of execution than hanging, although the humaneness of either method was highly questionable. Between 1924 when the first Texas electrocution occurred and 1964 when it ended, 361 people were electrocuted in the state.

After the Supreme Court required the states to revise their capital punishment laws, Texas reinstated the death penalty in 1974 and in 1977 switched to lethal injection as its execution method. In 1982, Texas executed its first inmate by lethal injection. Although lethal injection was considered a humane execution method, it has since been criticized for being inhumane.[44]

Today Texas is one of 31 states that have the death penalty. Of the 20 states (and the District of Columbia) that do not impose the death penalty, five have banned it since 2010. As of October 1, 2019, there were 2,639 people on death row throughout the nation, although over 60 percent of them are in five states—California with 727, Florida with 348, Texas with 219, Alabama with 177, and Pennsylvania with 152.[45] In Texas one is subject to the death penalty for the murder of a public safety officer, fireman, or correctional employee; murder during commission of a kidnapping, burglary, robbery, aggravated rape, or arson; murder for hire; multiple murders; murder during a prison escape; murder by a prison inmate serving a life sentence; or murder of a child under the age of 6. Texas executed 570 people from 1976 through January 15, 2020.[46]

As Figure 13.4 shows, though Texas has led the nation in the number of executions since the death penalty was reinstated by the Supreme Court, the imposition of the death penalty has declined in Texas and other states. National polling data show an increase in opposition to the death penalty—from 25 percent in October 2002 to 42 percent in October 2019.[47] That 371 Texas inmates have been exonerated from 1989 through December 2019 and that 11 Texas death row inmates have been exonerated during that time period has perhaps contributed to reducing the number of executions in Texas.[48] More important is that death penalty cases have become very expensive and time-consuming for the state. A life without parole sentence is far less costly, while ensuring that the defendant will not pose a future danger to the public.

Political scientists Paul Brace and Brent Boyea found that judges tend to affirm death penalty sentences in states where judges are elected and where there is strong public support for the death penalty.[49] Texas judges are elected, and polls show much stronger public support in the Texas for the death penalty than in the nation as a whole. One 2018 poll, for example, showed that 65 percent of Texas voters either somewhat or strongly supported the death penalty and that only 25 percent were opposed.[50]

FIGURE 13.4

Executions in Texas Compared with Other States

SOURCE: Death Penalty Information Center.

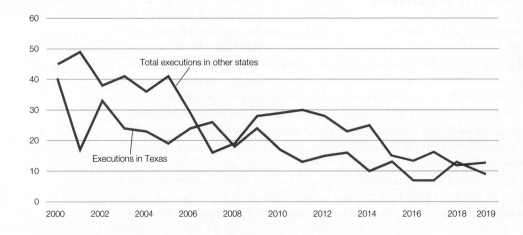

How Does Criminal Justice in Texas Compare with Other States?

Incarceration Rate, 2017 (per 100,000 adult residents)

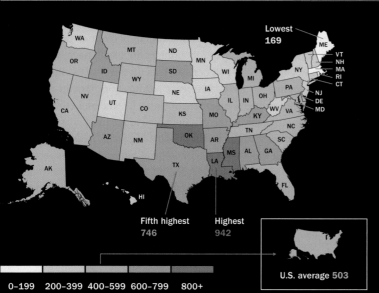

Lowest
169

Fifth highest
746

Highest
942

0–199   200–399   400–599   600–799   800+

U.S. average 503

Although the incarceration rate in Texas has declined in recent years, it still has a high rate—the fifth highest in the nation. In 2017, Texas incarcerated 746 out of every 100,000 adults, which is far higher than the national average of 503 per 100,000 adults. It is also higher than the incarceration rate of other large states such as California, Florida, and New York. Texas is also known for its use of the death penalty. Since the U.S. Supreme Court reinstated the death penalty in 1976, 37.5 percent of all executions within the United States have occurred in Texas, although the number of executions in the state has declined.

SOURCES: Jennifer Bronson and E. Ann Carson, "Prisoners in 2017," Bureau of Justice Statistics, April 2019, pp. 11–12; Death Penalty Information Center, "Executions in the United States (1977–2020)."

Total Executions, 1976–2017

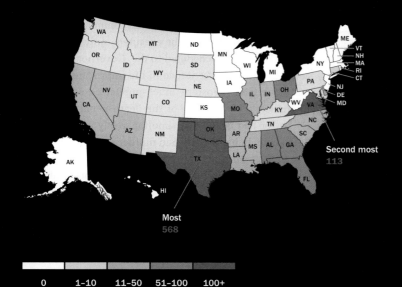

Second most
113

Most
568

0   1–10   11–50   51–100   100+

CRITICAL THINKING

- Which elements of Texas political culture or public opinion may contribute to the willingness to use the death penalty and to have high incarceration rates?

- Examine the regional patterns on the two maps. Do certain regions of the country have higher incarceration rates and death penalty usage? What do you think explains these regional patterns?

Kenneth Foster's father and wife celebrate after hearing that Governor Perry had commuted Foster's sentence only hours before Foster was to receive the death penalty. Foster was convicted of murder despite only driving the getaway car.

A stay on death row can be a lengthy one, even in Texas. In Texas the average time spent on death row prior to execution was 10.87 years, although the time varied considerably. One inmate waived his appeals and spent only 252 days. On the other hand, David Lee Powell spent 31 years on death row before his execution in 2010.[51]

One of the issues involving the death penalty is whether all offenders are treated fairly and equally. Racial and ethnic minorities, especially African Americans, are disproportionately represented on death row. As of January 31, 2020, 94 death row inmates were African American, 57 were Latino, 57 were White, and 6 were classified as "other."[52]

Although African Americans constituted only about 13 percent of Texas's population in 2019, 36 percent of those executed from December 7, 1982, to January 16, 2020, have been African Americans. Of the 568 persons executed from December 7, 1982, to January 16, 2020, 250 were White, 206 African Americans, 108 Latinos, and 4 members of "other" racial and ethnic groups.[53]

A bias may exist in the criminal justice system that makes people of color disproportionately subject to the death penalty, although a counterargument is that the murder rate is higher among people of color. When the bias issue was presented to the U.S. Supreme Court, the Court refused to strike down the death penalty on the basis of statistical generalizations—essentially saying that there had to be evidence of racial bias in the specific case presented to the Court.[54]

The Texas Board of Pardons and Paroles votes on clemency for death row inmates. The board was originally created as a remedy for possible corruption in clemency granted by the governor. Prior to 1936 the governor essentially had unlimited power to grant clemency—a power often abused, especially by Governor Miriam Ferguson, who granted 4,000 requests for commutations of sentences in 1922 alone. It was widely believed that payments were made for many of these acts of executive clemency. In reaction, a constitutional amendment was passed in 1936 that charged the board with giving the governor recommendations on clemency. Without such a recommendation, the governor can grant only a single 30-day reprieve. No other state limits the powers of the governor in this way.

In 2007 the board recommended commutation of Kenneth Foster's sentence to be executed—only seven hours before Foster was scheduled to die. Governor Rick Perry commuted Foster's sentence to life imprisonment about one hour later.[55] Foster's much-publicized case seemed to challenge two aspects of the death penalty in Texas: (1) Foster had been tried simultaneously with the other defendants in his robbery and murder case rather than in a separate trial, and (2) he was the getaway driver in the crime and not the actual shooter. Simultaneous trials with other defendants in murder cases can be a huge disadvantage for a defendant like Foster, who was not the shooter but was nevertheless tried with the shooter. Foster was tried in this way because Texas has the law of parties—

a person involved in a crime that leads to a murder is guilty of murder even though that person is not actually the person who committed the murder.

Self-Defense and Concealed/ Open Carry of Handguns

In any examination of crime in Texas, the enormous concern Texans have with self-defense cannot be ignored. One of the most controversial issues in the state over the past few years has concerned concealed and open carry of handguns. Advocates of concealed and open carry argue that the U.S. Constitution's Second Amendment provides them with a constitutional right to bear arms. Article 1, Section 28, of the Texas Constitution provides a similar right with the caveat that carrying arms is subject to state regulation. It states:

> Every citizen shall have the right to keep and bear arms in lawful defense of himself or the state; but the Legislature shall have the power, by law, to regulate the wearing of arms with a view to prevent crime.

To a large degree the wording in the Texas Constitution sums up the long-standing political debate over carrying firearms: does it provide protection against crime, or does it lead to crime?

In 1871, during Reconstruction, Texas passed legislation against both concealed and open carry. That law was not substantially changed until, in 1995, the legislature passed its first bill legalizing concealed carry, which was signed by Governor George W. Bush in fulfillment of a campaign promise. In the 2011 legislative session, concealed carry of handguns on college campuses became a major issue, and there clearly were enough votes to pass a bill allowing it, but the bill failed because of a parliamentary challenge. At the same time, legislation was passed and signed into law that prohibited employers from banning guns secured in employees' vehicles in company-owned parking lots.[56]

In the 2015 legislative session a bill allowing open carry of firearms passed despite concern that it would increase violence and lead to intimidation of others. The handgun must be in a hip or shoulder holster but no longer needs to be concealed. A concealed handgun license is still required, however, which means the license holder must be 21, pass a criminal and psychological record check, and undergo classroom and shooting training.[57] In 2015 campus carry was also passed, which allowed licensed gun holders to conceal carry on parts of Texas's public universities.

Campus carry has been one of the most controversial aspects of Texas handgun legislation. It required public universities to allow concealed handgun license holders to carry, except in some restricted locations, on their campuses. Some faculty, especially at the University of Texas at Austin, expressed concern that campus carry would lead to campus violence. At least one senior professor resigned over the policy, and three professors filed a lawsuit in an unsuccessful effort to stop it.

To date, however, campus carry, concealed carry, and open carry have not led to the violence their opponents predicted. Open carry has proven rare in the state's urban centers, and the number of students who can carry handguns on campus is limited by the requirement that concealed carry license holders be 21. The greatest problems have been in determining the specific locations where bans on carrying handguns can be legally implemented. During the shootings of Dallas police officers on July 7, 2016, described at the start of the chapter, bystanders and the police had some difficulty in distinguishing the shooter from demonstrators who were carrying long guns, but carrying a long gun in Texas has long been lawful and has never been part of the debate over concealed carry, open carry, or campus carry of handguns.

What is clear is that Texas's handgun legislation has led to a large number of concealed carry licenses being issued. In 2017 there were 1,200,747 concealed carry license holders in Texas.[58]

Currently, some lawmakers are pushing for legislation commonly called "constitutional carry," which would make the licensing process and the gun training classes optional. Supporters of constitutional carry argue that bearing arms is a constitutional right and that licenses and training classes burden that right.[59]

The Integrity of the Texas Criminal Justice System

 Explain why Texas's criminal justice system is controversial and how it is being reformed

In recent years, numerous controversial issues and cases have raised questions about how criminal justice works in Texas. Here, we consider whether the integrity of the criminal justice system is compromised. At the end of this section, we consider some of the reforms designed to improve the fairness of the criminal justice process.

How Fair Is the Criminal Justice System?

Ideally, the criminal justice system should hold the guilty accountable and protect the innocent from punishment. That has not always been the case in Texas. There seem to be problems with the fairness of the system. The question is how common those abuses are and what, if anything, can be done about them.

Texas is the home of more verified wrongful convictions than any other state.[60] There is a registry that lists wrongful convictions, generally known as exonerations,[61] in Texas and throughout the nation from 1989 through 2019. Two thousand five hundred and forty-nine exonerations have occurred nationally, and 366 of those exonerations have occurred in Texas. Many of the exonerations have resulted from scientific advances in DNA technology, and a number of wrongful convictions have received widespread public attention. Randall Dale Adams, for example, was the subject of an acclaimed movie, *The Thin Blue Line*. Adams was sentenced to death in 1977 for the murder of a police officer. In 1989, largely as a result of the 1988 movie, Adams was released from prison. His conviction was the result of perjury, mistaken witness identification, and official misconduct.[62]

Still another widely publicized exoneration was that of Tim Cole, who was convicted in 1986 of sexual assault. Though his conviction was for one rape, he was believed to be the "Texas Tech rapist," a serial rapist who had assaulted women near Texas Tech University. He was sentenced to twenty-five years in prison and died in prison in 1999. In 2009 he was exonerated—the first posthumous exoneration in the state. Largely owing to efforts by Cole's mother and brother, Texas enacted the Timothy Cole Act, which increased compensation for exonerated persons to $80,000 per year wrongfully served in prison and which expanded services to exonerated persons. In addition, the Timothy Cole Advisory Panel on Wrongful Convictions was created in 2009 to study the causes and prevention of wrongful convictions.[63] In December 2016, the panel issued an extensive final report detailing numerous recommendations on how wrongful convictions could be prevented.[64]

One of the most recent highly publicized exoneration cases involved Michael Morton, who was convicted of murdering his wife. On August 13, 1986, Christine Morton was beaten to death at her home in Austin. Her husband, Michael Morton, was charged with the murder and was prosecuted by Williamson County district attorney Ken Anderson. Michael received a life sentence for the murder, though he persisted in claiming his innocence and argued that some unknown intruder must have killed his wife after he had gone to work. The day after the murder, Christine's brother had found a bloodstained blue bandana near the crime scene, and he had turned it over to detectives. In 2005, Michael asked for DNA testing on several items including the blue bandana.

John Bradley, the district attorney at the time, and known as a tough prosecutor, opposed the requests for DNA testing, claiming there was no way the testing would lead to some "mystery killer." He said that Michael Morton's lawyers were "grasping at straws." Morton's lawyers suspected that key evidence had been withheld, and so they sought investigative materials in the case. Bradley opposed those requests as well. In 2008, Bradley was forced to turn over the investigative materials, and Morton's defense lawyers discovered that Eric Morton, who was three years old at the time of his mother's murder, had seen the murder and described the killer as a "monster" who had red gloves and a big mustache. He also had said that the killer was not his father.

Defense lawyers discovered other information as well from the newly released files of the case. Police reports noted there was a check to Christine that was cashed with a forged signature after her death. There were reports of fraudulent use of her credit card after her death. There were also neighbors' statements to police that a man was seen parked in a green van near the Morton home on several occasions before the murder. Contrary to a legal requirement that prosecutors share exculpatory materials, this information had not been provided to the defense lawyers.

Then, in 2010, DNA testing on the blue bandana was allowed. DNA was found on the bandana to belong to the victim, Christine, and to a man whose DNA was in a national database as a result of an arrest in California. That man was Mark Alan Norwood. On October 4, 2011, Michael Morton was released from prison—he had been convicted in 1987. Mark Alan Norwood was convicted of the murder of Christine Morton on March 27, 2013. He is believed to have murdered another woman in 1988.

High-profile exonerations like Morton's can have political consequences. District Attorney Bradley was defeated for re-election in the Republican primary in 2012. His opponent, Williamson County attorney Jana Duty, hammered Bradley for blocking the postconviction DNA testing for Morton and won with 55 percent of the vote. Bradley's resistance to that testing meant that Morton spent six additional years in prison.[65] Judge

In 2011, Michael Morton was released from prison based on new DNA testing in his case. He served nearly 25 years in prison before another man was arrested for the crime. DNA evidence has revealed a series of wrongful convictions raising questions about criminal justice in Texas.

Ken Anderson, the original district attorney, was sentenced to 10 days in jail, a $500 fine, and 500 hours of community service for criminal contempt in telling the Morton trial judge that he had no evidence favorable to Morton.[66] He has also lost his judgeship and law license. Morton is free and will receive financial restitution from the state for the quarter century that he spent in prison for a murder he did not commit. He was present when the Texas legislature passed a bill, the Michael Morton Act, which established a uniform policy for district attorneys to make material that can help defendants' cases available to defense attorneys.[67] Perhaps even more important than the Michael Morton Act, for the first time in Texas a prosecutor was held criminally responsible for actions that resulted in a wrongful conviction, and another prosecutor was held accountable by the electorate for his actions that delayed Morton's efforts to prove his innocence.

Reforms

Despite widely publicized abuses, improvements in the Texas criminal justice system have occurred. Texas is no longer handling its crime problem solely by incarceration. The number of drug treatment programs has increased, and there is greater emphasis on imprisonment as a last response to criminal behavior and more emphasis on alternatives such as requiring increased reporting to probation officers, community service, electronic monitoring of offenders, and mandatory treatment for alcohol or drug addiction. The result has been a decline in prison construction and even the beginning of prison closings. Texas has the most generous compensation system in the nation for exonerated persons.

Some police departments are modifying their procedures for obtaining eyewitness evidence. For example, the Dallas Police Department has changed the way photographic spreads for identification of suspects are conducted so that the police officer handling the photographs does not know who the actual suspect is and thus cannot provide cues to the witness as to which photo to pick. Prosecutors often call on scientific experts, such as arson investigators, to help prove their cases. However, fields such as arson science are rapidly evolving, and some scientific theories used to convict defendants in the past have now been debunked. Certain indicators once considered signs of arson are now known to appear in accidental fires.[68] Similarly, the Texas Forensic Science Commission has recommended that testimony that connects bite marks to a specific defendant's teeth is junk science and should not be used as evidence against a defendant. A new Texas law makes it much easier for an inmate to challenge a conviction if it was based on bad science.

Some Texas district attorneys have recognized the problem of wrongful conviction and have appointed prosecutors who review wrongful conviction claims and take a cooperative approach toward lawyers working with the claimants. In 2016 the Harris County district attorney announced major programs to divert first time felony drug offenders into treatment programs rather than jail; to divert class B theft offenders to treatment programs; and to provide treatment rather than jail for the mentally ill.[69] These changes are a recognition that not all crimes are best handled by jailing the offenders.

For the first time in Texas, prosecutors are suffering significant consequences for actions that deny rights to defendants. Michael Morton's prosecutor lost his law license and served brief jail time for his actions in the Michael Morton case, in which he failed to turn over exculpatory evidence to the defense. Since then, the former district attorney of Burleson County has failed in his effort to retain his law license. He had used false testimony and withheld evidence from the defense in a case where the defendant was sent to death row and later exonerated.

During the 2017 legislative session, one of the recommendations of the Timothy Cole Advisory Panel on Wrongful Convictions was made law. The law, the strictest in the nation regarding jailhouse informants, was in response to the recognition that one of the biggest causes of wrongful convictions was an inmate falsely testifying against another inmate in exchange for leniency in reference to his own crime. Such false testimony by inmates will become much more difficult because prosecutors will now be required to document their use of jailhouse

Does Texas's criminal justice system need to be reformed? Some observers feel that, beyond problems with wrongful convictions, the emphasis on imprisonment and the large number of inmates in Texas are major concerns, though incarceration rates are declining.

PERSONAL RESPONSIBILITY: WHAT WOULD YOU DO?

- **Are wrongful convictions inevitable? Overall, is the Texas criminal justice process working as it should?**

- **Do you think the reforms discussed here will make a difference in the fairness of the Texas criminal justice system? What are some other changes you think need to be made?**

informants, and they will have to share with defense lawyers information about the jailhouse informants' criminal histories. Additionally, prosecutors will have to notify defense lawyers of anything offered to the jailhouse informants in exchange for their testimony.

COVID-19 and Criminal Justice in Texas

The coronavirus pandemic created significant problems for the criminal justice system. Jails and prisons were hot spots for the coronavirus, and numerous inmates and staff at jails and prisons were stricken by the virus and some died. That led judges and district attorneys in parts of the state to avoid jailing those accused of minor crimes by releasing them without imposing money bail. In some cities, police departments were asked to avoid making arrests for minor crimes. Focusing on crime control in the face of the pandemic, however, Governor Abbott banned the release of those accused of violent crimes or who have a record of violent crime unless they pay money bail.

In the state prison system, inmates who tested positive for COVID-19 were no longer transferred to other prisons. Additionally, the state prison system no longer accepted transfers from county jails to the state prison, although that practice ultimately led to greater crowding and a greater COVID-19 risk in the county jails. The pandemic also caused delays in the release of thousands of inmates in the prison system who were granted parole, but who had not completed requirements prior to release such as life skills classes or a drug abuse course. As a result, jails and prisons took only limited actions in response to the coronavirus and remained major sources of infection for the disease.

Criminal Justice and the Future of Texas

PERHAPS THE CRIMINAL justice system in Texas works well overall, but is the system working as well as it should?

Will Texas decide, for example, that the accused need higher-quality legal representation so that problems in the system can be identified and resolved before a person is convicted and imprisoned? Former Dallas County district attorney Craig Watkins received national acclaim by offering a new perspective on his role of prosecutor, which he saw as not only convicting the guilty but also protecting the innocent charged with crime.

While Texas remains the major death penalty state and the state that holds the most offenders within its criminal justice system, its correctional policies are changing. The death penalty is imposed far less often than in the past—in large part because of a new alternative punishment of life without parole—although politically it is here to stay. Texas is also sending fewer people to prison than in earlier years. Today, the old corrections model of "Lock 'em up" seems to have been replaced by a more economically efficient approach in which nonviolent offenders, especially, are often given alternatives to prison, such as community supervision. The state is recognizing the strong connection between alcohol and drug addiction and crime, and more resources are being expended in addiction treatment programs. The issue of the future will be whether Texas will continue pursuing alternatives to prison for offenders. Finally, many states are reducing penalties for crimes such as possessing small amounts of marijuana. Will Texas join the movement toward decriminalization? Crime and corrections have always been a major issue in Texas politics, and the state appears on the cusp of major changes in this area.

Use **InQuizitive** to help you study and master this material.

Policing in Texas

- **Describe the characteristics of policing in Texas and analyze the controversies surrounding it (pp. 449–54)**

Law enforcement in Texas is a dangerous occupation with a large number of peace officers spread throughout a large number of local, county, and state agencies. The size and resources of these police agencies vary widely. Additionally, there are problems with public impressions of the fairness of police behavior and the use of violence by the police.

Key Terms
licensing (of law enforcement officials) (p. 450)
use of force (p. 450)
Sandra Bland Act (p. 453)

Practice Quiz
1. The agency responsible for licensing peace officers is the
   a) Texas Peace Officers Association.
   b) Police Licensing Board.
   c) Texas Commission on Law Enforcement.
   d) FBI.
   e) Texas Department of Public Safety.

2. One important requirement of the Sandra Bland Act is that
   a) jail deaths must be investigated by an independent agency.
   b) families of those who die in jail will have the right to sue for monetary damages.
   c) jailers will be legally liable if a person dies in a county jail.
   d) persons cannot be jailed if their offense is only punished by a fine.
   e) persons must give written consent for their vehicle to be searched by the police.

3. Officer-involved shootings in Texas
   a) create questions of racial bias in the use of violence by police.
   b) have never involved shootings of unarmed suspects.
   c) are always examined by the Texas Commission on Law Enforcement to determine if correct procedure was followed.
   d) are rarely controversial.
   e) will lead to the arrest of the police officer who did the shooting.

Categorizing Crime in Texas

- **Identify the major classifications of crime under Texas law and the types of punishments that may be imposed (pp. 454–57)**

Crimes are categorized along a number of dimensions. The more serious crimes are felonies. The less serious crimes are misdemeanors. Within each classification are various degrees of crime based upon the severity of the offenses. The more serious the crimes, the greater the penalties.

Key Terms
felony (p. 454)
misdemeanor (p. 455)
probation (p. 456)
parole (p. 456)
"three strikes" provision (p. 456)

Practice Quiz
4. The most serious crimes are classified as
  a) felonies.
  b) misdemeanors.
  c) trial-eligible crimes.
  d) grand jury felonies.
  e) county-court-at-law crimes.

5. Probation refers to
  a) a judge's initial term in office.
  b) a suspension of the jail or prison sentence.
  c) a court in the state court system.
  d) release into the community after time in prison.
  e) failure to pay bail.

6. Which of the following is true?
  a) Parole is rarely granted in Texas.
  b) Members of the Texas Board of Pardons and Paroles are chosen by the legislature every two years.
  c) People convicted of capital crimes are not eligible for parole.
  d) The death penalty is required in all serious felonies.
  e) Texas does not enhance the sentence of repeat felony offenders.

The Criminal Justice Process

- **Outline the procedural steps that occur after a person is arrested (pp. 457–65)**

There are a number of stages in the criminal justice process, including arrest, arraignment, possible posting of bail, possible grand jury indictment, pretrial hearings, and either plea bargaining or trial. If a person is found guilty, he or she will be sentenced, after which there may be appeals. Within this process, the most important actor is probably the district attorney, who is the key decision maker with regard to charging a suspect, presenting evidence to a grand jury, plea bargaining, or recommending a sentence to a jury or judge.

Key Terms
bail (p. 457)
grand jury (p. 460)
plea bargain (p. 460)
county attorney (p. 463)
district attorney (p. 463)
assigned counsel (p. 464)
public defender (p. 464)

Practice Quiz
7. Grand juries
  a) review all decisions made by a trial judge.
  b) determine if witnesses are telling the truth by voting "true bills" or "false bills."
  c) determine if there is probable cause to prosecute an individual for a crime.
  d) hear trials involving the death penalty.
  e) hear trials in district court.

8. District attorneys may have the most important roles in the criminal justice process because
   a) they have the power to charge people with crimes.
   b) they have the power to plea bargain with defendants.
   c) they usually make the only presentation before grand juries.
   d) all of the above
   e) none of the above

9. Which of the following statements about plea bargaining is true?
   a) Plea bargaining threatens to overwhelm the limited resources of a prosecutor's office.
   b) Plea bargaining does not benefit defendants.
   c) Plea bargains are made by defendants with district attorneys and agreed to by a judge.
   d) Most Texas district attorneys oppose plea bargaining.
   e) Most Texas criminal defense attorneys oppose plea bargaining.

10. Indigent defendants charged with serious crimes in Texas
    a) must represent themselves.
    b) are usually represented by private attorneys pro bono as part of their ethical obligation to help others.
    c) most commonly are represented by public defenders.
    d) most commonly are represented by assigned counsel.
    e) are usually represented by legal clinics at law schools.

Crime, Corrections, and the Texas Prison System

- **Describe prisons and corrections policy in Texas (pp. 465–76)**

The Texas prison system is one of the largest in the nation. A major federal court decision (*Ruiz v. Estelle*) found serious overcrowding in the prison system. A series of reforms have been implemented to address the concerns raised by the decision. There has been an effort to lessen the number of people in prison through community supervision. While Texas remains the death penalty capital of the United States, fewer death penalties have been imposed recently than in earlier years.

Practice Quiz

11. The Texas prison system
    a) was vastly affected by a federal court decision, *Ruiz v. Estelle*, which declared that the overcrowded system was unconstitutional.
    b) holds mostly persons convicted of violent crimes.
    c) is a very costly way of dealing with crime as opposed to community supervision such as drug and alcohol programs, and probation and parole.
    d) is beginning to contract in size after a long period of expansion.
    e) All of the above are true of the Texas prison system.

12. The Texas Department of Criminal Justice
    a) is run by a nine-member board appointed by the governor.
    b) is run by an elected body.
    c) runs the criminal court system.
    d) establishes sentencing guidelines for crimes.
    e) grants probation to those convicted of crimes.

13. The death penalty
    a) has now been banned in Texas.
    b) has been imposed less frequently since Texas allowed juries to sentence a defendant to life without parole.
    c) is opposed by most Texas voters.
    d) is carried out disproportionately against Whites.
    e) is imposed by a majority vote of the Texas Board of Pardons and Paroles.

The Integrity of the Texas Criminal Justice System

- Explain why Texas's criminal justice system is controversial and how it is being reformed (pp. 476–80)

Texas has had a significant number of people who have been wrongfully convicted. Numerous recent cases in which convictions were overturned have raised questions about the criminal justice system in Texas. Recent reforms that have been enacted may help reduce the number of wrongful convictions in Texas and improve the fairness of the criminal justice system. Reforms also may rely more on rehabilitation programs and less on incarceration as a solution to crime.

Practice Quiz

14. People have been wrongfully convicted in Texas because of
    a) police misconduct.
    b) bad or outdated forensic science.
    c) mistaken identifications.
    d) prosecutorial misconduct.
    e) All of the above are reasons for wrongful convictions.

15. An advance in which technology has conclusively proved the innocence of a large number of convicted people is
    a) drug testing.
    b) ballistics testing.
    c) DNA analysis.
    d) fire science.
    e) fingerprinting.

16. Reforms in the criminal justice process include
    a) financial compensation for people wrongfully convicted.
    b) changes to suspect lineups so that the police officer in charge of the lineup does not know who the actual suspect is.
    c) expanding drug treatment programs.
    d) showing photos in photo identifications to witnesses sequentially rather than at the same time to reduce the danger of witnesses comparing photos and choosing the one that best fits their memory of the assailant.
    e) All of the above are reforms to the criminal justice process.

17. Probation costs are
    a) about the same as prison costs.
    b) 10 percent higher than prison costs.
    c) considerably less than prison costs.
    d) extremely expensive because of costs of drug treatments.
    e) double the cost of prison.

The Santa Fe Bridge is a busy border crossing between Ciudad Juárez, Mexico, and El Paso, United States. Immigration to Texas from Mexico, Latin America, and elsewhere has transformed the state's demographics and increased its population in urban centers. What effects does this change have on the culture, politics, and public policies in Texas?

Building the Future: Public Policies for a Changing Texas

WHY PUBLIC POLICIES MATTER FOR THE FUTURE OF TEXAS The Texas of the early twenty-first century is far different from the Texas of the nineteenth and twentieth centuries. One of the most significant changes is the fact that Texas has become a majority-minority state. That is, non-Hispanic Whites now constitute a minority in the state. Latinos, African Americans, and Asian Americans combine to form a majority statewide, with Latinos now composing 40 percent of the entire state population. This new reality has led to a wide variety of responses at the state level, as well as in many local communities. In particular, the issue of immigration has become more salient and will undoubtedly continue to dominate the headlines.

Immigration has long affected Texas because it is a border state with Mexico. In recent years, because of national politics, state politicians have turned their attention to dealing with public policy issues related to the border. For example, in 2014 former governor Rick Perry sparred with the Obama administration by claiming that the federal government was not adequately protecting the border from illegal immigration and smuggling. He used his authority as governor to push for "Operation Strong Safety," a program aimed at investing $18 million per month of state funds to increase security along the border.[1] The people of Texas, despite the high numbers of Latinos in the state, seem to favor stricter controls on immigration and harsher punishments for undocumented immigrants. In an October 2019 poll of Texans conducted by the *Texas Tribune*, 50 percent of respondents agreed that undocumented immigrants should be deported immediately, while 44 percent disagreed.

Donald Trump's 2016 presidential campaign brought the issue of immigration even more prominently into the American political dialogue. With slightly over 11 million undocumented immigrants living in the United States (3.6 percent of the population), Trump called for efforts to remove and deport people living in the United States illegally. According to the Pew Research Center, in 2020 Texas had 1,600,000 illegal immigrants living in the state (about 6 percent of the state population). Specifically, Trump also called for the construction of a border wall and the deportation of undocumented immigrants. President Trump was ultimately unable to secure funding from Congress to build the wall, which is estimated to cost up to $22 billion to construct.[2] During the campaign, Trump suggested that Mexico would pay for the construction for the wall, but Mexico has said unequivocally this will not ever happen.

Legal and illegal immigration continue to have an enormous impact on the state's politics, but the state is also changing in other profound ways. Texas has become more demographically, economically, and politically diverse. Population growth has strained the state's infrastructure, leading to proposals to make transportation more efficient. Higher education in the state also faces important challenges, given that state funding for higher education has not kept up with the state's booming population growth. Droughts have also challenged the ability of local governments to provide safe, clean, and reliable water to residents.

This chapter will explore the challenges Texas faces in transportation, demographic change (including immigration), education, and water. These are just some of the growing issues that Texas will face in the coming years, but they are the most critical. These challenges strain state and local bureaucracies and budgets and raise important questions of federalism. They are the issues that will continue to dominate Texas elections for the foreseeable future and tackling them is likely to expose the deep divisions within and between the political parties that dominate Texas government today. In other words, we hope this chapter will answer the question, How will state and local politics shape, and be shaped by, a rapidly changing Texas?

CHAPTER GOALS

- Explain the major issues facing transportation policy in Texas (pp. 489–96)

- Analyze how immigration and border issues will change Texas in the coming years (pp. 497–507)

- Analyze the challenges facing Texas's system of higher education (pp. 507–18)

- Explain the challenges facing Texas's water supply (pp. 518–22)

Transportation Policy in Texas

Explain the major issues facing
transportation policy in Texas

The growth of Texas, especially the growth of the state's cities, has led to major issues
involving transportation. The pressure on the transportation system is one felt by nearly
every Texan. How will the state respond to keep Texas moving?

Texas Roads and Highways

Texas is a driving state. One survey found that 93 percent of Texans had a personal automobile or motorcycle as their primary means of transportation. Only 1 percent of Texans relied on public transportation, 1 percent on bicycling, and 2 percent on walking.
On average, Texans drive their personal vehicles an astounding 17,321 miles a year, an
increase of 3,970 miles per year since 2014. While 73 percent of Texans agree that there
is a need to increase transportation funding in the state, there is not strong support for
an increase—it's simply not a critical issue for most Texans.[3] Moreover, there is no agreement among Texans as to how an increase in transportation funding should be spent.

There are nearly 17.4 million licensed drivers in Texas. Only California, with over
27 million licensed drivers, has more.[4] The Texas highway network is the nation's largest,
and Texas has a massive and expensive obligation to maintain a wide variety of roads and
highways that people drive on approximately 455 million miles a day (see Table 14.1).
Texas roads are usually measured in one of two ways: **centerline miles**, which is the
total length of a road or a road segment, and **lane miles**, which are the centerline miles

centerline miles total length of
a road or road segment

lane miles centerline miles
multiplied by the number of lanes

TABLE 14.1

State-Maintained Roads and Highways in Texas

CLASSIFICATION	NUMBER OF CENTERLINE MILES	NUMBER OF LANE MILES	DAILY VEHICLE MILES TRAVELED
Interstate highways	3,417	16,376	167,083,705
U.S. highways	11,905	35,326	104,644,771
State highways, spurs, loops, business routes	16,390	42,726	112,992,589
Farm or ranch-to-market roads	40,910	84,925	69,154,237
Park roads	348	771	706,312
Total	72,970	180,124	454,581,614

SOURCE: Ginger Lowry and T. J. Costello, "Texas Road Finance (Part 1), Paying for Highways and Byways," *Fiscal Notes*, May 2016.
Data are from the Texas Department of Transportation.

---

multiplied by the road's number of lanes. Another measure commonly used is **vehicle miles traveled**, which is an estimate of road usage. Vehicle miles traveled are calculated by multiplying average daily amount of traffic on a road by its length in centerline miles.[5]

The Problem with Texas Roads and Highways

The American Society of Civil Engineers has determined that 24 percent of Texas's major roads are in poor condition. In addition, Texas has about 53,000 bridges. Half of those bridges have been in service for over 40 years and 20 percent over 60 years. Many of the state's bridges cannot meet increased traffic volume and loads.[6]

Congestion of roadways has become a major problem in the state's urban areas, a situation that is only expected to get worse as the state's urban areas continue to grow.[7] The Texas A&M Transportation Institute compiled a list of the 100 most congested roads in the state, most of which were in Austin, the Dallas–Fort Worth area, Houston, and San Antonio. Six of the 10 most congested roadways in the state were in Harris County, three were in Dallas County, and one was in Travis County. The American Transportation Research Institute listed the top 100 highway bottlenecks for commercial trucks in the United States. Table 14.2 shows that 13 of those traffic bottlenecks were in Texas, including 9 in Houston.

Road congestion is more than an irritant; it is expensive. A study of highway congestion estimated that the average automobile commuter in Houston was delayed about 75 hours a year as a result of traffic congestion and that the estimated cost of that congestion in time and fuel for the average Houston automobile commuter was $1,508. Other major cities in Texas also were estimated to have substantial costs associated with congestion. The congestion costs for Houston alone came to over $4.5 billion per year.[8] Costs of congestion for all Texas metropolitan areas is estimated to be $14 billion per year.[9]

The Costs of Texas Roads and Highways Funding for roads and highways comes from federal and state sources, and much of that funding comes from taxes on motor fuels. Federal taxes for roads and highways are deposited in the federal Highway Trust Fund, which provides money for highways and mass transit programs. The Texas Department of Transportation requested $32.68 billion for 2020–21, with 88 percent of that amount for the development, delivery, and maintenance of state highway projects. As substantial as this sum is, those funding sources have been insufficient to meet needs. Part of the problem has been that the vast new production of oil and gas from shale in Texas has led to an increase in heavy trucks, which have damaged roads. Another problem has been that the costs of road construction and repair have vastly outpaced the rate of inflation, so tax dollars for roads do not purchase what they did even a few years ago. Finally, there have been significant increases in fuel efficiency of vehicles, so people are not buying as much gasoline as they once did. Because motor fuels taxes are based on amount of fuel sold on a cents-per-gallon basis, less fuel purchased means less tax revenue.

Texas's gasoline tax is 20 cents per gallon, and the federal gasoline tax is 18.4 cents per gallon. When all fuel taxes on gasoline and diesel are considered, Texas's taxes are

TABLE 14.2

Top Trucking Traffic Bottlenecks in Texas

NATIONAL RANK OF BOTTLENECK	CITY	BOTTLENECK LOCATION
#5	Houston	I-45 at I-69/US 59
#13	Houston	I-10 at I-45
#16	Dallas	I-45 at I-30
#22	Austin	I-35
#24	Houston	I-45 at I-610 North
#27	Houston	I-10 at I-610 West
#42	Dallas	US 75 at I-635
#57	Houston	I-10 at I-610 East
#61	Houston	I-610 at US 290
#69	Fort Worth	I-35W at I-30
#79	Houston	I-610 at US 59 West
#89	Houston	I-45 at I-610 South
#100	Houston	I-10 at US 59

SOURCE: American Transportation Research Institute, "2019 Top Truck Bottlenecks" (2019).

the lowest among the 10 largest states. Combining state and federal taxes, Texans pay 38.4 cents in taxes for every gallon of gasoline and 44.4 cents per gallon for diesel. In contrast, Pennsylvanians pay 70 cents in taxes for every gallon of gasoline and 89.7 cents per gallon for diesel (the highest in the nation).[10]

In recognition of the fact that tax revenues dedicated to roads and highways were no longer sufficient, funding for transportation has been increased several times—by increased appropriations in 2013, an amendment to the Texas Constitution in 2014, reallocation of expenditures from the Economic Stabilization Fund, and another constitutional amendment in 2015. However, the demand for transportation expenditures is greater than the available supply of money even with these additional funds. And unless more money through taxation or tolls is spent on transportation, there will be greater congestion in the state.

The coronavirus pandemic, of course, adds to the financial stresses on transportation in the state. The budget problems created by the coronavirus will eventually reduce the funds for highway maintenance and construction, although in the early stages of the pandemic $3.4 billion in discretionary funds were authorized by the Texas Department of Transportation commissioners for an I-35 expansion through Austin. That decision was in spite of efforts by some legislators to delay the decision due to looming financial problems. It seems unlikely further decisions involving transportation will so readily ignore the economic effects of the pandemic.

Traffic in Texas has increased in recent years, causing commuters to experience significant delays and higher fuel expenses. The problem is expected to worsen as Texas's urban centers grow, posing problems for cities like Austin, which house some of the busiest stretches of highway in the state.

Highways and the Future

In 2040, Texas is expected to have 45 million people, and it is expected that Texans will drive 800 million daily vehicle miles. The Texas Department of Transportation estimates that just to maintain current conditions on the state's highways, it needs an additional $5 billion annually. With current reasonably expected revenues, the only way that existing highways and bridges can be maintained in "good" condition—meaning roadways with minimal cracking and smooth rides with structurally sound bridges—is to move all highway expansion dollars to preventive maintenance and rehabilitation of existing highways. With $5 billion additional funding annually, the condition of highways and bridges would be "good" and congestion and mobility in urban areas would be slightly worse than today, while mobility in rural areas would be comparable to today.[11] The question is how to provide the funds for the necessary continued expansion of Texas's roads and highways.

Toll Roads Tax increases are politically unpalatable, and so for about 20 years politicians have turned to tolls as a way to fund, build, and maintain roads in the state. By 2016 there were 25 toll roads in Texas, providing new driving lanes in the rapidly growing urban areas. Toll roads solved a huge problem for the conservative political leadership of the state. Funding for the roads was off-budget. The money would be borrowed for the roads based on the planned tolls that would be collected, and the roads could be built without raising the gasoline tax, which would have been overwhelmingly unpopular among voters.

The problem was that as more and more roads in urban areas became toll roads, tolls became more and more unpopular. The result was that political leaders such as Governor Greg Abbott and Lieutenant Governor Dan Patrick responded to that unpopularity of tolls by opposing additional toll roads. This led to the state to scrap plans for toll roads in some key congested areas. Without tolls, by 2040 the Dallas–Fort Worth area can expect to see an 80 percent increase in travel time, a 44 percent decrease in average speeds, and a $50 billion annual increase in the cost of congestion.[12]

Stunned by the opposition to toll lanes, the Regional Transportation Council chair, Rob Franke, noted, "The RTC [Regional Transportation Council] has successfully utilized innovative finance tools such as tolled managed lanes to complete a dozen projects worth over $12 billion since 2005. These are projects that would still be waiting in line for pay-as-you-go funding to be available."[13] Nevertheless, the problem for highway transportation policy is that without tolls, and with political opposition to tax increases, especially increases in the gasoline tax, there seems no funding mechanism to adequately meet the future needs for Texas roads and highways.

The Bullet Train At first glance, Texas might not seem an ideal place for a high-speed rail project: Texas's urban areas have a history of low public transportation use, Texans are very oriented toward the use of automobiles, and there is no significant

WHAT DO TEXANS THINK? ★★★★★★★★★★★★★★★★★★★★★★★★★

Support for Revenue Increases for Transportation

Many people acknowledge that Texas faces major transportation challenges. Solutions, however, are hard to come by, and the public doesn't seem very supportive of raising revenue for transportation. Of all suggested revenue increases, the strongest support (and that support is very weak) is for small increases in vehicle registration fees and for increases in the gasoline tax. How would an urban, rural, or suburban Texas legislative candidate campaign for improvements in the state's transportation system? Given the generally low support for additional revenue for transportation, what is the likely state response to the increasing congestion on the state's roads?

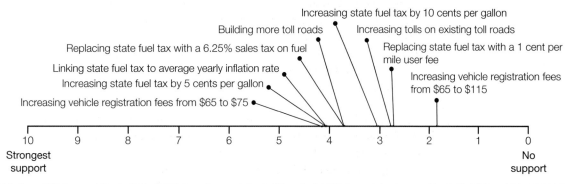

SOURCE: Texas A&M Transportation Institute, "2016 Texas Transportation Poll" (a poll of 4,805 Texans taken between March 10, 2016, and July 28, 2016).

intercity rail traffic in the state. Yet, a high-speed rail project between Dallas and Houston is only one of three such projects in the United States that is in advanced stages of development. (The other two are in California and Florida.) In contrast to the California train, the Texas train will not be subsidized but will instead rely on private investment and federal loans. And the Texas train will travel at twice the speed of the Florida train.[14]

Relying on Japanese train technology, it is claimed the Texas train will travel at speeds as fast as 205 mph. It will make the 240-mile trip between Dallas and Houston in 90 minutes, and trains will run every 30 minutes. This massive project will take at least a $12 billion investment and possibly as much as $20 billion. It will require the purchase of thousands of parcels of land. Supporters of the train believe it will be an economic engine that will spur development in the Dallas-Houston corridor as well as generate jobs needed for the railway's construction and operation. It is also claimed the train will generate substantial tax revenues. Supporters argue that the dramatic growth of Houston and the Dallas–Fort Worth Metroplex provides justification for construction of the train. They point to air travel between Dallas and Houston being one of the most heavily traveled air routes in the United States, and they point to the flat and largely rural land between the cities as making construction of high-speed rail fairly easy and relatively inexpensive.

There is, however, major opposition to the high-speed rail proposal.[15] Opponents believe it cannot be profitable and that taxpayers will wind up paying its costs. When COVID-19 led to the layoffs of 28 Texas Central employees, several state lawmakers asked the Secretary of Transportation to put an end to the bullet train on the grounds that the layoffs showed the project did not have sufficient financial resources. Some opponents even oppose the reliance on Japanese train technology, believing the train will primarily benefit Japan. Most significantly, many landowners in the 240 miles between Dallas and Houston are opposed to the train. As Figure 14.1 shows, the train's path will run through miles of rural countryside, and many of those rural landowners do not want to sell their land in order to speed the travel of urban dwellers. For those who do not want to sell, their land will have to be seized under the governmental power of eminent domain, in which government may take property for a public purpose as long as just compensation is paid. Opponents of the train have argued that the power of eminent domain does not extend to the Texas Central Railway (the corporate entity for the bullet train) because, though private entities such as railroads have the power of eminent domain, the Texas Central is not a railroad, since it currently operates no trains. That position was unsuccessful at the Court of Appeals level and it seems doubtful that argument will prevail in a further appeal, but without that power of eminent domain, it is clear that the right of way for the bullet train cannot be obtained.[16] Still, opposition to the project is strong. Supporters of the bullet train, however, did successfully oppose numerous bills in the 2019 legislative session that were designed to prevent or hinder the bullet train project. While further regulatory and legal hurdles remain, Texas Central passed two significant federal regulatory requirements in September 2020, which moves the project much closer to construction.

Texas plans to use Japanese bullet train technology to construct a route between Houston and Dallas to both develop that corridor and ease transportation issues between the two cities. Debates continue over the cost of the project, as some worry taxpayers will shoulder the burden of the cost.

FIGURE 14.1

Dallas to Houston Bullet Train

SOURCE: The Texas Bullet Train, "County Alignment Maps for Proposed Routes," Texas Central, www.texascentral .com/project (accessed 9/20/18).

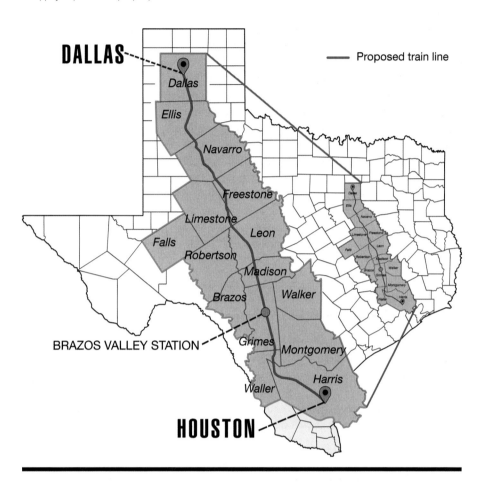

Public Transit in Texas

No part of Texas is known for its public transit or its use. Texas is a car-centered culture, and its sprawling cities are poorly designed for public transportation. Generally, larger cities in Texas have the best public transit, with the greatest availability of transit being at the city core and with less availability as the city spreads into the suburbs. In fact, many suburban cities see no advantage in participating in the public transit programs of central cities or in paying the taxes necessary to operate public transit programs. Houston is a special problem for the provision of public transit. The city was developed with cars in mind, and the city's territory extends over 1,285 square miles—an area so large that service is spread thin and that widespread transit coverage would be costly. Many public transit advocates believe bus and rail service is doomed in the city. For about

70 percent of the population in Harris and surrounding counties, transit access is poor, and more than half the population has no meaningful bus service.[17] Extreme as Houston's problems in providing public transit are, other cities in Texas face similar problems for similar reasons.

Table 14.3 offers a sense of how limited public transit and its use in Texas's major cities and metropolitan areas are compared with other major American cities and metropolitan areas. The Center for Neighborhood Technology has designed an overall transit score from 0 to 10, which considers the connectivity of public transit (the ease of reaching one's destination), access to land area, access to jobs, and the frequency of transit service. A score of 0 is the lowest possible score, and a score of 10 is the highest possible score. In terms of public transit, New York City is the highest-rated city, with a score of 9.6 (a rating tied with San Francisco) and with 59 percent of the city's commuters using public transit. The New York City metropolitan area has a score of 6.9 with 32.54 percent of the area's commuters using public transit.[18]

The Texas cities and metropolitan areas shown in Table 14.3 have relatively low transit performance scores and also a low percentage of commuters who use public transit. This leads one to question the overall value of public transit as a solution to the increasing traffic congestion problems in Texas urban areas. Perhaps if there were more public transit available, more people would use it. And perhaps as congestion increases, there will be more use of public transit. For now, however, public transit seems to be having little effect on driving habits in Texas.

TABLE 14.3

Public Transit in Major Texas Cities and Metropolitan Areas

CITY	OVERALL TRANSIT SCORE*	TOTAL COMMUTERS	COMMUTERS USING TRANSIT (%)
Houston	5.9	1,130,049	3.90%
Houston metro area	2.8	2,984,353	2.28
San Antonio	6.6	644,980	3.24
San Antonio metro area	4.5	1,038,068	2.22
Dallas	6.8	605,121	4.35
Dallas metro area	2.8	3,283,802	1.55
Austin	5.2	460,593	4.33
Austin metro area	2.8	954,575	2.45
El Paso	4.9	265,671	1.89
El Paso metro area	4.1	339,798	1.53

*An overall score ranging from 0 to 10 that looks at connectivity of transit, access to land area and jobs, and frequency of service.

SOURCE: Center for Neighborhood Technology, AllTransit, 2019, alltransit.cnt.org.

Demographic Change in Texas

Analyze how immigration and border issues will change Texas in the coming years

The Texas population continues to grow. This population boom is changing Texas socially and politically. These changes raise important questions that Texans are likely to be grappling with for generations: Who is coming to Texas, and why? Are rates of immigration to Texas too high? Are immigrants enhancing Texas's economy and society, or are they taking away jobs and social services from American citizens? Should undocumented immigrants be prosecuted, deported, or provided a path to citizenship?

Who Are Texas's Immigrants?

Americans from other parts of the country are flocking to Texas for economic opportunities. The state's oil and gas industry has largely recovered from the 2008 recession. Oil prices have gone up, and major companies have continued to expand and hire. This benefits the Houston region as well as other regions in the state with opportunities for natural gas exploration. In addition, migrants from all over the world continue to come to Texas, both legally and illegally. As Figure 14.2 shows, Texas and New York are essentially tied in terms of total number of immigrants in the state. Only California has a larger immigrant population.

The state demographer estimated that in 2018, 17 percent of the state population was foreign-born, as opposed to only 9 percent of the state population that was foreign-born in 1990.[19] Foreign-born individuals can go through the process of becoming

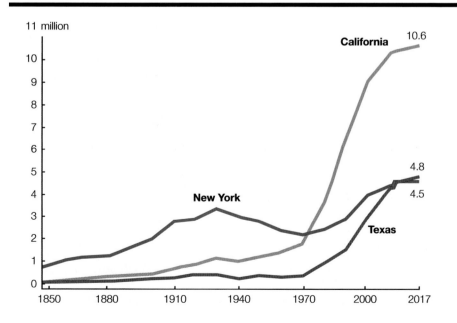

FIGURE 14.2

Immigrant Population in Texas, California, and New York

SOURCE: Renee Stepler, "Texas . . . Size," April 21, 2016, www.pewresearch .org/fact-tank/2016/04/21/texas -immigrant-population-now-rivals-new -yorks-in-size/.

naturalized citizen a foreign-born individual who becomes a citizen through a process involving examinations and demonstration of good moral character

naturalized citizens. This process can only happen if a person immigrated legally and has been a resident of the United States for at least five years. Individuals must also demonstrate good moral character, knowledge of American government, and a basic command of English.

Immigrants have come to Texas from all over the world. Sixty-six percent of immigrants in Texas are from Latin America, and 23 percent are from Asia. The rest of the immigrants in the state come from other countries. This diversity is most reflected in the state's major metropolitan areas. In fact, Fort Bend County, just southwest of Houston, is considered the most ethnically diverse county in the United States.[20] Native-born Texans have deep connections to the immigrant experience. The American Immigration Council estimates that 15 percent of native-born U.S. citizens in Texas have at least one immigrant parent. In the United States, even if someone is born to an immigrant parent, he or she will be a U.S. citizen.[21]

Immigrants in Texas also come from all educational backgrounds. The American Immigration Council estimates that 25 percent of adult immigrants in the state have a college degree, while almost 40 percent have less than a high school diploma. As in every state, public education at the K–12 level is available to all Texans regardless of their immigration status. In terms of higher education, in 2001, Texas passed a law allowing undocumented immigrants the ability to pay in-state tuition at the state's public universities. This bill was known as the **Texas Dream Act**. When he ran for president in 2008, Governor Rick Perry received criticism for signing this legislation, but he defended his position during the presidential debates. In 2017 some Republican legislators attempted to repeal this law, but they were ultimately unsuccessful. Other bills addressing immigration, however, were successful, such as SB 4, the bill targeting sanctuary cities (see p. 501).[22]

While most immigrants in Texas are legal residents, nearly 1.7 million of the total population is undocumented. This equates to 35 percent of the total immigrant popula-

Texas Dream Act law passed in 2001 allowing undocumented immigrants living in Texas to pay in-state tuition rates at public universities

While debates over immigration policies continue in Texas and throughout the United States, it is clear that immigrants have a large impact on the business and economy of Texas. In 2017 many people in Texas and the nation held "A Day Without Immigrants" to underscore the importance of immigrants to businesses across the country.

tion in the state, and 6 percent of the total state population.[23] Because these individuals are not legally present in the United States, they are subject to deportation if caught by the Border Patrol or Immigration and Customs Enforcement (ICE). With the failure of Congress to pass immigration reform, states have filled the policy void by enacting policies aimed at border security.

The labor force in Texas largely depends on immigrants. The American Immigration Council estimates that nearly 3 million immigrant workers composed 22 percent of the state labor force in 2015, and the Pew Research Center estimates that 8.5 percent of the workforce in the state is composed of undocumented immigrants. Certain occupation groups have high immigrant shares in the state. Forty-five percent of all building and grounds cleaning and maintenance employees are immigrants. Forty-three percent of all construction and extraction employees are immigrants. Forty percent of farming, fishing, and forestry employees are immigrants, and nearly 30 percent of all food preparation workers and servers in the state are immigrants.

Studies show that immigrants in Texas have paid tens of billions of dollars in taxes. In Texas, most revenue the state collects is from sales taxes. Everyone residing in the state has to pay these taxes when they purchase goods and services. In 2014 the Institute on Taxation and Economic Policy estimated that undocumented immigrants in Texas paid $1.6 billion in state and local taxes.[24] In addition, many undocumented immigrants also indirectly pay taxes through rents that defray the cost of property taxes.

Immigrants contribute tens of billions of dollars to the Texas economy. One estimate reported by the American Immigration Council concluded that immigrant households had nearly $90 billion in after-tax income in 2014. Another estimate in 2018 by New American Economy concluded that immigrant households in Texas had $112.8 billion in after-tax income that year. This income is used to purchase goods and services, which improve the state's economy and provide work for many Texans.[25]

Immigrants are also disproportionately business owners in the state, especially in the large cities. In the Houston metropolitan area, 42 percent of business owners are immigrants, in Dallas–Fort Worth 23 percent, and in the San Antonio area 19 percent, according to the American Immigration Council. Small business owners are the engine of today's economy, and they provide jobs for native-born workers as well.

The large metropolises in the state have also seen explosive growth of immigration. Indeed, it is estimated that 24 percent of the population in the Houston metropolitan area is foreign born (including legal and undocumented immigrants).[26] Most immigrants are migrating to Harris County (Houston), Dallas County, Bexar County (San Antonio), Tarrant County (Fort Worth), and Travis County (Austin).[27]

Immigration Policy in Texas

With the growth of immigration in Texas and the United States, one key policy debate is how to deal with the undocumented population. In particular, conflict has emerged between local officials and state officials on whether to cooperate or not with federal immigration authorities when undocumented immigrants are arrested for violation of local ordinances or state laws.

Who Is Responsible for Immigration Policy?

The federal government is ultimately responsible for securing the borders of the United States and regulating entry of goods, services, and individuals. Land crossings between Texas and Mexico are monitored by the U.S. Border Patrol, an agency first created in 1924. The Border Patrol is now part of the U.S. Customs and Border Protection agency, which was created in 2003 following the terrorist attacks of September 11, 2001, to consolidate the functions of separate agencies into one department. Border Patrol agents engage in a practice known as *linewatch* to guard against illegal immigration and smuggling of narcotics. The Border Patrol also operates checkpoints well within U.S. territory. These checkpoints are another line of defense against undocumented immigrants who may have crossed the border illegally outside of a designated entry point.

Recent Texas governors have sought to address what they consider a crisis on the border by deploying members of the Texas National Guard to assist the Border Patrol in its mission. Members of the Texas National Guard patrolling the border cannot arrest or apprehend individuals, but they can notify the Border Patrol if they encounter situations requiring the attention of federal authorities. Sheriffs and local law enforcement along the border with Mexico also cannot enforce immigration laws, but they can communicate with federal immigration authorities regarding individuals they apprehend who are not legally present, as well as individuals smuggling contraband.

While the federal government is responsible for securing the border, cities and localities have attempted to deal with undocumented immigration by passing local ordinances aimed at addressing this issue. For example, the city of Farmers Branch, Texas, passed an ordinance in 2006 requiring property owners to verify that their tenants were legal residents.

Sanctuary Cities

In Texas, perhaps the most controversial issue dealing with immigration had to do with the extent to which local law enforcement cooperated with federal immigration authorities. Some city and county police departments, such as Austin, refused to cooperate with federal immigration authorities regarding apprehended individuals who were not legal residents. This led to a prolonged policy debate in the state legislature regarding how best to deal with these cities and counties, known as **sanctuary cities**: localities where sheriffs have decided not to share information regarding the arrests of undocumented persons with federal immigration authorities.

During the 2016 presidential campaign, Donald Trump declared that he would order his attorney general and secretary of homeland security to stop federal funding of sanctuary cities. In April 2017 the Trump administration followed through on this campaign promise when then–attorney general Jeff Sessions sent letters to nine cities warning them that if they did not cooperate with Immigrations and Customs Enforcement (ICE), they would lose funding from the Department of Justice. A few cities, including Seattle, have sued the federal government, and a federal court issued an injunction barring the removal of funding until a court could hear the dispute. Lawsuits have continued in this policy area and in February 2020, the Department of Justice targeted sanctuary cities by challenging local ordinances that, in the judgment of the attorney general, limit the ability of federal immigration officials to deport unauthorized immigrants.

sanctuary cities localities where sheriffs have decided not to share information regarding the arrests of undocumented persons with federal immigration authorities

In the 2017 Texas state legislative session, state senator Charles Perry (R-Lubbock) introduced **Senate Bill 4 (SB 4)**, a bill that would end state funding of sanctuary cities. The bill would make it a crime for localities in Texas to refuse to cooperate with federal officials on immigration matters. Local sheriffs and law enforcement refusing to honor ICE holds would be subject to criminal prosecution. Local police departments of the major cities were largely opposed to this bill because they saw it as a way to deputize local law enforcement to enforce federal immigration laws in addition to city ordinances and state laws. In fact, Travis County sheriff Sally Hernandez was singled out by Governor Abbott for refusing to comply with ICE hold requests, and Abbott took executive action to prevent state funds from going to the Travis County sheriff's office. Houston police chief Art Acevedo opposed SB 4 by stating that it would go after "cooks and nannies, not hardened criminals."[28] However, Lieutenant Governor Patrick strongly pushed the bill through the state Senate, arguing that the bill was necessary to ensure that "no liberal local official can flaunt the law," by "allowing criminal aliens who have committed a crime to go free."[29] The state Senate acted first by passing SB 4 in February 2017 by a party line vote of 20–11.[30]

In late April 2017 the Texas House of Representatives took up SB 4. There it was met with more sustained opposition from the Democratic minority. Dallas state representative Rafael Anchía led a series of speeches against the measure in the chamber along with other members of the Mexican American Legislative Caucus (MALC). Of note were speeches by representatives Ana Hernandez (D-Houston) and Gene Wu (D-Houston). Hernandez spoke about her experience as an undocumented child and how the bill would instill fear in undocumented Texans. In particular, she and many local sheriffs opposing the bill argued that the new law would lead to an underreporting of crimes in the state as well as make it more difficult to solve crimes because of lack of cooperation with law enforcement. Undocumented immigrants would become less likely to

Senate Bill 4 (SB 4) law passed in 2017 by the Texas legislature enacting penalties for sanctuary cities that refused to cooperate with federal immigration authorities

In 2017 protesters gathered to demonstrate their opposition to SB 4, a bill that empowers police to question anyone's citizenship during routine stops. While the bill went into effect September 1, 2018, some expect it to increase instances of racial profiling and be eventually overturned by the courts.

cooperate with police or report crimes for fear of being reported to federal immigration authorities. Wu spoke about how the bill reminded him of the Chinese Exclusion Act of 1882, which he argued was inspired by fear and hatred of minorities.[31] Speaker Joe Straus, a moderate Republican from San Antonio, did not publicly support SB 4 yet allowed the bill to come to the floor given the support of both the lieutenant governor and governor. Despite fervent Democratic opposition, the bill passed the chamber on a party line vote of 93 in support and 54 against.

Abbott had signaled his support of SB 4, and once the measure passed the state House it was only a matter of time before the bill would become law. On a Sunday evening in early May, much to the consternation of opponents, Abbott broadcast his signature of the measure on Facebook Live. Critics accused Abbott of ignoring the bishops of his Catholic church, who voiced opposition to the measure, and for signing the legislation on a day of worship for many Texans.

Before anyone had the opportunity to sue over SB 4, Texas attorney general Ken Paxton asked a federal court for a declaratory judgment the first week of May 2017. In other words, the state asked the U.S. District Court in Texas to rule that the law is not a violation of the Fourth or Fourteenth Amendment to the U.S. Constitution.[32] Nevertheless, the measure was immediately challenged in court by several border towns and the League of United Latin American Citizens (LULAC). They charged that the new law, which took effect September 1, 2018, should be struck down because it would lead to racial profiling and have a disparate impact on the state's Latino population.[33] Critics argue that the measure targets Latinos similar to how Arizona's unconstitutional SB 1070 "Show me your papers" law targets Latinos. Defenders of the law claim that it will make communities safer by deterring illegal immigrants from committing crimes.

Civil rights groups have continued to protest the sanctuary cities law. On Mother's Day in 2017, hundreds gathered in Austin to protest the new law by marching from the state capitol building to the governor's mansion. Resistance to the law will also take place in the courts, where a long fight is inevitable. On May 21, 2017, El Paso County, along with the Texas Civil Rights Project, filed a lawsuit in federal court asking for the impending law to be ruled unconstitutional. The lawsuit alleges that SB 4 violates the equal protection clause and due process clause of the Fourteenth Amendment, as well as the Fourth Amendment's protection against unreasonable searches and seizures.[34] Other cities have joined El Paso in filing lawsuits against the state. In Houston, protesters interrupted Mayor Sylvester Turner at an event to demand that the city join a lawsuit against the legislation. In early June 2018, Turner asked the city council to join other Texas cities' lawsuits against the new law.

The American Civil Liberties Union (ACLU) has also joined in litigation against the new law, created a "travel alert" for Texas, and developed a bilingual website to inform Texans about their constitutional rights.[35] The website includes information about how to respond if stopped by police or questioned by law enforcement offers with respect to immigration status.

Governor Abbott and Attorney General Ken Paxton have vowed to defend the law in court, claiming it is constitutional and necessary to ensure public safety. They point to the case of Kate Steinle, a woman who was killed by an undocumented immigrant in California. The argument is that this happened in a sanctuary city and that the person who committed this crime would have been off the streets had this happened in a city that fully cooperated with federal law enforcement.

The politically charged and controversial issue of sanctuary cities will likely continue to be debated nationally and in Texas. California became a sanctuary state in 2018, and some localities in that state wanting to cooperate with federal immigration authorities have filed lawsuits demanding that they should retain the ability to collaborate with the federal government. Conflicts among states, localities, and the federal government strike at the heart of federalism, and no doubt the courts will issue rulings further outlining the proper role of each in the realm of immigration policy.

Deferred Action for Childhood Arrivals (DACA)

Toward the end of his presidency, President Obama issued an executive order known as **Deferred Action for Childhood Arrivals (DACA)**, which shielded from deportation an estimated 800,000 young adults enrolled in college who were born abroad but brought to the United States as children by immigrant parents. With the decision of President Trump early in his presidency to rescind the program, the fate of these "dreamers" had remained uncertain. After Trump's decision, many immigrant rights groups joined a lawsuit urging the federal courts to reinstate the program. While the lawsuit was pending, a federal judge allowed DACA permits to continue to be issued. In May 2018, Texas attorney general Ken Paxton joined six other states to sue the federal government, calling for an end to DACA.[36] Paxton and other opponents of DACA have argued that the program should be declared unconstitutional because President Obama effectively made a new law without congressional approval. In addition, they argue that the policy sets a bad precedent because individuals considering illegal entry to the United States might believe they will be granted amnesty in the future. They argue it is also unfair to those who have waited in line and immigrated legally to the United States. In June 2020, the U.S. Supreme Court weighed in on the controversial DACA program and ruled that the Trump administration did not follow proper procedures when it attempted to rescind the program. In a close 5–4 decision, Chief Justice John Roberts wrote for the majority in a narrowly worded opinion that provided a temporary reprieve for DACA recipients, but also gave the administration the ability to attempt to rescind the program again following another legal framework.

Deferred Action for Childhood Arrivals (DACA) executive order implemented by President Obama, which shielded certain undocumented immigrants from deportation if they were enrolled in school, had no criminal records, and were making educational progress

According to the Migration Policy Institute, nearly 1.3 million undocumented immigrants were eligible for DACA in 2020, with the largest share of DACA-eligible recipients from California and Texas.[37] In Texas, nearly 106,000 residents were DACA recipients as of 2020. According to the Migration Policy Institute, 55 percent of DACA-eligible immigrants in Texas had applied for DACA. In addition, more than 57,000 people living in Texas would be eligible for DACA but are not only because they do not meet the educational requirements. An additional 37,000 are estimated to become eligible as they grow older, according to the American Immigration Council.

An estimate by the Hobby School of Public Affairs at the University of Houston found that the DACA-eligible population in the state was 270,366 individuals, or 1 percent of the entire state population. Nearly 24 percent of the total DACA-eligible population (65,202 people) resides in Harris County. The Who Are Texans? feature illustrates where DACA-eligible Texans have come from, where they live, their educational achievements, and language skills.

Border Security One of the most contentious areas of immigration policy is border security, and Texas is at the center of these controversies and debates. Because of its 1,254-mile border with Mexico, Texas is the first point of entry for many land crossings between Mexico and the United States.[38] While many land crossings involve Mexican nationals, a significant number of unaccompanied minors from Central America as well as other migrants fleeing gang violence in Central America are also crossing the border.

Governor Abbott deployed the Texas National Guard to the border in April 2018. His rationale for doing so was that illegal crossings had increased 200 percent in the prior year and that increased National Guard presence would help stem this increase.[39] Governor Abbott's plan called for 1,000 personnel to assist the Department of Homeland Security in securing the border. As members of the military, however, Texas National Guard troops cannot detain and arrest undocumented immigrants crossing the border, or drug smugglers. They can contact the U.S. Border Patrol and the Drug Enforcement Agency, who can decide to take action.

A vivid picture of the complexity of border security emerged in 2018 when reports arose of undocumented children being separated from their parents after being apprehended trying to cross the border into the United States. This resulted from the Trump administration's "zero tolerance" policy aimed at discouraging illegal immigration by demanding that anyone who attempts to cross the border illegally will be detained and prosecuted. Critics noted that the policy is inhumane because it separates children from their parents. The Border Patrol has detention centers in many states, including Texas, and although the normal holding period is 72 hours, children were being detained for much longer periods in facilities that lacked adequate medical care and bedding.[40] Normally, the process calls for the Department of Health and Human Services to match unaccompanied children with foster families, but the backlog in the system prevented timely transfers. Although this is a national issue, many of the Border Patrol stations are located in south Texas.

In the 2018 gubernatorial election, Democratic candidate Lupe Valdez accused Abbott of being President Trump's "puppet," especially on issues relating to the border. Though Abbott deployed his Hispanic mother-in-law in his 2014 race for governor to appeal to the Latino vote, Valdez accused the Republican governor of enacting policies, such as SB 4, which she argued have been harmful to Latinos in the state.[41] The issue of

Who Is Eligible for DACA?

DACA and DACA-eligible individuals were born abroad and arrived undocumented in the United States with their immigrant parents. These individuals were granted relief from deportation in 2012 under an executive order signed by President Obama, but their status is in limbo under the Trump administration and the failure of Congress to take action on the issue. But who are these individuals? Where are they from? How connected are they to the United States and Texas?

Regions of Birth for DACA Eligible Population in Texas*

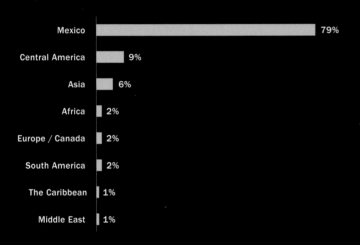

Region	%
Mexico	79%
Central America	9%
Asia	6%
Africa	2%
Europe / Canada	2%
South America	2%
The Caribbean	1%
Middle East	1%

DACA-Eligible Population by Regions in Texas

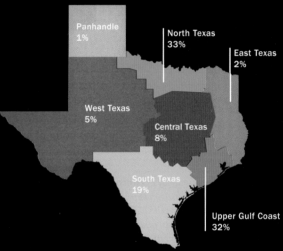

Panhandle 1%
North Texas 33%
East Texas 2%
West Texas 5%
Central Texas 8%
South Texas 19%
Upper Gulf Coast 32%

Note: There is no information about residential areas for 27,420 respondents. Therefore, the above figure is based on information for 242 946 respondents.

*Numbers may not add up to 100 percent due to rounding.

SOURCE: Hobby School of Public Policy, University of Houston.

Profile of DACA Eligible Population in Texas*

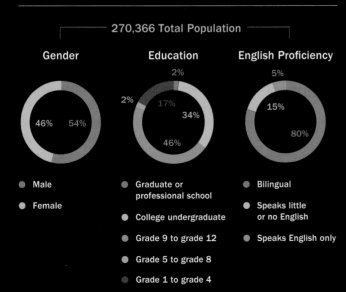

270,366 Total Population

Gender
46% Male
54% Female

Education
2%
2%
17%
34%
46%

- Graduate or professional school
- College undergraduate
- Grade 9 to grade 12
- Grade 5 to grade 8
- Grade 1 to grade 4

English Proficiency
5%
15%
80%

- Bilingual
- Speaks little or no English
- Speaks English only

QUANTITATIVE REASONING

- While all DACA recipients and DACA-eligible individuals are foreign born, what does their English proficiency and level of education say, if anything about their connection to the United States?

- Based on the map, where are most DACA-eligible individuals residing in Texas? Why do you think most DACA-eligible people live in those areas?

The Trump administration's "zero tolerance" policy on illegal immigration created controversy in 2018 when reports emerged that children were being separated from their families. This photo, taken in McAllen, was seen by millions around the world.

border security remained a salient issue in the 2018 campaign largely because of President Trump's repeated efforts to keep the issue on the national agenda.

One of the major promises of President Trump in his 2016 election was the construction of a wall along the border with Mexico. Because of Texas's 1,254-mile-long border with Mexico, this policy is of obvious concern to Texans and has become an issue in statewide campaigns. Proponents of the wall argue that it is needed to keep smugglers, narcotics, and unauthorized individuals from entering the United States. Without a secure border, any other efforts at immigration reform are bound to fail, according to proponents of rigorous border security. Opponents of the wall argue that it would be expensive, disrupt commerce, and antagonize many immigrants. The wall would also not prevent a large source of entry of illegal immigrants: those who simply overstay a tourist visa. In April 2018, Congress approved $1.6 billion to build a border wall spanning 100 miles in parts of California, Texas, and New Mexico. Current plans are to build 33 miles of a wall in Texas, but it is still unclear precisely where the wall will be built.[42] Specific locations are being considered along the border with Mexico, as landowners reported receiving letters in July 2018 requesting consent to survey their land for possible construction.[43]

One of the key goals of President Trump's administration is to build a wall along the U.S. border with Mexico to quell the flow of undocumented immigrants into the country.

In July 2018, Mexico elected a new president, Andrés Manuel López Obrador, who has been an outspoken critic of President Trump and his policies on immigration. Bilateral relations between Mexico and the United States were already strained because of Mexican opposition to the border wall. Nevertheless, during the pandemic in July 2020, President López Obrador visited President Trump in Washington, D.C., in celebration of the new trade agreement among the United States, Mexico, and Canada. Any significant policy changes regarding immigration are bound to have important effects on the Texas economy and will continue to impact the state in coming years. As a result of COVID-19 and the closing of essential travel to and from Mexico, as well as most other countries, immigration levels have undoubtedly dropped significantly. At the same time, immigration officials continue to apprehend, detain, and deport undocumented immigrants even during the pandemic. Detention centers have been in the news during the pandemic for conditions under which the coronavirus has spread due to close quarters and unsanitary practices.

Higher Education Policy in Texas

Analyze the challenges facing Texas's system of higher education

A third challenge facing Texas in coming decades is in higher education. Higher education is an important link between an expanding and diversifying population and a rapidly transforming economy. Businesses in the modern world economy demand a highly skilled workforce. For Texas to compete nationally and internationally, the next generation of Texans must have the skills and training to thrive in an ever-changing high-tech economy. Earning a high school diploma is no longer enough to prepare oneself for the rigors of the job market in the twenty-first century. Associate degrees from community colleges and bachelor's degrees from four-year colleges and universities are seen by employers as prerequisites for applying for good jobs. Increasing numbers of master's degrees in fields such as engineering, computer sciences, and business, as well as Ph.D.s and other professional degrees in medicine, dentistry, and law, are seen by policy makers as the hallmark of an educated population.

A number of factors have structured the evolution of higher education policy in Texas and continue to define it today. First, there was the enormous expansion of higher education in the number of both schools and enrollments since the end of World War II. In 2018, 1.71 million students were enrolled in colleges or universities in Texas. Only California had more enrolled at 2.4 million. In a year when two-year and four-year enrollments were dropping in the United States, Texas added over 20,000 new students. The number of high school graduates in Texas is expected to grow, adding 22.6 percent between the 2011–12 academic year and 2024–25.[44] The demand for college and university slots during this period is expected to grow correspondingly.

A second factor is that universities and colleges exist in a distinct geographic area. They are products of their local environment, and thus they address the educational needs of local as well as state workforces. They are also important local economic actors in their own right, being a source for jobs and personal income. Not surprisingly, local

The Texas university system has expanded rapidly as the number of high school graduates seeking higher education has increased in the last several decades. As that population increases and the working world demands a more skilled workforce, the two most prominent systems, Texas A&M University and the University of Texas at Austin, have become extremely crowded.

Higher Education and Immigration

1 How immigration laws affect higher education in Texas

In most discussions of immigration, pundits and the media often talk about unskilled immigration or undocumented immigration. To be sure, this is an important and pressing issue, especially the issue of unaccompanied minors immigrating to the United States. This citizen's guide addresses a lesser-known but important issue: the intersection of immigration and higher education.

Institutions of higher education in Texas admit students from all over the world to enroll in undergraduate and graduate programs. While many students receive scholarships, others pay for out-of-state tuition, which is a crucial source of revenue for such institutions.

International students wishing to enroll in universities must apply for a student visa from the federal government. These visas allow foreign nationals to enroll in institutions of higher education for the purpose of studying for a degree. In many cases, once the degree is conferred, such students return to their homelands. These arrangements benefit students since U.S. higher education is seen worldwide as an important signal of the acquisition of skills in a variety of fields. The universities benefit through tuition revenue as well as attracting the world's best and brightest students to work with scholars, thereby enhancing the ability of researchers to advance scientific discoveries.

2 What's the debate?

In June 2020, the Trump Administration initiated a new policy that would prevent the entry of most Chinese nationals to study in graduate schools in the United States. In particular, any Chinese nationals associated with any institution supporting China's "military-civil fusion strategy" would no longer be eligible to study in the United States.[a] The order would not apply to Chinese nationals wishing to study in the humanities or social sciences, or other fields that do not "contribute to China's military advancement." The key reason for this change was the concern that these Chinese nationals could potentially engage in espionage and divulge American technology to the Chinese government.

Students from all over the world come to Texas for graduate school. Here, a post-doctoral fellow performs an experiment in a biomedical engineering lab at the University of Texas at Austin.

Because of heightened tensions between China and the United States in the aftermath of the coronavirus pandemic, U.S. officials had become increasingly concerned about the theft of intellectual property, which could adversely affect U.S. national security.

Opponents of this new policy argue that this crackdown is an overreach because it would unfairly prevent talented researchers from a variety of fields who could advance scientific progress. The details of how this policy is implemented are critical, because if only Chinese nationals who attend military establishments are excluded, then this would only affect a small number of students. However, if the definition is broad, then many Chinese nationals would be prevented from studying in the United States.

In addition, a large majority of Chinese nationals currently pay tuition, and if lower numbers attend graduate school, then this could adversely impact already strained budgets due to the coronavirus pandemic.

3 What do the numbers say?

According to data from the Institute of International Education, there were a total of 1,095,299 international students in the United States in 2018–19, including 377,943 graduate students. Overall, the majority of these students

TOP FIVE PLACES OF ORIGIN FOR INTERNATIONAL STUDENTS IN TEXAS

PLACE OF ORIGIN	PERCENT (%) TOTAL
India	24.3%
China	18.9
Mexico	7.6
Vietnam	5.8
Nepal	4.1

INSTITUTIONS WITH THE HIGHEST NUMBER OF INTERNATIONAL STUDENTS

INSTITUTION	TOTAL
University of Texas at Dallas	9,401
Texas A&M University	7,163
University of Texas at Arlington	6,435
University of Texas at Austin	6,395
Houston Community College System	5,645

SOURCE: Institute of International Education. Data includes students in Optional Practical Training programs (OPT), who are graduates of these institutions on work visas.

Communicating Effectively: What Do You Think?

- Do you support the policy of not allowing some Chinese nationals to attend graduate school in the United States because of national security concerns?

- Should other countries be considered for similar policies, such as Iran or Russia? Why or why not?

- Should foreign nationals who receive graduate degrees in the United States be allowed to stay when they finish their degrees? Why or why not?

WANT TO LEARN MORE?

To learn more about international students on your campus, contact your university's global engagement office. For national level information, you may consult the Institute of International Education at http://www. iee.org.

majored in engineering, math, computer science, or business. In 2018, Texas hosted 81,893 international students, making it the state with the third most international students in the country, just behind New York and California. The table shows the countries sending the most, and the universities enrolling the most, international students in Texas.

TABLE 14.4

Public Higher Education in Texas, 2018

STATEWIDE FOUR-YEAR INSTITUTIONS	
Total enrollment	658,219
Average tuition and fees	$8,031
Total degrees awarded	156,348
Bachelor's degrees awarded	110,030
Master's degrees awarded	40,473
Ph.D. research degrees awarded	3,877
Doctoral professional degrees awarded	1,952
STATEWIDE TWO-YEAR COMMUNITY AND JUNIOR COLLEGES	
Total enrollment	758,133
Average tuition and fees	$2,506
Part-time	76.7%
Full-time	23.3%
Academic program	75.0%
Technical program	25.0%

SOURCE: Texas Higher Education Coordinating Board, *2019 Texas Public Higher Education Almanac.*

governments and state representatives have a strong interest in expanding the size and reach of universities and colleges located in their communities.

Third, higher education policy in Texas has long been defined by the University of Texas at Austin and Texas A&M University. Both have grown rapidly over the past fifty years to become nationally and internationally recognized institutions. The University of Texas at Austin enrollment stood at 51,684 in 2019. At the same time, Texas A&M enrolled 63,694 students at its flagship campus in College Station, a far cry from the 8,000 students enrolled there in 1963.[45] These institutions have been specially positioned to use their financial resources to expand their operations. Their large alumni bases enable both schools to mobilize much-needed political support inside and outside the legislature. On the other hand, their prominent place in the state's educational hierarchy often has made it difficult for other higher education institutions in the state to attain national and international prominence.

In Texas in the fall of 2018, 658,219 students were enrolled in four-year public and private institutions (see Table 14.4). Another 758,133 were enrolled in two-year public community and junior colleges.

Higher education is big business in Texas. Public higher education comprises 37 general academic institutions, 3 lower division institutions, 6 technical college system schools, 50 community and junior college districts with multiple campuses, 1 technical college system, and 10 health-related institutions. In addition, there were 38 private colleges or universities, 1 private junior college, 1 private health-related institution, and 2 private chiropractic schools.[46]

Funding these institutions is a complicated affair. For the 2020–21 biennium, $18.7 billion was appropriated by the legislature to support public higher education in Texas, a 0.9 billion increase from 2018–19. An additional $1.9 billion was appropriated to support two-year public community and junior colleges, which were also funded by local property taxes in their respective communities. Aggregated appropriations by the state alone do not capture the policy issues facing higher education in the state. For that we must briefly understand how institutions of higher education were built and funded in the state.

Building a System of Higher Education in Texas

Public higher education was slow in coming to Texas. The Republic of Texas had set aside 50 acres of land for the establishment of a university, but little substantively was done.

The Constitution of 1876 contained a number of important provisions for the future development of higher education in the state. A **Permanent University Fund (PUF)** was created out of the income from and sale of certain public lands. The Constitution of 1876 also called for the establishment of a University of Texas. Texas A&M was mandated to be part of the University of Texas. Prohibitions also were put into place forbidding the use of general revenue monies for the construction of buildings for the University of Texas. In 1881 a statewide popular vote chose Austin to be the site of the University of Texas. At the same time, the legislature created a governing board of eight regents who were empowered to oversee the affairs of the university. Galveston also was selected to be the site of the medical college for the University of Texas. The University of Texas formally opened in 1883.[47]

Texas's two most prestigious public universities—the University of Texas and Texas A&M University—thus have their historical origins in the state constitution. Other state colleges and universities, however, emerged from the needs of local communities. Normal colleges or schools were established across the United States in the nineteenth and early twentieth centuries out of local and regional demands to increase the number of primary and secondary teachers. Normal colleges were the predecessors to twentieth-century teachers colleges.

Paralleling the expansion of normal schools in Texas was the community college movement. Early community colleges were often church sponsored and offered first year and second year courses. In 1922 the first publicly supported junior college was established in Wichita Falls. As with normal schools, junior colleges were seen as an appendage to local school districts. In 1929 the legislature provided a process for establishing community colleges and supporting them with local tax dollars. In 1941 the state began providing direct funding to community and junior colleges and made the Texas Education Agency the supervising agency, confirming their close connections to the public-school system.

New institutions of higher learning were added across the state throughout the mid-twentieth century as the demand for higher education increased. Along with the former normal schools and community and junior colleges, these schools began competing for the state resources once monopolized by the two flagship institutions.

Unlike other states, such as California, that had a comprehensive plan for expanding higher education in the second half of the twentieth century, Texas followed a more haphazard strategy. Decisions were made often on a case-by-case basis in the legislature, addressing the needs of local communities and institutions rather than those of the state as a whole. Ultimately, policy makers adopted two strategies to bring coordination and efficiency to higher education.

First, six **university systems** were created around the state. The general idea of a system was to have a chancellor who would administer colleges and agencies through a president or director. In 1911 a Board of Regents of State Colleges was created to oversee the operations of normal schools and teaching colleges. This became the Texas State

Permanent University Fund (PUF) a fund created by the state of Texas from the proceeds of public lands to finance public higher education in the state at selected institutions

university systems organizations in the state that coordinate the activities of various universities, medical schools, and special agencies involved in higher education and research

University System. Today this system includes seven flagship institutions and 12 campuses and enrolls over 86,000 students. The Texas A&M System was created in 1948, bringing together the flagship school with other smaller agricultural schools around the state. Today Texas A&M University System schools enroll over 153,000 students. The University of Texas (UT) System was established in 1950, bringing together universities in Austin and El Paso along with medical branches in Galveston, Houston, Austin, and Dallas (see Figure 14.3). Today UT System Schools enroll over 240,000 students, the most in the state. The University of Houston System was established in 1977 and today enrolls over 70,000 students. The University of North Texas System was established in 1980 and today enrolls over 36,000 students. The Texas Tech University System was established in 1946 and today enrolls over 36,000 students.

A second strategy adopted by the legislature to bring cohesion to higher education policy in Texas was to create an administrative agency that could develop rules and regulations to coordinate the policies being developed at Texas's many state universities and community colleges. Before 1955 public colleges and universities (and existing systems) had to rely on their own efforts to secure funding from the legislature. Universities had to forge close connections with local state representatives and senators to make sure their financial interests were not lost in the state budgetary process. The

FIGURE 14.3

Texas's University Systems

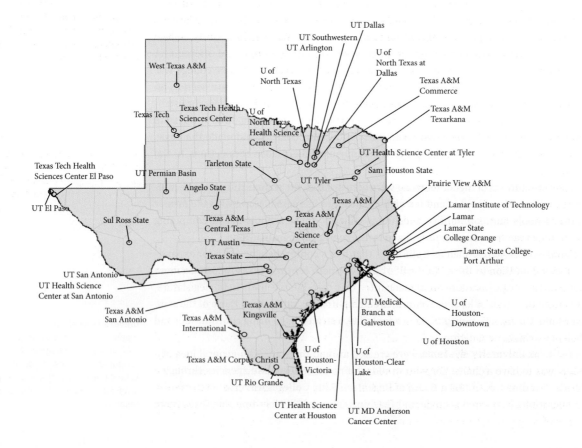

Texas Commission on Higher Education was established by the legislature in 1955 to try to coordinate the development of new institutions of higher education. The commission had little regulatory or financial authority and was largely ignored by the legislature and higher education institutions. In 1965 a new regulatory body was created by the legislature—the Coordinating Board, Texas College and University System. This body was renamed the **Texas Higher Education Coordinating Board (THECB)** in 1987.

The THECB has guided the expansion of higher education in Texas into the second decade of the twenty-first century. Its functions are largely regulatory. Among its many activities are monitoring academic program development and reviews, establishing success goals across all universities, working on a standardized common core across all public institutions of higher learning, and providing for coordination across universities and community colleges. Significantly, however, it did not have the authority to coordinate or make authoritative decisions about how universities and colleges were to be financed. Financing higher education remained a highly decentralized affair decided elsewhere.

Texas Higher Education Coordinating Board (THECB) state agency that oversees all public postsecondary education in the state

Financing Higher Education

Funding higher education in Texas is complicated. One source of funds is "formula funding" based upon enrollments and semester credit hours.[48] The THECB makes recommendations for formula funding for various state institutions, and the state legislature makes the final decision.

A second source is **tuition and fees**. These are set by the respective university system board of regents, based on requests from university presidents. The legislature reserves the right to stop or even roll back the tuition and fee schedule proposed by a university system board of regents. As noted in the introduction to Chapter 11, tuition and fees increases have become contentious affairs in the twenty-first century. As in other states, Texas is relying less on general revenue funding of higher education and more on tuition and fees. Students are having to spend more of their own money to attend public universities, and many are going into serious debt. One study in 2016 found that the average student debt in Texas was $26,292.[49]

tuition and fees amounts charged to students for the cost of attending a particular institution; varies by university or community college

A third source of funding for higher education has been so-called **special items**, which involve money designated to particular university programs outside the standard appropriation formulas for higher education. Over the years, universities have come to rely upon these special items as a way to initiate new programs and expand others. A fourth source of funding has been special funds established to promote higher education in the state: the Permanent University Fund, the Higher Education Fund, and the National Research University Fund.[50]

special items special pieces of legislation passed to support particular programs or building projects at state universities outside normal funding mechanisms

Today the PUF consists of 2.1 million acres of lands dedicated to it and the return on the investment of revenues from those lands.[51] The PUF endowment is managed by the University of Texas Investment Management Company (UTIMCO) under the authority of the UT System Board of Regents, with the land itself being managed by the Land Office. The Available University Fund (AUF) consists of the revenue from the PUF and is used to guarantee bonds issued by the University of Texas System for various projects. Bonds can benefit all 14 UT System schools but only to finance capital expenditures. AUF money is also distributed to benefit A&M and UT System institutions. AUF money can be used for operational expenses of UT Austin and the UT System Administration, but not of other UT System institutions.

PUF and AUF operations have been complicated affairs and have influenced the growth and expansion of higher education in the state throughout the nineteenth and twentieth and into the twenty-first centuries. The University of Texas and Texas A&M University have become world-class research universities because of the large amounts of monies made available to them above and beyond state appropriations or the tuition and fees paid by students. These funds have also been used to finance the building of a large number of capital construction projects across the UT and A&M System schools, although the flagship schools have been the primary beneficiaries of these construction projects. In 2019, $1.0 billion was distributed from the PUF through the AUF.[52]

In an attempt to address the needs of non-PUF schools, constitutional amendments passed in 1984 and 1993 establishing a second fund for higher education for universities, health-related institutions, and the Texas State Technical College that were not included in PUF funding. The idea for the **Higher Education Fund (HEF)** mirrored that of the PUF. But instead of revenues from public lands, general revenue appropriation funds would be used to build a fund for backing and servicing bonds used for capital expenditures. By 2009 a decision was made by the legislature to repurpose the HEF permanent endowment to the newly established National Research University Fund (see Chapter 11). NRUF funds would be used to promote and encourage the emergence of new national research institutions among a small group of universities. The HEF would continue to be funded by general revenues.

The 2017 Texas legislative session was a watershed year for higher education. At the beginning of the session some policy makers projected a 6 to 10 percent cut in higher education funding. Early Senate drafts of the budget all but eliminated special item funding. In the end, special items remained in the budget. And although drastic cuts were not passed, there was enough pain to go around. Sixteen of the state's public universities and administrative offices saw decreases in state funding, while the funding of many others could not keep up with inflation or enrollment growth. A special Joint Interim Committee on Higher Education Formula Funding was established to report back to the legislature on overhauling the funding of higher education.[53]

The Coronavirus Challenge to Higher Education

Many legislators expected the 2021 legislative session to be the higher education session, much as earlier sessions had focused on water, transportation, and public schools. These expectations were dashed with the public health and economic crises brought on by the coronavirus pandemic in the winter and spring of 2020. As was the case with public schools throughout the state, universities and colleges closed their doors following spring break in March and taught their courses online. Dorms were cleared out, except for the few domestic and foreign students who had nowhere else to live. By the beginning of May most schools had canceled graduation events, pushing them into the next academic year, and planned to offer summer classes online. Faculty were given a week or two to begin delivering classes virtually and to finish the semester. As with the public schools, valuable lessons were learned by universities and colleges as to what worked and what didn't work online. Not all faculty or students had access to good computer equipment or online services as they did at school. Laboratory classes were all but impossible to deliver on short notice. Assessment and exams became challenges that few faculties

Higher Education Fund (HEF) a fund supported by general revenue monies to finance public higher education for non-PUF institutions

Higher Education Spending and Outcomes

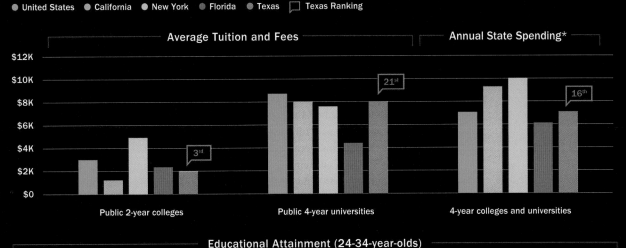

- United States - California - New York - Florida - Texas ▢ Texas Ranking

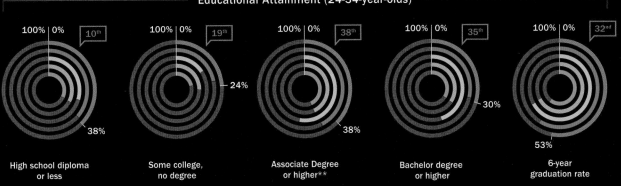

Texas contains the full range of institutions of higher education, from community colleges to private universities and liberal arts colleges, to major public research universities. How does the experience of higher education in Texas compare to other states? What does the state spend on students and faculty, and how far do Texans progress in their education compared other states and the country?

CRITICAL THINKING

- What factors might explain the differences in tuition and fees at public 2-year and 4-year universities and colleges across the five states? If you were a state legislator would you increase funding for higher education by raising tuition and fees or by appropriating more general revenue funds? What are the costs and benefits of either strategy?

- Higher education is considered to be a key factor in preparing a workforce for the dynamic world of the twenty-first century. Given the above data, which state do you believe is doing the best job creating an educated workforce through higher education?

* State spending on higher education, per full time enrolled student

**Includes bachelor and graduate degrees

SOURCE: 2018 Teas Higher Education Almanac: A Profile of State and Institutional Performance and Characteristics. Austin: Texas Higher Education Coordinating Board, 2018. Pp. 6-7.

were prepared to offer. And then there was the problem of cheating and the added stress that taking courses from home would have on students' emotional well-being. Hiring freezes were put into place at colleges and universities. Travel and study abroad were canceled. By the beginning of May most schools had canceled graduation events until the fall and planned to offer all summer classes online.

But questions remained: What would happen in the fall? Would universities fully reopen? Would students be allowed in the dorms? How many students would be allowed to live on campus under social distancing guidelines? How many students could be put safely into classrooms? Would students be willing to come back if campus life was seriously constrained by new public health rules and regulations and the ongoing threat of another coronavirus outbreak in the winter? Would there be football in the fall?

That last question might seem out of place, but it is not. Football is an important part of the social and cultural life on the modern university campus. More importantly, at larger schools, football has generated tens of millions of dollars in revenue. For many schools, big-time sports have been important parts of their business model. Brand new stadiums had to be paid off through ticket sales and television revenues just like newly built dorms had to be paid off through room and board fees. Without students on campus, stadiums and dorms were a drain on universities' financial health.

Entering the new academic year, most universities adopted a cautious reopening strategy. Social distancing and masks became common features of campus life. Social life was seriously curtailed. Classes were offered in a variety of formats, including in-person classes in a traditional classroom, fully online classes, virtual classes held online at a specific time, and a variety of mixed formats incorporating online and in-person features. Some fall sports were canceled, although a modified football season took place before greatly reduced or no-spectator crowds.

The hope of many university and political leaders entering the 2020–21 academic year was that the coronavirus pandemic would be brought under control and become a blip in the life of higher education in the state. Some feared, however, that the crisis facing higher education could extend into late 2021 or even 2022. The financial fallout of the pandemic could become something more ominous than anyone thought possible in the spring of 2020, forcing unwanted changes in higher education, its goals, and its delivery.

Setting Goals for the Future: 60x30TX

In 2000 the THECB drafted a 15-year plan called "Closing the Gaps by 2015." The plan identified a number of broad goals and benchmarks for the state's higher education system in regard to participation, success, excellence, and research. At the heart of the plan was finding ways to serve the higher education needs of all Texans, particularly those ethnic and racial minorities who were underrepresented in higher education.

In 2015 a new 15-year strategic plan called "60x30TX" was released by the THECB for higher education in Texas. Like "Closing the Gaps," the plan identified four targeted goals reflecting concerns about student success and the establishment of a globally competitive workforce in the state:

- The number of Texans between 25 and 34 with a certificate or degree will rise from 41 percent in 2015 to 60 percent in 2030.

- The number of individuals with a higher education degree or certificate will rise from 311,340 in 2015 to 550,000 in 2030.
- All graduates by 2030 will have completed programs with identified marketable skills.
- By 2030 undergraduate loan debt will not exceed 60 percent of first-year wages for graduates of public institutions.[54]

The goals of the report were laudable, calling upon universities to develop regional and statewide strategies to meet these goals and offering much-needed data that would track out comparative institutional and statewide performance indicators. What 60x30TX didn't do (and really couldn't do), however, was spell out how public universities might manage the institutional and financial constraints in Texas that made it difficult for other universities to become recognized as topflight universities in the image of the University of Texas at Austin or Texas A&M University. Nor did the report emphasize the significance of how much less Texas spends on higher education compared with states such as California and New York (see the Texas and the Nation graphic). It will be hard to meet the goals of 60x30TX without a significant rethinking of how to coordinate and fund higher education in the state. Without additional state funding (or significantly higher tuition) it likely will be difficult to compete with the educated workforces of other states.

When the THECB was established in 1965, Governor John Connally warned how mediocrity threatened higher education in Texas if resources were spread too thinly around the state and all universities and community colleges tried to be all things to all people. He hoped the Texas Higher Education Coordinating Board would bring some needed coordination to higher education policy in the state. The challenge today is less regulatory and more political. Reducing state funding and increasing tuition and fees may have worked in the past. Today, with growing student debt, Texas may be reaching

The 60x30TX plan seeks to create a well-educated and highly skilled generation of Texas graduates but fails to outline how schools should accomplish this goal. The financial constraints on Texas colleges and universities pose considerable challenges.

a point where significant increases in tuition and fees are no longer politically acceptable either in the public's mind or in the state legislature. The legislature needs to find a better way to finance higher education than it has over the past 20 years.

Water Policy in Texas

 Explain the challenges facing Texas's water supply

Water is the lifeblood of Texas. Access to plentiful water supplies over the past 100 years has been a necessary precondition for a thriving economy and an expanding urban population in the state. Approximately 59 percent of the water used in Texas comes from aquifers (underground pools of water), and the vast majority of that water (60 percent) is used in irrigation, particularly in the arid Panhandle region (Figure 14.4). The remainder of the state's water supply comes from surface sources, including rivers and reservoirs. Twenty-seven percent of the state's water use is in metropolitan areas. Individual cities rely on various amounts of aquifer and surface water, but, overall, aquifers are the source for more than one-third of the water consumed by metropolitan areas.

FIGURE 14.4

Water Usage by Sector, 2018

About 8.42 million acre-feet of water used in Texas (62 percent) came from groundwater sources. About 5.27 million acre-feet (38 percent) came from surface water sources. These two charts illustrate how these waters were used in various activities in Texas.

SOURCE: Texas Water Development Board, Texas Water Use estimates, 2018 Summary, June 15, 2020.

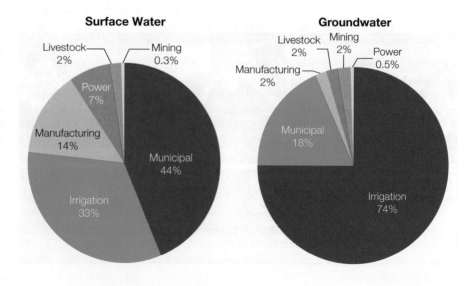

Texas's water consumption is projected to increase from about 18 million acre-feet per year in 2010 to about 22 million acre-feet per year in 2060.[55] (An acre-foot is a volume measurement used by water planners, comprising an acre of land—43,560 square feet—one foot deep.)[56] At the same time, existing supplies under current systems of production and conservation are expected to decrease by 10 percent, largely as a result of the depletion of the Ogallala Aquifer in the Texas Panhandle and reduced reliance on the Gulf Coast Aquifer. By 2060 experts project that an additional 8.3 million acre-feet per year will be needed for the state to continue to thrive.

Formulating a coherent water policy in Texas to address these and other issues is difficult for many reasons. As noted in Chapter 1, Texas is a large state with a diverse climate. The water-related issues along the Gulf Coast in southeast Texas near Houston, which is subtropical and humid, are quite different from those in the high plains Panhandle, which is semiarid savanna, or in the El Paso desert. For example, along the southeastern border with Louisiana, average annual rainfall is more than 80 inches per year, while near El Paso it is only 10 inches per year.[57] There are 15 major river basins and 8 coastal basins across the state, as well as 9 major and 21 minor aquifers.

Water policy is further complicated by the fact that various regions of the state have periodically experienced severe droughts and devastating floods. Throughout the twentieth century, reservoirs were built to more effectively distribute water during times of shortage and to control flooding. In 1913, when the Texas Board of Water Engineers was established, there were only 8 major reservoirs in the state. By 1950 the number had grown to 53, and today there are 188.[58]

Water Law in Texas

Underlying water policy in Texas is a complicated system of private property rights derived from three sources: Spanish law, traditional English common law, and statutory law. Texas law recognizes several legal classes of water rights for surface water and groundwater, classes that are governed by different rules. Historically, these variations in the law have made the forging of water policy an arduous and at times a politically charged matter.

In 1967 the law covering surface water and relatively well-defined underground streams was clarified when the state legislature passed the Water Rights Adjudication Act. This legislation essentially merged the various water rights doctrines dating back to the nineteenth century into a unified water permit system. It requires individuals seeking water rights to file a claim with the Texas Commission on Environmental Quality (originally called the Texas Water Commission) before using the water. A complex administrative and judicial process was put into place that essentially grants to holders of water rights certificates demonstrating that the rights have been adjudicated. The 1967 act thus greatly expanded the state's ability to control and manage surface water use.[59]

Groundwater law—that is, law regarding water flowing, or "percolating," underground—differs significantly from surface water law.[60] In *Houston and Texas Central Railroad Company v. East* (1904), the Texas Supreme Court adopted a strict common-law notion of property law for percolating underground water, one called the **law of capture**. This standard, which is also found in Texas oil and gas law, essentially says that the first person to "capture" the water by pumping it out of the ground and using it owns it. Landowners have the right to capture as much groundwater lying under their property as

law of capture the idea that the first person to "capture" water or oil by pumping it out of the ground and using it owns that water or oil

they wish without regard to the interests of other owners whose land may also lie on top of the same pool of underground water. Because it encourages landowners to take as much water as possible from groundwater sources without considering the needs of other consumers, the law of capture can work against conservation efforts of private individuals who are trying to protect the water under their lands. It can also undercut efforts of planning authorities to develop a water plan for a particular area that takes into account the short-term and long-term availability of water as well as the competing uses for available water.

Finding a balance between the law of capture and the need to plan has troubled policy makers for much of the last 65 years. *Houston and Texas Central Railroad v. East* was reaffirmed by the Texas Supreme Court in 1955. In its ruling, the court stated that "percolating waters are regarded as the property of the owner of the surface who may, in the absence of malice, intercept, impede and appropriate such waters while they are on their premises, and make whatever use of them they please, regardless of the fact that use cuts off the flow of such waters to adjoining land and deprives the adjoining owner of their use." Nevertheless, the court also accepted the state's authority to regulate groundwater. In 1949 the state legislature passed the Texas Groundwater Act, which created water districts to manage groundwater supply.

Today there are 99 groundwater districts in Texas, with varying powers. The smallest district is the Red Sands Groundwater Conservation District in Hidalgo County, covering 31 square miles. The largest is the High Plains Underground Water Conservation District, covering 12,000 square miles over the Ogallala Aquifer. Generally, the groundwater districts are able to develop regulations to protect the water supply provided by groundwater sources, including rules that may restrict pumping, require well permits, delineate well spacing, and establish rates of water use. The rules and regulations generated by these districts, however, can come into direct conflict with the law of capture, as we will see in the next section.[61]

Planning Authorities and Water Policy

The history of water planning in Texas stretches back to the early twentieth century. A constitutional amendment in 1904 paved the way for the development of various agencies and authorities concerned with water planning. Among the most important innovations put into place by the state legislature in the early 1900s were drainage districts (1905); conservation and reclamation districts, later referred to as "river authorities" (1917); and water control and improvement districts (1925).

In the 1960s the state established new agencies to address various water issues. Today the Texas Water Development Board (TWDB) is the state's primary water planning and financing agency. Enforcement of the state's environmental regulations regarding water is the job of the Texas Commission on Environmental Quality.[62]

The TWDB is composed of a six-member board serving staggered six-year terms. Each member comes from a different part of the state. The board has had a number of important responsibilities, including the following:

- Supporting the development of 16 regional water plans
- Developing a state water plan every five years

- Providing financial assistance to local governments for (1) water supply and waste management projects, (2) flood protection and control projects, (3) agricultural water conservation projects, and (4) the creation of groundwater districts
- Administering the Texas Water Bank, which facilitates the transfer, sale, and lease of water and water rights throughout the state
- Administering the Texas Water Trust, which holds water rights for environmental flow maintenance purposes
- Collecting data for the state's freshwater needs[63]

A number of strategies for meeting the short- and long-term water needs in the state were articulated in the 2012 State Water Plan. Two elements of the plan stand out. First, there is a notable focus on the importance of conservation. One of the most important elements is a strategy throughout all regions that seeks a more efficient use of current water supplies. Second, there is an emphasis on the importance of expanding and developing available surface water throughout Texas. The plan calls for the building of 26 new major reservoirs by 2060 and new pipeline infrastructure from existing sources to new points of use. Such projects represent an important shift in existing water policy in some planning areas, as they shift the focus from flood control or hydroelectric power generation to the provision of water.

The plan's groundwater strategies include the expansion of production by drilling more wells or building treatment plants for water quality. Conservation efforts also play a major part in groundwater initiatives, as some of the aquifers are experiencing overuse. The TWDB estimates that total groundwater supplies available to Texans will decline by 30 percent between 2010 and 2060. The Ogallala Aquifer (which runs from the Texas High Plains up through western Kansas and into Nebraska) and the Edwards Aquifer (which runs along the Balcones fault line near San Antonio) are estimated to decline by 50 percent by 2060.

The total capital needs of these initiatives proposed by regional water planning groups were estimated to be $53 billion, along with annual operating and maintenance costs. But cost is not the only challenge facing water policy makers. Some environmental groups in the state are opposed to further expansion of the reservoir system, arguing that the costs to the ecosystem far outweigh the advantages provided by more water. On the other hand, some property owners, particularly in west Texas, are opposed to any new conservation restrictions put upon them by the state. Texas water law itself may be one of the most intractable problems that water planners may have to face in coming years.

In 2012 the Texas Supreme Court ruled on the case *The Edwards Aquifer Authority v. Burrell Day and Joel McDaniel*, which has important implications for future attempts to regulate water use in Texas, particularly in areas that rely heavily upon aquifers. The case involved two farmers who had applied to the Edwards Aquifer Authority for permission to pump 700 acre-feet per year of water to irrigate their 350-acre ranch in Van Ormy, a small town south of San Antonio. The farmers argued that they had rights to water from the aquifer based on their ownership of land above it. Maintaining that the farmers were unable to prove "historical use" of water from the aquifer, the authority granted them a permit for pumping only 14 acre-feet.

The court sided with the farmers. Writing for the 9–0 court majority, Justice Hecht ruled that using "historical use" as a criterion for granting a permit to pump water was

The Texas water supply faces many challenges. The drought of 2011–14 was the worst in the history of Texas. It damaged the state's prosperity, causing dust storms in the Texas Panhandle (top), and drying lake beds throughout the state. Many of the state's cities were put on various levels of water emergencies that restricted use.

a departure from the Texas Water Code. "Unquestionably," Hecht wrote, "the state is empowered to regulate groundwater production . . . [but] groundwater in place is owned by the landowner on the basis of oil and gas law."[64] Texas regulatory authorities thus had the power to reasonably regulate in the public interest the use of water drawn from an aquifer, but they may have to pay property owners with a stake in that water any damages that are incurred by the regulation.

The ruling sparked a firestorm of controversy. Landowners celebrated the decision as vindication of their ownership of water under their lands. In contrast, state planning authorities and environmentalists were aghast at the implications that the case could have for their attempts to efficiently allocate and conserve water in Texas. The court's ruling also raised an important question: Which policy-making body would dominate water policy in the foreseeable future in Texas? Would it be the courts, working through judicial interpretations of the applicability of water property law? Or would it be the regulatory bodies whose job was to plan and to allocate water based on their assessment of available water supplies and the competing needs for water? Developing regulatory rules for the use of aquifer water that both protect property rights and promote the public interest through reasonable and efficient regulations will be a challenge facing these policy makers in years to come.[65]

A major step toward planning for water in the future took place in 2013, when voters approved a constitutional amendment to create a $2 billion water fund. The bulk of the fund came from a onetime transfer of money from the Rainy Day Fund to the State Water Implementation Fund for Texas (SWIFT). Proponents claimed that the two accounts could fund over $25 billion in water development projects over the next 50 years.

The basic idea behind this water initiative is that SWIFT projects would generate revenue that would go into another account (the State Water Implementation Revenue Fund for Texas or SWIRFT) that could be used to fund more water projects. Proposals for projects to be funded by SWIFT and SWIRFT would come from regional water planning groups and could include such things as building new reservoirs, fixing pipes, and developing groundwater. A number of provisos were attached to the legislation that put forward the constitutional amendment, including requirements that 20 percent of the funds had to be directed to conservation and 10 percent had to serve rural areas. Interestingly, concerns were also raised about the fact that the agency managing the program, the TWDB, might be too close to the governor given that the board would be appointed by him or her. The authorizing legislation thus established a separate committee to oversee how SWIFT and SWIRFT funds are managed. The committee would be appointed by the Speaker of the House and the lieutenant governor and be composed of the comptroller, three state representatives, and three state senators. Planning for Texas's water future did not mean that traditional concerns over too much executive power in public policy matters would be ignored.[66]

Facing Texas's Future

IN THIS CHAPTER, we have explored four of the most important challenges that are confronting Texas policy makers today. How Texas leaders address transportation problems, immigration and border issues, higher education policy, and water needs in the coming years will determine a large part of Texas's future.

Most policy makers and legislators recognize that each of these challenges is important in its own right. There is less agreement on the importance of these issues among the general public. Prior to the outbreak of the coronavirus in Texas in March 2020, polls of registered voters in Texas consistently showed that Texans thought that border control and immigration were the most important issues facing the state. The next greatest issue—a concern with political leadership and political corruption in the state—was not even close to border control and immigration as a perceived problem. Interestingly, transportation, higher education, and water were not perceived by voters as important problems at all.

The coronavirus pandemic has come to dominate policy discussions involving the future of Texas. In June 2020, 27 percent of voters thought that the most important issue facing the state was the coronavirus (see Table 14.5). Nothing else was even close. The poll also discovered that Texans of all political persuasions were dissatisfied with how the pandemic was being addressed by state officials. How long will the pandemic continue to dominate political, economic, and cultural life in the state? How long will other policies central to the future of Texas continue to be pushed into the background?

TABLE 14.5

What Is Important to Texas Voters Today?*

ISSUE	ALL VOTERS (%)	REPUBLICANS (%)	DEMOCRATS (%)	INDEPENDENTS (%)
Coronavirus	27%	35%	19%	26%
Border security	9	16	1	7
Immigration	8	13	2	7
The economy	7	9	3	6
Health care	6	1	11	6

University of Texas/Texas Politics Projects Poll. Texas Statewide Survey. June 19-29, 2020. N=1200 registered Voters. Margin of Error: +/−2.83% (3.28% adjusted for weighting).

*February 2020.

Texas may be in for a difficult time in coming months and years as governing officials try to develop a strategy for containing the pandemic. Once the pandemic is brought under control and the state's economy stabilizes, the problems of transportation, immigration, higher education, and water will no doubt remain. Unless forward-thinking officials take the lead to highlight these problems and mobilize Texans to deal with them, the future of Texas will be a less educated citizenry facing gridlock in its urban areas and water shortages outside the Gulf Coast. ★

Use **INQUIZITIVE** to help you study and master this material.

Transportation Policy in Texas

- **Explain the major issues facing transportation policy in Texas (pp. 489–96)**

Texas transportation policy primarily involves maintaining and expanding Texas's roads and highways and designing a public transportation system that can lessen the state's reliance on automobiles. The major problems facing transportation in Texas are developing a politically acceptable funding system for roads and highways and developing a public transportation system that will be used by a reasonable proportion of commuters in Texas's major metropolitan areas.

Key Terms
centerline miles (p. 489)
lane miles (p. 489)
vehicle miles traveled (p. 490)

Practice Quiz
1. Opposition to the bullet train comes primarily from
   a) persons in rural areas.
   b) bus companies.
   c) the aviation industry.
   d) taxpayers.
   e) persons concerned with its safety.

2. Roads and bridges in Texas
   a) will need billions of dollars in new funding by 2040.
   b) can be maintained with funds from motor fuels taxes.
   c) will be paid for with tolls.
   d) will be maintained with the new federal infrastructure law.
   e) will be paid for with the new production of oil and gas from shale.

3. The solution to transportation congestion in Texas is
   a) more toll roads.
   b) the bullet train.
   c) public transportation.
   d) uncertain.
   e) raising motor fuels taxes.

4. Public transportation
   a) tends to be more available in central cities.
   b) is more available in wealthy suburbs.
   c) is more popular in small towns.
   d) has been most effective in Houston.
   e) is widely used in El Paso.

5. The most likely response to the need for transportation funding is to
   a) increase the gasoline tax.
   b) increase motor vehicle fees.
   c) impose a state income tax.
   d) delay dealing with the problem.
   e) build more toll roads.

6. Texas roads and bridges are *not* funded by
   a) tolls.
   b) gasoline taxes.
   c) vehicle registration fees.
   d) shale oil taxes.
   e) diesel taxes.

7. Texans pay this amount per gallon in gasoline taxes:
   a) 70 cents
   b) 20 cents
   c) 18.4 cents
   d) 6.25 percent of price per gallon
   e) 38.4 cents

Demographic Change in Texas

- Analyze how immigration and border issues will change Texas in the coming years (pp. 497–507)

Because of its long border with Mexico, Texas has always been familiar with immigrants from Mexico and Central America. In recent years the issue of border security has taken center stage, as has the issue of how to respond to the state's large population of undocumented immigrants. Texas has passed laws taking aim at sanctuary cities, which have refused to cooperate with federal immigration authorities. In addition, Texas has a large population of DACA recipients, who are undocumented individuals brought to the United States at a very young age.

Key Terms
naturalized citizen (p. 498)
Texas Dream Act (p. 498)
sanctuary cities (p. 500)
Senate Bill 4 (SB 4) (p. 501)
Deferred Action for Childhood Arrivals (DACA) (p. 503)

Practice Quiz
8. The Texas economy is *most* affected by which industry?
  a) the film industry
  b) the high-tech industry
  c) the oil and gas industry
  d) the farming industry
  e) the tourism industry

9. Which of the following industries is *most* reliant on immigrant labor in Texas?
  a) construction
  b) manufacturing
  c) retail trade
  d) health care
  e) accommodation and food services

10. Who initially signed the DACA executive order?
  a) President George W. Bush
  b) President Ronald Reagan
  c) President Barack Obama
  d) President Donald Trump
  e) President Bill Clinton

11. Which state has the largest DACA population?
  a) New Mexico
  b) Florida
  c) Texas
  d) Wisconsin
  e) New York

12. Senate Bill 4 addressed the issue of sanctuary cities by
  a) mandating that every city in Texas cooperate with federal authorities.
  b) enacting penalties for local police and sheriffs who refused to cooperate with federal authorities.
  c) creating a commission to study the issue.
  d) requiring that all cities create sanctuaries for undocumented immigrants.
  e) providing additional state money for cities that did not cooperate with federal authorities.

13. To become a naturalized citizen, an individual must
  a) have lived in the United States for 10 years.
  b) demonstrate a perfect command of English.
  c) have arrived to the United States illegally.
  d) demonstrate good moral character.
  e) pay an additional tax on their income.

Higher Education Policy in Texas

- Analyze the challenges facing Texas's system of higher education (pp. 507–18)

Higher education is an important link between an expanding and diversifying population and a rapidly transforming economy. Businesses in the modern world economy demand a highly skilled workforce. For Texas to compete nationally and internationally and thrive in an ever-changing high-tech economy, the next generation of Texans must have the necessary advanced skills and training. Finding new ways to finance higher education across the state's many universities and colleges will be difficult.

Key Terms

Permanent University Fund (PUF) (p. 511)

university systems (p. 511)

Texas Higher Education Coordinating Board (THECB) (p. 513)

tuition and fees (p. 513)

special items (p. 513)

Higher Education Fund (HEF) (p. 514)

Practice Quiz

14. The Permanent University Fund
   a) is a major source of funding for community colleges.
   b) is open to all universities and colleges across the state.
   c) allocates revenue for selected University of Texas and Texas A&M University system schools.
   d) has recently been replaced by the Higher Education Fund.
   e) none of the above

15. Which of the following revenue sources do *not* play a role in funding 4-year colleges and universities in Texas?
   a) local property taxes
   b) tuition and fees
   c) special items legislation
   d) the Permanent University Fund
   e) none of the above (all play a role)

16. The Texas Higher Education Coordinating Board
   a) manages the affairs of elementary and secondary schools.
   b) is a subcommittee of the Texas House Committee on Education.
   c) controls the sales tax rates for money going to public higher education.
   d) watches over and coordinates higher education policy in the state.
   e) none of the above

Water Policy in Texas

> • **Explain the challenges facing Texas's water supply (pp. 518–22)**

A looming threat to Texas's further economic development is access to freshwater. Over the next 50 years, water consumption is expected to vastly increase, while existing supplies may decrease. Current water law in Texas adds complexity to the development of rational water policies for the state.

Key Term

law of capture (p. 519)

Practice Quiz

17. Which of the following is *true*?
   a) Texas water consumption will decrease as the population expands.
   b) The idea of planning for future water provision has been rejected by the Texas state legislature as being too socialistic.
   c) Water law in Texas distinguishes between surface water and groundwater.
   d) Providing water in Texas is primarily a federal responsibility.
   e) Current state water policies do not emphasize conservation.

18. The law of capture concerns
   a) property rights in underground percolating water.
   b) the right of the state to regulate rivers and estuaries.
   c) political control of the legislature by a particular policy interest.
   d) the Corps of Engineers's various attempts to direct the flow of the Rio Grande.
   e) the federal government's ability to override Texas water laws.

19. Which of the following is *true*?
   a) The Texas Supreme Court rejects the idea that the state can regulate *surface* water.
   b) Texas is empowered by the state constitution to seize without compensation an individual's right to use underground water.
   c) Aquifers provide a negligible supply of water to Texas.
   d) Attempts to regulate groundwater access frequently come into conflict with property rights.
   e) The Water Rights Adjudication Act of 1967 prohibits the state from regulating surface water permits.

Appendix

Here we include a series of documents that capture the nature of philosophical and practical problems the people of Texas confronted during their lengthy founding period. For each text we provide short introductions to guide the reader from the Texas Revolution, through statehood and the Civil War, to the Constitution of 1876. Copies of the various constitutions of Texas are available online at www.tarlton.law.utexas.edu/constitutions.

The Declaration of Independence (1836)

The Texas Declaration of Independence was the product of the Convention of 1836.[1] Drawing upon John Locke's Two Treatises of Government (1689) and Thomas Jefferson's Declaration of Independence (1776) for inspiration, it lays out an explanation of the nature of government, lists the grievances that Texas's people hold against the Mexican government, and declares independence and the establishment of a new "free, sovereign, and independent Republic." Note the appeals to "the first law of nature, the right to self-preservation," "the inherent and inalienable right of the People to appeal to first principles," and the "sacred obligation" that people have to their posterity to create a government that will "secure their future wealth and happiness." In addition to presenting the Texas Constitution of 1836, the Texas Declaration of Independence lays down the republican principles that would define government and politics in Texas from 1836 to 1845, when Texas joined the United States of America.

To the Public.

The undersigned, Plenipotentiaries from the Republic of Texas to the United States of America, respectfully present to the American People the unanimous DECLARATION OF INDEPENDENCE, made by the People of Texas in General Convention, on the 2d day of March, 1836; and, also, the CONSTITUTION framed by the same body.

Robert Hamilton,
GEO. C. CHILDRESS.
WASHINGTON CITY, May 22, 1836.

Unanimous Declaration of Independence, by the Delegates of the People of Texas.

In General Convention, at the town of Washington, on the 2d day of March, 1836.

When a Government has ceased to protect the lives, liberty, and property of the People from whom its legitimate powers are derived, and for the advancement of whose happiness it was instituted, and so far from being a guarantee for the enjoyment of their inestimable and inalienable rights, becomes an instrument in the hands of evil rules for their oppression: when the Federal Republican Constitution of their country, which they have sworn to support, no longer has a substantial existence, and the whole nature of their Government has been forcibly changed, without their consent, from a restricted Federative Republic, composed of sovereign States, to a consolidated central military despotism, in which every interest is disregarded but that of the army and the priesthood, both the eternal enemies of civil liberty, the ever-ready minions of power, and the usual instruments of tyrants: when, long after the spirit of the constitution

---

[1] "Unanimous Declaration of Independence, by the Delegates of the People of Texas," *Laws of the Republic of Texas, in Two Volumes* (Houston: Printed at the Office of the Telegraph, 1838), 1:3–4; Thomas W. Streeter, *Bibliography of Texas, 1795–1845* (5 vols.; Cambridge, MA: Harvard University Press, 1955–60). Errors in the original document are retained.

has departed, moderation is at length so far lost by those in power, that even the semblance of freedom is removed, and the forms themselves of the Constitution discontinued; and so far from their petitions and remonstrances being regarded, the agents who bear them are thrown into dungeons and mercenary armies sent forth to force a new Government upon them at the point of the bayonet.

When, in consequence of such acts of malfeasance and abdication on the part of the Government, anarchy prevails, and civil society is dissolved into its original elements: in such a crisis, the first law of nature, the right of self-preservation, the inherent and inalienable right of the People to appeal to first principles, and take their political affairs into their own hands in extreme cases enjoins it as a right towards themselves, and a sacred obligation to their posterity, to abolish such Government, and create another in its stead, calculated to rescue them from impending dangers, and to secure their future welfare and happiness.

Nations, as well as individuals, are amenable for their acts to the public opinion of mankind. A statement of a part of our grievances is therefore submitted to an impartial world, in justification of the hazardous but unavoidable step now taken, of severing our political connexion with the Mexican People, and assuming an independent attitude among the nations of the earth.

The Mexican Government, by its colonization laws, invited and induced the Anglo-American population of Texas to colonize its wilderness, under the pledged faith of a written constitution, that they should continue to enjoy that constitutional liberty and republican Government to which they had been habituated in the land of their birth, the United States of America.

In this expectation they have been cruelly disappointed, inasmuch as the Mexican nation has acquiesced in the late changes made in the Government by General Antonio Lopez de Santa Ana, who, having overturned the Constitution of his country, now offers us the cruel alternative, either to abandon our homes, acquired by so many privations, or submit to the most intolerable of all tyranny, the combined despotism of the sword and the priesthood.

It hath sacrificed our welfare to the State of Coahuila, by which our interests have been continually depressed, through a jealous and partial course of legislation, carried on at a far-distant seat of Government, by a hostile majority, in an unknown tongue; and this too notwithstanding we have petitioned in the humblest terms for the establishment of a separate State Government, and have, in accordance with the provisions of the National Constitution, presented to the General Congress a Republican Constitution, which was, without just cause, contemptuously rejected.

It incarcerated in a dungeon, for a long time, one of our citizens, for no other cause but a zealous endeavor to procure the acceptance of our Constitution and the establishment of a State Government.

It has failed and refused to secure, on a firm basis, the right of trial by jury, that palladium of civil liberty and only safe guarantee for the life, liberty, and property of the citizen.

It has failed to establish any public system of education, although possessed of almost boundless resources, (the public domain,) and although it is an axiom in political science that, unless a People are educated and enlightened, it is idle to expect the continuance of civil liberty, or the capacity for self-government.

It has suffered the military commandants stationed among us to exercise arbitrary acts of oppression and tyranny, thus trampling upon the most sacred rights of the citizen, and rendering the military superior to the civil power.

It has dissolved by force of arms the State Congress of Coahuila and Texas, and obliged our Representatives to fly for their lives from the seat of Government, thus depriving us of the fundamental political right of representation.

It has demanded the surrender of a number of our citizens, and ordered military detachments to seize and carry them into the interior for trial; in contempt of the civil authorities, and in defiance of the laws and the Constitution.

It has made piratical attacks upon our commerce by commissioning foreign desperadoes, and authorizing them to seize our vessels and convey the property of our citizens to far-distant ports for confiscation.

It denies us the right of worshipping the Almighty according to dictates of our own conscience, by the support of a national religion calculated to promote the temporal interests of its human functionaries rather than the glory of the true and living God.

It has demanded us to deliver up our arms, which are essential for our defence, the rightful property of freemen, and formidable only to tyrannical Governments.

It has invaded our country, both by sea and by land, with intent to lay waste our territory, and drive us from our homes; and has now a large mercenary army advancing, to carry on against us a war of extermination.

It has, through its emissaries, incited the merciless savage, with the tomahawk and scalping-knife, to massacre the inhabitants of our defenceless frontiers.

It has been, during the whole time of our connexion with it, the contemptible sport and victim of successive military revolutions, and hath continually exhibited every characteristic of a weak, corrupt, and tyrannical government.

These and other grievances were patiently borne by the People of Texas, until they reached that point at which forbearance ceases to be a virtue. They then took up arms in defence of the National Constitution. They appealed to their Mexican brethren for assistance. Their appeal has been made in vain: though months have elapsed, no sympathetic response has yet been heard from the interior. They are, therefore, forced to the melancholy conclusion that the Mexican People have acquiesced in the destruction of their liberty, and the substitution therefor of a military despotism; that they are unfit to be free, and incapable of self-government.

The necessity of self-preservation, therefore, now decrees our eternal political separation.

We, therefore, the Delegates, with plenary powers, of the People of Texas, in solemn Convention assembled, appealing to a candid world for the necessities of our condition, do hereby resolve and DECLARE that our political connexion with the Mexican nation has forever ended, and that the People of Texas do now constitute a FREE, SOVEREIGN, AND INDEPENDENT REPUBLIC, and are fully invested with all the rights and attributes which properly belong to independent States; and, conscious of the rectitude of our intentions, we fearlessly and confidently commit the issue to the decision of the Supreme Arbiter of the destinies of nations.

RICHARD ELLIS,
President.

C. B. Stewart,	R. M. Coleman, of Mina,	Geo. W. Smith, of Jasper,
Thomas Barnett, of Austin,	Robert Potter,	Elijah Stapp, of Jackson,
James Collinsworth,	Thos. J. Rusk,	Claiborne West,
Edwin Waller,	Charles S. Taylor,	Wm. B. Scates, of Jefferson,
Asa Brigham	Jno. S. Roberts, of Nacogdoches	E. O. Legrand,
J. S. D. Byrom, of Brazoria,	Robert Hamilton,	S. W. Blount, of San Augustine,
Francisco Ruis,	Collin McKinnee,	Syd. O. Bennington,
Antonio Navaro,	Alb. H. Lattimer, of Red River,	W. C. Crawford, of Shelby,
Jesse B. Badgett, of Bexar,	Martin Palmer,	J. Power,
Wm. D. Lacy,	W. Clark, jr., of Sabine,	Sam. Houston,
Wm. Menifee, of Colorado,	John Fisher,	David Thomas,
James Gains,	Matt. Caldwell, of Gonzales,	Edward Conrad, of Refugio,
M. B. Menard,	Wm. Motley, of Goliad,	John Turner, of San Patricio,
A. B. Hardin, of Liberty,	L. de Zavala, of Harrisburg,	B. Briggs Goodrich,
Baily Hardiman, of Matagorda,	S. C. Robertson,	G. W. Barnett,
J. W. Bunton,	Geo. C. Childress, of Milam,	James G. Swisher,
Thos. J. Gazeley,	Steph. H. Everett,	Jesse Grimes, of Washington.

Ordinance of Annexation Approved by the Texas Convention on July 4, 1845

The independent Republic of Texas ceased to exist in 1845 following the implementation of a new state constitution and Texas's formal admission into the Union as a state. Resolutions passed by the U.S. Congress stated the conditions under which Texas was to be admitted into the Union.[2] Note that the resolutions demand a republican form of government be adopted by the people through a constitutional convention (via a new constitution) and that the existing government consent to this action. Passage of this ordinance by the convention is an expression of the consent of the people of Texas to this new political configuration.

An Ordinance

Whereas,

the Congress of the United States of America has passed resolutions providing for the annexation of Texas to that Union, which resolutions were offered by the President of the United States on the first day of March, 1845; and

Whereas,

the President of the United States has submitted to Texas the first and second sections of said resolutions, as the basis upon which Texas may be admitted as one of the States of the said Union; and

Whereas,

the existing Government of the Republic of Texas, has assented to the proposals thus made,—the terms and conditions of which are as follows:

"Joint Resolutions for annexing Texas to the United States.

Resolved by the Senate and House of Representatives of the United States of America in Congress assembled, That Congress doth consent that the territory properly included within and rightfully belonging to the Republic of Texas, may be erected into a new State to be called the State of Texas, with a republican form of government adopted by the people of said Republic, by deputies in convention assembled, with the consent of the existing Government in order that the same may by admitted as one of the States of this Union.

2nd. And be it further resolved, That the foregoing consent of Congress is given upon the following conditions, to wit: First, said state to be formed, subject to the adjustment by this government of all questions of boundary that may arise with other governments,—and the Constitution thereof, with the proper evidence of its adoption by the people of said Republic of Texas, shall be transmitted to the President of the United States, to be laid before Congress for its final action on, or before the first day of January, one thousand eight hundred and forty-six. Second, said state when admitted into the Union, after ceding to the United States all public edifices, fortifications, barracks, ports and harbors, navy and navy yards, docks, magazines and armaments, and all other means pertaining to the public defense, belonging to the said Republic of Texas, shall retain funds, debts, taxes and dues of every kind which may belong to, or be due and owing to the said Republic; and shall also retain all the vacant and unappropriated lands lying within its limits, to be applied to the payment of the debts and liabilities of said Republic of Texas, and the residue of said lands, after discharging said debts and liabilities, to be disposed of as said State may direct; but in no event are said debts and liabilities to become a charge upon the Government of the United States. Third—New States of convenient size not exceeding four in number, in addition to said State of Texas and having sufficient population, may, hereafter by the consent of said State, be formed out of the territory thereof, which shall be entitled to admission under the provisions of the Federal Constitution; and such states as may be formed out of the territory lying south of thirty-six degrees thirty minutes north latitude, commonly known as the Missouri Compromise Line, shall be admitted into the Union, with or without slavery, as the people of each State, asking admission shall desire; and in such State or States as shall be formed out of said territory, north of said Missouri compromise Line, slavery, or involuntary servitude (except for crime) shall be prohibited."

Now in order to manifest the assent of the people of this Republic, as required in the above recited portions of said

---

[2] *Journals of the Constitution Convention of Texas, 1845* (Austin: Miner and Cruger, Printers to the Constitution, 1845), 367–70.

resolutions, we the deputies of the people of Texas, in convention assembled, in their name and by their authority, do ordain and declare, that we assent to and accept the proposals, conditions and guarantees, contained in the first and second sections of the Resolution of the Congress of the United States aforesaid.

In testimony whereof, we have hereunto subscribed our names.

THOMAS J. RUSK
President

followed by 61 signatures

Attest
JAMES H. RAYMOND
Secretary of the Convention

Sam Houston's Address on Secession (1860) and Declaration of Causes (1861)

Texas joined the Union in 1845 and left it in 1861. Following the lead of other southern states after the election of Lincoln, Texas called a Secession Convention that met in January 1861. Despite the efforts of Governor Sam Houston to keep Texas in the Union, the convention passed an Ordinance of Secession *on February 1 and a* Declaration of Causes *on February 2, 1861.*[3] *Texas joined the Confederacy as a state on March 1, 1861. Following a four-year conflict, as a practical matter the war ended in April 1865 with the surrender of Lee's Army of Northern Virginia. The last battle of the war (the Battle of Palmito Ranch) was fought May 12–13, 1865, near Brownsville.*

Sam Houston's address captures the minority pro-Union position in Texas. A disciple of Andrew Jackson who rigorously opposed the attempts of South Carolina to reject the dominance of the national government during the Nullification Debates of the 1830s, Houston argued that leaving the Union was a dangerous action for the South. Note that Houston does not reject slavery as an institution but argues that the best way to defend Texans and Texas's interests is within the existing constitutional structure.

The Declaration of Causes *presents the pro-secession argument in Texas, the one that ultimately carried the day. Note this document expresses the fear that southern proslavery states will become a minority in the Union. It also rejects the northern abolitionist contention that there is a "higher law" operating above the U.S. Constitution.*

From Sam Houston's Address on Secession, Austin, Texas, 1860

. . . [I]n 1836, I volunteered to aid in transplanting American liberty to this soil, it was with the belief that the Constitution and the Union were to be perpetual blessings to the human race,—that the success of the experiment of our fathers was beyond dispute, and that whether under the banner of the Lone Star or that many-starred banner of the Union, I could point to the land of Washington, Jefferson, and Jackson, as the land blest beyond all other lands, where freedom would be eternal and Union unbroken. . . . Power, wealth, expansion, victory, have followed in its path, and yet the aegis of the Union has been broad enough to encompass all. Is not this worth perpetuating? Will you exchange this for all the hazards, the anarchy and carnage of civil war? Do you believe that it will be dissevered and no shock felt in society? You are asked to plunge into a revolution; but are you told how to get out of it? Not so; but it is to be a leap in the dark—a leap into an abyss, whose horrors would even fright the mad spirits of disunion who tempt you on.

. . . What is there that is free that we have not? Are our rights invaded and no Government ready to protect them? No! Are our institutions wrested from us and others foreign to our taste forced upon us? No! Is the right of free speech, a free press, or free suffrage taken from us? No! Has our property been taken from us and the Government failed to interpose when called upon? No, none of these! The rights of the States and the rights of individuals are still maintained. We have yet the Constitution, we have yet a judiciary, which has never been appealed to in vain—we have yet just laws and officers to administer them; and an army and navy, ready to maintain any and every constitutional right of the citizen. Whence then this clamor about disunion? Whence this cry of protection to property or disunion, when even the very loudest in the cry, declared under their Senatorial oaths, but a few months since, that no protection was necessary? Are we to sell reality for a phantom?

There is no longer a holy ground upon which the footsteps of the demagogue may not fall. One by one the sacred things placed by patriotic hands upon the altar of our liberties, have been torn down. The Declaration of our Independence is jeered at. The farewell counsels of Washington are derided. The charm of those historic names which make glorious our past has been broken, and now the Union is no longer held sacred, but made secondary to the success of party and the adoption of abstractions. We hear of secession—"peaceable secession." We are to believe that this people, whose progressive civilization has known no obstacles, but has already driven back one race and is fast Americanizing another, who have conquered armies and navies,—whose career has been onward and never has receded, be the step right or wrong, is at last quietly and calmly to be denationalized, to be rent into fragments, sanctioned by the Constitution, and there not only be none of the incidents of revolution, but amid peace and happiness we are to have freedom from abolition clamor, security to the institution of slavery, and a career of glory under a Southern Confederacy, which we can never attain in our present condition! When we deny the right of a State to secede, we are pointed to the resolves of chivalric

[3] Edwin Anderson Alderman, *Library of Southern History*, ed. Joel Chandler Harris (Atlanta: Martin and Hoyt, 1909).

South Carolina and other States; and are told, "Let them go out and you can not whip them back." My friends, there will be no necessity of whipping them back. They will soon whip themselves, and will not be worth whipping back. Deprived of the protection of the Union, of the aegis of the Constitution, they would soon dwindle into petty States, to be again rent in twain by dissensions or through the ambition of selfish chieftains, and would become a prey to foreign powers. They gravely talk of holding treaties with Great Britain and other foreign powers, and the great advantages which would arise to the South from separation are discussed. Treaties with Great Britain! Alliance with foreign powers! Have these men forgotten history? Look at Spanish America! Look at the condition of every petty State, which by alliance with Great Britain is subject to continual aggression! And yet, after picturing the rise and progress of Abolitionism, tracing it to the Wilberforce movement in England, and British influence in the North, showing that British gold has sustained and encouraged Northern fanaticism, we are told to be heedless of the consequences of disunion, for the advantages of British alliance would far over-estimate the loss of the Union!

. . . It is but natural that we all should desire the defeat of the Black Republican candidates. As Southern men, the fact that their party is based upon the one idea of opposition to our institutions, is enough to demand our efforts against them; but we have a broader, a more national cause of opposition to them. Their party is sectional. It is at war with those principles of equality and nationality upon which the Government is formed, and as much the foe of the Northern as of the Southern man. Its mission is to engender strife, to foster hatred between brethren, and to encourage the formation here of Southern sectional parties equally dangerous to Southern and Northern rights. The conservative energies of the country are called upon to take a stand now against the Northern sectional party, because its strength betokens success. Defeat and overthrow it, and the defeat and overthrow of Southern sectionalism is easy.

I come not here to speak in behalf of a united South against Lincoln. I appeal to the nation. I ask not the defeat of sectionalism by sectionalism, but by nationality. These men who talk of a united South, know well that it begets a united North. Talk of frightening the North into measures by threats of dissolving the Union! It is child's play and folly. It is all the Black Republican leaders want. American blood, North nor South, has not yet become so ignoble as to be chilled by threats. Strife begets strife, threat begets threat, and taunt begets taunt, and these disunionists know it. American blood brooks no such restraints as these men would put upon it. I would blush with shame for America, if I could believe that one vast portion of my countrymen had sunk so low that childish threats would intimidate them. . . .

The error has been that the South has met sectionalism by sectionalism. We want a Union basis, one broad enough to comprehend the good and true friends of the Constitution at the North. To hear Southern disunionists talk, you would think the majority of the Northern people were in this Black Republican party; but it is not so. They are in a minority, and it but needs a patriotic movement like that supported by the conservatives of Texas, to unite the divided opposition to that party there and overthrow it. . . .

I came not here to vindicate candidates or denounce them. They stand upon their records. If they are national, approve them; if they are sectional, condemn. Judge them by the principles they announce. Let past differences be forgotten in the determination to unite against sectionalism. I have differed with all three of the candidates; but whenever I see a man at this crisis coming boldly up to the defense of the Constitution of the country, and ready to maintain the Union against its foes, I will not permit old scores to prejudice me against him. Hence I am ready to vote the Union ticket, and if all the candidates occupy this national ground, my vote may be transferred to either of them. This is the way to put Mr. Lincoln down. Put him down constitutionally, by rallying the conservative forces and sacrificing men for the sake of principles.

But if, through division in the ranks of those opposed to Mr. Lincoln, he should be elected, we have no excuse for dissolving the Union. The Union is worth more than Mr. Lincoln, and if the battle is to be fought for the Constitution, let us fight it in the Union and for the sake of the Union. With a majority of the people in favor of the Constitution, shall we desert the Government and leave it in the hands of the minority? A new obligation will be imposed upon us, to guard the Constitution and to see that no infraction of it is attempted or permitted. If Mr. Lincoln administers the Government in accordance with the Constitution, our rights must be respected. If he does not, the Constitution has provided a remedy.

No tyrant or usurper can ever invade our rights so long as we are united. Let Mr. Lincoln attempt it, and his party will scatter like chaff before the storm of popular indignation which will burst forth from one end of the country to the other. Secession or revolution will not be justified until legal and constitutional means of redress have been tried, and I can not believe that the time will ever come when these will prove inadequate. . . .

Declaration of Causes: February 2, 1861[4]
A declaration of the causes which impel the State
of Texas to secede from the Federal Union.

The government of the United States, by certain joint resolutions, bearing date the 1st day of March, in the year A.D. 1845, proposed to the Republic of Texas, then a free, sovereign and independent nation, the annexation of the latter to the former as one of the co-equal States thereof,

The people of Texas, by deputies in convention assembled, on the fourth day of July of the same year, assented to and accepted said proposals and formed a constitution for the proposed State, upon which on the 29th day of December in the same year, said State was formally admitted into the Confederated Union.

Texas abandoned her separate national existence and consented to become one of the Confederated States to promote her welfare, insure domestic tranquility [sic] and secure more substantially the blessings of peace and liberty to her people. She was received into the confederacy with her own constitution, under the guarantee of the federal constitution and the compact of annexation, that she should enjoy these blessings. She was received as a commonwealth holding, maintaining and protecting the institution known as negro slavery—the servitude of the African to the white race within her limits—a relation that had existed from the first settlement of her wilderness by the white race, and which her people intended should exist in all future time. Her institutions and geographical position established the strongest ties between her and other slave-holding States of the confederacy. Those ties have been strengthened by association. But what has been the course of the government of the United States, and of the people and authorities of the non-slave-holding States, since our connection with them?

The controlling majority of the Federal Government, under various pretences and disguises, has so administered the same as to exclude the citizens of the Southern States, unless under odious and unconstitutional restrictions, from all the immense territory owned in common by all the States on the Pacific Ocean, for the avowed purpose of acquiring sufficient power in the common government to use it as a means of destroying the institutions of Texas and her sister slave-holding States.

By the disloyalty of the Northern States and their citizens and the imbecility of the Federal Government, infamous combinations of incendiaries and outlaws have been permitted in those States and the common territory of Kansas to trample upon the federal laws, to war upon the lives and property of Southern citizens in that territory, and finally, by violence and mob law, to usurp the possession of the same as exclusively the property of the Northern States.

The Federal Government, while but partially under the control of these our unnatural and sectional enemies, has for years almost entirely failed to protect the lives and property of the people of Texas against the Indian savages on our border, and more recently against the murderous forays of banditti from the neighboring territory of Mexico; and when our State government has expended large amounts for such purpose, the Federal Government has refused reimbursement therefor, thus rendering our condition more insecure and harrassing [sic] than it was during the existence of the Republic of Texas.

These and other wrongs we have patiently borne in the vain hope that a returning sense of justice and humanity would induce a different course of administration.

When we advert to the course of individual non-slaveholding States, and that [of] a majority of their citizens, our grievances assume far greater magnitude.

The States of Maine, Vermont, New Hampshire, Connecticut, Rhode Island, Massachusetts, New York, Pennsylvania, Ohio, Wisconsin, Michigan and Iowa, by solemn legislative enactments, have deliberately, directly or indirectly violated the 3rd clause of the 2nd section of the 4th article of the federal constitution, and laws passed in pursuance thereof; thereby annulling a material provision of the compact, designed by its framers to perpetuate amity between the members of the confederacy and to secure the rights of the slaveholding States in their domestic institutions—a provision founded in justice and wisdom, and without the enforcement of which the compact fails to accomplish the object of its creation. Some of those States have imposed high fines and degrading penalties upon any of their citizens or officers who may carry out in good faith that provision of the compact, or the federal laws enacted in accordance therewith.

In all the non-slave-holding States, in violation of that good faith and comity which should exist between entirely distinct nations, the people have formed themselves into a great sectional party, now strong enough in numbers to control the affairs of each of those States, based upon the unnatural feeling of hostility to these Southern States and their beneficent and patriarchal system of African slavery,

[4] Ernest William Winkler, ed., *Journal of the Secession Convention of Texas 1861, Edited from the Original in the Department of State by Ernest William Winkler, State Librarian* (Austin: Texas Library and Historical Commission, 1912), 61–65.

proclaiming the debasing doctrine of the equality of all men, irrespective of race or color—a doctrine at war with nature, in opposition to the experience of mankind, and in violation of the plainest revelations of the Divine Law. They demand the abolition of negro slavery throughout the confederacy, the recognition of political equality between the white and the negro races, and avow their determination to press on their crusade against us, so long as a negro slave remains in these States.

For years past this abolition organization has been actively sowing the seeds of discord through the Union, and has rendered the federal congress the arena for spreading firebrands and hatred between the slave-holding and non-slave-holding States.

By consolidating their strength, they have placed the slave-holding States in a hopeless minority in the federal congress, and rendered representation of no avail in protecting Southern rights against their exactions and encroachments.

They have proclaimed, and at the ballot box sustained, the revolutionary doctrine that there is a "higher law" than the constitution and laws of our Federal Union, and virtually that they will disregard their oaths and trample upon our rights.

They have for years past encouraged and sustained lawless organizations to steal our slaves and prevent their recapture, and have repeatedly murdered Southern citizens while lawfully seeking their rendition.

They have invaded Southern soil and murdered unoffending citizens, and through the press their leading men and a fanatical pulpit have bestowed praise upon the actors and assassins in these crimes, while the governors of several of their States have refused to deliver parties implicated and indicted for participation in such offences, upon the legal demands of the States aggrieved.

They have, through the mails and hired emissaries, sent seditious pamphlets and papers among us to stir up servile insurrection and bring blood and carnage to our firesides.

They have sent hired emissaries among us to burn our towns and distribute arms and poison to our slaves for the same purpose.

They have impoverished the slave-holding States by unequal and partial legislation, thereby enriching themselves by draining our substance.

They have refused to vote appropriations for protecting Texas against ruthless savages, for the sole reason that she is a slave-holding State.

And, finally, by the combined sectional vote of the seventeen non-slave-holding States, they have elected as president and vice-president of the whole confederacy two men whose chief claims to such high positions are their approval of these long continued wrongs, and their pledges to continue them to the final consummation of these schemes for the ruin of the slave-holding States.

In view of these and many other facts, it is meet that our own views should be distinctly proclaimed.

We hold as undeniable truths that the governments of the various States, and of the confederacy itself, were established exclusively by the white race, for themselves and their posterity; that the African race had no agency in their establishment; that they were rightfully held and regarded as an inferior and dependent race, and in that condition only could their existence in this country be rendered beneficial or tolerable.

That in this free government all white men are and of right ought to be entitled to equal civil and political rights; that the servitude of the African race, as existing in these States, is mutually beneficial to both bond and free, and is abundantly authorized and justified by the experience of mankind, and the revealed will of the Almighty Creator, as recognized by all Christian nations; while the destruction of the existing relations between the two races, as advocated by our sectional enemies, would bring inevitable calamities upon both and desolation upon the fifteen slave-holding States.

By the secession of six of the slave-holding States, and the certainty that others will speedily do likewise, Texas has no alternative but to remain in an isolated connection with the North, or unite her destinies with the South.

For these and other reasons, solemnly asserting that the federal constitution has been violated and virtually abrogated by the several States named, seeing that the federal government is now passing under the control of our enemies to be diverted from the exalted objects of its creation to those of oppression and wrong, and realizing that our own State can no longer look for protection, but to God and her own sons—We the delegates of the people of Texas, in Convention assembled, have passed an ordinance dissolving all political connection with the government of the United States of America and the people thereof and confidently appeal to the intelligence and patriotism of the freemen of Texas to ratify the same at the ballot box, on the 23rd day of the present month.

Adopted in Convention on the 2nd day of Feby, in the year of our Lord one thousand eight hundred and sixty-one and of the independence of Texas the twenty-fifth.

Ordinance of Secession Null (1866) and Texas v. White et al. (1869)

Once the South and Texas had been defeated in the Civil War, the question arose as to the constitutional status of the secessionist states, including Texas. From the perspective of law and constitutional thought, had the southern states ever left the Union? Were the actions of state governments under the Confederacy legal or not? Two documents help clarify this issue.[5]

The ordinance declaring secession null and void answers these questions directly. By the expressed declaration of the Texas people in convention, the ordinance proclaims the 1861 act of secession to be null and void. Texas may have been in rebellion, but it never left the Union. Actions by the Confederate state of Texas thus were not legal.

The Texas v. White et al. *case answers this question further by exploring the legality of specific actions of the Confederate legislature in Texas. In 1850, Congress authorized $10 million in bonds to Texas. In 1862 the Confederate legislature authorized using the bonds for war supplies. In 1866, after the war, the Reconstruction government of Texas tried to reclaim the bonds on the grounds that the Confederate state government had illegally sold the bonds. Note the constitutional theory about the nature of the Union and the rebellion that is developed in the Chief Justice's opinion. The union established under the Articles of Convention and the U.S. Constitution is "perpetual" and "indissoluble." Once Texas joined the Union, Texas and Texans became part of this Union. Texas may have been in rebellion against the Union, but it had never left the Union. The actions of the Confederate government, like the act of secession, were thus null and void. The bonds thus had not been legally sold.*

An Ordinance, Declaring the Ordinance of Secession Null and Void (*March 15, 1866*)

Be it ordained by the people of Texas in Convention assembled, That we acknowledge the supremacy of the Constitution of the United States, and the laws passed in pursuance thereof; and that an Ordinance adopted by a former Convention of the people of Texas on the 1st day of February, A.D. 1861, entitled "An Ordinance to Dissolve the Union between the State of Texas and the other States, united under the compact styled 'Constitution of the United States of America,'" be and the same is hereby declared null and void; and the right heretofore claimed by the State of Texas to secede from the Union, is hereby distinctly renounced. Passed 15th March, 1866.

From TEXAS v. WHITE ET AL. (*1869*)
Supreme Court of United States.

The CHIEF JUSTICE delivered the opinion of the court.

. . . If, therefore, it is true that the State of Texas was not at the time of filing this bill, or is not now, one of the United States, we have no jurisdiction of this suit, and it is our duty to dismiss it.

We are very sensible of the magnitude and importance of this question, of the interest it excites, and of the difficulty, not to say impossibility, of so disposing of it as to satisfy the conflicting judgments of men equally enlightened, equally upright, and equally patriotic. But we meet it in the case, and we must determine it in the exercise of our best judgment, under the guidance of the Constitution alone. . . .

. . . [T]he word . . . [state is] used in the clause which provides that the United States shall guarantee to every State in the Union a republican form of government, and shall protect each of them against invasion. . . .

The Republic of Texas was admitted into the Union, as a State, on the 27th of December, 1845. By this act the new State, and the people of the new State, were invested with all the rights, and became subject to all the responsibilities and duties of the original States under the Constitution.

From the date of admission, until 1861, the State was represented in the Congress of the United States by her senators and representatives, and her relations as a member of the Union remained unimpaired. In that year, acting upon the theory that the rights of a State under the Constitution might be renounced, and her obligations thrown off at pleasure, Texas undertook to sever the bond thus formed, and to break up her constitutional relations with the United States. . . .

The governor and secretary of state, refusing to comply, were summarily ejected from office.

The members of the legislature, which had also adjourned and reassembled on the 18th of March, were more compliant. They took the oath, and proceeded on the 8th of April

---

[5] The Constitution of the State of Texas, as Amended by the Delegates in Convention Assembled, Austin, 1866 (Austin: Printed at the Southern Intelligencer Office, 1866), 32.

to provide by law for the choice of electors of president and vice-president of the Confederate States.

The representatives of the State in the Congress of the United States were withdrawn, and as soon as the seceded States became organized under a constitution, Texas sent senators and representatives to the Confederate Congress.

In all respects, so far as the object could be accomplished by ordinances of the convention, by acts of the legislature, and by votes of the citizens, the relations of Texas to the Union were broken up, and new relations to a new government were established for them.

The position thus assumed could only be maintained by arms, and Texas accordingly took part, with the other Confederate States, in the war of the rebellion, which these events made inevitable. During the whole of that war there was no governor, or judge, or any other State officer in Texas, who recognized the National authority. Nor was any officer of the United States permitted to exercise any authority whatever under the National government within the limits of the State, except under the immediate protection of the National military forces.

Did Texas, in consequence of these acts, cease to be a State? Or, if not, did the State cease to be a member of the Union? . . .

The Union of the States never was a purely artificial and arbitrary relation. It began among the Colonies, and grew out of common origin, mutual sympathies, kindred principles, similar interests, and geographical relations. It was confirmed and strengthened by the necessities of war, and received definite form, and character, and sanction from the Articles of Confederation. By these the Union was solemnly declared to "be perpetual." And when these Articles were found to be inadequate to the exigencies of the country, the Constitution was ordained "to form a more perfect Union." It is difficult to convey the idea of indissoluble unity more clearly than by these words. What can be indissoluble if a perpetual Union, made more perfect, is not? . . .

When, therefore, Texas became one of the United States, she entered into an indissoluble relation. All the obligations of perpetual union, and all the guaranties of republican government in the Union, attached at once to the State. The act which consummated her admission into the Union was something more than a compact; it was the incorporation of a new member into the political body. And it was final. The union between Texas and the other States was as complete, as perpetual, and as indissoluble as the union between the original States. There was no place for reconsideration, or revocation, except through revolution, or through consent of the States.

Considered therefore as transactions under the Constitution, the ordinance of secession, adopted by the convention and ratified by a majority of the citizens of Texas, and all the acts of her legislature intended to give effect to that ordinance, were absolutely null. They were utterly without operation in law. The obligations of the State, as a member of the Union, and of every citizen of the State, as a citizen of the United States, remained perfect and unimpaired. It certainly follows that the State did not cease to be a State, nor her citizens to be citizens of the Union. If this were otherwise, the State must have become foreign, and her citizens foreigners. The war must have ceased to be a war for the suppression of rebellion, and must have become a war for conquest and subjugation.

Our conclusion therefore is, that Texas continued to be a State, and a State of the Union, notwithstanding the transactions to which we have referred. And this conclusion, in our judgment, is not in conflict with any act or declaration of any department of the National government, but entirely in accordance with the whole series of such acts and declarations since the first outbreak of the rebellion. . . .

These new relations imposed new duties upon the United States. The first was that of suppressing the rebellion. The next was that of re-establishing the broken relations of the State with the Union. The first of these duties having been performed, the next necessarily engaged the attention of the National government.

The authority for the performance of the first had been found in the power to suppress insurrection and carry on war; for the performance of the second, authority was derived from the obligation of the United States to guarantee to every State in the Union a republican form of government. . . . It follows that the title of the State was not divested by the act of the insurgent government in entering into this contract. . . .

From Governor Richard Coke's Second Inaugural Address (1876)

Following the Civil War, Texas operated under two constitutions (the Constitution of 1866 and 1869). The return to power of the Democratic Party in the elections of 1872 and 1873 effectively ended reconstruction in Texas. A Constitutional Convention dominated by the Democrats in 1875 drafted a new constitution for the state that took effect in 1876.

Governor Richard Coke's second inaugural address in 1876 captures how many people thought of the new constitution. For Coke the 1876 Constitution was not meant to be a reworking of the earlier state constitutions. The people of Texas had become dissatisfied with the power granted to governmental institution over the last decade and were seeking to limit the powers and reach of government. The new constitution was to be unabashedly conservative in design and intent.

After years of trial and struggle, the people of Texas have at length inaugurated a government made in all its parts by themselves. Its faults and errors, as well as its blessings, have no uncertain paternity. The highest exercise of sovereign power of which a State in the American Union is capable, is that through which the people of Texas have swept out of existence the old government and enacted in its stead that which today has been put in operation in all its departments. Thus has a great revolution been accomplished, without violence or disorder, and with no other conflict than the attrition of opposing opinions in the field of argument and discussion, preparatory to the grand arbitrament of the peaceful ballot.... This is the sixth time in the history of Texas that this sovereign right has been exercised....

In the more recently framed constitutions we plainly see a wide departure from the beaten track of constitutional structure, and in none of them is this more apparent than in the new Constitution of Texas.

The accepted theory of American constitutional government is that State constitutions are limitations upon, rather than grants of power; and, as a general rule, not without its exceptions, that powers not prohibited exist in State government. Hence, express prohibitions are necessary upon the powers the people would withhold from the State government, and as time and circumstances and experience suggest their wisdom, these restrictions upon the powers of government have multiplied in the more recently created instruments of fundamental law. Many causes have conspired to produce these great changes of constitutional theory, and prominent among them are the enormous amounts of capital concentrated in few hands, operating under charters which perpetuate its power; immense railroad systems, which drive off competition and monopolize the carrying trade of the country; the wonderful growth of towns and cities, whose immediate local governments are peculiarly subject to abuses and malign influences, general extravagance, and frequent corruptions of all departments of government, of late years becoming so alarming—all producing results which necessitate a clearer definition and closer guardianship of the rights of the people; and, for their protection, constitutional barriers not demanded by the conditions of society a quarter of a century ago.—

In this instrument we see mirrored the result of issues made in the politics of the State, in the halls of legislation, and in the primary assemblies of the people during the last decade; and we see faithfully reflected in its restrictions upon the power of government, as in its assertion of powers, the dangers of the past, a recurrence of which is so well guarded against in the future. The instrument presents in its fundamental and leading features a basis on which a government may be reared, eminently conservative of all the purposes for which government is instituted; adapted to a sound and healthy growth and development of the State. It may possibly be, in some respects too restrictive, but when such is the case, the error is on the safe side, and while temporary inconvenience may ensue, no permanent injury will result....

The country and people whose welfare depends upon our deliberations and action need and expect a government light in its burdens, effective in administration, and certain in its securities for person and property. Naught else is necessary to ensure prosperity and continued progress and advancement. With such government the elements of greatness so abundant in the noble State we represent, in the hands of our intelligent adventurous and enterprising people, will combine, and evolve from the womb of the future a destiny of grander proportions than the most gorgeous dream of the enthusiast now pictures....

The Texas Constitution's Bill of Rights (1876 plus amendments)

One of the distinguishing features of the Texas Constitution is a lengthy Bill of Rights. Here the Texas Constitution protects Texans from the actions of state government. Unlike the U.S. Constitution where the Bill of Rights comprising the first ten amendments is located at the end of the document, the Texas Bill of Rights is placed at the beginning as Article 1.

The Texas Bill of Rights articulates a distinctive governing philosophy about the "principles of liberty and free government" that underlies the Texas Constitution. Power comes from the people and Republican government is guaranteed. The people reserve "at all times the inalienable right to alter, reform or abolish their government in such a manner as they may think expedient." Texas is a free and independent state, "subject only to the Constitution of the United States." But the Texas Bill of Rights also declares that the "perpetuity of the Union" depends upon the preservation of unimpaired local self-government. Today such a statement might seem to be uncontroversial. Put in the proper historical context, however, this philosophy signals a rejection of the 1869 Constitution's explicit affirmation of the supremacy of the U.S. Constitution in matters of federalism. Such a philosophy reflects the return to power of traditional secessionist political elites in Texas. This philosophy would dominate (and haunt) Texas politics and government from 1876 until the 1960s when federal civil rights legislation would redefine what local self-government would mean, particularly in regard to the protections afforded minorities by the U.S. Constitution.

Some of the rights in Article 1 echo the protections provided by the U.S. Bill of Rights. Freedom of worship is guaranteed (Sec. 6), as is freedom of speech (Sec. 8), freedom of the press (Sec. 8), freedom of assembly and petition (Sec. 27), and freedom from the quartering of soldiers (Sec. 25). Texans are protected in the Bill of Rights from unreasonable searches and seizures (Sec. 9), and the accused has certain due process rights (for example, Secs. 10, 12, 13, 14, 15, and 19). The Texas Bill of Rights explicitly bans religious tests for public office or appropriations for sectarian purposes (Sec. 7).

Some protections provided by the Texas Bill of Rights seem strange to the modern ear. Monopolies are outlawed (Sec. 26). Primogeniture (limiting the inheritance of land to the first born) and entails (conditions put on the inheritance of land) are forbidden. No one can be found guilty due to corruption of blood (guilt by family association) or be punished in their inheritance by the suicide of a family member.

The Texas Bill of Rights most sharply diverges from the U.S. Bill of Rights in the amendments that have been added over the years. Many of these reflect the ebb and flow of political and cultural concerns in the state. In contrast to the federal government, Texas added an Equal Rights Amendment to the Bill of Rights in 1972, protecting people from discrimination because of sex, race, color, creed, or national origin (Sec. 31). Between 1956 and 2007, complicated provisions were added to the Bill of Rights allowing the denial of bail for multiple convictions (Secs. 11a, 11b, and 11c). Lengthy provisions were added to the Bill of Rights granting rights to crime victims in 1989 (Sec. 30) and providing for compensation for crime victims in 1997 (Sec. 31). Provisions protecting traditional marriage were added in 2005 in Section 32, although these are now inoperable due to a recent Supreme Court ruling. Access to public beaches is guaranteed to individuals in 2009 (Sec. 33) as is the right to hunt, fish, and harvest wildlife by traditional methods such a guns (Sec. 34). In 2009, an amendment was added to the Bill of Rights clarifying when property could be seized by the state under eminent domain. These protections were added to the Bill of Rights largely in response to the furor created by cities taking land from individuals and giving it to others for development projects, like the building of modern sports stadiums.

The extensive list of rights contained in Article 1 of the Texas Constitution shows the ongoing concerns of people and politicians in Texas to limit what government does through constitutional mandate. These rights will likely be expanded in the future.

ARTICLE 1. BILL OF RIGHTS

That the general, great and essential principles of liberty and free government may be recognized and established, we declare:

Sec. 1. FREEDOM AND SOVEREIGNTY OF STATE. Texas is a free and independent State, subject only to the Constitution of the United States, and the maintenance of our free institutions and the perpetuity of the Union depend upon the preservation of the right of local self-government, unimpaired to all the States.

Sec. 2. INHERENT POLITICAL POWER; REPUBLICAN FORM OF GOVERNMENT. All political power is inherent in the people, and all free governments are founded on their authority, and instituted for their benefit. The faith of the people of Texas stands pledged to the preservation of a republican form of government, and, subject to this limitation only, they have at all times the inalienable right to alter, reform or abolish their government in such manner as they may think expedient.

Sec. 3. EQUAL RIGHTS. All free men, when they form a social compact, have equal rights, and no man, or set of men, is entitled to exclusive separate public emoluments, or privileges, but in consideration of public services.

Sec. 3a. EQUALITY UNDER THE LAW. Equality under the law shall not be denied or abridged because of sex, race, color, creed, or national origin. This amendment is self-operative.

(Added Nov. 7, 1972.)

Sec. 4. RELIGIOUS TESTS. No religious test shall ever be required as a qualification to any office, or public trust, in this State; nor shall any one be excluded from holding office on account of his religious sentiments, provided he acknowledge the existence of a Supreme Being.

Sec. 5. WITNESSES NOT DISQUALIFIED BY RELIGIOUS BELIEFS; OATHS AND AFFIRMATIONS. No person shall be disqualified to give evidence in any of the Courts of this State on account of his religious opinions, or for the want of any religious belief, but all oaths or affirmations shall be administered in the mode most binding upon the conscience, and shall be taken subject to the pains and penalties of perjury.

Sec. 6. FREEDOM OF WORSHIP. All men have a natural and indefeasible right to worship Almighty God according to the dictates of their own consciences. No man shall be compelled to attend, erect or support any place of worship, or to maintain any ministry against his consent. No human authority ought, in any case whatever, to control or interfere with the rights of conscience in matters of religion, and no preference shall ever be given by law to any religious society or mode of worship. But it shall be the duty of the Legislature to pass such laws as may be necessary to protect equally every religious denomination in the peaceable enjoyment of its own mode of public worship.

Sec. 7. APPROPRIATIONS FOR SECTARIAN PURPOSES. No money shall be appropriated, or drawn from the Treasury for the benefit of any sect, or religious society, theological or religious seminary; nor shall property belonging to the State be appropriated for any such purposes.

Sec. 8. FREEDOM OF SPEECH AND PRESS; LIBEL. Every person shall be at liberty to speak, write or publish his opinions on any subject, being responsible for the abuse of that privilege; and no law shall ever be passed curtailing the liberty of speech or of the press. In prosecutions for the publication of papers, investigating the conduct of officers, or men in public capacity, or when the matter published is proper for public information, the truth thereof may be given in evidence. And in all indictments for libels, the jury shall have the right to determine the law and the facts, under the direction of the court, as in other cases.

Sec. 9. SEARCHES AND SEIZURES. The people shall be secure in their persons, houses, papers and possessions, from all unreasonable seizures or searches, and no warrant to search any place, or to seize any person or thing, shall issue without describing them as near as may be, nor without probable cause, supported by oath or affirmation.

Sec. 10. RIGHTS OF ACCUSED IN CRIMINAL PROSECUTIONS. In all criminal prosecutions the accused shall have a speedy public trial by an impartial jury. He shall have the right to demand the nature and cause of the accusation against him, and to have a copy thereof. He shall not be compelled to give evidence against himself, and shall have the right of being heard by himself or counsel, or both, shall be confronted by the witnesses against him and shall have compulsory process for obtaining witnesses in his favor, except that when the witness resides out of the State and the offense charged is a violation of any of the anti-trust laws of this State, the defendant and the State shall have the right to produce and have the evidence admitted by deposition, under such rules and laws as the Legislature may hereafter provide; and no person shall be held to answer for a criminal offense, unless on an indictment of a grand jury, except in cases in which the punishment is by fine or imprisonment, otherwise than in the penitentiary, in cases of impeachment, and in cases arising in the army or navy, or in the militia, when in actual service in time of war or public danger.

(Amended Nov. 5, 1918.)

Sec. 11. BAIL. All prisoners shall be bailable by sufficient sureties, unless for capital offenses, when the proof is evident; but this provision shall not be so construed as to prevent bail after indictment found upon examination of the evidence, in such manner as may be prescribed by law.

Sec. 11a. MULTIPLE CONVICTIONS; DENIAL OF BAIL. (a) Any person (1) accused of a felony less than capital in this State, who has been theretofore twice convicted of a felony, the second conviction being subsequent to the first, both in point of time of commission of the offense and conviction therefor, (2) accused of a felony less than capital in this State, committed while on bail for a prior felony for which he has been indicted, (3) accused of a felony less than capital in this State involving the use of a deadly weapon after being convicted of a prior felony, or (4) accused of a violent or sexual offense committed while under the supervision of a criminal justice agency of the State or a political subdivision of the State for a prior felony, after a hearing, and upon evidence substantially showing the guilt of the accused of the offense in (1) or (3) above, of the offense committed while on bail in (2) above, or of the offense in (4) above committed while under the supervision of a criminal justice agency of the State or a political subdivision of the State for a prior felony, may be denied bail pending trial, by a district judge in this State, if said order denying bail pending trial is issued within seven calendar days subsequent to the time of incarceration of the accused; provided, however, that if the accused is not accorded a trial upon the accusation under (1) or (3) above, the accusation and indictment used under (2) above, or the accusation or indictment used under (4) above within sixty (60) days from the time of his incarceration upon the accusation, the order denying bail shall be automatically set aside, unless a continuance is obtained upon the motion or request of the accused; provided, further, that the right of appeal to the Court of Criminal Appeals of this State is expressly accorded the accused for a review of any judgment or order made hereunder, and said appeal shall be given preference by the Court of Criminal Appeals.

(b) In this section:

(1) "Violent offense" means:
  (A) murder;
  (B) aggravated assault, if the accused used or exhibited a deadly weapon during the commission of the assault;
  (C) aggravated kidnapping; or
  (D) aggravated robbery.
(2) "Sexual offense" means:
  (A) aggravated sexual assault;
  (B) sexual assault; or
  (C) indecency with a child.

(Added Nov. 6, 1956; amended Nov. 8, 1977; Subsec. (a) amended and (b) added Nov. 2, 1993.)

Sec. 11b. VIOLATION OF CONDITION OF RELEASE PENDING TRIAL; DENIAL OF BAIL. Any person who is accused in this state of a felony or an offense involving family violence, who is released on bail pending trial, and whose bail is subsequently revoked or forfeited for a violation of a condition of release may be denied bail pending trial if a judge or magistrate in this state determines by a preponderance of the evidence at a subsequent hearing that the person violated a condition of release related to the safety of a victim of the alleged offense or to the safety of the community.

(Added Nov. 8, 2005; amended Nov. 6, 2007.)

Sec. 11c. VIOLATION OF AN ORDER FOR EMERGENCY PROTECTION INVOLVING FAMILY VIOLENCE. The legislature by general law may provide that any person who violates an order for emergency protection issued by a judge or magistrate after an arrest for an offense involving family violence or who violates an active protective order rendered by a court in a family violence case, including a temporary ex parte order that has been served on the person, or who engages in conduct that constitutes an offense involving the violation of an order described by this section may be taken into custody and, pending trial or other court proceedings, denied release on bail if following a hearing a judge or magistrate in this state determines by a preponderance of the evidence that the person violated the order or engaged in the conduct constituting the offense.

Sec. 12. HABEAS CORPUS. The writ of habeas corpus is a writ of right, and shall never be suspended. The Legislature shall enact laws to render the remedy speedy and effectual.

Sec. 13. EXCESSIVE BAIL OR FINES; CRUEL AND UNUSUAL PUNISHMENT; REMEDY BY DUE COURSE OF LAW. Excessive bail shall not be required, nor excessive fines imposed, nor cruel or unusual punishment inflicted. All courts shall be open, and every person for an injury done him, in his lands, goods, person or reputation, shall have remedy by due course of law.

Sec. 14. DOUBLE JEOPARDY. No person, for the same offense, shall be twice put in jeopardy of life or liberty; nor shall a person be again put upon trial for the same offense after a verdict of not guilty in a court of competent jurisdiction.

Sec. 15. RIGHT OF TRIAL BY JURY. The right of trial by jury shall remain inviolate. The Legislature shall pass such laws as may be needed to regulate the same, and to maintain its purity and efficiency. Provided, that the Legislature may provide for the temporary commitment, for observation and/or treatment, of mentally ill persons not charged with a criminal offense, for a period of time not to exceed ninety (90) days, by order of the County Court without the necessity of a trial by jury.

(Amended Aug. 24, 1935.)

Sec. 15-a. COMMITMENT OF PERSONS OF UNSOUND MIND. No person shall be committed as a person of unsound mind except on competent medical or psychiatric testimony. The Legislature may enact all laws necessary to provide for the trial, adjudication of insanity and commitment of persons of unsound mind and to provide for a method of appeal from judgments rendered in such cases. Such laws may provide for a waiver of trial by jury, in cases where the person under inquiry has not been charged with the commission of a criminal offense, by the concurrence of the person under inquiry, or his next of kin, and an attorney ad litem appointed by a judge of either the County or Probate Court of the county where the trial is being held, and shall provide for a method of service of notice of such trial upon the person under inquiry and of his right to demand a trial by jury.

(Added Nov. 6, 1956.)

Sec. 16. BILLS OF ATTAINDER; EX POST FACTO OR RETROACTIVE LAWS; IMPAIRING OBLIGATION OF CONTRACTS. No bill of attainder, ex post facto law, retroactive law, or any law impairing the obligation of contracts, shall be made.

Sec. 17. TAKING, DAMAGING, OR DESTROYING PROPERTY FOR PUBLIC USE; SPECIAL PRIVILEGES AND IMMUNITIES; CONTROL OF PRIVILEGES AND FRANCHISES. (a) No person's property shall be taken, damaged, or destroyed for or applied to public use without adequate compensation being made, unless by the consent of such person, and only if the taking, damage, or destruction is for:

> (1) the ownership, use, and enjoyment of the property, notwithstanding an incidental
> use, by:
>> (A) the State, a political subdivision of the State, or the public at large; or
>> (B) an entity granted the power of eminent domain under law; or

> (2) the elimination of urban blight on a particular parcel of property.

(b) In this section, "public use" does not include the taking of property under Subsection (a) of this section for transfer to a private entity for the primary purpose of economic development or enhancement of tax revenues.

(c) On or after January 1, 2010, the legislature may enact a general, local, or special law granting the power of eminent domain to an entity only on a two-thirds vote of all the members elected to each house.

(d) When a person's property is taken under Subsection (a) of this section, except for the use of the State, compensation as described by Subsection (a) shall be first made, or secured by a deposit of money; and no irrevocable or uncontrollable grant of special privileges or immunities shall be made; but all privileges and franchises granted by the Legislature, or created under its authority, shall be subject to the control thereof.

(Amended Nov. 3, 2009.)

Sec. 18. IMPRISONMENT FOR DEBT. No person shall ever be imprisoned for debt.

Sec. 19. DEPRIVATION OF LIFE, LIBERTY, ETC.; DUE COURSE OF LAW. No citizen of this State shall be deprived of life, liberty, property, privileges or immunities, or in any manner disfranchised, except by the due course of the law of the land.

Sec. 20. OUTLAWRY OR TRANSPORTATION FOR OFFENSE. No citizen shall be outlawed. No person shall be transported out of the State for any offense committed within the same. This section does not prohibit an agreement with another state providing for the confinement of inmates of this State in the penal or correctional facilities of that state.

(Amended Nov. 5, 1985.)

Sec. 21. CORRUPTION OF BLOOD; FORFEITURE; SUICIDES. No conviction shall work corruption of blood, or forfeiture of estate, and the estates of those who destroy their own lives shall descend or vest as in case of natural death.

Sec. 22. TREASON. Treason against the State shall consist only in levying war against it, or adhering to its enemies, giving them aid and comfort; and no person shall be convicted of treason except on the testimony of two witnesses to the same overt act, or on confession in open court.

Sec. 23. RIGHT TO KEEP AND BEAR ARMS. Every citizen shall have the right to keep and bear arms in the lawful defense of himself or the State; but the Legislature shall have power, by law, to regulate the wearing of arms, with a view to prevent crime.

Sec. 24. MILITARY SUBORDINATE TO CIVIL AUTHORITY. The military shall at all times be subordinate to the civil authority.

Sec. 25. QUARTERING SOLDIERS IN HOUSES. No soldier shall in time of peace be quartered in the house of any citizen without the consent of the owner, nor in time of war but in a manner prescribed by law.

Sec. 26. PERPETUITIES AND MONOPOLIES; PRIMO-GENITURE OR ENTAILMENTS. Perpetuities and monopolies are contrary to the genius of a free government, and shall never be allowed, nor shall the law of primogeniture or entailments ever be in force in this State.

Sec. 27. RIGHT OF ASSEMBLY; PETITION FOR REDRESS OF GRIEVANCES. The citizens shall have the right, in a peaceable manner, to assemble together for their common good; and apply to those invested with the powers of government for redress of grievances or other purposes, by petition, address or remonstrance.

Sec. 28. SUSPENSION OF LAWS. No power of suspending laws in this State shall be exercised except by the Legislature.

Sec. 29. PROVISIONS OF BILL OF RIGHTS EXCEPTED FROM POWERS OF GOVERNMENT; TO FOREVER REMAIN INVIOLATE. To guard against transgressions of the high powers herein delegated, we declare that everything in this "Bill of Rights" is excepted out of the general powers of government, and shall forever remain inviolate, and all laws contrary thereto, or to the following provisions, shall be void.

Sec. 30. RIGHTS OF CRIME VICTIMS. (a) A crime victim has the following rights:

> (1) the right to be treated with fairness and with respect for the victim's dignity and privacy

throughout the criminal justice process; and

> (2) the right to be reasonably protected from the accused throughout the criminal justice process.

(b) On the request of a crime victim, the crime victim has the following rights:

> (1) the right to notification of court proceedings;
> (2) the right to be present at all public court proceedings related to the offense, unless the victim is to testify and the court determines that the victim's testimony would be materially affected if the victim hears other testimony at the trial;
> (3) the right to confer with a representative of the prosecutor's office;
> (4) the right to restitution; and
> (5) the right to information about the conviction, sentence, imprisonment, and release of the accused.

(c) The legislature may enact laws to define the term "victim" and to enforce these and other rights of crime victims.

(d) The state, through its prosecuting attorney, has the right to enforce the rights of crime victims.

(e) The legislature may enact laws to provide that a judge, attorney for the state, peace officer, or law enforcement agency is not liable for a failure or inability to provide a right enumerated in this section. The failure or inability of any person to provide a right or service enumerated in this section may not be used by a defendant in a criminal case as a ground for appeal or post-conviction writ of habeas corpus. A victim or guardian or legal representative of a victim has standing to enforce the rights enumerated in this section but does not have standing to participate as a party in a criminal proceeding or to contest the disposition of any charge.

(Added Nov. 7, 1989.)

Sec. 31. COMPENSATION TO VICTIMS OF CRIME FUND; COMPENSATION TO VICTIMS OF CRIME AUXILIARY FUND; USE OF FUND MONEY. (a) The compensation to victims of crime fund created by general law and the compensation to victims of crime auxiliary fund created by general law are each a separate dedicated account in the general revenue fund.

(b) Except as provided by Subsection (c) of this section and subject to legislative appropriation, money deposited to the credit of the compensation to victims of crime fund or the compensation to victims of crime auxiliary fund from any source may be expended as provided by law only for delivering or funding victim-related compensation, services, or assistance.

(c) The legislature may provide by law that money in the compensation to victims of crime fund or in the compensation to victims of crime auxiliary fund may be expended for the purpose of assisting victims of episodes of mass violence if other money appropriated for emergency assistance is depleted.

(Added Nov. 4, 1997.)

Sec. 32. MARRIAGE. (a) Marriage in this state shall consist only of the union of one man and one woman.

(b) This state or a political subdivision of this state may not create or recognize any legal status identical or similar to marriage.

(Added Nov. 8, 2005.)

Sec. 33. ACCESS AND USE OF PUBLIC BEACHES. (a) In this section, "public beach" means a state-owned beach bordering on the seaward shore of the Gulf of Mexico, extending from mean low tide to the landward boundary of state-owned submerged land, and any larger area extending from the line of mean low tide to the line of vegetation bordering on the Gulf of Mexico to which the public has acquired a right of use or easement to or over the area by prescription or dedication or has established and retained a right by virtue of continuous right in the public under Texas common law.

(b) The public, individually and collectively, has an unrestricted right to use and a right of ingress to and egress from a public beach. The right granted by this subsection is dedicated as a permanent easement in favor of the public.

(c) The legislature may enact laws to protect the right of the public to access and use a public beach and to protect the public beach easement from interference and encroachments.

(d) This section does not create a private right of enforcement.

(Added Nov. 3, 2009.)

Sec. 34. RIGHT TO HUNT, FISH, AND HARVEST WILD-LIFE. (a) The people have the right to hunt, fish, and harvest wildlife, including by the use of traditional methods, subject to laws or regulations to conserve and manage wildlife and preserve the future of hunting and fishing.

(b) Hunting and fishing are preferred methods of managing and controlling wildlife.

(c) This section does not affect any provision of law relating to trespass, property rights, or eminent domain.

(d) This section does not affect the power of the legislature to authorize a municipality to regulate the discharge of a weapon in a populated area in the interest of public safety.

(Added Nov. 3, 2015.)

Endnotes

CHAPTER 1

1. Ben Sisario and Julia Jacobs, "South by Southwest Is Cancelled as Coronavirus Fears Scuttle Festival," *New York Times*, March 6, 2020.

2. James Barragán, "DPS: No Checkpoints at Louisiana Border to Screen Road Travel During Coronavirus," *Dallas Morning News*, March 31, 2020, p. 9B.

3. Alan Rosenthal, "On Analyzing States," in *The Political Life of the American States*, ed. Alan Rosenthal and Maureen Moakley (New York: Praeger, 1984), 11–12.

4. Political scientist Daniel Elazar has created a classification scheme for state political cultures that is used widely. He uses the concepts of *moralistic*, *individualistic*, and *traditionalistic* to describe such cultures. These three state political cultures are contemporary manifestations of the ethnic, socioreligious, and socioeconomic differences that existed among America's original thirteen colonies. Daniel Elazar, *American Federalism: A View from the States*, 2nd ed. (New York: Crowell, 1971), 84–126. See also John Kincaid, "Introduction," in *Political Culture, Public Policy and the American States*, ed. John Kincaid (Philadelphia: Center for the Study of Federalism, Institute for the Study of Human Issues, 1982), 1–24.

5. Rosenthal, "On Analyzing States," 13.

6. An excellent discussion of the problem of characterizing Texas political culture is found in Chandler Davidson, *Race and Class in Texas Politics* (Princeton, NJ: Princeton University Press, 1990), chap. 2.

7. Texas General Land Office, *History of Texas Public Lands* (Austin: Texas General Land Office, revised January 2015), 9–17.

8. The following is drawn from the *Texas Almanac 2014–2015* (Denton: Texas State Historical Association, 2014), 78–84.

9. The following is drawn from Karen Gerhardt Britton, Fred C. Elliott, and E. A. Miller, "Cotton Culture," *Handbook of Texas Online*, www.tshaonline.org/handbook/online/articles/afc03 (accessed 5/2/18).

10. See Cecil Harper, Jr., and E. Dale Odom, "Farm Tenancy," *Handbook of Texas Online*, www.tshaonline.org/handbook/online/articles/aefmu (accessed 5/2/18).

11. *Texas Almanac 2014–2015*, 687; see Cecil Harper, Jr., and E. Dale Odom, "Farm Tenancy," *Handbook of Texas Online*, www.tshaonline.org/handbook/online/articles/aefmu (accessed 5/2/18).

12. Texas Department of Agriculture, "Texas Ag Stats," www.texasagriculture.gov/About/TexasAgStats.aspx (accessed 2/26/20).

13. T. C. Richardson and Harwood P. Hinton, "Ranching," *Handbook of Texas Online*, www.tshaonline.org/handbook/online/articles/azr02 (accessed 5/2/18).

14. *Texas Almanac* online, "Principal Crops of Texas" (Texas State Historical Association); *Texas Almanac 2020–2021* (Denton: Texas State Historical Association, 2019), 660–61; Southern Plains Regional Office, U.S. Department of Agriculture, National Agriculture Statistics Service, "Texas Cotton Production," Issue No. PR-123-14 (Austin: May 2014).

15. *Texas Almanac 2018–2019* (Denton: Texas State Historical Association, 2017), 693.

16. The following is drawn from Mary G. Ramos, "Oil and Texas: A Cultural History," *Texas Almanac 2000–2001* (Dallas: *Dallas Morning News*, 1999), 29–35; Roger M. Olien, "Oil and Gas Industry," *Handbook of Texas Online*.

17. See Texas Legislative Budget Board, "Fiscal Size-Up: 2018–19 Biennium" (September 2018), 31; Texas Legislative Budget Board, *Fiscal Size-Up: 2020–21 Biennium* (May 2020), 33.

18. Permanent University Fund, "Report on Certain Specified Data as Required by Art. 4413 (34e) of the Civil Statutes" (June 30, 2019), 1.

19. Simone Sebastian, "New Data Show 'Meteoric' Rise of Texas Oil," *Houston Chronicle*, December 3, 2013. See

James Osborne, "Texas Oil Production Hits 2 Million Barrels a Day, the Most Since 1986," *Dallas Morning News*, April 25, 2014. See Texas Railroad Commission, "Texas Permian Basin Oil Production 2008 through March 2016." For a more detailed discussion of the new technology of fracking and its impact on the oil boom in Texas and the United States, see Russell Gold, *The Boom: How Fracking Ignited the American Energy Revolution and Changed the World* (New York: Simon & Schuster, 2014).

20. See "Texas Manufacturing Facts" at www.nam.org /state-manufacturing-data/2019-texas-manufacturing -facts/.

21. U.S. Census Bureau, "State Exports Texas 2019" and "State Imports for Texas 2019." See also Texas economy online report from the office of the governor, "Overview of the Texas Economy" (June 2014).

22. Bruce Wright, "Military Installations Worth Billions for Texas," *Fiscal Notes* (Texas Comptroller Office, September 2016).

23. See Robert Plocheck, "American Indians in Texas," *Texas Almanac* online, http://texasalmanac.com/topics /culture/american-indian/american-indian. The revival of the American Indian population in Texas was fostered by a federal government program between 1950 and 1980 that encouraged Indians to leave reservations (some in other states) and integrate themselves in post–WWII urban communities.

24. See census data analysis on www.governing.com, Governing Data, "State Population Census Estimates: 2013 Births, Deaths, Migration Totals," www.governing.com /gov-data/census/census-state-population-estimates -births-deaths-migration-totals-2013.html.

25. See Alexa Ura and Ryan Murphy, "Texas Population Grew to 28.3 Million in 2017," *Texas Tribune*, December 20, 2017.

26. How the U.S. Census counts individuals in certain demographic groups is a complicated affair and is getting more complicated. The U.S. Census did not provide data for non-Hispanic whites, Hispanics, or Latinos as separate groups prior to 1970. Beginning in the 2000 census the term *Hispanic* was included. See U.S. Census Bureau, "QuickFacts Texas 2019."

27. See Arnoldo De León, "Mexican Americans," *Handbook of Texas Online*.

28. See U.S. Census Bureau, "QuickFacts Texas 2019" and "State & County QuickFacts"; U.S. Census Bureau, 2010 Census; Sharon R. Ennis, Merarys Ríos-Vargas, and Nora G. Albert, "The Hispanic Population: 2010" (2010 Census Briefs, May 2011); *Texas Almanac 2014–2015*, 15.

29. See National Association of Latino Elected and Appointed Officials (NALEO), "2016 Latino Primary Profile: Texas" (NALEO Educational Fund, 2016).

30. See W. Marvin Dulaney, "African Americans," *Handbook of Texas Online*; Chandler Davidson, "African Americans and Politics," *Handbook of Texas Online*.

31. See John R. Ross, "Lynching," *Handbook of Texas Online*, www.tshaonline.org/handbook/online/articles/jgl01 (accessed 10/31/17).

32. See U.S. Census Bureau, "QuickFacts: The Asian Population in Texas," 2019.

33. See *Texas Almanac 2014–2015* for county-by-county data. The Asian population of Texas counties can be found at www.indexmundi.com.

34. U.S. Census Bureau, "QuickFacts Texas."

35. U.S. Census Bureau, "QuickFacts Texas."

36. The definition used to measure the urban/rural dichotomy has shifted over time. For a more detailed discussion, see U.S. Census Bureau, "2012 Census Urban Area FAQs."

37. Estimates are drawn from the U.S. Census Bureau, "State & County QuickFacts."

38. The following is drawn from Jackie McElhaney and Michael V. Hazel, "Dallas, Texas," *Handbook of Texas Online*.

39. The following is drawn from Janet Schmelzer, "Fort Worth, Texas," *Handbook of Texas Online*.

40. The following is drawn from T. R. Fehrenbach, "San Antonio, Texas," *Handbook of Texas Online*.

41. Estimates are drawn from the U.S. Census Bureau, "State & County QuickFacts."

42. See Census Reporter, "Austin, TX," www.census reporter.org/profiles/16000US4805000-austin-tx/.

43. See The University of Texas at Austin, "Facts & Figures," www.utexas.edu/about/facts-and-figures.

44. See "City of Austin Population History, 1840–2016" at www.austintexas.gov/sites/default/files/files/Plan ning/Demographics/population_history_pub.pdf.

45. See David C. Humphrey, "Austin, TX (Travis County)," *Handbook of Texas Online*; and Anthony M. Orum, *Power, Money and the People: The Making of Modern Austin* (Austin: Texas Monthly Press, 1987), 235–36, 312–16.

46. Austin put in a competitive bid for Amazon's HQ2 location. See Kelly O'Halloran, "Meet Austin's Top 100 Tech Companies: Employee Count Up 11 Percent in 2017,"

Built in Austin, October 31, 2017, www.builtinaustin.com /2017/10/31/austin-top-100-tech-companies-2017-prd.

CHAPTER 2

1. The following is drawn from Proposition 10, deleting constitutional references to county Office of Inspector of Hides and Animals; Eric Aasen, "Round 'Em Up: Hide Inspectors Abolished," *Dallas Morning News*, November 8, 2007; John Council, "Richmond Lawyer Has Personal Stake in Hide Inspector Position," *Texas Lawyer*, November 2, 2007; Mark Lisheron, "Prop. 10 Would Abolish Office That No One Holds," *Austin American-Statesman*, October 15, 2007.

2. See Dick Smith, "Inspector of Hides and Animals," *Handbook of Texas Online*, June 15, 2010, www.tsha online.org/handbook/online/articles/mbi01 (accessed 5/11/18).

3. Harriett Denise Joseph and Donald E. Chipman, "Spanish Texas," *Handbook of Texas Online*, modified on January 23, 2017, www.tshaonline.org/handbook/online /articles/nps01 (accessed 5/11/18); Donald E. Chipman, *Spanish Texas, 1519–1821* (Austin: University of Texas Press, 1992).

4. S. S. McKay, "Constitution of 1824," *Handbook of Texas Online*, modified February 29, 2016, www.tshaonline .org/handbook/online/articles/ngc02 (accessed 5/11/18).

5. S. S. McKay, "Constitution of Coahuila and Texas," *Handbook of Texas Online*, June 12, 2010, www.tsha online.org/handbook/online/articles/ngc01 (accessed 5/11/8).

6. See Ralph W. Steen, "Convention of 1836," *Handbook of Texas Online*.

7. The following is drawn from Joe E. Ericson, "Constitution of the Republic of Texas," *Handbook of Texas Online*, June 12, 2010, www.tshaonline.org/handbook /online/articles/mhc01 (accessed 5/11/18).

8. Randolph B. Campbell, "Slavery," *Handbook of Texas Online*, modified October 30, 2017, www.tshaonline.org /handbook/online/articles/yps01 (accessed 5/11/18).

9. For a brief summary of the war, see Eugene C. Barker and James W. Pohl, "Texas Revolution," *Handbook of Texas Online*, modified March 30, 2017, www.tsha online.org/handbook/online/articles/qdt01 (accessed 5/11/18).

10. S. S. McKay, "Constitution of 1845," *Handbook of Texas Online*, June 12, 2010, www.tshaonline.org/handbook /online/articles/mhc03 (accessed 5/11/18).

11. The Texas Ordinance of Secession (February 2, 1861).

12. See Walter L. Buenger, "Secession Convention," *Handbook of Texas Online*; Walter L. Buenger, *Secession and the Union in Texas* (Austin: University of Texas Press, 1984).

13. See Claude Elliott, "Constitutional Convention of 1866," *Handbook of Texas Online*; S. S. McKay, "Constitution of 1866," *Handbook of Texas Online*; Charles W. Ramsdell, *Reconstruction in Texas* (New York: Columbia University Press, 1970).

14. See S. S. McKay, "Constitution of 1869," *Handbook of Texas Online*; Ramsdell, *Reconstruction in Texas*.

15. See John Walker Mauer, "Constitution Proposed in 1874," *Handbook of Texas Online*; John Walker Mauer, "State Constitutions in a Time of Crisis: The Case of the Texas Constitution of 1876," *Texas Law Review* 68, (June 1990): 1615–46.

16. Texas Legislative Council, "Amendments to the Texas Constitution since 1876" (Austin: March 1912).

17. For a further discussion, see George D. Braden et al., *The Constitution of the State of Texas: An Annotated and Comparative Analysis* (Austin: University of Texas Press, 1977), 707–10.

18. "Texas Voters Approve 7 Constitutional Amendments," CBS DFW, November 9, 2011, http://dfw.cbslocal.com /2017/11/07/texans-amendments-state-constitution/.

CHAPTER 3

1. Ken Silverstein, "Will Undoing the Stream Protection Rule Really Help Coal?" *Forbes*, February 3, 2017.

2. Brad Plumer, "Why Trump Just Killed a Rule Restricting Coal Companies from Dumping Waste in Streams," *Vox*, February 16, 2017.

3. Melissa C. Lott, "Strip-Mining Coal in the Heart of Texas," *Scientific American*, August 26, 2015.

4. Kiah Collier, "Texas Sues Federal Government One More Time over Coal Rule," *Texas Tribune*, January 17, 2017.

5. "AG Paxton Hails Victory over Stream Protection Rule," Ken Paxton, Attorney General of Texas, May 2, 2017, www.texasattorneygeneral.gov.

6. Collier, "Texas Sues Federal Government."

7. This discussion is taken from David Brian Robertson, *Federalism and the Making of America* (New York: Routledge, 2012), 1–3.

8. Robertson, *Federalism and the Making of America*, 20–21.

9. Robertson, *Federalism and the Making of America*, 20–22.

10. Robertson, *Federalism and the Making of America*, 27.

11. Robertson, *Federalism and the Making of America*, 31.

12. Robertson, *Federalism and the Making of America*, 29–30.

13. "Full Faith and Credit Clause," *The Heritage Guide to the Constitution*, www.heritage.org.

14. *McCulloch v. Maryland*, 17 U.S. 316 (1819).

15. *Gibbons v. Ogden*, 22 U.S. 1, 2 (1824).

16. *Gibbons*, 22 U.S. 1, 2.

17. Robert F. Nagel, *The Implosion of American Federalism* (New York: Oxford University Press, 2001), 5.

18. *Texas v. White*, 74 U.S. 700 (1869).

19. *McDonald v. Chicago*, 561 U.S. 742 (2010).

20. *Sweatt v. Painter*, 339 U.S. 629 (1950).

21. *Brown v. Board of Education of Topeka*, 347 U.S. 483 (1954).

22. Morton Grodzins, *The American System: A New View of Government in the United States*, ed. Daniel J. Elazar (Chicago: Rand McNally, 1966).

23. Equal Justice Initiative, "Lynching in America: Confronting the Legacy of Racial Terror," 2017, https://lynchinginamerica.eji.org/report/.

24. *Gamble v. United States* 587 U.S. __ (2019).

25. *Wickard v. Filburn*, 317 U.S. 111 (1942).

26. *Wickard*, 317 U.S. 111.

27. Susan B. Garland, "Getting Stuck with the Check," *Bloomberg Businessweek*, www.businessweek.com/stories/1994-05-29/getting-stuck-with-the-check (accessed 3/24/14).

28. Clyde Wayne Crews Jr., "Unfunded Mandates on the States Rising Again," *Forbes*, July 28, 2016; Congressional Budget Office, "CBO's Activities under the Unfunded Mandates Reform Act," www.cbo.gov/publication/51335.

29. *Villas at Parkside Partners v. City of Farmers Branch*, Texas, 726 F.3d 524 (2013).

30. "State Officials Warn White House against Enforcing New Gun Regulations," Fox News, January 15, 2013, www.foxnews.com/politics/2013/01/15/ore-sheriff-says-wont-enforce-new-gun-laws/ (accessed March 24, 2014).

31. Greg Abbott, "Lawsuits against Obama Are Taxpayer Bargain," *Dallas Morning News*, September 25, 2012, www.dallasnews.com/opinion/latest-columns/2012 0925-greg-abbott-lawsuits-against-obama-are-tax payer-bargain.ece (accessed 3/24/14).

32. Jill D. Weinberg, "Remaking Lawrence," 98 *Virginia Law Review in Brief* 61, 66 (2012).

33. *San Antonio v. Rodriguez*, 411 U.S. 1 (1973).

34. *Edgewood Independent School District v. Kirby*, 777 S.W.2d 391, 398 (Texas, 1989).

35. *Shelby County, Alabama v. Holder*, Brief of the State of Texas, p. 2.

36. *Veasey v. Abbott*, 888 F.3d 792 (2018).

37. San Antonio Chamber of Commerce, "2019 Healthcare Issue Paper," www.sachamber.org; Alex Arriaga, "Fewer Texans Were Uninsured in 2016, but State Still Has Largest Health Coverage Gap," *Texas Tribune*, September 12, 2017.

38. Ken Paxton, "It's Time to Bury ObamaCare Once and for All and Deliver REAL Health Care Reform," Fox News, July 9, 2019.

39. Emma Platoff and Edgar Walters, "Texas Is Going to Court to End Obamacare. It Hasn't Produced a Plan to Replace It," *Texas Tribune*, July 8, 2019.

40. *National Federation of Independent Business v. Sebelius*, 567 U.S. 519 (2012).

41. *Texas v. United States*, 352 F. Supp. 3d 665 (2018).

42. Paxton, "It's Time to Bury ObamaCare."

43. Emma Platoff, "Federal Judge Rules Obamacare Unconstitutional, Handing Texas an Early Win," *Texas Tribune*, December 14, 2018.

44. Platoff and Walters, "Texas Is Going to Court."

45. National Immigration Law Center, "Status of Current DACA Litigation," June 7, 2019, www.nilc.org/issues/daca/status-current-daca-litigation/.

46. These states were later joined by Kansas and the governors of Maine and Mississippi.

47. National Immigration Law Center, "DACA Litigation Timeline," July 3, 2019, www.nilc.org/issues/daca/daca-litigation-timeline/.

48. *Texas v. United States*, 328 F. Supp. 3d 662 (2018).

49. Seung Min Kim, Josh Dawsey, and Brady Dennis, "Trump's Inaccurate Assertion of 'Total' Authority Sparks Challenge from Governors," *Washington Post*, April 14, 2020.

50. Todd J. Gillman, "Trump Retreats, Defers to States," *Dallas Morning News*, April 17, 2020, pp. 1, 11A.

51. Josh Dawsey, Seung Min Kim, Felicia Sonmez, and Colby Itkowitz, "Trump's Guidelines for Reopening States amid Coronavirus Pandemic Will Leave Decisions to Governors," *Washington Post*, April 16, 2020.

52. Shane Harris, Felicia Sonmez, and Mike DeBonis, "Governors Plead for Federal Help on Coronavirus Testing, Contradicting Trump's Claims that Testing is Widely Available," *Washington Post*, April 19, 2020.

CHAPTER 4

1. Jeffrey M. Jones, "Special Report: Many States Shift Democratic during 2005," Gallup, January 23, 2006, www.gallup.com.
2. Use of party affiliation as an ideological cue is discussed in Philip L. Dubois, *From Ballot to Bench: Judicial Elections and the Quest for Accountability* (Austin: University of Texas Press, 1980).
3. University of Texas, "Texas Statewide Survey," *Texas Tribune*, February 2019.
4. University of Texas, "Texas Statewide Survey," *Texas Tribune*, 2016.
5. Taylor Hatmaker, "Democrats Are Using a Data Scientist's Secret Sauce to Flip Texas Blue," *TechCrunch*, March 12, 2020.
6. Quoted in Chandler Davidson, *Race and Class in Texas Politics* (Princeton, NJ: Princeton University Press, 1990), 198.
7. Davidson, *Race and Class in Texas Politics*, 24–25.
8. Jones, "Special Report: Many States Shift Democratic during 2005."
9. James R. Soukup, Clifton McCleskey, and Harry Holloway, *Party and Factional Division in Texas* (Austin: University of Texas Press, 1964), 22.
10. Mark P. Jones, "Guest Column: The 2013 Texas House, from Right to Left," *Texas Tribune*, October 15, 2013.
11. Robert T. Garrett, "2 Major GOP Donors Show Rift in Party," *Dallas Morning News*, February 3, 2006, p. 2A.
12. Robert T. Garrett, "PAC's Late Aid Altered Races," *Dallas Morning News*, March 10, 2006, pp. 1A, 16A.
13. Dante Chinni and James Gimpel, *Our Patchwork Nation: The Surprising Truth about the "Real" America* (New York: Gotham, 2011).
14. Anthony Champagne, "The Selection and Retention of Judges in Texas," 40 *Southwestern Law Journal* 80 (1986).
15. The lone Democratic survivor, Ron Chapman, became an appellate judge. Democratic judges who did not switch to the Republican Party were defeated.
16. Terri Langford, "District Judge Fends off Democratic Rival's Challenge," *Dallas Morning News*, November 9, 2000, p. 36A.
17. Anthony Champagne and Greg Thielemann, "Awareness of Trial Court Judges," 75 *Judicature* 271–72 (1991).
18. Langford, "District Judge Fends off Democratic Rival's Challenge."
19. David Koenig, "Democrats' Dream Team Falters," *Laredo Morning Times*, November 10, 2002, pp. 1A, 19A.
20. In 1994 it was estimated that there were between 420,000 and 460,000 illegal immigrants in Texas. Many of those illegal immigrants were Hispanic. See Leon F. Bouvier and John L. Martin, "Shaping Texas: The Effects of Immigration, 1970–2020," Center for Immigration Studies, April 1995. The Federation for American Immigration Reform cites the Immigration and Naturalization Service for a January 2000 estimate that there were 1,041,000 illegal immigrants then in Texas. See its report, "Texas: Illegal Aliens." An April 2006 study by the Pew Hispanic Center estimated that between 1.4 and 1.6 million unauthorized individuals were living in Texas: "Estimates of the Unauthorized Migrant Population for States Based on the March 2005 CPS," Pew Hispanic Center, April 26, 2006. Jeff Salamon reports 10.8 million undocumented immigrants in the United States and 1.68 million in Texas. Jeff Salamon, "Everything You Ever Wanted to Know about Illegal Immigration (But Didn't Know Who to Ask)," *Texas Monthly*, November 2010.
21. Seth Motel and Eileen Patten, "Latinos in the 2012 Election: Texas," Pew Research Hispanic Trends Project, October 1, 2012. See also U.S. Census Bureau, "The Diversifying Electorate—Voting Rates by Race and Hispanic Origin in 2012 (and Other Recent Elections)," May 2013.

CHAPTER 5

1. Sam Hanna Acheson, *Joe Bailey: The Last Democrat* (New York: Macmillan, 1932), 354.
2. Joe Robert Baulch, "James B. Wells: South Texas Economic and Political Leader" (PhD diss., Texas Tech University, 1974), 358–59.
3. Sue Tolleson-Rinehart and Jeanie R. Stanley, *Claytie and the Lady: Ann Richards, Gender, and Politics in Texas* (Austin: University of Texas Press, 1994), 18–19.
4. *United States v. Texas*, 384 U.S. 155 (1966).
5. *Beare v. Smith*, 321 F. Supp. 1100 (1971).
6. *Newberry v. United States*, 256 U.S. 232 (1921).
7. *Nixon v. Herndon*, 273 U.S. 536 (1927).
8. *Nixon v. Condon*, 286 U.S. 73 (1932).
9. *Grovey v. Townsend*, 295 U.S. 45 (1935).
10. *Smith v. Allwright*, 321 U.S. 649 (1944).
11. *Terry v. Adams*, 345 U.S. 461 (1953).
12. Gary Scharrer, "Holder Issues Challenge to Texas on Voter Rights," *Houston Chronicle*, December 13, 2011, www.chron.com/news/article/Holder-issues-challenge-to-Texas-on-voter-rights-2401340.php (accessed 8/2/18).

13. National Conference of State Legislatures, "Voter Identification Requirements," April 30, 2014.

14. Texas Secretary of State, "Turnout and Voter Registration Figures, 1970–Current."

15. See U.S. Census Bureau, "Voting and Registration in the Election of November 2018—Detailed Tables," and Texas Secretary of State, "Turnout and Voter Registration Figures, 1970–Current." It is important to recognize how easily different studies can produce different registration rates or voting rates for different racial and ethnic groups. The Texas secretary of state's office uses hard data on the number of registered voters and divides by an agreed-upon number of people in the voting-age population given by state and federal demographers. But the secretary of state's office has no information on how people from different racial and ethnic groups actually voted. The statistics cited here were based upon a survey done after the election asking individuals to self-identify their race or ethnicity, whether or not they were registered to vote, and if they voted. Registration rates and voting rates were built up from the survey rather than being based on hard data provided by outside authorities. Different methodological approaches to the same question can lead to different numbers without any of the numbers being "wrong."

16. Jolie McCullough, "Gov. Abbott Signs Bill to Eliminate Straight-Ticket Voting Beginning in 2020," *Texas Tribune*, June 1, 2017, www.texastribune.org/2017/06/01/texas-gov-greg-abbott-signs-bill-eliminate-straight-ticket-voting/ (accessed 8/2/18).

17. University of Texas, "Texas Statewide Survey," *Texas Tribune*, February 2013.

18. University of Texas, "Texas Statewide Survey," *Texas Tribune*, February 2018.

19. United States Elections Project, "2016 November General Election Turnout Rates," 2016, www.electproject.org/2016g (accessed 8/2/18).

20. Kevin Diaz, "Texas Latino Vote Splits," *Houston Chronicle*, November 6, 2014.

21. Wayne Slater, "Strayhorn Gets Democratic Cash," *Dallas Morning News*, January 26, 2006, pp. 1A, 17A.

22. Pete Slover, "Independents' Day Is a Bid for the Ballot," *Dallas Morning News*, March 8, 2006, p. 14A.

23. Ryan Murphy and Jay Root, "Texas Republicans Getting Almost 90 Percent of Money Flowing into State Elections," *Texas Tribune*, February 19, 2018, www.texas tribune.org/2018/02/19/texas-republicans-getting-almost-90-percent-money-flowing-state-electi/ (accessed 6/1/18).

24. Julian Aguilar, "Abbott Defends Corruption Remarks, Border Security Plan," *Texas Tribune*, February 10, 2014; Jens Manuel Krogstad and Mark Hugo Lopez, "Hispanic Voters in the 2014 Election," Pew Research Hispanic Trends Project, November 7, 2014.

25. Don Willett (@JusticeWillett), "When You're Tired of Cornbread Shaped like Colorado and Wyoming," Twitter, March 22, 2016, 8:41 P.M., https://twitter.com/justicewillett/status/712484343298457600.

26. Jordan Rudner and Lauren McGaughy, "Texas Ag Commissioner Sid Miller Blames Staffer for Tweet That Called Hillary Clinton the C-Word," *Dallas News*, November 2016, www.dallasnews.com/news/texas-politics/2016/11/01/texas-ag-commissioner-sid-miller-calls-clinton-c-word-twitter.

27. Alexa Ura, "Davis Renews Equal Pay Attack on Abbott," *Texas Tribune*, March 24, 2014.

Chapter 5 Citizen's Guide

a. Alexandra Jaffe, "GOP Hits Back at Hillary Clinton on Voting Rights," CNN, June 5, 2015, www.cnn.com/2015/06/05/politics/gop-responds-clinton-voting-rights/index.html.

b. Alyssa Dizon, "Passage of Voter ID Bill Stirs Strong Reaction, Pro and Con," *Lubbock Avalanche-Journal*, May 17, 2011.

c. Charles Stewart III, "Voter ID: Who Has Them? Who Shows Them?" 66 *Oklahoma Law Review* 21–52 (2013).

CHAPTER 6

1. The above is drawn from Jeffrey Weiss, "One Mom's Ire Becomes a Cause," *Dallas Morning News*, March 30, 2014; Jeffrey Weiss, " 'The Heart of the Vampire,' " *Dallas Morning News*, March 31, 2014; Jeffrey Weiss, "Testing System Shaken to Its Core," *Dallas Morning News*, April 1, 2014; Dax Gonzalez, "Finding the Funding," *Texas Lone Star*, August 2013; see also www.tam satx.org.

2. Mancur Olson, *The Logic of Collective Action: Public Goods and the Theory of Groups*, Harvard Economic Studies (Cambridge, MA: Harvard University Press, 1971).

3. James W. Lamare, *Texas Politics: Economics, Power and Policy*, 3rd ed. (St. Paul, MN: West, 1988), 82. See George Norris Green, *The Establishment in Texas Politics: The*

Primitive Years, 1938–1957 (Norman: University of Oklahoma Press, 1984).

4. Jon Herskovitz, "Texas Lawmakers Clear Way for Uber, Lyft Return to Major Cities," Reuters, May 21, 2017, www.reuters.com/article/us-texas-ridesharing/texas-lawmakers-clear-way-for-uber-lyft-return-to-major-cities-idUSKBN18H0IJ (accessed 8/2/18).

5. Ballotpedia, "United States Senate Election in Texas 2020," https://ballotpedia.org/United_States_Senate_election_in_Texas,_2020 (accessed 11/15/20).

6. Morgan Smith, "Texas Advocacy Group Wields Charter-Policy Power," *New York Times*, May 11, 2013.

7. Smith, "Texas Advocacy Group."

8. See Phillip Martin, "Progress Texas Releases ALEC Exposed in Texas," *Progress Texas*, January 17, 2012, http://progresstexas.org/blog/progress-texas-releases-alec-exposed-texas (accessed 8/2/18).

9. Texans for Public Justice, "Power Surge: TXU's Patronage Grid Plugs All but Seven Lawmakers," *Lobby Watch*, March 1, 2007.

10. Matt Stiles, "Lobbyist Gives 'Shocking' Gift to Lawmaker," *Texas Tribune*, February 15, 2010.

11. Chris Marquette, "Sen. Ted Cruz Gifted Houston Rockets Tickets Worth $12k," *Roll Call*, August 14, 2019, www.rollcall.com/news/congress/ted-cruz-houston-rockets-tickets (accessed 4/7/2020).

12. Chuck Devore, "Texas Taxpayers Shouldn't Have to Pay for Lobbyists Who Work to Raise Their Taxes," Texas Public Policy Foundation, November 29, 2017, www.texaspolicy.com/texas-taxpayers-shouldnt-have-to-pay-for-lobbyists-who-work-to-raise-their-taxes/ (accessed 4/7/2020).

13. Johnny Kampis, "Senate Big Spender #4: John Whitmire," *Texas Monitor*, June 14, 2017, https://texasmonitor.org/senate-big-spender-4-john-whitmire/.

14. Texas Ethics Commission, 2017 Lobby Registration Lists, www.ethics.state.tx.us/dfs/loblistsREG.htm #R2017 (accessed 8/6/18).

15. Texas Ethics Commission, Summary of Lobby Expenditures Sorted by Government Recipient, November 29, 2017, www.ethics.state.tx.us/data/search/lobby/LobbyExpendituresByGovernmentRecipient.pdf (accessed 8/6/18).

16. Andy Pierrotti, "Lobbyist's Lavish Party," Kvue.com, February 21, 2013.

17. Texas Ethics Commission, 2017 Registered Lobbyists with Clients, www.ethics.state.tx.us/data/search/lobby/2017/2017LobbyistGroupByClient.pdf (accessed 8/6/18).

18. Texas Monthly, Dave Mann, Eric Benson, and R. G. Ratcliffe, "Flush with Power," *Texas Monthly*, February 2017, www.texasmonthly.com/politics/flush-with-power/ (accessed 8/6/18).

19. Ross Ramsey, "Legislature Is a Training Ground for Lobbyists," *Texas Tribune*, June 10, 2010.

20. Ramsey, "Legislature Is a Training Ground."

21. Texans for Public Justice, "Draft Season: Is Joe Straus' House a Lobby Farm Club?" *Lobby Watch*, May 4, 2017.

22. Texans for Public Justice, "Ten New Lawmaker Retreads Merge into the 2009 Lobby," *Lobby Watch*, May 20, 2009.

23. Jason Cherkis and Paul Blumenthal, "Rick Perry's Former Staffers Made Millions as Lobbyists," *Huffington Post*, September 16, 2011.

24. Cherkis and Blumenthal, "Rick Perry's Former Staffers."

25. Ramsey, "Legislature Is a Training Ground."

26. Texans for Public Justice, "Texas Revolvers: Public Officials Recast as Hired Guns," *Lobby Watch*, February 1, 1999.

27. Tim Eaton, "Greg Abbott Looks to 2017 for Ethics Reform," *Austin American Statesman*, September 23, 2016; W. Gardner Selby, "Greg Abbott Strikes Out on His Ethics Campaign Promises," Politifact, July 5, 2015.

28. Texans for Public Justice, "Special-Interests Spend Up to $180 Million on Lobby Services in 1999 Legislative Session," June 1, 1999.

29. Transparency USA, "Political Action Committees," www.transparencyusa.org/tx/pacs (accessed 11/15/20).

30. Anthony Champagne, "Campaign Contributions in Texas Supreme Court Races," *Crime, Law and Social Change* 17, no. 2 (1992): 91–106.

31. Texans for Public Justice, "Texans for Lawsuit Reform Sustains Pricey Primary Hits," *Lobby Watch*, March 5, 2010; Julián Aguilar, "Primary Color: HD-43," *Texas Tribune*, February 26, 2010.

32. Dick Weekley, "A Good Night for Lawsuit Reform in Texas," Texans for Lawsuit Reform PAC.

33. "Texans for Lawsuit Reform," Transparency USA, May 17, 2017, www.transparencytexas.org/texans-for-lawsuit-reform/ (accessed 8/6/18).

34. National Institute on Money in Politics, "Contributions to Texas State House/Assembly and State Senate 2020," www.followthemoney.org/show-me?dt=1&y=2020&s=TX&f-fc=1,2#[{1|gro=c-r-ot,y (accessed 11/23/20).

35. Patrick Svitek, "Latest Texas Fundraising Totals Shed Light on Key Races," *Texas Tribune*, July 18, 2017, www

.texastribune.org/2017/07/18/tec-report-fundraising
-roundup/ (accessed 8/6/18).

36. Kristen Mack, "New Lawmakers Learn to Juggle Hectic Lives; Everybody—Lobbyists, Family—Wants a Moment of Their Time," *Houston Chronicle*, February 6, 2005, p. 1B.

37. Jason Embry, "Most Powerful Group in Texas Politics Has Wentworth in Its Sights," *Austin American Statesman*, December 7, 2011; John W. Gonzalez, "Campbell Upsets Wentworth for Texas Senate," *San Antonio Express-News*, August 1, 2012.

38. Texans for Public Justice, "Operation Vouchsafe: Dr. Leininger Injects $5 Million into Election; Many Candidates Fail on His Life Support," *Lobby Watch*, n.d.

39. Texans for Public Justice, "Texas PACs: 2012 Election Cycle Spending" (2013), p. 20.

40. Jay Root and Ryan Murphy, "Does Business Group's Use of 'Dark Money' for Its Political Action Committee Follow State Ethics Rules?" *Texas Tribune*, January 29, 2018, www.texastribune.org/2018/01/29/does-texas
-business-groups-use-dark-money-follow-state-ethics
-rules/ (accessed 8/6/18).

41. Sunset Advisory Commission Staff Report, "Railroad Commission of Texas," November 2012, p. 12.

42. Public Citizen, "Drilling for Dollars: How Big Money Has a Big Influence at the Railroad Commission," December 2010.

43. Public Citizen, "Drilling for Dollars," p. 4.

44. National Institute on Money in Politics data.

45. Jim Malewitz, "GOP Railroad Commission Hopefuls Split on Donations," *Texas Tribune*, February 8, 2016.

46. Sunset Advisory Commission, "Railroad Commission of Texas," p. 2.

47. Brett Shipp, "Attempt to Overhaul Texas Railroad Commission Fails, Again," WFAA, May 31, 2013.

48. Ryan May Handy, "Gov. Abbott Signs Bill Reauthorizing the Railroad Commission," *Houston Chronicle*, May 23, 2017, http://fuelfix.com/blog/2017/05/23/gov-abbott
-signs-bill-reauthorizing-the-railroad-commission/.

49. Emily Ramshaw, "Fighting for Fair Warning: Man Who Lost Wife, Kids in Blaze Seeks Visual Smoke Alarms for Deaf," *Dallas Morning News*, April 17, 2009; "Tragedy Leads to Improved Fire Safety in Texas," National Association of the Deaf, July 1, 2009.

50. Regina Lawrence, Deborah Wise, and Emily Einsohn, *Texas Civic Health Index* (Austin: Annette Strauss Institute for Civic Life, 2013), 5–14.

51. Lawrence, Wise, and Einsohn, *Texas Civic Health Index*, 22.

Chapter 6 Citizen's Guide

a. Kelley Shannon, "Former Legislators Kicking Off New Careers as Texas Lobbyists," *Dallas Morning News*, March 7, 2013.

b. Ross Ramsey, "Legislature Is a Training Ground for Lobbyists," *Texas Tribune*, June 10, 2010.

c. Randy Lee Loftis, "State of Neglect: Revolving Door Lets Lawmakers Profit from Capitol Floor Time," *Dallas Morning News*, January 6, 2009.

d. James Drew, "Corruption in State Governments? Researchers Turn to Reporters for Answers," *Houston Chronicle*, August 22, 2017, www.chron.com/news/politics/texas/article/Corruption-in-state-governments
-Researchers-turn-11948127.php (accessed 4/7/20).

e. Ross Ramsey, "Texas Voters' Biggest Concerns for the Country? Immigration and Political Corruption, UT/TT Poll Says," *Texas Tribune*, June 20, 2019, https://www
.texastribune.org/2019/06/20/texas-voters-say-immigration-corruption-top-issues-ut-tt/ (accessed 4/7/20).

CHAPTER 7

1. Ann Marie Kilday, "Equal Measure," *Dallas Morning News*, May 24, 2001, p. 31A.

2. Texas Legislature, "Legislative Statistics," February 8, 2018.

3. Ross Ramsey, "Will Texas Lawmakers Cut Their Own Benefits?" *Texas Tribune*, March 11, 2011.

4. Anthony Champagne and Rick Collis, "Texas," in *The Political Life of the American States*, ed. Alan Rosenthal and Maureen Moakley (New York: Praeger, 1984), 138.

5. *Baker v. Carr*, 369 U.S. 186 (1962); *Reynolds v. Sims*, 377 U.S. 533 (1964).

6. *Wesberry v. Sanders*, 376 U.S. 1 (1964).

7. See, generally, Steve Bickerstaff, *Lines in the Sand: Congressional Redistricting in Texas and the Downfall of Tom DeLay* (Austin: University of Texas Press, 2007).

8. "Texas Redistricting Battle Headed Back to Federal Courts," *Lubbock Avalanche-Journal*, June 21, 2013.

9. LegiScan, "Texas Legislature, 2019–2020, 86th Legislature, in Recess," legiscan.com, https://legiscan.com/TX.

10. Kelley Shannon, "Doctor Twice Honored by the Texas Legislature Registered as Sex Offender," *Sulphur Springs News-Telegram*, June 22, 2007, p. 1.

11. Frank M. Stewart, "Impeachment in Texas," *American Political Science Review* 24, no. 3 (August 1930): 652–58; George D. Braden et al., *The Constitution of the State of Texas: An Annotated and Comparative Analysis* (Austin: University of Texas Press, 1977), 707–18.

12. Dave McNeely, "Impeachment in Texas History," *Port Aransas South Jetty*, August 23, 2007.

13. Edgar Walters, "Texas Governor Signs $217 Billion Budget, Vetoes $120 Million," *Texas Tribune*, www.texastribune.org/2017/06/12/texas-governor-signs-217-billion-budget-vetoes-120-million/.

14. Terrence Stutz, "Texas Senate at Odds over Voter ID Legislation, Two-Thirds Rule," *Dallas Morning News*, January 14, 2009.

15. Joe Straus, letter to Sachi Dave, March 12, 2014.

16. Joe Straus, letter to Sachi Dave, March 12, 2014.

17. Paul Burka, "Partisanship Ranking: The Texas Tribune List," *Texas Monthly*, July 17, 2010.

18. Mark P. Jones, "Guest Column: The 2013 Texas House, from Right to Left," *Texas Tribune*, October 15, 2013.

19. Mark P. Jones, "Guest Column: The 2013 Texas Senate, from Left to Right," *Texas Tribune*, November 26, 2013.

20. Paul Starr, *Remedy and Reaction: The Peculiar American Struggle over Health Care Reform*, rev. ed. (New Haven, CT: Yale University Press, 2013), 162–63.

21. "Thus Spake Joe: Texas Politics after Joe Straus," *The Economist*, November 4, 2017.

Chapter 7 Citizen's Guide

a. Jay Jennings and Emily Einsohn Bhandari, *2018 Texas Civic Health Index* (Austin: Annette Strauss Institute for Civic Life, 2018), https://moody.utexas.edu/sites/default/files/2018-Texas_Civic_Health_Index.pdf (accessed 4/20/20).

CHAPTER 8

1. Alexa Ura, " 'Someone Did Not Do Their Due Diligence': How an Attempt to Review Texas' Voter Rolls Turned into a Debacle," *Texas Tribune*, February 1, 2019.

2. Ura, "Someone Did Not Do Their Due Diligence"; Alexa Ura, "Former Secretary of State David Whitley Back at Gov. Greg Abbott's Office," *Texas Tribune*, May 31, 2019.

3. Ura, "Former Secretary of State."

4. Ura, "Former Secretary of State"; Ura and Platoff, "After Blocking."

5. Ura and Platoff, "After Blocking."

6. Margaret Ferguson, "Governors and the Executive Branch," in Virginia Gray, Russell L. Hanson, and Thad Kousser (eds.), *Politics in the American States* (Thousand Oaks, CA: CQ Press, 2017), pp. 235–74.

7. Brian McCall, *The Power of the Texas Governor: Connally to Bush* (Austin: University of Texas Press, 2009), 5.

8. McCall, *Power of the Texas Governor*, 131–39.

9. Sam Kinch, in Government by Consent—Texas, a Telecourse (Dallas: Dallas County Community College District, 1990).

10. Governor's Office, Texas State Directory.

11. Jamie Knodel, "Gov. Greg Abbott Gives Most of His Appointments to Whites," *Dallas Morning News*, April 17, 2016.

12. Jolie McCullough, "Dozens of Abbott Appointees Surpass Donor Threshold Targeted by Stalled 'Pay for Play' Bill," *Texas Tribune*, May 23, 2017.

13. Peggy Fikac, "Abbott Makes Scores of Political Appointments," *Houston Chronicle*, July 4, 2015.

14. "Abbott Altered His Message on Jade Helm," *Houston Chronicle*, May 28, 2015; Cassandra Pollock and Alex Samuels, "Hysteria over Jade Helm Exercise in Texas Was Fueled by Russians, Former CIA Director Says," *Texas Tribune*, May 3, 2018.

15. Office of the Governor Greg Abbott, "Governor Abbott Delivers State of the State Address," February 5, 2019, www.gov.texas.gov.

16. Legislative Reference Library of Texas, "Legislation, Vetoed Bills, 1846–2019."

17. Madlin B. Mekelburg, "What Actually Passed the Texas Legislature," *Houston Chronicle*, June 2, 2015, www.chron.com/news/politics/article/What-actually-passed-the-Texas-legislature-6301754.php.

18. Legislative Reference Library of Texas, "Vetoes Overridden, 1860–2013."

19. Office of Governor Rick Perry, "Governor Perry Signs State Budget That Reduces GR by $1.6 Billion," press release, June 19, 2009.

20. Edgar Walters, "Texas Governor Signs $217 Billion Budget, Vetoes $120 Million," *Texas Tribune*, June 12, 2017.

21. Riane Roldan, "Texas Gov. Greg Abbott Signs $250 Billion Budget with No Line-Item Vetoes," *Texas Tribune*, June 15, 2019.

22. Jolie McCullough, "Minutes Before Execution, Texas Gov. Greg Abbott Commutes the Sentence of Thomas Whitaker," *Texas Tribune*, February 22, 2018.

23. Andrea Valdez, "The Worst: Senator Dan Patrick," *Texas Monthly*, June 16, 2013.

24. Tim Eaton, "Joe Straus Avoids Hot-Button Issues, in Contrast to Dan Patrick," *Austin American Statesman*, September 4, 2016.

25. Catherine Marfin, "Lt. Gov. Dan Patrick Defeats Democrat Mike Collier," *Houston Chronicle*, November 6, 2018.

26. Office of the Attorney General of Texas, "About Texas Attorney General Ken Paxton."

27. Lauren McGaughy, "Ag Chief Posts Cartoon Mocking Trump Foe," *Dallas Morning News*, October 25, 2017, p. 3B.

28. Texas State Auditor's Office, "A Summary Report on Full-Time Equivalent State Employees for Fiscal Year 2018."

29. Texas State Auditor's Office, "A Summary Report on Full-Time Equivalent State Employees for Fiscal Year 2007."

30. Christy Hoppe, "Perry's Appointees Give Him Unprecedented Hold on Texas—Longest-Serving Governor Spreads Pro-Business View," *Dallas Morning News*, December 19, 2008.

31. Will Weissert, "Texas Rejects Allowing Academics to Fact-Check Public School Textbooks," *Christian Science Monitor*, November 18, 2015.

32. Texas Sunset Advisory Commission, "Frequently Asked Questions."

33. Robert T. Garrett, "In Crisis, Abbott Tests Power of His Office," *Dallas Morning News*, March 23, 2020, p. 5A.

34. James Barragàn and Allie Morris, "Abbott Clamps Down Statewide," *Dallas Morning News*, April 1, 2020, p. 1.

Chapter 8 Citizen's Guide
a. Miriam Seifter, "Understanding State Agency Independence," 117 *Michigan Law Review* 1537 at 1552, 1554 (2019).

b. Miriam Seifter, "Gubernatorial Administration," 131 *Harvard Law Review* 483 at 497–98 (2017).

CHAPTER 9
1. Andrew Schneider, "Meet 'Black Girl Magic,' the 19 African-American Women Elected as Judges in Texas," NPR, NPR.org, January 16, 2019.

2. Stefan Haag and William R. Young, "The Effects of Eliminating Straight-Ticket Voting in Texas," Austin Community College, Center for Public Policy and Political Studies, Report #15, August 2019.

3. United States Census Bureau, QuickFacts, census.gov, July 1, 2018.

4. Texas Secretary of State.

5. Haag and Young, "Effects of Eliminating Straight-ticket Voting."

6. Thomas Petzinger, Jr., *Oil & Honor: The Texaco-Pennzoil Wars* (New York: Putnam, 1987).

7. Task Force on Indigent Defense, "Evidence for the Feasibility of Public Defender Offices in Texas" (2006).

8. Mary Alice Robbins, "West Texas Plans Public Defender Office for Capital Cases," *Texas Lawyer* 1 (August 20, 2007): 19; "New Public Defender for Capital Cases," *Tex Parte Blog*, October 16, 2007.

9. Valerie Wigglesworth, "Attorney's Eye-Popping $460,000 in Earnings to Defend Indigent Clients in Collin County Prompting Changes," *Dallas Morning News*, November 12, 2018.

10. Zach Despart and Keri Blakinger, "Harris County Judges Criticized over Pace of Court-Appointed Lawyer Reform," *Houston Chronicle*, October 7, 2019.

11. Ken Anderson, *Crime in Texas: Your Complete Guide to the Criminal Justice System* (Austin: University of Texas Press, 1997), 40.

12. Lisa Falkenberg, "A Disturbing Glimpse into the Shrouded World of the Texas Grand Jury System," *Houston Chronicle*, July 16, 2014. A follow-up to Falkenberg's work is Dan Solomon, "Is the Grand Jury System in Texas Broken," *Texas Monthly*, July 29, 2014.

13. Johnathan Silver, "Texas Proposal Would Limit Prosecutors in Grand Jury Proceedings," *Texas Tribune*, March 15, 2017.

14. Anderson, *Crime in Texas*, 44; nationally, 95 percent of felonies are plea bargained.

15. Legislative Budget Board Staff, "Specialty Courts," July 2016.

16. Eric Dexheimer, "For Texas County Judges, a $25,000 Bonus with No Questions Asked," *Austin American-Statesman*, December 15, 2016.

17. Texas Office of Court Administration, "2017 Statistical Report for the Texas Judiciary."

18. Texas Office of Court Administration, "2017 Statistical Report for the Texas Judiciary."

19. Barbara Kirby, "Neighborhood Justice: Non-Lawyer Judges, Repeat Players and Institutional Reform in Texas Justice of the Peace Courts" (Ph.D. diss., University of Texas at Dallas, 2015), 70, 71, 74.

20. Kirby, "Neighborhood Justice," 56.

21. Ed Housewright, "Emotional Issues, Historical Pedigree," *Dallas Morning News*, April 9, 2001, p. 10A.

22. Texas Office of Court Administration, "2016 Statistical Report for the Texas Judiciary."

23. Of the 79 judicial appointments made by Governor William Clements, only 6 were either African American or Hispanic. In contrast, one-third of Governor Ann Richards's judicial appointees were minorities. See Michael Totty, "Is This Any Way to Choose a Judge?" *Wall Street Journal*, August 3, 1994, T1, T4.

24. Texas Office of Court Administration, "Profile of Appellate and Trial Judges," September 1, 2019.

25. Paul Burka, "Heads, We Win, Tails, You Lose," *Texas Monthly* (May 1987), 138, 139.

26. Wallace B. Jefferson, "Reform the Partisan System," 79 *Texas Bar Journal* 90 (2016).

27. Mary Flood and Brian Rogers, "Why Some Harris County Judges Lost Not Entirely Clear," *Houston Chronicle*, November 6, 2008.

28. Chuck Lindell, "Green vs. Green: State Supreme Court GOP Race a Study in Contrasts," *Austin American-Statesman*, September 4, 2016; Rick Carey, "Imperfect Paul Green Is a Better Choice than Rick Green," *San Antonio Express-News*, February 19, 2016; "Editorial: We Recommend Sid Harle in GOP Race for Texas Court of Criminal Appeals Place 5," *Dallas Morning News*, January 17, 2016; Bruce Davidson, "Bad Old Days Return to Criminal Appeals Court Races," *San Antonio Express-News*, December 10, 2015.

29. Data are from the National Institute on Money in State Politics.

30. Anthony Champagne and Kyle Cheek, "The Cycle of Judicial Elections: Texas as a Case Study," 29 *Fordham Urban Law Journal* 907, 914 (2002).

31. Kent Rutter & Natasha Breaux, "Reasons for Reversal in the Texas Courts of Appeals," 57 *Houston Law Review* ___ (2020).

32. Texas Ethics Commission, "Campaign Finance Guide for Judicial Candidates and Officeholders" (2013).

33. Professor Brest is quoted in Kevin R. Johnson and Luis Fuentes-Rohwer, "A Principled Approach to the Quest for Racial Diversity on the Judiciary," 10 *Michigan Journal of Race Law* 5 (2004).

34. Professor Ifill is quoted in Johnson and Fuentes-Rohwer, "A Principled Approach."

35. Office of Court Administration, "Profile of Appellate and Trial Judges," September 1, 2019.

36. State Bar of Texas, "State Bar of Texas Membership: Attorney Statistical Profile (2019-20)," www.texasbar.com.

37. Citizens' Commission on the Texas Judicial System, "Report and Recommendations: Into the Twenty-First Century" (1993), p. 3.

38. "Executive Summary: Report of the Court Administration Task Force," 71 *Texas Bar Journal* 888, 889 (2008).

39. Ray Blackwood, "Overlapping Jurisdiction in the Houston-Based Courts of Appeals—Could a Special En Banc Procedure Alleviate Problems?" 26 *Appellate Advocate* 277–81 (2013).

40. Nathan Hecht, "State of the Judiciary in Texas," February 6, 2019.

41. David A. Anderson, "Judicial Tort Reform in Texas," 26 *Review of Litigation* 7 (2007).

42. State Bar of Texas, "Annual Report 2018–2019."

43. John MacCormack, "Barratry Suit Names Corpus Lawyers," *San Antonio Express-News*, December 9, 2011.

44. State Bar of Texas website, "Find a Lawyer," www.texasbar.com; Brett Shipp, "Attorney, Accused of Multiple Crimes, Still Working Courthouse Halls," wfaa.com, September 7, 2017.

45. Taylor Goldenstein, "Ex-Members of Judicial Conduct Commission Say Abbott Ousted Them over Gay Marriage Case," *Houston Chronicle*, December 5, 2019; Shawn Cunningham, "Ex Judicial Panelists Say Texas Governor Ousted Them over Gay Marriage," WAGM TV.com, December 6, 2019, Wagmtv.com/content/news .Ex-Judicial-Panelists-Say-Texas-Governor-Ousted -Them-Over-Gay-Marriage-565880811.html.

46. Emma Platoff, "Texas Attorney General Ken Paxton Won't Defend State Agency in Gay Marriage Case," *Texas Tribune*, January 29, 2020.

47. State Commission on Judicial Conduct, "Annual Report for Fiscal Year 2019."

48. Commission on Judicial Conduct website, www.scjc .texas.gov; State Commission on Judicial Conduct, "Annual Report for Fiscal Year 2019."

49. State Commission on Judicial Conduct, "Public Admonition Honorable Nora Longoria Justice, Thirteenth Court of Appeals, Edinburg, Hidalgo County, Texas."

50. Ralph Blumenthal, "Texas Judge Draws Outcry for Allowing an Execution," *New York Times*, October 25, 2007; Christy Hoppe, "Criminal Appeals Court Creates Emergency Filing System," *Dallas Morning News*, November 6, 2007; "Texas Judge Fosters Tough-on-Crime Reputation," MSNBC, October 23, 2007; State Commission on Judicial Conduct, "Special Master's Findings of Fact, In Re: Honorable Sharon Keller,

Presiding Judge of the Texas Court of Criminal Appeals" (January 20, 2010); "Judge Who Refused Last-Minute Appeal Re-Elected," News 92 FM, November 6, 2012.

51. Emma Platoff, "Coronavirus Throws Texas Supreme Court Justices into the Spotlight—and into Democrats' Crosshairs," *Texas Tribune*, May 20, 2020.

Chapter 9 Citizen's Guide

a. Ross Ramsey, "Analysis: After This Election, Texas Judicial Races Might Never Be the Same," *Texas Tribune*, August 3, 2018.

b. Lauren McGaughy, "Should Voters Elect Judges Based on Political Party? Texas Supreme Court Chief Justice Says No," *Dallas Morning News*, February 6, 2019.

c. James Barragàn, "Texas House Passes Bill to End 'One Punch' Straight-Ticket Voting," *Dallas Morning News*, May 6, 2017.

CHAPTER 10

1. February 2018 University of Texas/*Texas Tribune* poll.

2. U.S. Census Bureau, 2012 Census of Governments. See www.governing.com/gov-data/number-of-governments -by-state.html.

3. The two states that don't use counties as units of local government are Connecticut and Rhode Island; Richard L. Cole and Delbert A. Taebel, *Texas: Politics and Public Policy* (Fort Worth: Harcourt Brace Jovanovich, 1987), 151.

4. Cole and Taebel, *Texas*, 155.

5. Laurence M. Crane, Nat Pinnoi, and Stephen W. Fuller, "Private Demand for Publicly Provided Goods: A Case Study of Rural Roads in Texas," *TAMRC Contemporary Market Issues Report No. CI-1-92* (1992).

6. Texas Association of Counties, "Debate Goes Back and Forth, Just like Overweight Trucks."

7. Texas Commission on Jail Standards, "Abbreviated Population Report," September 1, 2018.

8. Texas Association of Counties, "About Counties."

9. Cole and Taebel, *Texas*, 152.

10. Anthony Champagne and Rick Collis, "Texas," in *The Political Life of the American States*, ed. Alan Rosenthal and Maureen Moakley (New York: Praeger, 1984), 140.

11. Bob Palmer, "AG Supports Commissioners in Courthouse Dog Dispute," *Mount Pleasant Daily Tribune*, August 29, 2013.

12. Harvey Rice and Emily Foxhall, "Fort Bend Leaders Weigh in on Galveston Co. Political Fight," *Houston Chronicle*, October 14, 2015; David Yates, "Texas SC Sides with Galveston County Judge in Suit Brought by District Judge," *Southeast Texas Record*, May 22, 2017.

13. These are 2014 Census estimates. U.S. Census Bureau, "State and County QuickFacts."

14. Roma Vivas, "Presidio County Officials Tackling Budget Problems," NewsWest9.com, undated.

15. Russell Gold, "Counties Struggle with High Cost of Prosecuting Death-Penalty Cases," *Wall Street Journal*, January 9, 2002, p. B1.

16. "Capital Trial Could Be Costly for Franklin Co.," *Sulphur Springs News-Telegram*, June 27, 2007, p. 4.

17. Andrew Becker and G. W. Schultz, "Drug Busts Strain County Budget," *Dallas Morning News*, July 28, 2013, p. 10A.

18. Jamie Thompson, "The Untold Story of Susan Hawk," *D Magazine*, November 2015, pp. 46–51, 161–67; Sarah Mervosh, "Lawsuit to Remove Dallas DA Susan Hawk to Move Forward," *Dallas Morning News*, December 9, 2015; Ken Kalthoff, "Case to Remove Dallas DA Susan Hawk Dismissed," 5NBCDFW.com, January 8, 2016.

19. "Republican Appointed Dallas County DA Faith Johnson Loses," CBS Dallas–Fort Worth, November 7, 2018, https://dfw.cbslocal.com/2018/11/07/dallas-county-da -faith-johnson-john-creuzot/ (accessed 11/15/18).

20. Frank Heinz, "John Wiley Price Arrested, Accused of Taking $950,000 in Bribes," 5NBCDFW.com, July 25, 2014.

21. Jo DePrang, "After Shady Campaign, Houston Community College Foe Becomes Trustee," *Texas Observer*, November 12, 2013.

22. There is some disagreement among scholars over why the population figure was lowered from 10,000 to 5,000 in 1909. John Keith argued that the changes enabled smaller cities to obtain special charters tailored to their needs. See John P. Keith, *City and County Home Rule in Texas* (Austin: Institute of Public Affairs, University of Texas, 1951). George D. Braden suggests that the reason may have been the desire of certain cities to escape a property tax provision in the existing constitution. See George D. Braden et al., *The Constitution of the State of Texas: An Annotated and Comparative Analysis* (Austin: Texas Advisory Commission on Intergovernmental Relations, 1977), p. 681.

23. League of California Cities, "Charter Cities"; Ballotpedia, "Cities in Illinois"; Ballotpedia, "Cities in Texas."

24. Diane Lang, "Dillon's Rule . . . and the Birth of Home Rule," *Municipal Reporter*, December 1991.

25. Article 11, Section 5, of the Texas Constitution is concerned with home rule. For a further discussion of

home rule in Texas, see Terrell Blodgett, *Texas Home Rule Charters* (Austin: Texas Municipal League, 1994); Terrell Blodgett, "Home Rule Charters," *Handbook of Texas Online* (Texas State Historical Association).

26. The literature on preemption has grown significantly in recently years. For an overview of the issues, see Luke Fowler and Stephanie L. Witt, "State Preemption of Local Authority: Explaining Patterns of State Adoption of Preemption Measures," *Publius: The Journal of Federalism* 49, no. 3 (Summer 2019): 540–59, https://doi.org/10.1093/publius/pjz011; Richard Briffault, "The Challenge of the New Preemption," 70 *Stanford Law Review* 1995, 2018; Columbia Public Law Research Paper No. 14-580 (2018); Lydia Bean and Maresa Strano, *Punching Down: How States Are Supressing Local Democracy*, New America Report, July 11, 2019.

27. Correspondence with Terrell Blodgett, Wednesday, February 3, 2000; *Texas Almanac 2009–2010*, 500–510; League of California Cities, "Charter Cities"; Ballotpedia, "Cities in Illinois."

28. Jim Malewitz, "Dissecting Denton: How One City Banned Fracking," *Texas Tribune*, December 15, 2014; Max B. Baker, "Denton City Council Repeals Fracking Ban," *Fort Worth Star-Telegram*, June 16, 2015.

29. Patrick Svitek, "Abbott Wants 'Broad-Based Law' That Pre-empts Local Regulations," *Texas Tribune*, March 21, 2017; Patrick Svitek, "Gov. Abbott: This Country Isn't the 'United States of Municipalities,'" *Texas Tribune*, March 27, 2017.

30. See Lydia Bean, "Repel Attacks on Local Control in Texas," *Dallas Morning News*, July 27, 2019, p. 12A.

31. Dave Lieber, "It Just Got Easier for You to Speak Out at Public Meetings." *Dallas Morning News*, October 6, 2019, p. 1B.

32. Jonathan Tilove, "With Rejection of Special Session Core Agenda, Is GOP Civil War Next?" *Austin American-Statesman*, August 21, 2017; Jonathan Tilove, "Abbott Blames Straus for All That the Special Session Didn't Get Done," *Austin American-Statesman*, October 25, 2017.

33. Colorado Municipal League, "Forms of Municipal Government."

34. *Texas Almanac 2018–2019* (Austin: Texas State Historical Association, 2018).

35. The following is drawn from Bradley R. Rice, "Commission Form of City Government," *Handbook of Texas Online* (Texas State Historical Association).

36. *Texas Almanac 1996–1997* (Dallas: *Dallas Morning News*, 1995), 513.

37. Rice, "Commission Form of City Government."

38. Exactly what constitutes a municipality with a council-manager form of government is difficult to define. Local forms of governments are complex with many nuances in their power structures and positions. Here we are referring to municipalities that have some form of professional manager or city manager or city administrator or town manager listed in the survey conducted by the *Texas Almanac* survey in 2017. See *Texas Almanac 2018–2019*, 531–40.

39. For a further discussion, see Terrell Blodgett, "Council-Manager Form of City Government," *Handbook of Texas Online* (Texas State Historical Association); Blodgett, *Texas Home Rule Charters*.

40. For a history of the office of controller in Houston, see the City of Houston Office of the City Controller, "Controller's Office History."

41. W. Gardner Selby, "Austin Group Says Austin Is the Biggest U.S. City Lacking City Council Members Elected from Geographic Districts," PolitiFact Texas, August 17, 2012.

42. Sarah Coppola, "Grass-Roots Effort Drove Austin City Council District Plan to Victory, Observers Say," *Austin American-Statesman*, November 7, 2012; Mike Kanin and Elizabeth Pagano, "The Road to 10-1," *Austin Chronicle*, February 1, 2013.

43. The following paragraphs are drawn from Derek Okubo, "A Time for Change: El Paso Adopts the Council-Manager Form," *National Civic Review* 94, no. 3 (Fall 2005): 3–9.

44. Jack C. Plano and Milton Greenberg, *The American Political Dictionary*, 10th ed. (Fort Worth: Harcourt, Brace, 1997).

45. See "Number of Special Districts," United States Census Bureau, www.census.gov/govs/go/number_of_special_districts_by_county.html; *Texas Almanac and State Industrial Guide, 2000–2001* (Dallas: *Dallas Morning News*, 1999), 533; see Local Governments in Individual County-Type Areas: 2012, 2012 Census of Governments; U.S. Census, "Number of Special Districts," Lists and Structure of Governments; Laura Langham, *Invisible Government: Special Purpose Districts in Texas* (Research Spotlight, Texas Senate Research Center, 2008); there is no centralized database that provides information regarding special purpose districts in Texas, although the Comptroller's Office reports information related to their taxing authority. A legislative study in 2014 concluded that there were approximately 3,350 special

purpose districts in the state, of which 1,965 were reporting to the Comptroller's Office.

46. County Information Program, Texas Association of Counties. Data are for 2018.

47. County Information Program, Texas Association of Counties. Data are for 2018.

48. Brooks Egerton and Reese Dunklin, "Government by Developer," *Dallas Morning News*, June 10, 2001, p. 1A.

49. Richard Williamson, "Texas MUD Sinks toward Chap. 9; Others on Solid Ground," *Bond Buyer*, May 18, 2009.

50. Sara C. Galvan, "Wrestling with MUDs to Pin Down the Truth about Special Districts," 75 *Fordham Law Review* 3041–80 (2007).

51. See Texas Association of Regional Councils, "About TARC."

52. Chuck DeVore, "On Prohibiting the Issuance of Capital Appreciation Bonds: Testimony to the Senate Committee on Intergovernmental Relations," Texas Public Policy Foundation, March 20, 2013.

53. Shane Shifflet, Sharon Pieczenik, and Trey Bundy, "Controversial School Bonds Create 'Debt for the Next Generation,'" Reveal, January 2013, www.revealnews .org/article/controversial-school-bonds-create-debt -for-the-next-generation/.

54. DeVore, "On Prohibiting the Issuance of Capital Appreciation Bonds."

55. Chuck DeVore, "CAB Rides Can Be Extremely Costly," *Austin American-Statesman*, September 11, 2012.

56. James Estes, "Capital Appreciation Bonds: The Creation of a Toxic Waste Dump in Our Schools," *JAFR* 2, April 2013.

57. DeVore, "CAB Rides Can Be Extremely Costly."

58. Lisa Minton, "Capital Appreciation Bonds: Another Finance Option for Schools," *Fiscal Notes*, March 2016.

59. Minton, "Capital Appreciation Bonds."

60. Minton, "Capital Appreciation Bonds."

61. Susan Combs, "Your Money and Pension Obligations," Texas Comptroller of Public Accounts, 2012, 4.

62. Brandon Formby, "Billions in Pension Shortfalls Threatening Texas Cities' Budgets," *Texas Tribune*, December 2, 2016.

63. Combs, "Your Money and Pension Obligations," 7.

64. Doug Miller, "Mayor Cuts Firefighter Pension Deal; Experts Call It Bad Bargain," KHOU 11 News, March 6, 2015.

65. Joe Martin, "Bill King: 'If We Don't Fix Pension Problem, It's Game Over,'" *Houston Business Journal*, December 9, 2015.

66. This discussion of the Dallas pension crisis is from Tristan Hallman, "Retirees' Rich Perk Cut Off," *Dallas Morning News*, January 15, 2015, pp. 1B, 9B; Tristan Hallman, "Return of Only 2% Seen as Hole Deepens," *Dallas Morning News*, February 20, 2015, pp. 1B, 7B; Robert Wilonsky, "Moody's Lowers City's Bond Rating," *Dallas Morning News*, October 29, 2015, pp. 5A; Robert Wilonsky, "Police-Fire Fund Pursues Ex-Leaders," *Dallas Morning News*, December 3, 2015, pp. 1B, 4B.

67. Luke Ranker, "Ft. Worth Pension Fix Costs Taxpayers, Employees. But Was the Unknown Worse?," *Fort Worth Star-Telegram*, February 27, 2019.

68. S&P Global Ratings, "Rising U.S. States' OPEB Liabilities Signal Higher Costs Ahead," November 28, 2018; Mary Williams Walsh, "In Texas, Some Rare Good News About Cities with Pension Woes," *New York Times*, June 1, 2017.

69. Comparison of El Paso City Employees' Pension Fund, "Summary Plan Description First Tier for Persons Whose Participation Date Is before September 1, 2011," with "Summary Plan Description Second Tier for Persons Whose Participation Date Is after September 1, 2011."

Chapter 10 Citizen's Guide

a. Kim Haddow, Anthony Gad, and Katy Fleury, "The Growing Shadow of State Interference," Local Solutions Support Center, 2019.

b. Rebekah Allen and Lauren McGaughy, "6 Takeaways from Secretly Recorded Audio," *Dallas Morning News*, October 16, 2019, p. 15A.

c. Haddow, Gad, and Fleury, "Growing Shadow."

d. Peter Simek, "Texas State Government Not Alone in Stripping Cities of Political Power," *D Magazine*, August 1, 2019.

e. Allen and McGaughy, "6 Takeaways."

CHAPTER 11

1. Jeannie Kever, "As Texas Public College Tuition Rises, Legislators Feel Heat," *Houston Chronicle*, July 10, 2008; Texas Higher Education Coordinating Board, "Tuition Set-Aside House Bill 3013, 78th Texas Legislature," *Overview* (February 2010).

2. Shannon Najmabadi, "UT System Increases Tuition 2.6% for All Campuses for 2020 and 2021," *Texas Tribune*, November 14, 2019.

3. See Trends in College Pricing 2019, "Tuition and Fees by State: Public Four-Year," https://research.college board.org/pdf/2019-trendsincp-fig-6.pdf.

4. See collegeforalltexans.com and trends.collegeboard.org.

5. See Rebecca Hennes, "New Report Reveals How Much Debt Texas College Students Graduated with in 2018," *Houston Chronicle*, September 11, 2019, www.chron.com /news/houston-texas/article/Student-debt-at-Texas -colleges-class-of-2018-14428784.php.

6. See Ryan McCrimmon and Bobby Blanchard, "Deregulating Tuition Slowed Increase, Universities Say," *Texas Tribune*, March 17, 2016; Ross Ramsey, "Analysis: Raising Tuition for College Students, Deflecting the Blame," *Texas Tribune*, February 12, 2015; Lauren McGaughy and J. David McSwane, "Rise in Costs Not as Steep after Legislature Gave Reins to Schools," *Dallas Morning News*, April 10, 2016; Matthew Watkins, "Lt. Gov. Patrick Slams Universities for Tuition Increases," *Texas Tribune*, April 26, 2016; Stacy Fernández, "University of Texas Rio Grande Valley to Provide Free Tuition for Students with Household Income under $75,000," *Texas Tribune*, September 16, 2019.

7. The following discussion is drawn from Texas Legislative Budget Board, *Fiscal Size-Up: 2018–19 Biennium* (September 2018), pp. 1–8.

8. See Henry J. Kaiser Family Foundation, "Total State Expenditures per Capita," www.kff.org.

9. Texas Legislative Budget Board, *Fiscal Size-Up: 2020–21 Biennium* (May 2020), p. 27.

10. Texas Legislative Budget Board, *Fiscal Size-Up: 2016–17 Biennium* (May 2016), p. 27.

11. See WalletHub, "2020's Tax Burden by State," https:// wallethub.com/edu/states-with-highest-lowest-tax -burden/20494/.

12. Texas Legislative Budget Board, *Fiscal Size-Up: 2016–17 Biennium*, pp. 36–37.

13. Clay Robinson, "Bullock Paints a Grim Picture/Says Income Tax Needed to Avert Financial Crisis," *Houston Chronicle*, March 12, 1991; Clay Robinson, "Bullock Plan May Open Door to Tax Battle," *Houston Chronicle*, March 2, 1993.

14. Texas Legislative Budget Board, *Fiscal Size-Up: 2020–21 Biennium*, p. 35.

15. Texas Legislative Budget Board, *Fiscal Size-Up: 2020–21 Biennium*, p. 39

16. Texas Legislative Budget Board, *Fiscal Size-Up: 2020–21 Biennium*, p. 40.

17. Texas Permanent School Fund, "Comprehensive Annual Financial Report for the Fiscal Year Ending August 31, 2019"; Texas Legislative Budget Board, *Fiscal Size-Up: 2020–21 Biennium*, p. 223.

18. See Texas Legislative Budget Board, *Fiscal Size-Up: 2020–21 Biennium*, p. 44.

19. Gerard MacCrossan, "Rainy Day Fund 101," *Fiscal Notes*, February 2011; Texas Legislative Budget Board, *Fiscal Size-Up: 2020–21 Biennium*, p. 45.

20. See www.utimco.org/funds-managed/endowment -funds/permanent-university-fund-puf/; see also University of Texas System, "The Permanent University Fund and Available University Fund," www.utsystem .edu/sites/default/files/offices/governmental-relations /PUF%20%20and%20AUF%20Issue%20Brief_2018 %20Update.pdf.

21. www.lbb.state.tx.us/Documents/HAC_Summary_Recs /86R/Agency_795.pdf.

22. For the Higher Education Fund, see Texas Legislative Budget Board, *Fiscal Size-Up: 2020–21 Biennium*, p 285. For the National Research University Fund, see Texas Higher Education Coordinating Board, "National Research University Fund Eligibility: A Report to the Comptroller and the Texas Legislature" (March 2016).

23. Texas Legislative Budget Board, *Fiscal Size-Up: 2018–19 Biennium* (May 2020), p. 28.

24. Texas Legislative Budget Board, *Fiscal Size-Up: 2018–19 Biennium* (May 2020), p. 28.

25. The following is drawn from Senate Research Center, *Budget 101: A Guide to the Budget Process in Texas* (January 2011), p. 29.

26. Texas Legislative Budget Board, *Fiscal Size-Up: 2018–19 Biennium*, p. 32.

27. Texas Legislative Budget Board, *Fiscal Size-Up: 2018–19 Biennium*, p. 192

28. Adam McCann, "2020's Tax Burden by State," Wallet-Hub, June 24, 2020, https://wallethub.com/edu/states -with-highest-lowest-tax-burden/20494 (accessed 11/25/20).

29. See Senate Research Center, *Budget 101*, pp. 24–25.

30. Senate Research Center, *Budget 101*, p. 28; "40 Years of Comptroller Revenue Estimates (1974–2013)," *Fiscal Notes, Texas Transparency* (2015), window.texas.gov.

31. Edgar Walters, "Capitol Insiders: Texas Lt. Gov. Dan Patrick Is Letting the State's Budget Agency Fall Apart," *Texas Tribune*, October 29, 2019, www.texastribune .org/2019/10/29/texas-lt-gov-dan-patrick-wages-war -texas-legislative-budget-board/; Emma Platoff, "Jerry McGinty to Head Troubled Legislative Budget Board," *Texas Tribune*, March 5, 2020, www.texastribune.org /2020/03/05/jerry-mcginty-legislative-budget-board -director/.

32. Mitchell Ferman, "As Oil Price Crisis Grips the Globe, Small Texas Producers Feel the Ripple Effects," *Texas Tribune*, April 6, 2020.

33. Cary Cheshire, "Nelson Announces Zero-Based Budgeting for All Texas Agencies," *Texas Scorecard*, May 13, 2020.

34. See the discussion in Senate Research Center, *Budget 101*, pp. 34–35.

35. Aman Batheja, "Hegar: Revenue Estimate 'Based on Expectations of Moderate Expansion,'" *Texas Tribune*, January 12, 2015.

36. These paragraphs are drawn from Texas Taxpayers and Research Association, "84th Legislative Session Wrap-Up," *Fiscal Notes*, June 2015; Michael Gibson, Elizabeth Barrett, and Bruce Wright, "2015 Legislative Wrap-Up," *Fiscal Notes*, September 2015.

37. The material in this section is largely drawn from Brian Wellborn, "2017 Legislative Wrap-Up," *Fiscal Notes*, September 2017; Texas Taxpayers and Research Association, "Texas Budget Challenges Are Not Over," Research Report, August 2017.

38. Doha Madani, "Dan Patrick on Coronavirus: 'More Important Things than Living,'" NBCNews, www.nbcnews.com/news/us-news/texas-lt-gov-dan-patrick-reopening-economy-more-important-things-n1188911.

Chapter 11 Citizen's Guide

a. Carl Davis et al., *Who Pays? A Distributional Analysis of the Tax Systems in All 50 States*, 6th ed. (Washington, DC: Institute on Taxation and Economic Policy, January 2018).

b. For what follows, see Julia Kagan, "Regressive Tax" and "Progressive Tax," Investopedia.com; Carl Davis et al., *Who Pays? A Distributional Analysis of the Tax Systems in All 50 States*, 6th ed. (Washington, DC: Institute on Taxation and Economic Policy, January 2018).

CHAPTER 12

1. See www.dfps.state.tx.us. See also Edgar Walters and Emily Ramshaw, "Federal Judge: Texas Foster Care System Violates Children's Rights," *Texas Tribune*, December 17, 2015.

2. "M.D. vs. Greg Abbott," U.S. District Court, Southern District of Texas, Corpus Christi Division, December 17, 2015, p. 186.

3. "M.D. vs. Greg Abbott," p. 17.

4. Marissa Evans, "State Leaders Order Overhaul of Texas Child Protective Services," *Texas Tribune*, October 12, 2016; Marissa Evans, "Report Says Child Protective Service Workers Are Overloaded, Urges Overhaul," *Texas Tribune*, November 4, 2016.

5. Marissa Evans and Emma Platoff, "Federal Judge Says Texas Still Needs Oversight to Fix Its 'Broken' Foster Care System," *Texas Tribune*, January 19, 2018; Robert T. Garrett, "Appeals Court Temporarily Halts Federal Judge's Order that Texas Make Big Improvements in Foster Care," *Dallas Morning News*, January 19, 2018.

6. Robert T. Garrett, "Texas Pushes Back on Federal Judge's Foster Care Ruling, though Children's Lawyers Say Let It Rip," *Dallas Morning News*, February 15, 2018.

7. Robert T. Garrett, "Judge Slams Homes after Girl's Death," *Dallas Morning News*, February 25, 2020, p. 1A.

8. See Benjamin Ginsberg et al., *We the People: Texas Edition*, 9th ed. (New York: W. W. Norton, 2012), 643.

9. B. Guy Peters, *American Public Policy: Promise and Performance*, 9th ed. (Washington, DC: CQ Press, 2012), chaps. 2 and 3; Charles O. Jones, *An Introduction to the Study of Public Policy*, 3rd ed. (Monterey, CA: Brooks/Cole, 1984).

10. Roger Cobb and Charles Elder, *Participation in American Politics: The Dynamics of Agenda-Building* (Baltimore: Johns Hopkins University Press, 1983), 85.

11. See Herbert Simon, "Bounded Rationality and Organizational Learning," *Organizational Science* 2, no. 1 February 1991: 125–34; Kristen Renwick Monroe, *The Economic Approach to Politics: A Critical Reassessment of the Theory of Rational Action* (New York: HarperCollins, 1991).

12. See Texas Legislative Budget Board, *Fiscal Size-Up: 2020–21 Biennium*, pp. 209, 213.

13. See Texas Legislative Budget Board, *Fiscal Size-Up: 2020–21 Biennium*, 197–212. See also www.census.gov/newsroom/press-releases/2019/school-spending.html; https://worldpopulationreview.com/states; www.publicschoolreview.com/average-student-teacher-ratio-stats/national-data.

14. Data on public school enrollment are taken from Texas Education Agency, *Enrollment in Public Schools, 2018–19*, "July 2019."

15. See Texas Education Agency, *Enrollment in Public Schools, 2018–19*. See also https://schools.texastribune.org/states/tx/.

16. See Oscar Mauzy, "Gilmer-Aikin Laws," *Handbook of Texas Online* (Texas State Historical Association); Dick Smith and Richard Allen Burns, "Texas Educa-

tion Agency," *Handbook of Texas Online*; Max Berger and Lee Wilborn, "Education," *Handbook of Texas Online*.

17. See Anna Victoria Wilson, "Education for African Americans," *Handbook of Texas Online*.

18. Arnoldo De León and Robert A. Calvert, "Segregation," *Handbook of Texas Online*.

19. The following discussion of the *Rodríguez* and *Edgewood* cases is drawn from Texas Legislative Budget Board Staff, "Financing Public Education in Texas: Kindergarten through Grade 12," *Legislative Handbook* (February 1999); Berger and Wilborn, "Education"; Cynthia E. Orozco, "*Rodríguez v. San Antonio ISD*," *Handbook of Texas Online*; Teresa Palomo Acosta, "*Edgewood ISD v. Kirby*," *Handbook of Texas Online*.

20. See Texas Legislative Budget Board Staff, "Financing Public Education in Texas," 26–27.

21. Mark Wiggins, "Attorneys, Schools and 83rd Texas Legislature's Impact on Education," www.kvue.com; Morgan Smith, "Texas School Finance Trial Goes for Round Two," *Texas Tribune*, June 19, 2013; Terrence Stutz, "State Seeks to Remove School Finance Judge," *Dallas Morning News*, June 3, 2014, p. 3a.

22. See *Morath, et al. v. The Taxpayer and Student Fairness Coalition, et al.*, Supreme Court of Texas (No. 14-0776). See also Kiah Collier, "Texas Supreme Court Rules School Funding System Is Constitutional," *Texas Tribune*, May 13, 2016, www.texasxtribune.org.

23. See Texas Legislative Budget Board, *2018 Fiscal Size-Up: 2018–19 Biennium*, Figure 152, p. 205, for the increasing reliance on school funding through local property taxes rather than state general revenue funding. Alex Samuels, "Local Taxes in Texas Have Been Rising to Help Pay for Education. Who Is to Blame?" TEXplainer, *Texas Tribune*, February 16, 2018, www.texastribune.org; Texas Taxpayers and Research Association, "Texas Budget Challenges Are Not Over," Research Report (August 2017).

24. Aliyya Swaby, "Will Texas School Finance Panel Tell Schools to Do More with Less? Some Members Think It's Predetermined," *Texas Tribune*, March 16, 2018; Aliyya Swaby, "Texas Panel Set to Discuss School Finance Fix. Can They Iron Out Lawmakers' Disagreements?," *Texas Tribune*, January 22, 2018; Texas Classroom Teachers Association, "Around 120 Education Bills Passed in 2019"; Edgar Walters, "Texas House, Senate Approve Budget Deal with Agreements on School Finance, Property Taxes, Hurricane Harvey Recovery," *Texas Tribune*, May 26, 2019.

25. See Clark D. Thomas, "Education Reform in Texas," in *Texas Politics*, ed. Anthony Champagne and Edward J. Harpham (New York: W. W. Norton, 1998), 213–32.

26. National Commission on Excellence in Education, *A Nation at Risk: The Imperative for Educational Reform* (Washington, DC: Department of Education, 1983).

27. See Thomas, "Education Reform in Texas," 218.

28. See Thomas, "Education Reform in Texas," 221.

29. See Thomas, "Education Reform in Texas," 231; "Public Schools," *Texas Almanac 2000–2001*, Millennium Edition (Dallas: Dallas Morning News, 1999), 533. See also Terrence Stutz, "State's List Cites Sub-par Schools in Transfer Plan," *Dallas Morning News*, December 24, 1999, p. 1.

30. College Board, "Mean 2009 SAT Scores by State" (2009); College Board, "2009 College-Bound Seniors Total Group Profile Report" (2009), p. 3. See also Texas Education Agency, "College Admissions Testing of Graduating Seniors in Texas High Schools, Class of 2010" (October 2011) and Texas Education Agency, "2010 Comprehensive Annual Report on Texas Public Schools" (December 2010). See also Joshua Benton, "Legislators Left Unanswered Questions on New State Tests," *Dallas Morning News*, June 11, 2007, p. B1. See also Terrence Stutz, "Failing Tests, Passing Grades," *Dallas Morning News*, March 8, 2012, p. A1.

31. See Kate McGee, "Two Big Education Bills Gain Approval from Texas Legislature," KUTnews.org, May 27, 2013.

32. See Aliyya Swaby, "Legislature Unanimously Approves Last-Minute Overhaul of School A–F Ratings," *Texas Tribune*, May 28, 2017.

33. See College Board, https://reports.collegeboard.org/pdf/2019-texas-sat-suite-assessments-annual-report.pdf and https://reports.collegeboard.org/sat-suite-program-results/class-2019-results.

34. See Richard V. Reeves and Dimitrios Halikias, "Race Gaps in SAT Scores Highlight Inequality and Hinder Upward Mobility," Brookings, February 1, 2017.

35. See Milton Friedman, *Capitalism and Freedom* (Chicago: University of Chicago Press, 1962).

36. See Tawnell D. Hobbs, "As Charter Schools Rise, Dallas ISD Rues Loss of Students—and Millions in Funding," *Dallas Morning News*, January 21, 2016.

37. See University of Texas/*Texas Tribune*, "Texas Statewide Survey," February 2017 and earlier surveys.

38. Allie Morris and James Barragán, "Texas Gov. Greg Abbott Announces Temporary Statewide School, Restaurant, Gym Closures," *Dallas Morning News*, March 19, 2020; Aliyya Swaby, "Gov. Greg Abbott Keeps Texas Classrooms Closed for Remainder of School Year," *Texas Tribune*, April 17, 2020.

39. www.census.gov/quickfacts and Texas Poverty Facts, www.indexmundi.com. See also Texas Health and Human Services Commission, "Texas Medicaid Enrollment Statistics."

40. U.S. Census Bureau, "2019 Poverty Rate in the United States," September 17, 2020, www.census.gov/library /visualizations/interactive/2019-poverty-rate.html (accessed 11/25/20).

41. See data at Henry J. Kaiser Family Foundation, kff.org.

42. Texas Legislative Budget Board, *Fiscal Size-Up: 2020–21 Biennium*, p. 162; Texas Health and Human Services, "Blueprint for a Healthy Texas," HHS Business Plan September 2019–August 2020 (October 2019), p.7.

43. The following is drawn from Edward J. Harpham, "Welfare Reform and the New Paternalism in Texas," in Champagne and Harpham, *Texas Politics*, 233–49.

44. See Vivian Elizabeth Smyrl, "Texas Department of Human Services," *Handbook of Texas Online*.

45. Harpham, "Welfare Reform and the New Paternalism," 238.

46. See Charles Murray, *Losing Ground: American Social Policy, 1950–1980* (New York: Basic Books, 1984).

47. The following paragraphs are drawn from Harpham, "Welfare Reform and the New Paternalism," 244–47.

48. See Texas Legislative Budget Board, *Fiscal Size-Up: 2014–15 Biennium* (February 2014), 221–22; Texas Health and Human Services Commission, "Temporary Assistance for Needy Families (TANF): Frequently Asked Questions." See also Texas Health and Human Services Commission, "Presentation to the House Select Committee on Human Services: HHSC Overview" (February 12, 2013).

49. See Texas Legislative Budget Board *Fiscal Size-Up, 2020–21 Biennium*, p. 191.

50. See TANF Statistics for 2020 at hhs.texas.gov. See also Texas Health and Human Services System, *Consolidated Budget, Fiscal Years 2016–17* (October 2014), p. 21; "Temporary Assistance for Needy Families (TANF) Statistics," January 2018, Texas Health and Human Services; Alexa Ura, "How Texas Curtailed Traditional Welfare without Ending Poverty," *Texas Tribune*, November 30, 2017.

51. https://talkpoverty.org/state-year-report/texas-2019 -report/.

52. Center on Budget and Policy Priorities, "TANF Cash Assistance Should Reach Many More Families in Texas to Lessen Hardship," www.cbpp.org/sites/default/files /atoms/files/tanf_trends_tx.pdf.

53. See Ura, "How Texas Curtailed Traditional Welfare."

54. Nic Garcia, "Dallas County Official: Stay-at-home Order Will Remain in Place until April 30 (not May 20)," *Dallas Morning News*, April 3, 2020; Patrick Svitek, "Gov. Greg Abbott Resists Calls for Statewide Shelter-in-place; Moves to Expand Hospital Capacity," *Texas Tribune*, March 22, 2020.

55. Stacy Fernández, "230,000 Texas Families Filed for SNAP Food Assistance in March, Twice as Many as Same Month Last Year," *Texas Tribune*, April 13, 2020.

56. Texas Health and Human Services Commission, *Texas Medicaid and CHIP Reference Guide*, 12th ed. (2018). Medicaid and the Children's Health Insurance Program (CHIP) information and data for this section are taken from this document and from data for Texas on the Henry J. Kaiser Family Foundation website, www.state healthfacts.org.

57. See Texas Legislative Budget Board, *Fiscal Size-Up: 2020–21 Biennium*, p. 184; Texas Health and Human Services, *Texas Medicaid and CHIP Reference Guide*.

58. See Henry J. Kaiser Family Foundation, "Federal Medical Assistance Percentage for Medicaid," kff.org.

59. See Nancy Flake, "Combs: Texas in Great Shape, but Look Out for Medicaid," *Cypress Creek Mirror*, May 2, 2012.

60. In the Senate, 58 Democrats and 2 independents voted for the Patient Protection and Affordable Care Act. All 39 Republicans in the Senate were opposed. In the House of Representatives, the final vote was 219 to 212. All supporters of the bill were Democrats, with 34 Democrats and 178 Republicans opposing the bill.

61. See Texas Health and Human Services Commission, *Texas Medicaid and CHIP in Perspective*, 11th ed. (February 2017) for a further discussion of the impact of federal health care reforms on Texas.

62. See Henry J. Kaiser Family Foundation, "How Will the Uninsured in Texas Fare under the Affordable Care Act?" at kff.org/medicaid.

63. See Alex Arriaga, "Fewer Texans Were Uninsured in 2016, but State Still Has Largest Health Coverage Gap," *Texas Tribune*, September 12, 2017.

64. See Edgar Walters, "More Have Health Insurance, but Texas Lags," *Texas Tribune*, December 18, 2015. See also Episcopal Health Foundation at www.episcopal health.org.

Chapter 12 Citizen's Guide

a. Brief of respondents Kirk Cole, Commissioner, Texas Department of State Health Services, et al., *Whole Woman's Health v. Hellerstedt*.

b. Brief of amicus curiae of American College of Obstetricians and Gynecologists and brief for petitioners Whole Woman's Health, et al., *Whole Woman's Health v. Hellerstedt*.

CHAPTER 13

1. Matt Pearce and Jaweed Kaleem, "12 Officers Shot, 5 Fatally, by Snipers in Dallas During Protest over Police Shootings," *Los Angeles Times*, July 8, 2016; F. Brinley Bruton et al., "Dallas Police 'Ambush': 12 Officers Shot, 5 Killed During Protest," NBC News, July 8, 2016; Manny Fernandez, Richard Pérez-Peña, and Jonah Engel Bromwich, "Five Dallas Officers Were Killed as Payback, Police Chief Says," *New York Times*, July 8, 2016; Rye Druzin, "Texas Top State for Law Enforcement Deaths in Line of Duty," *PolitiFact Texas*, September 19, 2016.

2. Danielle Kaeble and Mary Cowhig, "Correctional Populations in the United States, 2015," Bureau of Justice Statistics, April 2018.

3. Alvaro 'Al' Ortiz, "Different Views on Additional Staffing for the Houston Police Department," Houston Public Media, January 16, 2017, www.houstonpublic media.org/articles/news/2017/01/16/183687/different -views-on-additional-staffing-for-the-houston-police -department/.

4. Sarah Rafique, "Rural Challenges: West Texas' Smallest Departments Face Difficulties Policing Rural Towns," *Lubbock Avalanche-Journal*, December 3, 2016.

5. "New Response Time Report," dallaspolice.net /resources/CrimeReports/New%20Response%20 Time%20Report.pdf; Cassandra Jaramillo and Hayat Norimine, "350 More Cops Sought," *Dallas Morning News*, January 29, 2020, p. 1.

6. Texas Commission on Law Enforcement website, www.tcole.texas.gov.

7. Rafique, "Rural Challenges."

8. Material is from the Texas Commission on Law Enforcement website, www.tcole.texas.gov.

9. Ayan Mittra, "T-Squared: The Launch of 'Unholstered,' a Look at Texas Police Shootings," *Texas Tribune*, August 30, 2016.

10. Tasha Tsiaperas, "No Witnesses Called for Ex-cop in Trial," *Dallas Morning News*, December 19, 2017.

11. John Sullivan et al., "Number of Fatal Shootings by Police Is Nearly Identical to Last Year," *Washington Post*, July 1, 2017.

12. Jolie McCullough, "Why the Murder Charge against the Texas Police Officer Who Killed Jordan Edwards Is Rare," *Texas Tribune*, July 18, 2017.

13. Eva Ruth Moravec, "Seven Unarmed Black Men Killed by Officers in Texas in 2016," *San Antonio Express-News*, May 18, 2017.

14. Moravec, "Seven Unarmed Black Men Killed."

15. The Sandra Bland case received widespread news coverage. See, for example, Dana Ford, "DA: Sandra Bland's Death Being Treated Like Murder Investigation," CNN, July 21, 2015; David Montgomery, "Sandra Bland Was Threatened with Taser, Police Video Shows," *New York Times*, July 21, 2015; "Texas Trooper Indicted over Sandra Bland Arrest Formally Fired," *Chicago Tribune*, March 2, 2016; St. John Barned-Smith, "DPS Director Affirms Firing of Trooper in Sandra Bland Case," *Houston Chronicle*, March 2, 2016.

16. James Barragán, "Session's Bills Back the Blue," *Dallas Morning News*, June 3, 2017.

17. Fred Dahr, "Crimes and Punishment in Texas State Court," texasdefenselaw.com; Texas Criminal Defense Lawyer, "Texas Criminal Laws and Penalties," mytexas defenselawyer.com.

18. Texas Board of Pardons and Paroles.

19. Texas Department of Criminal Justice, "Fiscal Year 2018 Statistical Report" (February 2019).

20. *O'Donnell v. Harris County*, 2017 WL 1735456 (2017).

21. Jolie McCullough, "Marijuana Prosecutions in Texas Have Dropped by More than Half since Lawmakers Legalized Hemp," *Texas Tribune*, January 3, 2020.

22. Information is from the Texas Association of Counties. The term *district attorney* will be used to encompass district attorneys, county attorneys, and criminal district attorneys.

23. Texas Indigent Defense Commission, "Indigent Defense Data for Texas."

24. Dottie Carmichael, "Judgement and Justice," Public Policy Research Institute, Texas A&M University, June 2013, pp. vii–x.

25. Texas Department of Criminal Justice, "Fiscal Year 2018 Statistical Report."

26. Johnathan Silver, "Texas Prisons Ponder Cutting $250 Million," *Texas Tribune*, August 3, 2016.

27. Harry Mika and Lawrence J. Redlinger, "Crime and Correction," in *Texas at the Crossroads*, ed. Anthony Champagne and Edward J. Harpham (College Station: Texas A&M University Press, 1987), 245–46.

28. Mika and Redlinger, "Crime and Correction," 245–46.

29. *Ruiz v. Estelle*, 503 F. Supp. 1265 (1980).

30. Mika and Redlinger, "Crime and Correction," 247.

31. Texas Department of Criminal Justice, "Texas Board of Criminal Justice."

32. Texas Jail Project, "What Is the Difference between State Jail and County Jail in Texas?," December 21, 2010; John Vander Werff, "Texas State Jails Typically House Lower-Level Classifications of Criminals," *Killeen Daily Herald*, February 26, 2016.

33. Texas Department of Criminal Justice, "Rehabilitation Programs Division, Substance Abuse Treatment Program."

34. See Associated Texans Against Crime, "Annual Report" (1998); Texas Department of Criminal Justice, "Fiscal Year 2011 Operating Budget and Fiscal Years 2010–2013 Legislative Appropriations Request" (August 16, 2010).

35. Brandi Grissom, "With Crime, Incarceration Rates Falling, Texas Closes Record Number of Prisons," *Dallas Morning News*, July 5, 2017.

36. See Associated Texans Against Crime, "Annual Report" (1998).

37. Texas Department of Criminal Justice, "Fiscal Year 2018 Statistical Report."

38. Texas Department of Criminal Justice, "Fiscal Year 2006 Statistical Summary" (December 2006).

39. *Texas Almanac 2010–2011* (Austin: Texas State Historical Association, 2010), 482.

40. E. Ann Carson, "Prisoners in 2018," Bureau of Justice Statistics bulletin (April 2020).

41. "Violent Crime Rate by State," *World Atlas*, August 25, 2017.

42. Texas Department of Criminal Justice, "Fiscal Year 2018 Statistical Report."

43. Texas Department of Criminal Justice, "Fiscal Year 2018 Statistical Report."

44. "Total Number on Death Row as of October 1, 2019," Death Penalty Information Center.

45. "Total Number on Death Row," Death Penalty Information Center.

46. "Execution Database," Death Penalty Information Center.

47. The Gallup poll question used in both time periods was: "Are you in favor of the death penalty for a person convicted of murder?" See "Death Penalty," Gallup, news.gallup.com/poll/1606/death-penalty.aspx.

48. Data come from the National Registry of Exonerations at www.law.umich.edu.

49. Paul Brace and Brent D. Boyea, "State Public Opinion, the Death Penalty, and the Practice of Electing Judges," *American Journal of Political Science* 52, no. 2 (April 2008): 360–72.

50. UT/*Texas Tribune* poll of 1,200 registered Texas voters, June 8–18, 2018. Margin of error is +/−2.83 percentage points.

51. Texas Department of Criminal Justice, "Death Row Information," January 31, 2020.

52. Texas Department of Criminal Justice, "Death Row Information."

53. Calculated from Texas Department of Criminal Justice, "Death Row Information," January 16, 2020.

54. *McCleskey v. Kemp*, 481 U.S. 279 (1987).

55. "Gov. Perry Commutes Sentences of Man Scheduled to Die Thursday," ABC 13, August 30, 2007.

56. Larry Arnold, "The History of Concealed Carry, 1976–2011," Texas Handgun Association.

57. Eric Aasen, "Here's What You Should Know about Open Carry in Texas," KERA, January 5, 2016.

58. Guns to Carry, "Active Concealed Carry Permits (2017)," www.gunstocarry.com/concealed-carry-statistics/.

59. Alex Samuels, "Lawmaker Seeks to Pass 'Constitutional Carry' Gun Bill in 2017," *Texas Tribune*, January 3, 2017.

60. National Registry of Exonerations.

61. Technically, an exoneration is an official finding of innocence from a court, whereas a wrongful conviction may not necessarily result in a formal determination of innocence by a court. All exonerations are wrongful convictions, but some wrongful convictions may not be exonerations.

62. National Registry of Exonerations.

63. National Registry of Exonerations.

64. Timothy Cole Advisory Panel on Wrongful Convictions, "Final Report," December 2016.

65. Jordan Smith, "WilCo D.A.: Duty Upsets Bradley," *Austin Chronicle*, June 1, 2012.

66. Claire Osborn, "Ken Anderson Begins Serving Jail Sentence in Michael Morton Case," *Austin American-Statesman*, November 14, 2013.

67. Will Weissert, "Bill Named for Michael Morton Passes House," May 13, 2013, kxan.com; "Perry Set to Sign Michael Morton Act," May 16, 2013, kxan.com.

68. Maurice Chammah, "Bill Aims to Address Changing Science in Criminal Appeals," *Texas Tribune*, February 4, 2013.

69. Brian Rogers, "Harris County Officials Outline Plan to Curb Jail Population," *Houston Chronicle*, January 7, 2016.

Chapter 13 Citizen's Guide

a. Paul Heaton, Sandra Mayson, and Megan Stevenson, 69 *Stanford Law Review* 711, 729–734 (2017); *O'Donnell v. Harris County*, 251 F. Supp. 3d 1052, 1058–1110 (2017).

b. Nathan L. Hecht, "The State of the Judiciary in Texas," February 6, 2019.

c. *O'Donnell v. Harris County*.

d. *O'Donnell v. Harris County*, 1,118.

e. It does appear that the current software that does risk assessments of those accused of crime is of limited value. See Megan Stevenson, "Assessing Risk Assessment in Action," 103 *Minnesota Law Review* 303 (2018).

f. Texas Alliance for Safe Communities, "Justice Reform Myth vs. Fact," www.texasallianceforsafecommunities.org/justice-reform-facts/.

CHAPTER 14

1. Antonio Olivo, "Deployed by Gov. Rick Perry, National Guard Adjusts to Its New Role on the Texas Border," *Washington Post*, September 1, 2014, www.washingtonpost.com/national/deployed-by-gov-rick-perry-national-guard-adjusts-to-its-new-role-on-the-texas-border/2014/09/01/24968056-2f90-11e4-994d-202962a9150c_story.html?utm_term=.2d719ca54a1b (accessed 8/13/18).

2. Julia Edwards Ainsley, "Trump Border 'Wall' to Cost $21.6 Billion, Take 3.5 Years to Build: Internal Report," *Reuters*, February 9, 2017, www.reuters.com/article/us-usa-trump-immigration-wall-exclusive/exclusive-trump-border-wall-to-cost-21-6-billion-take-3-5years-to-build-internal-report-idUSKBN15O2ZN (accessed 8/13/18).

3. Texas A&M Transportation Institute, 2016 Texas Transportation Poll.

4. "Total Number of Licensed Drivers in the U.S. in 2018, by State," Statista, January 2020, statista.com/statistics/198029/total-number-of-us-licensed-drivers-by-state/.

5. Ginger Lowry and T. J. Costello, "Texas Road Finance (Part 1): Paying for Highways and Byways," *Fiscal Notes*, May 2016.

6. "100 Most Congested Roadways in Texas," Texas A&M Transportation Institute, 2017.

7. Lowry and Costello, "Texas Road Finance (Part 1)."

8. David Schrank, Bill Eisele, and Tim Lomax, "2019 Urban Mobility Report," Texas A&M Transportation Institute (August 2019).

9. Jay Blazek Crossley, "How Much Do Traffic Crashes Cost the People of Texas? (A: $162 Billion)," Farm & City, September 5, 2017, farmandcity.org.

10. Texas Department of Transportation, "Transportation Funding in Texas, 2019 Edition," http://ftp.dot.state.tx.us/pub/txdot-info/fin/funding-sources.pdf; John Heleman and Bruce Wright, "Texas' Motor Fuels Taxes," *Fiscal Notes*, February 2016.

11. Texas Department of Transportation, "Texas Transportation Plan 2040" (2014).

12. Ray Leszcynski, "Officials Back Toll Lanes to Fix LBJ East," *Dallas Morning News*, January 16, 2018.

13. Leszcynski, "Officials Back Toll Lanes."

14. Aman Batheja and Stephen J. Smith, "The Bullet Train That Could Change Everything," *Texas Tribune*, August 18, 2014.

15. Batheja and Smith, "Bullet Train."

16. Brandon Formby, "Some Texans Dodge Bullet Train, Others Are Square in Its Path," *Texas Tribune*, December 15, 2017; "Starts and Stops: A History of the Texas Bullet Train Project," ABC13 Eyewitness News, December 18, 2017, abc13.com; Madeleine Rivera, "Texas Bullet Train Proposal Pits Rural Landowners against Urbanites," Fox News, January 4, 2018, foxnews.com.

17. Dug Begley, "Houston's Public Transit Challenges Highlighted in U.S. Analysis of Bus, Rail Networks," *Houston Chronicle*, June 10, 2016.

18. Center for Neighborhood Technology, All Transit, 2019, alltransit.cnt.org.

19. Office of the Texas Governor Advisory Council on Cultural Affairs, "Texas Demographic Trends & Characteristics" (January 31, 2020), https://demographics.texas.gov/Resources/Presentations/OSD/2020/2020_01_31_OfficeoftheGovernorAdvisoryCouncilonCultural.pdf.

20. Corrie MacLaggan, "Fort Bend County, the Picture of Ethnic Diversity," *Texas Tribune*, November 25, 2013, www.texastribune.org.

21. American Immigration Council, "Immigrants in Texas" (August 6, 2020), www.americanimmigrationcouncil.org/research/immigrants-in-texas.

22. Elena Mejia Lutz and Peggy Fikac, "All Bills Targeting the Texas Dream Died, but DACA Students Feel like They Didn't Dodge the Bullet," *San Antonio Express-News*, June 3, 2017, www.expressnews.com.

23. American Immigration Council, "Immigrants in Texas."

24. Institute on Taxation and Economic Policy, "Undocumented Immigrants' State and Local Tax Contributions" (March 2, 2017), https://itep.org/immigration/.

25. American Immigration Council, "Immigrants in Texas"; New American Economy, www.newamericaneconomy.org

26. Greater Houston Partnership, "Foreign-Born Population" (September 14, 2017), www.houston.org.

27. Office of the State Demographer, "The Foreign-Born Population in Texas: Sources of Growth" (October 2015), http://demographics.texas.gov.

28. Amanda O'Donnell, "Houston Police Chief Art Acevedo: 'Sanctuary Cities' Bill Targets 'Cooks and Nannies,' Not Criminals," *Austin American-Statesman*, September 22, 2018, www.statesman.com/news/local/houston-police-chief-art-acevedo-sanctuary-cities-bill-targets-cooks-nannies-not-criminals/CmdOjFrzxU9Hy6SuOzHoMM/ (accessed 10/10/18).

29. Lieutenant Governor Dan Patrick: Statement on SB4 Concurrence, "Sanctuary Cities Legislation Is on Its Way to the Governor's Desk," The State of Texas, Lieutenant Governor, May 3, 2017, www.ltgov.state.tx.us/2017/05/03/lt-governor-dan-patrick-statement-on-sb-4-concurrence/ (accessed 10/10/18).

30. Ashley Goudeau, "Texas Lawmakers Vote on 'Sanctuary Cities' Bill," KVUE, April 26, 2017, www.kvue.com/article/news/politics/texas-lawmakers-vote-on-sanctuary-cities-bill/434441733 (accessed 10/10/18).

31. Lyanne A. Guarecuco, "'Sanctuary Cities' Debate Brings Tears, Protests, Feuds to Texas House," *Texas Observer*, April 27, 2017, www.texasobserver.org/sanctuary-cities-tears-protests-feuds-texas-house/ (accessed 10/10/18).

32. Patrick Svitek, "Paxton Looks to Get Ahead of Legal Challenges to 'Sanctuary Cities' Ban," *Texas Tribune*, May 8, 2017, www.texastribune.org/2017/05/08/paxton-looks-get-ahead-legal-challenges-sb4/ (accessed 10/10/18).

33. Kelsey Jukam, "Border City & County Declare Legal War on Texas," *Courthouse News Service*, May 9, 2017, www.courthousenews.com/border-city-county-declare-legal-war-texas/ (accessed 10/10/18).

34. Julián Aguilar, "El Paso County Files Lawsuit Seeking to Halt Texas 'Sanctuary' Law," *Texas Tribune*, May 22, 2017, www.texastribune.org/2017/05/22/el-paso-county-files-lawsuit-seeking-halt-states-immigration-law/ (accessed 10/10/18).

35. "Know Your Rights under SB4," ACLU of Texas, March 13, 2018, www.aclutx.org/en/sb4 (accessed 10/10/18).

36. Madlin Mekelburg, "Texas Attorney General Ken Paxton Files 7-State Lawsuit Seeking to End DACA," *El Paso Times*, May 1, 2018, www.elpasotimes.com.

37. Maria Sacchetti, "Federal Judge Gives Respite to 'Dreamers,' Says DACA Can't End While Lawsuit Is Pending," January 10, 2018, www.washingtonpost.com.

38. Texas Department of Transportation, "Texas-Mexico Border Crossings," www.txdot.gov.

39. Texas Military Department, "Texas National Guard Deploys to Texas-Mexico Border to Enhance Border Security," April 10, 2018, https://tmd.texas.gov.

40. Julia Ainsley and Courtney Kube, "Hundreds of Migrant Kids Separated from Parents Are Stuck at Border Stations," NBC News, January 5, 2018, www.nbcnews.com.

41. Patrick Svitek, "Lupe Valdez Sees Texas Gov. Greg Abbott as President Donald Trump's 'Puppet,'" *Texas Tribune*, May 29, 2018, www.texastribune.org.

42. Molly Hennessy-Fiske, "The Great Test for Trump's Border Wall: Texas' Rio Grande Valley," *Los Angeles Times*, April 30, 2018, www.latimes.com.

43. "More South Texas Land Owners Getting Letters on Border Wall," *U.S. News & World Report*, July 8, 2018, www.usnews.com.

44. See Texas Higher Education Coordinating Board, *2019 Texas Public Higher Education Almanac: A Profile of State and Institutional Performance and Characteristics*. See also National Student Clearinghouse Research Center, "States with Largest Higher Education Enrollment, Fall 2019," www.asumag.com/research/top-10s/article/21118631/states-with-largest-higher-education-enrollment-fall-2019.

45. See Texas Higher Education Coordinating Board, *2019 Texas Public Higher Education Almanac*.

46. The education data used in this section are drawn from two sources: Texas Higher Education Coordinating

Board, *2018 Texas Public Higher Education Almanac: A Profile of State and Institutional Performance and Characteristics* and Texas State Historical Association, *Texas Almanac 2018–2019* (Austin: Texas, 2018). Community college data generally included information on the Lamar State Colleges and the Texas State Technical Colleges. See also www.txhighereddata.org/.

47. See Charles R. Matthews, *Higher Education in Texas: Its Beginnings to 1870* (Denton: University of North Texas Press, 2018). See Chapter 5 for a more detailed discussion.

48. See V. R. Cardozier, "Higher Education," *Handbook of Texas Online*, www.tshaonline.org/handbook/online/articles/khhxr (accessed 7/12/20). See also Texas Higher Education Coordinating Board, "Formula Funding Recommendations for the 2020–21 Biennium" (April 2018), www.thecb.state.tx.us.

49. Institute for College Access & Success, "Student Debt and the Class of 2016," (September 2017), Table 3.

50. See Texas Legislative Budget Board, "Agencies of Higher Education; Higher Education," May 2016, in *Fiscal Size-Up: 2016–17 Biennium*, pp. 220–24.

51. The following is drawn from "Understanding PUF: What Is the Permanent University Fund?," University of Texas System, August 22, 2016, www.utsystem.edu/offices/chancellor/blog/what-is-the-permanent-university-fund. See also "Permanent University Fund (PUF) Quick Facts," University of Texas System, www.utsystem.edu/puf.

52. Financial Statements and Independent Auditor's Report, Permanent University Fund, years ended August 31, 2019 and 2018, p. 5.

53. See Matthew Watkins, "Texas Universities Forced to Trim Their Budgets, Even with Big State Cuts Averted," *Texas Tribune*, July 27, 2017.

54. See Texas Higher Education Coordinating Board, *2018 Texas Public Higher Education Almanac*.

55. Peter G. George, Robert E. Mace, and Rima Petrossian, "Aquifers of Texas," Texas Water Development Board, Report 380 (July 2011).

56. An acre-foot is equal to 325,851.43 U.S. gallons. Planners typically assume that a suburban family will consume an acre-foot of water a year.

57. Texas Water Development Board, "Water for Texas 2012 State Water Plan" (January 2012), p. xii.

58. See Texas Water Development Board, "Water for Texas 2012," pp. 17–18.

59. See Otis W. Templer, "Water Law," *Handbook of Texas Online*; Otis W. Templer, "Water Rights Issues: Texas Water Rights Law: East Meets West," *Journal of Contemporary Water Research and Education* 85 (Spring 1991).

60. The following is drawn largely from Templer, "Water Law" and "Texas Water Rights." See also Terry L. Hadley, "Texas Water Commission," *Handbook of Texas Online*; Laurie E. Jasinski, "Texas Water Development Board," *Handbook of Texas Online*; Texas Water Development Board, "Water for Texas 2012," Executive Summary and chap. 1. See also Texas Water Development Board, "A Texan's Guide to Water and Water Rights Marketing"; Ronald A. Kaiser, *Handbook of Texas Water Law: Problems and Needs* (College Station: Texas Water Resources Institute, Texas A&M University, 1987). We also thank Benedict Voit for his useful summary of water policy issues. See Benedict Voit, "Texas Water Policy for the 21st Century" (unpublished paper, University of Texas at Dallas, April 10, 2008).

61. See Texas Water Development Board, "A Texan's Guide to Water."

62. See the historical timeline regarding environmental policy, Texas Commission on Environmental Quality, www.tceq.texas.gov.

63. See Texas Water Development Board, "About the Texas Water Development Board," www.twdb.texas.gov.

64. See Kate Galbraith, "Texas Supreme Court Hands Victory to Landowners in Landmark Water Case," *Texas Tribune*, February 24, 2012. See also Forrest Wilder, "The Texas Supreme Court Turns Water into Oil in a Landmark Groundwater Decision," *Texas Observer*, February 24, 2012; Chuck Lindell, "Supreme Court Delivers Major Water Ruling on Water Regulation," *Austin American-Statesman*, February 24, 2012.

65. For a good discussion of some of these issues, see a five-part series published by the *Texas Tribune*: Neena Satija, "Beneath the Surface," *Texas Tribune*, November 19, 2013–January 29, 2014.

66. Michael Marks and Terrence Henry, "Everything You Need to Know about Proposition 6, Texas' Water Fund," *State Impact: A Reporting Project of NPR Member Stations*, November 4, 2013.

Chapter 14 Citizen's Guide

a. Teresa Watanabe, " 'It's the New Chinese Exclusion Act': How a Trump Order Could Hurt California's Universities," *Los Angeles Times*.

AnswerKey

CHAPTER 1
1. B
2. A
3. C
4. D
5. B
6. D
7. E
8. A
9. E
10. C
11. B
12. C
13. A
14. A

CHAPTER 2
1. A
2. E
3. D
4. C
5. E
6. D
7. A
8. D
9. D
10. B
11. C
12. B
13. C
14. B

CHAPTER 3
1. C
2. D
3. A
4. C
5. A
6. B
7. B
8. A
9. D
10. A
11. C
12. A
13. B
14. C
15. D
16. A
17. B

CHAPTER 4
1. B
2. B
3. A
4. B
5. A
6. A
7. A
8. D
9. C
10. B
11. B
12. A

CHAPTER 5
1. C
2. C
3. D
4. E
5. C
6. C
7. A
8. C
9. A
10. A
11. D
12. A
13. C
14. B

CHAPTER 6
1. B
2. E
3. E
4. E
5. A
6. E
7. A
8. D
9. C
10. C
11. E
12. B
13. D
14. B
15. A
16. B

CHAPTER 7
1. A
2. A
3. D
4. B
5. E
6. B
7. C
8. B
9. D
10. D
11. C
12. A
13. D
14. A
15. A
16. D
17. B

CHAPTER 8
1. D
2. E
3. E
4. B
5. D
6. A
7. A
8. B
9. B
10. B
11. A
12. C
13. A
14. E

CHAPTER 9

1. B
2. B
3. C
4. C
5. C
6. E
7. E
8. D
9. A
10. A
11. E
12. A
13. A
14. C

CHAPTER 10

1. B
2. D
3. D
4. D
5. C
6. A
7. B
8. B
9. D
10. E
11. A
12. A
13. A
14. C
15. A
16. A
17. D
18. A

CHAPTER 11

1. A
2. B
3. A
4. C
5. B
6. B
7. C
8. A
9. B
10. D
11. D
12. B
13. A

CHAPTER 12

1. E
2. A
3. B
4. C
5. A
6. B
7. E
8. A
9. C
10. C

CHAPTER 13

1. C
2. A
3. A
4. A
5. B
6. C
7. C
8. D
9. C
10. D
11. A
12. A
13. E
14. E
15. C
16. E
17. C

CHAPTER 14

1. A
2. A
3. D
4. A
5. E
6. A
7. B
8. C
9. A
10. E
11. B
12. B
13. A
14. C
15. A
16. D
17. C
18. A
19. D

Credits

Gay; **p. 285:** Courtesy of Laura Skelding; **p. 287:** Larry W Smith/EPA-EFE/Shutterstock. **Chapter 9: p. 294:** Marie D. De Jesús/Houston Chronicle via AP; **p. 303 (Figure 9.2):** Courtesy of the Texas Legislative Council; **p. 304:** William Osler McCarthy/Supreme Court of Texas; **p. 306:** Courtesy of Court of Criminal Appeals of Texas; **p. 308:** SARGENT © Austin American -Statesman. Reprinted with permission of Andrews McMeel Syndication. All rights reserved; **p. 310:** Chine Nouvelle/SIPA/Newscom; **p. 313:** Twitter/@Brett-Busby; **p. 318 (left):** AP Photo/Erich Schlegel; **p. 318 (right):** Marie D. de Jesus/Houston Chronicle via AP; **p. 324:** Courtesy of Texas Law Center; **p. 325:** Courtesy of McAllen Police Department. **Chapter 10: p. 332:** Thomas B. Shea/AFP/Getty Images; **p. 340:** Caleb Pritchard; **p. 341:** Erich Schlegel; **p. 342:** AP Photo/Pat Sullivan; **p. 348:** J.G. Domke/Alamy Live News; **p. 352 (left):** Courtesy of the city of Houston; **p. 352 (right):** AP Photo/Eric Gay; **p. 353:** AP Photo/Tony Gutierrez; **p. 354 (top):** Drew Anthony Smith/Getty Images; **p. 354 (bottom):** Xinhua/Wang Ying/Alamy Stock Photo; **p. 356:** Adam Ziegenhals; **p. 362:** Charles O'Rear. **Chapter 11: p. 372:** NiKreative/Alamy Stock Photo; **p. 376 (Table 11.1):** From "Fiscal Size-Up 2020-21 Biennium." Used by permission of the Legislative Budget Board; **p. 377 (Figure 11.1):** From "Fiscal Size-Up 2020-21 Biennium." Used by permission of the Legislative Budget Board; **p. 378:** Courtesy of Texas Comptroller of Public Accounts; **p. 380 (Table 11.2):** From "Fiscal Size-Up 2020-21 Biennium." Used by permission of the Legislative Budget Board; **p. 383:** Dan Tian/Xinhua/Alamy Live News; **p. 386 (Table 11.3):** From "Fiscal Size-Up 2020-21 Biennium." Used by permission of the Legislative Budget Board; **p. 398:** Ralph Barrera/Austin American-Statesman via AP. **Chapter 12: p. 406:** AP Photo/The Daily Sentinel/Andrew D. Brosig; **p. 411 (top left):** AP Photo/Eric Gay; **p. 411 (top right):** Association of Texas Professional Educators; **p. 411 (bottom left):** Jason Hoekema/The Brownsville Herald via AP; **p. 411 (bottom right):** Darren Abate/AP Images for Boys & Girls Clubs of America; **p. 414:** AP Photo/Eric Gay; **p. 419:** AP Photo/Eric Gay; **p. 420:** Brett Coomer/Houston Chronicle via AP; **p. 423:** Cooper Neill/Bloomberg via Getty Images; **p. 425:** Robert Nickelsberg/Getty Images; **p. 426:** Russell Lee/Library of Congress; **p. 427:** Horizons WWP/TRVL/Alamy Stock Photo; **p. 434:** Mandel Ngan/AFP via Getty Images; **p. 436:** Mark Graham/The New York Times/Redux; **p. 440:** Sophie Novack. **Chapter 13: p. 446:** Paul Moseley/Fort Worth Star-Telegram/TNS via Getty Images; **p. 451:** Farmers Branch Police Department via AP–File; **p. 453 (left):** Aaron M. Sprecher/Epa/Shutterstock; **p. 453 (right):** Aaron M. Sprecher/Epa/Shutterstock; **p. 458:** Steve Snodgrass; **p. 459:** Republished with permission of Stanford Law Review, from Paul Heaton, Sandray Mayson, and Megan Stevenson, "The Downstream Consequences of Misdemeanor Pretrial Detention," Stanford Law Review 69(3), 2017; permission conveyed through Copyright Clearance Center, Inc.; **p. 462:** Rodger Jones/The Dallas Morning News Inc. All Rights Reserved; **p. 464:** Tamir Kalifa; **p. 466:** AP Photo; **p. 474:** Mona Reeder/MCT/Newscom; **p. 478:** AP Photo/Will Weissert; **p. 479:** AP Photo/The Daily Sentinel/Andrew D. Brosig. **Chapter 14: p. 486:** Brendan Smialowski/AFP/Getty Images; **p. 489 (Table 14.1):** "Exhibit 1: State-Maintained Roads and Highways in Texas, 2014" from Ginger Lowry and TJ Costello, "Texas Road Finance (Part I): Paying for Highways and Byways," Fiscal Notes, May 2016, comptroller.texas .gov; **p. 492:** AP Photo/Harry Cabluck; **p. 494:** Urbanmyth/Alamy Stock Photo; **p. 495 (Figure 14.1):** Texas Bullet Train Alignment Map from texascentral.com. Reprinted by permission of Texas Central; **p. 497 (Figure 14.2):** "Texas immigrant population now rivals New York's in size." Pew Research Center, Washington, D.C. (April 21, 2016) https://www.pew research.org/fact-tank/2016/04/21/texas-immigrant-popu lation-now-rivals-new-yorks-in-size/; **p. 498:** AP Photo/Eric Gay; **p. 501:** AP Photo/Eric Gay; **p. 502:** AP Photo/Eric Gay; **p. 506 (top):** John Moore/Getty Images; **p. 506 (bottom):** Robert DeDeaux/U.S. Army Corps of Engineers, South Pacific Border District; **p. 507:** AP Photo/Eric Gay; **p. 508:** AP Photo/Eric Gay; **p. 517:** Texas Higher Education Coordinating Board; **p. 522 (top):** AP Photo/Amarillo Globe-News/Michael Schumacher; **p. 522 (bottom):** AP Photo/Tony Gutierrez.

Glossary/Index

step in the legislative process, during which a bill is killed, amended, or heard by a standing committee

Consolidated Vultee Aircraft Corporation, 32

conspiracy theories, 267–68, *267*, 277

constable, 335–36 precinct-level county official involved with serving legal papers, serving as bailiff in justice of the peace courts, and, in some counties, enforcing the law

constituent, 221 a person who is represented by an elected official

constituent service, 221 nonlegislative activities legislators perform to assist people living in their districts, including writing letters of recommendation, giving speeches to civic groups, or working to solve a problem for someone in their community

constitution, 43 the legal structure of a government, which establishes its power and authority as well as the limits on that power. *See also* Texas Constitution; U.S. Constitution

constitutional amendments
    budget-execution authority and, 394
    elections for, 69–72, 76
    executive clemency and, 474
    governor's term and, 258
    important, listed, 73
    income tax and, 42, 66, 70, 73, 74–75, 383
    joint resolutions and, 228
    legislative salaries and, 220

medical malpractice suits and, 206
process for, 40, 41–42, 57, 69
state funds and, 388, 389, 390
transportation needs and, 400, 491
water policy and, 522
constitutional carry, 476
Constitutional Convention of 1787 (U.S.), 87
Constitutional Convention of 1875 (Texas), 55–56, 58, 190
Constitution of Coahuila y Tejas (1827), 46, 50
consumption taxes, 384. *See also* sales tax

contingent fee, 297 the presentation of a defendant's defense against an allegation in a civil case

contract, right to, 53
controller, 351–52
Convention of 1836, 47, *49*

cooperative federalism, 93, 94–96, 107, 109 a way of describing federalism where the boundaries between the national government and state governments have become blurred

corn pone, 6
Cornyn, John
    2020 race against Hegar, 122, *122*, 123, 151, 177, 178, 190
    Kirk's loss to, 144, 145
    Trump administration and, *106*
coronavirus pandemic of 2020
    2020 elections and, 147, 177, 178, 179
    Abbott and, 4, 267, 286–87, *286*, 289, 326, 334, 346–47, 402, 423, 430, 480

budgetary process and, 396–97
bullet train and, 494
campaigning during, *313*
college football and, 516
county judges and, 305
courts and, 326
economic crisis and, 16, 35–36, 368, 388, 402
executive branch and, 286–88
federalism and, 107–8, 109
gas prices and, *383*
governors and, 107
higher education and, 374, 508, 514–16
immigration and, 507
Johnson at briefing on, *353*
local government and, 2, 3–4, 35–36, 334, 346–47, 368
Medicaid and, 107, 432, 439–40, *440*
Patrick and, 347, 402
Paxton and, 347
police power and, 93
political culture and, 35–36
public education and, 423–24, *423*
public policy and, 523–24
tax revenue effects, 16, 279, 368, 374
transportation and, 491
uninsured rate and, 101
as voter priority, 523, *523*
Corpus Christi, *344*
corrections. *See* parole; probation; Texas prison system
corruption, 199, 200, *200*, 338
cosmopolitanism, 6
cotton industry, 10, 12–13, *13*, 14, 15, 24, 30, 31

council-manager form of government, 350–51, 352–54, 356–57 a form of city government in which public policies are developed by the

city council and executive and administrative functions are assigned to a professional city manager

council of government (COG), 363, *363* a regional planning board composed of local elected officials and some private citizens from the region

counties, 338–42, *341*, 368. *See also* county government; *specific counties*

county attorney, 336, 338, 463 an elected official in some counties who prosecutes misdemeanor cases

county auditor, 336 public official, appointed by the district judges, who receives and disburses county funds; in large counties, this official also prepares the county budget

county chair, 124 the county party official who heads the county executive committee

county clerk, 336 public official who is the main record-keeper of the county

county commissioner, 335, 337, 338, 347 government official (four per county) on the county commissioners' court whose main duty is the construction and maintenance of roads and bridges

county commissioners' court, 64, 335, 336, 337, ***337, 340*** the main governing body of each county; has the authority to set the county tax rate and budget

medical research in, 17, *17*
minority population in, *32*
nonschool special purpose districts in, 358
oil and gas industry in, 30, 32, 497
pension shortfalls, 365–67
property taxes in, 357–58
public transit and, 495–96, *496*
racial and ethnic composition of, 355
road congestion in, 490
San Antonio compared to, 34
SB 4 and, 503
urban political life, 5, 30–31, *35*
UT System and, 512
water policy and, 519
White liberals in, 122
Houston, Sam, 8, 50, 52
Houston and Texas Central Railroad Company v. East (1904), 519–20
Houston and Texas Central Railway, 31, 34
Houston Chronicle, 176, *176*, 299, 373
Houston Community College, 342, *342*, *509*
Houston County, 321
Houston Firefighters' Relief and Retirement Fund, 365–66
Houston Independent School District, 357
Houston Municipal Employees Pension System, 365
Houston Newsmakers (TV show), 176
Houston Police Department, 449
Houston Police Officers' Pension System, 365
Houston Ship Channel, 30
Howard, Donna, 198
Hubbard, Richard B., *259*
Huddle, Rebeca, *304*
Hudspeth County, 339, *341*
Huey, Mary Ann, 142
Hughes, Sarah, 317–18

Hughs, Ruth R., *271*
human trafficking, 268
Humphrey, Hubert, 126
Hunt, Wesley, 179
Hunter, Todd, 197
Huntsville, 466
Hurd, Will, 143, 144
Hurricane Harvey, 203, 248, 268, 277, *332*, 333, 334
Hurricane Katrina, 333
Hurricane Rita, 333–34
Hutchison, Kay Bailey, 116, 123, 116, 123

I
IBM, 35
ICE (Immigration and Customs Enforcement), 499, 500, 501
ideology, 119–20, 139, 246–47, *246*, 409
Ifill, Sherrilyn, 317
Illinois, *257*, *283*, 313, 343, 394
immigrants and immigration. *See also* undocumented immigrants and workers
business interests and, 210
coronavirus pandemic and, 507
Democratic Party and, 119, 139, *178*
domestic, 21, 22, 23, 34, 36
as election issue, 178, *178*
as a federalism issue, 105–7, 109
higher education and, 508–9
immigrant population, 497–99, *497*
international, 21, 32, 34, 36
from Latin America, 24, *26*
population growth and, 21, 497
preemption and, 97
provincialism and, 6
Republican Party and, 130, 178, *178*, 179
slavery and, 50
social conservatism and, 6–7
as voter priority, 523, *523*

Immigration and Customs Enforcement (ICE), 499, 500, 501
immigration law enforcement, 97–98, 399
immigration policy, 487–88, 498–507, *498*, *501*. *See also* sanctuary cities
immigration reform, 151, 506

impeachment, 68, 229, 260–62, 325 under the Texas Constitution, the formal charge by the House of Representatives that leads to trial in the Senate and possible removal of a state official

imperial presidency, 255
incarceration. *See* Texas prison system
income inequality, 384, *385*
income tax
   Article 8 of the Texas Constitution and, 66
   comparisons of states, 75, *385*
   prohibition of, 42, 66, 70, 73, 74–75
   property taxes and, 178
   question of, in Texas, 383, 384
   state revenue and, 378, 379, 384

incorporation of the Bill of Rights, 91 the Supreme Court ruling that rights that are deemed to be fundamental rights are considered part of "liberty" in the Fourteenth Amendment and apply to the states as well as the national government

independents, 119, 126–28, 139, 169–70

independent state grounds, 98 a constitutional concept allowing states, usually

under the state constitution, to expand rights beyond those provided by the U.S. Constitution

India, *509*
Indian Americans, 151
Indian Wars, 21

indictment, 300, 460, 464 a written statement issued by a grand jury that charges a suspect with a crime and states that a trial is warranted

indigent defense (2018), *465*

individual mandate, 104–5 a requirement of the Affordable Care Act that health insurance be purchased

individual rights, 43–44, 51, 53, 101
inheritance tax, *386*
Institute of International Education, 508
Institute on Taxation and Economic Policy, 384, 499
Instructional Materials Fund, 388
insurance companies, 281
insurance occupation taxes, *382*, *386*
intellectual property protections, 19

interest group, 187 an organization established to influence the government's programs and policies
   business dominance and, 6
   constitutional amendment elections and, 69–70
   contributions to Texas legislature candidates (2018), 203, *204*, 205
   corruption and, 200
   democracy and, 188–90
   election campaigns and, 171–72, 190–91, 201–8

future of Texas and, 210
importance of, 185–86
legislative process and, 240, *240*
lobbyists and, *191*, 192–93 (*see also* lobbyist)
party control and, 125
plural *versus* single executive and, 282
policy makers and, 190–91, *193*
political process and, 187–93
resources and strategies of, 187–88
tort cases and, 323
types of, 192–93

interest-group capture, 206–8, *207* process by which a government agency comes to serve the objectives of the interests that the agency is supposed to regulate

Interior Lowlands, 11, *11*
international students, 508–9, *509*
interstate commerce, regulation of, 89–90, *90*, 92–93, 94, 97
Interstate Highway System, 15, 140–41
intolerance, 6

introduction, 230 the first step in the legislative process, during which a member of the legislature drafts a bill and files a copy of it with the clerk of the House or secretary of the Senate

investigative power, 229 the power, exercised by the House, the Senate, or both chambers jointly, to investigate problems facing the state

Ireland, John, *259*
irrigation, 12

Irving, 31
Isaac, Jason, 215

issue advocacy, 202 independent spending by individuals or interest groups on a campaign issue but not directly tied to a particular candidate

J

Jack, Janis, 407, 408
Jack and Wise County joint judicial district, 465
Jackson, Andrew, 89
Jade Helm 15, 267–68, *267*
jailers, certification of, 450

Jaybird Party, 158 after the White primary was ruled unconstitutional, this offshoot Democratic Party preselected candidates for the Democratic primary and prohibited African Americans from participating

Jean, Botham, 451
Jefferson, Thomas, 47–48
Jefferson, Wallace, 144
Jenkins, Clay, 305, 334
Jester, Beauford H., *259*, 262
JOBS (a work-related training program), 428
Johnson, Andrew, 53
Johnson, Ann, 115
Johnson, Cliff, 198
Johnson, Eddie Bernice, 143
Johnson, Eric, *27*, 144, 353, *353*
Johnson, Faith, 341
Johnson, Ken, 450–51, *451*
Johnson, Lyndon, 20, 94, 135, 139, 159, 318, 426
Joint Committee on Prison Reform, 466
Joint Interim Committee on Higher Education Formula Funding, 514

joint resolution, 228 a resolution, commonly a proposed

amendment to the Texas Constitution or ratification of an amendment to the U.S. Constitution, that must pass both the House and Senate but that does not require the governor's signature

Jones, Anson, 51
Jones, Elizabeth Ames, 204–6
Jones, Jesse, 190
Jones, Mark, 138, 246
Jordan, Barbara, 28, 143
judges, 321, 323. *See also* judicial conduct; *specific types of judges*

Judicial Campaign Fairness Act, 317, 327 a judicial reform that places limits on judicial campaign contributions

judicial conduct, 324–26, *325*
judicial politics. *See also* Texas judiciary
changing the system for selecting judges, 309–14, 327
comparing selection of judges to other states, 315
electoral competition on courts of appeal (2018), *316*, 327
increasing representation of people of color, 317–20, 327
initial appointment of judges by the governor, 307
judicial campaign finance, *308*, 314–17, 327
judicial elections and straight-ticket voting, 310–11, *310*, 312, 327
judicial elections become highly partisan, 296, 308–9, 311, 312, 327

number of judicial races on 2018 ballot in urban counties, 311, *311*
state Supreme Court campaign contributions, *314*, 316, 327

judicial power, 64, 229 the power of the House to impeach and of the Senate to convict members of the executive and judicial branches of state government

Juneteenth, 27
junior colleges, 511

justice of the peace courts, 64, 305–6, 321, 325, 336, 337, 461 local trial courts with limited jurisdiction over small claims and very minor criminal misdemeanors

juvenile justice cases, 299

K

Kaiser Family Foundation, 425, 438, *439*
Kaiser Foundation Study (2019), 378
Kansas, 10, 32
Kaufman County, 365
Keller, Sharon, 325–26
Kendall County, 425
Kenedy County, 153, 339
Kent County, 305
Kent County Sheriff's Department, 449
Kerrigan, Patricia, 312
Kinch, Sam, 258
King, Bill, 366
King, Ken, 191
King Ranch, *14*
Kirby, Barbara, 306
Kirby, William, 416
Kirk, Ron, 144, 145
Kulkarni, Sri Preston, *150*, 151

L

labor segregation, 24
land, 7–12, 14, 15

land commissioner, 64, 68, 222, 271, *271*, 276–77 elected state official who is the manager of most publicly owned lands

land ownership, 49–50
land titles, 66

lane miles, 489–90 center-line miles multiplied by the number of lanes

Lanham, S. W. T., *259*

La Raza Unida, 26, 126 former political party created in 1970 in Texas in order to bring attention to the concerns of Mexican Americans

Laredo, *344*
Latin America, 6, 19, 23–24, *486*, 498
Latinos. *See also* minorities
    Abbott's 2014 campaign and, 174
    Austin city government and, 354
    in the Border region, 12
    Bush, George W., and, 178
    civil rights groups and, 192
    Confederate monuments debate and, 8
    in Congress, *26*, 123
    on Dallas city council, 353
    death penalty and, 474
    Democratic Party and, 6, 116, 119, 122, 127, 131, 139, 144–45, *144*, 175, 295–96
    demographic changes and, *22*, 23–26, *24*, 25, *26*, 34, 142, 180
    in El Paso, 354
    favorability toward courts and criminal justice system, *320*

    favorability toward police, *452*
    growing influence of, 26, 36, 126, 180, 221, 368
    in the judiciary, 317–18, *318*, 319
    media and, 176
    party politics and, 6, 116, 119, 122, 123, 130, 131
    as percentage of Texas electorate, 167
    in political parties in Texas, 144–45
    population growth and, 21, 123, 164, 180
    population in Texas, 119, 166, 487
    poverty among, 425, *425*
    in prison population, *467*
    racial diversity and, 33, 36
    SB 4 and, 502
    straight-ticket voting and, 310
    voter ID requirements and, 103, 162, 163, *163*
    voter registration and, 160–61, 166
    voting rates, 100, 123, 143, *143*, 145, 168, 173
    voting rights and, 159
law enforcement, *264*, 267, 335–36, 450, 501.
    See also criminal justice system; policing
lawmaking, 229–40, *232–233*
    additional players in, 238–40
    committee action, 230–31
    conference committee, 235–36, 244
    floor action, 231–35
    governor's action, *235*, 236–38
    introduction of bill, 230
    referral, 230, 244
    standing committees, 230, *231*
    voting by legislature, *236*

law of capture, 519–20 the idea that the first person

to "capture" water or oil by pumping it out of the ground and using it owns that water or oil

lawyer-legislators, 220–21
lawyers, 323–24

layer-cake federalism, 92–94, 107–8 a form of federalism in which the powers and responsibilities of the state and national governments are separate and distinct

LBB. *See* Legislative Budget Board (LBB)
League of United Latin American Citizens (LULAC), 192, 254, 502
League of Women Voters, 167, 279
Lee, Robert E., *9*, 53, 90
Lee, Sheila Jackson, 143, *143*
legal process, 297–300
legal profession, 323–24
Legislative Appropriation Request (LAR), 396
Legislative Audit Committee, 274

legislative budget, 266 the state budget that is prepared and submitted by the Legislative Budget Board (LBB) and that is fully considered by the House and Senate

Legislative Budget Board (LBB), 266–67, 274, 392–97, *391*, *395*, *398*, 399
Legislative Budget Estimates, 396
Legislative Education Board, 274
legislative powers, 63, 66, 74–75, 225–28, 236–38
legislative process. *See* budgetary process; lawmaking
Legislative Redistricting Board (LRB), 222–24

Legislative Reference Library, 268–69
legislative staff, 219
Leininger, James, 206
Leon County, 321
Lewis, "Gib," 200
LGBTQ Caucus in Texas House, 215
LGBTQ rights, 6–7, 72, 130, 131, *354*. *See also* same-sex marriage; transgender rights
liberal Democrats, 139
liberal politics, *35*
liberal Republicans, 139
Libertarian Party, 126, 130–31
liberty, right to, 46, 48, 91

licensing (of law enforcement officials), 450 in order to be a Texas peace officer, one must meet the requirements imposed by the Texas Commission on Law Enforcement, the regulatory body for peace officers and certain other officers in the state

licensing income, 380, 386
Lieber, Dave, 346

lieutenant governor, 241–44, 273–75 a statewide elected official who is the presiding officer of the Senate; the lieutenant governor is one of the most important officials in state government and has significant control over legislation in the state Senate; the second highest elected official in the state and president of the state Senate
    appointment power, 243–44, 265, 280
    bills and, 230, 236, 243
    budgetary process and, 397
    Legislative Budget Board and, 394
    Legislative Redistricting Board and, 222, 274

nonlegislative powers and, 229

plural executive and, 271, *271*, 273–75, *282*

political style of, 274–75

powers under Senate Rules, 242, 243, 274

succession and, 262

Texas Constitution and, 51, 62, 63, 64, 68

water projects committee and, 522

life, right to, 48, 91

lignite coal, 81

Limestone County, 321

limited government, 6, 59, 60, 126, 129, 130 a principle of constitutional government; a government whose powers are defined and limited by a constitution

Lin, C. Huie, *17*

Lincoln, Abraham, 52

line-item veto, 236, 255, 266, 269, 399 the power of the executive to veto specific provisions (lines) of an appropriations bill passed by the legislature

Ling-Temco-Vought (LTV), 32

Livestock Show and Rodeo, 3

Livingston, Robert, 89

lobbying reform, 198–99, *198*, 200

lobbyist, *191*, 192–93 an individual employed by an interest group who tries to influence governmental decisions on behalf of that group. *See also* interest group

access to policy makers, 193–94

activities of, 197–200

business groups and, 6, 192, 201, 210, 240

former legislators as, 196, 198, *198*

individuals as, 208–10, *208*, 240

interest-group capture and, 206

legislative process and, 240

PACs and, 201–2, 204

public interest and, 201

revolving door and, 196–97, 198

in Texas, compared to other states, 195

Texas Ethics Commission and, 170–71, 194

local bill, 225 a bill affecting only units of local government, such as a city, county, or special district

local elections, *154*

local government, 332–68

Articles 9 and 11 of the Texas Constitution and, 66

city government, 343–57

coronavirus pandemic and, 2, 3–4, 35–36, 334, 346–47, 368

councils of government, 363, *363*

county government, 335–42

favorability toward, *345*

financial issues facing, 364–67

future of Texas and, 367–68

Hurricane Harvey response and, *332*, 333–34

importance of, 333

local bills and, 225

number of, in Texas and other states, 359

pensions, 365–67

preemption and, 344–49, *348*, *349*

special purpose districts, 357–62

state constitutions and, 43, 45

state government relationship to, 87

Locke, John, 47–48

The Logic of Collective Action (Olson), 188

Lone Star College System, 357–58

Longoria, Nora, 325, *325*

López de Santa Anna, Antonio, 50

López Obrador, Andrés Manuel, 506–7

"Lost Cause," 8

lottery, 387

Louisiana, 91, 119, 146, 286, 333, 470

Loving County, 153, 338

Lower Rio Grande Valley, 10, 12

Low-Income Vehicle Repair Assistance Program, 269

LRB (Legislative Redistricting Board), 222–24

Lubbock, 12

LULAC (League of United Latin American Citizens), 192, 254, 502

Luther, Shelley, 287, *287*, 326, 347

Lyft, 190, *191*, 345

lynching, 27, 93

M

Madison, James, 43, 188

Mahendru, Ashish, 312

mail-in voting, 179, 326

Majcher, Dineen, *184*, 185, 186, 208

MALC (Mexican American Legislative Caucus), 254, 501

MALDEF (Mexican American Legal Defense and Education Fund), 159, 192, 416

manufacturing sector, 17, 32, 34

marble-cake federalism, 93, 94–96, 107, 109 a way of describing federalism where the boundaries between

the national government and state governments have become blurred

Margo, Dee, *354*

marijuana, 88, 131, 461–62, 462–63, *462*, 481

Marling, Robert, 193

marriage

Proposition 2, 71, 72

same-sex, 61, 71, 73, 88, 98, 131, 325, *354*

Supreme Court decision (2015), 41

traditional, 6, 41, 72

Marshall, John, 89–90

Marshall, Khambrel, 176

martial law, 267

Massachusetts, 98, 101

Matagorda Bay, *281*

matching funds, 386 federal monies going to a state based on states pending for a program

mayor-council form of government, 350, 351–52, 356–57 a form of city government in which the mayor is the chief executive and the city council is the legislative body; in the *strong mayor–council* variation, the mayor's powers enable him or her to control executive departments and the agenda of the city council; in the *weak mayor–council* variation, the mayor's power is more limited

mayors, 334, 346, 350–56, *354*

Mays, Richard, 142

McAllen, 12, 25, *84*, 325, *325*, *506*

McAllen, Roman, *172*, *272*

McCall, Brian, 255–56, 280

McCally, Sharon, 312

McCulloch v. Maryland (1819), 89

McDonald, Craig, 201

McGee, Josh, *265*

McKinney, 31, 454

McLennan County, 325

McWilliams, Andrea, 194, *194*

media, 176–77, 191, 238–39, *239*, 279. *See also* social media

mediation, 298

Medicaid, 425, 426, 428, 431–36 a federal and state program financing medical services to low–income people

    ACA and expansion of, 96–97, 101, 438, 439, 440, *440*

    administration and financing of, 432–36

    coronavirus pandemic and, 107, 432, 439–40, *440*

    Federal Funds and, 375, 386, 392

    participation in, 432, *433*

    state expenditures for, 393, 400, 436

medical malpractice suits, 206, 322, 323

medical research, 17, *17*, 34

Medicare, 95, 96, 430, 432

Meier, Bill, 234

mental health services, 268

merit selection, 309–12, 317, 327 a judicial reform under which judges would be nominated by a blue–ribbon committee, then be appointed by the governor and, after a brief period in office, run in a retention election

Mesquite, 31

mestizos, 23

Mexican American Legal Defense and Education Fund (MALDEF), 159, 192, 416

Mexican American Legislative Caucus (MALC), 254, 501

Mexican Americans, 23–24, 26, *26*, 34, 36, 119, 126

Mexican-American studies, *285*

Mexican-American War, 7–10

Mexican and Spanish land titles, 66

Mexican Constitution (1824), 46, 47

Mexican Revolution (1910), 34

Mexican War of Independence, 46

Mexico

    border wall and, 487

    immigration from, 36, *486*, 504

    independence from Spain, 46

    international students from, *509*

    NAFTA and, 18

    Texas's independence from, 26, 45, 46, 47–48, 50

    USMCA and, *18*, 19, *19*, 506–7

Miami, Florida, 356

Michael Morton Act, 478

Michigan, *314*, 364, 365

Middle East, 6, 284

middle schools, *411*, 420

Midland County, 136

Migration Policy Institute, 504

military and military bases, 20–21, *20*, 32, 34

military power, 88, 267–68

militias, 87

Miller, Bill, 179

Miller, Sid, *172*, 177, *271*, *272*, 277–78, *278*, 287, 289

mineral rights, 49–50

Minnesota, *385*, 454

minorities. *See also specific groups*

    at-large elections and, 351

    death penalty and, 474

    educational attainment and, 412, 421

    growing population and influence of, 6, *32*

    religious groups, 6

    voter ID law and, 160, 162–63

    voting and participation by, 166, 167

    minority rights, 96, 221, 224

misdemeanor, 298–99, 455 a minor criminal offense usually punishable by a small fine and/or short jail sentence

    bail system and, 457, 458, *459*, 462

    justice of the peace courts and, 305, 306, 307

    municipal courts and, 307

    prosecuting attorneys and, 463

    punishment for, *455*, 456

    trial and sentencing for, 461

Mississippi, 98, 119, 159

Missouri, 313

Mockingbird Elementary School, *423*

Monitor, *174*

monopolies, 62

Moody, Dan, *259*

Moody's, 365, 367

Morath, Mike, *411*

Morton, Christine, 477

Morton, Eric, 477

Morton, Michael, 477–78, *478*, 479

Moseley, Jeff, 240

motor fuels tax, 278, 378, 382, *382*, *383*, *386*, 388, 490–93, *493*

Motorola, 35

motor vehicle inspection, 267

motor vehicle sales and rental taxes, 382, *382*, *386*, 400

motor voter law, 160, 180 a national act, passed in 1993, that requires states to allow people to register to vote when applying for a driver's license

MUD. *See* municipal utility district (MUD)

municipal courts, 307, 461 local trial courts with limited jurisdiction over violations of city ordinances and very minor criminal misdemeanors

municipal utility district (MUD), 358–60, 362 a special district that offers services such as electricity, water, sewage, and sanitation outside the city limits

Muñiz, Ramsey, 126

Murray, Mekisha, 312

Murray, Robert, 81

N

NAFTA. *See* North American Free Trade Agreement (NAFTA)

Napoleonic Wars, 46

National Association for the Advancement of Colored People (NAACP), 159, 192

National Association of Latino Elected and Appointed Officials, 26

National Commission on Excellence in Education, *A Nation at Risk*, 418

National Council of State Legislators, 219

national defense, 87

National Federation of Independent Business v. Sebelius, 104, 438

National Research University Fund (NRUF), 389, 390, 513, 514 fund established in 2009 to provide funding to universities seeking to achieve national prominence as research institutions

National Rifle Association (NRA), 178

Native Americans. *See* American Indians

OPEC (Organization of Petroleum Exporting Countries), 284

open carry of personal firearms, 177, 475

open primary, 154 a primary election in which any registered voter can participate in the contest, regardless of party affiliation

ordinance, 307, 345–46 a regulation enacted by a city government in each of Texas's incorporated cities and towns

Oregon, 98, *283*

Organization of Petroleum Exporting Countries (OPEC), 284

O'Rourke, Beto
Democrats and, 116, 120, 122, 146–47, 202, 295–96, 310
demographics and voters for, *130*, 131, 177
race against Cruz in 2018, 116, 120, 123, 146–47, 202, 295–96

Other Funds, 375 consists of all other funds flowing into the state treasury that are not included in other state budgets; this includes the Texas Highway Fund, various trust funds operated by the state, and certain revenues held for local higher education accounts

Our Patchwork Nation (Chinni and Gimpel), 141

P

PAC. *See* political action committee (PAC)

Panhandle, 5, 24, 449, 518, 519, *522*

Panhandle Producers and Royalty Owners Association, 265

Paris, Texas, 454

Parks, Ursula, *398*

parole, 456 the conditional release of an offender who has served some prison time, under specified rules and under the supervision of a parole officer

partisan polarization, 118, 119, 246–47 the degree to which Republicans have become more conservative and Democrats have become more liberal

partisanship
Affordable Care Act and, 101–5
coercive federalism and, 97
in Congress, 118, 242
as cue used for voting, 153
in El Paso city government, 354–56
history in Texas, since the Civil War, 132
ideology and, 119–20, 246–47, *246*
in judicial elections, 308–9
plural executive and, 272
preemption of local laws and, 346, 347, 348
redistricting and, 224–25
at the state and local level, 118–19
state *vs.* national government and, 81–82
in Texas legislature, 139, 243, 244, 245–47, *245*
urban, rural, and suburban influences on, 140–42
A Partnership for Independence, 427–28

party platform, 117, 124–25 a statement of principles and

political philosophy that a political party promises to enact if elected to office

Patrick, Dan
abortion access and, *273, 274*
coronavirus pandemic and, 347, 402
CPS reform and, 407–8
educational reform and, 420
election for lieutenant governor 2014, 121, *121,* 140, 180, 239, 274, 275
election for lieutenant governor 2018, *172, 272,* 274, 275
immigration and, 210
LBB attacked by, 396, 397
legislative session 2019 and, 140, *235*
as lieutenant governor, 241, *241,* 242, 274–75, 289
partisanship and, 118, 244, *245*
plural executive and, *271,* 280
property taxes and, 418
regular order of business rule and, 235
Republican Party divisions and, 116
Sandra Bland case and, *453*
SB 4 and, 501
Senate rules and, 243, 274
social media blunder, 239
Tea Party and, 129, 130, 274
toll roads and, 493

patronage, 263 the resources available to higher officials, usually opportunities to make political appointments to offices and to confer grants, licenses, or special favors to supporters

Patterson, Jerry, 197, 273

Paul, Rand, 126

Paul, Ron, 126

Paxton, Ken
2014 attorney general's race and, 275
2018 attorney general's race and, *172, 272,* 275, 290
Affordable Care Act and, 101–5
campaigning by, *174*
coronavirus pandemic and, 347
CPS reform and, 408
DACA and, 503
felony charges against, 276, 289–90
plural executive and, *271*
SB 4 and, 502, 503
State Commission on Judicial Conduct and, 325
Stream Protection Rule and, 81–82
Tea Party and, 275
voter fraud claim and, 253
voter ID law and, 160

pay-as-you-go limit. *See* Article 3, Section 49a

payroll tax, 94, 96

PBS, 176

peak association, 187

Pearson publishing company, 186

Pelosi, Nancy, 137

Pennsylvania, 33, *314,* 472, 491

Pennzoil, 298

Penry, Johnny Paul, 339

pensions, 365–67, 368

People's Party, 132

per diem, 220 daily payment to a public official engaged in state business

Pereira, Andres, 312

Permanent School Fund (PSF), 51, 276, 387, 388, 414

fund created in 1854 that provides monies for primary and secondary schools

Permanent University Fund (PUF), 16, 276, 389, 511, 513, 514 fund established in 1876 and funded from the proceeds from land owned by the state; monies go to various universities in the University of Texas (UT) and Texas A&M systems

Permian Basin Producers Association, 265
Permian Basin region, 16
Perry, Charles, 501
Perry, Rick
 2006 election for governor and, 126–28, 170
 aides and lobbying, 196–97
 appointments of, *318*
 border security and, 487
 emergency transfer of funds and, 399
 expanded Medicaid program and, 438
 Foster's sentence commuted by, 474, *474*
 as governor, 121, 145, *256*, 258, *258, 259*, 262, 263, 266, 280
 redistricting and, 218, *222*
 Texas Dream Act and, 498
 tort law and, 323
 vetoes by, 236
 voter ID law and, 162
Personal Responsibility and Work Opportunity Reconciliation Act, 428
petrochemical industry, 10, 30
petroleum financing, 32
petroleum pipelines, 15
petroleum production, 12, 15. *See also* oil and gas industry
Pew Research Center, 487, 499
Phelan, Dade, *129*, 241, 248
physical regions of Texas, *11*

"pick-a-pal" system for grand jurors, 299, 460
Pierre, Goodwille, 312

pigeonholing, 230 a step in the legislative process during which a bill is killed by the chair of the standing committee to which it was referred, as a result of his or her setting the bill aside and not bringing it before the committee

Pilgrim, "Bo," 200
Pitts, Jim, 196
Planned Parenthood, 240, 346, 434, 435
Plano, 31, *344*, 449
Plano Independent School District, 357
plantation system, 10, 28

plea bargain, 300, 456, 460–61 negotiated agreement in a criminal case in which a defendant agrees to plead guilty in return for the state's agreement to reduce the severity of the charge or prison sentence the defendant is facing

Plessy v. Ferguson (1896), 91, 414–15

plural executive, 64, 255, *257*, 271–80, 282–83, 289 an executive branch in which power is fragmented because the election of statewide officeholders is independent of the election of the governor

pluralism, 188
pocket veto, 236
Pojman, Joe, 240

police power, 93, 267–68 the power of states to pass laws to promote health, safety, and public welfare

police reform, 454
policing, 447–54
 community relations and, 447–48, 449
 controversies surrounding, 450–54
 favorability toward police, *452*
 police departments, 449–50
 SB 4 and, 501, *502*
 Texas Commission on Law Enforcement, 450
policy legitimation, 410
policy-making process, 409–11, *411*
 evaluation, 410, *411*
 implementation, 410, *411*
 policy formulation, 409, *411*
 problem identification, 409, *411*
 rationality in policy making, 410–11

political action committee (PAC), *196*, 201–3, 204–6, 210 a private group that raises and distributes funds for use in election campaigns

political culture, 4, 5–7, 35–36 broadly shared values, beliefs, and attitudes about how the government should function and politics should operate; American political culture emphasizes the values of liberty, equality, and democracy

political elites, 5
political participation, 226–27, *227. See also* voter turnout
political parties in Texas. *See also* partisanship
 African Americans in, 143–44
 digital media and, 132
 election campaigns and, 172–74

 future of Texas and, 146–47
 Latinos in, 144–45
 party organization, 123–25, *124, 125*
 party system evolution, 132–39
 party unity and disunity, 139–40
 public attitudes about parties, 119–20
 Tea Party movement, 115, 116, 120–21, 129, 130
 Texas party politics, 118–19, 139–45
 third parties, 125–29
political power and constitutions, 43–45

political socialization, 119 the introduction of individuals into the political culture; learning the underlying beliefs and values on which the political system is based

Polk County, 339

poll tax, 26, 27, 73, 157, *158* a state tax imposed as a requirement for voting; poll taxes were rendered unconstitutional in national elections by the Twenty–Fourth Amendment, and in state elections by the U.S. Supreme Court in 1966

population growth, 21, 25, 164, 402, 488, 489, 497
Populist Party and movement, 13, 126, 132
Port of Houston Authority, 357–58

post-adjournment veto, 236, 269 a veto of a bill that occurs after the legislature adjourns, thus preventing the legislature from overriding it

poverty, 29, *29*, *96*, 409, 412, 424–26, *425*, 429, 441

poverty index, 425

Poway Unified School District, 365

Powell, David Lee, 474

Powered by People, 202

prayer in public schools, 139

precinct, 124, 153 the most basic level of political organization at the local level

precinct chair, 124, 125 the local party official, elected in the party's primary election, who heads the precinct convention and serves on the party's county executive committee

precinct convention, 124–25 a meeting held by a political party to select delegates for the county convention and to submit resolutions to the party's state platform; precinct conventions are held on the day of the party's primary election and are open to anyone who voted in that election

preclearance, 100–101, 102, 164, 221 provision under Section 5 of the Voting Rights Act of 1965 that required any changes to election procedures or district lines to be approved by the U.S. Department of Justice or the U.S. District Court for the District of Columbia

preemption, 97, 344–49, *348*, *349*, 368 an aspect of constitutional reasoning granting exclusive powers to act in a particular area to the national government; the legislature's power to overrule ordinances or actions of local home–rule cities

preexisting conditions and health care, 101–5, 179

preponderance of the evidence, 298 the standard of proof in a civil jury case, by which the plaintiff must show that the defendant is more likely than not the cause of the harm suffered by the plaintiff

Presidential Reconstruction, 53 a reconstruction plan for reintegrating former Confederate states back into the Union and freeing the enslaved people that placed mild demands upon the existing White power structure

presidential Republicanism, 134, *134* a voting pattern in which conservatives vote Democratic for state offices but Republican for president

president pro tempore of the Senate, 242, 397

Presidio County, 338–39

pretrial hearings, 460

Price, Four, 228

Price, John Wiley, 342

primary education. *See* elementary education

primary election, 153–54 a ballot vote in which citizens select a party's nominee for the general election

primogeniture and entail, 62

prison alternatives, 468, 478–79, 481

prisoners' rights, 466–68

prison reform, 466–68

prison system. *See* Texas prison system

private corporations, 66

privatization of public property, 7 the act(s) by

which Texas gave public land owned by the state over to private individuals for cultivation and development

probate, 298, 337 the supervision of the estates of deceased persons

probation, 456, 462 punishment where an offender is not imprisoned but remains in the community under specified rules and under the supervision of a probation officer

professional licensing policy, *264*

progressive tax, 383, 384, *385* type of tax where in the tax burden falls more heavily on upper–income individuals

Progress Texas, 193

Prohibition, 189

property crime rate, 469, 470

property rights, 41, 46, 48, 53, 73, 91

property tax, 361 a tax based on an assessment of the value of one's property, which is used to fund the services provided by local governments, such as education

  cuts to, 401

  housing prices and, 401

  income tax and, 178

  MUDs and, 360

  public education funding and, 384, 412, 415, 416–18

  special purpose districts and, 357–58, 360, 361–62

  Texas tax system and, 384

Property Tax Relief Fund, 375

proportional representation, 128–29 a multimember district system that allows each political party representation in proportion to its percentage of the total vote

Proposition 2, 71, 72

Proposition 12, 72

prosecutors, 298–300

prostitutes, 304

provincialism, 6, 22 a narrow, limited, and self–interested view of the world often associated with rural values and notions of limited government

PSF. *See* Permanent School Fund (PSF)

public, 226–27, 240, *240*, 346

public beach access, 41

Public Citizen, 192, 207

public defender, 464, 465 salaried lawyer who is funded by the government or by grants who represents indigents in Texas in some counties or for some types of cases

public defender offices, 299

public education. *See also* school district

  antitax policies and funding for, 129

  budget deficit and, 400

  budget surplus and, 400

  de facto segregation in, 415, 417

  Democratic Party and, 6, *422*, 423

  demographics and, 417

  educational reform and, 418–20

  evolution, teaching of, 139, 284

  Federal Funds for, 412

  general revenue funding of, 412, 416–18

  immigrants and, 498

coronavirus pandemic and revenues from, 368, 374, 397

cuts to, 401

immigrants and, 499

revenue in Texas and, 178, 378, 380, *382*, 384, 401, 402

State Highway Fund and, 400

same-sex marriage, 61, 71, 73, 88, 98, 131, 325, *354*

San Antonio

African Americans in, 143

city government in, 352–53, *352*, 355

coronavirus pandemic and, 347

cotton production and, 12

Democratic influence in, 123

demographic changes in, 24, *24*, 25, 34

as home-rule city, *344*

immigrants in, 499

Interstate Highway System and, 15

mayors in, 144, *352*

pension shortfalls, 365

preemption bills and, 346

public transit and, *496*

racial and ethnic composition of, 355

road congestion in, 490

school desegregation in, 415

urban political life, 34

White liberals in, 122

San Antonio de Béxar, 34

San Antonio Express-News, 176, *176*

San Antonio missions, 277

San Antonio Railroad, 34

San Antonio v. Rodríguez, 415

Sanchez, 145

sanctuary cities, 500–503 localities where sheriffs have decided not to share information regarding the arrests of undocumented persons

with federal immigration authorities

Cornyn and, 178

Democrats and, 130

preemption and, 345

Republicans and, 140

SB 4 and, 116, 131, 498, 501–3, *502*

Straus as Speaker and, 242

Tenth Amendment and, 98

Trump administration and, 500, *501*

Sandra Bland Act, 453–54 legislation in response to the arrest and jailing of Sandra Bland, who died in jail; the law requires independent investigation of jail deaths and alternatives to jailing those with mental or substance abuse problems

Sandra Bland case, 452–54, *453*

Sanlin, Max, 138

San Marcos, 34. *See also* Austin–San Marcos area

Santa Anna, 50

Santa Fe Bridge, *486*

Sawyer, Allison Lami, 115

Sayers, Joseph D., *259*

SB 4. *See* Senate Bill 4 (SB 4)

SB 1070 (Arizona), 502

SBOE. *See* State Board of Education (SBOE)

school choice, 6

school district, 357, 358, 361, 364–65, 387, 412, 415 a specific type of special district that provides public education in a designated area

school finance/funding, 66, 140, 218, 269, 275, 289, *411*, 415, *418*. *See also under* higher education; public education

school safety, 177, 178, 268

school vouchers, 191, 206

SCOPE (Select Committee on Public Education), 418–19

Scott, Winfield, 54

Seattle, Washington, 500

secession from the Union, 8, 20, 22, 52–53, *53*, 55, 90, 92

Second Amendment, 91, 475

secondary education, 7, 66, 185, 387, 419–20, *422*

Second Bank of the United States, 89

secretary of state, *252*, 253–54, 271, *271*, 279, 282 state official, appointed by the governor, whose primary responsibility is administering elections

Texas Constitution and, 52, 63, 64

secretary of the Senate, 236

sectarian purposes, appropriations for, 41

security, right to, 46

segregation

civil rights legislation and, 96

civil rights movement and, 8, 9

de facto, in public education, 415, 417

federal court decisions and, 28

federal government intervention and, 84

in Gulf Coastal Plains, 10

of labor, 24

public policy and, 27

of schools, 28, 414–15

third party candidates and, 126

of train cars, 91

Select Committee on Public Education (SCOPE), 418–19

self-defense, 475–76

self-government, 45, 48, 61–62

Seliger, Kel, 203

Sematech, 35

semiconductor industry, 17

Senate Bill 4 (SB 4), 116, 131, 498, 501–3, *502* law passed in 2017 by the Texas legislature enacting penalties for sanctuary cities that refused to cooperate with federal immigration authorities

Senate Concurrent Resolution 10, 228

Senate Finance Committee, *391*, 394, 397

Senate rules, 242, 243, 274

senatorial courtesy, 266 in Texas, the practice whereby the governor seeks the indication that the senator from the candidate's home district supports the nomination

sentencing enhancements, 456–57

"separate but equal", 91–92, *91*, 414–15 an interpretation of the Fourteenth Amendment's equal protection clause that held that states could segregate races as long as equal facilities were provided; it was overturned in 1954

separation of powers, 43, 51, 62–63, 269 the division of governmental power among several institutions that must cooperate in decision making

Sephra Burks Law, 209

Sessions, Jeff, 105, 500

severance taxes, 16, 278, 380, 397, 400, 401–2

sex discrimination, 98

sexual abuse scandal, 281

sexual assault survivors, 238

sharecroppers, 13, 28

Sharp, John, 145, 427
Shays, Daniel, 86
Shea, Brigid, *340*
Shelby County, Alabama v. Holder (2013), 100–101, 102, 159, 160, 164, 225
sheriffs, 335–36

Shivercrat movement, 134 a movement led by the Texas governor Allan Shivers during the 1950s in which conservative Democrats in Texas supported Republican candidate Dwight Eisenhower for the presidency because many of those conservative Democrats believed that the national Democratic Party had become too liberal

Shivers, Allan, 134, 139, 255, *259*, 262
Sibley, David, 197
Sierra Club, 192
Simmons, Ron, 310
Simon, Herbert, 411

simple resolution, 228, 229 a resolution that concerns only the Texas House or Senate, such as the adoption of a rule or the appointment of an employee, and that does not require the governor's signature

single executives, appointed, 281

single-member district, 128, 220, 350, 351, 352, 353, 354, 368 an electorate that is allowed to elect only one representative for each district

slavery
    abolition of, 53, 54, 91
    Coahuila y Tejas Constitution and, 46, 50
    Confederacy and, 8
    cotton industry and, 13

end of, in Texas, 27
    federalism and, 90
    Gulf Coastal Plains and, 10
    secession from the Union and, 52–53
    Texas population and, 21, 26
    textbook review and, 285
    White immigrants from the South and, 22, 26
Smith, Preston, *259*
Smitherman, Barry, 207
Smith v. Allwright (1944), 28, 158
SNAP (Supplemental Nutritional Assistance Program), 425, *427*, 428, 430
social conservatism, 6–7, 72, 130, 137, 146
social liberals, 126, 131
social media, 132, 174, 177, 186, 221, 226, 239, 277–78, 285
social programs, 94, 401, 425–27
Social Security, 94, 95
Social Security Act (1935), 94, 426, 432, 433
Social Security Amendments of 1965, 432
social services, 336
socioeconomic status (SES), 166
solar energy, 81
South by Southwest festival, 3, 334, 3, 334
South Carolina, 89, 127
South Dakota, 75, *385*
Southern Poverty Law Center, 159
South Plains, 449
Southwest Airlines, 298

sovereign, 87, 94 possessing supreme political authority within a geographic area

Spanish and Mexican land titles, 66
Spanish colonists and explorers, 13, 15, 23
Spanish language, 449

Spanish law, 519
Spanish-Mexican law, 49–50
Spanish rule, 46

Speaker, 241–44 the chief presiding officer of the House of Representatives; the Speaker is the most important party and House leader, and can influence the legislative agenda, the fate of individual pieces of legislation, and members' positions within the House
    appointment power, 243–44, 265, 280
    bills and, 230, 231, 236
    budgetary process and, 397
    investigative powers and, 229
    LBB and, 394
    LRB and, 222
    power of recognition and, 243
    spending limit and, 392
    water projects committee and, 522

special bill, 225 a bill that gives an individual or a corporation a special exemption from state law

special election, 156 an election that is not held on a regularly scheduled basis; in Texas, a special election is called to fill a vacancy in office, to give approval for the state government to borrow money, or to ratify or reject amendments to the Texas Constitution

special interests, 34, 59, 69, 153, 307. *See also* interest group

special items, 513, 514 special pieces of legislation passed to support par-

ticular programs or building projects at state universities outside normal funding mechanisms

specialized jurisdiction, 304, 305

special purpose district, 357–62 a unit of local government that performs a single service, such as education or sanitation, within a limited geographic area
    creating, governing, and paying for, 360–61
    nonschool special purpose districts, 358–60
    problems with, 361–62, 368
    school districts, 358, 360
    types of, 357–58

special session, 218–19, 229, 243, 256, 269 a legislative session called by the governor that addresses an agenda set by him or her and that lasts no longer than 30 days

specialty courts, 304 usually part of district courts and focusing on trying to resolve the underlying problems such as mental health, alcohol and drug abuse, and prostitution that lead to recurring criminal behavior

spending limit, 392–93
Spindletop, 15
spot market oil prices, 35
SSI. *See* Supplemental Security Income (SSI)
STAAR (State of Texas Assessments of Academic Readiness), 419–20, 421, 423
standardized testing, *184*, 185

standing committee, 230, *231*, 243–44, 274 a permanent committee with the power to propose and write legislation that covers a particular subject, such as finance or agriculture

Sunset Advisory Commission (SAC), 208, 286
a commission created in 1977 for the purpose of reviewing the effectiveness of state agencies

Sunset Review Act, 286
Supplemental Nutritional Assistance Program (SNAP), 425, *427*, 428, 430

Supplemental Security Income (SSI), 427, 432
a national welfare program passed in 1972 that provides assistance to low–income elderly or disabled individuals; replaced the federal–state programs that had offered assistance to the blind, the permanently and totally disabled, and the aged

supremacy clause, 44, 87, 97 Article VI of the U.S. Constitution, which states that the Constitution and laws passed by the national government and all treaties are the supreme law of the land and superior to all laws adopted by any state or any subdivision

surface coal mining, 81
surface water, 518, *518*, 519, 521
Sweatt, Heman, 91, *91*
Sweatt v. Painter (1950), 28, 91
SWIFT (State Water Implementation Fund for Texas), 522
SWIRFT (State Water Implementation Revenue Fund for Texas), 522

T
TAMSA (Texans Advocating for Meaningful Student Assessment), 185–86

TANF. *See* Temporary Assistance for Needy Families (TANF)
Tarrant County, 31, *31*, 295–96, 310–11, *311*, 499
TASER International, 193
tax burden, 378, 379, 383, 384, *385*, 437
Tax Cuts and Jobs Act (2017), 104
taxes. *See also specific taxes*
  2020 election and, 178
  Affordable Care Act and, 104
  Article 8 of the Texas Constitution and, 66
  Articles of Confederation and, 86
  budget surplus and, 399
  comptroller's duties and, 278, 279
  constitutional amendments and, 70
  elastic clause and, 88
  oil and gas production and, 16
  Republican Party and, 130, 379, 401
  state power to collect, 87
  Tea Party movement and, 129, 139
  Trump's 2017 reforms, 438, 439
Tax Foundation, 394
tax reform, *235*
Taylor, Ivy, 144, *352*
Taylor, Van, 197
TEA. *See* Texas Education Agency (TEA)
Teacher Retirement System, 388
teachers, 192, 248, 268, 284–85, 418–19, 420, 421–23
teachers colleges, 511
TEAMS (Texas Educational Assessment of Minimal Skills), 419

Tea Party movement, 129, 130 reaching prominence after Barack Obama's election, a political movement that advocates lower government spending, lower taxes, and limited government campaigns backed by, 206
  constitutional amendments and, 70–72
  division in the Republican Party and, 115–16, 120–21, 139, 140, 247
  education policy and, 421, 423
  "no new taxes" mantra of, 402
  PACs and, 202
  Patrick and, 129, 130, 274
  Paxton and, 275
  religious freedom *vs.* civil rights and, *61*

TEC. *See* Texas Ethics Commission (TEC)
Tejanos, 8, 119
telecommunications, 190
telecommunications, certification in, 450

Temporary Assistance for Needy Families (TANF), 393, 425, 428, 429, 432 a welfare program passed in 1996 to provide temporary assistance to families with needy children; replacing the AFDC program, TANF sought to make poor families self–sufficient and to give states greater flexibility in setting benefit levels, eligibility requirements, and other program details

tenant farmers, 13
Tennessee, 75, 378

Tenth Amendment, 87–88, 89 a provision in the Constitution's Bill of Rights that says, "The powers not delegated to the United States by the Constitution, nor prohibited by it to the States, are reserved to the States respectively, or to the people"; used by states to challenge actions of the national government
  federalism and, 44
  preclearance and, 100, 102
  sanctuary cities and, 98
  Stream Protection Rule and, 82
  U.S. Supreme Court and, 94, 97

terrorism, fear of, and NAFTA, 18, 19
Terry v. Adams (1953), 158
tetrahydrocannabinol (THC), 463
Texaco, 298
Texans Advocating for Meaningful Student Assessment (TAMSA), 185–86
Texans for Lawsuit Reform, 203, 204–6
Texans for Public Justice, 206
Texas
  demographics in (*see* demographics)
  economy of (*see* economy)
  founding of, 45–46, 50
  future of, 35–36
  "low service, low tax" reputation of, 377, 378
  as majority-minority state, 146, 173, 487
  movement into, 146
  myths of, 45
  size of, 10
  "travel alert" for, 503
Texas A&M system, 196, 389, 390, 512, 513, 514
Texas A&M Transportation Institute, 490
Texas A&M University, 16, 66, *507*, *509*, 510, 511
Texas Alcoholic Beverage Commission, 280
Texas Alliance for Life, 240
Texas Almanac, 350

Watergate, 143
water policy, 518–22
    governor's appointment
        power and, *264*
    planning authorities and,
        520–22
    special purpose districts
        and, 362
    water law, 519–20
    water usage by sector,
        518
water projects, 42, 363, 388,
    522
Water Rights Adjudication
    Act, 519
Watkins, Craig, 341, 481
Weber, Randy, 169
welfare policy, 424–30
    1935–1996, 426–27, *426*
    dependency, idea of, and
        welfare reform in
        1990s, 427–28
    evaluating welfare
        reforms, 429–30
    poverty and, 424–26, *425*,
        429, 441
    welfare and the
        coronavirus, 429–30
    welfare reforms, 96, 428
    welfare spending limit,
        393
Wells, Jim, 156
Wells, Tinie, 156–57
Wentworth, Jeff, 204–6

Wesberry v. Sanders (1964),
    222
West, Allen, 287
West, Royce, 122, 151, 209
West Texas Permian Basin, 16
West Texas Rolling Plains, 11
West Virginia, *314*
Whitaker, Thomas, 270–71
White, John, 134
White, Mark, *259*, 272
White flight, 140–41

**White primary, 26, 27, 28,
157** primary election in which
only White voters were eligible to participate

Whites
    achievement gap and, 421
    Confederate monuments
        and, 8
    Constitution of 1876 and,
        55–56, 57
    cotton cultivation and,
        12–13
    death penalty and, 474
    demographic changes
        and, 21, 22–23, *22, 23,*
        25, 34
    favorability toward courts
        and criminal justice
        system, *320*
    favorability toward police,
        452

    influence in Texas
        electorate, 168
    liberal, and Democratic
        Party, 6, 122–23, 127
    political status of Latinos
        and, 26
    poverty among, 425
    in prison population, *467*
    racial diversity and, 33
    rural, and Republican
        Party, 123
    school desegregation and,
        415, 417
    slavery and, 26
    voter ID requirements
        and, 103, 163, *163*
    voter registration and,
        160–61
    voting rates, 100, 143, *143*,
        173
Whitley, David, *252*, 253–54,
    271, 279
Whitman, Hank, 407–8
Whitmire, John, 193–94, *193*
*Whole Woman's Health v.
    Hellerstedt*, 434, 435
Wichita Falls, 511
Wickard v. Filburn (1942), 94
Willacy County, 425
Willett, Don, 177
Williams, Michael, 144
Williams, Tommy, 196
Williamson County, 425, 477
Wilson, David, 342, *342*

wind energy, 81
Wink Engineering, 190
Wisconsin, 162–63, *314*
women
    growing influence of, 6,
        221
    in the judiciary, 317–18,
        318, 319
    right to vote, 156–57
    in the Texas legislature,
        214, 215, 216, 221
workers' compensation laws,
    269
World Health
    Organization, 3
World War I, 13, 20, 32
World War II, 13, 20, 24, 32,
    94, 134
Wortham, Gus, 190
Wright, Jim, 284
Wu, Gene, 501, 502
Wyoming, 10, 75

Y
Yarborough, Ralph, 122, 135,
    139
Young, William, 295

Z
Zaffirini, Judith, 228, *228*
Zapata County, 425
Zavala County, 126, 425
zero-based budgeting, 397
Zwiener, Erin, *214*, 215, 216